Date Due

COMPARATIVE AND MULTINATIONAL MANAGEMENT

Wiley Series in International Business

International Business: Issues and Concepts
by Reed Moyer

Strategic Management of Multinational Corporations: The Essentials
by Heidi Vernon Wortzel
    Lawrence H. Wortzel

International Business, 2nd ed.
by R. Hal Mason
    Robert R. Miller
    Dale R. Weigel

Comparative and Multinational Management
by Simcha Ronen

COMPARATIVE AND MULTINATIONAL MANAGEMENT

Simcha Ronen
Graduate School of Business Administration
New York University

John Wiley & Sons
New York   Chichester   Brisbane   Toronto   Singapore

Library of Congress Cataloging in Publication Data:

Ronen, Simcha, 1935–
  Comparative and multinational management.

  (Wiley series in international business)
  Bibliography: p.
  Includes indexes.

  1. International business enterprises—Management.
2. Comparative management.   3. Management—Cross-
cultural studies.   I. Title.   II. Series.
HD62.4.R66   1986   658′.049   85-17971
ISBN 0-471-86875-2

Printed in the United States of America

10 9 8 7 6 5 4

To Raymond A. Katzell
A scholar, a mentor, a friend,
a model to so many of us

Preface

I recall an analogy (attributed to Douglas McGregor) that goes as follows. If managers build a channel running upwards, they cannot blame the water for refusing to flow up that channel. The water is neither lazy, nor stubborn, nor incompetent. Similarly, it is the duty of managers to determine and create the optimal conditions for developing and utilizing available resources, particularly human resources. This assertion is true for managers in any organization—whether they operate in relatively static conditions with low uncertainties or in complex conditions with high uncertainties. The latter demand more information, more sophisticated professional skills, and (above all) more awareness that high uncertainty and volatile environmental conditions require as much imagination as possible.

Many of the 500 leading enterprises in the world operate primarily outside their own countries. The Ford Motor Company has half its employees outside the United States; three-fourths of Philips employees work outside the Netherlands; Saint-Gobain employs over half its employees outside France; and more than half of Matsushita Electric's employees are outside Japan. And the trend is increasing. The world is no longer a tidy place where employees of each nationality work only in that nation for companies of the same origin.

Therefore, the challenge is to expand our knowledge about employees, management, and organizational behavior to encompass the entire world. This is obviously a vast endeavor; however, given current political, economic, and cultural realities, there is no escaping it. Fortunately, the social sciences are increasingly useful in pursuing the goal of increased cross-cultural understanding within the realm of management. For managers in the complex world of international management, *Comparative and Multinational Management* offers a starting point for reaching that goal.

In this book, my intention has been to heighten the awareness of managers and students of organizations to the complexity of operating in other cultures and in unfamiliar nations. The book provides a framework for understanding individuals' cultural differences and the implications of such differences in forming managerial policies. Moreover, it provides a guide for dealing with strategic issues associated with cross-national environments, organizational design, and adaptation.

It is sad to realize how badly these issues have been neglected. The reason may be that many managers find it preferable to analyze and manipulate products, machines, and numbers than people. Too often, managers expect people to respond to rules, regulations, and directives the same way in one context as in another. Yet people, whatever else they may be, are unpredictable. Hence, the common temptation to hope that managerial problems within challenging environments will simply resolve themselves if left alone.

As a psychologist, my interest in human behavior has followed a holistic view that transcends any single life domain, whether the family, the wider social context, or the work environment. As an organizational psychologist, however, I have chosen to deal with variables related to human effectiveness in the organizational setting. The combination of these two interests has prompted me to investigate the relationship between the antecedents of behavior (in all possible domains) to work behavior. The intriguing contribution of *culture* to behavior has been the highlight of that interest.

Researching the field of organizational behavior, interacting with colleagues, and doing consultation work with various organizations had led me toward the challenge of documenting the diversification of human affect, cognition, and behavior in organizational settings. But beyond the inherent individual differences, studying the diversification within the cultural environment has offered me the opportunity to fulfill this challenge. I have therefore invested the past few years in reviewing the literature on comparative management, and now summarize it for the students of organizations. The product is a bridge between the academic conceptualization and the application for the practicing executive.

Such a bridge may fully satisfy neither academicians nor executives. Yet it addresses what I perceive to be the appropriate integration of the field for the advanced business student. An integration does, in fact, offer the potential for practical application. It can provide a foundation from which the student can build once working in the field. Ultimately, my hope is that *Comparative and Multinational Management* will assist managers in achieving more effective interaction with subordinates and co-managers in cross-cultural settings, both within their country and overseas.

Acknowledgments

Every endeavor like this one is a result of contributions by many supporting individuals. This book is no exception. My deepest gratitude goes to my students, who have either challenged me in our classes or have worked with me as graduate assistants. Their contributions in literature surveys, in critical discussions, and in social settings often turned the laborious process of writing into an enjoyable and challenging process. Some of them are already professionals and academic colleagues, and others soon will be: Eli Weitz, Chuck Hosler, Nick Wasiliewski, B. J. Punnett, Susan Schneider, Barbara Ross, Rajesh Kumar, Eric Abramson, and Bob Krupnick. My colleagues at New York University—Stephen Kobrin, William Egelhoff, and Eric Walton—deserve special thanks for their valuable comments on earlier drafts. The intellectual climate and support services at the N.Y.U. Business School have provided the supportive environment that every author needs.

My deep gratitude goes to Ed Myers. Ed has contributed his special ability to make sense out of confusing paragraphs and has relentlessly kept improving the manuscript till its final deadline. His sensitivity, insight, and friendship I highly value. Miryam Farr has had her fingers on every word and punctuation sign. She has been a faithful and diligent co-worker throughout the last two years. At John Wiley, Rick Leyh, my Editor; Susan Giniger, Supervising Copy Editor; and Miriam Seda, Senior Production Supervisor, have lent their expertise and continuous support.

Finally, I now have the opportunity to give credit to those who have paid the highest price during the writing of this book. My children, Benzy and Vered, have been patient throughout the time of my preoccupation. However, my deepest gratitude goes to my wife, Freddy, whose vital emotional support, encouragement, and intellectual inspiration have made the whole endeavor possible in the first place.

Contents

PART I
Background Considerations

During the 1960s, Marshall McLuhan coined the phrase *global village* to describe the contemporary world. Technological developments in communications and transportation not only have diminished the size of what once seemed a vast planet but have also linked virtually every place with the rest of the world. In the twenty years since McLuhan coined his famous phrase, innovations in satellites, computers, fiber optics, and aerospace technology have shrunk the Earth still further. The world does indeed seem like a village, and all humanity the tribe living there.

Or does it? The image of a global village is beguiling, but is it accurate? Does the ease of communication and travel today give us a deceptive sense of unity? Unfortunately, even a quick glance at the world situation will answer these questions. The superficial sense of connection, of village coziness, is illusory. Wars, conflicts, and misunderstandings among nations and cultures are as common as before—if not more frequent. Even nations with shared backgrounds and amicable histories, such as Canada and the United States, often squabble over political and economic matters. Technology may facilitate communication, but it has never guaranteed insight, patience, or compassion.

The fact remains that the human population of this planet still encompasses many differences. We may lament or celebrate these differences, or both; in any case, they exist. They affect how nations, cities, companies, and individuals interact with each other. Likely as not, such differences will remain even as people of different origins travel more widely. The world will not end up as homogenized as Grade A milk. As a result, people must somehow learn to recognize each other's differences, understand them, and come to terms with them.

This situation holds true within the business world as in all others. Even relatively small companies now trade with countries on the other side of the globe. Corporations may end up dealing with dozens of nations, just as they once dealt with dozens of cities. And yet comparative and international management is still a relatively free-form discipline. Knowledgeable managers may assume they will face complex circumstances overseas, but the information available to them is new and somewhat unfamiliar. How should a manager contend with these complexities?

The three parts of *Comparative and Multinational Management* will address this issue and others—not only in theory but in their practical aspects as well. Part I examines the background of international management: historical developments, cultural and national perspectives, and cross-cultural research issues. Part II then proceeds to consider attitudinal and behavioral differences that affect management in different cultures. Finally, Part III explores the specific implications of cultural differences or managers in MNCs. In this manner, the three parts combine to form a comprehensive framework for coping with cultural change and diversity in the management domain today.

The situation facing cross-cultural managers is unquestionably one of personal and professional challenge. On the other hand, it may appear to be more difficult than it really is. Modern communications and transportation technology provide us with a feeling that we, alone, face culturally complex issues within a business context. As it happens, nothing could be farther from the truth.

But we are already getting ahead of ourselves. Chapter 1 will explain why.

CHAPTER 1
Historical Perspective of International Management

International and comparative management is clearly not a new field. The ancient Egyptians, Phoenicians, and Greeks traded with foreigners and learned to do business with different cultures. The Dutch, the English, and other Europeans established worldwide business empires during the Renaissance. Traders built vast enterprises within the New World. And whenever people have had to engage in commerce with groups outside their own environment, they have needed to be sensitive to differences in languages, beliefs, and customs. All of these people have been engaged in cross-cultural management and international business.

HISTORICAL DEVELOPMENT OF INTERNATIONAL BUSINESS (1500–1970)

How have economic historians charted the evolution of international business throughout the centuries? Robinson (1964) has identified four major eras in the period from 1500–1970, each characterized by a particular business emphasis: the Commercial Era, the Explorative Era, the Concessionary Era, and the National Era.

Robinson bases each historical era on a different business motivation. These motivations are personal fortune seeking, empire building, protectionism, and finally market development. Each of these business motivations was influenced by the relationship between a given business enterprise and a given political

Table 1.1 Historical Perspective of International Business

Era	Motivation	Business–Political Relationship
Commercial (1500–1850)	Personal fortune seeking	Company sovereignty
Explorative (1850–1914)	Empire building	Colonial rule
Concessionary (1914–1945)	Protectionism	Political concessions
National (1945–1970)	Market development	MNCs encounter nationalism and localization
Global (1970–1985)	High competition	Regional company–government interaction and co-operation, especially in European and Third World countries

system; the result was relationships that Robinson defines, respectively, as company sovereignty, colonial rule, political concessions, and nationalization and localization. (During all four of these eras, international business was almost entirely a Western phenomenon.) The various stages are summarized in Table 1.1.

The Commercial Era (1500–1850)

Columbus's voyage to the New World began a phase of international trade during which individual entrepreneurs went off to seek their personal fortunes. The Commercial Era started with the age of the great explorers (about 1500) and continued into the European industrial revolution (ending about 1850). Enterprising traders traveled to distant lands, purchased exotic goods—precious metals, spices, silk, and slaves—and sold them at home for large profits. The risks were great; success depended on a high degree of personal motivation and on superb navigational skill.

European monarchs soon realized that these transactions yielded regular profits, and they demanded direct involvement in the enterprise. They encouraged the development of national monopolies to secure maximum returns. Throughout this era, great chartered companies developed under English, French, and Dutch authority. Most of them possessed broad powers of both commercial and political natures. Thus, companies like the British India Company could (and did) claim to be "sovereign states": the Dutch East India Company was granted exclusive trading rights in the East Indies and was permitted to make alliances with native princes, appoint governors, and employ troops. The Levant Company in the Middle East, and the British Royal American Company and the Hudson's Bay Company in America all performed consular functions.

The Explorative Era (1850–1914)

Lasting from 1850 to just before World War I, this era was characterized by the building of industrial empires. The Industrial Revolution had changed the nature of overseas European enterprise, and the need for cheaper and more secure sources of raw materials prompted importers to move away from exotic goods toward industrial products such as mineral ores and plantation crops. By the mid-nineteenth century, numerous permanent, large-scale investments had developed in several industries. In Africa, mining was the major force that drew the colonial powers into the interior; in Southeast Asia and Latin America, both mining and agriculture were important factors. The number of European nationals participating in overseas ventures, the size of their economic and personal investments, and the vital importance of these investments to the European economies all forced the home governments to become involved in colonial rule.

European countries initially preserved their colonies' traditional political institutions, but these institutions became more and more dependent on foreign rule. Simultaneously, Western enterprises aimed more at political as well as industrial domination. This further weakened traditional political authority and, in turn, resulted in the dissolution of old loyalties and established political power.

In addition, local skills were often inadequate for the needs of running colonial enterprises. Western technicians and skilled workers were brought in to help; where unskilled labor was also inadequate, companies imported it as well. Alternatively, Western enterprises became involved in training workers. The overall effect was to dissolve both traditional political systems and cultural values, which Western systems and values replaced to some degree. The increasing political power of Western businesses provided the major influence during the next era.

The Concessionary Era (1914–1945)

During the period encompassing the two world wars, companies assumed many paternalistic responsibilities as traditional leadership continued to weaken. This trend resulted in an era during which host countries granted major concessions to Western enterprise. Within the limits of these concessions, each company tended to become all-powerful and all-providing. Typical of such concessions were the Lever Concession in the Congo, the early oil concessions in the Arab Middle East, and the United Fruit Company's agreements in Central America. These companies provided housing, health and sanitation services, finances, education, distribution of food and other goods, transportation, and protection for workers within their boundaries. For the most part, local governments could not provide these services themselves, and were therefore happy to let the companies provide them.

The many different ideas and approaches introduced through these major concessions resulted in a period of transition. Ironically, nationalism and economic development—often changes that Westerners themselves had introduced—would eventually doom the colonial system. The Great Depression of the 1930s prompted many companies to replace high-priced home nationals with trained locals; thus, the employment of Asians, Africans, and Latin Americans in Western enterprises increased. Cutbacks in public services accompanied such hiring policies, so that Western enterprise, which had previously replaced local political authority, now appeared to be failing in its paternalistic obligations. Host country nationals began to form new loyalties. Even where enterprises tried to consolidate their deteriorating position through long-term contracts, political changes were almost inevitable. Thus, the Concessionary Era finally ended with a rising tide of nationalism.

The National Era (1945–1970)

The outbreak of World War II ended the Concessionary Era, although some Western enterprises appeared unaware of changing political environments in Asia, Africa, and Latin America. Two new influential factors now emerged: locally responsible political leaders and—in the wake of the Cold War's political and economic polarization—an alternative source of capital and technical skills. Both developments increased the host countries' bargaining power with Western enterprises, particularly as the enterprises were no longer protected to Western political power.

Many countries now viewed the presence of Western foreigners as an intrusion into local affairs; in many instances, this became a source of irritation that led to hostility and antagonism toward Western enterprise. The emergence of ideas about sovereignty and self-government encouraged many countries to seek independence. Because of their previous dependence on foreigners, however, they were often ill-equipped for this change. Consequently, the National Era was characterized by major political instability. Eventually, however, most political forms of colonialism collapsed, and a large number of newly independent countries emerged. Many of these new nations, while still seeking private Western capital, now wanted it on their own terms.

The National Era, despite its instabilities and changes, was nevertheless a period of global expansion for businesses. It also laid the foundations for the functioning of today's multinational corporations (MNCs). Although trade across cultures and national boundaries had almost always existed, only since the 1940s has international trade been a dominant factor in the global industrial system. The years from 1954 to 1970 were years of global expansion for industry as businesses began seeking both markets and productive inputs on a worldwide scale. In part, expanded communications systems made this internationalization possible. Geographic distance had previously meant isolation, and thus a limit to the geographic dispersion that a company could effectively undertake. Once it was possible to communicate quickly and efficiently across large distances, however, a major barrier to internationalization had disappeared.

The 1950s and 1960s   During the 1950s and 1960s, American firms of all kinds went abroad. The multinational corporation was almost exclusively an American phenomenon at the time. The book value of American foreign direct investment rose from $12 billion in 1950 to almost $80 billion in 1970. The first movement abroad was generally defensive; American companies sought to overcome trade barriers that existed in the 1950s. As trade restrictions were eased, however, companies became more aggressive and tried to link technical, marketing, managerial, and financial advantages with cheap overseas labor. During this period, "going multinational" was the fashionable thing to do, and American companies felt a need to develop global product portfolios if they were to remain competitive.

In 1968, Jean-Jacques Servan Schreiber published *The American Challenge,* predicting that American MNCs would soon dominate world business. This was not exactly the case. By the mid-1960s, other countries had joined the international expansion. In 1965, large non-American companies were setting up or acquiring foreign manufacturing operations at the same annual rate as American multinationals. The 1965 value of foreign direct investment in the United States was about $7.5 billion; by 1972 it was almost $15 billion. Although foreign investment in the United States was still small compared to American investment abroad, the increase represented an important change in the makeup of multinational companies.

Exact data on overall international business are not always available; however, we can make rough estimates about the volume and makeup of this segment of business. Robock and Simmonds (1970) estimated that in 1966, 57% of total foreign direct investment worldwide was American-owned and 17% was British; but the expansion rate was lower for these two than for other European countries and Japan. Robock and Simmonds felt that Europe had settled into a mature pattern, whereas Japan, no longer preoccupied with domestic expansion, had entered a take-off phase of international investment. Rowthorn (1971) reported that from 1957 to 1967, Japan had been the leader in international growth, followed by continental Europe, with Canada, the United States, and the United Kingdom well behind. As of 1968, Japanese overseas investment totaled $1.4 billion and involved 1908 projects. By 1968, the United States foreign investment rate peaked, with 540 subsidiaries initiated. By 1968, the rate of growth of non-U.S. foreign direct investment had surpassed the U.S. rate of growth. In absolute terms there were still more American firms with foreign subsidiaries abroad than firms of any other single group of countries, but the number of continental firms was not far behind (Franko, 1978).

The 1970s   By the 1970s, some of the glamour of "internationalization" was wearing off, and increasing non-American participation in the international business scene (as well as growing host-government resentment toward foreign businesses) combined to change the pattern of international business. One result was a period of American divestment during the early 1970s. From 1971 to 1975, American companies sold 1359 of their foreign subsidiaries (almost 10%). During the same period, there was a substantial decline in the number of new subsidiaries being formed (3.3 for each divestment in 1971 compared to 1.4 in 1975). These divestments were largely in low-technology, high-competition industries such as textiles, apparel, leather, and beverages. Investment in high-technology industries such as pharmaceuticals, machinery, and office equipment increased during the same period (Rose, 1977).

Thus, both investment patterns and the makeup of the multinationals themselves were changing. European multinationals had largely caught up with American companies; Japanese firms were beginning to expand internationally; and even the developing countries were spawning their own multinationals.

In general, host countries were becoming increasingly aware of the economic, social, and political impact of foreign subsidiaries. The developing countries, meanwhile, were becoming increasingly nationalistic. A 1976 study by the Conference Board reported a wide variety of restrictions, particularly concerning MNC executives (see Table 1.2). As these concerns indicate, a number of countries had instituted various restrictions to curtail the MNCs power and to lessen what they saw as a threat to their national sovereignty. A major problem remains, however, in that multinationals are often seen as being supranational, and subject in only a limited degree to the laws of any one nation. (The Conference Board Reports, 1976, on the development of international guidelines and regulations may be beneficial in countering the MNCs increasing power.) Box 1.1 provides excerpts from the International Chamber of Commerce Guidelines regarding suggested investment policies for investors, home governments, and host governments. The International Confederation of Free Trade Unions (ICFTU) has also suggested a series of social obligations for MNCs, forming a voluntary code for individual corporations, which appears in Box 1.2.

Although no international body is capable of enforcing a general set of guide-

Table 1.2 Major Concerns of MNC Executives

Tariffs and duties
Import quotas
Export commitments
Export restrictions
Limits on expansion
Price controls
Financing restrictions
Restrictions on nationality of management
Foreign ownership limitations
Local sourcing requirements
Nationalization and expropriation
Local manufacturing requirements
Capital repatriation restrictions
Dividend remittance restrictions
Abrogation of right to royalties

Source: J. La Palombara and S. Blank, *Multinational Corporations and National Elites: A Study in Tensions,* New York: Conference Board Report No. 702, 1976.

Box 1.1

Social and Economic Guidelines for International Investment

1. The Investor

(a) Should ensure in consultation with the competent authorities that the investment fits satisfactorily into the economic and social development plans and priorities of the host country.

(b) Should be prepared in any negotiations with the government of the host country to make known his expectations concerning the expansion of the enterprise, employment and marketing prospects and the financing of its operations.

(c) Should in appropriate cases, where the government of the host country so wishes, be prepared to enter into contractual arrangements with that government.

(d) Should, in response to the interest shown by the public of the host country in his activities, take steps to provide relevant information about the operations of the enterprise, subject to any exclusions necessary for competitive reasons.

2. The Investor's Country's Government

(a) Should, in the formulation or modification of policies that affect foreign investments by its nationals, take the fullest possible account of the need of investors for stability, continuity, and growth in their operations as well as of the general interests of the host country.

(b) Should seek to enter into binding obligations under international law with other governments either on a bilateral or multilateral basis, in respect of the reciprocal treatment to be accorded to the property, rights, and interests of its nationals.

(c) Should offer, either nationally or through participation in an international investment insurance agency, guarantee facilities against noncommercial risks encountered by the investor.

(d) Should examine the possibility of providing special aid for relevant economic and social infrastructure projects in developing countries which will facilitate private investment of significance to the economic development of the host country.

3. The Host Country's Government

(a) Should, in the formulation or modification of policies that affect foreign investments, take the fullest possible account of the need of investors for stability, continuity and growth in their operations.

(b) Should, with regard to sectors not reserved to domestic ownership, make known to prospective investors its economic priorities and the general conditions that it wishes to apply to incoming direct private investment, and should provide an opportunity for consultation with the private sector during the development of national plans.

(c) Should make known the treatment that it will accord to the proposed investment and any limitations or financial charges that it will impose.

(d) Should not discriminate on the grounds of its foreign ownership in the treatment accorded to the enterprise, it being understood that the government has a right to accord special treatment to any enterprise or enterprises, whether domestic or foreign owned, in the interest of the economy.

(e) Should, in appropriate cases and where the foreign investor so wishes, be prepared to enter into contractual arrangements with the investor concerned.

(f) Should be prepared to enter into binding obligations under international law with other governments either on a bilateral or multilateral basis, in respect of the reciprocal treatment to be accorded to the property, rights, and interests of nationals of the other state or states.

Source: Excerpts from International Chamber of Commerce Guidelines, Paris, 1972.

Box 1.2

Social Obligations of Multinational Companies

Regarding employment and industrial relations the following obligations should be imposed on the multinational companies:

(a) multinational companies shall follow the laws, the rules and the practices of the host country regarding the labour market only if these are not inferior to the standards of the International Labour Organisation in which case those of the ILO shall be followed;

(b) multinational companies shall not offer working conditions inferior to those provided for in the United Nations Charter of Human Rights and ILO Conventions;

(c) multinational companies shall acknowledge the genuine trade unions of the host country as well as the right of negotiation of the employees, and shall endeavour to regulate the working conditions of the employees through collective agreements. Further the multinational companies shall not hinder, but facilitate, trade union work at the local as well as international level;

(d) multinational companies shall continuously inform the authorities and the trade unions of the home and host country regarding ongoing or planned activities for the purpose of adjusting these to the economic and social planning of both countries;

(e) multinational companies shall in their activities use such production methods and forms of cooperation as are in harmony with the economic and social conditions of the host country, and in a longer perspective contribute to a development consistent with the host country's interests. The criteria of such production methods shall be fixed by governmental authorities having regard for the worker's aspirations.

(f) in cooperation with the trade unions, multinational companies shall provide the necessary facilities for the promotion of the principles of industrial democracy, both at the local, as well as headquarter level;

(g) provision shall be made for the employees' representatives of the multinational to meet at least three times a year for consultation and exchanges of views;

(h) the operating expenses of the employees' representatives shall be met by the management of the relevant subsidiary of the multinational;

(i) no lay-off may be carried out by a multinational (in case of "rationalisation," transfer of production, etc.), without prior arrangement of a job, equivalent in income and skill, for the employee.

(j) multinational companies shall in cooperation with the authorities and trade unions in the host country provide ample opportunities for the employees to further their education;

(k) multinational companies, through active manpower planning, shall provide stable employment for their employees and accept negotiated obligations for job and social security;

(l) multinational companies shall not exercise any discrimination on racial, political or religious grounds regarding, for example, employment, wages, housing, etc.;

(m) multinational companies operating in a developing country shall make contributions to a fund for the development of that country's social infrastructure, the amount being fixed as a percentage (to be determined by the government in consultation with the company and the trade unions concerned) of the profits made by the company in that country. The fund shall be administered by a tripartite committee representing the government, trade unions and the company.

(n) multinational companies operating in a developing country shall pay wages and fringe benefits which give their employees a fair share of the fruits of the higher productivity resulting from their superior technology and managerial skills.

Source: Excerpts from International Confederation of Free Trade Unions, Multinational Charter, 1975.

lines or rules for MNCs, a number of United Nations agencies have been created to deal with specific aspects of MNC operations (for example, the United Nations Commission on Transnational Corporations—UNCTC—headquartered in New York).

Whether or not codes of conduct, suggestions for policy, or UN agencies have any noticeable impact on the operations of MNCs is debatable. However, since MNCs themselves are concerned with how national restrictions affect their operations, it is in their best interests to be sensitive to these monitoring devices. MNCs remain largely supranational. This movement toward monitoring activities, which may eventually exert control over the MNCs, is indicative of the widespread concern about the impact of multinational operations.

Resource scarcity has been a major factor in ending American hegemony in international business. American activity has been biased toward labor-saving convenience technologies that are energy, and material, intensive (Vernon, 1966). Europe and Japan, in contrast, have been more concerned with energy efficiency and conservation of resources. Thus, the energy crises of the 1970s and the global realization of the need for conservation have provided real advantages for non-American companies.

Another factor in declining American influence has been the realization by many countries that they need not depend on the United States for an entire investment package. Developing countries initially felt that if they were to reap the benefits of new technologies, they must accept the total package offered by those providing the technical knowledge. During the 1970s, however, the idea of "unbundling" became prevalent. As developing countries demanded more and more direct participation in enterprises, they often attempted to obtain resources from a variety of sources—for instance, technology from one source, capital from another, management from a third, and so on—and they would then put them all together on a local basis.

These trends have resulted in a relative decrease in American participation in international business and, concomitantly, a relative increase in non-American participation. A new but notable phenomenon is the rise of the Third World multinationals. According to a ranking by Ray S. Cline (of Georgetown University's Center for Strategic International Studies) of the twenty most powerful countries in the world today, eleven are developing nations. Multinationals are headquartered today in South Korea, the Philippines, India, and Brazil, among other countries. Korean companies, for example, have paved roads in Ecuador; there are Taiwanese steel mills in Nigeria; India's Hindustan Machine and Tool Company is involved in Algeria; and a Bangladeshi company made mattresses in the southern United States (Heenan & Keegan, 1979).

In the past, multinational corporations were primarily involved in two activities: distribution of raw materials and manufacturing. Today, however, multinationals perform a variety of tasks through a worldwide network of multinational service organizations: banks, advertising agencies, management consultants, and computer software companies. Nonprofit organizations, too, have followed the example of their profit-making counterparts. Labor unions, universities, hospitals, and philanthropic agencies have become part of the multinational scene (Heenan & Keegan, 1979).

The 1980s

The 1980s promise to bring more changes to the international business arena. Competition will almost certainly continue to increase; regulations appear to be on the rise; and technology transfer is in flux, with some parties pressing for unbundling and others emphasizing the efficiency of a total package. All signs indicate that the international business environment will become increasingly complex. This in itself justifies exploring more imaginative approaches to comparative management. Companies large and small, profit and nonprofit, manufacturing and service-oriented, in developed and developing nations alike will have a greater need to consider cross-cultural aspects of their environments. These aspects will greatly influence their ability to function effectively.

From a comparative management viewpoint, an additional consideration is the increasing wish for mobility across international borders; in some countries immigration laws have been liberalized—especially for skilled employees—and mass communication has increased people's awareness of opportunities in other countries and mass transportation has facilitated travel throughout the world. Thus, even a purely domestic firm often faces the necessity of dealing with employees of widely varied cultural backgrounds.

Comparative management research has demonstrated that employees' attitudes and cultural values differ. Such differences increase the need for flexible management practices. This holds true in situations in which immigrants make up a large proportion of the workforce. In fact, the problems in such situations might actually be magnified: managers anticipate differences when working in foreign countries, but they are probably less sensitive to such differences at home. Surveys have shown that executives perceive employee motivation and productivity as varying from country to country (Basche & Duerr, 1975); however, there is little documentation about these perceptions regarding immigrant groups. Meanwhile, all indicators suggest that the trend toward greater international mobility for workers will continue through the next decades (Daniels, 1980).

NATIONAL VERSUS WORLD VIEW

In his classic *Sovereignty at Bay* (1971), Raymond Vernon identifies a corporate "global outlook" as one that has "shed any non-rational preferences for U.S. money, personnel or markets." Although he emphasizes American multinationals, the same definition can apply to companies in any country.

The key concept in this definition is "non-rational preference." In other words, a national viewpoint involves ethnocentric preferences—home country money, personnel, and markets—that are not based on a rational analysis of the company's situation but rather on a categorical prejudice in favor of the home country. In contrast, a world view or global outlook focuses on analyzing the company's situation or rationally choosing the most appropriate inputs and outputs. Thus, a company using only local inputs and catering to a local market may reveal a rational outlook if it remains open to home country inputs and markets.

A company with a truly global outlook would consider the world its domain and make decisions accordingly. Because all companies retain some national biases, a completely global outlook is unrealistic; however, the acceptance of extranational possibilities is the characteristic differentiating a global view from a national view.

This global or national approach develops over time. Vernon (1966) has developed the product life cycle model to illustrate the early growth of multinational corporations. Vernon proposes four stages in a multinational company's development. This is a phased process that also illustrates the initial dominance of global commerce by American firms.

1. In the first stage, the enterprise develops labor-saving products for the American market; manufacturing takes place near its main markets even if costs might be lower elsewhere. Its initial monopoly position gives it greater flexibility in changing inputs, thus minimizing the importance of cost differences. Proximity ensures swift communication to facilitate product development.
2. In the second stage, the product has become more standardized. Overseas markets have expanded to the point at which exports are economically feasible.
3. In the third stage, costs become more important and flexibility and communication less important. Hence, production shifts to locations outside the United States but still within areas where the market is substantial (i.e., in advanced industrial countries).
4. In the fourth stage, cost pressure (especially for high labor–content products) becomes strong enough to shift production into the less developed countries, where factories produce primarily for export (Fayerweather, 1976).

This model provided a valid explanation of early multinational development. However, its usefulness diminishes in light of corporations' more global view today. The ease of communication and relative availability of information negates the necessity of following this development pattern; thus, companies may follow quite different paths. Today, it is not uncommon for a company to go from stage 1 directly to stage 4, or perhaps to begin at stage 3.

For our use, we have adopted Heenan and Perlmutter's (1979) definition of multinationalism, which may vary along three dimensions based on the structural, performance, and attitudinal criteria (see Figure 1.1).

MULTINATIONALS TODAY

U.S. foreign direct investment, as well as foreign direct investment in the United States, has increased steadily in recent years. In 1975, American investment abroad was about $124 billion; by 1983, it had increased to $226 billion—an increase of 84%. Foreign investment in the United States over the same time period had grown from $27 billion to $102 billion, a substantially greater increase of 280%. Although investment in all areas has increased, American

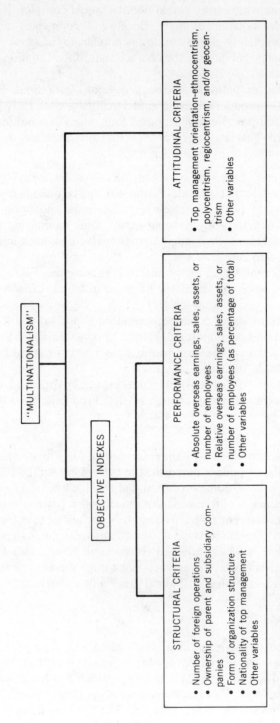

Figure 1.1   Definition of multinationalism.

Source: D. A. Heenan and H. V. Perlmutter, *Multinational Organization Development,* © 1979, Addison-Wesley, Reading, Massachusetts. Pg. 16. Reprinted with permission.

investment in the developing countries has increased at a faster rate than investment in the developed countries (96% vs. 86%); but investment in the developed countries was still three times greater than in the developing countries. In contrast, European investment in the United States had increased from $12.3 billion in 1975 to $68.5 billion in 1982. Japan's investment in the United States, though still relatively low in 1982 ($8.7 billion), was fifteen times what it has been in 1975. Canada's investment had grown by 81% and British investment by 90%. Table 1.3 provides further details of the changes in the investment picture, for the United States abroad and foreign investment in this country.

Several business periodicals publish annual reports on developments in international business. Among these are summaries compiled by *Fortune* and *Forbes* on American investment abroad, foreign investment in the United States, and the world's largest MNCs. These reports are of great value in understanding the makeup of today's international business world.

Of particular interest are the changes occurring over time. Between 1981 and 1982, there was a noticeable increase in British investment in the United States, with several British firms becoming more prominent. (Midland Bank, Consolidated Gold Fields, Grand Metropolitan, Northern Foods, and U.K. General Electric). Canada's Seagrams moved from 31st place to 3rd, but Genstar moved down substantially (from 38th to 53rd), as did Inco (from 22nd to 73rd) and Canada Development Corporation (27th to 64th). Kuwait Petroleum appeared on the list for the first time as the 29th largest foreign investor in the United States. Japan's Matsushita Electric dropped to 114th from 26th, and Sony to 109th from 49th. Among American multinationals, rankings remained relatively stable, but there were also some changes. For example, Philbro Salomon was 8th in 1982 but did not even appear in the top 100 in 1981. Nabisco appeared as 55th and also did not appear in 1981. In contrast, Engelhard Minerals was 8th in 1981, and Conoco was 12th, but neither appeared on the 1982 list. Among non-American companies, industrial changes were noticeable, and chemical companies generally improved their ranking (Kuwait Petroleum, Pe-

Table 1.3a   Comparisons of U.S. Foreign Direct Investment, 1975–1983—U.S. Investment Abroad, in Billions of Dollars

	1975	1976	1977	1978	1979	1980	1981	1982	1983
TYPE OF INVESTMENT									
Petroleum	25.97	28.4	28.0	30.5	39.1	47.5	53.2	56.6	59.7
Manufacturing	55.9	61.1	62.0	69.6	79.0	89.2	92.3	90.5	90.1
Other	42.2	46.8	55.9	62.5	69.7	78.4	82.7	74.2	76.2
Total	124.0	136.4	145.9	162.6	187.8	215.1	228.2	221.3	226.0
AREA OF INVESTMENT									
Developed countries	90.7	100.4	110.1	121.2	139.4	158.2	167.4	164.1	169.5
Developing countries	26.3	28.9	31.8	37.5	44.6	53.2	56.1	52.4	50.9
International	7.0	7.1	4.0	3.9	3.7	3.9	4.7	4.9	5.5

Source: U.S. Department of Commerce, Bureau of Economic Analysis, 1984.

Table 1.3b Comparisons of Foreign Direct Investment in the United States, 1975–1982—Foreign Investment in the United States, in Billions of Dollars

	1975	1976	1977	1978	1979	1980	1981	1982
TYPE OF INVESTMENT								
Petroleum	6.2	5.9	6.6	7.8	9.9	12.3	18.0	20.4
Manufacturing	11.4	12.6	13.7	17.2	20.9	24.1	29.9	32.1
Other	9.9	12.3	13.8	17.0	23.7	29.1	18.9	22.0
Total	26.7	30.8	34.1	42.5	54.5	65.5	90.4	101.8
AREA OF INVESTMENT								
Canada	5.4	5.9	5.9	6.2	2.7	9.8	9.8	9.8
Europe	12.3	14.4	16.3	21.5	27.6	32.1	60.5	68.5
U.K.	6.3	5.8	6.3	7.6	9.8	11.3	12.0	12.0
Japan	0.6	1.2	1.7	2.7	3.5	4.2	6.9	8.7
Other	3.1	3.5	3.7	4.4	6.4	8.0	13.0	14.7

Source: U.S. Department of Commerce, Bureau of Economic Analysis, 1984.

troleos Mexicanos, Petroeo Brasileiro, SA, Nippon Oil Company, The Electricity Council, and Tokyo Electric Power Company). However, the National Iranian Oil Company slipped from 19th to 59th.

As these brief comments indicate, major changes can occur among the corporations of the world from one year to the next. It is important to keep abreast of these changes by analyzing data according to country, industry, size, and so forth. It is particularly important to consider changes over relatively extensive time periods (e.g., increments of five, ten, or fifteen years) to gain a historical perspective.

CONCLUSION

The world of business is extremely varied and complex. The manager today faces not only normal business complexities, but also the implications of cultural differences within the international business community. Cross-cultural issues directly affect managerial practices. What works positively in one culture may have negative consequences in another. Managerial practices for different nationalities and cultures need to be examined in light of the behavioral sciences. The aim of this book is therefore to examine the knowledge amassed in the behavioral sciences, and, in light of this knowledge, to develop a practical understanding of other cultures and their effects on business.

To understand the manager's role in today's business, we cannot focus solely on multinationals, nor solely on individual cultures. Rather, our aim should be to combine comparative and international management and to examine both the intercultural differences in managerial practices and multinational companies' interactions with specific countries.

Accordingly, we should now consider the basis for our understanding of all cross-cultural management issues: the more general cultural and national perspectives that social sciences provide.

CHAPTER 2
Cultural and National Perspectives

In its most general sense, culture refers to a people's way of life. People have always followed certain customary ways of behaving, which give their lives a particular pattern, regularity, and meaning. Societies differ in their cultural patterns, yet cross-cultural comparisons are possible because we can identify similarities even in the midst of cultural differences. "The cultural patterns of societies, when placed side by side, are like the patterns of snowflakes, in that no two are exactly alike," write Edgerton and Langness (1974). "Yet a discerning eye can find similarities between aspects of one pattern and aspects of another" (p. 92).

But what do we really mean when we speak of *culture*? What constitutes culture? What are the effects of culture on people—both individually and collectively? And how does culture affect a manager's task in the field? The following discussions will attempt to answer these questions in the context of cross-cultural management.

Culture refers to the way that human beings understand the world. In the broadest sense, culture defines and expresses both attitudes and behavior. It represents a shared way of being, evaluating, and doing that is passed from one generation to the next. Culture embraces the concept of morality—determining for each group what is "right" and "proper"—and teaches individuals how things "ought" to be done. Culture is shared by all members of a particular group; as such, it forms the basis for social or communal life.

Culture is a phenomenon that develops over time. It provides a fluid continuity with the past. Social life depends to a large extent on individual conformity to the shared understandings that make up a given culture, but these shared understandings are continually evolving and changing. Even in the midst of the commonality of culture, individual motives and drives exert powerful influences on the culture-sharing group.

All human societies have a culture that includes at least those shared understandings that allow its members to live together. It is not necessary that all members share all understandings but only that some people share some understandings. Within a given cultural group, there will be smaller groups—whether vocational, religious, social, or other—and each of these groups may have its own distinct codes of attitudes and behavior. The dictates of each particular group will guide its members. In the United States, for example, a person may behave one way at work, another way at home, still another way at church, and yet another way at a party. This variation of behavior is acceptable within the specific subcultures and is governed by the overall understanding that such differences are acceptable and even desirable. But in other societies, such distinctions may be quite unacceptable.

People shape culture and at the same time are shaped by it. From our culture we learn which meanings to attach to events in our world and to the people who engineer events. And just as cultures differ, so do interpretations of it (Swartz & Jordan, 1980, p. 11). Understanding and evaluating others according to the frame of reference one's own culture provides is an unavoidable consequence of cultural identity. Humans are socialized to use their culture as an interpretive tool. But the danger is that one's own perspective may be too narrow to allow for a full, objective understanding of other people and other cultures. Triandis (1977) points out the well-recognized fact that people from other cultures often appear ''strange, peculiar, or even crazy.'' We frequently misunderstand or misinterpret people from other cultures. Culture controls human behavior in a nonrational (Hofstede, 1980) but nevertheless persistent fashion (Hall, 1959). Because we learn cultural behavior early in life, it frequently affects us on an unconscious level. Cultural conditioning resides so deep within us that we often recognize our own cultural attributes only after we face those in another culture.

CULTURE AND ANTHROPOLOGY

In the past, the study of culture and cross-cultural differences and similarities has been the almost exclusive concern of cultural anthropologists. Corporations paid only limited attention to cultural research. A ''known'' cultural environment, though always relevant to a company's decisions, was nevertheless considered a reasonably stable factor in the domestic business environment. The growing internationalization of business, however, has led to an increasing awareness of the cultural environment and its importance. As firms cross national boundaries, they are likely to encounter radically different attitudes and behavior. Such differences will probably challenge most managers' own cultural expectations. The challenge, however, need not be a source of frustration. Dealing with cultural differences can work out satisfactorily for all parties concerned. But before we turn to the study of cultural variables and how they affect the management field, we should first consider how cultural anthropologists view the meaning of culture, and how they analyze it.

Even cultural anthropologists debate the exact meaning of the theoretical concept "culture." In fact, some anthropologists have argued that culture, in the abstract, can be explained only by reference to specific cultures (White, 1949). White has proposed that every human culture can be divided into three parts: (1) economics and technology, (2) social structure, and (3) ideology. He argues that the economic and technological aspect is fundamental to the other two, and that social structure and ideology can be understood only through reference to that foundation. Thus, we should examine or explain culture in terms of other cultural constructs.

Despite this difficulty, however, we can make certain general statements about culture with which most cultural anthropologists would agree. The following is a brief synthesis of these major anthropological concepts.

Anthropology dates back to the ancient Greeks. Attempts to explain differences in culture have taken a variety of forms. The Renaissance held two opposing views: (1) that cultural differences resulted from non-Europeans having "fallen" from a higher state of cultural development and (2) that there were many distinct and separate species of humans, rather than only one, each following its particular way of life. In the eighteenth century it was thought that human progress, rather than human degeneration, accounted for cultural differences. In this evolutionary view, cultures were seen as developing from a single primordial beginning; as they became more complex and refined, they followed certain common cultural changes. Anthropologists espousing this theory believed that if universally applicable laws of human change could be found, these laws would make it possible to understand one's own cultural development as well as that of others.

This goal of understanding cultural development is still central to anthropology; there is, however, little evidence that all societies develop through similar states. In the early 1900s the "diffusion" view suggested that cultural change occurs because of cultural "borrowing," or the transmission of cultural traits from one society to another. Like the other theories previously discussed, this view focused largely on the past. Some anthropologists in the early 1900s, however, felt that observing actual relationships among individuals who together constituted a group would provide the best basis for understanding the principles underlying their social order.

Today's anthropologists still hold many of these different views, and the evolutionary school is still prominent. One branch, cultural ecology, emphasizes similarities among groups living in similar environments and having similar means of dealing with these environments; another emphasizes the importance of personality; still others concentrate on cognitive or linguistic approaches. These differing views are not mutually exclusive, but rather complementary, and each has contributed to the understanding of human cultures.

Comparative management studies have the same goal as anthropology: to understand culture. Management, however, needs to focus on cultural differences from a business viewpoint rather than from a purely anthropological one.

The ultimate goal of anthropology is "the understanding of man in all societies" (Edgerton & Langness, 1974). Such understanding evolves through a search for wider theories of human behavior that provide an understanding of how and why cultures take the forms that they do. In contrast, the goal of comparative management is to use such knowledge to design the most effective organizational strategy and structure possible and to make the most effective use of human resources in different cultures. Organizations must understand how and why cultures take the forms they do because the organization must function in these differing cultures. No organization can function effectively without understanding all aspects of its environment. In the past, organizations have paid attention to the political, technological, economic, and interorganizational aspects of their environments, but they have often ignored powerful cultural influences. This attitude is no longer productive. A major task of comparative management is therefore to make organizations more aware of their cultural environments.

There are three approaches to comparative management (Robinson, 1978). The *universalist approach* contends that few major differences exist among managers across cultures and that management theories and practices transfer easily from one culture to another. This school emphasizes the overall similarities among cultures rather than the differences. In contrast, the *economic cluster approach* emphasizes that the economic similarities and differences among nations, or among groups of nations, will determine management's tasks. Finally, the *cultural cluster approach* focuses on how behavioral and attitudinal differences among cultures determine these tasks. All three approaches contribute to our understanding of the management process from a comparative viewpoint.

International business has traditionally preferred the use of hard, easily quantifiable data (such as differences in currency, taxes, or regulations) over softer, more abstract data. Information about cultural and behavioral considerations are difficult, if not impossible, to measure with any exactitude. A 1976 Conference Board report (La Palombara & Blank) indicated that most multinationals do little to gather noneconomic data regarding host countries. However, most managers interviewed for the study felt that there was too much emphasis on quantifiable economic variables and not enough on the social, political, administrative, and related variables that deeply affect operations.

It is, indeed, difficult to measure culture; surely this is one of the central problems of comparative management. Yet the existence of this problem does not mean that we should ignore it. Nor does it mean that examining nonquantifiable variables will serve no purpose for managers. What, then, are the useful alternatives before us? We should examine the ways in which anthropologists approach culture and consider how well these approaches help managers in cross-cultural settings.

Cultural Universals Approach

One approach to this subject is the cultural universals approach. Whitely and England (1977) have analyzed 164 separate definitions of culture that Kroeber and Kluckhohn categorized in 1952. From this analysis, Whitely and England arrived at the following definition: culture is "the knowledge, beliefs, art, law, morals, customs and other capabilities of one group distinguishing it from other groups." In 1945, George P. Murdock compiled a list of 70 variables that he argues represent an exhaustive list of "cultural universals" common to all cultures. According to this theory, cultures could be examined in terms of each of these variables to suggest similarities and differences. Murdock's list may, in fact, provide an overall picture of the many variables that differ among cultures; however, it does not provide a very practical or structured method for analyzing such differences, nor does it identify the variables with significant implications for attitudes and behavior in the work environment. Consequently, we should explore approaches that may be more productive for our purposes (see Table 2.1).

Value Systems Approach

A more appropriate and potentially useful method for classifying cultures focuses on their value systems. The concept of culture is implicitly bound with the concept of values. A wide variety of anthropological literature views different cultures as reflecting different value systems. The two concepts appear together in statements such as "the dominant values of black culture," "man-

Table 2.1 Cultural Universals

age grading	food taboos	music
athletic sports	funeral rites	mythology
bodily adornment	games	numerals
calendar	gestures	obstetrics
cleanliness training	gift giving	penal sanctions
community organization	government	personal names
cooking	greetings	population policy
cooperative labor	hairstyles	postnatal care
cosmology	hospitality	pregnancy usages
courtship	housing hygiene	property rights
dancing	incest taboos	propitiation of
decorative art	inheritance rules	supernatural beings
divination	joking	puberty customs
division of labor	kingroups	religious rituals
dream interpretation	kinship nomenclature	residence rules
education	language	sexual restrictions
eschatology	law	soul concepts
ethics	luck superstitions	status differentiation
ethnobotany	magic	surgery
etiquette	marriage	tool making
faith healing	mealtimes	trade
family	medicine	visiting
feasting	modesty concerning	weaning
fire making	natural functions	weather control
folklore	mourning	

Source: G. P. Murdock, "The Common Denominator of Cultures," in *The Science of Man in the World Crises,* Ralph Linton, ed. New York: Columbia University Press, 1945, p. 77.

Box 2.1

Green, a popular color in many Moslem countries, is often associated with disease in countries with dense, green jungles. It is associated with cosmetics by the French, Dutch, and Swedes. Various colors represent death. Black signifies death to Americans and many Europeans, but in Japan and many other Asian countries, white represents death. (Obviously white wedding gowns are not popular with numbers of Asians.) Latin Americans generally associate purple with death, but dark red is the appropriate mourning color along the Ivory Coast. And even though white is the color representing death to some, it expresses joy to those living in Ghana. In many countries, bright colors such as yellow and orange express joy. To most of the world, blue is thought to be a masculine color, but it is not as manly as red in the United Kingdom or France. In Iran, blue represents a bad color. Although pink is believed to be the foremost feminine color by Americans, most of the rest of the world considers yellow to be the most feminine color. Red is felt to be blasphemous in some African countries but is generally considered to be a color reflecting wealth or luxury elsewhere. A red circle has been successfully used on many packages sold in Latin America, but it is unpopular in some parts of Asia. To them it conjures up images of the Japanese flag.

Source: D. A. Ricks, *Big Business Blunders*. Homewood, IL: Dow Jones–Irwin, 1983, p. 33.

agerial values as a reflection of culture,'' and ''the value-profiles of different cultures'' (Ford, 1976; Whitely & England, 1977; Kluckhohn & Strodtbeck, 1961). Many authors formally define cultures in terms of values. For example, Vickers (1968) states that ''a culture enshrines common patterns of evaluation.''

If we define culture in terms of values, then values and value systems become the analytic focus of cultural assessment. Thus, it becomes necessary to define their meaning clearly. Various writers have defined values as ''conceptions of the desirable'' (Morris, 1956), as ''the standards by which the importance of everything in society is judged'' (Steinger, 1971), and as ''enduring beliefs that specific modes of conduct or end states of existence are personally and socially preferable to opposite modes or end states'' (Rokeach, 1973).

It is important to differentiate between values that an individual holds and value as an attribute of an object or person. In economic terms, value is worth, whether in money or in the rate at which one commodity is exchangeable for another. The expectancy-valence motivational model (Vroom, 1964) postulates valence as the perceived positive or negative value ascribed to an outcome resulting from a particular action. Valence (the value attached to an object) describes the extent to which an outcome is either ''approach-evoking'' or ''avoidance-evoking.'' Values, on the other hand, rest within each individual. They serve to influence that individual's choice of valued ends, as well as the person's choice of how to attain those ends.

We must also distinguish between values and needs. Lewin's model of human behavior (1951), views needs as creating a state of tension that the individual attempts to relieve through appropriate action. Maslow's model (1954) views needs as structured in a hierarchy of prepotency; the individual's behavior attempts to satisfy the most potent need at a given time. Values concern how one ought to act, and therefore they affect the means chosen to satisfy a given need. The more abstract the need (e.g., the need for growth or self-realization), the more reflective it is of certain values. The distinction between needs and values is no longer easy to make when one focuses on this level.

We must also distinguish beliefs from values—although they are often considered identical. We may view values as a particular kind of belief. Values are either prescriptive of proscriptive (Rokeach, 1973, p. 7). According to Fishbein and Ajzen (1975, p. 12), a belief is composed of an object (a person, a group, an institution, a behavior, a policy, an event, etc.), and an associated attribute (any trait, property, quality, characteristic, outcome or event, etc.). For example, the belief that "the United States is a good place to live" links the object "United States" with the attribute "a good place to live." Fishbein's theory of attitude (1963) asserts that a person's attitude toward any object is a function of his or her beliefs about that object. Whereas a belief may change when the individual receives new information, values are relatively resistant to change. We can think of values as intervening between beliefs and attitudes in many instances; thus, a belief that New York is the cultural capital of the world may lead to a favorable attitude toward New York by someone who values culture.

And what of the distinction between attitudes and values? Fishbein and Ajzen (1975) feel that attraction, value, sentiment, valence, and utility can all constitute attitudes. Rokeach (1973), however, clearly distinguishes between values and attitudes: "Whereas a value is a single belief, an attitude refers to an organization of several beliefs that are all focused on a given object or situation" (p. 18).

Finally, we must distinguish norms from values. Social norms are standardized, distinctive ways of behaving. Norms prescribe or proscribe specific behavior in specific situations. Hackman (1976) defines norms as "structural characteristics of groups which summarize and simplify group influence processes" (p. 1495). Norms serve to regulate group-member behavior. They are represented in specific situations (what is an acceptable norm at a party, for instance, may not be acceptable at a funeral), whereas values are general concepts that apply to all situations. Most social norms evolve from the values of a given culture.

Values are major cultural variables. A culture, which we may consider a collective programming of the human mind (Hofstede, 1980), communicates its values to the individual through family, schools, churches, and other institutions. In this way, the culture perpetuates its unique value system from generation to generation. This ensures their relative permanence. Culture changes over time, of course, but such changes are generally slow.

Can we compare cultures? What are the similarities and differences among cultures, and how did they emerge? Kluckhohn and Strodtbeck (1961) theorize that all people face the same basic human problems. In solving these problems, they develop value systems to define how the problems can best be solved. Because these value systems are responses to essentially the same problems, they will be comparable. Pepper (1958) proposes a similar explanation. Pepper sees values as hierarchical: values concerning survival of the species are most important, followed by those ensuring group survival; least important are those based on personal needs. Such a hierarchy can be found cross-culturally. The explanation for differences in values rests on the assumption that the problems facing each culture, though basically the same, can be expected to differ in intensity and timing.

Research in the area of values has resulted in fairly convincing evidence that certain global values or "concepts of the desirable" do exist and that these values can, in fact, be measured. Cross-cultural research indicates that values differ from culture to culture, and that "value profiles" can be developed for various cultures. Such value profiles could be important to managers faced with the task of assessing different cultures. Unfortunately, however, researchers have used a great variety of different instruments to measure values; there is little agreement regarding any one definitive value scale suitable for managers.

Typically, researchers have developed questionnaires for use in assessing values. Analyzing these questionnaires produces groupings of similar concepts. To develop a value profile for a given culture, researchers administer questionnaires to a sample of the population (randomly selected, if possible) and determine average scores for each value grouping. Researchers have used many such instruments, and social scientists have proposed a number of different classification schemes for systematic comparison of values in different cultures.

The following discussion reviews some of these instruments. It should be stressed, however, that they have all been developed in the United States and, therefore, may be limited in application. Still, they may serve the student by indicating the conceptual usage of value constructs.

Allport, Vernon, and Lindsey developed one of the first value assessment instruments in 1951. This instrument was based on Spranger's classification of human ideas and activities as theoretical, economic, aesthetic, social, political, and religious (see Table 2.2). Researchers have used this instrument in several cross-cultural studies of values, although its cultural references and assumptions limit its usefulness. It is nevertheless important for comparative management because it provides evidence of a relationship between values and behavior. The main problem with this scale is its length and cumbersome questionnaire.

In 1956, Morris undertook a similar attempt to measure values as philosophical orientations by using a series of value scales defined as "ways to live" (see Table 2.3). Morris asked respondents to rate each category on a seven-point scale, ranging from "I like it very much" to "I dislike it very much," and then rank each category in order of preference from 1 to 13. Morris administered this instrument cross-culturally to students in the United States, India, Japan, China, Italy, Norway, Canada, and England. Using a factor-analytic approach, Morris found that reponses could be grouped into five categories. He identified these categories as follows:

Table 2.2 Allport, Vernon, and Lindzey's Values (1960)

a. *Theoretical man* values the discovery of truth. He is empirical, critical, and rational, aiming to order and systematize his knowledge.
b. *Economic man* most values what is useful. He is interested in practical affairs, especially those of business, judging things by their tangible utility.
c. *Aesthetic man* values beauty and harmony. He is concerned with grade and symmetry, finding fulfillment in artistic experiences.
d. *Social man* most values altruistic and philanthropic love. He is kind, sympathetic, unselfish, valuing other men as ends in themselves.
e. *Political man* most values power and influence. He seeks leadership, enjoying competition and struggle.
f. *Religious man* most values unity. He seeks communion with the cosmos, mystically relating to its wholeness.

Source: G. W. Allport, P. E. Vernon, and Q. Lindzey. *A Study of Values.* Boston: Houghton Mifflin, 1960.

1. Social restraint and self-control.
2. Enjoyment and progress in action.
3. Withdrawal and self-sufficiency.
4. Receptivity and sympathetic concern.
5. Self-indulgence.

In spite of methodological problems, Morris's research is of interest in comparative management because it provides distinct cultural profiles.

Another approach to cultural values assessment focuses on existential and evaluative beliefs. Kluckhohn and Strodtbeck (1961) studied variations in value orientation in five different communities—Spanish-American, Mormon, Texan, Zuni, and Navaho—and, not surprisingly, they found differing profiles. They assumed that these values guide concrete behaviors (see Table 2.4).

Sarnoff's conceptualization of Western society's values as "values of realization" and "values of aggrandizement" (see Table 2.5) was the basis for

Table 2.3 Morris's "Ways to Live" (1956)

1. Preserve the best that man has attained.
2. Cultivate independence of persons and things.
3. Show sympathetic concern for others.
4. Experience festivity and solitude in alternatives.
5. Act and enjoy life through group participation.
6. Constantly master changing conditions.
7. Integrate action, enjoyment, and contemplation.
8. Live with wholesome, carefree enjoyment.
9. Wait in quiet receptivity.
10. Control the self stoically.
11. Meditate on the Inner Life.
12. Chance adventuresome deeds.
13. Obey the cosmic purposes.

Source: C. Morris, *Varieties of Human Value.* Chicago: University of Chicago Press, 1956.

Table 2.4 Kluckhohn and Strodtbeck's Value Theory (1959)

Kluckhohn's five crucial questions common to all human groups are as follows:

1. What is the character of innate human nature?
2. What is the relation of man to nature?
3. What is the temporal focus of human life?
4. What is the modality of human activity?
5. What is the modality of man's relationship to other men?

Source: F. R. Kluckhohn and F. Strodtbeck, *Variations in Value Orientations.* Westport, CT: Greenwood Press, 1961.

Ronen's comparative study (1978) of industrial employees in Israel kibbutzim and in privately owned factories.

Finally, Rokeach compared samples of people from different ethnic and social origins in the United States, as well as samples of students from different countries, using a value survey instrument that classifies values as terminal or instrumental (see Table 2.6). Subjects rank these values (eighteen in each case) from most important to least important. Rokeach's research and that of others (e.g., Feather, 1970; 1971; 1977) suggest that this instrument can identify distinct cultural value profiles both for different groups within a country and for different countries and that these profiles correlate with a variety of measured attitudes. This instrument has been criticized methodologically, but it may be particularly useful because of its simple design.

It is important, however, to be aware of the inherent cultural bias in any approach to measuring cultural values. The researcher's own values shape every aspect of the research—design, data collection, analysis, and reporting of results. Most research to date contains a distinct Western bias; therefore, we might justifiably question its applicability to non-Western cultures. Awareness of this ethnocentric bias indicates that extensive research designs should be developed cross-culturally—that is, with input from individuals in different cultures. Because research is always anchored in the researcher's own culture, the only way to avoid a cultural bias is to incorporate a variety of cultural views into a given research design. This has happened rarely in the past; hence, much

Table 2.5 Sarnoff's Human Value Index (1966)

Aggrandizement is reflected in three areas:
Wealth. The desirability of acquiring goods, services, and legal tender that represent the material resources of one's society.
Prestige. The worthiness of obtaining the respect and admiration of others.
Power. Control over the actions and destinies of others.

Realization is reflected in four areas:
Humanitarian. Values advocating the worth of human life, which consequently motivate us toward our preservation and betterment.
Egalitarian. The advocation of basic equivalence of each person.
Aesthetic. The emphasis on beauty and artistic creation.
Intellectual. Values referring to the exercise of man's capacity for thought and reason.

Source: I. Sarnoff, *Society with Tears.* Secaucus, NJ: Citadel Press, 1966.

Table 2.6 Rokeach's Value Survey (1973)

The eighteen terminal values are as follows:

a comfortable life	family security	mature love
an exciting life	social recognition	pleasure
a sense of accomplishment	wisdom	salvation
a world at peace	freedom	self-respect
a world of beauty	happiness	true friendship
equality	inner harmony	national security

The eighteen instrumental values are as follows:

ambition	forgiveness	logic
broadmindedness	helping	loving
capability	honesty	obedience
cheerfulness	imagination	politeness
cleanliness	independence	responsibility
courage	intellectualism	self-control

Source: J. Rokeach, *The Nature of Human Values.* New York: Free Press, 1973.

previous research contains cultural biases. These instruments are still valid and useful, however. From a comparative management viewpoint, the results provide empirical evidence for the existence of cultural value systems that differ (at least in degree of importance of various values) across cultures, as well as evidence of their importance as one determinant of behavior.

Systems Approach

Another approach to analyzing cultural differences and similarities focuses on the systems that make up a given culture. A culture is itself a system and comprises various subsystems, which we can analyze to give a comprehensive picture of the overall structure. In this context a subsystem refers to a regularly interactive or interdependent group of components forming a unified whole. Harris and Moran (1979) identify eight such subsystems:

Kinship	Religion
Education	Association
Economy	Health
Politics	Recreation

Box 2.2

Pepsodent reportedly tried to sell its toothpaste in regions of Southeast Asia through a promotion which stressed that the toothpaste helped enhance white teeth. In this area, where some local people deliberately chewed betel nut in order to achieve the social prestige of darkly stained teeth, such an ad was understandably less than effective. The slogan "wonder where the yellow went" was also viewed by many as a racial slur.

Source: D. A. Ricks, *Big Business Blunders.* Homewood, IL: Dow Jones–Irwin, 1983, p. 65.

Box 2.3

The failure to consider specialized aspects of local religions has created a number of difficulties for firms. Companies have encountered problems in Asia when they incorporated a picture of a Buddha in their promotions. Religious ties are strong in this area, and the use of local religious symbols in advertising is strongly resented—especially when words are deliberately or even accidentally printed across the picture of a Buddha. One company was nearly burned to the ground when it ignorantly tried such a strategy. The seemingly minor incident led to a major international political conflict remembered for years.

Source: D. A. Ricks, *Big Business Blunders*. Homewood, IL: Dow Jones–Irwin, 1983, p. 66.

Although there may be other systems that we could include, a short synopsis of these eight systems should provide a reliable overview of any given culture and its implications for organizational behavior.

Kinship refers to the familiar patterns typical of a given culture. These systems range from the nuclear family (typical of the United States), which is relatively independent, to the extended family (found in many Eastern nations), in which several horizontal levels (cousins) as well as vertical levels (generations) live closely together, often under the same roof. A culture's kinship patterns may have a variety of implications for management. For example, a well-accepted practice in some countries is the placing of family members in desirable positions regardless of ability, whereas in other countries this is discouraged.

Education encompasses both the formal and informal methods of providing knowledge and skills. Educational systems vary in both level and content. Learning, for example, may be almost entirely formal or almost entirely informal; it may take place largely at home or entirely outside of the home; it may be very practical or very theoretical. The educational system of a particular society may have a major impact on the organization's choice of leadership styles and training programs. In addition, it is intricately tied to the level of industrialization.

Economy concerns the production and distribution of goods and services. The system may be individually oriented or group-oriented; there may be wide differences between rich and poor or a large middle class with few extremes; rewards may be based on status, accomplishment, equality, or need. The economic system can have important effects on the organization, particularly in terms of appropriate technology and reward systems, and it may also be important in making decisions about product marketing and distribution.

Politics focuses on government. It is particularly important to managers concerned with government–business interactions. First, overall political systems differ: there are dictatorships, democracies, communist states, and so on. These systems have obvious implications for business because they generally determine the amount of freedom that exists for doing business. Within this framework, companies also have to consider specific government–business relations. In some countries, government and business work closely together; in others, separation of government and business is considered ideal.

Religion concerns a culture's spiritual beliefs and its emphasis on these beliefs. Religion can have important repercussions for business. For example, the Protestant work ethic stems from Puritan religious beliefs that encourage hard work. In many countries, religious practices are an integral part of everyday life and must therefore be included in the work day. Separation of church and state is typical of some countries, whereas in others the church *is* the state.

Association refers to the network of social groupings in a society. Some cultures greatly emphasize organizations and create formal or informal associations for a wide variety of activities. Others avoid such associations. Understanding why and when such associations will occur can greatly facilitate the management process. Joining such associations may be important, because managers may find them a valuable source of information and support. It may also be important to allow for group associations to form within the company (if this is the normal practice).

Health concerns a culture's view of its overall well-being, as well as how the culture prevents and cures illness or cares for victims of disasters and accidents. The availability and type of health care service will affect the benefits available within the reward system. For example, it is becoming more common for American companies to provide facilities for physical fitness, which seems appropriate in a culture that considers physical fitness an important aspect of overall health.

Recreation focuses on how people use their leisure time. Some cultures focus on sports, others on aesthetic activities, and still others on entertainment. Within these differences further differences exist, such as whether recreational activities are group, family, or individually oriented. Cultural differences in recreational activity can have an important effect on people's behavior at work (Ronen, 1981).

Subcultures

Both the cultural value and system approaches emphasize the importance of viewing a culture as a whole. Both also emphasize the importance of analyzing similarities and differences among cultures. However, within a given culture major differences may exist. According to Nord (1976), subculture "provides the advantages of the concept of culture but allows the unit of social analysis to be smaller than the general society" (p. 205). Although many discussions about culture also apply to subcultures, we should consider some other dimensions along which we can distinguish subcultures. This can be done on the basis of a wide variety of factors, but we suggest the following as some of the most useful.

Age. The generation gap is a cross-cultural phenomenon; young people tend to share more closely the values and behaviors of other young people than of older people. Social scientists have attributed this gap to a variety of factors:

Box 2.4

A religious-type blunder occurred when a refrigerator manufacturer used a picture of a refrigerator containing a centrally placed chunk of ham. The typical refrigerator advertisement often features a refrigerator full of delicious food, and because these photos are difficult to take, the photos are generally used in as many places as possible. This company used its stock photo one place too many, though, when it was used in the Middle East where Moslems do not eat ham. Locals considered the ad to be insensitive and unappealing.

Source: D. A. Ricks, *Big Business Blunders*. Homewood, IL: Dow Jones–Irwin, 1983, p. 66.

technology, increased communication, and contemporary physical and psychological developments. Whatever the reasons, however, the implications for business may be profound because those in positions of authority will generally belong to the older subculture, and they must interact with the young subculture entering the organization.

Regionality. Members of regional subcultures (e.g., those from a rural rather than urban background) have been shown to exhibit different values. Dalton's study of high producers in industry (1971) suggested that "ratebusters" who were willing to violate group production norms were usually from rural backgrounds, whereas nonratebusters were more likely to come from urban backgrounds. In the United States, differences in values and attitudes are readily apparent between the Northeast, the South, the Midwest, and the West, but even in small countries differences are apparent—for example, between coastal people and mountain people.

Status. Most societies are stratified into a hierarchy of social groups based on caste, estate, or class (Terpstra, 1978). Each of these classes may have distinctive values, norms, and preferences that affect their behavior as members of an organization. In addition, a person's occupation in most countries is closely tied to social status, and both may be reinforced by the educational system. Thus, many countries have prestigious universities and schools that turn out professionals who are assured of high-level careers in government or industry.

Understandably, conflicts may arise when one subculture must interact regularly with another. In France, for example, graduates of the *grandes écoles* usually go into high-level government positions, and from there they may enter the ranks of a narrow class of top industrial managers. There, they have the task of dealing with middle managers, most of whom have been recruited from lesser institutions. The differences in social status and professional orientation often put these two groups at odds.

Most modern societies are divided along economic lines. The dividing lines mark off the familiar distinctions between the upper, middle, and lower classes. Economic variations appear to have a substantial impact on values and attitudes. For example, Rokeach (1973) found notable variations in the value profiles he developed when he considered economic status as an independent variable. These differences can influence the effectiveness of various organizational factors such as task design, leadership, or reinforcement.

Religion. Some societies contain different religious sects of varying sizes; others have essentially one religious group. Even in societies of limited religious diversity, however, there will likely be a number of minorities. Since religious training is a major aspect of the socialization process, it should not surprise us that various religious groups hold quite different values. Neither should it surprise us that such differences might affect their behavior. Terpstra (1978) suggests that religious heterogeneity within a nation may indicate a potential for strife and division. An example is the conflict between Hindus and Muslims that resulted in the establishment of two separate states—India and Pakistan—within the Indian subcontinent. Other examples are Lebanon and Ireland.

For the most part, organizations are nonsectarian and thus encompass many of the religious groups represented in any society, although some will claim that there is much "class" bias in the stratification. To avoid conflicts, however, managers must consider value differences among these groups and must also be alert to factors such as religious holidays, the role of religious institutions, and taboos or requirements for various groups. Every religion has holy days. These affect both consumption patterns and workers' behavior, and can thus have an important organizational impact. Where religion is important in a society, religious institutions will play a major role; organizations would do well to consider their impact. In Latin America, for example, the Catholic church has a major social role and in recent years has influenced social, political, and economic changes that could have a major impact on businesses.

A comprehensive description of cultural differences is desirable but not yet achievable. A few initial attempts have been offered, and Table 2.7 is offered as an example.

CULTURAL ASSESSMENT IN PRACTICE

In general, it appears that people are more favorably disposed toward those whose values resemble their own (Smith, 1957; Newcomb, 1963; Scott, 1965). This disposition has major implications for managers, because a favorable (or unfavorable) attitude between workers and managers, or between personnel from different cultures, can affect all aspects of a business.

Sitaram and Haapanen (1979) point out the tendency for people to regard their own values as superior to those of others. Lee (1966) sees this unconscious identity with one's own cultural values as the root of most international business problems. American organizations have long assumed that they are blameless in matters of chauvinism or nationalism; according to this view, others are the guilty party. However, members of most nationalities probably hold this view as well. For example, John Fayerweather (1959) traces the impasse between a Mexican and an American executive to conflicts in cultural attitudes, values, and objectives—all of which are deeply rooted in the two men's personalities.

Fortunately, value differences do not create an impenetrable barrier to understanding. Value differences can be overcome if people show a "tolerance

Table 2.7   Cultural Concerns for MNCs

1. The relationship between the central, regional and local governments, and particularly the capacity of the central government to have its policies carried out in various parts of the country.
2. Local or regional pressures for devolved political and/or administrative authority, with special reference to what these pressures might mean for the foreign investor.
3. The professionalism, technical capability, basic attitudes and values of national, regional and local public bureaucracies. In particular, how these matters help to describe the principal regulatory agencies with which the multinational will have to be involved on a regular or periodic basis.
4. The primary development goals of the host government; their degree of internal consistency; the amount of domestic controversy they engender; and the political and other organized groups favoring one set of priorities or another.
5. The nature and quality of the planning machinery of the central, regional or local governments, together with an assessment of their capacity to turn plans into legislation and legislation into actual practice.
6. Identification of sectors where the aspirations of indigenous governments and the activities—existing or planned—of the multinational affiliate might be made attractively complementary. By the same token, identification of those areas where corporate activities are not in harmony—or even conflict—with what is desired locally.
7. The basic attitudes and demands involving multinational corporate behavior held by the most significant groups in society, including those that do not wield power or influence today but may tomorrow.
8. Proposed policies and regulations affecting the foreign investor that may be in the pipeline, along with information regarding where and how—without violating local norms and corporate codes of conduct—the views of the multinational affiliate can be most effectively communicated.
9. Apparent misunderstandings, on either the corporate or host-country side, regarding failure to conform to expectations, and how these misunderstandings can be avoided in the first place and clarified and corrected when they occur.

Source: Multinational Corporations in Comparative Perspective Conference Board Report No. 725. New York, 1977.

for diversity'' (Scott, 1965). The lesson for comparative management is clear: understanding and accepting different values is essential to the success of any company that encounters different cultures.

In reviewing the actual practices among multinational corporations, however, La Palombara and Blank (1976) found few systematic approaches being used to gather noneconomic information. The major sources of information were old hands and wise men both inside and outside the firm: host-country nationals of political or social prominence; information brokers and lobbyists in host countries; government agencies and officials of the parent country; and public affairs and internal relations departments (see Table 2.8 for further details on each source.)

Table 2.8   Sources of Information on Host Countries

1. *Old hands and wise men inside the firm.* These are sometimes executives with extensive overseas experience. Their views about a given country may be of considerable value, provided they were based on indepth understanding in the first place, and provided the executive involved has kept current.

2. *Old hands and wise men outside the firm.* These would include bankers, businessmen, consultants and other persons whose presumed knowledge about host countries might be tapped.

3. *Host-country nationals of political or social prominence.* There is extensive, and possibly growing, use of such persons. In some instances, they serve as advisers, and are extensively used in this capacity in negotiations at the point of entry into the host country. Later such persons may become nonexecutive members of an affiliate's board. In Brazil and Nigeria, there are several figurehead presidents of foreign-based affiliates who represent but do not manage the firm. These persons are presumed to be highly knowledgeable about local politics. They are often well-connected and, therefore, able to open doors quickly when necessary—and generally are well able to represent the affiliate locally.

    There are obvious risks in this method. One is that the persons may themselves be heavily involved in host-country politics. Another is that they may, in fact, be working against the firm's primary interests, or have their own interests more in mind than the firm's.

4. *Information brokers and lobbyists in host countries.* During entry negotiations, lawyers are especially prominent in this category. Once a company is operational overseas, it may have recourse to individuals who know the political and administrative systems, can provide useful reports, and help the firm make contacts and representations and requests as occasions arise. By and large, corporate managers believe that these outsiders are of limited value and actually counterproductive in many settings.

5. *Governmental agencies and officials of parent country.* Both at home and in host countries government officials may be tapped for whatever expertise they possess about a host country. These same officials and agencies may be asked to be of assistance to the multinationals in a wide variety of ways, not all of them perhaps as well known or widely used as might be the case. Much depends here on the quality of governmental facilities and personnel at home and abroad, and on the relative capability of the multinational to conduct environmental analysis under its own power. There are quite notable differences in European and American propensities to utilize this resource.

6. *Public affairs and external relations departments.* A number of firms are clearly going considerably beyond earlier formats in which dealing with the environment was seen largely as *public relations.* The more directly operational sides of corporations tend to consider public relations units to be involved primarily in applying cosmetics to irritating disturbances from the outside. Public relations units have been expected to keep the outside world from interfering with management's more important task of getting on with business.

Source: Multinational Corporations in Comparative Perspective. Conference Board Report No. 725. New York, 1977.

Table 2.9 Critical Environmental Constraints

C_1: EDUCATIONAL–CULTURAL VARIABLES

$C_{1.1}$: Literacy level. The percentage of the total population and those presently employed in industry who can read, write, and do simple arithmetic calculations, and the average years of schooling of adults.

$C_{1.2}$: Specialized vocational and technical training and general secondary education. Extent, types, and quality of education and training of this kind not directly under the control or direction of industrial enterprises; the type, quantity, and quality of persons obtaining such education or training and the proportion of those employed in industry who have such education and training.

$C_{1.3}$: Higher education. The percentage of the total population and those employed in industry with post-high school education, plus the types and quality of such education; the types of persons obtaining higher education.

$C_{1.4}$: Special management development programs. The extent and quality of management development programs which are not run internally by productive enterprises and which are aimed at improving the skills and abilities of managers and/ or potential managers; the quantity and quality of managers and potential managers of different types and levels attending or having completed such programs.

$C_{1.5}$: Attitude toward education. The general or dominant cultural attitude toward education and the acquisition of knowledge, in terms of their presumed desirability; the general attitude toward different types of education.

$C_{1.6}$: Educational match with requirements. The extent and degree to which the types of formal education and training available in a given country fit the needs of productive enterprises on all levels of skill and achievement. This is essentially a summary category; depending on the type of job involved, different educational constraints indicated above would be more important.

C_2: SOCIOLOGICAL–CULTURAL VARIABLES

$C_{2.1}$: Attitude toward industrial managers and management. The general or dominant social attitude toward industrial and business managers of all sorts, and the way that such managers tend to view their managerial jobs.

$C_{2.2}$: View of authority and subordinates. The general or dominant cultural attitude toward authority and persons in subordinate positions, and the way that industrial managers tend to view their authority and their subordinates.

$C_{2.3}$: Interorganizational cooperation. Extent and degree to which business enterprises, government agencies, labor unions, educational institutions, and other relevant organizations cooperate with one another in ways conducive to industrial efficiency and general economic progress.

$C_{2.4}$: Attitude toward achievement and work. The general or dominant cultural attitude toward individual or collective achievement and productive work in industry.

$C_{2.5}$: Class structure and individual mobility. The extent of opportunities for social class and individual mobility, both vertical and horizontal, in a given country, and the means by which it can be achieved.

$C_{2.6}$: Attitude toward wealth and material gain. Whether or not the acquisition of wealth from different sources is generally considered socially desirable, and the way that persons employed in industry tend to view material gain.

$C_{2.7}$: Attitude toward scientific method. The general social and dominant individual attitude toward the use of rational, predictive techniques in solving various types of business, technical, economic and social problems.

$C_{2.8}$: Attitude toward risk taking. Whether or not the taking of various types of personal, collective, or national risks is generally considered acceptable, as well as the dominant view toward specific types of risk taking in business and industry;

Table 2.9 (*Continued*)

the degree and extent to which risk taking tends to be a rational process in a particular country.

$C_{2.9}$: Attitude toward change. The general cultural attitude toward social changes of all types which bear directly on industrial performance in a given country, and the dominant attitude among persons employed in industry toward all types of significant changes in enterprise operations.

Source: R. N. Farmer and B. M. Richman. *Comparative Management and Economic Progress.* Homewood, IL: Irwin, 1965, p. 29.

Based on their interviews with MNC managers, the researchers identified specific noneconomic environmental dimensions that are important to managers both at headquarters and in the field. They suggest that MNCs systematically analyze the following variables:

1. Relationships between central, regional, and local government.
2. Pressures for developed political authority.
3. Capabilities, attitudes, and values of public bureaucracies.
4. Developmental goals of the host government.
5. Government planning machinery.
6. Governing aspirations.
7. Societal demands on the MNC.
8. Proposed policies and regulation.
9. Areas of misunderstanding.

This list represents only a first assessment; it warrants considerable expansion. Nevertheless, it can help immensely to have answers—even if they are only tentative—to these questions in advance. This kind of information can help prevent surprises, misinterpretations, and overreactions. Farmer and Richman (1965) suggest that noneconomic environmental constraints, which they see as critical, fall into two broad categories: educational–cultural variables and sociological–cultural variables. They examine a variety of each type of variable, ranging from literacy levels to attitudes toward risk taking, that directly affect the MNCs. They also suggest ways of analyzing these variables (see Table 2.9).

The need for business to analyze cultural variables appears incontrovertible, particularly in the case of the MNC. In the past, the cultural aspect of the corporate environment has been neglected to a large degree. Today, however, this is changing. Although there are no well-developed, well-tested methods for conducting cultural analysis, social scientists have suggested different approaches. The use of these approaches, or some combination of them, is essential for effective functioning of any business.

As a final note, the value classification analysis prepared by Sitaram and Cogdell (1976) is presented in Table 2.10. It classifies various values according to their level of importance in different cultural groupings.

Table 2.10 Value Classification System

Value	Primary	Secondary	Tertiary	Negligible
Individuality	W	B	E	M
Motherhood	BE	MW	—	—
Hierarchy	WEMA	B	—	—
Masculinity	BMEWA	—	—	—
Gratefulness	EA	MB	W	—
Peace	E	B	WA	M
Money	WAB	M	E	—
Modesty	E	BAM	—	W
Punctuality	W	B	ME	A
Saviorism	W	M	—	EBA
Karma	E	—	—	MWBA
Firstness	W	B	—	EAM
Aggressiveness	WB	M	AE	—
Collective responsibility	EAM	B	—	W
Respect for elders	EAM	B	—	W
Respect for youth	W	MABE	—	—
Hospitality to guests	EA	B	MW	—
Inherited property	E	—	MWAB	—
Preservation of environment	E	BA	W	M
Color of skin	EWB	M	—	A
Sacredness of farm land	E	A	—	BMW
Equality of women	W	EB	A	M
Human dignity	WB	EAM	—	—
Efficiency	W	B	EM	—
Patriotism	BMAE	W	—	—
Religion	WBMAE	—	—	—
Authoritarianism	EMA	WB	—	—
Education	WB	EAM	—	—
Frankness	W	BEMA	—	—

Source: K. S. Sitaram and R. T. Cogdell, *Foundations of Intercultural Communication.* Columbus, OH: Merrill, 1976, p. 191. Used by permission.

Legend: W = Western cultures   E = Eastern cultures
B = Black cultures   A = African cultures
M = Muslim cultures

CONCLUSION

Culture is a vast subject—in some senses vast enough to encompass the entire human experience. No brief summary of culture can do justice to this subject. However, the preceding discussions have addressed the aspects of culture most crucial to our understanding of cross-cultural management issues today. We will consider other aspects and issues in succeeding chapters.

To summarize the salient points thus far: culture is essentially a people's way of life. Culture defines and expresses both attitudes and behavior. It provides continuity both through geographical space and over the passage of time. However, because cultures differ from place to place, and all people consider their own culture to be the most sensible, cultural disagreements and misunderstandings seem inevitable. At best, cultural differences can provide a marvelous sense of variety in how people choose to live. At worst, these differences can give rise to tremendous conflict. Cross-cultural managers must often deal with the consequences of many differences, but the ultimate result need not be traumatic either for the managers themselves or for their employees.

The social sciences cannot handily solve all cross-cultural problems. However, careful and thoughtful research can provide managers with a clearer sense of the problems they may face in dealing with other cultures; similarly, research can suggest possible solutions. Studies of values, attitudes, and work motivation, for example, can assist managers in determining how to accommodate workers most effectively and productively in a particular country. Studies can predict what aesthetic, ethical, or economic issues may influence a corporation's functions under specific circumstances. As the social sciences continue to develop, they will offer increasingly detailed information to cross-cultural managers.

For these reasons, we should now turn to an overview of cross-cultural research issues. Examining these issues will not only facilitate an understanding of later chapters but will provide further insights into cross-cultural management issues as well.

CHAPTER 3
Methodological Issues in Cross-Cultural Management

Cross-cultural methodology is currently receiving increased attention from researchers. Although methodological issues in the cross-cultural area have been widely discussed by researchers operating in the domains of political science (Ross & Homer, 1976), sociology (Bendix, 1969), anthropology (Naroll, 1968), and social psychology (Berry, 1979), theoretical and methodological reviews of comparative management research up to the early 1970s have been somewhat pessimistic in their conclusions (Roberts, 1970; Roberts & Snow, 1973; Triandis, 1972). Some recent developments, however, should make management researchers more sanguine in this regard. Bhagat and McQuaid (1982) and Sekaran and Martin (1982) have pointed out that the cross-cultural literature of the 1970s gives us reason for optimism concerning the future of research into organizational behavior. Recent international symposia and conferences in international management also attest to the importance of taking stock in the conceptual, theoretical, and methodological domains of cross-cultural research. The main challenge lies in the fact that even theoretically sound research projects are hampered by obstacles posed by methodological issues that make generalizations tenuous at best.

The importance of cross-cultural methodology is highlighted by researchers' greater willingness to perceive culture as a determinant of behavior. In a paper entitled "Culture, Contingency and Capitalism," Child (1981) concluded that while macro-level variables (organizational structure and technólogy) are tending to become more and more similar across various cultures, micro-level variables are tending to maintain their cultural distinctiveness. He argues that in this respect, culture is retaining its salience or importance as a determinant of behavior. Negandhi (1973) reached the same conclusion: he suggested that similarities may be explained in terms of industrialization, whereas differences may be explained in terms of cultural variables. Cross-cultural methodology is particularly important in terms of conceptualization, measurement, and interpretation of behavioral context. The importance of methodology does not stop there. Sorge (1982) and Jamieson (1980) have argued that there is no culture-free context of organizations; even if the various organizational solutions are similar, they are constructed in a cultural context and may be interpreted as a reaction to a given constraint.

The chapter will provide an overview of the various methodological problems arising in cross-cultural research. The emphasis will be primarily at a micro level—that is, the behavior of people in organizations across various cultures, as would occur in a multinational firm. We will also examine the problem of operationalizing culture and whether the nation or the culture should be the appropriate unit of analysis.

PROBLEMS OF DEFINING CULTURE

One of the fundamental problems in cross-cultural research is an inadequate definition of culture as a moderator. Goodman and Moore (1972) note that most studies fail to specify the role of culture as a moderator *exante* (i.e., in advance). The problem with this strategy is that there is no way to validate such post hoc explanations. For example, a researcher may test a specific hypothesis in several countries. In some countries, the hypothesis holds; in others, it does not. The researcher then uses the notion of culture to explain similarity or dissimilarity in results. But, in such a strategy, it is difficult to assess why and to what extent culture operates as a moderator. Goodman and Moore note that because culture is a complex multidimensional variable, its impact as a moderator tends to be ambiguous. To successfully demonstrate the role of culture, researchers must show which subcomponents of culture have the principal effects, which have no effect, and which lead to interactive effects.

Goodman and Moore cite a study by Zurcher (1965) to show how culture may be theoretically specified as a moderating variable. Zurcher had hypothesized that Mexican, Mexican American, and Anglo-American employees working in a similar financial organization will differ on particularism. The value orientation of particularism shows the influence of culture on an employee actor who must choose between duty toward a friend (particularism) and duty to an abstract society (universalism). The authors' hypothesis was that the impact of formal work organization will influence employee alienation differentially, depending on the amount of particularism found in the cultures. From a methodological perspective, Zurcher selected a particular dimension of culture, specified its form across five different societies, and related it to alienation from work. Because this study focused on a specific aspect of culture, it enhanced the potential for explanation and this prediction, as suggested by Goodman and Moore.

Operational specification is another important element. As variation in a culture is also likely, researchers should not only specify which element of culture moderates the relationship but also demonstrate the existence of variation in that element across two or more societies. One needs to operationalize the cultural dimension under consideration for both the research subjects and the modal population in the society. This enables us to see whether we are dealing with a select population or not.

The problem of adequately defining and measuring culture is one of the key challenges confronting cross-cultural methodology. It is a problem that has attracted considerable attention. Ajiferuke and Boddewyn (1970), for example, suggested that ''culture is one of those terms that defy a single all-purpose definition and there are almost as many meanings of culture as people using the term'' (p. 154). This statement suggests that culture, though used as an independent variable, has a rather obscure identity; it seems to be used as a residual variable. Negandhi (1983) also points out that the postulated relationship between culture and attitudes, attitudes and behavior, and behavior and organizational effectiveness raises a whole set of conceptual and methodological issues. According to Negandhi, many of these concepts are not well-defined and their operational measures are poor.

Kroeber and Kluckhohn's (1952, pp. 43–55) 164 definitions of culture are evidence of the confusion in the field. Negandhi (1983) suggests that Kluckhohn and Strodtbeck's (1961, p. 25) definition, which relies on the concept of value orientation, is useful for cross-cultural management research. The authors write, ''Value orientations are complex but definitely patterned (rank-ordered) principles, resulting from the transactional interplay of three analytically distinguishable elements of the evaluative process—the cognitive, the affective and the directive elements—which give order and direction to the ever flowing stream of human acts and thoughts as these relate to the solution of common human problem.'' As Negandhi (1983) points out this definition suggests a number of common human problems. These are (1) the character of innate human nature, (2) the relationship of humans to nature, (3) the temporal focus of human life, (4) the modality of human activity, and (5) the modality of an individual's relationship to others.

The basic idea is that limited variation is possible in the solution of these problems, resulting in a corresponding variation in society's value system. Table 3.1, which is also cited by Negandhi, shows the various value orientations and the range of variation associated with them.

Other definitions also exist in the literature. Triandis's definition (1972) is also useful: subjective culture is a group's characteristic way of responding to its social environment. Of particular interest, too, is Geertz's definition: ''Culture denotes an historically transmitted pattern of meanings embodied in symbols, a system of inherited conceptions expressed in symbolic forms by means of which men communicate, perpetuate and develop their knowledge about and attitudes towards life.'' The fact that many of these symbols are valued leads to

Table 3.1 The Five Value Orientations and the Range of Variations Postulated for Each

Orientation	Postulated Range of Variations					
	Evil		Neu-tral	Mixture of Good & Evil	Good	
Human nature	Muta-ble	Immuta-ble	Muta-ble	Immuta-ble	Muta-ble	Immuta-ble
Man–nature	Subjugation to nature		Harmony with nature		Mastery over nature	
Time	Past		Present		Future	
Activity	Being		Being-in-becoming		Doing	
Relational	Lineality		Collaterality		Individualism	

Source: F. R. Kluckhohn and F. Strodtbeck, *Variations in Value Orientations.* Westport, CT: Greenwood Press, 1961, p. 12.

ethnocentric thinking, especially on issues such as ideology, religion, morality, or law. Coming from differing cultural groups, people generally presume that what they do is appropriate, whereas members of other groups are irrational or unsophisticated, or both, in dealing with the same circumstances. Ethnocentrism may in turn lead to prejudice, which hinders effective cross-cultural interaction.

Although many of these definitions capture the essence of what culture is and how it influences behavior, many of these definitions—when perceived from a cross-cultural management perspective—are not precise enough to allow adequate operationalization of culture. Such precision may be attained when we consider the specific context of behavior under consideration. Different variables may be more or less important under varying circumstances. Triandis (1982; 1983) has broken down the dimensions of cultural differences into three categories: perceptual differentiations, utilization and evaluation of information, and patterns of action. The components of these dimensions appear in Table 3.2.

Triandis views cultural complexity as linked to pragmatism, situational use of many values, situational use of associative versus abstractive mental processes, and little sex differentiation. Many of these dimensions may also be linked with one another. We may view power distance, for example, as being linked with action patterns, with deference or superordination, depending on the status of actors and the target of action. Triandis demonstrates how the various managerial functions may be linked with the various dimensions of culture that he has identified. To the extent that this is true, such a dimension provides an important basis for conducting cross-cultural research.

Triandis notes, for example, that definition of goals is more likely in cultures that emphasize mastering the environment than in those that value subjugation. Planning is easier to facilitate in cultures in which there is an orientation toward

Table 3.2   Dimensions of Cultural Variation

PERCEPTUAL DIFFERENTIATIONS

1. What the other does vs. who the other is—focus on the family, ingroup, age, race, religion, tribe, or status of the other
2. Who is in the ingroup (professional group, tribe, nation, family, etc.)
3. Size of ingroup (small vs. large)
4. Ease of getting into ingroup

Emphasis on:

5. Age
6. Sex
7. Social class (power distance)

Self-concept:

8. High self-esteem
9. High power
10. High activity

UTILIZATION AND EVALUATION OF INFORMATION

11. Ideologism vs. pragmatism
12. Associative vs. abstractive communications; field dependent vs. field independent
13. Human nature is good vs. bad (ecosystem distrust)
14. Mastery over nature is good vs. subjugation to nature is good
15. Emphasis on past, present, future
16. Emphasis on doing, being, being-in-becoming
17. Individualism vs. collectivism (n-Ach vs. n-Aff, n-Ext) (absolute vs. situational ethics); individualism vs. conformism; familism
18. Uncertainty avoidance (tight vs. loose society)
19. Masculine–feminine goals

PATTERNS OF ACTION

20. Contact vs. no-contact (Dionysian vs. Appollonian)

Source: H. Triandis, "Dimensions of Cultural Variations as Parameters of Organizational Theories," *International Studies of Management and Organization.* 12(4):142–143, 1982–1983.

the future. Low power distance coupled with high uncertainty avoidance is likely to make planning effective. Triandis sees the selection, training, and controlling of people as being affected by age, sex, ingroup/outgroup status, and other factors. Controlling employees through criticism, for example, may be ineffective in cultures in which people have either a higher or low self-esteem. Triandis's typology is useful because it provides a good operational definition of culture. According to this definition cultures vary on the stated dimensions; accordingly cross-cultural differences may be explained in terms of the variables. (This typology thus resembles Goodman and Moore's.) We will now turn our attention to another important issue in cross-cultural analysis: should the nation or the culture be the unit of analysis?

NATION VERSUS CULTURE AS A UNIT OF ANALYSIS

In cross-cultural management research, this question is receiving increasing attention today. The general practice to date has been to use the nation-state as the unit of analysis (e.g., Haire, Ghiselli, & Porter, 1966; Granick, 1972; England, Dhingra, & Agarwal, 1974; England, 1978; Whitely & England, 1977; Sirota & Greenwood, 1971; Hofstede, 1980; Ronen & Kraut, 1977). This practice has come into increasing question lately, however; several authors have criticized it as potentially misleading (Roberts & Snow, 1973; Elder, 1976; Poortinga, 1977; Berry, 1979). The criticisms put forth by these researchers stem from Triandis's seminal work, which coined the term *subjective culture* and noted that differences in perception of the environment exist within a nation.

The notion that cultures and nations differ may also be seen on a more empirical level. There are several instances in which a culture has been divided into several nations (as in some African states); colonial powers arbitrarily drew national boundaries, so that there is little overlap between nation and culture. On the other hand, there is the case of a country like the Soviet Union, in which several cultures have been subsumed into a single political entity, thus encompassing great cultural diversity within a nation. The meanings of the concepts of "culture" and "nation" are also different. Webster, for example, defines a culture as "the customary beliefs, social forms and material traits of a group" and defines nation as "People inhabiting a country under the same government; an aggregation of persons of the same origin and language." A nation may contain several cultures, and a culture may be present in many nations. There is no reason that they should coincide. Hence, the appropriate unit of analysis should be the culture, not the nation.

Although these may be convincing reasons for separating these concepts, there are equally good reasons for merging them. Ronen and Punnett (1982) have recently addressed this issue. The authors argue that from a historical standpoint, nations are political expressions of cultural similarity. The early nations of Egypt and Greece were essentially defined by this similarity. Even today, when a nation consists of two or three cultures with little overriding or uniting values, it seems unlikely to survive. Either the nation breaks up into smaller units or, alternatively, a group imposes its culture on the rest. In nations with very diverse groups, the result has been more evolutionary, as different cultural groups become united on the basis of superordinate values. (An example of this phenomenon is the nationalism in many emerging nations of today.) These superordinate values bind the various groups together, stimulating the development of national culture.

Another argument supporting the notion of coincidence is that nation and culture have been defined in terms of similar variables. The variables associated with the nation are also the ones that are associated with cultures. Government, religion, language, geography, economy, education, and mass communication are some of the variables associated with both. Apart from these theoretical considerations, Ronen and Punnett also advance a number of practical reasons for the alleged coincidence. An important practical consideration derives from the fact that most multinational firms function in a nationalistic world. The implication is that the firm will use the nation-state in conducting its environmental analysis. More specifically, national laws, taxes, and tariffs, and differences among them across countries, will make firms adopt the nation as the unit of analysis. Exchange rates, interest rates, and credit availability are also determined to a large extent by national policy. Money supply and balance of payments surpluses or deficits are also under the control of local governments to some degree; thus, their decisions can have a major impact on these firm activities. Moreover, governments determine the size or length of investment permitted, and also have the power to nationalize or expropriate the company. For these reasons, the multinational firm should be viewed as being subservient to national sovereignty.

Human resource considerations also play an important part in determining a national focus. First, the organization's workforce is primarily national in nature. The majority of the corporation's employees come from the host country. Accordingly, the organization must design its system with the national makeup of the workforce as a major consideration. Legal requirements concerning minimum wages and benefits also vary from country to country. Of particular interest to the firm is workers' participation in management, as this represents varying degrees of loss of control for the parent. This varies from the self-management in Yugoslavia and Zambia to the codetermination in Germany and minority board participation in the European countries.

We may conclude by noting that because of largely national workforces and a nationally oriented legislation, pragmatically, the appropriate unit of analysis for the multinational corporation is the nation. There may be some justification for individual or group variation, but one should begin by analyzing national characteristics as a whole and then tailor organizational characteristics accordingly.

This discussion has delineated practical and theoretical considerations that make the nation an appropriate unit of analysis. We now turn to an overview of methodological problems encountered in cross-cultural and cross-national research from the perspective of experimental social psychology.

BENEFITS OF CROSS-CULTURAL RESEARCH

Cross-cultural research must be viewed more in terms of a methodology than as a content field. As suggested earlier, culture is an independent variable used to account for various dependent variables. To be maximally useful, cross-cultural research should follow a well-developed theory, with cultures selected on the basis of relevant theoretical variables rather than on the basis of expedience. This statement may represent more of a normative idea than a practical reality. Sekaran (1983) notes that cross-cultural research is time-consuming as well as expensive. Accordingly, she suggests that we should settle for less than ideal research designs. Instead of feeling undue concern about two-nation opportunistic studies, we should investigate ways of realizing maximum synergy.

Brislin (1983) has identified several advantages of cross-cultural research. Apart from enabling us to know how management practices differ across cultures and what specific cultural factors are responsible for such differences, this research can also help us realize what practices are culturally specific and which are culturally universal. In this way, we can develop a truly universalistic theory of management.

Among the advantages that Brislin identified are (1) an increase in the range of variables, (2) obtaining of different variables, (3) the unconfounding of variables, and (4) the opportunity to study the context in which behavior occurs.

A supposedly big advantage of cross-cultural research is that the range of independent variables is much wider, as are the responses. An implication of this is that a theory may have a better chance of support than if the range were not so wide. Aram and Piraino (1978), for example, found much greater support for Maslow's theory in Chile than is typical of research carried out in highly industrialized countries. In Chile, there is far less satisfaction of basic physiological and safety/security needs than in the United States. Considering a sample whose basic needs are unmet increases the range of the independent variables central to Maslow's theory.

It may also be possible to find variables in other cultures that are not found in countries where much empirical research has been done. For a multinational corporation, which has to function in many different cultures, knowledge of these variables is crucial. Hofstede's work (1980) represents a step in this direction. Similarly, the various elements identified by Triandis may have differential relevance in different cultures. Apart from finding variables in other cultures that are not obtained in the home country, the strength of the variables studied may also vary. This would also be helpful from a managerial perspective.

Another advantage is that it may be possible to untangle spurious relationships (i.e., appear to be related but are due to a common cause) and thus clarify confounded variables. Often, many variables occur together in one culture and hence are confounded in statistical analysis. In cross-cultural studies, it may be possible to disentangle this influence; thus, we can identify the variable responsible for the effect.

As suggested earlier, cultures vary in terms of the context within which behavior occurs. The context of behavior varies because values and attitudes differ across different cultures and because there are differences in economic, geographical, and other related factors. From a comparative management perspective, it is important to understand the context within which behavior occurs across different cultures. Knowledge of context is essential for devising an appropriate managerial policy. Brislin (1983) suggests that the study of context would be of greater advantage in other cultures, because researchers may be able to distance themselves from the cultures under scrutiny. Cross-cultural experiences, according to Brislin (1981), may lead to greater insights into the social contexts.

The potential advantages of this strategy are evident, but it is unclear whether or not the assessment of behavioral context can be achieved with the same degree of precision as the assessment of the behavior itself. Berry (1981) has tackled this problem. The context problem is most evident in the work of Whiting (1976), who describes it as that of the packaged variable. A packaged variable is an independent variable that is too global and diffuse to permit us to perform causal analysis. If culture is being specified as an independent variable, the question is *what* aspects of culture lead under *which* conditions to *what* kinds of behavior. Cole and his colleagues (1971; 1974), for example, have reviewed the context problem to specify precisely the situational context responsible for a given performance. Berry talks of an ecological context that provides a framework of human action and includes the various situations. Berry distinguishes between an individual's predisposition to behave in a particular way and his specific behavior as a function of the context that he finds himself in. The problem facing cross-cultural researchers is the difficulty in talking meaningfully about either behavioral dispositions or specific behaviors as functions of context when the only source of data is the experimental method. According to Berry, there has been insufficient concern with internal and external validity in the experimental methods. We will clarify these terms in the next section.

PROBLEMS OF INTERNAL AND EXTERNAL VALIDITY

One of the biggest problems in cross-cultural methodology is that of ensuring that the experimental results can be attributed to the operationalization of culture as an independent variable. Even in intracultural research, it is often difficult to ensure that variation. A good experimental design is one that can rule out various threats to the validity of an experiment.

We must be able to say not only that variation in a given variable causes changes in the other variable but also that results from the sample are generalizable to the population (i.e., to cultures as a whole). These two problems are called the problems of internal and external validity. An experiment must be internally valid before it can be externally valid. The discussion in this section will focus on the various threats to internal and external validity that may arise in the course of cross-cultural research. The factors that may affect the internal–external validity of an experiment are the following:

1. Emic versus etic distinction.
2. Problems of instrumentation—construction and validation.
3. Data collection techniques.
4. Sampling design issues.
5. Data analysis.
6. Problems of translation/stimulus equivalence.
7. Static group comparisons.
8. Lack of knowledge of others' way of seeing things.
9. Problems of resolving contradictory findings.
10. Administrative problems.

We will discuss each of these issues and its relevance from a cross-cultural perspective.

Emic Versus Etic Distinction

The emic versus etic distinction is by far one of the most frequently discussed issues in cross-cultural research. Whereas emics apply in only a particular culture, etics represent universality—they apply to all cultures in the world. The distinction between emics and etics can be best illustrated by the following comparison (Berry, 1980).

Emics	Etics
Studies behavior from within the system	Studies behavior from a position outside the system
Examines only one culture	Examines many cultures, comparing them
Structure discovered by the analyst	Structure created by the analyst
Criteria internal	Criteria considered absolute or universal

The objective of the emic approach is to see how the natives conceptualize the world. The etic approach, on the other hand, is distinguished by the presence of universality. The assumption of universality across cultures leads to the notion of an imposed etic, whereas a true etic is one that emerges from the given phenomena. The fundamental problem this distinction poses for us is our ability to describe behavior in terms that are meaningful to members of a given culture while retaining the ability to compare behavior in that culture with that in others. Malpass (1977) suggests a procedure by which the problem of conceptual equivalence, or emic–etic, can be dealt with. According to Malpass, one should explicitly state an abstract theory at the outset.

The abstract categories that then emerge do not supply the content of the research investigation. After these categories have been defined, one must operationalize the various categories in different cultures. The local contents of various categories should then be validated through reliability or internal consistency checks, or both. The use of emic and etic approaches is one to which anthropologists, too, have given a lot of attention. The importance of the emic approach has also been emphasized by researchers in the management field. In cross-cultural research, such emic approaches become even more important, because a shared frame of reference does not exist. The importance of the insider's viewpoint in organizations has been addressed by Weick (1979), who suggests the importance of studying cognitive variables in an attempt to understand the thinking patterns of people in organizations. Pfeffer (1981) also emphasizes the importance of cognitive approaches from the perspective of meaning. Morey and Luthans (1984) note that anthropologists use both etic and emic approaches, but as they move up the level, they become more etic in approach. This is similar to what Malpass has emphasized. Although an emic orientation would lead to an emphasis on qualitative research, such categories need to be recombined later for the purposes of nomothetic analysis and generalizations. Nomothetic analysis is one that uses quantitative methods to establish general laws. A detailed discussion of various research techniques used for emic research can be found in Morey and Luthans (1984).

Triandis and Martin (1983) note that a basic assumption in cross-cultural psychology has been that a "pseudoetic" approach must be avoided. A pseudoetic approach is one that assumes a dimension is etic when there is little evidence to support that assumption. In their study, Triandis and Martin tried to test whether or not an etic and emic approach yields better results than a pseudoetic one. The subjects tested were naval recruits of Anglo-European and Hispanic background. The study's results support the proposition that an etic and emic approach yields better results than a pseudoetic one. Interestingly, these authors found that even a pseudoetic approach was useful. This approach was able to identify more cultural differences than expected by chance. One implication of this study is that, instead of spending a great deal of time and money in developing instruments after pretesting, it may be better to use a pseudoetic approach.

This discussion has explored one of the most important issues in cross-cultural methodology. The distinction between emic and etic has considerable implications for measurement in cross-cultural research. Suppose we wish to measure aggressive behaviors in different cultures. What is viewed as aggressive behavior in one culture may not be so viewed in another. This, in a nutshell, describes the fundamental emic–etic dilemma.

Problems of Instrumentation

Sekaran (1983) has identified several types of equivalences, which should be considered in developing instruments to measure variables. Vocabulary equivalence, idiomatic equivalence, grammatical equivalence, and experimental equivalence are some of the important dimensions she identifies. Much of this equivalence may be ensured through good back-translation by people who have a facility with relevant languages and familiarity with relevant cultures. Although equivalence is important, one should not be so obsessed by it that we obliterate various cultural differences.

Scaling is another important aspect of instrument development that Sekaran identified. Barry (1969), for example, found that a five-point scale was more sensitive than a four-point scale. In a similar vein, Sekaran and Trafton (1978) and Sekaran and Martin (1982) found that a Job Characteristic Inventory had greater validity as a measure of job dimensionality in India than did the Job Diagnostic Survey, even though most of them used the same etics but with different scaling anchors. Some of the other biases that she identified include culturally sensitive topics (religion in Pakistan) and a courtesy or hospitality bias (whereby respondents give answers that may be pleasing to the researchers). This bias can be found in many Asian countries. Mitchell (1969) has also identified some other biases, such as underrating of achievement by the Japanese and exaggeration of achievement in some Middle Eastern countries. He also describes a so-called sucker bias in which all outsiders are viewed as fair game for deception.

The extent to which measures developed in the United States can be used elsewhere is also a matter of concern. Researchers are attempting to establish reliability and validity of measures. A measure is considered reliable if it is error-free; it is valid if it measures what it purports to measure. Sekaran and Martin (1982) sought to examine how well measures of individual differences, job, and organizational climate factors could transfer across cultures. Two hundred and sixty-seven bank employees in the United States and 307 similar employees in India completed a set of questionnaires. This study demonstrated that organizational climate measures were more reliable and related consistently to the criterion measures, whether within or across cultures. The authors conclude their discussion by noting that it may be possible to develop sound measures transferable across cultures. To the extent that this proves true, it will be a development for cross-cultural research.

Data Collection Techniques

Regarding data collection techniques, Sekaran identified four issues: response equivalence, timing of data collection in different cultures, status and other psychological issues, and cross-sectional versus longitudinal data collection. According to Sekaran, response equivalence could be ensured by adopting a set of uniform data collection procedures in all the cultures in which researchers are investigating a particular problem. She also observes that the timing of data collection in different countries is important as well. If too much time elapses, it may affect the comparability of data. Moreover, in societies with sharp status and authority cleavages, Western interviewing techniques may not be appropriate.

A critique of much cross-cultural research is that researchers view organizations statistically; accordingly they collect only cross-sectional data. Recent researchers such as Hofstede (1981) and Sekaran (1977; 1981b) have observed this criterion and are making amends for it. Furthermore, Heller (1969) notes that whether or not cultural effects are found depends on the format of the question. He suggests that broad questions that do not deal with specific behavior are the ones that predominate in studies showing cultural differences. Heller also notes that Haire and associates' study (1966), uses fairly broad questions. In his opinion, a broad question format may produce responses derived from the group's collective unconscious or from the group members' early upbringing and family-derived values. In data gathering, one should also guard against the effects that may emerge from the researcher's own cultural biases. Triandis (1972) suggests that a way out of this quandary may be achieved by the employment of multicultural research teams.

Sampling Issues

Sampling issues are also important from the perspective of cross-cultural research. The problems in this area stem from the number of cultures included, the choice between representative and matched samples, and whether or not the cultures included in the sample are independent. Brislin and co-workers suggest that the number of cultures selected should be sufficient to rule out alternative explanations and should also be sufficient to make variance random on nonmatched variables. Sekaran suggests that studies characterized by an insufficient number of samples should be viewed primarily as pilot studies. A decade ago, Kraut (1975) had already pointed out the progress that had been made in such studies included many more cultures than comparable studies a decade or two earlier.

A critical problem in cross-cultural research is the ability to select representative samples. This is often difficult because it is unclear which subjects best represent the nation's central tendencies. As a second best alternative, Sekaran (1983) proposes the use of matched samples. Matched samples are functionally equivalent but are not identical across various cultures. A further problem in this regard arises as the samples selected may not be independent. This is often referred to as Galton's problem. The problem arises because different cultures may adopt similar practices because of cultural diffusion. This would violate the condition of sample independence. We can minimize the problem if we select for study geographically dispersed cultures. However, in a highly interdependent, industrialized world, it may be difficult to select samples that are culturally, politically, and geographically independent. To that extent, comparative management researchers should be aware of the potential bias when they interpret their results.

Data Analysis

Since the 1960s there has been a movement toward a greater quantitative trend in cross-cultural research. Prior to the 1960s, the principal tool used in data analysis was the bivariate correlation. Such a simplistic technique could often lead us to spurious relationships among variables. In 1969, Boddewyn commented that many of the comparative management/marketing studies lacked analytical rigor. Since then, significant progress has been made in that multiple regression and multivariate techniques are in common use now. Also in common use are cluster analysis by Ajiferuke and Boddewyn (1970), factor analysis by Hofstede (1980), componential analysis by Tzeng and Osgood (1976), and multidimensional scaling by Raveed and Sekaran (1979). Apart from the ability to use significance tests, which are highly sensitive, quantification has helped the researchers to map the perceptions and cognitive schema of people in different cultures. This trend can only benefit comparative management research; but with greater theoretical precision, the benefits could increase further.

Box 3.1

Several brief examples of mistranslated English idioms or expressions can be cited to illustrate how often blunders have been made. One European firm certainly missed the point when it translated the expression "out of sight, out of mind" as "invisible things are insane" in Thailand. There is also the story of the phrase "the spirit is willing, but the flesh is weak" being translated to "the liquor is holding out all right, but the meat has spoiled." And consider, finally, a translation of "Schweppes Tonic Water" to the Italian "il water." The copy was speedily dehydrated to "Schweppes Tonica" because "il water" idiomatically indicates a bathroom.

Source: D. A. Ricks, *Big Business Blunders.* Homewood, IL: Dow Jones–Irwin, 1983, p. 86.

Problems of Translation and Stimulus Equivalence

Translation is yet another stumbling block in much cross-cultural research. The language used should be equivalent across cultures rather than identical in any literal sense. Plain and simple sentences are preferable. There is considerable debate about the extent to which language determines our thought processes (Whorf, 1956). In French, for example, there appears to be no word for achievement, whereas in Japanese there seems to be no word for decision making (Adler, 1982).

Researchers can employ four basic translation methods: (1) back translation, (2) bilingual technique, (3) the committee approach, and (4) pretest procedures (Brislin, 1980). The process of back translation involves translating research material back into the original language. An advantage of this technique is that it helps to provide literal accuracy. The second procedure involves bilingual assistants taking the same test or different halves of a test that they know. The items that lead to discrepant conclusions can be found fairly easily. In the committee approach, a group of bilinguals work together to translate from a source to a target language. The advantage of this procedure is that any particular individual's error can be caught by another group member. The pretest method, on the other hand, involves field testing the translation after completion to see if people comprehend all the material. Theoretically, each of these methods can yield conceptual equivalence.

Static Group Comparisons

From an experimental standpoint, one of the biggest problems in cross-cultural research is that most cross-cultural comparisons are essentially "static group comparisons." In other words, it is not possible to assign subjects randomly to different levels of a treatment variable, and the treatment variable is unclear. Malpass (1977) notes that this specification of culture as a treatment variable is not satisfactory because any other variable correlated with culture could help explain mean differences between two or more populations. To counteract this problem, Malpass suggests that we should try to obtain data on as many rival explanations as possible, and then demonstrate that they are less plausible than the ideal one. He suggests that most investigators fail to recognize that it is important to support one's favored interpretations of cultural difference in relation to other alternative explanations. He cites the work of Whiting and Child (1953), which attempted to cope with rival explanations. Malpass also refers to the work of Naroll (1962) on data quality control and on Galton's problem (Naroll, 1970) as examples of research giving attention to testing alternative explanations. The inability to assign people randomly to different levels of a treatment variable is one of the chief threats to the internal validity of an experiment.

Brown and Sechrest (1980) have also identified several other threats to internal validity. In experimental social psychological research, the use of a control group is common. A control group is one that is not exposed to the treatment variable whose influence is being tested. To the extent that there are differences between the control group and the treatment group, we can be confident that our independent variable has had an impact. Threat to internal validity may arise if some changes occur in the control group. If the control group learns that another group is getting a treatment, if knowledge about treatment becomes diffused, or if a compensatory equalization of treatment occurs in the control group, the internal validity of an experiment is threatened. Even when none of these problems exists, internal validity may still be in jeopardy if the direction of causal influence is uncertain. Problems may also arise as a result of confounding variables emanating from local history or when cultural hypotheses are tested, if treatment has not been applied at an equal strength in all cultures.

Lack of Knowledge of Others' Way of Seeing Things

Another fundamental methodological problem that Malpass identifies is the lack of knowledge of others' viewpoints. If people from different cultures view objects and events differently from the investigator, the investigator will not be able to manipulate the stimulus in a meaningful way for them, and he or she will not be able to attribute differences in their behavior to variations in the stimulus. Campbell (1964) has appropriately noted that differences among people can be interpreted only against a background of similarity. If the differences between the subject and the investigator are great, and if the extent of differences is unknown, the differences in data may not be interpretable. There may be a number of alternative explanations for such differences—differences we are unaware of. Subjects tend to present themselves in a socially desirable way

Box 3.2

A U.S. company was taken by surprise when it introduced its product in Latin America and learned that the name of the product meant "jackass oil" in Spanish. Another well-intentioned firm sold shampoo in Brazil under the name "Evitol." Little did it realize that it was claiming to be selling a "dandruff contraceptive." A manufacturing company sold its machines in the Soviet Union under the name "Bardak"—a word which signifies a brothel in Russian. An American product failed to capture the Swedish market; the product name translated to "enema," which the product was not. A Finnish brewery introduced two new beverages in the United States—"Koff" beer and "Siff" beer. Is it any wonder that sales were sluggish? Another name, unappealing to Americans, can be found on the package of a delicious chocolate and fruit product sold in the German or European deli. The chocolate concoction has the undesirable English name "Zit!"

Of course not all companies have been forced to change names. In fact, some of them have traveled quite well. Kodak may be the most famous example. A research team deliberately "developed" this name after carefully searching for a word which was pronounceable everywhere but had no specific meaning anywhere. Exxon is another such name which was reportedly accepted only after a lengthy and expensive computer-assisted search.

Source: D. A. Ricks, *Big Business Blunders.* Homewood, IL: Dow Jones–Irwin, 1983, pp. 40–41, 46.

and want to please the experimenter, and these tendencies often make differences hard to interpret. Malpass (1977) suggests several ways to overcome this problem. One can accept the help of a colleague who comes from the host country culture, design a task so that subjects' responses are fairly clear, or develop a theory about which aspects of subjects' world views threaten the experiment's validity. What Malpass suggests is to determine the utility of alternative acts for the subject; once such utilities are known, one can more easily eliminate many of the confounding factors in the research.

Problems of Resolving Contradictory Findings

Elder (1976) notes that when cross-national research leads to contradictory findings, the latter should be discarded. He believes that these contradictions arise simply as a consequence of differences in language patterns. Such differences may cause distortions, thus leading subjects to respond to different stimuli. If researchers find contradictions even within an identical set of people, these contradictions may be attributed to irrationality, evasiveness, or acquiescence. Before accepting these explanations, Elder suggests that researchers consider the possibility that contradictions exist in their own perceptions, not in the respondents'.

Administrative Problems

Psychological research is often intrusive. Research procedures often tend to affect the phenomena under scrutiny. Accordingly, an important aspect of cross-cultural studies is that the influence of the research across subjects be uniform across cultures. Administrative equivalence would entail an equivalence in subjects' responses to (1) the introduction of study, (2) introduction to the researcher, (3) task instructions, (4) closing remarks, and (5) research setting. Equivalence of response may be ensured if subjects are equally familiar with test instruments, format, and social situation; if they have similar levels of anxiety; and if the experiment's effect is equivalent across the cultures being studied. According to Adler (1982), demand characteristics—the subject's attempt to find out the researcher's hypothesis and to help or hinder the research process—vary across cultures. It is, therefore, imperative that the samples be either matched or controlled. Demand characteristics may be a consequence of either differential sensitivity to a research topic or a courtesy bias.

Considering these issues, should culturally similar or different people administer the study in each culture? In authoritarian cultures, subjects may respond better to people who have a higher status; where participation is widely hailed, subjects may prefer an administrator who has status similar to theirs. Adler and Kiggundu (1983) note that in developing countries, people may respond better to research administrators who come from developed countries than administrators from their own or other countries. Adler suggests that if the subjects' responses to the administrator, research, and setting are not clear, it may be preferable to use multiple administrative approaches. The advantage of this method is that we know which aspects of responses are a function of experimental variables and which represent an interactive effect between the administrative process and cultural variables.

In this section, we have surveyed some of the fundamental problems that plague cross-cultural research and how such problems can greatly affect the interpretation of data. Pointers for overcoming some of these problems are offered in Table 3.3. Although we know intuitively that cultural differences exist, methodological problems often prevent us from drawing firm conclusions about them. We will now review the trends in cross-cultural management research and examine the directions and implications of these trends.

TRENDS IN CROSS-CULTURAL RESEARCH

Nancy Adler (1982) has identified six alternative approaches to doing research in the cross-cultural area. The approaches differ in what issues they address, the assumptions they make about universality, and how they deal with similarities and differences. The six approaches are parochial, ethnocentric, polycentric, comparative management, geocentric, and synergistic studies. Table 3.4 describes the various studies and the kind of issues that they address.

The parochial approach deals with research conducted in a particular culture by members of that culture. The United States has reportedly produced the most parochial studies. Adler (1983) found during the period 1971–1980 that 80% of over 11,000 articles published in twenty-four management journals were studies of the United States conducted by Americans. A basic assumption implicit in these studies is that their results are universal. According to Adler, culture is viewed as neither an independent nor a dependent variable. Barrett and Bass (1976) observe, for example, that research confining itself to a particular cultural context is constrained by theory as well as practice.

The ethnocentric approach involves replicating in one culture a study already conducted in another. The primary research question addressed in these studies is whether a theory applicable in culture A can be extended to culture B. Such research seeks to demonstrate the universality of results and theories. Replication is probably the most common approach to this sort of research. In this form of research, similar findings are viewed as confirming as universal the theory being tested. One possible fallacy in such an interpretation, however, stems from the fact that a sample of two cultures is probably insufficient to demonstrate universality. Adler points out that it would be more appropriate to consider results as either not dependent on cultural factors or, alternatively, applicable to the second culture. The primary objective of such studies is to extend the universality of a particular set of results; consequently, any differences show a defect in experimental design. A central problem in this type of research is its failure to consider whether the results are important in the second culture.

Polycentric studies, on the other hand, try to explain management and organizational practices in specific foreign cultures. They are essentially individual domestic studies carried out in various countries. The implicit assumption is that institutions can be best interpreted in terms of their own culture. Such

Table 3.3 Methodological Issues in Comparative Management Research

Methodological Issue	Description
Sampling	Sampling issues involve size of sample, selection of cultures, representative versus matched samples, and the independence of samples: *Size of sample.* The number of cultures selected should be large enough to —Randomize variance on nonmatched variables —Eliminate rival hypotheses Studies with insufficient numbers of cultures (i.e., 2 or 3) should be treated as pilot studies *Selection of cultures.* The selection of cultures should be based on theoretical dimensions of the research, not on the opportunistic availability of access to particular cultures *Representative versus matched samples.* Is the research goal to have samples that are representative of each culture or is it to have matched samples that are equivalent on key theoretical dimensions across cultures? Matched samples should be functionally, not literally, equivalent *Independence of samples.* Given the interrelatedness of the industrialized world, culturally, politically, and geographically independent samples in management research are generally neither feasible nor desirable
Translation	*Equivalence of language.* The language used in each version of the research—instrumentation and administration—should be equivalent across cultures, not literally identical *Wording.* The wording of items and instructions should —Use a common vocabulary (e.g., high-frequency words) —Avoid idiomatic expressions —Use equivalent grammar and syntax —Use plain, short sentences —Include redundancy *Method of translation.* Recognizing the Whorfian hypothesis, the translation technique should aim at equivalence, not at literal translations *Whorfian hypothesis.* Different cultural and linguistic backgrounds lead to different ways of perceiving the world. Unless their linguistic backgrounds are similar or can be calibrated, people who speak 2 different languages will not perceive the world in the same way *Translation techniques.* To achieve equivalent translations, the material should be —Back translated. Translated and then back translated into the original language using a good bilingual target population, or —Translated by an expert. Translated independently by excellent bilingual translators who are (1) familiar with the linguistic and cultural backgrounds in both cultures, (2) familiar with the subject matter of the research, and (3) translating into his or her native language
Measurement and instrumentation	*Equivalence of instrumentation.* Are the test items, scaling, instrumentation and experimental manipulations equivalent across cultures?

Table 3.3 (*Continued*)

Methodological Issue	Description
	Equivalent variables. Across cultures, are the items or measures conceptually equivalent, equally reliable and equally valid? Have indigenous measures been created to operationalize conceptually equivalent variables? Are variables based on equally salient conceptual dimensions?
	Equivalent scaling. Differences in means are uninterpretable unless measured on equivalent scales that have been developed individually in each culture —Equivalent procedures. Researcher must use the same or equivalent procedures in each culture to develop scales, or —Similar patterns of correlations. Items must have similar patterns of correlations within each culture
	Equivalence of language. See translation above
	Equivalence of experimental manipulations. Interaction between experimental and cultural variables can confound interpretation. Therefore, experimental manipulations must be equivalent across cultures
Administration	*Equivalence of administration.* The research settings, instructions, and timing should be equivalent, not identical, across cultures
	Equivalence of response. Given that observation changes that which is observed (Heisenberg effect), the influence of the research on the subjects should be equivalent across cultures. The research should be designed and administered in such a way that the responses to the stimuli and to the situation are similar across cultures on such dimensions as
	Familiarity. Subject should have equal familiarity with test instruments, format, and the social situation of the research
	Psychological response. Subjects should have similar levels of anxiety and other psychological responses in the test situation
	Experimenter effect. The extent to which the researchers communicate their preferred hypotheses to subjects—both verbally and nonverbally—should be equivalent across cultures
	Demand characteristics. The extent to which subjects attempt to discover the researcher's hypotheses and thereafter attempt to help (usually) or hinder the research varies across cultures based on such things as (1) sensitivity to various topics (sex, religion, politics) and (2) the courtesy bias
	Characteristics of the person conducting the research. Depending on the culture, there can be a difference in response (respectfulness, indifference, hostility) to such characteristics of the research administrator as —Gender —Race —Origin: from an economically developed or developing country —Status relative to subjects: high versus low —Foreigner versus citizen

Continued on page 58

Table 3.3 (*Continued*)

Methodological Issue	Description
	Characteristics of the presentation. The response of the subjects can vary in reaction to the —Introduction of the research —Introduction and characteristics of the presenter —Task instructions —Closing remarks —Timing of the presentation and data collection —Setting of the presentation and data collection The goal in comparative management research is to have the administration and experimental conditions equivalent, not standardized in each culture. The approach to conducting the research may be identical, but the ways in which it is operationalized will vary from culture to culture

Source: Adapted and abbreviated from N. Adler, ''Understanding the Ways of Understanding: Cross Cultural Management Methodology,'' in R. N. Farmer, ed., *International Comparative Management,* JAI Press, 1984;N. J. Adler, *Journal of International Business Studies,* Fall 1983, pp. 38, 39.

studies attempt to produce theories applicable to the culture in question. The emphasis is cultural uniqueness. According to this approach, there is no one best way of doing things. The approach is essentially anthropological. The research approach is inductive rather than deductive and emphasizes specific descriptions of a particular situation—the individuality and the uniqueness of circumstances in that culture. There are potential problems here, however. These are descriptive rather than evaluative studies. Most management researchers do not accept the assumption that one way is no better than any other way.

Comparative studies are those that try to determine similarities and differences across two or more cultures. These studies try to identify some sort of universality. The emergent similarity is referred to as the universality. A basic assumption here is that a dominant culture does not exist. In such studies, the balance between culture-specific and culture-general features is something that comes out of research; it does not constitute an assumption.

Geocentric studies, on the other hand, deal with the management of multinational firms (i.e., those firms that operate in more than one country). This research implicitly tries to search for similarity across cultures. The assumption is that there are universally effective approaches in organizing and managing business. Miller observes that much traditional international business research falls into this category. According to Adler, this type of approach assumes cross-cultural universality and does not question the validity of this assumption. Noncultural variables are the primary independent variables of the study.

Last, synergistic studies try to understand the patterns of relationships that develop when people from different cultures interact in a work setting. The objective is to determine laws underlying interaction. Synergistic studies differ from other studies in a number of ways. To begin with, these studies emphasize interaction. Although the research strategies discussed earlier were concerned with determining natural patterns of organization and management, synergistic studies focus on creating such patterns. Earlier studies focused on understanding similarities and differences; however, the emphasis of synergistic research is on determining an optimum balance between culture-specific and culture-general patterns of management. Action research with which this research is concerned tries to create new solutions to existing problems. In other words, research is undertaken with the purpose of improving the effectiveness of the organizations. Another advantage of synergistic study is that it focuses on the interaction itself. Cross-cultural interaction is crucially relevant for a headquarters executive who must interact with managers from all over the world. Adler notes that few studies have addressed cross-cultural interaction in an organizational setting.

Although there has been some progress in the field—as exemplified by larger samples, use of multicultural teams, and better research designs—Adler finds that articles published in American management journals have not kept pace with the internationalization of corporate activity. Adler's 1983 survey of American management journals notes that the majority of articles published are noncultural. Of the articles emphasizing culture, the majority contain only studies of a single foreign culture or else try to compare two cultures' organizational practices. Cross-cultural studies—especially those focusing on interaction—are badly needed, yet many problems impede such research. These problems arise from lack of sufficient funding and from the methodological complexity referred to earlier. Many studies in this area cannot meet the rigor required of domestic studies.

Another research typology categorizing the level at which culture operates is that developed by Sechrest (1977). He identifies three kinds of cross-cultural organizational research.

The first kind of research seeks to examine the overall impact of culture on organizational behavior. An example of this kind of research is the study that documents the impact of culture on an organizational control system. In type II studies, the primary emphasis is on understanding what specific aspects of culture are responsible for the effects. The focus is on studying fundamental psychological processes. Type III studies, by contrast, are anthropologically oriented research whose objective is primarily to study culture per se rather than understand its impact on the dependent variable.

Sechrest observes that most of the studies conducted to date are of the type II variety. Type I studies, which seek to document the global importance of culture, are vulnerable to alternative hypotheses that reflect operations of either genetic, geographic, or ecological factors. Type II studies may also be hampered by alternative hypotheses that reflect the confounding effects of theoretical variables. These studies enable us to obtain knowledge about specific social systems but do not enhance our comparative understanding of

Table 3.4 Types of Cross-Cultural Management Research

Title	Culture	Approach to Similarity and Difference	Approach to Universality	Type of Study	Primary Question	Main Methodological Issues
Parochial research	Single culture studies	Assumed similarity	Assumed universality	Domestic management studies	What is the behavior of people like in work organizations? Study is only applicable to management in one culture and yet it is assumed to be applicable to management in many cultures	*Traditional methodologies.* All of the traditional methodological issues concerning design, sampling, instrumentation, analysis, and interpretation without reference to culture
Ethnocentric research	Second culture studies	Search for similarity	Questioned universality	Replication in foreign cultures of domestic management studies	Can we use home country theories abroad? Can this theory which is applicable to organizations in culture A be extended to organizations in culture B?	*Standardization and translation.* How can management research be standardized across cultures? How can instruments be literally translated? Replication should be identical to original study with the exception of language
Polycentric research	Studies in many cultures	Search for difference	Denied universality	Individual studies of organizations in specific foreign cultures	How do managers manage and employees behave in country X? What is the pattern of organizational relationships in country X?	*Description.* How can country X's organizations be studied without either using home country theories or models and without using obtrusive measures? Focus is on inductive methods and unobtrusive measures.
Comparative research	Studies contrasting many cultures	Search for both similarity and difference	Emergent universality	Studies comparing organizations in many foreign cultures	How are the management and employee styles similar and different across cultures? Which theories hold across cultures and which do not?	*Equivalence.* Is the methodology equivalent at each stage in the research process? Are the meanings of key concepts defined equivalently? Has the research been designed such that the samples, instrumentation, administration, analysis, and interpretation are equivalent with reference to the cultures included?

| Geocentric research | International management studies | Search for similarity | Extended universality | Studies of multinational organizations | How do multinational organizations function? | *Geographic dispersion.* All of the traditional methodological questions are relevant with the added complexity of geographical distance. Translation is often less of a problem since most MNOs have a common language across all countries in which they operate. The primary question is to develop an approach for studying the complexity of a large organization. Culture is frequently ignored |
| Synergistic research | Intercultural management studies | Use of similarities and differences as a resource | Created universality | Studies of intercultural interaction within work settings | How can the intercultural interaction within a domestic or international organization be managed? How can organizations create structures and processes that will be effective in working with members of all cultures? | *Interaction models and integrating processes.* What are effective ways to study cross-cultural interaction within organizational settings? How can universal and culturally specific patterns of management be distinguished? What is the appropriate balance between culturally specific and universal processes within one organization? How can the proactive use of cultural differences to create universally accepted organizational patterns be studied? |

Source: Adapted and abbreviated from N. Adler, ''Understanding the Ways of Understanding: Cross Cultural Management Methodology,'' in R. N. Farmer, ed., *International Comparative Management.* JAI Press, 1984; N. J. Adler, *Journal of International Business Studies,* Fall 1983, pp. 30, 31.

cultures. Bhagat and McQuaid (1982) note that it would be best to conduct type I research initially; this would allow us to make a general assessment of the global aspects of culture. Afterwards, we should proceed with type III studies, so that we can see what specific cultural features are important in relation to the dependent variables. Type II studies may be done next to show the importance of specific cultural variables on the pertinent dependent variables.

In order to do studies of this nature, we must be strongly committed to developing a theory (as emphasized earlier), and we must adopt suitable methodological strategies.

CONCLUSIONS

This survey has attempted to review the field of cross-cultural management research. It has identified the various problem areas and the various steps being taken to address them. One of the critical problems is that of defining culture. Lammers and Hickson prefer the term *cross-societal* because the term *culture* is ambiguous. Furthermore, they note that many cross-societal studies offer little more than educated guesses concerning the relative importance of contextual or cultural influences. They do observe, however, that Hofstede's work represents an advance. To separate the culture from contextual variables surrounding it would require an intimate knowledge of the country. The recent research trend toward mapping people's perceptions and cognition should aid us in this effort.

In conclusion, we should evaluate researchers' opinions of the issues warranting attention in the future. Karlene Roberts of Berkeley has surveyed researchers (primarily in the United States and United Kingdom, but in other countries as well). Most researchers have felt that organizational design and structure should receive the greatest priority. Motivation came second. Other issues singled out are the influences of culture on life in organizations, decision making, and communication and personnel issues.

Regarding the basic disciplines that contribute to research in this area, psychology got 33 nominations; anthropology, 32; economics, 31; sociology, 30; and political science, 29. Psychology received strong support because it focuses on cognitive/emotional processes that lie at the heart of cross-cultural interaction. The survey also revealed that different issues have priority in different countries. Thus, in the United States, macro-issues (power, structure, decision making) and micro-issues (motivation, leadership, job satisfaction) appear to be equally important. In the United Kingdom, there is more emphasis on macro-issues and on radical Marxist positions. Canada typically follows trends in the United States.

Cross-cultural issues are clearly receiving increased attention today. This is only appropriate, as interdependence is also increasing. Although many issues, both theoretical and methodological, remain to be investigated, significant progress appears to have occurred. We can thus be optimistic about further research in this area.

CASES FOR PART I

Case A: The Road to Hell . . .

John Baker, Chief Engineer of the Caribbean Bauxite Company of Barracania in the West Indies, was making his final preparations to leave the island. His promotion to production manager of Keso Mining Corporation near Winnipeg—one of Continental Ore's fast-expanding Canadian enterprises—had been announced a month before and now everything had been tidied up except the last vital interview with his successor, the able young Barracanian, Matthew Rennalls. It was vital that this interview be a success and that Baker should leave his office uplifted and encouraged to face the challenge of his new job. A touch on the bell would have brought Rennalls walking into the room but Baker delayed the moment and gazed thoughtfully through the window considering just exactly what he was going to say and, more particularly, how he was going to say it.

John Baker, an English expatriate, was forty-five years old and had served his twenty-three years with Continental Ore in many different places: in the Far East; several countries of Africa; Europe; and, for the last two years, in the West Indies. He hadn't cared much for his previous assignment in Hamburg and was delighted when the West Indian appointment came through. Climate was not the only attraction. Baker had always preferred working overseas (in what were termed the developing countries) because he felt he had an innate knack—better than most other expatriates working for Continental Ore—of knowing just how to get on with regional staff. Twenty-four hours in Bar-

racania, however, soon made him realize that he would need all of this "innate knack" if he was to deal effectively with the problems in this field that now awaited him.

At his first interview with Hutchins, the production manager, the whole problem of Rennalls and his future was discussed. There and then it was made quite clear to Baker that one of his most important tasks would be the "grooming" of Rennalls as his successor. Hutchins had pointed out that, not only was Rennalls one of the brightest Barracanian prospects on the staff of Caribbean Bauxite—at London University he had taken first-class honors in the B.Sc. Engineering Degree—but, being the son of the Minister of Finance and Economic Planning, he also had no small political pull.

The company had been particularly pleased when Rennalls decided to work for them rather than for the government in which his father had such a prominent post. They ascribed his action to the effect of their vigorous and liberal regionalization program which, since the Second World War, had produced eighteen Barracanians at mid management level and given Caribbean Bauxite a good lead in this respect over all other international concerns operating in Barracania. The success of this timely regionalization policy has led to excellent relations with the government—a relationship that had been given an added importance when Barracania, three years later, became independent, an occasion which encouraged a critical and challenging attitude toward the role foreign interests would have to play in the new Barracania. Hutchins had therefore little difficulty in convincing Baker that the successful career development of Rennalls was of the first importance.

The interview with Hutchins was now two years old and Baker, leaning back in his office

Source: This case was prepared by Mr. Gareth Evans for Shell–BP Petroleum Development Company of Nigeria, Limited, as a basis for class discussion in an executive training program. Distributed by the Intercollegiate Case Clearing House, Soldiers Field, Boston, MA 02163. All rights reserved to the contributors. Printed in the U.S.A.

chair, reviewed just how successful he had been in the "grooming" of Rennalls. What aspects of the latter's character had helped and what had hindered? What about his own personality? How had that helped or hindered? The first item to go on the credit side would, without question, be the ability of Rennalls to master the technical aspects of his job. From the start he had shown keenness and enthusiasm and had often impressed Baker with his ability in tackling new assignments and the constructive comments he invariably made in departmental discussions. He was popular with all ranks of Barracanian staff and had an ease of manner which stood him in good stead when dealing with his expatriate seniors. These were all assets, but what about the debit side?

First and foremost, there was his racial consciousness. His four years at London University had accentuated this feeling and made him sensitive to any sign of condescension on the part of expatriates. It may have been to give expression to this sentiment that, as soon as he returned home from London, he threw himself into politics on behalf of the United Action Party who were later to win the preindependence elections and provide the country with its first Prime Minister.

The ambitions of Rennalls—and he certainly was ambitious—did not, however, lie in politics for, staunch nationalist as he was, he saw that he could serve himself and his country best (for was not bauxite responsible for nearly half the value of Barracania's export trade?) by putting his engineering talent to the best use possible. On this account, Hutchins found that he had an unexpectedly easy task in persuading Rennalls to give up his political work before entering the production department as an assistant engineer.

It was, Baker knew, Rennalls's well-repressed sense of race consciousness which had prevented their relationship from being as close as it should have been. On the surface, nothing could have seemed more agreeable. Formality between the two men was at a minimum; Baker was delighted to find that his assistant shared his own peculiar "shaggy dog" sense of humor

so that jokes were continually being exchanged; they entertained each other at their houses and often played tennis together—and yet the barrier remained invisible, indefinable, but ever present. The existence of this "screen" between them was a constant source of frustration to Baker since it indicated a weakness which he was loath to accept. If successful with all other nationalities, why not with Rennalls?

But at least he had managed to "break through" to Rennalls more successfully than any other expatriate. In fact, it was the young Barracanian's attitude—sometimes overbearing, sometimes cynical—toward other company expatriates that had been one of the subjects Baker had raised last year when he discussed Rennalls's staff report with him. He knew, too, that he would have to raise the same subject again in the forthcoming interview because Jackson, the senior draftsman, had complained only yesterday about the rudeness of Rennalls. With this thought in mind, Baker leaned forward and spoke into the intercom. "Would you come in Matt, please? I'd like a word with you," and later, "Do sit down," proffering the box, "have a cigarette." He paused while he held out his lighter and then went on.

"As you know, Matt, I'll be off to Canada in a few days' time, and before I go, I thought it would be useful if we could have a final chat together. It is indeed with some deference that I suggest I can be of help. You will shortly be sitting in this chair doing the job I am now doing, but I, on the other hand, am ten years older, so perhaps you can accept the idea that I may be able to give you the benefit of my longer experience."

Baker saw Rennalls stiffen slightly in his chair as he made this point so added in explanation, "You and I have attended enough company courses to remember those repeated requests by the personnel manager to tell people how they are getting on as often as the convenient moment arises and not just the automatic 'once a year' when, by regulation, staff reports have to be discussed."

Rennalls nodded his agreement, so Baker went on. "I shall always remember the last job performance discussion I had with my previous boss back in Germany. He used what he called the 'plus and minus' technique. His firm belief was that when a senior, by discussion, seeks to improve the work performance of his staff, his prime objective should be to make sure that the latter leaves the interview encouraged and inspired to improve. Any criticism must, therefore, be constructive and helpful. He said that one very good way to encourage a person—and I fully agree with him—is to tell him about his good points—the plus factors—as well as his weak ones—the minus factors—so I thought, Matt, it would be a good idea to run our discussion along these lines."

Rennalls offered no comment, so Baker continued: "Let me say, therefore, right away, that, as far as your own work performance is concerned, the plus far outweighs the minus. I have, for instance, been most impressed with the way you have adapted your considerable theoretical knowledge to master the practical techniques of your job—that ingenious method you used to get air down to the fifth-shaft level is a sufficient case in point—and at departmental meetings I have invariably found your comments well taken and helpful. In fact, you will be interested to know that only last week I reported to Mr. Hutchins that, from the technical point of view, he could not wish for a more able man to succeed to the position of chief engineer."

"That's very good indeed of you, John," cut in Rennalls with a smile of thanks. "My only worry now is how to live up to such a high recommendation."

"Of that I am quite sure," returned Baker, "especially if you can overcome the minus factor which I would like now to discuss with you. It is one which I have talked about before so I'll come straight to the point. I have noticed that you are more friendly and get on better with your fellow Barracanians than you do with Europeans. In point of fact, I had a complaint only yesterday from Mr. Jackson, who said you

had been rude to him—and not for the first time either.

"There is, Matt, I am sure, no need for me to tell you how necessary it will be for you to get on well with expatriates because until the company has trained up sufficient people of your caliber, Europeans are bound to occupy senior positions here in Barracania. All this is vital to your future interests, so can I help you in any way?"

While Baker was speaking on this theme, Rennalls had sat tensed in his chair and it was some seconds before he replied. "It is quite extraordinary, isn't it, how one can convey an impression to others so at variance with what one intends? I can only assure you once again that my disputes with Jackson—and you may remember also Godson—have had nothing at all to do with the color of their skins. I promise you that if a Barracanian had behaved in an equally peremptory manner I would have reacted in precisely the same way. And again, if I may say it within these four walls, I am sure I am not the only one who has found Jackson and Godson difficult. I could mention the names of several expatriates who have felt the same. However, I am really sorry to have created this impression of not being able to get on with Europeans—it is an entirely false one—and I quite realize that I must do all I can to correct it as quickly as possible. On your last point, regarding Europeans holding senior positions in the Company for some time to come, I quite accept the situation. I know that Caribbean Bauxite—as they have been doing for many years now—will promote Barracanians as soon as their experience warrants it. And, finally, I would like to assure you, John—and my father thinks the same too—that I am very happy in my work here and hope to stay with the company for many years to come."

Rennalls had spoken earnestly and, although not convinced by what he had heard, Baker did not think he could pursue the matter further except to say, "All right, Matt, my impression *may* be wrong, but I would like to remind you about the truth of that old saying, 'What is important is not what is true but what is believed.' Let it rest at that.''

But suddenly Baker knew that he didn't want to ''let it rest at that.'' He was disappointed once again at not being able to ''break through'' to Rennalls and having yet again to listen to his bland denial that there was any racial prejudice in his makeup. Baker, who had intended ending the interview at this point, decided to try another tack.

''To return for a moment to the 'plus and minus technique' I was telling you about just now, there is another plus factor I forgot to mention. I would like to congratulate you not only on the caliber of your work but also on the ability you have shown in overcoming a challenge which I, as a European, have never had to meet.

''Continental Ore is, as you know, a typical commercial enterprise—admittedly a big one—which is a product of the economic and social environment of the United States and Western Europe. My ancestors have all been brought up in this environment for the past two or three hundred years and I have, therefore, been able to live in a world in which commerce (as we know it today) has been part and parcel of my being. It has not been something revolutionary and new which has suddenly entered my life. In your case'' went on Baker, ''the situation is different because you and your forebears have only had some fifty or sixty years' experience of this commercial environment. You have had to face the challenge of bridging the gap between fifty and two or three hundred years. Again, Matt, let me congratulate you—and people like you—once again on having so successfully overcome this particular hurdle. It is for this very reason that I think the outlook for Barracania—and particularly Caribbean Bauxite— is so bright.''

Rennalls had listened intently and when Baker finished, replied, ''Well, once again, John, I have to thank you for what you have said, and, for my part, I can only say that it is gratifying to know that my own personal effort has been so much appreciated. I hope that more people will soon come to think as you do.''

There was a pause and, for a moment, Baker thought hopefully that he was about to achieve his long awaited ''breakthrough,'' but Rennalls merely smiled back. The barrier remained unbreached. There remained some five minutes' cheerful conversation about the contrast between the Caribbean and Canadian climate and whether the West Indies had any hope of beating England in the Fifth Test before Baker drew the interview to a close. Although he was as far as ever from knowing the real Rennalls, he was nevertheless glad that the interview had run along in this friendly manner and, particularly, that it had ended on such a cheerful note.

This feeling, however, lasted only until the following morning. Baker had some farewells to make, so he arrived at the office considerably later than usual. He had no sooner sat down at his desk than his secretary walked into the room with a worried frown on her face. Her words came fast. ''When I arrived this morning I found Mr. Rennalls already waiting at my door. He seemed very angry and told me in quite a peremptory manner that he had a vital letter to dictate which must be sent off without any delay. He was so worked up that he couldn't keep still and kept pacing about the room, which is most unlike him. He wouldn't even wait to read what he had dictated. Just signed the page where he thought the letter would end. It has been distributed and your copy is in your 'in tray.' ''

Puzzled and feeling vaguely uneasy, Baker opened the ''Confidential'' envelope and read the following letter:

From: Assistant Engineer
To: The Chief Engineer, Caribbean Bauxite Limited
14th August, 196_

ASSESSMENT OF INTERVIEW BETWEEN MESSRS. BAKER AND RENNALLS

It has always been my practice to respect the advice given me by seniors, so after our interview, I decided to give careful thought once again to its main points and so make sure that I had understood all that had been said. As I promised you at the time, I had every intention of putting your advice to the best effect.

It was not, therefore, until I had sat down quietly in my home yesterday evening to consider the interview objectively that its main purport became clear. Only then did the full enormity of what you said dawn on me. The more I thought about it, the more convinced I was that I had hit upon the real truth—and the more furious I became. With a facility in the English language which I—a poor Barracanian—cannot hope to match, you had the audacity to insult me (and through me every Barracanian worth his salt) by claiming that our knowledge of modern living is only a paltry fifty years old whilst yours goes back 200–300 years. As if your materialistic commercial environment could possibly be compared with the spiritual values of our culture. I'll have you know that if much of what I saw in London is representa-tive of your most boasted culture, I hope fervently that it will never come to Barracania. By what right do you have the effrontery to condescend to us? At heart, all you Europeans think us barbarians, or, as you say amongst yourselves we are "just down from the trees."

Far into the night I discussed this matter with my father, and he is as disgusted as I. He agrees with me that any company whose senior staff think as you do is no place for any Barracanian proud of his culture and race—so much for all the company "clap-trap" and specious propaganda about regionalization and Barracania for the Barracanians.

I feel ashamed and betrayed. Please accept this letter as my resignation which I wish to become effective immediately.

c.c. Production Manager
Managing Director

Case B: Bougainville Copper Ltd.

Bougainville Copper Ltd., in November 1973, operated one of the world's largest open pit copper mines, located on the remote South Pacific island of Bougainville (see map). The mine began production in April 1972 under the terms of a mining concession agreement signed in 1967 with the Australian Government, administrator of the territory of Papua and New Guinea on behalf of the United Nations. As the mine's profitability grew far beyond initial estimates, several factions in the government of Papua New Guinea came to regard the agreement as one-sided in the company's favor and began to exert considerable pressure on the

Source: Copyright © 1974 by the President and Fellows of Harvard College. This case was prepared by Gerald B. Allan under the supervision of John S. Hammond as the basis for class discussion rather than to illustrate either effective or ineffective handling of an administrative situation. Reprinted by permission of the Harvard Business School.

more conservative or uncommitted legislators and officials for its renegotiation. These events were taking place against a background of escalating world copper prices, chaotic international monetary relationships, widespread metal and energy shortages, and the threat of a worldwide recession in 1974. The territory was approaching nationhood, with full independence due December 1, 1974.

Papua New Guinea

Pressure for renegotiation of the Bougainville mining agreement originated among the diverse interests that coexisted within the territories of Papua and New Guinea (or Papua New Guinea [PNG], as the combined area was becoming known), Papua and New Guinea were governed by Australia under a territorial administration headquartered in the Papuan city of Port Moresby. Papua had been under British and

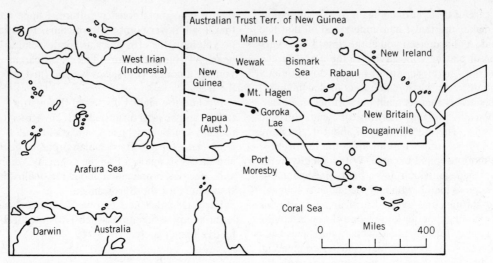

Source: The Economist, August 22, 1970. Reprinted by permission.

Australian rule since 1884, while New Guinea, formerly German New Guinea, had been an Australian-administered Trust Territory since World War I, first under the League of Nations and later under the United Nations. Bougainville Island, largest of the Solomon Island chain, had been included in the New Guinea Trust Territory.

The colonial union of Papua, New Guinea, and nearby islands could not obscure the region's fundamental characteristic—ethnic and cultural diversity. Separated by a violent landscape, impenetrable jungles, and mangrove swamps, tribes remained isolated from each other over the centuries and came to regard the next valley as another nation. Reinforcing the topographical separation were striking variations in appearance—ranging from the tall, light-skinned coastal inhabitants to the short, dark, inland peoples of the main island, to New Britain's blond-haired, black-skinned Tolains and finally, to the ebony-black Bougainvillians. In fact, Bougainvillian indigenes were so dark that they commonly referred to mainland Papua New Guineans as contemptible "redskins."

Over half of Papua New Guinea's population of 2.5 million survived by subsistence farming.

Many tribes continued to live in the Stone Age and considered white man's technology a magical "cargo" produced by sorcery rather than by education and work. For most of Papua New Guinea, there was little contact with Western cultures until the late 1800s when the influence of Catholic missionaries increased significantly and spread into most of the territories' more accessible and hospitable regions. In coastal areas and in New Britain and Bougainville particularly, contact with traders, which had begun about 1850, led gradually to a widespread hostility toward whites. Through the efforts of labor recruiters and as the result of a tax later imposed on all male indigenes, many were forced into indentured labor on plantations owned by whites. This hostility, exacerbated by recent acute land shortages due to the area's explosive birthrate, reportedly gave rise to talk of a Biafra-type war in PNG after independence.

Language and cultural differences were a significant factor in dealings between PNG and the English-speaking mining interests. The labor indenture system was largely responsible for the spread of a common language—Pidgin English—throughout the territory. Prior to this, communication had been made extremely difficult by the existence of some 700 languages—about one quarter of the world's total—in the territory. Pidgin, one of the three official languages of PNG, was developed by the indigenes mostly around English words learned from Europeans. Thus, the English "this is our country" would become, in Pidgin, "dis pela kantri bilong yumi," and Prince Charles of Britain, during the visit to the islands was described locally as "numba wan pikinini bilong misis kwin."

From shortly after World War II until 1964, a group of Australian officials administered both the Crown territory of Papua and the Trust Territory of New Guinea under direction from the Australian government in Canberra. In 1962 the United Nations produced a report highly critical of the Australian administration and urged immediate self-government for the Trust Territory (New Guinea). The report, along with armed conflicts in adjoining West Irian (West New Guinea) between the remnants of Dutch colonialism and the increasingly militant Indonesian nation, prompted Australia to take immediate steps toward that end.

A legislative House of Assembly was formed in 1964 and, following elections that year, began steadily to absorb the duties of a national government. Indigenous representation in the House grew from 60% of the seats in 1964 to 92% after the election in 1972. Several political parties emerged during this period, leading to the formation of a coalition government in 1972 of the comparatively radical Pangu party (once considered a club for educated radicals, it included Paul Lapun from South Bougainville) and the more conservative elements representing coastal New Guinea and many of the islands. Despite a growing number of educated Papua New Guineans, generated primarily by the University of Papua and New Guinea's 200 graduates a year, most of the electorate was illiterate and responsive only to magic and superstition: one political candidate reportedly promised to turn a basket of eggs into American soldiers bearing gifts. Thus, there was considerable doubt that British-style democracy could operate effectively in PNG for long without solid administrative and economic support from Australia.

Uncertainty also existed over the extent to which cultural differences between the mining and PNG interests might influence arrangements for and conduct of a renegotiation of the Bougainville mining agreement. In addition to this potential source of conflict, the cultural diversity—which more than any other feature characterized the peoples of PNG—was expected to give rise to divergent objectives within PNG itself.

Two examples of traditional social interaction between Bougainvillians might serve to illustrate the differences between PNG and Western cultures. Although commercially inexperienced by Western standards, Bougainvillians nevertheless had gained some familiarity with matters of trade and business through centuries of intertribal bartering and years of labor in the island's Catholic missions and European-run plantations. The normal state of intertribal hostilities was sometimes attenuated, or even absent, in tribes with well-developed trading habits. An interesting feature of barter negotiations had been the display of force made by each participating group prior to, and often during, the bargaining process. Since exchange terms were commonly determined by custom, extensive negotiation was an infrequent occurrence and the displays of force became the central feature of the exchange meeting. Following the exchange of goods, however, fights often broke out and hostilities resumed until the next bartering contact.

Another aspect of traditional interaction between Bougainvillians concerned the exchange process itself. Gifts in the Western sense, without expectation of repayment, were offered only to immediate kin. With persons outside the family group, "generosity" was treated quite differently. A gift always carried with it the obligation to provide an equivalent gift in return. Responding with an inferior gift, or with no gift at all, was regarded as an insult. Even in feast-giving, a favorite means of displaying generosity, guests were obliged to repay the hosts with prestige-enhancing verbal praise. A lack of appreciation of this facet of the local culture had undoubtedly contributed to the conflict with European interests, particularly over the sensitive issue of land acquisition for plantations.

Bougainville Copper

Bougainville Copper Ltd. was owned by Conzinc Riotinto of Australia (CRA), Australia's second largest company in gross revenues in 1972. It was broadly diversified in natural resources, having interests in iron ore, copper, aluminum, lead, zinc, uranium, coal, timber, oil, and natural gas. Directly, and through various subsidiaries and joint ventures, CRA was active in exploration for minerals throughout Australia, New Zealand, Papua, New Guinea, and Malaysia. Bougainville Copper was CRA's first large-scale mining venture in a less-developed nation.

CRA itself was owned by the United Kingdom's Rio Tinto–Zinc Corp., an organization primarily in the extraction, processing, and marketing of minerals through a large number of subsidiaries and affiliated companies. Although concentrated in Australia through CRA, Rio Tinto–Zinc also had major operations in North America, Europe, and South Africa. Its gross revenues exceeded US$1.4 billion in 1972.

Bougainville Island's copper deposits were initially discovered during the New Guinea gold rush of the 1920s and 1930s. However, they lay unexplored until the development of large-scale mining and concentrating equipment during the 1950s made feasible the commercial development of large deposits of low-grade copper ores. On the strength of a report made in 1960 by an administration geologist, CRA and an affiliated mining company in 1964 formed a joint venture, CRA Exploration Pty. Ltd., to evaluate the potential of the deposit. By late 1966

a very large copper orebody (subsequently proven to be a billion tons) containing significant amounts of gold and silver had been proven in the rugged Panguna Valley of the island's mountainous southern interior.

Bougainville Copper Pty. Ltd. (BCP), the operating subsidiary of Bougainville Mining Ltd., was subsequently formed to finance, develop, and operate the mine. The company then entered into a mining agreement with the territorial administration under which, in return for permission to mine the Panguna deposits, the company agreed to a special arrangement of production royalties, income taxation, land rents, and PNG participation. (Details of the agreement are covered in a later section.) In 1970 the Papua New Guinea government took a 20% equity interest in BCP and in 1971 Bougainville Mining made a public issue. A reorganization in 1973 eliminated Bougainville Mining from the ownership structure and BCP, renamed Bougainville Copper Ltd., was established as a public company. Exhibit 1 summarizes the resulting distribution of ownership.

In order to obtain financing for the A$300 million[1] project, Bougainville Copper entered into long-term sales contracts with smelters in Japan, West Germany, and Spain. These contracts, covering deliveries for a period of fifteen years, provided for the sale of 2.2 million tons of copper concentrate. Japanese smelters contracted for a total of 1.15 million tons over the life of the contract, with the remainder going to the Europeans. Annual contracted deliveries in the first five years were to be 182,000 tons, reducing in the next five years to 166,000 tons, and in the final five-year contract period, to 100,000 tons.

Payments under the sales contracts were to be based on contained metal weight priced at the London Metal Exchange spot market prices upon delivery. A floor price of US$0.30 per

---

[1] Rising to A$400 million by completion in 1972. The exchange rate in November 1973 between Australian dollars (A$) and U.S. dollars (US$) was A$1.00 = US$1.49.

Exhibit 1

Ownership and Capital Structure of Bougainville Copper Ltd.

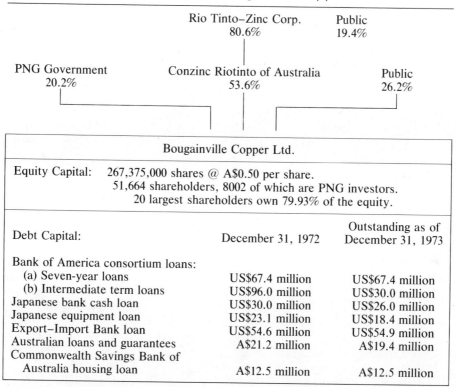

Bougainville Copper Ltd.

Equity Capital:	267,375,000 shares @ A$0.50 per share.
	51,664 shareholders, 8002 of which are PNG investors.
	20 largest shareholders own 79.93% of the equity.

Debt Capital:	December 31, 1972	Outstanding as of December 31, 1973
Bank of America consortium loans:		
(a) Seven-year loans	US$67.4 million	US$67.4 million
(b) Intermediate term loans	US$96.0 million	US$30.0 million
Japanese bank cash loan	US$30.0 million	US$26.0 million
Japanese equipment loan	US$23.1 million	US$18.4 million
Export–Import Bank loan	US$54.6 million	US$54.9 million
Australian loans and guarantees	A$21.2 million	A$19.4 million
Commonwealth Savings Bank of Australia housing loan	A$12.5 million	A$12.5 million

Sources: Annual Reports, 1972 and 1973, Bougainville Mining Ltd.

pound for copper was guaranteed in the contracts. From payments due under these pricing arrangements, the smelters would deduct so-called "realization costs" to arrive at the amount actually payable to the mining company. Realization costs, which cover transportation, insurance, marketing, smelting, and refining of the concentrate, averaged 11.6% of the gross value of metals in the concentrate during the first half of 1973.[2]

Long-term financing for the mine was obtained through a variety of international loans and supplier credits. Exhibit 1 summarizes these. Interest rates on most of the fixed-rate

[2]Gross value of metals shipped was estimated at A$111 million using data given in Exhibit 2.

loans exceeded 8% while approximately half of the loans had a variable interest rate tied to six-month Eurodollar rates. Repayment of these loans was concentrated in the period 1973 to 1978 with most of the remainder becoming due by 1982. The majority of the loan agreements imposed limits on dividend payments during the term of the loans; increased dividend payments required acceleration of debt repayment.

The Mine

The Panguna minesite was located some sixteen miles inland in a mountainous region of thick, rainforest vegetation. Rainfall averaging 240 inches per year, often occurring in downpours of 10 inches within little more than an hour,

Exhibit 2
Bougainville Mining Ltd.
Operating Results for the Six Months Ending June 30, 1973

Production Statistics

Ore milled		13,230,000 tons
Concentrate produced		304,285 tons
Metal content: Copper		85,861 tons
Gold		252,226 ounces
Silver		531,062 ounces
Average L.M.E. prices:		
Copper		A$1,050 per ton
Gold		A$78.42 per ounce
Silver		A$2.00 per ounce

Financial Results (in thousands of A$)

Net value of products		98,136
Less: Production costs		
and interest	47,960	
PNG government royalty	1,155	(49,115)
Add: Exchange gain on loan		
repayments*		2,935
Net income—Bougainville Copper		51,956
Less: PNG government interest in		
Bougainville Copper		
earnings (20%)		(10,391)
Add: Bougainville Mining Ltd.		
net earnings (loss)		(12)
Less: Dividend withholding tax[†]		(3,209)
Consolidated net income—		
Bougainville Mining Limited		38,334

*Loan repayments during 1973 were expected to exceed A$60 million.
[†] Bougainville Copper had announced its intention to declare an interim dividend before the end of 1973 at a rate of A$0.10 per share.
Source: Bougainville Mining Limited press release dated 24 August 1973.

made transportation, construction, and the mining itself both difficult and hazardous.

Exceeding 900 million tons, the orebody averaged 0.48% copper, 0.11 ounces of gold per ton of ore, and about 0.2 ounces of silver per ton.[3] There was some evidence that additional commercial-grade mineralization existed beyond the limits of the proven reserves. Mine life was estimated to be around thirty years based on known ore reserves.

[3] The units "tons" and "ounces" appearing in the case are metric tons and troy ounces, respectively. A metric ton is 2205 pounds and there are 12 troy ounces in 1 pound.

Large electric power shovels mined the ore from the surface, creating a pit that would eventually extend more than 1½ miles across and over ½ mile in depth. Diesel-electric trucks, carrying 100 tons of ore in a load, hauled the ore out of the pit to an extensive crushing and concentration complex set into the mountainside just above the pit. Approximately 80,000 tons of ore were removed from the pit each day, ore which would ultimately produce some 400 tons of copper metal.

The ore was first crushed in a three-stage crushing plant. Pieces as large as two feet across were reduced to gravel-sized chunks in preparation for grinding to powder size. After crushing, the ore was pulverized by hardened steel balls in nine large grinding mills where water was added to form a slurry. In the concentration stage, the slurry was mixed with various chemicals and aerated in many rectangular tanks, or flotation cells. Mineral-containing ore particles floated to the top, to be skimmed off for additional stages of concentration by flotation. At each stage, weakly mineralized and nonmineral particles would sink to the bottom of the cells and be drawn off for disposal as tailings. About 95% of the ore mined ended up as tailings. Tailings disposal, which can create mountainous and occasionally dangerous piles or can silt up rivers and ruin fishing, is a serious and often political problem for many mines.[4]

The ore concentrate, in the form of a slurry, was then pumped through a pipeline over the coastal mountains to a portsite on the island's east coast. At the portsite, water was removed from the slurry and the concentrate dried in large, horizontal rotating kilns. It was finally conveyed to a storage area to await shipment to overseas smelters where the remaining non-metallic components of the ore would be removed and copper metal produced.

The company had, at various times, considered the addition of smelting and refining facilities. Existing long-term contracts for the mine's output, however, were thought to present a serious obstacle to any such forward integration for at least a decade. A feasibility study for such a smelter was to be conducted by the company by 1977.

---

[4]The ore concentrate shipped from the mine contained about 30% copper metal by weight, the remainder being iron, oxide, and sulfide constituents of the copper ore minerals. Thus, of the 200 tons of ore mined to obtain 1 ton of copper metal, 197 tons of ore waste (tailings) were removed at the mine to produce the concentrate and the remaining 2 tons of mineral waste were removed at the smelter and refinery. Gold and silver were recovered from the mineral waste in subsequent refining stages.

Impact on Bougainville's Social and Political Structure

The mine's earliest and greatest impacts were considered to be those on the Bougainville islanders themselves. Beginning with conflicts over the company's land acquisition policies, the problems expanded to include damage to agricultural lands and fishing grounds as the result of construction and mining activities, and finally, the discontent over the distribution within Papua New Guinea of government revenues from the mine.

One of the main points of contention between Bougainvillians and the mining company involved land acquisitions. In the Bougainvillian culture, ownership or control over land tracts was handed down through innumerable generations, normally through the female line of each tribe, and the land often had deep religious significance for its owners. Land was almost never transferred by sale; land or some of its more important features was sometimes offered as a gift or as compensation for some service, but always between kinfolk. Various features of a land tract, such as soil (including subsurface materials), plants and streams, might be owned by several different individuals, or more often by groups, and transfer normally required consent of the majority.

Consequently, the government's issuing a license for land use, which involved removal (or *sale*, in effect) of a part of the land itself, ran counter to the traditional handling of land in the Bougainvillian culture. Under the territory's mining ordinance, companies were obliged to pay an "occupation fee" to landowners for land "used" in the mining operation. This fee, A$6.50 per acre per year, on the 50,000 acres under use, was completely unrelated to the value of land in the indigenous culture. In addition, under the Bougainville Copper agreement, the government received A$1 per acre per year rental. Bougainvillians reacted strongly to the removal of valuable resources, which they regarded as their own and not the state's, in return for this payment. The fact that revenue derived from these resources was to be spent mostly in the "foreign" lands of Papua and New Guinea gave rise to even greater resentment. Ill feelings grew over this issue until, through the efforts of Paul Lapun,[5] the administration amended the mining ordinance in 1967 to allocate 5% of mine royalty payments to owners of land leased to mining companies. While Bougainvillians were not particularly satisfied with this solution, it did succeed in reducing the importance of this issue.

Related problems arose in connection with damage to agricultural land and trees. Compensation payments by the company, reported to be quite generous, had little meaning to a people who did not value these things in monetary terms. Other problems grew out of the removal and relocation of a small village from the mine pit and plant areas and out of the relocation of residents in river valleys where silt from the mining operations had begun to raise river levels significantly. Claims were also being made over damage to coastal fishing grounds where silt from tailings fanned out from the rivers into the Pacific.

The mine quickly became a central feature of the island's economic social structure. Employment in the mine and in the growing number of conventional businesses supporting it had given many Bougainvillians ready access to cash for the first time in their lives. Prior to the mine, occupations had been limited mainly to subsistence agriculture or to labor in European-run plantations. But now, in addition to becoming avid consumers of imported goods such as radios, bicycles, and trucks, Bougainvillians sought ownership of productive land with which to carry on cash-cropping in copra, cocoa, and vegetables. Growing numbers of Bougainvillians who preferred to be self-employed led to the formation of cooperatives—a radically new social structure in the indigenous culture—and to the starting of many family-owned businesses. Increasing opportunities for wage work in these businesses were drawing many residents from their traditional regions in the island's interior to the coastal commercial areas. At the same time, the islanders' dependence on medical facilities operated by the Catholic missions was sharply reduced by the construction of modern hospital facilities at the mine port town of Arawa. The mine thus offered the opportunity for both financial and medical independence from the traditional and mission-centered ways of life in Bougainville.

Despite rising incomes, however, both ownership of arable, accessible land and consumption of imported goods were still beyond the reach of the great percentage of Bougainville's population. More significant was the fact that unless the PNG economy was able to grow at a relatively high rate, problems of labor oversupply were almost certainly in store for both Bougainville and other areas of PNG as a result of the rapidly growing population (3.5% increases annually in Bougainville in 1966) and the shift of more of the population into the money labor market.

Pressures developing as a result of these changes had an almost immediate impact on Bougainvillian politics. Efforts were directed initially toward obtaining a better deal for landowners affected by the mine. As this issue faded into the background following the granting of a portion of mine royalties to landowners, Bougainvillians began to make demands for a larger share of mine profits and ownership. In September of 1972, Paul Lapun called for renegotiation of the mining agreement. Shortly afterward, Father John Momis, another Bougainville MHA, proposed in the House a set of guidelines for future mining agreements; these guidelines were adopted almost unanimously late in 1972. Later, Chief Minister Michael Somare appointed three of the four Bougainville MHAs to high posts in his coalition govern-

---

[5] Paul Lapun, MHA (member of the PNG House of Assembly) from South Bougainville, was Minister of Mines at the time of the case.

ment. Lapun became Minister of Mines; Father Momis, Deputy Chairman of the Constitutional Planning Committee; and Donatus Mola (MHA from North Bougainville), Minister for Business Development (see Exhibit 3). Bougainville, as a result, assumed a position of importance in PNG politics far in excess of what its relatively small population might otherwise justify. This situation did not appear to improve relations between Bougainville and the remainder of Papua New Guinea.

Social and Political Policies of Bougainville Copper

Early recognition of the mine's potential impact on Bougainvillians and their way of life led Bougainville Copper to adopt social and employment policies unusual for mining companies in less-developed countries at that time. Of greatest concern was the employment and training of as many Papua New Guineans as possible when mining operations commenced, followed closely by the replacement over a ten-year period of most of the mine's expatriate employees and professional staff. Plans were also made to ease the transition of indigenes from their traditional ways of life into the large-scale, Western industrial production culture of the mine.

Employment in the mining operations was expected to level off at about 3500, down from the 10,000 workers involved in construction activities in 1971. These, together with about 500 apprentices, trainees, and students, comprised a significant proportion of the adult male population of Bougainville (21,000 males in June 1971). The company had begun a training program for mine workers several years before the mine's initial production in April 1972. As a result of this early effort, about 70% of the mine's first employees were from the PNG indigenous population. Although Bougainville Copper had made no firm commitment to the PNG government regarding the rate at which indigenes would be brought into the mining operation, the

company was reported to have adopted the ten-year plan given in Table 1.

High turnover in the skilled and semiskilled worker groups, who averaged over 35% of the workforce in 1973, made it necessary for the company to continue with an extensive training program. Its Mine Training Center by the end of 1972 had trained 2459 equipment and plant operators and 363 repairmen and tradesmen. Another 410 workers received administrative training or further education at company expense. Although the training program was costing Bougainville Copper about A$1.5 million each year, replacement of high-salaried expatriate employees by newly trained indigenes over the next few years was expected to more than offset this training expenditure. The high turnover rate among trained and experienced workers did, however, provide a significant indirect benefit to PNG by contributing to productive efforts in other sectors of the PNG economy. (Prior to the mine, expatriates supplied nearly all of the required technical skills since few Bougainvillians had skills other than those useful in manual, agricultural activities.)

Bougainville Copper also attempted to equalize expatriate and indigenes' wage levels for equivalent jobs but had been constrained in doing so by the difference in general wage levels between PNG and the developed nations supplying most of the expatriates. Equalization of wage levels in PNG's copper industry, if forced by political pressures for wage equalization, would likely have spread through trade union and government pressure to other sectors of the PNG economy which were highly labor-intensive. Probable results were thought to include reduced development rates and lower export production, creating a severe unemployment problem, particularly as workers accelerated their abandonment of traditional subsistence activities for the high money wages of the restricted labor market.

Other social policies adopted by the company included integrated eating, housing, and recreational facilities and the threat of immediate

Exhibit 3
Effects of the Bougainville Copper Project on PNG Government Receipts and Expenditures (in millions of Australian dollars)

A. Government Receipts and Expenditures Related to Bougainville Copper as Estimated by the PNG Government in 1970.*

Fiscal Year‡	1969–1970 to 1971–1972	1972–1973 to 1976–1977	1977–1978 to 1981–1982	Total
Receipts				
Internal revenue§	22.0	159.5	251.2	432.7
Loans (for equity and infrastructure)	45.0	—	—	45.0
Total receipts	67.0	159.5	251.2	477.7
Expenditures				
Equity in Bougainville Copper	25.0	—	—	25.0
Debt redemption	4.3	15.2	19.3	38.8
Capital and recurrent (infrastructure investment and operation)	45.9	45.7	73.4	165.0
Total expenditures	75.2	60.9	92.7	228.8
Excess of receipts over expenditures	− 8.2	98.6	158.5	248.9

B. PNG National Budget Estimate (made in 1973)†

	1973–1974
Receipts	
Internal revenue:	
Bougainville Copper	36
Corporate taxes	12
Personal taxes	24
Dividend withholding tax	5
Import duties	20
Excise duties	12
Total internal revenue	109
Australian aid:	
Grant-in-aid	25
Development grant	52
Staffing assistance	49
Special aid for transfer of functions including civil aviation, broadcasting, and banking	63
Total Australian aid	189
Borrowing:	
International loans	21
Other loans	33
Total borrowing	54
Total receipts	353
Expenditures (inclusive of Australian staffing assistance and payments for transfer of functions from Australia)	353

* M. L. Treadgold, "Bougainville Copper and the Economic Development of Papua-New Guinea," *The Economic Record*, June 1971, p. 202.
† Philip Bowring, *op. cit.*, p. 55.
‡ Figures tabulated in each column are for the entire period (i.e., 3, 5, 5 and 13 years, respectively).
§ Based on a copper price of US$0.55 per pound.

Table 1 Indigenization Program of Bougainville Copper Ltd.

	Percentage of Indigenes, by Job Category		
	1972	1975	1980
Managerial and professional	1	7	30
Subprofessional	4	25	70
Supervisory and skilled	36	75	95
Semiskilled	95	100	100
Unskilled	100	100	100
Overall	70	87	94

Source: Douglas Oliver, *Bougainville.* Melbourne, Australia: Melbourne University Press, p. 160.

dismissal for interethnic fighting. Conflicts developed not only between expatriates and indigenes but among indigenes from the many tribes represented in the mine's workforce. To ease the transition between traditional ways of life and Western ways in an industrial setting, the workforce was broken into three groups. Indigenes who were unskilled, spoke little or no English, and were unfamiliar with Western customs were housed in simple, segregated barracks and were served native foods. Those with sufficient language facility and social flexibility, and who were in the skilled or semiskilled worker category, lived in the integrated quarters with expatriates at similar job levels. Indigenes who spoke some English but who were not yet comfortable in an integrated setting were housed and fed in special "transit" facilities.

While not overtly participating in Bougainville's political activities, the company had sought to develop good community relations in the mine area. A well-financed, many-faceted community relations program was undertaken, involving village meetings designed to make the villagers aware of what the mine was and how it might benefit them, and agricultural assistance and training for mine area farmers. This program became especially important as a means of offsetting the effects of Father Momis' in-

creasingly radical position with respect to the mine.

Impact on PNG's Economy

An indication of the impact of Bougainville Copper on Papua New Guinea's economy may be found in the export and budget estimate figures given in Table 2 and Exhibit 3. The 1972–73 export total represented a 300% increase over 1969–70 exports of A$65 million—due almost entirely to the addition of the mine's output—while the A$109 million internal revenue projected for the fiscal year 1973–74 was nearly four times the 1969–70 internal revenues of A$29 million.

As large as they appeared, however, PNG government revenues under the terms of the existing concession agreement, added to tax revenues from other sources and to the expected continuation of Australian aid following independence, were not generally considered to be sufficient to cover both debt repayments and the nation's anticipated growth needs. A major cash drain until about 1983 was the relatively heavy amortization schedule of the A$40 million in borrowing used to finance the A$27 mil-

Table 2 Principal Exports of Papua New Guinea (in millions of Australian dollars)

	June 1972 to June 1973	June 1971 to June 1972
Copra	8.8	9.3
Copra oil & products	6.1*	7.9
Coffee	23.2	20.4
Cocoa	11.4	11.1
Rubber	2.0	1.9
Tea	2.0	1.5
Timber	10.4	8.7
Fish	2.6*	4.8
Copper ore & concentrate	125.6	22.2
	192.1	87.8

*Ten months only.
Source: Philip Bowring, "Papua New Guinea: The Price of Economic Freedom," *Far Eastern Economic Review* 83(2):55 (January 14, 1974).

lion equity investments in Bougainville Copper and an estimated A$41 million for infrastructure (housing for government officials in the area, power systems, communications systems, and similar public facilities) associated with the mine. In addition, funds would be needed for public facilities to serve PNG's rapidly growing and urbanizing population and for possible large infrastructure expenditures required for other mining projects which were expected to develop in PNG over the next decade.

Two terms of the concession agreement were regarded as responsible for the inadequate cash flow to the PNG government prior to 1979. Direct tax revenue was minimized by the three-year tax holiday provision,[6] and a further tax-free period of several years while the mine's A$400 million investment was written off. Consequently, the government was left with a comparatively small revenue from royalties, dividends, important duties, mine employee income taxes, and the dividend withholding tax until about 1979. Without the tax holiday and investment writeoff provisions, the estimated A$36 million in revenues from the above sources would have been increased by mine income taxes to approximately A$86 million in 1973, based upon indicated 1973 pretax earnings and a 50% tax rate.

The mine also contributed significantly to the private sector of PNG's economy. Wages, salaries, and supplements paid to mine employees totaled over A$20 million in 1972–73 while local purchases of goods and services were estimated to be about A$10 million during the same period. Lease payments and fees paid to Bougainville landowners amounted to somewhat more than A$200,000, and the landowners' share of government royalties was estimated to be about A$100,000 annually.

[6] A tax holiday is a period during which there are no income taxes payable on mine profits. It is designed to accommodate the heavy and relatively short-term debt repayment schedules normally required by lenders for high-risk mining ventures.

The Concession Agreement

Negotiated by the Australian government on behalf of PNG, and reported to have been "rubber-stamped" by the PNG House of Assembly, the Mining Ordinance 1967 (known as the "Bougainville Copper Agreement") clearly reflected the eagerness of the Australian administration to attract a large mining investment in the face of several major uncertainties. The size and grade of the ore deposit, the future price of copper on world markets,[7] the size of investment required, and the financing of a project of this magnitude were all uncertain to a large extent at the time of signing. A summary of the important features of the Bougainville agreement is presented in Exhibit 4.

Factors influencing the terms of mining agreements could include project risk, the need for the mine to generate high revenues to the investors' company in early years to satisfy lenders, the country's desire to use a particular mine to gain new markets or additional market strength, and its near-term need for funds. In rapidly developing countries, high revenues during a mine's early years might be most important. Other countries might be willing to accept low revenues in years of low copper prices in order to share heavily in earnings when prices were high. Still others might wish to trade immediate revenues for development of related industry within their country. Historically, however, mining agreement terms rarely remained unchanged over long periods. Once a mining venture became successful, and especially after debts were repaid and equity investments recovered, agreement renegotiations were often initiated. The resulting changes were almost invariably in favor of the host country.

To provide some indication of the range of terms offered in mining agreements, major concession terms, very much simplified, have been tabulated in Table 3 for several copper-

[7] Metal prices in 1967 averaged US$0.35 per pound for copper, US$35 per ounce for gold and US$1.50 per ounce for silver.

Exhibit 4

Principal Terms of the Bougainville Copper Agreement of June 1967 and Applicable PNG Tax Law

Royalty:	1.25% of net revenue, deductible for tax purposes.
Income Tax:	(i) *Tax holiday* (zero tax rate) for 3 years beginning April 1972.
	(ii) *Depreciation,* normally straight line, over 25 years or the mine's life, whichever was less.
	(iii) *Accelerated depreciation,** allows all capital expenditures to be deducted from income for tax purposes in the year expenditures were incurred. The Bougainville Agreement extended forward so that the entire mine investment could be written off against income in the early years of operation, beginning at the end of the tax holiday.
	(iv) *Exempt income:*[†] 20% of net income was tax exempt.
	(v) *Tax rate:*[‡] 25% in the first year the company has a taxable income, rising gradually to 50% over the subsequent 3 years, where it would remain through year 26. Beginning in year 27, the tax rate would rise at 1% per year to a maximum rate of 66%.
Participation:	PNG was allowed to purchase at par up to 20% of the shares issued.
Dividend Tax:	A 15% withholding tax applies to dividend payments to nonresidents of PNG.[§]
Infrastructure:	PNG was obliged to construct at its own expense all required public facilities not directly connected with the mining operations.
Term:	42 years; renewable for successive 21-year terms at the company's option, with modifications only to the royalty and rents in the first and second such renewals.

* To encourage investment in agriculture, mining, and manufacturing, Australian and PNG tax law allowed firms to deduct a certain percentage of capital outlays made each year. The allowance was 20% for manufacturers but 100% for mining enterprises, which served in lieu of a depletion allowance and made it possible for mines to generate the large cash flows needed early in their lives for debt retirement and expansion.

[†] This exemption was subsequently dropped by both Australia and PNG but remained in effect for Bougainville Copper because of the freezing of tax laws provided for in the Agreement as of the date of signing.

[‡] The wording in the Agreement is ambiguous. An alternative interpretation is that the tax rate was to be 25% in year 4, after the tax holiday ended, and rising to 50% in year 7. The ambiguity hinges on whether "taxable income" includes accelerated depreciation deductions or is simply reduced by them.

[§] The dividend withholding tax was imposed by PNG after the concession agreement was signed. To eliminate double taxation of dividends paid to Australian firms such as CRA, Australian tax law provided for a tax rebate rather than a foreign tax credit. This rebate was computed using the firm's average tax rate on total income with dividends included and had the effect of virtually eliminating Australian taxation of such dividend income.

producing countries. Bougainville Copper and Freeport Sulphur concession terms are typical of those offered to the first producer in a region, while mining terms in mature copper-producing areas are reflected in those of Chile, Zambia, and Zaire. Further comparisons are difficult without taking the goals and resources of the host country into account.

Subsequent Developments in PNG Mining Policy

Many government officials felt that increasing mineral exploration activity in the territory made imperative the establishment of mining concession principles which, while more favorable from PNG's standpoint, would still be at-

Table 3 Major Mining Concession Terms in Various Copper-Producing Countries*

	Bougainville Copper	West Irian (Indonesia) Kennecott	West Irian (Indonesia) Freeport Sulphur†	Chile (After 1969)	Zambia (After 1969)	Zaire (Formerly Belgian Congo)	Peru Cuajone Project
Income tax	25% in year 4, rising to 50% in year 7	35% in first ten years; 42% thereafter	35% in years 4–11; 41.7% thereafter	52.5%	22.5%	45.5% minimum; increases with return on capital	47.5% initially, rising to 54.5% after 10 years
Tax holiday	3 years	None	3 years	None	None	None	None
Royalties	1.25% of net revenues	Copper: 3.6%; gold and silver: 1%	None	None	None	None	4% of metal value
Participation by host country	20% of equity for cash, at par	Equity available at 2% per year up to 20%	None	Participation of 54% of income for US$0.40/lb copper, rising to 70% as copper price rises	51% equity to be paid for out of future dividends	Major producer has been nationalized and is being operated under service contracts	None
Other taxes	Dividend withholding tax of 15% of dividends paid outside of country	None	Minimum tax of 5% of net revenues in years 4–11; 10% thereafter	Variable surtax on income tax of 33%, reducing as production exceeds a specified base	Minerals tax of 51% of net profits before income taxes	Additional tax of from 5% to 40% of copper price increase above US$0.45 per pound	None

Tax credits and depreciation	Entire capital investment may be deducted from income, after tax holiday ends	8% investment tax credit up to 50% of tax payable. Depreciation up to 12½% per year, straightline	Depreciation at up to 12½% per year, postponable to year 4	N.A.	N.A.	N.A.	Depreciation at 3% to 12%/year based on asset life
Transactions with affiliated companies	Covered in PNG tax laws	Limitation on interest payments to affiliates	Interest paid to affiliates must be approved by Ministry of Finance. Royalty and technical fees not deductible	N.A.	Limitation on management and sales fees paid to affiliates	N.A.	Limitation on technical assistance fees paid to affiliates
Agreement term	42 years	30 years	30 years	N.A.	N.A.	N.A.	10 years

N.A. = not available.

*Concession terms tabulated here include relevant terms from associated tax laws as well as terms in the mining agreements themselves. The gross simplifications required to present this comparison do not reflect the highly complex nature of nearly all mining agreements and tax laws relating to mining company operations.

†The first producer in a country normally receives more favorable terms than are offered to subsequent producers. Bougainville Copper and Freeport Sulphur were the first producers in Papua New Guinea and West Irian, respectively.

Source: The Wells Report.

tractive enough to draw foreign exploration and mining investment. Consequently, pending formulation of a general mining code, the PNG House of Assembly in November 1972 adopted a motion outlining a set of principles under which future mining agreements would be negotiated. In the ensuing months, elaborations and additions were made which gave rise to the following general mining policy proposal:

1. Large mining companies would be obliged to pay about 50% of their earnings to PNG through taxation.
2. PNG's equity position would be as high as possible, although not necessarily 50%, and it would be paid for out of future dividends rather than immediately in cash. Infrastructure provided by the government might be used as part of the payment for its equity share.
3. Long tax-free periods would not be offered.
4. Agreements would provide for training and maximum employment of Papua New Guineans in accordance with a definite timetable.
5. Landowners would be paid a proportion of royalties rather than a nominal, fixed annual sum per acre.
6. Development of industries which might supply the mine and further process its output would be sought along with the mine itself.
7. Agreements would include provision for review by the PNG government every ten years and for adjustment of terms if profitability exceeded initial estimates. In particular, the government would have to share in any profit increases that arose from increased world metal prices.
8. Disputes between mining companies and the government should be settled in PNG courts and not by resort to outside arbitrators.

The Situation in Late 1973

On December 1, 1973, Papua New Guinea was scheduled to gain independence from Austra-

lian administration except in the matters of defense and foreign affairs. A year later, full independence would be granted. Considered one of the world's most primitive societies only a relatively few years earlier, Papua New Guinea faced independence with an inexperienced government, a growing exodus of whites with much-needed skills, a division of opinion within the country itself as to whether independence now was desirable, and rising separatist movements in both Papua and Bougainville.

Under these unsettled conditions, pressures for renegotiation of the Bougainville agreement were increasing rapidly. Release in August of the company's operating results for the first half of 1973 (see Exhibit 2) had contributed significantly to these pressures. Continued escalation of metal prices in world markets led to the expectation of enormous full-year profits. Mine output, 124,000 tons of copper in 1972, was expected to rise in 1973 to 175,000 tons. Production in 1973 would also include about 500,000 ounces of gold and 1 million ounces of silver. At metal prices received during the first half of 1973, the mine's 1973 output would represent about A$200 million in net revenues, and approximately A$105 million in operating profits before taxes, to Bougainville Copper.

Complicating the situation was the need for the government to act on a set of mining proposals submitted more than a year earlier by Kennecott Copper Corp. for the development of its huge Ok Tedi copper prospect in northwestern Papua. Although the terms proposed offered more benefits to PNG than did the Bougainville agreement, the PNG government decided to seek advice from other major copper-producing countries before dealing with Kennecott on Ok Tedi. In June, Peru responded by sending a delegation of mining experts to PNG for the purpose of examining both the Ok Tedi deposits and the Kennecott proposals.

In addition to seeking advice from other producing countries, the PNG government commissioned Professor Louis T. Wells, Jr., of Harvard University to examine the appropriateness of the terms of the Bougainville agreement with respect to circumstances existing in 1973. Professor Wells had advised on mineral agreements and national mining policy in a number of developing countries, including several copper-producing nations. In contrast to the secrecy under which such advice is normally sought from abroad, the PNG government decided to publicize widely both Wells' role and that of the Peruvian officials.

Australia's part in any future negotiations was uncertain at that point. It was not clear whether the mining agreement involved only internal policy (and was therefore entirely within the jurisdiction of the PNG government) or whether it involved foreign policy as well, in which case Australia could insist on taking part until full independence in 1975. Because of this situation, and because the PNG mining officials had little previous involvement in negotiation of mining agreements, there was a possibility that PNG might obtain further outside assistance for any renegotiation of the Bougainville agreement.

The Wells Report

In a consulting report prepared for the PNG government, Professor Wells suggested that PNG should seek terms closer to those of the traditional copper producers (Chile, Zambia, and Zaire) and that, in order not to discourage future investment in the region's substantial undeveloped resources, changes should be implemented gradually. Implicit in this recommendation was a cautionary note with regard to the forthcoming negotiations with Kennecott Copper.

Four basic changes in the agreement were recommended:

1. Allow either a tax holiday or accelerated depreciation, but not both as the existing agreement allowed, to provide for rapid recovery of mine investment. Rather than eliminate one or the other, it was suggested that they run concurrently so that the maximum benefit would be the greater of the two rather than their sum.

2. Eliminate the income tax ordinance provision which excluded 20% of the income from PNG taxation. Both Australia and PNG had dropped this provision from their taxation laws so that it remained in effect for Bougainville Copper only as the result of a freezing of tax laws through the agreement.

3. Remove a potential loophole in the agreement whereby it appeared that interest payments made during the tax holiday would not be deducted from income until after the tax holiday.

4. Include specific, enforceable provisions for indigenization of the enterprise.

The first three changes were directed at increasing tax inflows and getting substantial tax revenues several years earlier than allowed under the existing agreement. The requirement for a firm indigenization commitment was designed to make enforceable a general provision in the existing agreement for training and maximum employment of local people.

With regard to an increase in ownership, Professor Wells suggested that the desired increase in the government's share of mine earnings might be achieved more directly and effectively through increased taxation. Additional equity, if required for political or other reasons, could then be purchased at market prices using a portion of future dividends. It was also noted that holding equity would subject the government to normal investment risks whereas taxation to obtain equivalent revenues would be comparatively riskless and would free PNG funds for use elsewhere in the nation's development.

The control aspect of ownership was considered to have only a political appeal at that point. Until it became clear where and to what degree control might be needed, it was suggested that the PNG government simply seek to ensure through its seats on the company's board that it became aware of any areas where the interests of the company and Papua New Guinea might diverge.

Commenting on proposals that ore be left

Exhibit 5
A Note on the World Copper Industry

Copper mining, smelting, and fabrication in 1973 was dominated by less than a dozen major firms, a growing number of which were integrated from exploration through fabrication. Industry concentration was slowly but steadily decreasing as the seven firms responsible for most of the world's production prior to World War II were joined by many new producers that had been formed to exploit the low-grade copper deposits found in many areas of the globe.

Organized into well-defined geographical market areas until about 1950, the industry subsequently underwent a series of changes as the new producers began to compete aggressively for markets without regard for traditional market boundaries or trading patterns. Shaken from their previously secure market positions by this competition and by the postwar conditions of rapidly changing supply and demand, the older large firms began vertically integrating to provide the degree of flexibility needed to meet these challenges. Copper, like most other major primary metals, was subject to periods of insufficient supply, as industry capacity limits were strained and producers began to construct new capacity, and to periods of oversupply when these plants began production, usually within a short time of one another. An integrated firm was better able to respond to government pressures for stable concentrate or metal prices as the supply–demand balance shifted since it had the profit margins from many stages of production with which to accommodate falling metal prices or large labor cost increases.

Few of the new producers were integrated to any extent. Most were subsidiaries of large companies in other industries which were diversifying or attempting to gain control over a source of an important raw material. The differences in structure between the integrated copper producers and firms involved only at a single stage in the process led to the development of a two-price copper market. Major producers sold the copper to their fabricating subsidiaries and to large buyers at a stable "producers price" which was supposed to reflect long-term trends in the industry. Small buyers and sellers, and occasionally the large firms during periods of excess production or shortages, would deal on a free market operated by the London Metal Exchange (L.M.E.). Although price fluctuations on this market reflected its function as a short-term, marginal supply–demand balancing mechanism, L.M.E. prices frequently influenced producer prices to such an extent that by 1966, following Chile's lead, major producers throughout the world had begun to tie their pricing to L.M.E. forward prices. Only U.S. producers continued to maintain a separate, but world-market dependent, producer price system.

Most major industrialized countries except the U.S. were heavily dependent on copper concentrate imports, purchased from developing countries under long-term contracts, and on free market concentrate and metal purchases during periods of oversupply. Like petroleum, copper played a crucial role in the industrial economies—one which seemed certain to continue despite replacement in many applications by aluminum and plastics. Thus, to the extent that copper remained in short supply, producing nations such as Zambia, Chile, and Peru held considerable bargaining leverage over major importers such as Japan, the U.K., and West Germany.

Against the long-term consumption growth rate of about 4%, Western world consumption grew at rates of 7% and 10% in 1972 and 1973, respectively. During this period, supply growth suffered from increasing government control and involvement in copper production, especially in Peru and Zambia, widespread labor disturbances, and production difficulties at several of the largest producers. This extremely tight situation was expected to ease during 1974 as large capacity additions came on stream, as labor problems diminished somewhat, and as current production problems were overcome.

in place until it could be developed without foreign assistance or until better terms could be obtained, Professor Wells provided three reasons for not doing so. To reduce its dependence on foreign aid and investment, PNG needed an internal source of funds such as the mine. Second, metal prices might decrease rather than increase: lower prices in the future would conceivably result from the development of substitutes or from new technologies which would open up major sources of the metal. And third, agreement terms would tend to shift in the host country's favor as its bargaining position improved with time, thus compensating to some degree for better terms that might be obtained by delaying.

Timing was also considered to be crucial. Professor Wells felt that both Kennecott and others exploring actively in PNG would be reluctant to begin negotiations until they had assessed the effects of changes in the Bougainville agreement on their own positions. In addition, he noted that further delay would serve only to increase political pressures for immediate ac-

tion without adding significantly to an understanding of the basic issues.

Careful preparation for the negotiations was another strong recommendation. Agreement beforehand on goals and a clear understanding of its negotiating tactics were stressed as prerequisites for the government's negotiating team.

Bougainville Copper's Position

In contrast to the publicity surrounding actions and statements by the PNG government with respect to renegotiation of the agreement, there

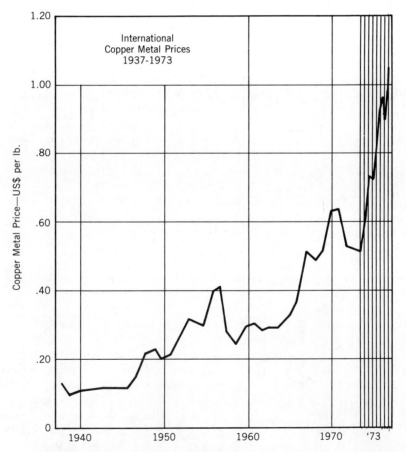

Sources: "Average Annual Metal Prices—1910 to 1973," *Engineering & Mining Journal,* March 1974, p. 63.
Louis Perlman, "Copper—There Has Never Been a Year Like 1973," *Engineering & Mining Journal,* March 1974, p. 65.

Exhibit 6
Estimated Cash Flow from Bougainville Copper Operations at Different Copper Price Levels ($A millions)

	Years from Start of Operation										Total 10 Years
	1	2	3	4	5	6	7	8	9	10	
I. Cooper at US$0.68/lb.*											
Bougainville Copper:											
Net revenue†	196	196	196	196	196	196	196	196	196	196	1,960
Less: Production costs	(62)	(62)	(62)	(62)	(62)	(62)	(62)	(62)	(62)	(62)	(620)
Interest	(18)	(14)	(10)	(7.5)	(5)	(0)	(0)	(0)	(0)	(0)	(54.5)
Royalty	(2.5)	(2.5)	(2.5)	(2.5)	(2.5)	(2.5)	(2.5)	(2.5)	(2.5)	(2.5)	(25)
Net operating income before tax shelter or depreciation	113.5	117.5	121.5	124.0	126.5	131.5	131.5	131.5	131.5	131.5	1,260.5
Less: Tax holiday shelter†	(113.5)	(117.5)	(121.5)								(352.5)
Accelerated depreciation				(124.0)	(126.5)	(131.5)	(18.0)				(400)
Taxable income	0	0	0	0	0	0	113.5	131.5	131.5	131.5	508.0
Income tax‡							(22.7)	(32.9)	(39.5)	(46.0)	(141.1)
After-tax income§	113.5	117.5	121.5	124.0	126.5	131.5	90.8	98.6	92.0	85.5	1,101.4
CASH FLOW	113.5	117.5	121.5	124.0	126.5	131.5	108.8	98.6	92.0	85.5	1,119.9
Dividends**	58.0	60.0	62.0	63.3	64.5	107.2	74.6	91.0	85.1	76.9	743.3
PNG government:											
Royalties	2.5	2.5	2.5	2.5	2.5	2.5	2.5	2.5	2.5	2.5	25.0
Dividends**	11.6	12.0	12.4	12.7	12.9	21.4	14.9	16.2	17.0	15.4	146.5
Income tax	0	0	0	0	0	0	22.7	32.9	39.5	46.0	141.1
Withholding tax††	7.0	7.2	7.4	7.6	7.7	12.9	9.0	9.7	10.2	9.3	88.0
CASH FLOW	21.1	21.7	22.3	22.8	23.1	36.8	49.1	61.3	69.2	73.2	400.6
II. Copper at US$0.30/lb.‡‡											
Bougainville Copper:											
Net revenue	110	110	110	110	110	110	110	110	110	110	1,100
Net operating income before tax shelter or depreciation	28.6	32.6	36.6	39.1	41.6	46.6	46.6	46.6	46.6	46.6	411.5
Less: Tax holiday shelter	(28.6)	(32.6)	(36.6)								(97.8)
Accelerated depreciation				(39.1)	(41.6)	(46.6)	(46.6)	(46.6)	(46.6)	(46.6)	(313.7)
Taxable income	0	0	0	0	0	0	0	0	0	0	0
After-tax income	28.6	32.6	36.6	39.1	41.6	46.6	46.6	46.6	46.6	46.6	411.5
CASH FLOW	28.6	32.6	36.6	39.1	41.6	46.6	46.6	46.6	46.6	46.6	411.5
Dividends	15.0	17.0	19.0	20.3	21.5	24.0	24.0	24.0	24.0	24.0	212.8

PNG government:

											Total
Royalties	1.4	1.4	1.4	1.4	1.4	1.4	1.4	1.4	1.4	1.4	14.0
Dividends	3.0	3.4	3.8	4.0	4.3	4.8	4.8	4.8	4.8	4.8	42.5
Income tax	0	0	0	0	0	0	0	0	0	0	0
Withholding tax	1.8	2.3	2.3	2.4	2.6	2.9	2.9	2.9	2.9	2.9	25.9
CASH FLOW	6.2	7.1	7.5	7.8	8.3	9.1	9.1	9.1	9.1	9.1	82.1

III. Copper at US$1.00/lb.

Bougainville Copper:

											Total
Net revenue	270	270	270	270	270	270	270	270	270	270	2,700
Net operating income before tax shelter or depreciation	186.6	190.6	194.6	197.1	199.6	204.6	204.6	204.6	204.6	204.6	1,991.5
Less: Tax holiday shelter	(186.6)	(190.6)	(194.6)								(571.8)
Accelerated depreciation				(197.1)	(199.6)	(3.3)					(400)
Taxable income	0	0	0	0	0	201.3	204.6	204.6	204.6	204.6	1,019.7
After-tax income	186.6	190.6	194.6	197.1	199.6	161.0	153.4	143.2	133.0	123.2	1,682.8
CASH FLOW	186.6	190.6	194.6	197.1	199.6	164.3	153.4	143.2	133.0	123.2	1,685.6
Dividends	95.0	97.0	99.0	100.3	162.4	131.5	141.1	128.9	122.8	113.9	1,191.9

PNG government:

											Total
Royalties	3.4	3.4	3.4	3.4	3.4	3.4	3.4	3.4	3.4	3.4	34.0
Dividends	19.0	19.4	19.8	20.1	32.5	26.3	28.2	25.8	24.6	22.8	238.5
Income tax	0	0	0	0	0	40.3	51.2	61.4	71.6	81.4	305.9
Withholding tax	11.4	11.6	11.9	12.0	19.5	15.8	16.9	15.5	14.7	13.7	143.0
CASH FLOW	33.8	34.4	35.1	35.5	55.4	85.8	99.7	106.1	114.3	121.3	721.4

* For the first half of 1973, copper prices averaged A$1050 per metric ton (A$0.47/lb); this is equivalent to US $0.68/lb at the exchange rate US$1.49 = A$1.00.

† Copper, gold, and silver production levels were assumed to remain fixed at the 1973 figures given in Exhibit 3. However, no allowance has been made for the added cost due to reduction in grade of ore as the mine deepened. (The higher grade ore was on top.) To maintain constant output of metal required mining greater quantities of ore and would require additional capital investments sometime during the first decade. However, these additional costs and investments were extremely difficult to estimate.

‡ Income tax was calculated on a base of 80% of taxable income (due to 20% tax exclusion). Rates used were 25% in the first year of taxable income; 31.25%, the second; 37.5%, the third; 43.75%, the fourth; and 50% from the fifth year onward.

§ CRA, in 1973, had consolidated net earnings after taxes and minority interests, of LA$95.9 million, while RTZ had earnings of A$109.2 million (69.6 million). CRA's interes in Bougainville Copper's earnings was 53.6% of net earnings; RTZ's interest, 42.3%.

** Through year 5 (for copper at US$0.68/lb), year 4 (at US$1.00/lb), and after year 10 (at US$.03/lb), when most of the mine's debt will have been repaid, dividend payout was assumed to be 50% of net income before royalty deduction and before provisions of the tax holiday and accelerated depreciation are applied. Payout was assumed to rise to 80% for the next two years and to 90% thereafter. CRA and the public receive 80% of the dividends and the PNG government, 20%.

†† The 15% withholding tax was applied to 80% of dividends (assumes all CRA and public share of dividends is remitted to Australia).

‡‡ Based on the change in copper metal prices alone, net revenues were estimated to be A$110 million and A$270 for prices of US$0.30 and US$1.00 per lb, respectively. Depreciation, production costs, and interest for copper at US$0.68 lb were used to arrive at the cash flow estimates for the other price levels. Gold and silver prices were held fixed at 1973 levels.

Source: The Wells Report and casewriters' calculations.

was almost no published information on the company's position. Vague statements, such as ". . . The company, however, would probably resist [a hefty royalty increase or export tax], whereas it appears more readily prepared to accept less fundamental tax changes . . . ," appeared from time to time but the company seemed to be maintaining a cautious silence.

Its position, however, would likely develop around the need to recover its equity investment and repay its debt as quickly as possible, the need to protect its profits in the event of falling copper prices (being predicted by some observers for the mid-1970s), and the desire to retain as much bargaining power as possible for the future. Information in Exhibit 5 (copper industry note) and Exhibit 6 (cash flow projections for three copper price levels) appeared relevant in relating those needs to the fundamental requirement of maintaining satisfactory relations with the PNG government.

PART II
Attitudinal and Behavioral Differences

The first part of this book has dealt with the most general background to comparative and international management. By examining the relevant historical, cultural, and research issues, Chapters 1 through 3 have provided an overview of what managers face in today's complex business environment. However, these chapters provide *only* an overview. The most obvious and potentially challenging aspect of comparative and international management is precisely its complexity. Cultures differ from each other in many ways. Each culture contains still other differences within its own nature and structure. To understand cross-cultural management in general, we must understand cross-cultural differences in detail.

What are these differences? What are their effects on cross-cultural management? And how can a manager predict when he or she will encounter particular differences (and potential management problems) in another culture?

These questions provide the focus for Part 2. Answering them, we can then proceed to specific recommendations for managers in the field.

Accordingly, we will begin by considering the interactions between communication and interpersonal relations. Chapter 4 examines these interactions in detail. The relevant issues are more complex and more significant than they might appear at first glance. After all, communication lies at the heart of most human relationships, and it influences them for better or worse. Communication also causes most cross-cultural difficulties in the business world and elsewhere. The reason for this powerful influence is that communication involves not only verbal exchanges—speech and writing—but also nonverbal behaviors such as gestures, facial expressions, posture, and even people's use of space and time. All of these aspects differ from one culture to another. To understand the difficulties that managers may face in other cultures, we should explore these issues carefully.

Chapter 5 then considers another intricate subject: employee attitudes and motivation. This initially appears to be a matter unrelated to communication. Like communication, however, attitudes and motivation are aspects of people's lives that vary greatly according to the cultural conditioning within a given society. This is true as well for the meanings that people give to their work. By investigating motivational models and the dimensions underlying them, however, we can gain a much better sense of why employees' behavior differs in various cultures.

What do these differences mean for management in an MNC? Obviously, managers must respond to employees according to specific circumstances in specific cultures. Yet even the concept, role, and function of management may vary overseas. For this reason, Chapter 6 explores the differences in managerial attitude and behavior. The salient issues here are theories of leadership, determinants of leadership style, the degree of democracy, and decision making in different cultures.

But having grasped these issues—communication, attitudes and motivation, and managerial style—how can we assemble them into a guide to assist managers in the field? How can we relate the abundance of available data into a device or instrument suitable for understanding today's complicated world? Fortunately, that guide, that instrument, already exists. Researchers have attempted to identify criteria that exists in various societies, regardless of location, history, or cultural background. By comparing these criteria, researchers can determine how cultures converge or diverge. Marking off the contours of convergence and divergence produces a kind of "map" of cultural differences. Chapter 7, therefore, discusses the maps and what they tell us about cross-cultural management.

Before dealing with the implications of cultural maps, however, we should first consider the research that makes them possible.

CHAPTER 4
Communication and Interpersonal Relations

Communication is a crucial factor in understanding cross-cultural management. First, communication is intricately bound with all other aspects of organizational functions. It is integral, for instance, to areas such as leadership and group decision making. Second, culture and communication are so closely related that some anthropologists consider them synonymous. They believe that it is impossible to understand culture without first understanding local modes of communication (including language). Samovar et al. (1981) describe how culture and communication are inextricably linked to each other:

Culture and communication are inseparable, because culture not only dictates who talks with whom, about what, and how the communication proceeds, it also helps to determine how people encode messages, the meanings they have for messages, and the conditions and circumstances under which various messages may or may not be sent, noticed, or interpreted. In fact, our entire repertory of communicative behaviors is dependent largely on the culture in which we have been raised. Culture, consequently, is the foundation of communication. And, when cultures vary, communication practices also vary. (p. 24)

Communication is an attempt to share meaning through the transmission of messages. Its aim may be to convey specific information, to motivate, to instruct, to give pleasure, or simply to interact with others. But no matter what the intent, meaning is shared. Meaning is the content of communication. As we will see, it is a complex mix of personal, historical, and contextual factors that affect the meaning an individual generates and attaches to a given message.

Communication also takes specific forms. The same meaning can be transmitted through a variety of channels (sometimes referred to as modality). Moreover, methods or channels of communication vary in impact and effectiveness. Written communication seems most effective for relaying factual information, while oral (face-to-face) communication seems best for relaying emotional nuances and matters of opinion. Since face-to-face communication is often limited or impossible across cultures because of language barriers, communication may be confined to written or other indirect means (e.g., through a translator). As a result, communication may lose subleties of meaning or may reduce the influence of the source characteristics—especially credibility and authenticity.

THE COMMUNICATION PROCESS
A Model of the Communication Process

To understand the communication process in an intercultural setting, we must first consider the basic stages of the process. Figure 4.1 diagrams these stages in their simplest form.

Encoding   A sender decides to share a specific item of information—a specific meaning—with another individual. With the possible exception of telepathic communication, however, meaning cannot be transmitted directly. A particular meaning must first be encoded into the set of stimuli we call a message. It is this message that is transmitted to the receiver. Under no circumstances should the message (the set of stimuli), be equated with the meaning. Messages are not meaning; rather, they symbolize meaning.

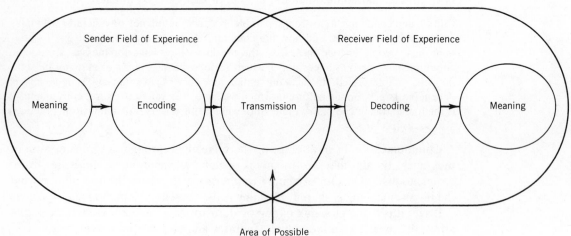

Area of Possible
Interpersonal Communication
(Modality or Channel of Verbal and Nonverbal Communication)

Figure 4.1   The communication process.

Box 4.1

Everyone is familiar with the Pepsi-Cola advertising slogan "Come Alive with Pepsi." When the campaign was reportedly introduced in Germany, the company was forced to revise the ad because it discovered that the German translation of "Come Alive" became "Come out of the grave." And in Asia, the same phrase translated to "Bring your ancestors back from the dead." The intended meaning of this famous slogan was definitely lost somewhere in the translation.

Source: D. A. Ricks, *Big Business Blunders*. Homewood, IL: Dow Jones–Irwin, 1983, p. 84.

The Choice of Channel and Transmission   We can transmit meaning by encoding it into various types of stimuli. Words, gestures, facial expressions, even dress and the physical setting in which the communication takes place can serve, alone or in conjunction, as channels of encoding meaning into messages.

Decoding   Decoding refers to the process by which the receiver interprets the message and recreates for himself or herself the meaning that is being transmitted.

In summary, a meaning is encoded into verbal or nonverbal stimuli and transmitted to a receiver, who in turn decodes the stimuli and ends up with the subjective meaning. The field of experience of each of the participants is an integral part of the process.

Two-Way Communication

The communication framework we have just described can be extended to include a two-way interaction—for example, a conversation. Both individuals engaged in communication must encode and decode messages. The feedback resulting from the two-way communication can help to clarify the transmittal of meaning. Ambiguities in meaning that result from the first round of communication can be resolved in the next (see Figure 4.2). From this perspective, the communication process seems to present no difficulties. However, we all know that difficulties *do* arise. We should now consider why.

Ineffective Communication—Statement of the Problem

Effective communication takes place only when the receiver ends up with the same meaning that the senders created. Unfortunately, there are numerous opportunities for confusing the meaning. For example, it may be badly encoded, faultily transmitted, incorrectly decoded, or interrupted by some sort of interference. Any factors that affect the effectiveness of the communication process we refer to as *noise*; we will show that in cross-cultural communication, cultural antecedents can generate noise at each stage of the communication process.

Situations in which the meaning ends up improperly encoded or decoded are particularly interesting to the student of cross-cultural communication. Some-

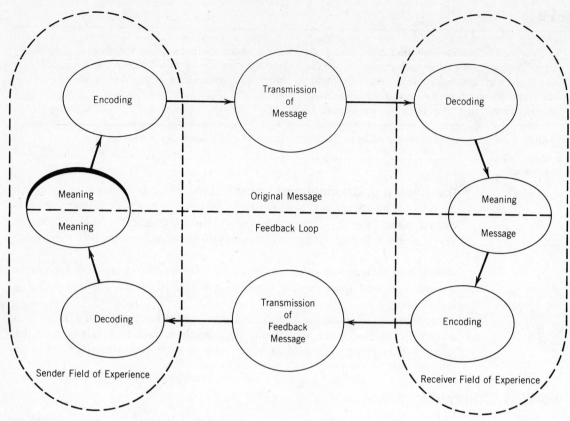

Figure 4.2 Two-way communication.

how, the meaning that the sender encodes differs radically from the meaning that the receiver assimilates on decoding the message. The meaning was properly encoded and adequately transmitted without interference; yet the receiver does not understand the message, or may even misconstrue its meaning completely. How can we start to understand this communicative breakdown?

Overlap Between Universes of Meaning   To understand how cultural noise affects the encoding and decoding process, we should look to the source of the meaning that we encode and decode into messages. A complex mix of personal, historical, contextual, and cultural factors—sometimes called the individual's field of experience—constitute the source of encoded and decoded meaning. To the extent that the fields of experience are similar, meanings grounded in an experiential base common to both communicators can be shared unambiguously. However, when such an overlap in the fields of experience does not exist, the receiver's repertoire of possible meanings lacks the one that should be assigned to a specific message; therefore, the correct meaning cannot be ascribed to the message. The message has no meaning for this receiver. He or she may ascribe to the message a meaning grounded in a personal

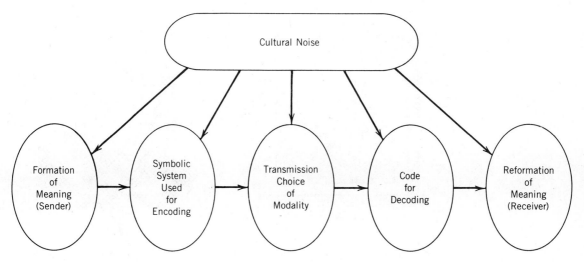

Figure 4.3   Communication and cultural noise.

field of experience, but this meaning is to some degree inconsistent with the sender's intended meaning. Clearly, the more the communicator's worlds overlap, the more effective their communication is. The further apart their worlds, the less effective their communication is. Think of the problems that can easily arise in trying to communicate across cultures (see Figure 4.3).

Noncongruence of Symbolic Systems   Another general source of noise is in the transmission, due to the noncongruence between a system of signs used to encode meaning and the codes necessary to interpret the meaning. Although two communicators' fields of experience may overlap, the system of signs and symbols utilized to encode and transmit meaning—not to mention the rules used to decode these symbols—may differ. As a result, a receiver may decode what appears to be a familiar set of signs and unwittingly misinterpret the meaning that the sender wanted to symbolize through these signs.

Figure 4.4 presents a model of intercultural communication suggesting that a message is transmitted in the ''language'' of one culture and decoded in the context of the receiving culture. Three cultures use three distinct geometric shapes. Cultures A and B are more similar to each other than to culture C, as represented by the similarities in geometric shapes and distance between shapes. Within each culture is another shape representing the individual; this shape is similar to, but not an exact duplication of, the culture's shape. This suggests that ''although culture is the dominant shaping force on an individual, people vary to some extent from each other within every culture (Samovar et al., 1981, p. 28). The arrows represent the transmission of the message. According to these researchers,

The meaning content of the original messages becomes modified during the decoding phase of intercultural communication because the culturally different repertory of com-

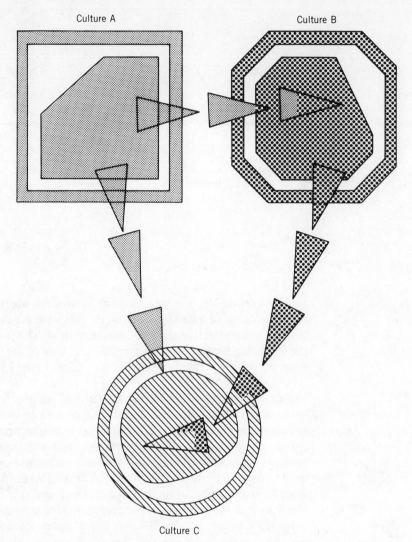

Figure 4.4 Model of intercultural communication.

Source: L. A. Samovar, R. E. Porter, and N. C. Jain, *Understanding Intercultural Communication.* Belmont, CA: Wadsworth, 1981, p. 29. Reprinted by permission.

municated behaviors and meaning possessed by the decoder does not contain the same cultural meanings possessed by the encoder. (p. 28)

This model helps us to understand how thoroughly communication is embedded in culture. Thus, given the inseparability of culture and communication, and given the integral nature of communication to all organizational processes, we must understand communication in a cross-cultural context.

The importance of communication lies in the accuracy with which it transmits meaning. When communicating, individuals usually assume that the message they have communicated has been received as intended. This assumption is often mistaken. Individual differences in perceptions, values, and attitudes often mean that one participant's meanings, signs, and behavior in the communication process will be different from others'. Such discrepancies directly relate to the degree and amount of both individual and cultural differences. Thus, a major cause for concern in intercultural communication is the failure to transmit the intended meaning. If meaning is to be transmitted effectively across cultures, one must pay particular attention to the communication process.

LANGUAGE—VERBAL AND NONVERBAL

Language can be an important source of noise in cross-cultural communication. Samovar et al. (1981, p. 141) define language as "an organized, generally agreed upon learned symbol-system used to represent the experiences within a geographic or cultural community." This definition suggests that language is a process for encoding or "symbolically representing" reality. Language, as the tool of communication, is consequently not an objective, impartial instrument. Rather, it is subject to the perceptual biases of its cultural environment. The important things have more generalized names that must be modified through additional words to be made specific. Linguists have catalogued over fifty distinct words for "snow" in the Eskimos' vocabulary—an impressive array next to our own meager supply.

Each culture uses language to convey the ideas central to its values, filtering perceptions of the environment through the labeling process. Two researchers, Edward Sapir and Benjamin Whorf, studied Indian languages. They theorized that language provides a guide to social reality as well as a means of communication (Samovar et al., 1981, p. 49). The Sapir–Whorf hypothesis maintains that language influences perceptions and transmits thoughts, as well as helping pattern them. Thus, language provides a frame of reference that determines the perceptions and thoughts of cultural members. The implications of the Sapir–Whorf hypothesis for intercultural communications are profound. Differences in language represent more than just differences in the particular labels assigned to an object or concept; in addition, differences mean that individuals who speak different languages also think different thoughts and generate different meanings. Individuals presented with the same physical evidence may draw very different conclusions unless they share a common language (Almaney, 1974).

Although people generally understand that language differences provide a major barrier to communication (hence the need for translation), there is less recognition that nonverbal communication may create other barriers. Nonverbal communication can also occur through a variety of distinct channels. Kinetics, for instance, is the analysis of nonverbal communication using body movements as its medium. The use of social and personal space (proxemics) and the use of communicative artifacts (object language) constitute two other channels of nonverbal communication. Paralanguage—which is concerned with *how* something is said rather than what is said—is yet another channel.

We should now consider some of the important varieties of nonverbal communication.

The Nonuniversality of Kinetics

The early research on kinetics begun a century ago focused primarily on establishing the universality of body movements across cultures (Darwin, 1872). Later research established that certain facial expressions (interest, joy, surprise, fear, sadness, anger, disgust) that are primarily determined biologically, and are therefore common characteristics across cultures, have a universal meaning (Ekman, Friesen, & Ellsworth, 1971). However, even these biologically determined stimuli are not reliable messages for the cross-cultural communication; they can lead to decoding mistakes. These universal stimuli, although they signify the same *dimension* of meaning, may indicate a different *intensity* of meaning across cultures. What appears to be a look of slight annoyance in one culture may convey murderous intent in another. Moreover, under certain circumstances, universal expressions are modified and qualified in certain social situations according to display rules. For instance, American and Japanese subjects in an experiment shared similar facial affects when watching a film alone; however, when an audience was present, the Americans showed more facial affects than did the Japanese (Boucher, 1974).

In general, kinetic systems of meaning are culturally specific and learned. Moreover, most concerted facial expressions simply cannot be generalized across cultures. It seems unlikely, for instance, that Americans would correctly decode the following expressions described in a review of the Chinese literature: sticking out the tongue to express surprise, widening of the eyes for anger, and scratching the ears and cheek to show happiness (Klineberg, 1983).

Gestures and Posture

Gestures and posture also function as channels for nonverbal communication. Within a culture, body movements used in communication are frequently analogous to the meanings that they signify. For instance, in interpersonal communication, spacial proximity among Americans symbolizes a degree of emotional closeness. South Americans perceive close proximity without such emotional involvement. Although some of these analogies hold across cultures and could therefore be used by the cross-cultural communicator, it remains true that if one is using a different logic, quite different analogical expressions can express the same meaning (Condon & Yousef, 1975, p. 33). Conversely, similar analogical expressions can have radically different analogical meanings. Yousef (1974) relates an example of the serious cross-cultural problems these discrepancies can produce.

The problem occurred in October, 1952 at Ain Sham in Egypt. In the midst of a discussion of a poem in the sophomore class of the English Department, the professor, who

Box 4.2

Advertisements that somehow fail to reflect the local life-style often wind up a wasted effort. When General Mills made its attempt to capture the English market, for example, its breakfast cereal package showed a freckled, red-haired, crew-cut grinning kid saying, "See kids, it's great!"—a promotional package that could not be more typically American. General Mills failed to recognize that the British family is not as child-centered as the U.S.; the stereotyped U.S. boy and near banal expression had no appeal to the more formal and aristocratic ideal of the child upheld by the English. As a result, the cereal package repelled the British housewife and wound up almost untouched on retail shelves.

Source: D. A. Ricks, *Big Business Blunders.* Homewood, IL: Dow Jones–Irwin, 1974, p. 13.

was British, took up the argument, started to explain the subtleties of the poem, and was carried away by the situation. He leaned back in his chair, put his feet up on the desk, and went on with the explanation. The class was furious. Before the end of the day, a demonstration by the University's full student body had taken place. Petitions were submitted to the deans of the various faculties. The next day, the situation even made the newspaper headlines. The consequences of the act, that was innocently done, might seem ridiculous, funny, baffling, incomprehensible, or even incredible to a stranger. Yet, to the native the students' behavior was logical and in context. The students and their supporters were outraged because of the implications of the breach of the native behavioral pattern. In the Middle East, it is extremely insulting to have to sit facing two soles of the shoes of somebody.

Other Channels for Nonverbal Communication

Many channels for nonverbal communication other than kinetics exist. A comprehensive list of various forms of nonverbal gestures and symbols is presented in Table 4.1 (Birdwhistell, 1970; Condon & Yousef, 1975). Cross-cultural communicators should familiarize themselves with the possible channels of nonverbal communication to be more sensitive to the stimuli that they might otherwise unconsciously and incorrectly interpret.

Nonverbal communication occurs simultaneously with verbal processes, although the sender is usually unaware of the nonverbal message being transmitted. In fact, the nonverbal may contradict the verbal message, indicating (or interpreted as) the deeper feelings of the persons sending the message.

Birdwhistell, who has extensively researched this subject, estimates that only about 30% of the message communicated in a conversation is verbal—even between two people sharing the same culture and language. Condon and Yousef suggest that in the intercultural context, in which a common language is not shared, the impact of nonverbal communication may be even greater. Furthermore, because we are generally unaware of the nonverbal messages we transmit, and because we are usually ignorant of how these messages are decoded and interpreted, the potential for serious communication problems increases. Familiarity with verbal language certainly enhances the communica-

Table 4.1   Various Forms of Nonverbal Communication

1. Hand gestures, both intended and self-directed (autistic), such as the nervous rubbing of hands
2. Facial expressions—such as smiles, frowns, yawns
3. Posture and stance
4. Clothing and hair styles (hair being more like clothes than like skin, both subject to the fashion of the day)
5. Walking behavior
6. Interpersonal distance (proxemics)
7. Touching
8. Eye contact and direction of gaze, particularly in "listening behavior"
9. Architecture and interior design
10. "Artifacts" and nonverbal symbols, such as lapel pins, walking sticks, jewelry
11. Graphic symbols, such as pictures to indicate "men's room" or "handle with care"
12. Art and rhetorical forms, including wedding dances and political parades
13. Somatypes of bodies; ectomorphs, endomorphs, mesomorphs
14. Smell (olfaction), including body odors, perfumes, incense
15. Paralanguage (though often in language, just as often treated as part of nonverbal behavior—speech rate, pitch, inflections, volume)
16. Color symbolism
17. Synchronization of speech and movement
18. Taste, including symbolism of food and the communication function of chatting over coffee or tea, oral gratification—such as smoking or gum chewing
19. Thermal influences, such as influences of temperature on communication, sensitivity to body heat
20. Cosmetics: temporary—powder, lipstick; permanent—tattoos
21. Drum signals, smoke signals, factory whistles, police sirens
22. Time symbolism: what is too late or too early to telephone or visit a friend, or too long or too short to make a speech or stay for dinner
23. Timing and pauses within verbal behavior
24. Silence

Source: J. C. Condon and F. S. Yousef, *An Introduction to Intercultural Communication.* Indianapolis: Bobbs-Merrill, 1975, pp. 123–124. Reprinted by permission.

tion process and gives insight into the perceptual and thought processes it defines, yet we often find little help for interpreting nonverbal communications.

Through our own and others' experience, we can learn to encode and decode verbal and nonverbal messages. However, we must temper experience with empathy and sensitivity toward others' feelings and circumstances. "To communicate effectively with other people, we must be able to create inner images that give us some insight into their feelings and characteristics" (Samovar et al., 1981, p. 197). In unfamiliar situations, stereotypes and ethnocentrism may influence those images. To the extent that we have empathy, however, we can override stereotypes and negative expectations and make more appropriate predictions about each other's attitudes, feelings, and values. According to Almaney (1974),

Successful empathy in intercultural communication will . . . depend on our ability to engage continually in a process of role-playing and inferences. If we make inferences and discover that they are invalid, we should go back to role-playing (analyzing and imitating behavioral patterns) and then make more inferences. We keep doing this until the inferences coincide with, or come close to, the actual behavior of those we attempt to communicate with. (p. 27)

CULTURAL FACTORS AFFECTING COMMUNICATION

As we have seen, cultural similarities and differences are a key factor in the communication process, and they influence the degree of correspondence between the meaning before and after decoding. Hall (1959) suggests that culture permeates all aspects of communication. His seminal book, *The Silent Language,* discusses the relationships between culture and communication. In particular, he notes that difficulties in intercultural communication are seldom seen for precisely what they are because people are not conscious of the elaborate patterns of behavior that they demonstrate in dealing with time, spatial relationships, and attitudes toward work, play, and learning. Our response to a sharp rebuke from a supervisor will depend in large measure on whether we think such a rebuke is warranted or unwarranted. We respond to the others' actions and communication more according to the perceived causes of these messages than to the message itself (Lowe & Goldstein, 1970).

The attribution process—the way in which people search out causes for others' behavior—plays an important role in intercultural communication. Research indicates that people tend to attribute others' actions to their personalities or dispositions whereas they attribute their own behavior to external factors (Triandis, 1977). When it becomes apparent to individuals from different cultures that they do not understand each other, each blames it on the other's "stupidity, deceit, or craziness" (Hall, 1959, p. 15). Moreover, individuals from different cultures make very different attributions about the more specific causes of the behavior or message, depending on their respective values, perceptions, and expectations. We tend to interpret the actions of others in terms of our own cultural framework. For example, Triandis (1977) describes a situation in which "an American supervisor who favors employee participation interacts with a Greek subordinate who expects and wants a 'bossy boss' " (p. 248).

Behavior	Attribution
American: "How long will it take you to finish this report?"	American: I asked him to participate. Greek: His behavior makes no sense. He is the boss. Why doesn't he tell me?
Greek: "I don't know. How long should it take?"	American: He refuses to take responsibility. Greek: I asked him for an order.
American: "You are in the best position to analyze time requirements."	American: I press him to take responsibility for his actions. Greek: What nonsense: I'd better give him an answer.

Behavior	Attribution
Greek: "10 days."	American: He lacks the ability to estimate time; this time estimate is totally inadequate.
American: "Take 15. Is it agreed? You will do it in 15 days?"	American: I offer a contract. Greek: These are my orders: 15 days.

In fact, the report needed 30 days of regular work. So the Greek worked day and night, but at the end of the 15th day, he still needed to do one more day's work.

Behavior	Attribution
American: "Where is the report?"	American: I am making sure he fulfills his contract. Greek: He is asking for the report.
Greek: "It will be ready tomorrow."	(Both attribute that it is not ready.)
American: "But we had agreed it would be ready today."	American: I must teach him to fulfill a contract. Greek: The stupid, incompetent boss! Not only did he give me the wrong orders, but he doesn't even appreciate that I did a 30-day job in 16 days.
The Greek hands in his resignation.	The American is surprised. Greek: I can't work for such a man.

From this example, we can see that attributions have a powerful effect on intercultural communications by providing a source of "noise" that interferes with the transmission and decoding process.

To summarize, cross-cultural communication is characterized by differences rather than by similarities. Individuals from different cultures bring different perceptions, values, norms, beliefs, and attitudes to the communication process. Because we interpret each other's messages in the context of these culturally determined factors, we must consider how differences in these factors can affect attributions. We should now examine the three most significant factors: perception, stereotyping and ethnocentrism.

Perception

Our discussion of cultural values and attitudes thus far has emphasized that different cultures view vocabulary differently and that each culture classifies its experiences in ways that are functional for its particular environment. This process of classification produces a kind of "map" of reality. Because environments differ, these maps also differ. A detailed analysis of the perceptual process (Gibson, 1969) suggests that both the familiarity and the distinctiveness of stimuli influence perception.

As perceptual learning takes place, previously generalized stimuli become increasingly differentiated and meaningful. When dealing with people from another culture, perceptions will be unfamiliar, thus largely undifferentiated. The lack of familiarity will result in an inability to interpret stimuli correctly. For example, Westerners may notice Orientals bowing. This behavior is distinctive; it has no counterpart in Western culture. The Westerner, however,

Box 4.3

One laundry detergent company certainly wishes now that it had contacted a few locals before it initiated its promotional campaign in the Middle East. All of the company's advertisements pictured soiled clothes on the left, its box of soap in the middle, and clean clothes on the right. But, because in that area of the world people tend to read from the right to the left, many potential customers interpreted the message to indicate the soap actually soiled the clothes.

Source: D. A. Ricks, *Big Business Blunders*. Homewood, IL: Dow Jones–Irwin, 1983, p. 55.

while perceiving that Orientals bow upon meeting, may fail to recognize the variations in depth of bows as a form of status differentiation.

Moreover, the perception of environmental cues varies not only with culture but also with other factors. Triandis (1977) suggests that race, social class, religion, and nationality all account for differing degrees of importance in social perceptions, depending on an individual's native culture. Persons working in unfamiliar cultures face a complex task in responding appropriately to these many factors.

Researchers have directed a great deal of attention to the study of perceptual accuracy. In summarizing the research, Triandis concludes that humans are poor judges of people who are dissimilar to them. If a person is very similar to us, we can judge that person accurately, not so much because we can accurately judge another, but because we can accurately judge ourselves. Triandis further states that the greater the dissimilarity is between the sender and the receiver, the more likely that distortion of the message will occur. Thus, communication between individuals of different cultures often emerges from inaccurate perceptions unless people make a conscious attempt to understand the differing cultural factors, and unless they show a real desire to communicate across cultural boundaries (Samovar et al., 1981, p. 32).

Stereotyping

Stereotyping is another factor that influences communication. Individuals exhibit countless characteristics; each individual is unique in many ways. Because no one can process all this information adequately, people simplify the perception of complexity by various means. One way is to assign a set of traits to an entire group and act as though all regular members of that group possess those particular traits. This assignment of characteristics to a group without conscious regard for the individual members is called stereotyping. The process of stereotyping helps individuals to screen the countless verbal and nonverbal messages transmitted, thus simplifying the task of information processing (Huseman et al., 1976). Stereotyping is particularly common in the intercultural setting.

We tend to stereotype people and groups based on very little knowledge or contact. It is both effortless and comfortable to be able to quickly say "All Jews are . . ." or "He is a

Mexican, therefore he must . . . ." Such conclusions take little energy, and also exonerate the individual from any other reflection or observation. He is able, often without ever knowing a Jew or a Mexican, to act as if he knows all about the person who stands before him. It is, in short, a lazy method of interaction. (Samovar et al., 1981, p. 200)

Stereotyping not only helps an individual to process the many and often conflicting cues received from a different culture; it may also help to reduce culture shock (Samovar et al., 1981). In a situation with few familiar symbols or behaviors, stereotypes provide a defense mechanism to avoid being overwhelmed. Among the most common stereotypes are those regarding sex, race, ethnic origin, and national identity. Nevertheless, Triandis (1977) carefully distinguishes between stereotypes and sociotypes. Traits that accurately describe a group constitute a sociotype, whereas arbitrary and often inaccurate ideas about a particular group make up a stereotype.

Ethnocentrism

Ethnocentrism refers to our sense of superiority as members of a particular culture. Ruhly (1976) defines ethnocentrism as "the tendency to interpret or judge all other groups, their environments, and their communication according to the categories and values of our own culture" (p. 22).

All people undergo a socialization process that encourages the development of ethnocentric attitudes: people are taught certain ways of doing things, observe those around them behaving in certain ways, and become familiar with certain systems. It would seen irrational to assume that a culture would choose any but the "best" way to do things from the point of view of that culture. Thus, from our earliest years we have negative implications for communication between culturally divergent individuals (Almaney, 1974).

A U.S. executive, for instance, who considers English to be the "best" or the "most logical" language will not apply himself to learn a foreign language which he considers "inferior" or "illogical." And if he considers his nonverbal system to be the most "civilized" system, he will tend to reject other systems as "primitive." In this sense, ethnocentrism can constitute a formidable block to effective empathy and can lead not only to a complete communication breakdown but also to antagonism, or even hostility. (p. 27)

To interact effectively with people whose cultural conditioning has been different, a person must be aware of this ethnocentric bias. Being aware does not necessarily mean that one can eliminate one's own ethnocentrism; rather, one must take it into account and, moreover, make allowances for it in others.

ORGANIZATIONS AND COMMUNICATION

Up to this point, we have examined primarily how cultural factors (language, attribution, perceptions) not only shape people but also shape their capacity to communicate effectively in situations requiring intercultural communication.

However, culture can also affect the communication process by shaping its context. Communication within an organization is profoundly affected by certain aspects of that organization. Its social composition, goal orientation, division of labor, system of coordination, and continuity through time all exert powerful influences. We should examine each aspect of this situation in turn.

Social Composition

An organization's social composition produces a complex communication environment: communicators (whether senders or receivers of information) act both as individuals and as members of the organization. In this latter capacity, they tend to communicate within and between groups. A given group's norms and values will necessarily influence both the form and the content of the information transmitted, as well as the way in which it is received and interpreted. The more overarching cultural norms will influence not only informal group norms but also formal group objectives and structure. An example will make these notions more concrete.

One study (Barrett & Frank, 1969) revealed that across cultures, managers' preference for one-way versus two-way communication was not uniform (Table 4.2). For instance, 20.6% of "senders" in India preferred one-way communication, yet only 3.4% of Norwegians preferred this mode of communication. For the "receiver" position, the differences were even more extreme; 11.8% of Indians and 10% of Danish managers preferred one-way communication whereas none of the Italian or American managers preferred this mode. These findings revealed that the norms controlling whether or not managers' and subordinates' conversation should be two-way varied in different cultures. Imagine the problems arising when a superior from a culture preferring two-way superior–subordinate conversation interacts with a subordinate from a culture preferring strictly one-way exchange.

Table 4.2   Attitudes in One-Way and Two-Way Communication

	Belgium	Denmark	India	Italy	Norway	U.K.	U.S.	Total
No. of managers	47	30	34	47	88	36	31	313
No. of groups	5	5	6	7	18	4	6	51
Percent preferring as sender*								
1-way communication	6.4	10.0	20.6	6.4	3.4	13.9	6.5	8.3
2-way communication	87.2	83.3	79.4	91.5	95.5	86.1	93.5	89.5
Percent preferring as receiver[†]								
1-way communication	2.1	10.0	11.8	0.0	1.1	8.3	0.0	3.8
2-way communication	95.7	90.0	88.2	95.7	97.7	91.7	100.0	94.9

*Percentages may not total 100; the remainders represent those expressing no difference in their attitude.
[†]Found significant at the 0.05 level, chi-square analysis.
Source: G. V. Barrett and R. H. Frank, *Communication Preference and Performance: A Cross Cultural Comparison.* MRC Technical Report No. 29, August 1969.

Goal Orientation

Another aspect that affects communication within an organization is goal orientation. One conception of business organizations is that they are goal-oriented social units. To function effectively, they must set organizational goals that specify the purpose of the organization, they must divide the organizational tasks necessary to meet these goals, and they must coordinate the different subtasks in a way that allows the organization to function effectively. Culture has an impact on each of these separate functions (see Figure 4.5). Yet workers from different cultures may have different conceptions of the organization's goals and of how the organization's activities are divided and coordinated. Such differences may become problematic in two contexts, however.

First, within an MNC's subsidiaries, there may be different conceptions of the attributes we have discussed. Failure to consider these differences will probably result in unsuccessful communication. Second, if employees from one culture are transferred to an organization in another, they should realize that their culturally determined conception of the organization's functioning may be very different from its actual circumstances.

Porter and Roberts (1976) describe goal orientation and goal acceptance as structural variables. Within the cross-cultural context, goal orientation is also important as a reflection of orientation toward activity. According to Samovar et al. (1981), acceptance of goals may be affected by the extent to which members of a culture believe that a goal can be achieved through activity and work.

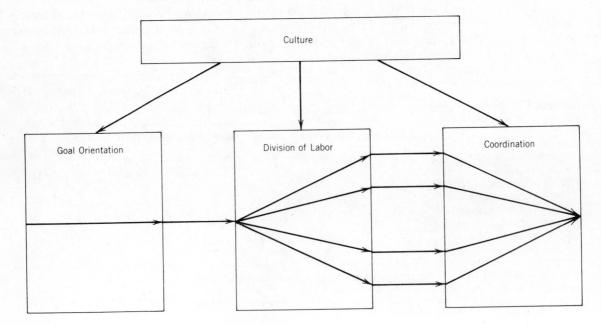

Figure 4.5   Effects of culture on managerial tasks.

Westerners tend to believe that through their deeds and acts they can cause things to happen. Eastern people may be more content with waiting for events to happen rather than trying to cause their occurrence. While Western people are prone to actively pursue truth, many Easterners more commonly share the view that truth will present itself when the time is appropriate. How different views toward world and activity manifest themselves in different cultures is reflected in the following anecdote:

If you ask a Hindu why he got only ten bags of corn from his land while nearby farmers got much more he would say it was the wish of God. An American farmer's answer to the same question would be: "Hell, I didn't work hard enough."

The Hindu's explanation that it was God's wish is indicative of a passive activity orientation. And the American's perception of not having worked hard enough reflects a maximum doing activity orientation. (p. 94)

This anecdote suggests that although individuals or groups may have goals in common, differences in goal orientation may interfere with communication in this regard. We should examine the factors influencing goal orientation. The most significant factors are division of labor, coordination, patterns, and continuity.

Division of Labor   Division of labor (differentiation of function) makes certain patterns of interactions possible, but it also limits these same patterns. Workers' perspectives, attitudes, and goals are dramatically affected by work tasks and functions—a situation that facilitates communication among those performing similar functions but inhibits it among individuals from different functional areas. In the context of an MNC's operations, it is easy to see how goal differences, arising from the division of labor and reinforced by cultural differences, may seriously impede the communication process.

Coordination   Coordination ensures that subgoals are complementary and that the division of labor does not lead to dysfunctional conflict. One such coordination mechanism is the communication network through which employees combine their discrete tasks.

Patterns of Communication   Much communication in organizations takes place within a subunit or work group. Figure 4.6 and Table 4.3 present different types of communication networks, grouped according to whether they are centralized or not. As we can see, the centralized networks have focal individuals through whom communication must pass; the decentralized networks do not. Generally speaking, centralized networks will be more prevalent in authoritarian cultures, and decentralized networks more common in democratic cultures. Each network leads to a drastically different pattern of communication. Such differences account for employees' difficulties in adjusting from one pattern to another.

Continuity   Finally, organizations are characterized by continuity through time. By continuity through time, Porter and Roberts (1976) mean that organizations have a past, a present, and a future. Individuals are thus aware that

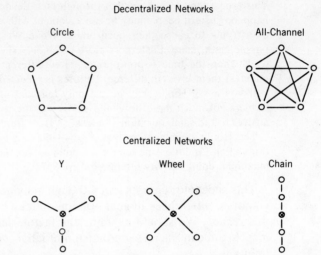

Figure 4.6 Basic small-group communication networks.

their activities and interactions are not likely to be singular, one-time occurrences; they are more likely to be repeated through time. This awareness affects communication sent, received, and interpreted to conform to this concept of continuity. For instance, an individual may choose to transmit to a superior a message criticizing job performance in a particular situation, because he or she knows that the situation and performance are likely to be repeated in the future with similar resulting problems.

Samovar et al. (1981) describe how a culture's concept of time may vary:

Most Western cultures think of time in lineal spatial terms. We are timebound and well aware of the past, present and future. Countries such as Germany and Switzerland are even more aware of time. Trains, planes, and meals must always be on time. In contrast, the Hopi Indians pay very little attention to time as we know it. They believe that each thing, whether a person, plant, or animal, has its own time system. (p. 53)

To the extent that perceptions of time vary between cultures, they will vary in institutions across cultures—something MNCs would do well to notice. For example, an individual whose culture places a greater emphasis on the present than on the past or future may see little need to document important communications "for the record," viewing a verbal transaction as perfectly sufficient. Differences in time orientation may also affect such processes as planning, especially long-range planning, hiring, staffing, training, appraising, and so on.

Two other structural variables important to communication in the cross-cultural context are status (the relative importance of a position) and power (the relative ability to control other people and events). These are key variables that affect both the direction and content of communication. Differential power and status lead to substantial screening and shaping of information at all levels of the organizational hierarchy—activities that can be broadly interpreted as

Table 4.3 Comparisons Showing Differences Between Centralized (Wheel, Chain, Y) and Decentralized (Circle, Comcon) Networks as a Function of Task Complexity

	Simple Problems*	Complex Problems†	Total
Time			
Centralized faster	14	0	14
Decentralized faster	4	18	22
Messages			
Centralized sent more	0	1	1
Decentralized sent more	18	17	35
Errors			
Centralized made more	0	6	6
Decentralized made more	9	1	10
No difference	1	3	4
Satisfaction			
Centralized higher	1	1	2
Decentralized higher	7	10	17

*Simple problems: symbol-, letter-, number-, and color-identification tasks.
†Complex problems: arithmetic, word arrangement, sentence construction, and discussion problems.
Source: L. W. Porter and K. H. Roberts, ''Communication in Organizations,'' in M. D. Dunnette, ed., *Handbook of Industrial and Organization Psychology.* Chicago: Rand McNally, 1976, p. 1578.

attempts at self-protection, self-enhancement, and gratification. Status and power are important determinants of communication between superior and subordinate, as well as across groups at the same organizational level.

We have considered how culture affects communication throughout the organization. We should now examine what managers can do to facilitate communication in a cross-cultural setting.

MANAGING CROSS-CULTURAL COMMUNICATION

An organization needs to consider two distinct yet interrelated aspects of communication. On the one hand, organizational communication networks are designed to move messages throughout the organization; on the other hand, individual interactions involving communication on a day-to-day, personal basis also take place within these networks. These two aspects are distinct because communication networks are largely formal and designed to achieve specific objectives, whereas day-to-day communication is essentially informal and spontaneous.

As already noted, different cultures exhibit different communication patterns. These differences affect both networks and daily interpersonal communication. Previous discussion has stressed the cultural factors that affect interpersonal communication at all levels. Some cultural factors, however, are also significant because they influence the direction, amount, and type of communication. Organizations within a given culture exhibit differences in communication styles, depending on their purpose as well as their personnel, but they are also likely to exhibit similarities as a function of work-related values. Let's examine these implications.

Communication Networks

Intercultural communication takes place in organizations for a variety of reasons and in a variety of situations. Multinational corporate managers of one nationality may have to interact with their counterparts in other countries, or with subordinates or superiors, or both, of another nationality. Furthermore, they often negotiate with salespeople, customers, and suppliers of various nationalities. And when working in a foreign country, they inevitably interact with host-country nationals who are service personnel, civil servants, and government officials.

Robinson (1978) has investigated various kinds of communication networks typically found in multinational corporations. He suggests that the key element to maintaining an effective communication network is a skillful communicator in both the home country and the host country. He proposes five alternative channels of communication that represent a continuum over time as individual abilities develop. These five alternatives appear in Figure 4.7.

Channel 5 is typical of the MNC that has a cadre of international managers of different nationalities communicating effectively in all directions. Robinson considers this unusual, however, and contends that many MNCs must stop at channel 3. This is adequate as long as someone at headquarters is really knowledgeable about the situation in the host country. Channel 1 is characteristic of the newly internationalized firm: it achieves communication largely through a host-country national who has been trained in the home country and is thus able to communicate effectively with the home-country management.

Brandt and Hulbert (1976) conducted an empirical study of the communications systems in sixty-three MNCs with subsidiaries in Brazil. Their intention was to identify those characteristics of a communication system associated with better understanding between headquarters and the field, as perceived by field managers. They found significant differences between European, Japanese, and American communication practices. American field managers, for example, generally reported more often to headquarters, held more regularly scheduled regional or worldwide meetings, and relied more on personal visits between the subsidiary's chief executive and his home-office superior. Japanese and European companies, by contrast, were found to prefer ''management by exception,'' responding only when a problem or opportunity arose.

Brandt and Hulbert emphasize that exchange of information between home office and subsidiary management plays a crucial role in coordinating and controlling multinational operations, and they conclude that home offices clearly need to give more thought to planning their information flows and communication systems. Their findings suggest that home-office personnel need to have

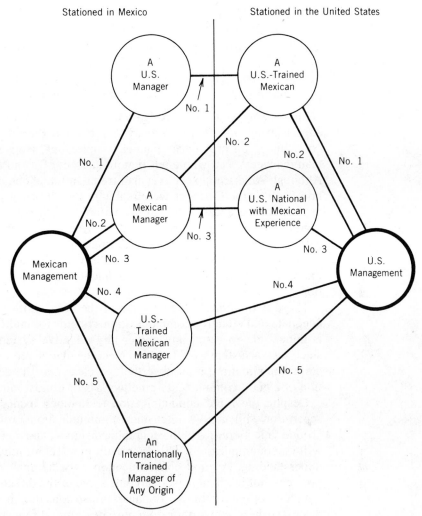

Figure 4.7 Alternative channels of communication between a U.S. firm and an associated Mexican enterprise.

Source: R. D. Robinson, *International Business Management.* Hinsdale, IL: Dryden, 1978, p. 296.

firsthand knowledge of subsidiary operations to ensure effective communication. Unfortunately, this is often not the case.

A survey that included thirty-two North American as well as English, French, and Japanese MNCs (Murray, 1972) reveals major communication challenges:

1. Increasing the communication system's ability to process information from more than one source, and communicating this in composite form.
2. Directing governmental resources to collect pertinent information.

3. Mechanizing international system flows to allow managers greater freedom from documentation.
4. Increasing the capacity to incorporate decision rules into strategic planning.
5. Convincing foreign operations of the limited capacities available in currently utilized information processing systems.

Similarly, a study of German and American general managers working in American subsidiaries in Germany (Hildebrand, 1973) identified three recurring communication problems: channel complexities, language, and culture. German managers as a whole felt remote and cut off from their parent company. Although American executives had frequent telephone conversations with the home office, the Germans were reluctant to call because of cost and language problems. There was great dissatisfaction with formal channels of communication; as a result, they were frequently bypassed. Several managers noted that getting translated reports from German-speaking, lower-level management through to headquarters and back again was such a time-consuming process that German nationals who were not fluent in English had little hope of promotion.

These two studies indicate some of the complexities involved in designing adequate and effective communication systems for multinational companies. It is impossible to detail any universally effective system for communication, since such a system would need to meet the unique requirements of a particular corporate situation; it is, nevertheless, clear that the design and implementation of a good communication network is of utmost importance to the MNC.

Despite the rapid communication technology available today, geographic separation still greatly intensifies communication problems. Message turn-around time increases with geographic distance, and more reliance is placed on written communication. This can result in a lack of integration and decreased understanding. A good communication network may not entirely solve the problem, but it will at least overcome some of the difficulties inherent in multinational communications. Managers must consider the interpersonal factors discussed here: perceptions, stereotypes, and ethnocentrism, as well as language and nonverbal processes. Moreover, corporate characteristics, including ownership, size, age diversity, and industry, all deserve close attention if an effective communication network is to be designed.

Training for Intercultural Communication

Given these communication problems, selection and training of international personnel for overseas assignments becomes critically important. In a later chapter, we shall elaborate on this issue. Here we will concentrate on communication training.

Several training methods have been suggested as useful. However, Moran and Harris (1982) sound a cautionary note. They point out that in many cases, communication training methods have been developed according to American priorities and assumptions about other cultures. Such culture-bound training

Box 4.4

Companies have even been known to promote their products in the wrong language. In Dubai, for example, only 10 percent of the population speaks Arabic. The remaining 90 percent originate from Pakistan, India, Iran, or elsewhere. Several European and American firms, however, have assumed that all Middle Eastern countries are primarily populated with Arabic-speaking people and so have only promoted their products in Arabic.

Source: D. A. Ricks, *Big Business Blunders*. Homewood, IL: Dow Jones–Irwin, 1983, p. 53.

methods are neither realistic nor acceptable from an intercultural perspective. Specifically, Moran and Harris note several instances in which American suggestions to improve communication that would be appropriate in the United States are, in fact, totally inappropriate from an Arab viewpoint. For example, they criticize the performance goals of a five-day management training program used by a major American multinational corporation in the Middle East: given the context, the seminar precludes rather than encourages trust. Table 4.4 provides some specific data from this program, relating the accepted norms of building a climate of trust.

Moran and Harris claim that all of the factors listed under the heading of behaviors that preclude a trust climate do, in fact, help preclude the development of trust in the Middle East. They are all unfavorable traits.

However, Moran and Harris offer the following list of norms predominant in the Middle East (which does not reflect the cultural approach of Christian Arabs or Israelis) and delineate the inappropriateness of the "managing-climate" (helping to build a trust climate) instrument in reference to the Middle East:

1. It is stated that an expression of doubt and concern and feelings in an open and natural way would be a behavior which facilitates the building of a trust climate. This may be so from a Western perspective; however, this behavior might become a barrier to effective communication in the Middle East. Middle Easterners are sensitive, especially when it comes to the expression of doubt and concern in an open manner, in a non-familiar setting. Middle Easterners cherish honesty, but tact is extremely important when expressing doubt. This could be viewed as disagreement or disharmony that might cloud the trust climate between persons. Middle Easterners are generally very temperamental, and therefore they try to avoid arguments. Once there is an argument, it tends to be heated because each one in the discussion wants to be right.

2. The management style in the Middle East tends to be much more authoritative than in the United States. This is a cultural characteristic that can be explained by the following:

● Governments in the Middle East generally are much more authoritative than governments in the West with the absolute authority being vested in the hands of the ruling class.

Table 4.4 Managing Climate

Behaviors That Help *Build* a Trust Climate	Behaviors That Help *Preclude* a Trust Climate
1. Express your doubts, concerns, and feelings in an open, natural way. Encourage your subordinates to do so also.	1. Look on expressions of feelings and doubts as signs of weakness.
2. When subordinates express their doubts, concerns, and feelings, accept them supportively and discuss them thoroughly.	2. Be sarcastic, but cleverly so.
3. Set honesty as one standard that will not be compromised. Demand it from yourself and from your staff.	3. Let your subordinates know that you expect them to "stretch the truth" a little if it will make the organization look good.
4. Be clear about your expectations when assigning work or eliciting opinions. Explain your reasons, wherever possible, behind requests and directions.	4. Be secretive. Never let them really be sure what's on your mind. This keeps them on their toes.
5. Encourage subordinates to look to you as a possible resource in accomplishing results, but develop and reinforce independence.	5. Discourage subordinates from coming to you for help. After all, they should be "stem-winders" and "self-starters."
6. When something goes wrong, determine what happened, not "who did it."	6. When something goes wrong, blow up, hit the ceiling, and look for the guilty party.
7. Encourage active support and participation in corrective measures from those involved.	7. Gossip about and disparage others on the staff when they are not present. Overrespond to casual comments by others about your people.
8. Share credit for successes: assume the bulk of responsibility for criticism of your unit.	8. Take credit for successes. Plan vendettas and other ploys to make other organizations look bad. Draw on subordinates for carrying these out. Always insist on plenty of documentation to protect yourself.

Source: R. T. Moran and P. R. Harris, *Managing Cultural Synergy.* Houston: Gulf Publ., 1982, p. 81.

● The social structure—Older persons are highly respected in the Middle East, and this stems from religious teachings.

● The family structure—The father in a family in the Middle East is generally the most respected and authoritative person. He is the highest authority and his children look up to him for guidance.

● The manager in the Middle East enjoys his power and exercises his authority. Possessing power and authority in the Middle East is generally relished by those who possess it. To give in to subordinates would be viewed by them as possessing weakness.

3. Honesty as a standard—Honesty is highly regarded in the Middle East, yet it is coupled with the concept of saving face and preserving one's honor. Middle Easterners are introverted and shy until a mutual trust is built, and at that time a person will share his concerns. The process of developing mutual trust takes a long time when compared with the establishment of relations in the United States. Honesty is also a word that has many meanings depending on the situation.

Box 4.5

General Motors was . . . . troubled by the lack of enthusiasm among the Puerto Rican auto dealers for its recently introduced Chevrolet "Nova." The name "Nova" meant "star" when literally translated. However, when spoken, it sounded like "no va" which, in Spanish, means "it doesn't go."

The naming of a new automobile model to be marketed in Germany by Rolls Royce was a difficult undertaking. The company felt that the English name "Silver Mist" was very appealing but discovered that the name would undoubtedly not capture the German market as hoped. In German, the translated meaning of "mist" is actually "excrement," and the Germans could not possibly have found such a name appealing.

Source: D. A. Ricks, *Big Business Blunders.* Homewood, IL: Dow Jones–Irwin, 1983, pp. 38, 39.

4. Clarity of expectations—Clarity in expectations is extremely important. It is very difficult to read another person's mind, but stating clearly what one wants is western. Another way would be to anticipate the needs or expectations of another (i.e., as Middle Easterners often do).

5. Encouragement of subordinates to look up to their superiors as a possible resource for accomplishing results. However, the people in the Middle East like to be independent, especially persons who are educated. If the superior is a foreigner, they probably would resent referring to him at all times for accomplishing tasks or results because it might make them feel inferior. The job might get done, but if not enough responsibility is given to the person from the Middle East, the trust climate would be stifled. They may also adapt the attitude of carelessness and simply do what is required from them without further incentive.

6. When things go wrong—It is sometimes necessary to tell someone that an error was made by someone in the organization, but this must be done very tactfully.

7. Active support and participation—This is a good point in helping subordinates realize and develop responsibility.

8. Sharing credit—This is considered generosity and would win the respect and support of persons one is working with. (Moran & Harris, 1982, pp. 86–87)

Moran and Harris suggest a list of values and social norms that captures the Arab employees' attitude. This is presented in Table 4.5.

Although no single training program can realistically expect to prepare people fully for effective communication across a wide range of different cultures, a manager's appreciation of cultural factors, along with empathy, can substantially improve his or her chances for success (Samovar et al., 1981). Two training programs that attempt to accomplish these goals warrant our attention.

- The Society for International Education, Training and Research (SIETAR) has developed a number of training programs focusing on the communication process. These programs stress communication as a creative art that requires both patience and skill. Excerpts from these exercises are presented at the end of this chapter (Appendix A).

Table 4.5 Norms in the Middle East

Assume a company's representatives are assigned to an Arab culture in the Middle East. The following points are presented as they relate specifically to comments made in the critique* of the communicating section:

1. The person with whom a Middle Easterner is working is more important than the mission, product, or job.
2. Quiet strength is a greater value than an obvious use of power.
3. Patience is a virtue.
4. Friendship and trust are prerequisites for any social or business transactions and are slowly developed.
5. Confrontation or criticism in the presence of others should be avoided.
6. Middle Easterners love the spoken word, tend to ramble and don't get to the point quickly.
7. Middle Easterners are masters at flattery and appreciate compliments.
8. Middle Easterners find bluntness very disrespectful, which is why they usually respond in the most agreeable manner, regardless of truth.
9. Middle Easterners are very emotional people and are easily outraged by even slight provocations.
10. Middle Easterners are proud and their dignity is important to them.

*"Middle East" is a broad term and refers here to the Arab countries in the region generally referred to as the Middle East. However, the presentation does not reflect the cultural approach of Christian Arabs or Israelis.
Source: R. T. Moran and P. R. Harris, *Managing Cultural Synergy.* Houston: Gulf Publ., 1982, pp. 81, 82.

● As noted earlier, Triandis (1977) suggests that attributions—explanations of certain behaviors in other people—often differ from culture to culture. (Recall the example of the Greek subordinate and the American manager.) These differences in attributions can produce serious breakdowns in the communication process. Triandis has therefore devised a training program that he calls the "Cultural Assimilator" as a means of identifying and understanding other people's likely attributions. This training program is described in Exhibit 4.1.

The cultural assimilator rewards judgments reflecting the correct attribution. Specifically, it provides the following information about another culture:

1. Norms for different kinds of situations;

2. Role structures and, in particular, the way role perceptions differ from role perceptions in the learner's culture;

3. The way behaviors express general intentions;

4. Self-concepts frequently found;

5. Behaviors valued and disvalued;

6. Antecedents and consequences frequently associated with valued and disvalued behaviors;

7. Differentiations common among types of people, within modes of exchange, and between modes of exchange, as well as across time and place;

8. Strengths of the norms, roles, self-concept, general intentions, affect toward the behavior—that is, the weights of the model;

9. Amplitude of the responses that people generally make in various social situations; and

10. Reinforcements that people expect in different situations and the appropriateness of the exchange of particular reinforcements—for example, that you can exchange love for status but not money for love. (Triandis, 1977, p. 254).

The cultural assimilator program is only one way of fostering more astute perception in cross-cultural settings; others address the same issues in different ways. However, this program suggests how a laboratory exercise can heighten participants' awareness.

Exhibit 4.1
An Example of a Cultural Assimilator

Briefly, the student of intercultural events is presented with one or two hundred "items" that give information about the other culture. Each item consists of six sheets of paper. On page 1 there is a journalistic description of an intercultural episode in which P, a member of culture A, interacted with O, a member of culture B, and there was some sort of interpersonal difficulty or misunderstanding. Page 2 presents four interpretations of what went wrong. These interpretations can be considered attributions of the observed behavior. Only one of these attributions is correct, from the perspective of culture B. Thus, a member of culture A has to find the one correct attribution; the other three are plausible and usually consistent with the attributions made by naive members of culture A, but they are unacceptable and inaccurate from the point of view of the other culture. The trainee selects the alternative that he or she considers correct and is then instructed to turn to the corresponding one of the remaining four pages. If the correct answer was selected, the appropriate page will praise the trainee and tell why the answer was correct. If the wrong answer was selected, the trainee finds on the appropriate page a mild criticism, such as "You did not read the episode sufficiently carefully," and he or she is instructed to read it again and select another answer.

This procedure clearly increases the extent to which a member of culture A makes attributions that are isomorphic with the attributions made by members of culture B. Furthermore, as the trainee learns to make "correct" attributions, it is probable that he or she becomes more and more able to predict the behavior of members of culture B.

As an illustration of the culture assimilator, here is one item from an assimilator prepared by Slobodin and his associates (1972) to train white supervisors of black hard-core unemployed male workers.

Exhibit 4.1 (*Continued*)

On page 205–1, we find the following:

> Several hard-core unemployed blacks had been hired by Jones Tool and Die Company. Mac Grove was one of the supervisors who was supposed to train the blacks in the procedures of their new jobs. After he had explained the use of one machine, he asked:
>
> "Are there any questions?"
>
> One of the black workers replied: "Yes, Mr. Grove . . ." At which time Mac interrupted, saying: "Oh, call me Mac. Everybody does."
>
> The group moved on to another machine and Mac explained its function. He was surprised when one of the other black workers again addressed him as Mr. Grove.

On page 205–2, we find the following:

> Why did the black workers call him Mr. Grove?
> 1. They thought whites in positions of authority expect to be called Mr. by blacks.
>
>   Please go to page 205–3.
> 2. They felt that Mr. was more appropriate under the circumstances.
>
>   Please go to page 205–4.
> 3. They didn't feel comfortable about calling a white by his first name.
>
>   Please go to page 205–5.
> 4. They didn't believe that Mac really wanted to be called Mac. They thought he was just saying the expected thing.
>
>   Please go to page 205–6.

Persons studying the assimilator would turn to the page indicated after their selected answer and would find the following feedback:

On page 205–3:

> You selected 1: They thought whites in positions of authority expect to be called Mr. by blacks.
>
> While this might be true, it doesn't explain why they continued to call him Mr. after he told them to call him Mac.
>
> Please go back to page 205–1.

Source: H. C. Triandis, *Interpersonal Behavior*. Monterey, CA: Brooks/Cole, 1977, pp. 248–253.

Exhibit 4.1 (*Continued*)

On page 205–4:

> You selected 2: They felt that Mr. was more appropriate under the circumstances.
> Yes.
> Our data indicate that hard-core unemployed blacks feel that formal speech indicates mutual respect and provides status. They also feel that establishing this mutual respect indicates friendship and trust. It is a good thing to keep in mind that hard-core blacks may prefer the more formal use of Mr. until they have established a good relationship with another person. They may prefer to be called Mr. themselves, at first, if the situation is at all formal. Take your cues from the black workers and maintain formality until it seems appropriate to do otherwise.
>
> Please go to page 206.

On page 205–5:

> You selected 3: They didn't feel comfortable about calling a white by his first name.
> This is not necessarily true. Hard-core blacks call friends, white or black, by their first names. However, they may have felt uncomfortable about calling the foreman Mac until they got to know him better.
>
> Please go back to page 205–1.

On page 205–6:

> You selected 4: They didn't believe that Mac really wanted to be called Mac. They thought he was just saying the expected thing.
> This is not the best answer. There is no evidence given in the incident to assume this.
>
> Please go back to page 205–1.

On page 206:

> SUMMARY
> In this section, we saw that some black workers believe . . . formality is a desirable way to achieve mutual respect between [themselves] and the foreman.

Summary statements, such as the one on page 206, usually include several related points and follow the presentation of half a dozen or so assimilator items.

Box 4.6

Ford encountered translation problems with some of its cars. It introduced a low cost truck, the "Fiera," into some of the less-developed countries. Unfortunately the name meant "ugly old woman" in Spanish. Needless to say, this name did not encourage sales. Ford also experienced slow sales when it introduced a top-of-the-line automobile, the "Comet," in Mexico under the name "Caliente." The puzzlingly low sales levels were finally understood when Ford discovered that "caliente" is slang for a streetwalker.

Additional headaches were reportedly experienced when Ford's "Pinto" was briefly introduced in Brazil under its English name. The name was speedily changed to "Corcel" (which means "horse" in Portuguese) after Ford discovered that the Portuguese slang translation of "pinto" is "a small male appendage."

Source: D. A. Ricks, *Big Business Blunders*. Homewood, IL: Dow Jones–Irwin, 1983, p. 39.

CONCLUSION

The cultural factors influencing the communication process are varied and complex. It is hardly surprising that intercultural communication is a hazardous process. Yet today it is an increasingly common one—especially for managers in multinational corporations. Although it is difficult to generalize about improving intercultural communication, the one cardinal rule applicable to intercultural communication is sensitivity both to one's own culture and to "foreign" cultural patterns.

To summarize, communication is an attempt to share meaning through the transmission of messages. As simple as that attempt may seem, it is inevitably fraught with difficulties. Even communication between persons of similar cultural backgrounds involves a complex process of encoding, transmitting, and decoding messages—a process that few people will notice consciously but that all of us undertake whenever we communicate with others. If this process is complex under relatively simple intracultural circumstances, then it is all the more so between cultures.

What complicates the situation is the variety, subtlety, and multifaceted nature of human communication. Each person communicates not just as an individual, but as a member of a society, a nation, a large or small group with linguistic, racial, and historical affiliations or influences. These affiliations or influences constitute the person's field of experience. Depending on the differences between their fields of experience, communicators may find themselves misunderstanding each other, misreading each other, even resenting each other for imagined slights and insults. What complicates the situation still further is that cultural differences affect not just what we say and how we say it, but also our gestures, posture, and use of space.

Moreover, these differences in verbal and nonverbal communication run the risk of further misinterpretation because of another intercultural force: attribution. Perception, stereotyping, and ethnocentrism incline all people to attribute meanings to what others do. Attribution is, in fact, one of the most powerful forces that affects (and sometimes disrupts) communication between human beings.

At times it seems remarkable that people manage to communicate with each other as well as they do. The additional differences between organizations in different cultures—differences in structure, division of labor, coordination, and continuity—present the risk of further obstacles to good communication. Yet organizations can overcome these obstacles. Three kinds of effort make this possible. One is establishing effective communication networks, particularly through the use of well-planned channels. The second is training for intercultural communication—specific programs to provide information about dealing with another culture.

The third kind of effort deserves special note. It is the most obvious kind, yet the most often forgotten. It is simply the constant effort to remind oneself that one's own culture is not the yardstick by which all others are measured; that one's own way of living and working is not the source of all human meaning; that one's own words for describing the world are not the only eloquence. This effort is both the means to good intercultural communication and its goal.

Appendix A Communication Exercise

1. *Aim:* To analyze a set of communication styles, see how intercultural communication can be practically improved and used to help people adjust to new cultural environments.

2. *Objectives:* Participants will:

(1) Analyze four value orientations and their impact on communication styles (self-assessment exercise);

(2) Learn how to switch from one style to another (exercise);

(3) Learn how to cope with different styles (exercise and conceptual framework: input 1);

(4) Practice four listening and responding styles (exercise and conceptual framework: input 2);

(5) Examine five communication skills and their use across cultures (conceptual framework: input 3).

3. *Process:*

(a) Participants fill out the self-assessment exercise on communication styles:

COMMUNICATON VALUE ORIENTATIONS:
A SELF-ASSESSMENT EXERCISE

Please select in each pair of attributes the one which is most typical of your personality. No pair is an either-or proposal. Make your choice as spontaneously as possible. There is no wrong answer.

1. I like action.
2. I deal with problems in a systematic way.
3. I believe that teams are more effective than individuals.
4. I enjoy innovation very much.
5. I am more interested in the future than the past.
6. I enjoy working with people.
7. I like to attend well-organized group meetings.
8. Deadlines are important for me.
9. I cannot stand procrastination.
10. I believe that new ideas have to be tested before being used.
11. I enjoy the stimulation of interaction with others.
12. I am always looking for new possibilities.
13. I want to set up my own objectives.
14. When I start something I like to go through until the end.
15. I basically try to understand other people's emotions.
16. I do challenge people around me.
17. I look forward to receiving feedback on my performance.
18. I find the step-by-step approach very effective.
19. I think I am good at reading people.
20. I like creative problem solving.
21. I extrapolate and project all the time.
22. I am sensitive to others' needs.
23. Planning is the key to success.

Appendix A (*Continued*)

24. I become impatient with long deliberations.
25. I am cool under pressure.
26. I value experience very much.
27. I listen to people.
28. People say that I am a fast thinker.
29. Cooperation is a key word for me.
30. I use logical methods to test alternatives.
31. I like to handle several projects at the same time.
32. I always question myself.
33. I learn by doing.
34. I believe that my head rules my heart.
35. I can predict how others may react to a certain action.
36. I do not like details.
37. Analysis should always precede action.
38. I am able to assess the climate of a group.
39. I have a tendency to start things and not finish them.
40. I perceive myself as decisive.
41. I search for challenging tasks.
42. I rely on observation and data.
43. I can express my feelings openly.
44. I like to design new projects.
45. I enjoy reading very much.
46. I perceive myself as a facilitator.
47. I like to focus on one issue at a time.
48. I like to achieve.
49. I enjoy learning about others.
50. I like variety.
51. Facts speak for themselves.
52. I use my imagination as much as possible.
53. I am impatient with long, slow assignments.
54. My mind never stops working.
55. Key decisions have to be made in a cautious way.
56. I strongly believe that people need each other to get work done.
57. I usually make decisions without thinking too much.
58. Emotions create problems.
59. I like to be liked by others.
60. I can put two and two together very quickly.
61. I try out my new ideas on people.
62. I believe in the scientific approach.
63. I like to get things done.

Appendix A (*Continued*)

64. Good relationships are essential.
65. I am impulsive.
66. I accept differences in people.
67. Communicating with people is an end in itself.
68. I like to be intellectually stimulated.
69. I like to organize.
70. I usually jump from one task to another.
71. Talking and working with people is a creative act.
72. Self-actualization is a key word for me.
73. I enjoy playing with ideas.
74. I dislike to waste my time.
75. I enjoy doing what I am good at.
76. I learn by interacting with others.
77. I find abstractions interesting and enjoyable.
78. I am patient with details.
79. I like brief, to-the-point statements.
80. I feel confident in myself.

(b) *Scoring the self-assessment exercise:* Each *selected item* has to be reported on the four scales reproduced below. In other words, if items 1, 4, 6, have been selected, the same numbers on the four scales should be circled again.

Style 1 = 1—8—9—13—17—24—26—31—33—40—41—48—50—53—57—63—65—70—74—79

Style 2 = 2—7—10—14—18—23—25—30—34—37—42—47—51—55—58—62—66—69—75—78

Style 3 = 3—6—11—15—19—22—27—29—35—38—43—46—49—56—59—64—67—71—76—80

Style 4 = 4—5—12—16—20—21—28—32—36—39—44—45—52—54—60—61—68—72—73—77

Circled items should be added up (not the figures but the number of selected items). The maximum is 20 per style and the total for the four styles should be 40.

(c) *Describing the value orientations:*
Four value orientations have been used to construct this self-assessment exercise. Two assumptions underlie the theory.

☐ The four value orientations can be found in any culture or individual;
☐ The four value orientations have a tremendous impact on the way one communicates.

Style 1 is influenced by the *ACTION* value orientation. People who are strong on this style like action, doing, achieving, getting things done, improving, solving problems.

Style 2 is related to the *PROCESS* value orientation. People who are strong on this style like facts, organizing, structuring, setting up strategies, tactics.

Style 3 is typical of the *PEOPLE* value orientations. Individuals who are people-oriented like to focus on social processes, interactions, communication, teamwork, social systems, motivation.

Style 4 is characterized by the *IDEA* value orientation. People with the idea orientation like concepts, theories, exchange of ideas, innovation, creativity, novelty.

Appendix A   (*Continued*)

SUMMARY OF THE FOUR VALUE ORIENTATIONS

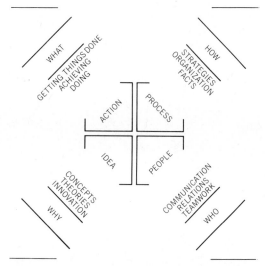

The following remarks should be made at this stage of the process:

(1) Everybody possesses the four value orientations (check with the participants to be sure that nobody has a zero score on any style).

(2) People have a dominant value orientation or a value orientation they feel more comfortable with (ask the participants to focus on their highest score, which reflects this dominant value orientation *for the time being!*).

(3) The importance of the value orientations changes according to the *situations* in which people are involved.

(4) Value orientations are influenced by (a) the personality of the individual, (b) his or her cultural background, (c) past experiences, and (d) present situations.

(5) Each individual has the capability to switch from one value orientation to another. However, it has been shown that when a crisis occurs, most individuals switch back to the value orientation they are most used to.

(6) People with even scores have to choose the style they feel is more relevant for themselves. Even scores mean the people have already some flexibility in shifting from one style to another. They can also appear as confusing to other people.

(d) *Analyzing the impact of the four value orientations on communication styles:*
Participants who share the same dominant value orientation meet together (the group is split into four subgroups) and identify the main characteristics of their communication style. They try to answer the following two questions:

▫ What do we talk about when we communicate? (Content)
▫ How do we do it? (Process)

Table 1 gives a summary of those characteristics (to be distributed at the beginning of this part of the exercise).

(e) Each subgroup is now asked to prepare a set of guidelines that could be used when one has to cope with different styles:

▫ The action orientation group prepares guidelines to adjust to the process-oriented people.

Table 1 Communication Styles (Description of Their Main Characteristics)

Styles	Content		Process
	Features		
ACTION	**They talk about:**		**They are:**
	—Results	—Feedback	—Pragmatic (down to earth)
	—Objectives	—Experience	—Direct (to the point)
	—Performance	—Challenges	—Impatient
	—Productivity	—Achievements	—Decisive
	—Efficiency	—Change	—Quick (jump from one idea to another)
	—Moving ahead	—Decisions	—Energetic (challenge others)
	—Responsibility		
PROCESS	**They talk about:**		**They are:**
	—Facts	—Trying	—Systematic
	—Procedures	—Analysis	—Logical (cause and effect)
	—Planning	—Observations	—Factual
	—Organizing	—Proof	—Verbose
	—Controlling	—Details	—Unemotional
	—Testing		—Cautious
			—Patient
PEOPLE	**They talk about:**		**They are:**
	—People	—Sensitivity	—Spontaneous
	—Needs	—Awareness	—Empathetic
	—Motivations	—Cooperation	—Warm
	—Teamwork	—Beliefs	—Subjective
	—Communications	—Values	—Emotional
	—Feelings	—Expectations	—Perceptive
	—Team spirit	—Relations	—Sensitive
	—Understanding	—Self-development	
IDEA	**They talk about:**		**They are:**
	—Concepts	—New ways	—Imaginative
	—Innovation	—New methods	—Charismatic
	—Creativity	—Improving	—Difficult to understand
	—Opportunities	—Problems	—Ego-centered
	—Possibilities	—Potential	—Unrealistic
	—Grand designs	—Alternatives	—Creative
	—Issues	—What's new in the field	—Full of ideas
	—Interdependence		—Provocative

☐ Process-oriented people do the same for people-oriented individuals,
☐ People-oriented individuals for idea oriented persons, and
☐ Idea-oriented persons for action-oriented people.

The groups share their findings and compare them with the guidelines below (Table 2), to be distributed when the groups have had a chance to present their guidelines.

(f) *Practicing other styles:*
Participants work in pairs practicing the styles they feel less comfortable with.

Table 2 Coping with Other Communication Styles

A. Communicating with an idea-oriented person:
☐ Allow enough time for discussion.
☐ Do not get impatient when he or she goes off on tangents.
☐ In your opening, try to relate the discussed topic to a broader concept or idea (in other words, be conceptual).
☐ Stress the uniqueness of the idea or topic at hand.
☐ Emphasize future value or relate the impact of the idea on the future.
☐ If writing to an idea-oriented person, try to stress the key concepts which underlie your proposal or recommendation right at the outset. Start off with an overall statement and work toward the more particular.

B. Communicating with a process-oriented person:
☐ Be precise (state the facts).
☐ Organize your presentation in logical order:
  Background
  Present situation
  Outcome
☐ Break down your recommendations.
☐ Include options (consider alternatives) with pros and cons.
☐ Do not rush a process-oriented person.
☐ Outline your proposal (1, 2, 3 . . .).

C. Communicating with a people-oriented person:
☐ Allow for small talk (do not start the discussion right away).
☐ Stress the relationships between your proposal and the people concerned.
☐ Show how the idea worked well in the past.
☐ Indicate support from well-respected people.
☐ Use an informal writing style.

D. Communicating with an action-oriented person:
☐ Focus on the results first (state the conclusion right at the outset).
☐ State your best recommendation (do not offer many alternatives).
☐ Be as brief as possible.
☐ Emphasize the practicality of your ideas.
☐ Use visual aids.

(g) *Helping others through intercultural communication skills:*
When trying to help a foreigner ease the cross-cultural adjustment process, it is helpful to keep in mind that:

(1) One cannot solve someone else's problem for him or her. The other person has to come up with his or her own solution to the problem at hand;

(2) What is good for one individual is not necessarily good for another;

(3) What is effective in one situation is not automatically so in another;

(4) People and situations are different. Consequently, decisions about what one should do have to be tailored to the reality of the moment (a *contingency* approach seems to be appropriate);

(5) To learn how to learn is the key to success when trying to adjust to another culture.

Source: P. Casse, *Training for the Cross-Cultural Mind.* Washington, DC: The Society for Intercultural Education, Training and Research, 1981, pp. 125–136.

CHAPTER 5
Employee Attitudes and Motivation

CULTURAL CONDITIONING

Hofstede (1980) describes an exercise that he uses in his classes on organizational behavior: he shows the class an ambiguous picture—one that can be interpreted in two different ways. Viewers can perceive the picture either as an attractive young girl or as an unattractive old woman. What the observers see depends on how they look at it. The experiment shows how different people may perceive strikingly different things in the same situation.

In a variation on this experiment, Hofstede and his colleagues first ask half the class to close their eyes. To the other half, they show (for five seconds) a slightly changed version of the picture—a version in which only the young girl can be seen. Then they ask the other half to close their eyes. To the first half they show (also for five seconds) a version in which only the old woman can be seen. After this preparation, they show the ambiguous picture to everyone at the same time. The results are amazing. The vast majority of those first conditioned by seeing the young girl now see only the young girl in the ambiguous picture; those conditioned by seeing the old woman first can usually see only the old woman afterward. Hofstede then asks one of the students who perceives the old woman to explain to one of those who perceives the young girl what he or she sees, and vice versa, until everyone can see both pictures. But these explanations often prove difficult. Sometimes the students express irritation at the other party. How can they be so stupid? How can they be so blind to reality?

This experience illustrates two crucial issues. First, it shows that even five seconds of conditioning can influence one's perception of reality. This is important. If five seconds can make such a difference, then certainly a lifetime of conditioning will have great impact on how people from different cultures perceive the same environment. Second, it seems significant that students see the opposing group as "stupid," and that they sometimes become irritated with them. This succinctly illustrates the development of negative attitudes toward those who seem different.

Researchers have often found that cultural patterns influence how people perceive reality. Segall, Campbell, and Herskovitz (1966) found that Westerners are more accustomed to straight lines and right angles in three-dimensional structures than non-Westerners, and this influences how they "see" obtuse angles in a two-dimensional drawing. Language is also an important factor in perception. For example, the Eskimo language has many words for snow. This enables Eskimos to discriminate among different types of snow, whereas non-Eskimos see no differences (Whorf, 1956). If people's perceptions of reality are so thoroughly conditioned by the cultural context of their socialization, it should come as no surprise that differing attitudes can also be attributed to cultural differences.

The concept of attitudes is complex and difficult to define. Fishbein and Ajzen (1975) describe attitudes as complex systems comprising the person's beliefs about the object and his or her action tendencies with respect to the object (a person, physical object, place, etc.). To consider attitude differences across cultures, we should look at broad issues in which we might expect attitudes to differ. The following pages briefly discuss a number of such issues in terms of how and why attitudes may differ. These issues are chosen from a large group of attitudes that may affect individuals' work behavior and attitudes in cross-cultural situations. These issues are conformity, achievement, sex order, time, space, and ethnocentrism.

Conformity

To some extent, all societies encourage both conformity and individuality. Every society puts forth laws and requires respect for authority. Every society discourages deviant behavior. On the other hand, every society allows individuals some degree of autonomy. To what degree one or the other of these societal dimensions is emphasized can vary greatly. This variable emphasis can, in turn, greatly influence individual behavior. It would be unreasonable, for instance, to expect most people to work creatively on their own where attitudes toward conformity are positive and those toward individuality are negative. At the opposite extreme, it would be ineffective to emphasize group cooperation in a society in which individuality is highly prized and attitudes toward conformity are largely negative.

Studies in different parts of the world have tended to confirm that societies emphasize compliance training when they require cooperative social action for subsistence. Pressures toward conformity consistently appear to be greater in agricultural societies than in hunting and fishing societies. For example, Berry (1967) found that (as expected), Eskimos were much less conformist on a judgment task than the Temme; this seemed predictable, given the Eskimos' hunting and fishing life-style, which emphasizes independence. In contrast, Temme agricultural practices demand group cooperation and stress conformity.

Anastasi (1983) has written recently about the diverse meanings of intelligence in different cultural settings. She emphasizes that observations of such diversity are increasingly associated with typical differences in cognitive behavior. She concludes that each culture demands, fosters, and rewards a somewhat different set of cognitive skills. "Cultures vary in the extent to which behavior is linked to context and situations," she writes. "These differences are in turn reflected in the development of abstract thinking and in the breadth and nature of the concepts that are formed" (p. 170). If cultural conditioning holds true for cognitive skills, it has also been shown to influence attitudes and selective perception. Levinson (1964) has compared child-rearing practices with typical managerial behavior in Western societies such as Germany, England, and the United States. In Germany, the father is viewed as authoritative and directive; he is the primary source of socialization. This is paralleled by authoritarian and directive management practices. In England, the mother plays a more important role; similarly, management practices are more "feminine" in that they are often protective and aimed at preventing open competition. In the United States, socialization tends to be child-centered, with children having considerable freedom; this, in turn, is paralleled by organizations that stress the value of the individual. Although Levinson warns that these analogies are only suggestive, observing socialization processes may provide valuable insights into appropriate organizational structure and practice. For example, we could extend this analysis to Japan, where child-rearing practices emphasize protection and conformity—an emphasis paralleled by lifetime tenure and group decision making within organizations.

To summarize, all societies must foster some degree of conformity and some degree of individuality among its members. The relative degrees of conformity and individuality tend to vary. Some societies encourage cooperation; others reward competitiveness. Researchers hypothesize that in societies in which the socioeconomic system encourages individual initiative, competitiveness will emerge as part of the dominant life-style. By comparison, a system that encourages less initiative will tend to produce a life-style stressing conformity. Such differing degrees of conformity can cause organizational difficulties. For example, the emphasis on cooperation within the Japanese work setting can be confusing to someone unfamiliar with the system—hence, the difficulty in indiscriminately applying Japanese management style in the United States.

Achievement

As with conformity, achievement is an attribute that some societies recognize and encourage, whereas other societies lack the concept altogether. McClelland (1961) has argued that a society must have a certain level of need for achievement (nAch) before the economic development characteristic of a modern industrial society will take place. McClelland analyzed folk tales to assess a culture's collective level of nAch and found support for his theory. McClelland bases his thesis on the idea that entrepreneurial characteristics are important to successful industrialization and that people who have a strong need for achievement tend to exhibit these characteristics. (The characteristics in question are an affinity for taking personal responsibility, a desire for concrete feedback, and a tendency to take calculated risks.) Although some support has been generated for this view, the difficulty of translating the achievement concept makes the results questionable.

From a managerial perspective, it is probably more important to consider how differences in need for achievement will manifest themselves in behavior. Modern Western management theories emphasize the importance of giving employees the opportunity to satisfy their higher-level "growth" needs, including the need for achievement. Societies that underemphasize (or actually disparage) individual achievements, however, will consider these opportunities useless.

Such cultural emphases are not simply a result of attitudes toward business. They are often considerably more fundamental. Religion accounts for many of the most basic differences. The Protestant work ethic, for example, emphasizes earthly achievement as part of a person's religious duty. In contrast, Hinduism teaches that concern with earthly achievements is a snare and a delusion. Buddhism similarly sees the worldly life as antithetical to religion. Individual-achievement-oriented societies often assume that the desire for higher levels of wealth and material gain is inherent and universal, but in many societies the reverse may be encouraged by religious and ideological views. As a result, Western managers must be alert to cultural conditioning in other countries.

Sex Roles

Another major difference is how societies view the appropriate roles for men and women. Division of labor by sex as a means of dealing with practical tasks is almost universal. Traditional cultures base this division on assumptions about men's and women's capabilities. Recent movements toward greater equality have occurred in industrialized nations, where division of labor by sex is less relevant. Modern technology makes differences in physical strength largely irrelevant, and as the number of hours spent at work diminishes, both men and women have more time for domestic chores. Nevertheless, even industrialized societies may view as negative a woman's success in traditionally male roles.

Certainly traditional, nonindustrialized societies have more distinctly sex-linked, adult roles. Socialization practices include obvious and effective efforts to produce behavioral differences between the sexes. These are accepted as normal, natural, and appropriate. In most agricultural societies, for example, females are particularly subject to training that encourages nurturant, compliant behavior. Thus, they are more likely to conform and submit to male authority. In societies in which women's role in the basic subsistence activity is integral, their contribution is more valued; men are likely to expect less subservience.

Understanding a society's view of sex roles is important in dealing with its workforce. If a particular attitude toward "men's work" and "women's work" originates in the entire socialization process, managers must accommodate this attitude in the workplace.

Time

There are diverse attitudes toward time, but two general categories are most useful for our purposes. We can label these categories traditional and modern (Terpstra, 1978). A traditional attitude can be associated with preindustrial, agricultural societies. This attitude measures time by the long view. It governs life through regular, unhurried natural events. Time is perceived as a cycle: "If today is lost or wasted, there is no concern, for it will return tomorrow." There is always another chance. This attitude toward time, however, differs from that common in the modern world. The modern sense of time originates in a mechanical perception of the world as mathematically divided into hours, minutes, and seconds. The emphasis is on precision and the future (Ronen, 1981; 1984). Industry follows this artificial, mechanical pace: This modern approach is the converse of the traditional. It views time as a straight line. Yesterday is gone forever; today is here only briefly. There are no second chances.

Some specific examples will clarify this difference in attitudes. Americans, for instance, are socialized to be very sensitive to time. They plan for weeks or months ahead (as evidenced by the ubiquitous appointment book) and arrive promptly for appointments. In contrast, Middle Easterners lump all time beyond a week into one category—the future (Nord, 1976). Latin Americans are similar; they do not consider it impolite to keep someone waiting for hours. Each of these attitudes toward time represents different kinds of cultural conditioning. Obviously, each attitude seems natural when everyone works according to its assumptions. But of course when people from different cultures work together, the possibilities for misunderstanding increase. Americans tend to regard Latin Americans as unpunctual and indifferent to schedules and to the clock. Latin Americans, on the other hand, often consider Americans to be compulsive about time—much as the French or Italians regard the Swiss. Time is clearly an issue that can cause real problems for managers in MNCs.

Space

Culture also affects how people view and use space. The normal distance individuals maintain when interacting often varies from culture to culture. For example, Hall (1959) noted that people in Latin America stand closer together when talking than people in the United States; as a result, Americans may feel Latin Americans are "pushy" because they stand "too close." From the Latin American viewpoint, however, Americans seem "standoffish" because they maintain "too much distance." Hall also noted that different approaches to space affect the physical arrangement of offices. In the United States, for example, desks are positioned around the walls, leaving space in the middle. In contrast, the French place a key figure in the middle and divide the remaining space unequally. These variations in spatial arrangements and interactions can result in individuals from one culture feeling uncomfortable in another and, moreover, perhaps misinterpreting the implications of unfamiliar spatial arrangements.

Ethnocentrism

In analyzing behavior, we must acknowledge another problem as well: the innate ethnocentrism that exists in all people. Ethnocentrism is the belief that "our way" of doing things is the best way. Several studies have shown that people usually think of their home as disproportionately important in the world; for example, the Chinese character for China means "the country at the center of the earth." Other countries and cultures manifest the same attitude. A study asked university students in various parts of the world, for instance, to draw world maps. These maps almost always depicted the home country as disproportionately large and usually located at or near the center of the world. People tend to know most about their own country and progressively less about more and more distant countries. Studies by Piaget (1970) and Tajfel et al. (1970) showed that children learn which countries are "good" and "bad" before they learn anything else about the particular countries. Coupled with pervasive ethnocentrism, this lack of knowledge about other countries results in a definite bias when attempting to understand how and why behavior differs across cultures. It is true that people are most comfortable with those who resemble them; nevertheless, this does not mean that efforts to overcome ethnocentrism are futile. Rather, the realization that this view pervades human thinking alerts us to it not only in other people but in ourselves as well.

The recognition of ethnocentrism is a key factor in understanding cultural differences in behavior. With awareness one does not necessarily eliminate one's own ethnocentrism but rather can take it into account. Similarly, awareness does not usually make it possible to overcome ethnocentrism in others, but one can at least make allowance for it.

Having examined these individual issues of cultural conditioning, we should now consider an integrative approach to this subject.

Integrative Approach

In a review of a variety of studies, Barrett and Bass (1976) begin by noting that what motivates people to work depends on what they will lack if they do not work. They conclude that when the motivation to work is closely tied to basic survival, the pattern and diversity of motives that induce people to work are restricted. Thus, in the developed countries, employees often express the desire for more challenging work and autonomy, but most people elsewhere in the world still work for basic survival. For them, job security is paramount.

We cannot, however, explain the situation in these terms alone. A study by Aronoff (1967; 1970) illustrates some of the interacting factors that we must also consider. This study began as field research on a West Indian island. It was designed to test the proposition that personality and sociocultural structures result from the interactions of the environment and past social–cultural institutions as well as from basic psychological needs. The subjects of the study all came from the same village. Virtually all were descendants of Negro slaves. Yet the researchers could isolate two quite distinct groups: the cane cutters and the fishermen. The fishermen were independent businessmen living by their personal efforts, whereas the cane cutters were dependent on the plantations for work. (In addition, the cane cutters had lost more family members in the first twelve years of life than had the fishermen.) Based on interviews, Aronoff derived need-level scores for the two groups. These scores reflected important differences. The cane cutters scored high on the physiological and safety levels, while the fishermen were low in these need levels; in contrast, the fishermen scored higher in needs for affection and esteem.

The original results (1967) appeared at a time when health conditions on the island were a major problem. The cane cutters' work was organized in a very authoritarian manner. In 1970, the situation had changed dramatically: health conditions had improved, and the cane cutters' work had been reorganized to directly reward individual productivity. The second survey found that the new group of cane cutters were functioning at a higher motivational level focused on affiliative and self-esteem needs.

This study indicates the need to consider a wide variety of factors (e.g., medical) in analyzing need levels in different countries, and it illustrates the possibility of making overly facile interpretations based solely on economic factors.

In an attempt to provide an integrated approach to cross-cultural issues, Barrett and Bass suggest the following sequence for understanding the world of work cross-culturally:

1. Understanding national socialization patterns. If the nation in question is highly fragmented, a number of socialization patterns may be operating at the same time; each must be addressed.
2. Examining institutions peculiar to the country. For example, educational institutions may concentrate on preparation of a technical elite or, alternatively, may promote universal literacy.
3. Considering individual traits that distinguish the nation from others. Included here would be distinct perceptual styles, intellectual reasoning, educational qualifications, values, and so on.
4. Focusing on the predominant technology: for example, handicraft or unit, batch or mechanized, automated or process. This information should give a picture of viable organization objectives, predominant compensation policies, and other management function and control considerations.

Both the individual and the organization operate in a larger environmental context. Barrett and Bass (1976) are advocating a very large contingency model that takes a multitude of disparate elements into account. This model, despite its seeming complexity, can facilitate our understanding of cultural conditioning.

Employees' Expectations

Understanding work value systems and expectations in various societies has become increasingly relevant in recent years. Particularly for managers in multinational companies, such understanding means better design or management policies, training programs, reward systems, and decision-making processes in diverse cultural milieus.

The study of work motivation is especially crucial in this regard. First, it assumes that human beings are universally need-fulfilling and goal-achieving organisms. Furthermore, it assumes that people strategize behavior that will fulfill their needs and achieve their goals. The choice of behavior and the impetus with which people engage in it is termed *motivation*. Motivation is therefore a result of variables stemming from a combination of individual needs, value system, and environmental conditions. Although intrasocietal individual differences clearly exist, the question remains whether or not we can observe differences between societies (cultures, nations, etc.) that can explain the differences in terms of identifiable variables. Studies of motivation offer an effective tool for understanding these differences and their consequences.

In the work environment, the motivational process is relevant to organizational effectiveness. It is a management task to induce employees to strive toward organizational objectives. Various motivational models and theories have been developed in the Western world, all with some limitations. (Otherwise we would have had one inclusive, exhaustive theory). The student is by now well versed in and acquainted with these theories; a detailed description is unnecessary. What seems most relevant at present to cross-cultural studies of work motivation, however, is not the process theories (e.g., expectancy theory) but rather the content theories (e.g., need theories). This is so because the available field research has stressed comparisons of attitudes, needs, values, and managerial approaches among various societies, all based on the individual employees' self-report.

These studies have often employed the attractive structure of the five needs proposed by Maslow or the three needs proposed by McClelland to facilitate a systematic basis for cross-cultural comparison. We shall therefore examine research on four topics in cross-cultural perspective:

1. The meaning of work.
2. The derivation of cultural dimensions based on work values.
3. Motivational theories.
4. The underlying dimensions in the comparative management literature (or country vs. culture as an independent variable).

Figure 5.1 describes the relationship between the attitudinal and behavioral variables relevant to the individual employee's motivational process. The fol-

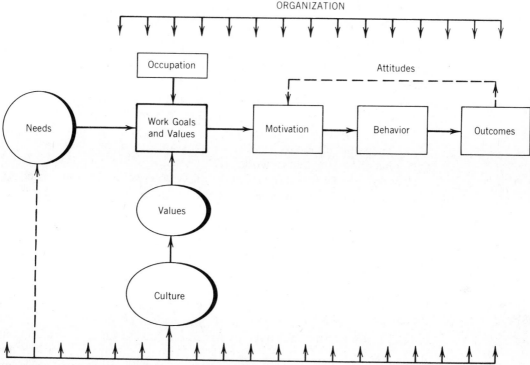

Figure 5.1 Cultural antecedents of work motivation.

lowing discussions elaborate on the relationships of work goals, motivational theories, and culturally independent variables.

THE MEANING OF WORK

Why is research into the meaning of work fundamental to understanding motivation? Very simply, it is the prospect of attaining a favorable outcome that motivates an individual to act. To understand motivation, we must understand not only the psychological mechanism that drives individuals to reach positive outcomes but also the specific outcomes they seek. Understanding workers' motivation in the workplace, therefore, requires that we comprehend the specific facets of the work that trigger or inhibit motivational mechanism. The meanings individuals attach to work are good indicators of the valued work outcomes. For instance, if the meaning of work for an individual is making money, the promise of a pay raise will motivate him or her to work harder.

Cross-cultural research into the meaning of work rests on a fundamental assumption that work itself has no meaning other than what individuals attach to it. The notion that the meaning of work is subjectively constructed can easily be overlooked because it is inconsistent with our predominantly "objective" conception of work. Research has shown that in the United States, the meaning of work is generally equated with its objective economic function for society and the individual (Kaplan & Tausky, 1980). People work to make money or to produce something of value for society. Surveys on the meaning attached to work cite the more subjective conceptions less frequently (Kaplan & Tausky, 1980). We reflect less on how work provides fulfillment, social contacts, or status than on how much money our work will bring us. However, it is only if we start considering the multiplicity of subjective meanings attached to work that we can expose the true nature of our objective economic conception of work. Then our "objective" notion of work appears as only one more subjective conception attached to work.

In cross-cultural research, it is imperative to develop this multifaceted and subjective approach to the study of work meanings. The predominant conception of work in the United States may not be universal. It may, therefore, be necessary to understand how individuals in other cultures or nations subjectively perceive work if we are to understand what facets of work motivate them. Work can take on very different meanings in different cultures.

History

A brief history of the meaning of work in the Judaeo-Christian tradition highlights just how the meaning of work in Western culture has varied, and it provides an indication of how different the meanings attached to work can be across countries and cultures.

In ancient Greece, a small elite leisure class owned the large slave population that performed most physical labor. Within this leisure class, a negative perception of work emerged. Work was considered punishment and drudgery imposed by the gods. Moreover, the Greek elite believed that work corrupted the individual because it interfered with the pursuit of truth and virtue, and with the development of mind and spirit carried out in leisure time. Consequently, work was relegated to a class of slaves—"animated instruments" as Aristotle called them. Over time, the Greeks' highly negative perception of work migrated, through the writings of Greek philosophers, to the Roman Empire, whose society—which also relied on a large slave labor force—adopted this perception.

Obviously, the Greco-Roman conception of work depended on a specific social structure (a small elite group and a large slave class) and also on a specific culture at a particular point in history. Only an idle elite, shielded by a large slave class from the rigors of work, could afford the luxury of devaluing work so extensively. Working every day with such a negative conception of work would have rapidly become unbearable for the elite. It should not be surprising that divergent conceptions of work have emerged in different historical and cultural contexts.

Some Hebrew philosophers were influenced by the Greco-Roman perception of work, and their writings preserve many of its negative connotations. There were, however, some notable differences between the Greco-Roman and Hebraic conceptions of work. For Hebrew philosophers, work was both a product of original sin and a way to atone for it. Therefore, although work itself had negative connotations, it also had positive potential.

Early and medieval Christians accepted and developed this simultaneously positive and negative style of work. Work itself remained neutral. However, the goals to be achieved through work took on strong positive connotations. A surplus of goods generated through work could be shared with the needy, thereby allowing the merchant or craftsman a chance to do a good deed and advance his chances for salvation. Conversely, hoarding surplus goods was avarice—a transgression of divine law.

The medieval Christian conception of work did not remain fixed. With the ascendance of Luther's theology, many Christians began to value work in its own right. For Luther, work itself was a path to salvation. Engaging oneself in a particular profession was a calling—something one had to accept as a divine ordinance. The best way to serve God was to follow this calling and to perform most perfectly the work of one's profession. Consequently, work was a duty to God; not working, or failing to follow one's calling, was considered immoral.

Calvin developed these ideas further. He believed that he could prove his faith through good works but that the individual could not buy salvation with good deeds. Salvation was entirely in divine hands. By exercising unrelenting self-control in work, the individual could only prove to himself that he was worthy of salvation. This self-control involved difficult and ceaseless mental and physical labor and a renunciation of the fruits of labor. The accumulation of wealth, then, became an objective symbol of this self-renunciation and a signal to the individual that he was favored by God. Work had itself become intrinsically good, as had the accumulation of wealth that it permitted.

Max Weber has speculated that the emergence of capitalism—a system of production requiring large outlays of capital to purchase machinery—was possible only because of Protestant religious values and the consequent drive to work and to accumulate wealth. This Protestant work ethic is the basis of a conception of work that many individuals hold in American society today.

The above discussion shows that a host of factors—cultural, sociostructural, and historical—determine the meaning of work. The meaning of work, therefore, will vary greatly across cultures and nations at different stages of development. However, pointing out that work can take on many meanings still leaves us with the question: What practical use does the study of the meaning of work have for managers in MNCs?

Practical Applications of Research

Throughout this chapter it is assumed that individuals have a universal drive to fulfill needs and achieve goals. To understand what motivates employees in a culturally specific work setting, however, it is not sufficient to know that individuals seek to attain goals and to satisfy needs through their work. These are only mechanisms of the human psyche. They are totally devoid of content in their own right and are therefore insufficient for understanding human motivation. We must also know what specific goals the individual seeks and what specific needs he or she is satisfying. Research into the meaning of work is helpful in making such a determination. The meaning of work for an individual also tells us what specific outcomes an individual seeks from working and what functions work performs for the individual (referred to as valences by instrumentality theory).

These insights into the meaning of work have practical applications for managers in MNCs. A perception of work as meaningful for people is grounded in certain philosophical assumptions. People construct or create certain specific meanings for their work; they do not simply let work determine what meaning it holds for them. The meanings attached to work are what guide employees' actions in the workplace. In fact, what work means to individuals becomes a predictor of their behavior at work, because people are motivated to work by what they understand work to be. By understanding the meaning of work, managers can understand their subordinates' goals and needs. Managers can, in fact, understand why their subordinates work and why they exert a particular level of effort at work. Conversely, overlooking what work means to employees can produce negative consequences for managers.

The average adult in the United States spends much of his or her life working. Much of this work, of course, is a matter of necessity; yet studies have shown that people would go on working even if they suddenly became independently wealthy (Kaplan & Tausky, 1980). Work obviously provides individuals with something more than just the means for basic biological sustenance. Working fulfills other human needs, and fulfilling these needs can be a strong force driving and motivating employees. On the other hand, frustrating these needs—by a manager insensitive to the meaning employees attach to work, for example—can result in a real loss to an organization. The MNC manager should therefore understand and respect the meanings employees attach to their work.

The meaning of work is also a good indicator of why subordinates find work satisfying and work situations attractive. Because the meaning of work provides insights into workers' values and the resultant motivational structures in different cultures, it becomes very important in making decisions about the design of work organizations. Information concerning the meaning of work should be used in designing organizations and organizational units that are responsive to workers' motives and needs, and which therefore take full advantage of the natural motivation individuals bring to their work.

Finally, work does not have meaning only at an individual level, but also at a social and legal level. In the United States, the meaning of work has changed drastically at a societal and legal level. Women, minorities, and certain age groups now have legally protected rights in the workplace. Discrimination or harassment on the basis of sex, for instance, is now not only socially unacceptable within organizations but also punishable by law. The legal and social meanings of work in the host country should also concern managers of MNCs.

Empirical Research

Empirical evidence for the United States shows that the meaning of work can be measured, and many of the important dimensions on which it varies have been isolated. Recently, scholars have attempted to explore the meaning of work cross-culturally. One of the more comprehensive programs of cross-cultural research into this area has been undertaken by a group of scholars led by George England. They have carried out a comparative study of the meaning of work (MOW) for employees in eight countries. The research is geared toward identifying and understanding the meanings that individuals and groups attach to work in industrial societies across the globe.

What also interests these researchers is how the meanings have emerged and developed, and how they will affect individuals', organizations', and societies' development. They have also developed methods for using the information collected to aid in policy decisions. The researchers are interested in identifying problems and opportunities for work force management given certain meanings of work patterns.

England and his colleagues have developed a three-level model to describe and explain the formation, existence, and impact of work meanings (Figure 5.2). The "conditional variable" level is concerned with the forces (personal, job history, economic) that influence or cause certain patterns of meaning to emerge. The second level, "central variables," concerns variables utilized to measure different patterns of meaning when they have emerged. Five different "central variables" are used to capture different facets of these patterns of meaning. At the third level, "consequences," the authors measure the impact of different MOW patterns on two variables. One variable measures the expectations of individuals or groups when they hold a particular pattern of work meaning and also measures the action of these individuals' behavior.

The three levels of analysis in Figure 5.2 allow the researchers to answer questions concerning how work meanings emerge, what they are, and what their consequences are on expectations and behavior.

We should look at some of the results to get a sense of how they can help us understand motivation in the workplace cross-culturally.

Work centrality is one variable in the cluster of five variables that constitute the central variable dimension. Work centrality is defined as "the degree of general importance that working has in the life of an individual at any given point in time" (England et al., 1984, p. 4). Researchers determine the centrality of work by assessing the importance of work in an individual's life in relation to other life roles and by measuring the centrality of work in absolute terms.

England used two methods to assess work centrality. For the first measure he and his colleagues asked individuals in each of eight countries to assign a total of one hundred points to five categories or life roles (leisure, community,

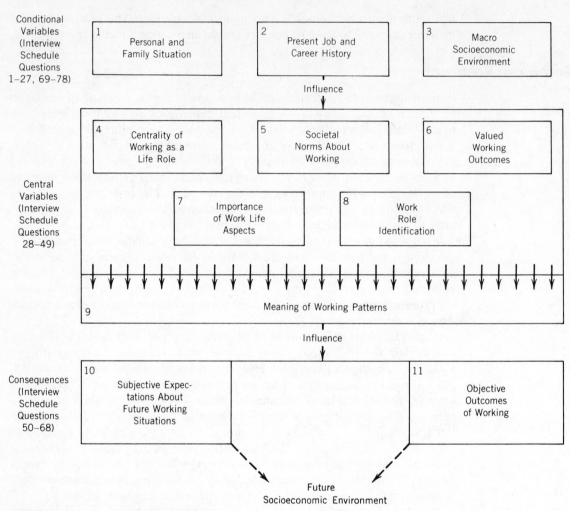

Figure 5.2 Heuristic research model.

Source: I. H. Harpaz, ''The Meaning of Working: MOW International Research Team,'' in G. Olugos, N. Weiermair, and W. Dorow, eds. *Management under Differing Value Systems: Political, Social and Economical Perspectives in a Changing World.* New York: Walter de Gruyter, 1981, p. 577.

work, religion, and family) according to the importance they attached to them. England could then rank these different life roles. He obtained a second measure of work centrality by having individuals locate the importance they attached to work on a continuum from low to high. The two measures of work centrality were combined into one score. The researchers calculated an average for individuals in each country. The rank ordering of the result is shown in Figure 5.3.

Particularly interesting are the major differences in work centrality separating a country like Japan from countries like Germany or the United Kingdom.

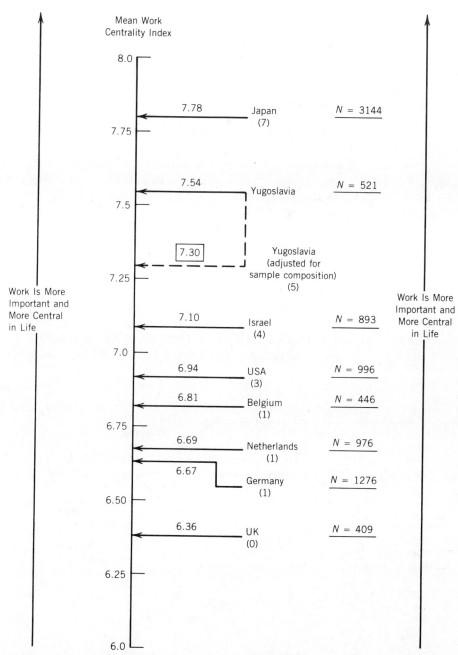

Figure 5.3 Work centrality index (mean score) for each country. The numbers in parentheses indicate the number of countries significantly lower ($P < 0.05$) in work centrality than the country designated. For example, Israel is not significantly higher than the United States but is significantly higher than the four lowest-scoring countries.

Source: MOW International Research Team. 1985 (in Press) *The Meaning of Working: An International Perspective.* London · New York: Academic Press.

These differences become especially clear when we look at the data from another perspective. If the work centrality scores for each country are divided into three groups (high, medium, low), a country like Japan has roughly twelve times as many high scorers as low scorers. The same proportion of high to low scorers in the United Kingdom is only two to one.

The practical implications of these findings could be wide ranging. If work meanings are actually indications of the goals individuals seek, then we would predict that a high score on the work centrality measure would relate causally and positively to involvement and commitment to work and more generally to individuals' motivation of work. One indication of work motivation is the average number of hours spent working. It should therefore not surprise us that the mean number of hours in Japan (the highest on the work centrality scale) is a whopping 48.9 hours per week as opposed to only 39.9 hours per week in Germany (which is next to last on the scale).

The "valued working outcome" variable in the central variable cluster (see Figure 5.2) is also helpful in understanding the practical implications of the MOW research for understanding workers' motivation across cultures. The variable elucidates the individual's general outcomes or opportunities sought from work, or both, and their relative importance. This variable can therefore help us understand the goals that individuals will be motivated to pursue.

Individuals in each of eight countries were asked to assign one hundred points to categories in Table 5.1. Table 5.1 represents the average number of

Table 5.1 Mean Number of Points Assigned to Working Functions (Q28) by Country Samples

Country	N	Working Provides You with an Income That Is Needed	Working Is Basically Interesting and Satisfying to You	Working Permits You to Have Interesting Contacts with Other People	Working Is a Useful Way for You to Serve Society	Working Keeps You Occupied	Working Gives You Status and Prestige
Japan	3180	45.4	13.4	14.7	9.3	11.5*	5.6
Germany	1264	40.5	16.7	13.1	7.4	11.8	10.1
Belgium	447	35.5	21.3	17.3	10.2	8.7	6.9
United Kingdom	471	34.4	17.9	15.3	10.5	11.0	10.9
Yugoslavia	522	34.1	19.8	9.8	15.1	11.7	9.3
United States	989	33.1	16.8	15.3	11.5	11.3	11.9
Israel	940	31.1	26.2	11.1	13.6	9.4	8.5
Netherlands	979	26.2	23.5	17.9	16.7	10.6	4.9
All countries combined	8792	35.0†	19.5	14.3	11.8	10.8	8.5

*Working keeps you occupied was incorrectly translated in Japan.
†The combined totals weigh each country equally, regardless of sample size.
Source: MOW International Research Team. 1985 (in Press) *The Meaning of Working: An International Perspective.* London New York: Academic Press.

points assigned to each category by these individuals. England and his colleagues found that individuals perceive the income-producing function of working to be work's most important function. However, Table 5.1 suggests that other aspects of work motivate individuals as well and that certain combinations of different dimensions of work are a more important motivation than earning money. In Israel, for instance, the value placed on work as a source of interest and social contact combine to outweigh its value as a source of income. In such a country, it might be dangerous to motivate workers only with financial incentives. As England and his colleagues have asserted, "the economic underpinning of work and working is powerful but not all-powerful" (England et al., 1984). The following section further discusses the implication of MOW in terms of specific work goals and motivational models.

CROSS-NATIONAL STUDY OF EMPLOYEES' WORK GOALS AND MOTIVATION

Organizational behavior literature has lately reflected the increasing rate of information exchange about the quality of work life in various Western societies. However, a prerequisite for comparing work milieu is to determine whether employees from different national settings share similar needs and motivational systems. The question is whether or not cultural norms significantly influence employees' expectations, values, and motives. The extent that this is so may restrict generalization from studies within a single country.

Large-scale comparative studies in employees' values, perceptions, and leadership styles have emphasized the existence of cross-national differences (e.g., England, Dhingra, & Agarwal, 1974; Haire, Ghiselli, & Porter, 1966; Hofstede, 1980; Sirota & Greenwood, 1971; Triandis, 1977; England et al., 1984; Ronen & Kraut, 1977). Bass (1981) points out that to understand managers' decision processes, one must examine their objectives. If these objectives systematically differ from country to country, knowledge of them is useful in understanding cross-national managerial behavior. Variations in managerial style and leadership models will be discussed in Chapter 6.

Nations differ in the level of importance that employees attach to different needs, and how well employees' needs are met through work and, as a result, employees' satisfaction vary from one country to another. Haire and colleagues (1966) have concluded that the percentage of difference in managerial job attitude attributed to nationality is 28%. Hinrichs (1975) has studied sixty-four countries and concludes that a country's wealth is an important summary variable in understanding employees' goals and satisfaction. However, Hinrichs recommended cross-national research to understand and legitimize organizational and industrial psychologists' basic theories. In other words, the studies referred to above have dealt with variables based on individuals' internal perception of expectations and attitudes, assuming *universal* dynamic processes of motivation and behavior. These assumptions allow one to investigate and compare levels of employee needs or satisfaction in different countries.

However, researchers have assumed that the basic structure of goals and needs is generalized. The issue of the universality of kinds of needs and their pattern is still unanswered; therefore, the legitimacy of cross-national comparisons of behavioral and attitudinal data is questionable. For example, cross-national comparisons of managerial behavior and perception have been reported by different researchers, all employing a questionnaire developed by Porter (1961) based on Maslow's need hierarchy conceptualization (Haire et al., 1966—14 countries; Mozina, 1969—Yugoslavia; Clark & McCabe, 1970—Australia). These researchers' underlying assumption was that Maslow's theory is universal, despite the lack of validation for it even within the U.S. borders (Miner & Dachler, 1973; Wahba & Bridwell, 1976; Wofford, 1971).

Other researchers reporting large cross-national studies also assumed similarity in employees' need structure in different countries; they questioned only the level of importance of work values or level of satisfaction from different job rewards (Hinrichs, 1975—64 countries; Sirota & Greenwood, 1971—25 countries; Hofstede, 1976—37 countries; Ronen & Kraut, 1977—29 countries). Invariably, all the cited studies referred to Maslow's needs categories or to the popular extrinsic–intrinsic dichotomy, and they all considered the models to be universal.

Motivational Models—Need Theories

One of the most popular conceptualizations of work motivation is Maslow's need hierarchy (1954). Maslow's model stipulates that, although people strive toward self-actualization, they do so only after fulfilling lower-level needs. Maslow therefore hierarchically categorizes human needs according to their priority for satisfaction. Lowest in the hierarchy are physiological needs, followed by security needs, social (affiliation) needs, self-esteem (ego) needs, and finally, self-actualization needs. Maslow claims that these five types of needs are instinctive; they should therefore be universal across cultures. More recently, however, other researchers have questioned the validity of this assumption of universality. There are convincing arguments on both sides of this question.

Tannenbaum (1980), discussing the potential difficulty of cross-cultural analysis, suggests that even the assumption that members of an organization are motivated by the organization's rewards and incentives (money, social approval, promotion, etc.) may not apply in all cultures. Redding (1977) questions the applicability of Western "ego-centered paradigms" that focus on the individual (through concepts such as achievement and self-actualization) to non-Western cultures in which the focus is on relationships. Along these lines, Hofstede (1980) argues that many Western concepts (e.g., "achievement") cannot even be translated into other languages, thus indicating their lack of appropriateness for use in those cultures.

Other models have been popular as well, however. Some are nonhierarchical models of motivation. One is the intrinsic–extrinsic model of employees' needs (also labeled content–context or hygiene–motivators). These models suggest that the contribution of either intrinsic or extrinsic factors to overall job satisfaction is, in part, a function of nationality and occupational level (Simonetti & Weitz, 1972; Kraut & Ronen, 1975). Still, it is an empirical question whether or not these theories should be considered universal. Ronen (1979), for example, undertook a research project that directs itself to several questions at the heart of these motivational models:

1. Does the grouping of work goals into clusters differ among nations?
2. Do the interrelationships between the various goals and the pattern of the goal clusters differ among nations?
3. Are the clusters and goal interrelationships consonant with the two motivational models under consideration (intrinsic–extrinsic distinction and Maslow's hierarchy of needs)?

The data consist of the rating of fourteen work goals by employees of the national affiliates of a multinational electronic company in five different industrialized countries. The sample from all five countries includes highly trained male employees, none of whom are in managerial positions (Germany, $N = 2720$; Canada, $N = 1088$; France, $N = 1966$; United Kingdom, $N = 1535$; Japan, $N = 1695$). It is felt that doing cross-national research in affiliates of a large multinational firm has its advantages as well as disadvantages. On the one hand, the sample may have a value system, transcending national borders, that may obscure national differences. On the other hand, the differences found will have a higher validity because of the ability to control for errors resulting from interorganizational factors (e.g., climate, size, management policy, etc.).

The results of Ronen's study produced the Smallest Space Analysis (SSA) maps for employees from Germany, Canada, the United Kingdom, France, and Japan. These are presented in Figures 5.4, 5.5, 5.6, 5.7, and 5.8, respectively. The location of the fourteen goals on the diagram is determined by their similarities to each other, based on employee ratings; the computer-output locations are based on an intercorrelational matrix of the work-goal ratings. The results of this study analyzing fourteen work goals provide an empirical basis for understanding three issues.

Universality in Goal Clusters

The first issue is whether or not the structures of work-related value systems are similar, regardless of the employees' nationality and their work settings. According to these results, such a structural similarity does exist—at least for the industrialized nations. Across countries, certain needs and goals tend to cluster together and to be relatively distant from others. Whatever the employees' nationality, the workers group together job goals such as working area, work time, physical working conditions, fringe benefits, and job security. For all five countries, relationships with co-workers and supervisors generally appear as another cluster, with work challenge and opportunity for utilization of skills forming a third group. Thus, even before we interpret the clusters, we can

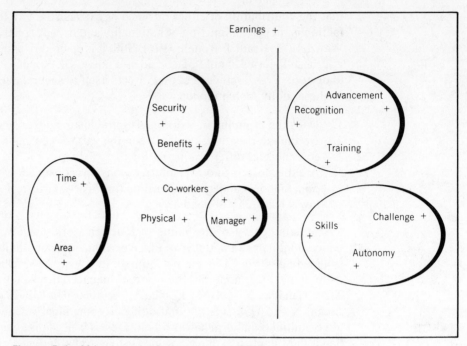

Figure 5.4 SSA of goals. Germany; N = 2720.

Source: S. Ronen, ''Cross-National Study of Employees' Work Goals.'' *International Review of Applied Psychology* 28(1):6, 1979.

see them as relatively constant across the different subject samples. However, some variability of clusters showed up as well.

Support for Motivational Models

The next issue concerns whether or not we can consider the clusters present in the data as falling within the intrinsic–extrinsic dichotomy and Maslow's five-fold categorization of needs. This study found the intrinsic–extrinsic dichotomy and Maslow's five-need hierarchy to be good approximations of the cross-national clusters. These results affirm the utility of both taxonomies as conceptual tools in studying work motivation and value systems.

Certain job goals, however, emerged as border cases, which could conceivably fall into more than one cluster, according to both the intrinsic–extrinsic dimension and Maslow's five needs. The existence of border cases requires us to reexamine the nature of these conceptualizations to avoid oversimplifying either taxonomy. In discussing this aspect of the results, we will consider the intrinsic–extrinsic dichotomy first, and then Maslow's five categories of needs.

Intrinsic–Extrinsic Model   For all countries, goals such as physical working conditions, work area, time, security, benefits, and interpersonal relations with managers and co-workers clustered together in one-half of the figures. Simi-

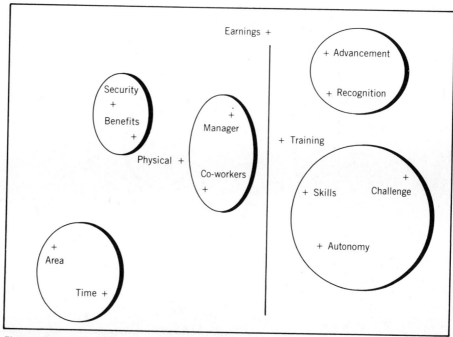

Figure 5.5 SSA of goals. Canada; $N = 1088$.

Source: S. Ronen, "Cross-National Study of Employees' Work Goals." *International Review of Applied Psychology* 28 (1):6, 1979.

larly, goals such as opportunities for training, utilization of skills, autonomy, and challenge clustered in the other half. These goals may therefore be ordered from left to right along a continuum that represents the extrinsic–intrinsic dimension.

However, there are certain border cases—goals that make it difficult to draw a conclusive line separating these two poles for all countries. As a goal, opportunity for higher earnings does not seem to appear distinctly in any cluster; an arbitrary division may associate it with either the intrinsic or the extrinsic pole. In most cases it appears close to security and benefits in the extrinsic (tangible) category and to recognition and advancement in the more abstract goal cluster. This example and others suggest that in a strict sense the intrinsic–extrinsic conceptualization is difficult to apply to the case of borderline variables.

Maslow's Model The fourteen goals cluster much as one would predict from the Maslow conceptualization. The basic needs (area, time, security, benefits, and physical conditions) cluster in one group. Social needs—here represented by co-worker relations and relationships with the supervisor—cluster in another. Higher-level needs, though clustered together, show a separation between self-esteem needs (recognition, opportunities for advancement) and self-actualization needs (autonomy, challenge, and utilization of skills). As for the interrelationships of the clusters, self-esteem and self-

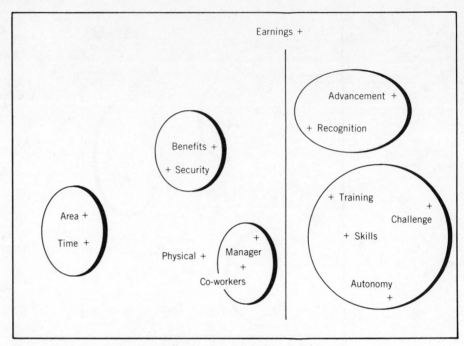

Figure 5.6 SSA of goals. Great Britain; N = 1535.

Source: S. Ronen, ''Cross-National Study of Employees' Work Goals.'' *International Review of Applied Psychology* 28(1):7, 1979.

actualization needs are equally distant from social needs and further from the basic needs. It appears, then, that there is an order to the mappings of goals for all countries. At one extreme are basic physical and security goals; at the other are ego and self-actualization goals.

Certain findings, however, lead us to question any literal application of Maslow's categorization to studies of employee attitudes, especially for international comparisons (e.g., Haire, Ghiselli, & Porter, 1966; Mozina, 1969; Clark & McCabe, 1970).

Two borderline cases call into question the nature of the distinction between self-esteem and self-actualization needs. First, autonomy emerges as a work goal that is included in the intrinsic category by all employees, but with different relations to ego and self-actualization needs in different countries.

The second variable on the border between self-esteem and self-actualization is employees' expectation of training opportunities aimed at improving their skills or learning new ones. This goal seemed to be perceived as potentially fulfilling both ego and self-actualization needs. Unless the need categories of self-esteem and self-actualization can include borderline variables such as autonomy and training, there may be misapplication of Maslow's schema to empirical situations. This would also be a problem when earnings are too readily

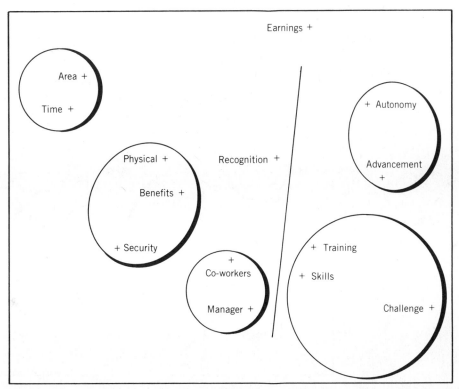

Figure 5.7 SSA of goals. France; N = 1966.

Source: S. Ronen, "Cross-National Study of Employees' Work Goals." *International Review of Applied Psychology* 28(1):7, 1979.

considered a low-level, basic variable without consideration of the higher-level-need aspects of pay.

These findings do not rule out the idea of environmental influence on goal formation, nor do they invalidate the available evidence supporting the organizational climate's contribution to the individual's perceived need hierarchy. The results suggest, however, that when an employee orders the importance of work goals—whether as a result of environmental and organizational climate or perceived attainability of rewards—his or her choices tend to go toward similar rather than disparate goals. And (as stated before), there is support for Maslow's contention that needs of different order do not appear simultaneously but rather in some sort of sequence.

Intersection of the Two Models

Having examined both the intrinsic–extrinsic dichotomy and Maslow's categorization of needs, we may now address a third issue to which the results of Ronen's study could contribute—that is, the question of how these two

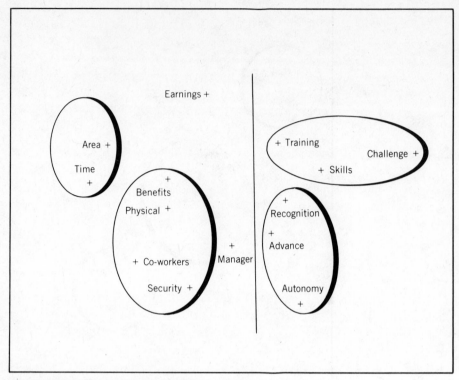

Figure 5.8 SSA of goals. Japan; N = 1695.

Source: S. Ronen, "Cross-National Study of Employees' Work Goals." *International Review of Applied Psychology* 28(1):8, 1979.

conceptualizations intersect. What overlap exists between intrinsic or extrinsic needs and the five needs proposed by Maslow?

According to these data, extrinsic aspects overlap significantly with Maslow's basic needs, whereas intrinsic aspects subsume the higher-order needs of self-esteem and self-actualization, or—as termed by Alderfer (1972)—growth needs. This parallels the division promoted by the hygiene-motivator theory (Herzberg et al., 1959), which includes Maslow's ego needs in the intrinsic aspects of work (King, 1970). However, as mentioned earlier, we must take care not to oversimplify either of these conceptualizations in applying them to empirical situations, especially in light of the borderline variables.

In conclusion, Ronen's (1979) study has shed light on three issues basic to any consideration of employee value systems, perceptions, and work motivation. First, it began to provide evidence that there are substantial clusters of work goals and needs that can be found across national boundaries, and that we can generalize these results to industrialized Western countries. Second, we can interpret these clusters as representing the theoretical dimensions suggested by the intrinsic–extrinsic dichotomy and by Maslow's categorization of needs. Third, we can meaningfully relate these two taxonomies to each other because of significant overlap in their data.

Other Motivational Theories

McClelland has provided conclusive evidence that individuals' levels of achievement motivation in a society are directly related to that society's economic growth.

Confirming studies have been done of the importance for the high need for achievement, not only in American corporations but also in diverse entrepreneurial activities in countries as widely separated as Nigeria, India, and South Africa (LeVine, 1966; Singh, 1970; Morsbach, 1969). As developed by McClelland (1961) and his associates, this construct usually employs a special scoring of the Thematic Apperception Tests (TATs), a projective technique. Alternatively, when studying the need achievement of a whole culture or nation, researchers may use children's readers or other literary or graphic material to determine the need achievement themes.

McClelland (1961) has presented evidence that the achievement motive is a fairly consistent trait developed in early childhood and persisting into adult life. This is not to say, however, that proper training cannot modify or increase adults' need for achievement. With the growing interest in cross-national studies, a number of scholars set about examining the generalizability of McClelland's theory to other countries and cultures. Would countries whose workers have had a high need for achievement also be leaders in the world economy? Bhagat and McQuaid provide a comprehensive review of research in this area. They cite a number of studies that provided good empirical support for generalizing the theory cross-culturally (Hines, 1973; 1974; Melikian et al., 1971). As is apparent in Table 5.2, these studies used survey methods to test the theory with a variety of workers in various countries. The theory seemed to be equally applicable to developing countries, such as Turkey or Brazil (Melikan et al., 1971), as well as to more developed countries, such as Britain or Japan (Iwawaki & Lynn, 1972).

However, this last study posed a serious challenge to the notion that individual needs for achievements relate to a society's economic development. Iwawaki and Lynn found that English and Japanese workers had roughly the same need for achievement. The theory predicts that the two countries' economic development should be roughly equivalent, but this was not the case. Japan's economic development since WWII has far surpassed England's. Following Iwawaki and Lynn's study, a rash of studies seemed to disprove McClelland's theory. Krus and Rysberg (1976) found, for instance, that need for achievement motives of Czechoslovakian executives was half those of American executives; yet, contrary to the theory's predictions, the rate of economic development of these countries was not nearly as disparate.

These studies were interpreted as refuting McClelland's theory. However, the studies made one crucial assumption—that motivation is manifested simi-

Table 5.2 Post-1970 Empirical Studies on Work Motivation

Author(s)	Countries/ Cultures	Primary Focus	Sample Size and Type	Research Methodology	Theoretical Base
Eden, 1975	Israel	Emic	375 kibbutz workers	Survey	Atkinson's version of expectancy theory
Hines, 1973	New Zealand	Etic	315 entrepreneurs	Survey	McClelland's achievement motivation theory
Hines, 1974	New Zealand	Etic	677 mixed sample of entrepreneurs, midmanagers, educators	Survey	McClelland's achievement motivation theory
Iwawaki & Lynn, 1972	Britain, Japan	Etic	622 British students, male, and 281 Japanese students, male and female	Survey	McClelland's achievement motivation theory
Krus & Rysberg, 1976	Czechoslovakia	Emic	83 upper management males	Projective technique (i.e., TAT) and survey	McClelland's achievement motivation theory
Melikian et al., 1971	Turkey, Brazil, Saudi Arabia, Afghanistan	Etic	622 male and female students	Survey	McClelland's achievement motivation theory
Salili, 1979	Iran	Emic	235 male and 288 female Iranian students	Survey	Vocational and achievement related motivation
Singh, 1970a, 1970b	India	Emic	80 farmers and 80 business entrepreneurs	Projective technique and survey	Atkinson's version of achievement motivation theory
Yuchtman, 1972	Israel	Emic	104 kibbutz workers & 26 kibbutz managers	Survey	Adam's equity theory

Source: R. S. Bhagat and S. J. McQuaid, "Role of subjective culture in organizations: A review and direction for future research." *Journal of Applied Psychology Monograph,* 67(5): 667 (1982).

larly across cultures—which is not necessarily correct. Perhaps achievement motivation takes on different forms in different cultures (Kornadt, Eckensberger, & Amminghaus, 1980). Perhaps, too, the American tendency to define achievement strictly in terms of entrepreneurial success is questionable elsewhere (Maehr, 1977). For instance, the Japanese have a high need for affiliation, and many Japanese workers' need for achievement expresses itself as a need to belong and to cooperate with others (DeVos, 1968). The motive for achievement, then, is not "I did it for myself" but rather "I did it for others." In Latin countries, the need for achievement expresses itself partly as family success. Bhagat and McQuaid (1982) conclude that the mix of "culture-specific experiences, cognitive structure, and the values of each person will ultimately determine the area in which achievement motivation will develop, the causal attributions of success and failure, and the learned pattern of reacting to them'' (p. 669).

These conclusions have practical as well as theoretical implications. The mistaken notion that the need for achievement manifests itself identically across cultures has led to some misinterpretations concerning the results of training programs in non-American countries to boost workers' levels of achievement. Training programs to increase Indian managers' need for achievement, for instance, have had virtually no effect (McClelland & Winter, 1969). Moreover, a follow-up study by a team of two Indian psychologists (Pareek & Kumar, 1969) showed that the training, indeed, affected Indian managers' needs, but not the one anticipated. It increased their need for experiencing status. (This is a significant need among Indians.)

Other theories of motivation have seldom been tested cross-culturally (Bahgat & McQuaid, 1982), although there are a few exceptions. Equity theory, which predicts that perceived job inequity will result in dissatisfaction, was validated in an Israeli kibutz (Yuchtman-Yaar, 1972). Another study (Eden, 1975) validated Atkinson's expectancy theory, which hypothesizes that the strength of the tendency to act in a certain way is determined by a multiplicative function of expectancy, motive, and incentive. Ideally, more validation studies along these lines should be made.

What can the cross-cultural manager learn from this research? It should be apparent that motivating subordinates from another culture can be markedly different from motivating American employees. The cross-cultural manager should remain sensitive to this possibility for three reasons: first, to avoid attributing a *lack* of motivation to someone who is only *differently* motivated; second, so that the manager may use methods to motivate subordinates that are consistent with their motives and structure-appropriate reward systems; finally, to help managers perform a ''self-diagnosis'' of their motive structure. Only by being acutely aware of our own cultural biases can we become aware of others'.

OPERATIONALIZING CROSS-CULTURAL AND CROSS-NATIONAL DIMENSIONS IN STUDYING EMPLOYEE ATTITUDES

Although there have been many varied and all-inclusive definitions of *culture* in many scientific disciplines, comparative management researchers have not reached a consensus regarding how to define this concept. In fact, most studies purporting to measure cross-cultural differences are actually cross-national in scope (Bhagat & McQuaid, 1982). Most researchers assume that there are cultural variables that explain cross-national variance, but these have not been empirically identified.

For the academic community, one of the first tasks at hand is what Dymsza and Negandhi (1983) refer to as ''dimensionalizing the variable 'country' in cross-cultural organizational studies'' (p. 15). Two major issues arise from this statement. First, the assumption that the cultural environment influences individuals' attitudes, beliefs, values, and needs in that society should be investigated. Second, the assumption that these predispositions are related to individuals' behavior in organizations should be explored. In short, there is a need to identify universal dimensions that will serve to distinguish systematically between cultural entities and that can serve as independent variables to replace the more commonly used discrete variable of the nation-state. Various theorists speak of this situation as the need for operational definitions of the independent variable in cross-cultural or cross-national studies, or both (Negandhi, 1983; Adler, 1983; Ronen & Shenkar, 1985; Ronen & Punnett, 1982; Kluckhohn & Strodtbeck, 1961; Schollhammer, 1969). Indeed, the task of comparative management is to "reveal the extent to which the particular behavior being studied depends on cultural factors" (Adler, 1983, p. 41).

We can identify two approaches to resolve this issue in the literature. The first, the "armchair approach"—implicitly employed by most researchers—is the assumption, often accepted as an axiom, that certain variables underlie cultural and national differences and that these variables account for the observed differences in attitudes and behavior among the aggregated individuals of different societies. The most frequent variables cited are religion, language (as cultural representation), political systems and level of industrialization (as national representation), and geographical location (as a reflection of both). The other approach, which may be termed the "empirical approach," is best represented by Hofstede's work (1980). Rather than assume causal cultural variables, Hofstede derived salient dimensions empirically from employees' attitudinal differences. He then attempted to show an association between these four dimensions and various national or cultural observed (objective) differences [e.g., gross national product (GNP) per capita, geographical location].

The following discussion attempts to examine the applicability of the first approach. It examines the assumed causal relationship of the armchair dimensions to various employees' attitudes. The aim is to identify dependent variables reported in comparative studies that can be systematically categorized, and then to investigate whether the main armchair variables of religion, language, geography, and level of industrialization (defined here by GNP per capita) can account for reported between-nation differences. We shall next turn to the empirical approach, which is best represented by Hofstede's work.

Religion, Language, GNP, and Geography

An initial review of the literature carried out by Punnett and Ronen (1984) identified thirty-four studies that included organizational behavior attitudinal variables and were comparative in nature. These are presented in Table 5.3. The student may find this table helpful in locating sources of research on the variables that are depicted in the columns describing the studies' purpose and results. Most of these studies will be covered later in the discussions of leadership, attitudes, and country clustering. For our present discussion, however, we have selected from this list only those studies that have the criteria neces-

Table 5.3   Summary of Comparative Studies

Author & Date	Sample & Number of Countries	Purpose	Results
Ajiferuke & Boddewyn (1970)	14 countries 3641 managers	Tests validity of various economic and cultural indexes as explanatory of differences in attitudes and motivations	Religion, health, and education most salient explanatory variables
Badawy (1979)	6 countries 248 managers	Explores attitudes and motivations in Mid-Eastern countries (Not explicitly comparative)	Mid-Eastern managers have modern approach to individual's capacity for leadership and a classic approach to participation
Bass & Burger (1979)	13 countries 3082 managers	Examines life-goal ranking and rate of advancement	Rankings follow Maslow's hierarchy. Country and rate of advancement explained from 4–15% of variance in goals. Country was the most significant factor
Cummings, Harnett, & Stevens (1971)	5 countries 451 managers	Compares attitudes toward risk, conciliation, and trust in bargaining behavior	Country accounts for 5% of variance in attitude
England (1974; 1978)	5 countries 2556 managers	Studies personal value systems and their relationship to behavior and success	Country accounts for 30–45% of variance in value systems. Value systems stable and predict behavior and success
England & Lee (1971)	3 countries 1688 managers	Studies importance of organizational goals	Cultural effects dominate economic development variable as explanatory of variation
England & Lee (1974)	4 countries 1991 managers	Examines relationship of value systems to success	Success implies pragmatic, dynamic, and achievement-oriented values. Other values important depending on country. Causation seems to run from values to success
England & Negandhi (1979)	2 countries 529 managers	Examines national differences in employee perceptions of social issues, job factor importance, and managerial style	Real national differences found in perceptions of social issue. Little differences in job factor importance and managerial style
Granick (1978)	4 countries case studies	Examines differences in executive reward systems	Significant national differences found
Griffeth, Hom, De-Nisi, & Kirchner (1980)	15 countries 1768 managers	Compares organizational attitudes and satisfaction	Country accounted for 52% of variance. Four clusters identified: Anglo-Saxon, Northern European, Southern European I & II

(Continued)

Table 5.3 (Continued)

Author & Date	Sample & Number of Countries	Purpose	Results
Gruenfeld & Mac-Eachron (1975)	22 countries 329 managers & technicians	Examines differences in field articulation cognitive style	Developed countries more field independent. National and cultural variables correlate significantly with field articulation cognitive style
Haire, Ghiselli, & Porter (1966)	14 countries 3641 managers	Examines differences in attitudes and motivation	Country accounts for approximately 30% of variance. Five clusters identified: Anglo, Nordic, Latin European, developing, Japan. Language, religion, and level of development explain clusters
Heller & Porter (1966)	2 countries 150 managers	Compares perceptions of need and management style	England and the U.S. very similar
Herbert, Popp, & Davis (1979)	2 countries 58 male MBAs	Examines work reward preferences	High similarity between Australia and U.S. Ranking supports Maslow's hierarchy; higher for employees
Hinrichs (1975)	46 countries 27,997 blue-collar, technical, and marketing employees	Examines differences in work goals and satisfaction as a function of economic development	Per capita GNP correlates negatively with importance of work goals and satisfaction with work goals
Hofstede (1976)	15 countries 372 managers	Examines value profiles as related to national and age differences	Five clusters found: Anglo, Nordic, Germanic, Latin, Asian. Age differences found only for conformity and benevolent concepts
Hofstede (1980)	40 countries 60,000 employees & managers	Identifies dimensions that explain differences in goals and attitudes. Relates these to geographical, economic, and cultural variables	Four dimensions found: power distance, uncertainty avoidance, individualism, masculinity, geographic latitude. Wealth, health, education, religion, all important explanatory variables. 68% of variance in individualism accounted for by GNP per capita. Six clusters identified: Anglo, Nordic, Latin, Eastern, Germanic, Asian
Ivancevich & Baker (1970)	2 countries 150 middle & top level managers	Compares perceived need satisfaction of U.S. managers in Europe and the U.S.	U.S. managers in Europe less satisfied than those in the U.S. Ranking follows Maslow for the U.S., not Europe

Table 5.3 (*Continued*)

Author & Date	Sample & Number of Countries	Purpose	Results
Kanungo & Wright (1981)	4 countries 449 lower & middle level managers	Compares reward expectations and job satisfaction	Significant country differences found in job factor importance. Smaller differences in satisfaction
Kao & Levin (1978)	5 countries 100 employees	Tests applicability of Maslow's need hierarchy and Herzberg's 2-factor theory	Some support for Maslow, none for Hertzberg. Preference order most similar for countries at similar level of industrialization
Kelley & Worthley (1981)	2 countries 130 managers	Examining cultural and national effects on attitudes, separately	National differences more important than cultural differences
Kraut & Ronen (1975)	5 countries 8707 employees	Examines relationship between job satisfaction and overall satisfaction, intent to stay, work tensions, and performance ratings	Country is best predictor of performance ratings. Adds little to prediction of intent to stay, work tension, or overall satisfaction, which is better predicted by occupations
Lee & Larwood (1983)	2 countries 212 managers	Examines effect of socialization on managerial attitudes	Concludes Korean & U.S. managers' attitudes different. Expatriates in between
Orpen (1976)	5 countries England's data plus 92 managers from South Africa	Compares relationship between values and success to that found in other countries	Value-success relationship most similar to that found in Anglo countries
Poblador (1975)	2 countries 47 banks in U.S. and Philippines	Compares structure of rewards and authority	Culture and wealth differences affect both. Philippine banks have taller hierarchies and more concentration in income distribution
Redding (1976)	8 countries 736 managers	Examines satisfaction and motivation in Southeast Asia and compares with European countries	Unlike in European countries, social needs more important than esteem needs. Need importance similar in the studied countries
Reitz (1975)	8 countries 3527 managers	Examines relative importance of need levels and its relationship to education	Educational level explains some variance in importance of security and self-actualization. Need hierarchy similar for all countries
Ronen (1979)	5 countries 8934 employees	Clusters work goals and compares structures across countries (levels of needs not compared)	Supports intrinsic–extrinsic dichotomy and Maslow's need categorization

(*Continued*)

Table 5.3 (*Continued*)

Author & Date	Sample & Number of Countries	Purpose	Results
Ronen & Kraut (1977)	(a) 15 countries 4000 technicians (b) 14 countries 3641 managers (c) 25 countries 13,000 employees	Uses smallest space analysis to establish cluster of countries based on two samples from published research and their own sample	Six clusters identified: Anglo-American, Latin, European, Nordic, Central European, Latin American, and independent countries. Language, religion, and industrialization suggested as explanatory variables
Ross (1976)	6 countries 36 sales engineers & marketing managers	Examines relationship of values and success	Pragmatism associated with success. Country appears to affect value systems
Schaupp & Kraut (1975)	8 countries 800 employees	Examines employee work values	No significant country differences in work values found
Simonetti & Weitz (1972)	3 countries 342 employees	Examines relative contribution of intrinsic and extrinsic factors to satisfaction	Nationality differences important for level of satisfaction with extrinsic but not intrinsic factors
Singh & Wherry (1963)	2 countries 200 factory workers	Compares ranking of job factors	Factory workers from both countries rank-order job factors similarly; nonfactory workers were different
Sirota & Greenwood (1971)	25 countries 13,000 employees	Examines differences and similarities in work goals	Similarity of work goals across countries: 5 clusters identified: Anglo, French, Northern European, Western Latin American, Southern Latin American
Slocum, Topichak, & Kuhn (1971)	2 countries 177 employees	Examines cultural differences using Maslow's need hierarchy	Large differences in work-goal ratings and need preference between countries
Whitehill (1964)	2 countries 2000 production workers	Compares reciprocal obligations felt by employees in Japan and U.S. regarding employment continuity, economic and personal involvement	Culture effects reciprocity. Job security differently defined
Whitely & England (1977)	5 countries 2090 managers	Relating value system to level of industrialization and cultural differences	Both culture and level of industrialization explain differences in personal values

Source: B. J. Punnett and S. Ronen, ''Operationalizing Cross-Cultural Variables.'' Paper delivered at the 44th Annual Meeting of the Academy of Management, Boston, 1984.

sary for identifying the basic cultural and national operational dimensions. These criteria (and constraints) are described below.

Several studies, although implicitly comparative, did not explicitly compare the differences of different countries but concentrated instead on their similarities (e.g., Badawy, 1979). We retained for further analysis only those that made explicit between-national comparisons. (We have also reported whether the differences found were significant and retained these studies for further analysis.) In addition, we excluded those studies that examined the universality of various accepted models or theories (e.g., Maslow's need structure) but did not compare the level of attitudes or behavior cross-nationally (e.g., Ronen, 1979). We then grouped the remaining studies into descriptive categories according to their dependent variables.

A wide variety of such variables appeared. For example, Harnett and Cummings (1980) measured risk, conciliation, and trust, whereas Haire et al. (1966) compared Maslow's need hierarchy. Descriptive categories were selected to be broad enough to include several studies. These were work values, attitudes and needs, personal values, leadership style, and organizational culture. Even with broad categories, however, a fairly large number of studies unfortunately had to be categorized as miscellaneous. As a result, the number of studies in each group was rather small. Only the group dealing with values, attitudes, and needs in a work-related setting contained an adequate number to make further analysis worthwhile. This group consisted of twenty-five studies.

We considered several further subdivisions of this group based on organizational and personal characteristics of the samples. For example, some studies included only managers and others only nonsupervisory employees; some contained technical personnel and others sales people; some used a single organization or industry and others used many. These differences might show up in work values, attitudes, and needs, and ideally they should be controlled for. Unfortunately, demographic and organizational information on all of these variables was not always reported. Consequently, subdivisions of managers and subordinates were the only groupings made, as this information was available for all studies.

We then analyzed the results of these studies to determine whether or not they reported a significant between-nation difference and their dependent variables. Those that did report such a difference were used in the next stage of the analysis. We identified seventeen such studies. These are designated with an asterisk in Table 5.4, which also reports the between-nation variations found in these studies. This table summarizes the studies that investigated mainly attitudes, needs, and work values.

The second part of this research focused on the independent variables assumed to explain differences in organizational variables between nations. The variables used for this analysis were language, religion, GNP per capita, and geographical location. We selected these (based on the initial review) as the variables most frequently used to operationalize culture. In addition, these have all been proposed as variables representing both nations and cultures (Ronen & Punnett, 1984). If one or more of these variables could explain much

Table 5.4 Summary of Results of Twenty-five Studies Investigating Work Values, Attitudes, and Needs

Authors	Conclusions
Ajiferuke & Boddewyn (1970)*	42–63% of variance attributable to culture
Bass & Burger (1979)*	15% of variance attributable to country
England (1974; 1978)*	30–45% of variance attributable to country
England & Lee (1971)*	Cultural effects dominant
England & Lee (1974)*	Unclear if national differences significant
England & Negandhi (1979)	Within-country variation greater than between-country
Griffeth et al. (1980)*	52% of variance attributable to country
Haire et al. (1966)*	28% of variance attributable to country
Heller & Porter (1966)	England and United States very similar
Hinrichs (1975)*	GNP correlates with work goals
Hofstede (1980)*	National differences significant
Hofstede (1976)*	Groupings possible on basis of national differences
Hofstede (1972)	Occupational differences greater than national
Kao & Levin (1978)*	Level of industrialization important in need preferences
Kelley & Worthley (1981)	Significant differences between countries
Lee & Larwood (1983)*	Korean and U.S. attitudes significantly different
Redding (1976)	Need importance similar
Reitz (1975)	Relative importance of needs similar
Ronen & Kraut (1977)*	Countries can be clustered based on similarities and differences
Schaupp & Kraut (1975)	No significant differences
Simonetti & Weitz (1972)*	Nationality significant for extrinsic factors, for intrinsic
Slocum et al. (1971)*	Culture has significant effect
Sirota & Greenwood (1971)	Country rankings similar
Whitely (1979)*	Values affected by country
Whitely & England (1975)*	Culture and level of industrialization explain differences

*These studies report significant between-nation variance on work values, attitudes, and needs.
Source: B. J. Punnett and S. Ronen, "Operationalizing Cross-Cultural Variables." Paper delivered at the 44th Annual Meeting of the Academy of Management, Boston, 1984.

of the between-nation variation found in the studies, this should show up in diversity of that variable (or variables) within each study. Hofstede (1980) and Hinrichs (1975) had both reported GNP per capita as having a significant relationship to work values. We therefore excluded their studies in this analysis, as they could bias the results in that direction. Their finding will later be reincorporated into the results. Moreover, the massive data of Hofstede's work may obscure rather than illuminate the intent of this section.

To incorporate the variables into the analysis, we categorized each country in each study according to its major language, religion, geographic location, and GNP per capita. In addition, we identified each country as belonging to one of the following geographical areas: North America, South and Central America, Africa, the Near East, Europe, Australia and New Zealand, and the

Far East. Several social disciplines have already identified these areas as meaningful groupings. In addition, we used Ronen and Shenkar's (1985) clusters of countries, which were based on a survey of related findings. A consistent relationship between the clusters appearing in a given study and the other variables being examined could therefore provide further insight into the relative importance of these underlying dimensions.

There is marked diversity in all the underlying dimensions examined. Table 5.5 summarizes these results for the fifteen studies analyzed. Note that the first eleven studies investigated predominantly managerial samples, and the last four used nonmanagerial employees. Frequencies were calculated for each variable over all the studies. Overall, there are a total of forty-seven geographical locations, forty-two languages, thirty-nine levels of GNP per capita, thirty-five religions, and fifty clusters. The rank order for both managers and subordinates is the same as for the overall group.

As it was possible to have more variation in some categories than in others, we also examined diversity as a ratio of the numbers appearing in each category to the number possible. This approach shows the GNP per capita to be a most diverse factor; religion remains the least diverse. These results suggest that all of these underlying dimensions may be important but they do not provide clear evidence of their relative importance. We should now review these results.

It is particularly interesting that fifteen studies concluded that there were significant differences in dependent variables among nations. This is especially noteworthy because these studies often use different variables, different subject populations, different instruments, and different methodologies. Unintentionally, comparative management researchers have employed a multitrait/multimethod approach in their work. The consistency of their results, within this framework, clearly supports the hypothesis that national differences in work values, attitudes, and needs are significant.

It seems plausible that managers might be more cosmopolitan in outlook than their subordinates because of their more extensive exposure to other cultures. Their values, attitudes, and needs might be more similar to those of their peers in other nations than to those of their subordinates. In addition, the variables influencing their values, attitudes, and needs might differ. The analysis does not support this hypothesis, however. Studies of managers are as likely to show significant between-nation differences as studies of nonsupervisory employees. We should note, however, that only twelve studies were aggregated; of these, only three dealt with skilled workers. This is, of course, a rather small sample on which to base any conclusions.

Although these studies all support the hypothesis that there are differences between societies, it is unfortunately still unclear what causes these underlying differences, or exactly how these differences are manifested in the workplace. The present synthesis supports the findings of Hofstede (1980) and Hinrichs (1975) to some extent. Clearly, a diversity of GNP per capita is evident in most studies in which significant between-nation differences appeared. However, diversity in the other variables is also evident. One possible conclusion is that all of these variables may be important contributors to between-nation varia-

Table 5.5 Summary of Underlying Variables Appearing in Fifteen Studies Reporting Significant Between-Nation Differences

Author	# Countries	Cluster										Religion							Language										GNP per Capita						Geographical Location							
		Near Eastern	Nordic	Germanic	Anglo	Latin European	Latin American	Far Eastern	Arab	Independent	Total #	Christian	Hindu	Judaic	Shinto	Buddhist	Islam	Total #	Romance	Germanic	Finno-ugric	Hellenic	Iranian	Malay-Polynesian	Semitic	Japanese	Sino-Tibet	Total #	Very High	High	Medium	Low	Very Low	Total #	North American	South & Central American	Africa	Near East	Europe	Australia & New Zend	Far East	Total #
MANAGERS																																										
Ajiferuke & Boddewyn (1970)	14		x	x	x	x	x			x	6	x	x	x				3	x	x			x					3	x	x	x	x		4	x	x		x	x		x	4
Bass & Burger (1979)	13		x	x	x	x				x	4	x	x	x				3	x	x			x			x		3	x	x	x	x		4	x	x		x	x		x	5
England (1978)	5				x			x		x	3	x	x	x				3	x	x						x		3		x	x	x		3	x					x	x	3
England & Lee (1974)	4			x	x	x		x		x	3	x	x					2	x	x						x		2	x	x				2	x					x	x	3
England & Lee (1971)	3			x	x	x				x	2	x						2		x		x				x		2	x	x				3						x	x	3
Griffeth et al. (1980)	15		x	x	x	x	x			x	5	x	x	x	x	x		6	x	x	x					x		4	x	x	x	x		4	x	x		x	x	x	x	5
Naire et al. (1966)	14		x	x	x	x				x	6	x	x		x			2	x	x						x		2	x	x		x		2	x	x		x	x		x	2
Kelley & Worthley (1981)	2				x			x		x	2	x			x			2		x						x		2	x		x			1	x						x	1
Lee & Larwood (1983)	2				x					x	2	x			x			2		x						x		2	x		x			2	x						x	2
Whitely (1979)	2			x	x					x	2	x					x	2		x		x						2		x		x		2				x	x			2
Whitely & England (1975)	5			x	x	x		x		x	3	x			x		x	3	x	x			x			x		3		x	x		x	3					x	x	x	3
Total											38							25										31						27								35
EMPLOYEES																																										
Kao & Levin (1978)	5				x			x		x	1	x			x	x		3						x		x		3	x		x			2						x	x	1
Ronen & Kraut (1977)	29		x	x	x	x	x			x	6	x		x	x	x		3	x	x					x	x		3	x	x	x	x		4	x	x		x	x	x	x	6
Simonetti & Weitz (1972)	3			x	x	x				x	3	x		x				2	x	x						x		2	x		x			3	x				x	x	x	3
Slocum et al. (1971)	2				x	x				x	2	x		x				1	x									1	x					2						x	x	2
Total											12							9										11						12								12
Grand Total											50							34										42						39								47

tion, but their importance may differ from nation to nation. For example, it seems possible that the effect of religion is more notable at low levels of industrialization, or, alternatively, that the level of industrialization has more impact in a nation where religion is a dominant force in everyday life. In other words, the regression equation that would explain the differences among one set of countries is not necessarily the same as that which would explain the differences within another set. In addition, explanatory variables (other than those included in this analysis) may be important independent variables; and a more complex, interactive model is probably necessary for the understanding of the relationships involved.

The issue of the dimensions underlying cross-cultural and cross-national differences is still a major challenge to researchers in the field. It seems that employing "country" as the independent variable is still a worthwhile alternative in the current state of such studies.

Having considered the value of the overview in examining cross-cultural and cross-national differences, we should now examine the role of empirical studies in such an inquiry.

Empirically Derived Dimensions

Hofstede's (1980) massive project using survey data from 116,000 employees of a major multinational corporation is a major contribution to cross-cultural study. This systematic and scientific study is important both because of its impressive magnitude and because of the investigator's well-thought-out conceptual analysis of the data. The study reflects the appreciation in the last decade by organizational scientists that cultural differences influence management and restrict the generalizability of certain organizational theories. Hofstede underscores the significance of culture, or the "collective mental programming," in determining attitude and behavior. In his study, he sets out, in particular, to discover the criteria that determine national cultural differences.

A dominant issue in comparative management theory is the impact of culture on management. Hofstede views culture as a sort of collective mental programming of people in an environment. Such programming is often difficult to change, and if it changes at all, it changes slowly. Such programming tends to be crystallized in the institutions people build together. The various institutions, in turn, tend to constrain and reinforce people's ways of thinking.

With a view to examining the impact of culture—particularly the ways in which culturally determined thinking perpetuates itself as a kind of self-fulfilling prophecy—Hofstede studied differences in work-related values in fifty countries. He undertook this study by utilizing two chronologically different questionnaire surveys of employees of a multinational firm operating in these countries collected during the period 1967–1973. These dealt with the work-related value patterns of matched samples of industrial employees. The data consisted of responses by individual employees to standardized paper-and-pencil attitude and value questionnaires.

Although the data bank set consisted of 116,000 questionnaires, with about

150 questions each, Hofstede gave primary emphasis to questions about how the respondents looked at the work environment. These showed relatively stable differences among countries during the period 1968–1972. The questions utilized for analysis dealt with perceptions of the organizational regime and of the organizational climate and values in terms of the desirable and of the desired. Perception of the organizational regime deals with the extent to which superiors consult their subordinates. Perception of the organizational climate concerns feeling such as job-induced stress. Values in terms of the desirable refers to ideological orientation—such as "competition among employees usually does more harm than good." Desired values, on the other hand, represents the importance attached to various aspects of a job.

Originally, the number of countries included in the analysis was forty. Later, Hofstede added countries for which data were available on at least two occupational groups; this increased the data base to fifty. Hofstede studied the relationship among the country scores on the set of thirty-two questions for the original forty countries.

The researchers put the various questionnaire items into different groups depending on their theoretical relevance and the statistical relationships. A factor analysis, in which countries constituted the cases (i.e., unit of analysis) and the variables were the mean scores for the country on the different questions, showed the existence of four dimensions—power distance, uncertainty avoidance, individualism versus collectivism, and masculinity versus femininity. The position of each of the forty countries on these dimensions was shown on an index. A factor analysis showed, for example, that 50% of variance between countries on the value questions could be explained by three factors. Factor 1 includes an individualism–power distance factor; factor 2 is a masculinity factor; and factor 3 corresponds to the uncertainty–avoidance factor. Table 5.6 shows the various dimensions that are loaded on different factors.

Power Distance   An important dimension of national culture that Hofstede identified is *power distance*. This is a reflection of the degree to which power in organizations is unequally distributed. More specifically, power distance is associated with the degree of centralization of authority and the extent of autocratic leadership. Power distance reflects the degree to which centralization and autocratic leadership are inherent in the mental programming of members of a society—not only among those who have power but also among those who are at the bottom of the power hierarchy.

As Hofstede suggests, subordinates are accessory to the exercise of power in such a system. The functioning of the system is a reflection of their collective complicity. Societies in which power is distributed unequally can continue to maintain this inequality because such a situation satisfies the psychological need for dependence among people who do not have power. The Phillipines and Mexico have the highest score on this dimension, whereas Austria and Israel have the lowest. Mulder's work (1976; 1977) inspired the conception of power distance; this dimension is measured by a three-item country index (fear of disagreement with the superior, perceived and preferred leader styles). An

Table 5.6 Factors Resulting from Work Goal Importance Data

FACTOR 1 (FACTOR VARIANCE 24%)

.82	A18	Importance personal time
.82	B53	Interesting work *not* as important as earnings
.78	B52	Corporation *not* responsible for employees
−.76	A55	Low percentage perceived manager 1 or 2
.75	B46	Employees *not* afraid to disagree
.74	A54	High percentage preferred manager 3 (1967–1969)
.69	B59	Staying with one company *not* desirable
.63	B56	Employees should *not* participate more
−.62	A12	Low importance physical conditions
−.61	A9	Low importance training
.59	A13	Importance freedom
.59	B55	Employees *don't* lose respect for consultative manager
.59	B24	Does *not* prefer foreign company
−.58	A17	Low importance use of skills
.41	A5	Importance challenge (second loading)
.37	B58	Corporation *not* responsible for society
−.35	A15	Low importance advancement (third loading)

FACTOR 2 (FACTOR VARIANCE 13%)

−.71	A16	Low importance manager
.68	A7	Importance earnings
−.67	A8	Low importance cooperation
.60	A11	Importance recognition
.54	A5	Importance challenge
−.53	A6	Low importance desirable area
−.51	A14	Low importance employment security
−.46	A37	High stress (second loading)
−.45	B57	Individual decisions better (second loading)
.43	A17	Importance use of skills (second loading)
.39	A15	Importance advancement (second loading)
−.35	B52	Corporation responsible for employees (second loading)
−.35	B58	Corporation responsible for society (second loading)

FACTOR 3 (FACTOR VARIANCE 12%)

.76	B60	Company rules may be broken
.62	A37	Low stress
.59	A43	Continue less than five years
.56	B9	Prefers manager rather than specialist career
−.50	B57	Individual decisions better
.49	B44	Does *not* prefer manager of own nationality
.49	A58	Low overall satisfaction
.46	A15	Importance advancement
−.46	B55	Employees lose respect for consultative manager (second loading)
.45	B54	Competition *not* harmful
−.43	A9	Low importance training (second loading)
−.35	A10	Low importance benefits

Source: G. Hofstede, *Culture's Consequences. International Differences in Work Related Values.* Beverly Hills: Sage, 1980, pp. 83–84. Reprinted by permission.

Table 5.7 Consequences for Organizations from Power Distance Index

Low PDI	High PDI
Less centralization	Greater centralization
Flatter organization pyramids	Tall organization pyramids
Smaller proportion of supervisory personnel	Large proportion of supervisory personnel
Smaller wage differentials	Large wage differentials
High qualification of lower strata	Low qualification of lower strata
Manual work same status as clerical work	White-collar jobs valued more than blue-collar jobs

Source: G. Hofstede, *Culture's Consequences. International Differences in Work Related Values.* Beverly Hills: Sage, 1980, p. 135. Reprinted by permission.

interesting aspect of power distance is that the greatest tendency for its reduction will be found in people whose power striving is partly satisfied. One implication of this is that people can become addicted to "power distance reduction." This hypothesis has been verified by Mulder (1977) in a series of laboratory as well as field experiments undertaken in the West. Various sociological studies, such as Michel's (1962) iron law of oligarchy, seem to support Mulder's hypothesis.

The power distance norm is culturally determined; its origins lie in the early socialization by the family, the school, and various other institutions. Once instilled as a component of a people's culture, its influence spills over into other sectors. To the extent that it is an important aspect of culture, power distance is likely to have pervasive influence within work organizations. An interesting finding is that lower-education and lower-status occupations are associated with high power distance values and that occupations characterized by higher education and higher status have low power distance values. Country differences appear to be the greatest for the more educated than for the less-educated occupations, whereas occupational differences appear to be much larger in small power distance countries than in large power distance countries.

Hofstede has spelled out some behavioral implications of differences in power distance. He suggests that in systems where superiors maintain a great power distance, subordinates tend to polarize toward either dependence or counterdependence. At the same time, where superiors maintain a lesser power distance, subordinates have a preference for the consultative style.

Table 5.7 shows the consequences for organizations arising from differences in power distances. Although this table illustrates the consequences for organizations in particular, Table 5.8 shows the operation of a general societal norm of power distance. Table 5.8 is useful because it shows specific societal parameters that affect the power distance dimension. From societal and organizational standpoints, one implication of differences in power distance is that some cultures require less legitimization of power than others.

Hofstede finds that, across the sample of countries studied, about 43% of the variance is predicted from the country's geographical lattitude; 51% from a

Table 5.8 Power Distance Dimension

Small Power Distance	Large Power Distance
Inequality in society should be minimized.	There should be an order of inequality in this world in which everybody has a rightful place; high and low are protected by this order.
All people should be interdependent.	A few people should be independent; most should be dependent.
Hierarchy means an inequality of roles, established for convenience.	Hierarchy means existential inequality.
Superiors consider subordinates to be "people like me."	Superiors consider subordinates to be a different kind of people.
Subordinates consider superiors to be "people like me."	Subordinates consider superiors as a different kind of people.
Superiors are accessible.	Superiors are inaccessible.
The use of power should be legitimate and is subject to the judgment as to whether it is good or evil.	Power is a basic fact of society that antedates good or evil. Its legitimacy is irrelevant.
All should have equal rights.	Power-holders are entitled to privileges.
Those in power should try to look less powerful than they are.	Those in power should try to look as powerful as possible.
The system is to blame.	The underdog is to blame.
The way to change a social system is to redistribute power.	The way to change a social system is to dethrone those in power.
People at various power levels feel less threatened and more prepared to trust people.	Other people are a potential threat to one's power and can rarely be trusted.
Latent harmony exists between the powerful and the powerless.	Latent conflict exists between the powerful and the powerless.
Cooperation among the powerless can be based on solidarity.	Cooperation among the powerless is difficult to attain because of their low-faith-in-people norm.

Source: G. Hofstede, "National Cultures in Four Dimensions." *International Studies of Management and Organization,* 13(2):60 (1983).

combination of latitude and population; and about 58% from latitude, population size, and wealth. According to Hofstede, in the latitude–power distance relationship, the key intervening variable is need for technology as a condition for survival. In cold climates, the need for technology was greater than in warmer climates. This sets up a causal chain leading to the emergence of a certain kind of social structure.

To summarize, power distance is an important variable that varies cross-culturally. Such cross-cultural variation, in turn, has important positive and normative implications from the standpoint of organizations—as alluded to earlier. Let us now turn to an examination of another variable that Hofstede identified as central—namely, uncertainty avoidance.

Uncertainty Avoidance This dimension identifies the extent to which a society tends to consider itself threatened by uncertain and ambiguous situations. To this degree, it tends to avoid such situations by establishing greater career stability, formal rules, intolerance of deviant ideas or behaviors, and a belief in absolute truths. At the same time, such societies have a high level of anxiety and aggressiveness, which creates a strong inner urge to work hard.

The uncertainty avoidance norm is also a kind of value system shared by the majority of the middle class. The primary focus of this norm is on the prevention of anxiety. As Hofstede suggests, technology, rules, and rituals provide the means for such anxiety reduction. In countries where uncertainty avoidance is high, anxiety is released through aggressiveness and emotions for which society has created an outlet. In countries where uncertainty avoidance is low, anxiety is released through passive relaxation; overt demonstration of aggressiveness and emotion is not socially approved. In a similar vein, tolerance toward people who have different ideas is more often present in countries that have a low uncertainty avoidance.

Plotting the uncertainty avoidance index for fifty countries against the power distance, several clusters of countries are found that are characterized by strong uncertainty avoidance and large power distance. (More information on clustering appears in Chapter 7 of this book.) A large cluster of countries with strong uncertainty avoidance and large power distance comprises the Latin countries (Latin Europe and Latin America), Mediterranean countries such as Yugoslavia, Greece, and Turkey, plus Japan and Korea. On the other hand, the Asian countries appear in two clusters with large power distance and medium-to-weak uncertainty avoidance. Denmark, Sweden, Great Britain, and Ireland are typical of small power distance and weak uncertainty avoidance countries.

Hofstede (1980) notes that the origin of the uncertainty avoidance norm is much less clear than that of the power distance norm. Differences in uncertainty avoidance among countries may reflect differences in religion, population diversity, and a high rate of societal change. This dimension is measured by a three-item index that deals with the importance of not breaking rules, staying with the company, and the amount of job stress experienced. Table 5.9 shows the consequences of uncertainty avoidance on organizations; Table 5.10 shows the various societal parameters that affect this dimension.

From an organizational perspective, this norm probably most significantly affects the structuring of activities. Thus, in countries where uncertainty avoidance is high, there may be more structuring of activities as manifested by written rules. Management in high uncertainty avoidance countries may also be relatively task oriented. This dimension may also affect the exercise of power in organizations. Various forms of ritual behavior found in high uncertainty avoidance countries are also likely to show up in these societies.

Individualism–Collectivism   Individualism–collectivism is another dimension that Hofstede identified—one that is an important component of culture. This describes the relationship between an individual and society as a whole. Although some cultures view individualism positively, others view it with disapproval or even contempt. Issues of collectivity versus individualism carry strong moral overtones. Thus, Americans view individualism as a contributor to greatness, but the Chinese (for example) do not (Hofstede, 1980).

The degree of individualism or collectivism present will probably have sev-

Table 5.9 Consequences of Uncertainty Avoidance for Organizations

Low VAI	High VAI
Less structuring of activities	More structuring of activities
Fewer written rules	More written rules
More generalists or amateurs	Larger number of specialists
Organizations can be pluriform	Organizations should be as uniform as possible (standardization)
Managers more involved in strategy	Managers more involved in details
Managers more interpersonal oriented and flexible in their style	Managers more task-oriented and consistent in their style
Managers more willing to make individual and risky decisions	Managers less willing to make individual and risky decisions
High labor turnover	Lower labor turnover
More ambitious employees	Less ambitious employees
Lower satisfaction scores	Higher satisfaction scores
Less power through control of uncertainty	More power through control of uncertainty
Less ritual behavior	More ritual behavior

Source: G. Hofstede, *Culture's Consequences. International Differences in Work Related Values.* Beverly Hills: Sage, 1980, p. 187. Reprinted by permission.

Table 5.10 The Uncertainty Avoidance Dimension

Weak Uncertainty Avoidance	Strong Uncertainty Avoidance
The uncertainty inherent in life is more easily accepted and each day is taken as it comes.	The uncertainty inherent in life is felt as a continuous threat that must be fought.
Ease and lower stress are experienced.	Higher anxiety and stress are experienced.
Time is free.	Time is money.
Hard work, as such, is not a virtue.	There is an inner urge to work hard.
Aggressive behavior is frowned upon.	Aggressive behavior of self and others is accepted.
Less showing of emotions is preferred.	More showing of emotions is preferred.
Conflict and competition can be contained on the level of fair play and used constructively.	Conflict and competition can unleash aggression and should therefore be avoided.
More acceptance of dissent is entailed.	A strong need for consensus is involved.
Deviation is not considered threatening; greater tolerance is shown.	Deviant persons and ideas are dangerous; intolerance holds sway.
The ambiance is one of less nationalism.	Nationalism is pervasive.
More positive feelings toward younger people are seen.	Younger people are suspect.
There is more willingness to take risks in life.	There is great concern with security in life.
The accent is on relativism, empiricism.	The search is for ultimate, absolute truths and values.
There should be as few rules as possible.	There is a need for written rules and regulations.
If rules cannot be kept, we should change them.	If rules cannot be kept, we are sinners and should repent.
Belief is placed in generalists and common sense.	Belief is placed in experts and their knowledge.
The authorities are there to serve the citizens.	Ordinary citizens are incompetent compared with the authorities.

Source: G. Hofstede, "National Cultures in Four Dimensions." *International Studies of Management and Organization,* 13(2): 46–74 (1983).

eral consequences for organizational functioning. In countries where collectivism predominates, people's involvement is likely to be moral; by contrast, it will tend to be calculative where an individualistic ethos exists. Both moral and social orientations may be discerned in the same relationship, but one orientation may tend to dominate. In addition, people may transfer part of their extended family allegiances to the organizations to which they belong. Japan is an example of this phenomenon. The individualism–collectivism dimension has become associated with the normative organization theories coming from different countries. Hofstede notes that the United States' extreme position on the individualism dimension causes doubt concerning the relevancy of its theories cross-culturally.

Hofstede states that a country's degree of individualism is related statistically to its wealth. There is a 0.82 correlation between individualism and wealth as measured by GNP per capita. Figure 5.9 shows the relationship between individualism and national wealth. Apart from wealth, Hofstede has noted that geographical latitude and the organization's size also play a role in predicting individualism. Like the dimensions already mentioned, the individualism norm resembles a value system shared by the majority of a country's middle class. The nuclear family is often considered a central element in fostering the development of this norm. Where the nuclear family dominates, there is less emphasis on broader social groupings. Table 5.11 shows the organizational consequences arising out of differences on this dimension.

Table 5.12, on the other hand, is an indication of how the societal norm of individualism affects various dimensions of behavior. Many of the indexes identified by Hofstede are also related to each other. The power distance index, for example, correlates negatively with individualism. There are some exceptions, though. Latin European countries such as France, Belgium, and Italy have a combination of high power distance and high individualism. Hofstede suggests that in these countries people have a need for dependence on superiors; at the same time, they stress their personal independence from the organization to which they belong.

Masculinity–Femininity   This dimension considers the degree of masculinity of a society's dominant values—values such as assertiveness, acquisition of money, and not caring for others. As Hofstede defines it, this dimension deals with the respondents showing a more or less traditionally masculine pattern. His findings reveal that countries closer to the equator tend to be more masculine; countries closer to the poles are more feminine. The relationship becomes stronger when the poorer and wealthier countries are considered separately.

Hofstede explains differences in this dimension in terms of the necessity for men and women to master complex skills in moderate climates. The masculinity–femininity index is also related to population growth: it is negative for the wealthier countries and positive for the poorer ones. Although these ecological indicators explain a portion of the variance, much of the societal masculinity–femininity difference must be historically and traditionally determined. Histor-

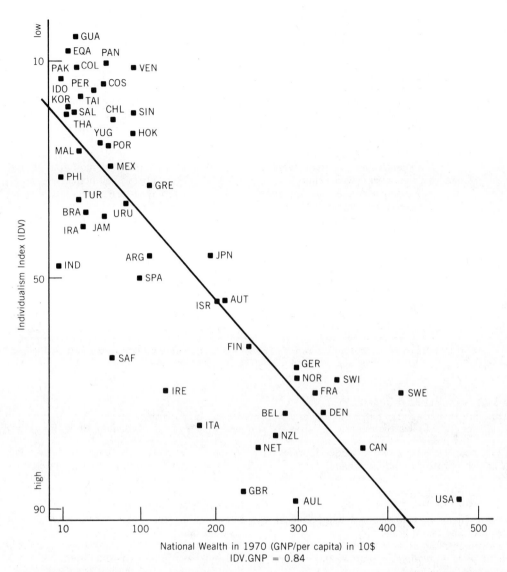

Figure 5.9 The position of the fifty countries on their individualism index (IDV) versus their 1970 national wealth.

Source: G. Hofstede, "The Cultural Relativity of Organizational Practices and Theories." *Journal of International Business Studies* 14(2):80, 1983.

ical factors play an important role, but among modern nations, there is no trend toward convergence in the direction of masculinity or femininity. From an organizational perspective, this dimension indicates the importance of earnings, recognition, achievement, and challenge in a particular country. This dimension is measured by a factor derived from the work importance scores.

Advancement and earnings correlate positively with this factor, whereas

Table 5.11 Consequences of Individualism–Collectivism Dimension for the Organization

Low IDV Countries	High IDV Countries
Involvement of individuals with organizations primarily moral.	Involvement of individuals with organizations primarily calculative.
Employees expect organizations to look after them like a family—and can become very alienated if organization dissatisfies them.	Organizations are not expected to look after employees from the cradle to the grave.
Organization has great influence on members' well-being.	Organization has moderate influence on members' well-being.
Employees expect organization to defend their interests.	Employees are expected to defend their own interests.
Policies and practices based on loyalty and sense of duty.	Policies and practices should allow for individual initiative.
Promotion from inside.⎫ Promotion on seniority.⎬ (localism)	Promotion from inside and ⎫ (cosmo- outside. ⎬ poli- Promotion on market value.⎭ tanism)
Less concern with fashion in management ideas.	Managers try to be up-to-date and endorse modern management ideas.
Policies and practices vary according to relations (particularism).	Policies and practices apply to all (universalism).

Source: G. Hofstede, *Culture's Consequences. International Differences in Work Related Values.* Beverly Hills: Sage, 1980, pp. 238–239. Reprinted by permission.

Table 5.12 Individualism Dimension

Collectivist	Individualist
In society, people are born into extended families or clans who protect them in exchange for loyalty.	In society, everybody is supposed to take care of himself/herself and his/her immediate family.
"We" consciousness holds sway.	"I" consciousness holds sway.
Identity is based in the social system.	Identity is based in the individual.
There is emotional dependence of individual on organizations and institutions.	There is emotional independence of individual from organizations or institutions.
The involvement with organizations is moral.	The involvement with organizations is calculative.
The emphasis is on belonging to organizations; membership is the ideal.	The emphasis is on individual initiative and achievement; leadership is the ideal.
Private life is invaded by organizations and clans to which one belongs; opinions are predetermined.	Everybody has a right to a private life and opinion.
Expertise, order, duty, and security are provided by organization or clan.	Autonomy, variety, pleasure, and individual financial security are sought in the system.
Friendships are predetermined by stable social relationships, but there is need for prestige within these relationships.	The need is for specific friendships.
Belief is placed in group decisions.	Belief is placed in individual decisions.
Value standards differ for in-groups and out-groups (particularism).	Value standards should apply to all (universalism).

Source: G. Hofstede, "Motivation Leadership and Organization: Do American Theories Apply Abroad? *Organizational Dynamics,* Summer 1980, p. 48.

Table 5.13 Consequences of National Masculinity Index Differences

Low MAS Countries	High MAS Countries
Some young men and women want careers, others do not.	Young men expect to make a career; those who don't see themselves as failures.
Organizations should not interfere with people's private lives.	Organizational interests are a legitimate reason for interfering with people's private lives.
More women in more qualified and better-paid jobs.	Fewer women in more qualified and better-paid jobs.
Women in more qualified jobs not particularly assertive.	Women in more qualified jobs are very assertive.
Lower job stress.	Higher job stress.
Less industrial conflict.	More industrial conflict.
Appeal of job restructuring permitting group integration.	Appeal of job restructuring permitting individual achievement.

Source: G. Hofstede, *Culture's Consequences. International Differences in Work Related Values.* Beverly Hills: Sage, 1980, p. 296. Reprinted by permission.

social and environmental factors are negatively related. One aspect of this dimension is its implications for work reform. The concept of a humanized job depends on one's definition of what is human. In a masculine culture, a humanized job should lead to opportunities for recognition, advancement, and challenge; in a feminine culture, the emphasis will be more on cooperation and a good working atmosphere. The masculinity index shows Japan as the country that leads the index. German-speaking countries (Austria, Switzerland, and Germany) also score high. Table 5.13 shows the organizational consequences arising out of differences in masculinity, and Table 5.14 shows the societal consequences of differences in masculinity.

The main finding emerging from the work of Hofstede and his colleagues is that organizations are very heavily culture-bound. This not only affects people's behavior within organizations; such cultural influences also limit how much (and how well) theories developed in one culture can be used in another. The dimensions that Hofstede identified affect different facets of organizational functioning. From a leadership perspective, individualism and power distance are the most important phenomena. In the United States, the various leadership theories are based on the premise that each individual seeks his or her own self-interest. Leadership in the Third World, on the other hand, is primarily a group phenomenon. A working group that does not coincide with the natural in-group will require conversion into an in-group before it can become effective. People in many of these countries bring considerable loyalty to their jobs if they feel that the employer returns the loyalty through protection. The problem of appropriate leadership behavior, in particular, is likely to be aggravated in multicultural organization settings. Although the adaptation of the manager to a high power distance environment does not pose as many problems, the operation of a manager in a country where the power distance norm is less than his

Table 5.14 Masculinity Dimension

Feminine	Masculine
Men needn't be assertive, but can also assume nurturing roles.	Men should be assertive. Women should be nurturing.
Sex roles in society are more fluid.	Sex roles in society are clearly differentiated.
There should be equality between the sexes.	Men should dominate in society.
Quality of life is important.	Performance is what counts.
You work in order to live.	You live in order to work.
People and environment are important.	Money and things are important.
Interdependence is the ideal.	Independence is the ideal.
Service provides the motivation.	Ambition provides the drive.
One sympathizes with the unfortunate.	One admires the successful achiever.
Small and slow are beautiful.	Big and fast are beautiful.
Unisex and androgyny are ideal.	Ostentatious manliness ("machismo") is appreciated.

Source: G. Hofstede, "Motivation Leadership and Organization: Do American Theories Apply Abroad?" *Organizational Dynamics,* Summer 1980, p. 49.

own is likely to pose greater problems. French and Latin managers are said to have problems in Anglo or Nordic countries unless they are particularly culturally sensitive. Leadership behavior may also be affected by a country's ranking on the masculinity index. Thus, Hofstede cites the cases of a U.S. consulting firm which, in analyzing the decision-making process in a large Scandinavian firm, emphasized the importance of fact-based rather than intuitive management. The consulting firm was oblivious to the notion that concern with intuition and consensus reflect the feminine aspects of Scandinavian culture. Table 5.15 reflects the standing of various countries according to these dimensions.

Power distance and uncertainty avoidance affects how members of different organizational groups respond to management issues. A study by James Stevens of INSEAD, cited by Hofstede (1983), discussed the implications of power distance from the perspective of leadership behavior. Management students from France, West Germany, and England were given a problem involving a conflict between two departments. Researchers asked the students to find out what was wrong and what actions might be taken to solve the problem. The French students recommended transferring the problem to the next highest authority level. Germans wanted to set up rules to solve such problems in the future. The British wanted to improve communications among respective groups by instituting a human relations training program.

Note that the dominant organizational model for the French was a hierarchical structure; the Germans emphasized a well-oiled machine; and the British structure was characterized by a lack of hierarchy, flexible rules, and resolution of problems by negotiating. People from different cultures create different solutions to the problem, thus reflecting the different design structures appropriate in their cultures.

Table 5.15 Index Values and Rank of Fifty Countries and Three Regions on Four Cultural Dimensions

Country	Abbre-viation	Power Distance Index (PDI)	Rank	Uncertainty Avoidance Index (UAI)	Rank	Individualism Index (IDV)	Rank	Masculinity Index (MAS)	Rank
Argentina	ARG	49	18–19	86	36–41	46	28–29	56	30–31
Australia	AUL	36	13	51	17	90	49	61	35
Austria	AUT	11	1	70	26–27	55	33	79	49
Belgium	BEL	65	33	94	45–46	75	43	54	29
Brazil	BRA	69	39	76	29–30	38	25	49	25
Canada	CAN	39	15	48	12–13	80	46–47	52	28
Chile	CHL	63	29–30	86	36–41	23	15	28	8
Colombia	COL	67	36	80	31	13	5	64	39–40
Costa Rica*	COS	35	10–12	86	36–41	15	8	21	5– 6
Denmark	DEN	18	3	23	3	74	42	16	4
Equador*	EQA	78	43–44	67	24	8	2	63	37–38
Finland	FIN	33	8	59	20–21	63	34	26	7
France	FRA	68	37–38	86	36–41	71	40–41	43	17–18
Germany (F.R.)	GER	35	10–12	65	23	67	36	66	41–42
Great Britain	GBR	35	10–12	35	6– 7	89	48	66	41–42
Greece	GRE	60	26–27	112	50	35	22	57	32–33
Guatemala*	GUA	95	48–49	101	48	6	1	37	11
Hong Kong	HOK	68	37–38	29	4– 5	25	16	57	32–33
Indonesia*	IDO	78	43–44	48	12–13	14	6– 7	46	22
India	IND	77	42	40	9	48	30	56	30–31
Iran	IRA	58	24–25	59	20–21	41	27	43	17–18
Ireland	IRE	28	5	35	6– 7	70	39	68	43–44
Israel	ISR	13	2	81	32	54	32	47	23
Italy	ITA	50	20	75	28	76	44	70	46–47
Jamaica*	JAM	45	17	13	2	39	26	68	43–44
Japan	JAP	54	21	92	44	46	28–29	95	50
Korea (S.)*	KOR	60	26–27	85	34–35	18	11	39	13
Malaysia*	MAL	104	50	36	8	26	17	50	26–27
Mexico	MEX	81	45–46	82	33	30	20	69	45
Netherlands	NET	38	14	53	18	80	46–47	14	3
Norway	NOR	31	6– 7	50	16	69	38	8	2
New Zealand	NZL	22	4	49	14–15	79	45	58	34
Pakistan	PAK	55	22	70	26–27	14	6– 7	50	26–27
Panama*	PAN	95	48–49	86	36–41	11	3	44	19
Peru	PER	64	31–32	87	42	16	9	42	15–16
Philippines	PHI	94	47	44	10	32	21	64	39–40
Portugal	POR	63	29–30	104	49	27	18–19	31	9
South Africa	SAF	49	18–19	49	14–15	65	35	63	37–38
Salvador*	SAL	66	34–35	94	45–46	19	12	40	14
Singapore	SIN	74	40	8	1	20	13–14	48	24
Spain	SPA	57	23	86	36–41	51	31	42	15–16
Sweden	SWE	31	6– 7	29	4– 5	71	40–41	5	1
Switzerland	SWI	34	9	58	19	68	37	70	46–47
Taiwan	TAI	58	24–25	69	25	17	10	45	20–21
Thailand	THA	64	31–32	64	22	20	13–14	34	10
Turkey	TUR	66	34–35	85	34–35	37	24	45	20–21
Uruguay*	URU	61	28	100	47	36	23	38	12
U.S.A.	USA	40	16	46	11	91	50	62	36
Venezuela	VEN	81	45–46	76	29–30	12	4	73	48
Yugoslavia	YUG	76	41	88	43	27	18–19	21	5– 6
Regions:									
East Africa*	EAF	64	(31–32)	52	(17–18)	27	(18–19)	41	(14–15)
West Africa*	WAF	77	(42)	54	(18–19)	20	(13–14)	46	(22)
Arab Ctrs.*	ARA	80	(44–45)	68	(24–25)	38	(25)	53	(28–29)

*Based on data added later.
Source: G. Hofstede, "National Cultures in Four Dimensions," *International Studies of Management and Organization,* 13(2):52 (1983).

The dimensions that Hofstede identified have additional implications for two other issues: management development programs and the structuring of work in different cultures. As mentioned earlier, some cultures have a tendency to avoid uncertainty. Organizational development processes, however, create insecurity. These processes may create stress in high uncertainty avoidance cultures. Organizational development may have to take shape as a kind of counterculture in such countries. From the perspective of structuring schedules, flexible working hours may provide a useful device for encouraging change. The notion of flexible working hours emerged in Germany and has had its greatest success in that country and Switzerland. It has not caught on in France, Britain, or the United States, however. Hofstede suggests that in high uncertainty avoidance–low power distance countries, time is a source of great stress. Hence, a system that allows people relief from rules about time is often attractive to employees.

Hofstede also links industrial democracy with the dimensions that he identified. By industrial democracy, he means the degree to which lower-level participants are involved in making certain decisions. Power distance and uncertainty avoidance are the cultural dimensions that determine such a system's successful functioning. Power distance is linked with industrial democracy because it is a way of reducing precisely that distance. Accordingly, these factors are much more natural in cultures with low power distance than in other cultures. The formal or informal acceptance of industrial democracy in turn is dependent on the countries' levels of uncertainty avoidance. In the Anglo-American countries, Scandinavia, and the Netherlands, the greatest stress tends to be on informal and spontaneous forms of participation. In German-speaking countries, on the other hand, more stress is likely to be placed on formal legal participation. In Sweden, both sorts of approaches may well appear.

Hofstede's work can also aid in our understanding of motivational dynamics. Hofstede suggests that the individualism–collectivism dimension is related to motivation. In an individualistic society, motivation is a consequence of a need to fulfill obligations toward oneself. Accordingly, self-actualization becomes an important motivator. In a collectivist society, however, people try to fulfill their obligations toward the in-group, which may be the family, the enterprise, or the country. These individuals do not seek self-actualization or self-respect, but primarily seek respect in relationships with in-group members. Hofstede suggests that different combinations of uncertainty avoidance and masculinity lead to different motivational patterns. Low uncertainty avoidance and low masculinity should lead to an emphasis on belonging over self-actualization.

Note that these dimensions, though seemingly abstract, have specific and concrete consequences within particular countries. Achievement and challenge, for example—both of which are present as sources of motivation in the United States—have two implications: (1) Americans are willing to take risks, which reflects their weak uncertainty avoidance, and (2) they have a need to perform, which is related to the dimension of masculinity. Hofstede also identifies Japan and Germany as masculine; but because they are characterized by stronger uncertainty avoidance, there is less willingness to take risks. This implies that security is a powerful motivator as well. Other combinations of these dimensions will affect other countries in other ways.

We should also note that these dimensions are not static. They change as people and cultures change. Hofstede reports that during the period from 1968 to 1972, the largest universal shift occurred in the individualism dimension. This shift occurred in all countries except Pakistan. In the dimensions of masculinity–femininity, there was an average shift toward the masculine dimension, although generally speaking this did not affect all countries. Concerning the dimension of power distance, the preference for a more consultative or democratic manager increased, yet only in low power distance countries did the increased preference accompany a corresponding shift in managers' behavior. Only the question of stress showed a distinct worldwide trend, with a tendency toward increased stress in most countries.

To summarize, the cultural relativity of management practices has profound implications for multinational organizations. Similar policies may have different effects in different countries depending on the countries' relative positions on these dimensions. A fundamental dilemma confronting an organization operating abroad is whether to adapt to the local culture or to change it. Hofstede suggests that some companies have succeeded in changing local habits. He cites the example of a firm that successfully introduced matrix organization in France. Such changes may be more feasible within Anglo-European countries. Third World countries present another situation. Many Third World countries are trying to import technologies from advanced countries, yet successful adaptation often presupposes acquiring values that run counter to local traditions. Generally, it appears that both adaptation and maintenance of traditions are necessary.

Hofstede's work has implications for training. For managers sent to work overseas, training based on home-country theories may be of limited use. In the United States, much effort has been devoted since the early 1960s to developing cross-cultural training and orientation programs. A motivating force toward the development of such training has been the high rate of failure of personnel sent abroad. From a training perspective, the main difference is between a culture-specific and a culture-general approach. We will discuss these issues further in the section on training.

This survey has attempted to provide an overview of Hofstede's work. His work is of prime importance because it documents in detail the role of culture in organizations. As he points out, organizing is culturally dependent: it consists of manipulating symbols that have meaning for the people who are managed or organized. The meanings we associate with symbols are heavily affected by what we have learned in the course of our socialization.

COUNTRY SPECIFICS

The following brief paragraphs, written on the basis of selective sources, should give the reader a flavor of the country-specific characteristics identified in Hofstede's work. Readers who wish to supplement their information on a particular area should consult the bibliography of comparative management literature at the end of this text.

Australia

This country is moralistic, with a high emphasis on political and social value as well as on achievement, success, and risk. There are major regional differences. It is relatively low in power distance and somewhat high on masculinity and uncertainty avoidance, but essentially moderate on these indexes.

Turkey

Emphasis in Turkey is on revealed truths. Centralized decision making, highly personalized, strong leaders, and little delegation or task orientation exist. Emphasis is on family and status. The country is strong on uncertainty avoidance and relatively high in power distance, but surprisingly low on masculinity.

France

In France there is strong emphasis on logic and rationality, with stress on individual opinions, and elan is important to organizational success. It is important to be sharp witted as well as mature, steady, and reliable. One-way communication is relatively acceptable. Self-perception is one of tolerance of conflict. France is high on uncertainty avoidance, relatively low on masculinity, and high on power distance. Managers are generally from the *grandes écoles*.

Italy

Italy is low in risk tolerance and high on uncertainty avoidance. Italians are willing to accept affection and warmth but are high on masculinity. They are highly competitive but prefer use of group decision making and are moderate on the power distance index.

Latin America

Concern with prestige and self-realization is strong here, with less interest in independence, security, and pleasure. The area is moderate in masculinity, with relatively strong uncertainty avoidance and high power distance. Rapid decision making, little conscious planning, reliance on intuition, and emotional judgments are dominant.

Japan

Japan is high on both masculinity and uncertainty avoidance and relatively high in power distance. In contradiction, it is high in empathy and risk-taking indicators as well as in wanting to accept warmth and affection from others. Prestige, service, security, and pleasure are considered less important. There is a high element of pragmatism, with a low value placed on conflict and its open expression. Objectivity is desired.

United States

The United States is high in pragmatism, emphasizing profit maximization, organizational efficiency, and productivity. It is individualistic and action-oriented, with a high tolerance for risk and a low uncertainty avoidance. Need for achievement is high, with stress on individual self-realization, leadership, and wealth as life goals. Emphasis is on democratic leadership, favoring group decision making and participation, with a low score on power distance. One-way communication is disliked. The masculinity index score is moderate, with a preference for considerate, relations-oriented leaders. Americans believe in self-determination, resulting in decisions based on precise, accurate data, and an emphasis on planning. Rewards based on merit are considered appropriate because the individual is seen as being responsible for outcomes.

Germany/Austria

These countries are low in tolerance for risk, with an emphasis on self-realization, leadership, and independence as life goals. They are highly competitive, with little regard being placed on patience and reliability. They are relatively high on the masculinity index but low on power distance.

Scandinavia

Scandinavia is above average in risk tolerance; emphasis here is on maturity and steadiness, with a premium placed on tolerance and sociability. Femininity is combined with weak uncertainty avoidance and low power distance.

The Netherlands

The Dutch are concerned with expertness and duty, and less concerned with self-realization. They are high in tolerance of risk and content to be reactive rather than proactive, with an emphasis on being sharp witted.

Belgium

Emphasis is on duty but risk tolerance is low. Importance is placed on being sharp witted; less importance is placed on tolerance or thoughtfulness. Belgians are high on uncertainty avoidance, moderate in masculinity, and relatively high in power distance.

Britain

Strong social class traditions exist in Britain. Security is an important goal, yet pleasure is emphasized as a life goal. Resourcefulness, logic, and adaptability are considered important goals; the people are highly competitive. They are low on indexes of power distance and uncertainty avoidance, high on individualism, and relatively high on masculinity.

India

India is autocratic and paternalistic, with a centralized decision-making style and strong task orientation. The people are concerned with rules and emphasize patience and modesty; concomitantly they are low in risk tolerance and deemphasize pleasure. Scores on power distance and masculinity indexes are high. They are relatively satisfied with an uninvolved subordinate and see compensation as a potential motivator of improved performance. Strong emphasis is placed on family and status, with little concern for individual independence. Indians are idealistic in their personal concerns but are cynical about businessmen in general, who they see as cold and calculating. Stress is placed on loyalty over personal growth.

WORK MOTIVATION IN DEVELOPING NATIONS

As multinationals continue to expand their operations to many *developing* nations, we must emphasize the importance of understanding how workers in these countries are motivated. Indeed, to address the issue of worker productivity, there must be an acknowledgment of the cultural and societal values that affect employee motivation. Although there is a plethora of theories and models regarding motivation in Western industrialized countries, we must question whether such theories as Maslow's need hierarchy theory and Herzberg's two-factor theory are applicable to these developing nations. For example, Kanungo (1983), in his study of work alienation, concluded that the measurement devices and intervention strategies used in the West to increase work involvement and to improve the quality of working life have limited applicability for many Third World countries that do not adhere to an "individualistic" value orientation.

This lack of cross-cultural applicability of the Western models has spurred research into worker motivation in these countries. Studies have revealed that although needs often motivate employees, these needs may vary dramatically from country to country and from culture to culture. Moreover, workers have a variety of needs, some more salient than others. The saliency of any one person's needs is determined by his or her past socialization in a given culture. It is also constantly modified by present job conditions. For these reasons, multinational corporations cannot merely transplant American management techniques to subsidiaries in developing nations without taking into account the local socioeconomic setting and culture. Foreign subsidiaries must be allowed enough flexibility to adjust their management practices to the local environment.

Cross-Cultural Motivation Studies

Most research on motivation in work settings has studied people in industrially advanced nations; very little has been conducted in developing countries.

However, those studies that have been done—both multinational and one-country studies—have revealed a common theme in developing countries' work motivation: in Third World countries, work motivation can be attributed to culture strength (lack of dilution by other cultures), as well as to the level of industrialization.

Cultural Environment and Socialization

Since an individual's cultural milieu exerts a powerful influence over his or her attitude toward most objects in the physical and social world (Wrightsman, 1976), researchers have often looked to this factor when attempting to assess worker motivation. Additionally, socialization (by which one generation's frame of reference is transmitted to another) also appears to affect employee motivation.

Kanungo (1983) points out that Eastern and Western cultures differ in the values their socialization processes impart. Unlike Eastern cultures, Western cultures value individualism and promote the importance of autonomy and personal achievement needs. In contrast, socialization in many Eastern and Third World nations promotes a strong sense of collectivism and the importance of social and security needs. For example, the Hindu religion imparts a type of work ethic that considers work central to one's lfe but maintains that it must be performed as a service to others, not for one's own personal achievement.

In his study of Western and tribal black employees' work values in South Africa (all of whom held first-level supervisory jobs), Orpen (1978) studied the potential effect of the relative Westernization of black African employees on the relationship between employee performance and job satisfaction. Orpen's research showed that a widely held assumption—that work does not mean the same to "modern" and "traditional" black employees—had some validity. The author did so by demonstrating that these two groups' cultural environment has a powerful impact on individuals' attitudes. For example, Orpen found that the Western-oriented employees accept the major tenets of the Protestant work ethic to a greater extent than the tribal-oriented employees. Orpen concluded that the main reasons for the different work values were the different cultural backgrounds of the two groups' members.

In another study of African countries, Chukwumah (1974) found the various countries to be all basically alike in employees' work motivation despite the nations' differing levels of industrialization. In short, similar motivations attributable to the importance of these cultures' psychological and social factors stemmed from the specific attitudes of the tribal backgrounds.

In their study of spinning workers in Hong Kong, Taiwan, Malaysia, the Philippines, and Thailand, Kao and Levin (1978) demonstrated the impact of culture on worker motivation. They concluded that although preindustrial cultural systems may affect worker motivation in the early stages of industrialization, such influence will probably diminish as countries move toward more advanced levels of development. Hence, culture may have its strongest effect on worker motivation before it is diluted by other cultures (in this case, that of the Western industrialized countries). The introduction of new "cultures" may alter workers' needs, and hence their motivation as well.

Culture as a prime motivator is the theme of another Asian study by Redding and Martyn-Johns (1979). In a study of Hong Kong, Malaysia, Indonesia, Thailand, the Philippines, and South Vietnam, the authors conclude that different cultural thought processes (e.g., fatalism and guilt) lead to different attitudes and motivations. Oriental cultures, the authors say, yield less individualistic employees who are more susceptible to authority and formal control. Redding and Martyn-Johns also found that motivation of leaders in these cultures (i.e., managers and supervisors) stem from self-actualization and autonomy needs.

In his study of Arab countries (Saudi Arabia, Kuwait, Abu Dhabi, Bahrain, Oman, and the United Arab Emirates), Badawy (1979) found the greatest need was autonomy, a function of historical and cultural values. Badawy found that culture has a greater effect on motivation than Westernization of job content. The author found Middle Eastern executives to have a traditional (i.e., stemming from their culture) approach to management, an offshoot in turn of their kinship-oriented society. Thus, a significant cultural value is the importance of interpersonal relations. Arabs prefer to deal with people they know, with whom they have established relations, rather than with less well-known people. Another important cultural value is religion. Arabs place a high value on religion. Some will not do business with people who do not believe in God. In conclusion, Badawy suggests that motivational development programs should target the ingrained culture; management should work with employees' heritage of culture to bring forth useful qualities in the subordinate's abilities.

An Indian study by Sinha (1969) found cultural values to be a primary motivator as well. The author, who compared motivations in developed and underdeveloped communities (differentiated by the level of industrial progress), found very little difference between them. Sinha attributes this lack of difference to values rooted in cultural and religious traditions. Traditionally, Indian religion sanctions destruction of wants, so psychological transformation does not necessarily follow economic development; economic differences of communities did not significantly change the motivational structure.

In conclusion, differences in workers' motivation can be explained in part by the fact that people belonging to different cultures tend to develop different salient needs as a result of different cultural and group norm influences.

Industrialization and Westernization

Culture is an important variable in employee motivation, but in the developing countries we must also examine other factors. Among these are the level of industrialization and the stage of development. Indeed, many studies have found that while culture may be of primary importance in determining what motivates employees, other forces—such as the process of industrialization and the infiltration of Western values—affect cultural values as well. Consequently, culture viewed in the context of changing economic conditions and the effects of industrialization may prove to be the best indicator of worker motivation.

In Nambudiri and Saiyadain's cross-cultural management study of India and Nigeria (1978), the authors concluded that the conflict between traditional values and modern industry results in changing motivational factors for managers in those two countries. In Nigeria, the workers became less loyal to traditional values and more pay oriented. In India, where the culture is still rather pure, managers appeared to be loyal but somewhat distrustful of employees. However, tradition affected both cultures in that both sets of managers held authoritarian views of leadership. This study viewed motivation as a function of the contribution of a strong culture and the advent of industrialization. Low-level needs (according to Maslow's hierarchy) were still important but were in the process of changing as a result of industrialization.

In a study of employees in Indian pharmaceutical companies, Richman and Orpen (1973) found that the least successful companies were those that continued to use traditional Indian values and ignored the Westernization process. As the Indian companies moved closer to American firms in their management values, the successful firms employed more participative techniques and emphasized individualism. Also, as these firms became more Westernized, they put more emphasis on intrinsic job satisfaction and changing work and less on traditional Indian autocracy.

Emphasis on higher-order needs such as self-actualization resulting from the industrialization process is also supported by Salmans's study (1978) of garment accessory workers in Thailand. In her study, Salmans found that need for self-actualization (as defined by Maslow) motivated their workers. The company responded by using employee participation to motivate them.

Yet another study that advances the theory that industrialization will affect workers' needs is Machungwa and Schmitt's (1983). In their study of work motivation in Zambia—a study of (among others) managers, technical personnel, secretaries, and semiskilled and general workers—the authors found that the nature of work and the opportunity for growth and advancement were the most important elements when reporting what motivates hard work. Demotivators included poor interpersonal relations with superiors, co-workers, and subordinates, unfair organizational practices, and personal problems. It is interesting to note that, overall, the author's data were roughly supportive of Herzberg's two-factor theory in that hygiene variables were more frequently mentioned as demotivators by the respondents; likewise, employees' motivating variables were those that Herzberg identified as motivators—that is, growth opportunities and the nature of the work performed.

Finally, Laaksonen (1977) states that in developing countries such as China, the motivating needs are the lower-level type, for example, physical needs, security needs, and so on. The author writes that in the industrialized Western nations, managing individuals demands investing time and other resources to provide motivation, and that the constant acquisition of knowledge results in satisfying higher-level needs. In this light, Laaksonen suggests that cultural values may be the prime motivator until a time of greater industrialization arrives.

The scarcity of systematic data from the developing countries makes it difficult to draw generalized conclusions. What seems to be true is that both cultural differences are distinct, but a low economic level overrides these cultural differences. The need for survival and security predominate.

CONCLUSION

This chapter has explored the interrelationships between cultural conditioning, motivation, and work in different cultures. These interrelationships are highly complex; this chapter, despite its detail, provides only an overview of a world-wide situation. But grasping the relevant issues is crucial for researchers and managers alike.

Whatever else, cultural conditioning is powerful. All societies condition their members in one way or another. Such conditioning affects not only behavior, but actual perceptions of reality. Small wonder, then, that business interactions between nations often produce disagreements, misunderstandings, and a sense that the other party is counterproductive, incompetent, or even bizarre. The attitudinal differences that affect human behavior stem from a variety of influences found within all cultures. Among the most important of these influences are conformity, achievement, sex roles, time, space, and ethnocentrism. Awareness of these issues does not mean that managers can easily overcome their effects; however, knowledge at least provides a chance to compensate for such differences.

Consequently, understanding social conditioning is an important aspect of cross-cultural management. Perceiving differences in work motivation is especially crucial. A number of studies have attempted to explain differences in motivation, their sources, and their effects. Among these studies are Maslow's hierarchy of needs, McClelland's theory, Hofstede's cross-national study, and others. Some of these studies have employed the so-called armchair approach. Others are empirically based. Examined collectively, these studies reveal patterns of work motivation—sometimes according to culture, sometimes according to nation—and offer managers a useful device for structuring jobs overseas.

Managers should consider both the general and the specific influences that affect work motivation in particular cultures. The general influences include not only the "armchair" dimensions (e.g., religion, language, political systems, etc.) but also empirically derived dimensions (e.g., Hofstede's power distance, uncertainty avoidance, individualism–collectivism, etc.). The specific influences included idiosyncrasies in particular cultures (historical aftermaths, specific traditions, etc.).

These are, of course, complex issues to analyze; responding to them is often difficult. Understanding another culture's work motivation is a crucial step for the overseas manager, but motivation alone does not settle all the relevant issues. Accordingly, we should now proceed to another important consideration in the overall context of cross-cultural management: managerial behavior and leadership style.

CHAPTER 6
Managerial Behavior and Leadership Style

COMPARATIVE MANAGEMENT MODELS

Comparative management literature recognizes the importance of culture in determining managerial attitudes and practices. Researchers nevertheless disagree about which aspects of culture are most important and to what degree.

Harbison and Myers (1959), for instance, who performed the initial studies in modern comparative management, proposed the notion that managerial beliefs reflect a country's level of industrial development. This notion suggests that as differences in the level of industrial development diminish, managerial beliefs and practices should become more similar. It seems possible that such differences will virtually disappear over the long term. We can only speculate, however, on how long the long term might be. For this reason, we must recognize how significantly culture affects managerial behavior for at least the immediate future. We must also spell out both the sources of cultural influence and the mechanisms by which it affects managerial behavior, because behavior, in turn, affects managerial and organizational effectiveness.

Farmer and Richman (1965) have developed a model that considers culture as an important variable influencing such effectiveness (see Figure 6.1). This model views cultural as well as national antecedents as external constraints (educational, legal, political, economic) that affect the management process. Among the cultural variables that influence managerial style are such variables as attitudes toward achievement, risk-taking preferences, and needs. This model has several advantages. To the extent that relevant cultural factors can be identified and systematically analyzed, it can help trace the impact of such factors on managerial and organizational effectiveness.

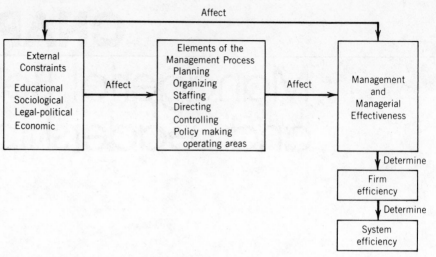

Figure 6.1   Farmer and Richman model.

Source: R. N. Farmer and B. M. Richman. *Comparative Management and Economic Progress.* Homewood, IL: Irwin, 1965, p. 35. Copyright © 1971 by Cedarwood Press, Bloomington, IN.

Farmer and Richman suggest that their model is relevant on a micro- as well as a macro-level. At a micro-level, the model can help improve an enterprise's awareness of the cultural effects on the performance of individuals and groups. This, in turn, can enable the firm to lessen the impact of cultural constraints. For example, if the firm finds that employees are not sufficiently achievement oriented, and if this orientation strongly influences the employees' effectiveness, then the firm can either try to institute appropriate training or select people who are more achievement oriented. For the MNC, such awareness may help to limit unwarranted expectations about the local personnel.

Although Farmer and Richman's model has these positive attributes, it has some limitations as well. One possible criticism is that the model is static—it does not consider the environmental factors (e.g., cultural or legal factors) that industrialization may influence. Another possible criticism is that the model views the firm as adapting passively to external constraints (Schollhammer, 1969). In a critique of this model, Negandhi and Prasad (1971) argue that if environmental and cultural factors were the main determinants of management practices, the management practices of comparable industrial firms in a culture would tend to resemble each other. However, this is not so. Compare, for instance, two American retail chains—Montgomery Ward and Sears Roebuck. Both are in the same business and face similar environmental conditions, but they have adopted different managerial practices. Negandhi and Prasad provide the model shown in Figure 6.2.

Although it incorporates culture as a variable, Negandhi and Prasad's model does not seem to accord as much importance to culture as it does to management philosophy (Kelley & Worthley, 1981). By management philosophy, we mean management's attitudes toward and beliefs regarding consumers,

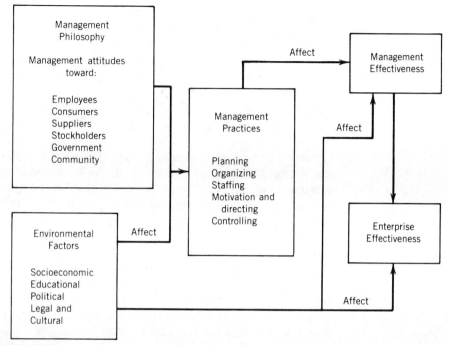

Figure 6.2 Comparative management construct: Negandhi and Prasad model.

Source: A. R. Negandhi and S. B. Prasad. *Comparative Management.* New York: Appleton-Century-Crofts, 1971, p. 23.

suppliers, stockholders, the community, and, particularly, their employees. Negandhi and Prasad (1971) studied American subsidiaries in Argentina, Brazil, India, the Philippines, and Uruguay, along with local firms to explore how management philosophy and environmental factors affect management practice. They found that managers in the American subsidiaries were much more likely to delegate than managers in the locally owned firms. There was little difference between the managerial style and effectiveness of U.S. subsidiaries and of those local firms classified as the most sophisticated in management philosophy.

To test the Farmer and Richman model against that of Negandhi and Prasad, Kelley and Worthley (1981) designed a study comparing similarities and differences in the managerial attitudes of Japanese, Caucasian American, and Japanese–American managers working in financial institutions. Previous research (Kitano, 1968) suggests that the Japanese–Americans in Hawaii tend to retain many Japanese attitudes and values. Accordingly, one would expect that if culture were important, Japanese–American managers' responses would be more similar to the Japanese responses than to those of the Caucasian Americans. Because national differences arising out of differences in legal/political systems were also present, the researchers predicted that the Japanese–Americans' responses would lie between those of the other two groups. On nine out of fifteen items, the responses were in the predicted order. Kelley and Worthley conclude that their study supports Farmer and Richman's position (1965) on the role of culture in shaping managerial attitudes. They believe that the Negandhi and Prasad model is not supported. Negandhi and Prasad include culture as a variable, but they do not accord it as much importance as Farmer and Richman.

Although Farmer and Richman's study certainly supports the presence of both cultural and national differences in the formation of managerial beliefs and attitudes, it appears that the role of management philosophy as an independent variable has not been explicitly tested. Management philosophy is the variable that Negandhi and Prasad consider to be of major importance. Kelley and Worthley's study, in contrast, demonstrates the importance of culture, but it does not adequately differentiate between the effects of culture and those of management philosophy. Consequently, their study makes a useful contribution, although it would have been still more useful if they had made this distinction.

We suggest that managerial philosophy may be an important independent variable and that philosophy and culture may not necessarily coincide. To the extent that the philosophy fits well into the prevailing culture, both variables should yield similar behavioral consequences. To the extent that philosophy does not fit in with the prevailing culture, the impact of culture may diminish. Culture may be the primary variable from a theoretical standpoint, but its impact depends on precisely this fit. The Farmer and Richman and Negandhi and Prasad models may thus *complement* each other—the relative importance of either model may be expected to vary from country to country.

These models address the issue of the importance of culture by attempting to understand managerial behaviors. Alternative approaches have focused on the importance of macroorganizational-level variables (e.g., organizational structure and technology) in influencing behaviors. Consistent with this perspective, Child (1981) stressed the role of culture in a different way. He considers the relevant question not *whether* culture is important, but rather *when* it is important. Child suggests that macro-level variables such as organizational structure and technology are becoming more and more similar while micro-level variables continue to retain their cultural identity. (By micro-level variables he means people's behavior in work settings.) One implication of Child's distinction is that leadership behaviors will remain culturally specific despite the convergence of organizational structures.

Having explored how management activity can vary when culture and management philosophy differ, we should now consider another issue: how leadership and decision-making styles reflect management activity.

LEADERSHIP STYLES

Leadership is important because a particular leadership style can affect the motivation and behavior of an organization's members—not to mention the organization's whole climate. Leaders, in a sense, are agents of change who can have a significant impact on the behavior of others.

Anthropological studies indicate that leadership is a universal phenomenon. The universality of leadership does not, however, imply a similarity of leadership style throughout the world. Bass's review (1981) of Margaret Mead's studies shows that the pattern of appropriate leader–subordinate behavior varies across cultures. For example, he cites the following contrasts in appropriate leadership behavior that can be discerned from Mead's studies.

- In central Africa, the Bachiga were characterized by individualism, lack of political integration and noncompliance with their leaders. The Bathonga, on the other hand, emphasized obedience, respect for the chief, and cooperative effort, with little room for rivalry.

- Among traditional Eskimos, one person's importance in relation to others was not emphasized. The Samoans, however, ranked individuals in a clear hierarchy and enforced conformity to these ranks.

- Among Native Americans, the Iroquois achieved leadership through behavior that was socially rewarding to others, such as generosity, cooperation, and hospitality. In contrast, among the Kwakiutl, the ideal chief was one who could successfully compete financially against other chiefs.

- The Arapesh of New Guinea did not consider ownership of land as a basis for leadership; however, the Ifugao of the Philippines considered the landowner the ideal of success.

These examples indicate the variation of specific leadership behaviors across cultures. Differences in values, attitudes toward authority, achievement motivation, and risk taking are among the factors determining such differences. At the same time, we should stress that the *functions* of leadership in organizations are largely similar across cultures. Different leadership behaviors will have different implications for the success of the organization in fulfilling its managerial functions. Because leaders' behaviors have an impact on such functions, we should analyze them.

Traditionally, the functions of management have been planning, controlling, and organizing the firm's activities. The planning function is responsible for establishing organizational or departmental objectives and determining appropriate means for achieving them. The organizing function deals with how to allocate activities among various groups to meet organizational goals. The control function concerns measuring how well the organization realizes its stated objectives and controls subordinates' activities. To realize the goals of effectiveness and efficiency in any culture, management must emphasize these functions. Effectiveness depends on how well the organization can achieve its stated goals; efficiency depends on the organization's cost-effectiveness. The process of realizing these goals varies from culture to culture. Content differences affect the nature of the process but not its basic function.

The functionality of leadership behaviors can be well-illustrated by examining the model of Schriesheim, Mowday, and Stogdill (1979), with Bass adopted for his review (1981). This model appears in Figure 6.3.

The figure shows how leadership behaviors affect group productivity, which in turn influences its effectiveness and efficiency. The various stages in the

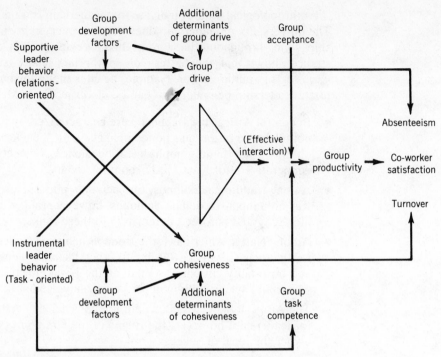

Figure 6.3 Linking leadership to group outcomes.

Source: B. M. Bass. *Stogdill's Handbook of Leadership.* New York: Free Press, a Division of Macmillan Inc. © 1981, p. 420. Adopted from C. A. Schriesheim, R. T. Mowday, and R. M. Stogdill. "Crucial Dimensions of Leader-Group Interactions," in J. G. Hunt and L. L. Larson, eds. *Cross-Currents in Leadership.* Carbondale: Southern Illinois University Press, 1979.

model are (1) the development of a group structure, (2) the development of group cohesiveness, and (3) the completion of the group task. The basic idea here is that leadership functions depend on the group's stages of development. If a group needs to develop cohesiveness, relations-oriented behavior might be the appropriate function; at a stage in which task achievement is the central objective, task-oriented behavior may be appropriate instead.

One important aspect of such leadership behaviors is the extent to which democratic or autocratic styles are a major characteristic of the relationship between leaders and subordinates. A democratic or autocratic style will be influenced largely by that culture's prevalent attitude toward authority. For example, Whyte and Williams (1963) found that Peruvian workers were happy with their supervisors to the extent that they perceived them to be exercising close rather than general supervision. In American firms, the situation was exactly the opposite.

Thus far, we have considered the nature of leadership and its functionality for organizations. The most salient issue here is that specific behaviors vary across cultures, but their ultimate objective remains the same. We should now examine the most significant theories of leadership.

Theories of Leadership

First, we should look at various theories as they have developed in the West. This will indicate the universality of these theories in explaining behavior.

A major conceptualization of leadership—which has been dominant for a long time—views it as a personality trait distributed throughout the population. According to this theory, some people have more of the leadership trait than others and thus become effective leaders. In a review of the various traits associated with leadership in the United States, Bass (1981) has observed that a leader possesses the following characteristics: persistence, self-confidence, a strong drive for responsibility and task completion, the ability to influence others' behavior, and originality. Other studies have also shown that leaders have superior physical attributes (height and weight) as well as intelligence and extroversion (Vroom, 1976).

Although some of these traits certainly may be found in leaders, their importance depends to a large extent on their context. Certainly some traits are more important in one situation than in another, and if a trait varies in its importance, then the notion of universal leadership traits is not valid. Viewing leadership as a personality characteristic therefore proves to be simplistic. Later in this chapter, we will examine how situations affect leadership style. From a cross-cultural perspective as well, it appears that some traits may be more important in some societies than in others. In a society that espouses democratic values, for instance, an autocratic individual may not make a successful leader.

An alternative to the personality approach is one that focuses on effective leadership behavior. The basic idea underlying this theory is that we can distinguish between effective and ineffective leaders by means of their underlying behavioral patterns. For example, studies conducted during the 1960s at Ohio State University and the University of Michigan revealed two important facets of leadership behavior: (1) consideration (employee-centeredness) and (2) initiation of structure (job-centeredness). Consideration refers to how much a leader is concerned with his or her group members' well-being. Consideration may be manifested in many different ways: enhancing subordinates' self-esteem, accepting their suggestions and advice, or praising them for good work. The initiation of structure deals with how leaders organize subordinates' work group activity. The emphasis here is on maintaining standards, meeting deadlines, and deciding what task to perform or how to do it.

The results of studies conducted in the United States have not been clear-cut. It appears that in this country, subordinates tend to be more satisfied with a considerate leader, but a leader's effectiveness appears to vary with the situation. Similar results emerged from the Michigan and Ohio studies (Likert, 1961; Fleishman, 1973). These studies focused on supervisory behavior as employee-centered (compared to production-centered), and they have generally concluded that more effective leaders are supportive of their subordinates, use group methods of supervision and decision making, and set high performance goals. This essentially translated into a managerial style that is both employee- and production-centered. In Blake and Mouton's terminology (1964), this is 9.9 style—it embodies maximal concern for both production and people. Blake and Mouton (1970) report uniform agreement among managers from various cultural areas (United States, South Africa, Canada, Australia, the Middle East, South America, and Japan) that the 9.9 style is the ideal managerial style.

There are several problems with these theories, however. For instance, Bass (1981) reports that much of this uniformity across countries is apparent rather than real. When describing their actual behavior, managers from Japan and South America expressed a greater concern for production than for people. (Bass also notes the possible presence of artifact in Blake and Mouton's work.) Vroom (1976) raises another issue: the employee-centered/production-centered principle is very broad. Broad leadership principles do not cover the complexities of situational differences nor implications of these differences for leadership behavior. The two-factor distinction that Blake and Mouton postulate is not helpful to managers who wish to choose an appropriate response for concrete situations they face daily.

More recently, researchers have focused specifically on contingency aspects that influence effective leadership. These approaches have particularly important implications for comparative management, which by definition concerns leadership in different situations. A general integrative model of leadership appears in Figure 6.4.

This model shows how leaders' behavior is affected by situational, leader, and subordinate characteristics and how such behavior affects performance outcomes. The model also easily captures the role of culture. Leader characteristics, subordinate characteristics, and the nature of the situation are all culturally determined. Differences in these dimensions across cultures will yield different behaviors and different performance outcomes. Although this model is a general one, there are more specific contingency models as well. Three well-known situational theories are Fiedler's contingency theory (1967), Vroom and Yetton's normative model (1973), and the path-goal theory of leadership (House & Mitchell, 1974).

Fiedler's model of leadership, one of the best-known models, has generated a considerable amount of research. This is a contingency model because the situation is considered along with the leader's personality as a determinant of the leader's effectiveness. According to Fiedler, his model can help predict which leaders would be most effective in which situations. The model, thus, has many implications for recruiting, selecting, and placing leaders. A central aspect of this theory is that leaders differ in a personality variable (called LPC) that indicates the extent of their social responsiveness. The LPC score measures the leaders' feelings about an individual with whom they work least effectively.

Leaders with low LPC scores see their least-preferred co-worker in negative terms, whereas the high LPC leaders do not impute negative attributes to those with whom they have difficulty working. The correlation between a leader's LPC score and group effectiveness is highly related to the favorableness of the situation. (A very favorable situation is one in which the task is structured, the leader has high position power, and leader–member relations are good.)

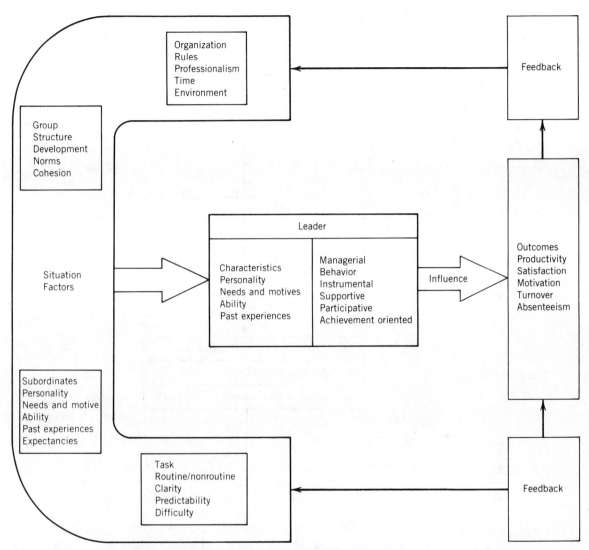

Figure 6.4   An integrative model of leadership.

The basic thesis is that low LPC leaders do well in extremely favorable and unfavorable situations whereas high LPC leaders do well in moderately favorable situations. It is unclear exactly what the LPC scale measures and whether such differences would also be apparent in non-Western societies, however, this line of research has clearly demonstrated the importance of the situation in determining leader effectiveness. From a cross-cultural perspective, a contingency theory seems appealing. Conditions vary across cultures; a theory that has some applicability in one culture may be irrelevant in another. For example, Bennett (1977) found that high-performing bank managers in the Philippines are low on Fiedler's LPC scale, whereas comparable managers in Hong Kong

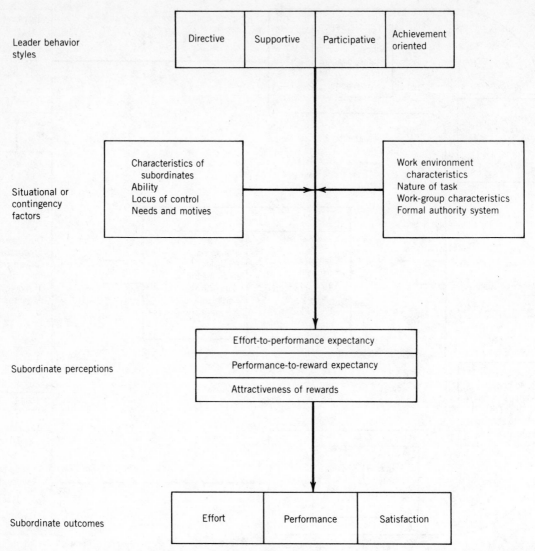

Figure 6.5   A summary of path-goal relationships.

score high on it. Just as contingencies vary across cultures, so does the relationship between LPC scores and performance.

The path-goal theory is another contingency theory that seeks to explain the leadership style most conducive to group satisfaction and effectiveness. Figure 6.5 summarizes the various path-goal relationships.

In recent years, Evan (1970) and House (1971) have popularized this theory. It postulates that leaders must try to influence their subordinates' perception of the paths for achieving goals and of the goals' desirability. The leadership style most appropriate for increasing motivation depends as well on the subordinates' personal characteristics and on the nature of the task demands. The leadership model (see Figure 6.5) shows the nature of the various leadership styles—instrumental, supportive, participative, and achievement oriented. It also shows how subordinates' characteristics and the nature of the work environment influence these styles. A cultural dimension exists within this theory: after all, cultures are likely to differ in terms of subordinates' and leaders' personal characteristics, thus implying that different managerial styles will be appropriate in dealing with them.

The path-goal theory is not explicitly normative, but, because the optimal style depends on the nature of the contingency, it does have normative implications. Vroom and Yetton's model (1973), on the other hand, is prescriptive and is based on the assumption that no single leadership style is applicable to all situations.

This model's focus is the degree of subordinate participation that is appropriate in a given situation. Vroom and Yetton have developed a series of problem attributes that together determine the appropriate managerial style, ranging from no subordinate participation to group decision making. Again, it is questionable whether these problem attributes are transferrable to non-Western cultures; however, the significant conclusion (from a comparative management point of view) is that styles ranging from highly autocratic to highly democratic can be effective in particular situations. This clearly implies that managers must fit the decision-making process to a particular situation and that a leadership style that is effective in one culture may be ineffective in another.

Although all these theories are useful in emphasizing the various important facets of leadership, we must remember that much of the underlying research took place within a particular country. Moreover, reporting of cultural differences in leadership in the business literature before 1966 was almost entirely anecdotal. The formal study of such differences had been the domain of cultural anthropologists; it was hardly considered an area of legitimate concern for international business research. The systematic study of cross-cultural variations in leadership began with the publication of major research findings by Haire, Ghiselli, and Porter in 1966. Since the publication of their book, *Managerial Thinking—An International Study*, the volume of research in cross-cultural leadership has increased dramatically; as a result, more is now understood regarding both similarities and differences in leadership styles across cultures (in particular, see Bass, 1981; Heller & Wilpert, 1981; Tannenbaum, 1980; Bass & Burger, 1979; and Barrett & Bass, 1976).

Having examined leadership theories within the literature, we should now focus on the determinants of leadership style.

Determinants of Leadership Style

In addition to situational variables, the chief factors influencing leadership style in different cultures are differences in values, needs, beliefs, risk taking, cognitive styles, and the managers' backgrounds. Differences in some variables are likely to be much more pronounced than in others. Moreover, countries will be much more similar to certain other countries than to others. Differences, to the extent that they exist, are relative.

Let us now turn to how values, needs, beliefs, and other variables differ across cultures.

Values Let us begin by considering the role of values. Values form a central part of the human personality and therefore may significantly influence the various facets of one's performance.

England and Lee (1974) discuss the impact of values on performance and suggest several reasons for their effect on leadership. Values help to shape the leader's perception of a situation, influence decisions and solutions to problems, affect interpersonal relationships, define what may or may not be ethical behavior, and help to determine how well a leader will accept or resist various organizational pressures.

Figure 6.6 shows the various kinds of values an individual may hold. Potential values include all possible values and can be divided into two subgroups: (1) *nonrelevant* or *weak values* and (2) *conceived values*. Nonrelevant or weak values have no impact on behavior. Conceived values, on the other hand, have the potential of influencing behavior. These, in turn, can be further broken down into *operative values, intended values,* and *adopted values.* Operative values are values that will probably influence behavior. Intended values are only moderately likely to influence behavior. Adopted values may also affect behavior, but they are a less important constituent of an individual's personality structure. In short, operative and intended values affect behavior more than adopted or weak values do. This is well demonstrated in Figure 6.6.

Figure 6.7 summarizes England's notion that values can influence behavior through either behavior channeling or perceptual screening, or both. The former has a direct impact on behavior, the latter, an indirect impact through the individuals' selection, filtering, and interpretation of what they see and hear. England's notion that value systems influence behavior has received support from a study of Indian and Australian managers carried out by Whitely (1979). The choice of behavior was found to be highly related to their values.

A characteristic of value systems is that they are relatively stable and do not change rapidly. Moreover, as one ages, one's value system becomes less flexible and less susceptible to change. The stability of value systems may help

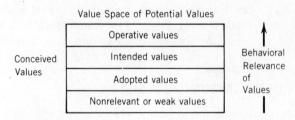

Behavior is more influenced by operative and intended values than by adopted or weak values.

Figure 6.6 Value framework.

Source: G. W. England. "Managers and Their Value Systems: A Five Country Comparative Study," *Columbia Journal of World Business,* 13(2):36, Summer 1978. Reprinted with permission.

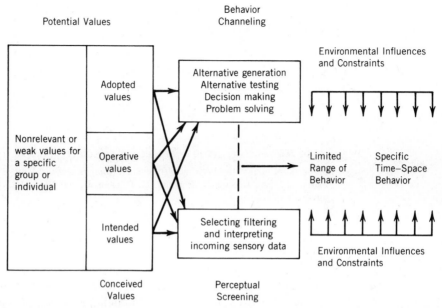

Figure 6.7 Theoretical model of the relationship of values to behavior.

Source: Reprinted with permission from *The Manager and the Man: A Cross-Cultural Study of Personal Values,* George W. England, O. P. Dhingra, and Naresh C. Agarwal, The Kent State University Press, 1974, p. 7.

explain why managerial styles exhibit a lagged response to changing environmental conditions.

In a survey of over 2500 managers, England (1974) found a high degree of pragmatism among managers in all countries (India was the only exception). Figure 6.8 shows England's results. We might expect that pragmatic managers would generally attain better outcomes for their organizations, and in the process would further their careers as well. Empirical work has confirmed this assumption. Pragmatic values emphasizing productivity, profitability, and achievement correlate positively with career success (measured as pay/age) in all the countries studied.

Bass and Burger (1979) came to similar conclusions based on managerial exercises administered to approximately 5000 managers. In particular, they found that in a specific exercise—"exercise objectives" focusing on budgeting decisions—a majority of the managers from all the countries (the United States, Britain, the Netherlands, Belgium, Germany, Austria, Scandinavia, France, Italy, Iberia, Latin America, India, and Japan) favored pragmatic solutions. These pragmatic managers chose not to spend money for safety, to settle a strike, to improve management morale, to improve the quality of a product, or to clean up a stream that the company was polluting. According to Bass (1981), a study by Palmer, Veiga, and Vora (n.d.) showed that the incidence in the exercise objectives of American and Indian managers who decided to reject expenditures was greater among those higher in pragmatic values (economic,

Managers	Sample Size	Moralistic	Pragmatic	Affect	Mixed
		%	%	%	%
India	623	44	34	2	20
United States	1071	31	58	1	9
Japan	394	11	66	8	15
Australia	351	40	40	5	14
Korea	223	12	61	9	18

Figure 6.8 Primary value orientation of selected groups of managers.

Source: Reprinted with permission from *The Manager and the Man: A Cross-Cultural Study of Personal Values,* George W. England, O. P. Dhingra, and Naresh C. Agarwal. The Kent State University Press, 1974, p. 20.

political, theoretical) and lower in altruistic or idealistic values (social, aesthetic, religious).

Pragmatism also seems to be associated with a high rate of advancement (Bass and Burger, 1979). In most of the countries studied, an individual who advanced rapidly was more willing than his slower-rising counterpart to break a strike rather than to grant wage increases, and less willing to control pollution. In short, a manager with a high rate of advancement did not want to spend money for unproductive purposes. At the same time, though, he or she valued generosity and fair-mindedness. Such an individual did not tolerate conflict and did not prefer the group decision-making mode.

Note that the managers whose rate of advancement is high are those who have acquired authority, responsibility, and decision-making influence within an organization over a relatively short period of time. Their values are conducive to effective managerial performance. Values thus play an important role in determining organizational effectiveness.

We have discussed the importance of values in general and their effects on managerial behavior; now let us look at specific value differences among managers from various countries.

These differences are important because they definitely affect managers' degree of pragmatism. To examine these differences, we should first turn back to England and his colleagues' work. Figures 6.9 and 6.10 show the scores attained by Indian, American, and Australian managers on dimensions such as job satisfaction, achievement, and creativity.

England's study reveals that Indian managers give much more importance to organizational stability than managers from other countries. Compared with American managers, Indian and Australian managers attach more importance to employee welfare than to the goal of profit maximization. The authors suggest that Indian managers regard organizational stability as an end in itself; profit maximization is more of a means to the goal. For American managers, the relationship is exactly the opposite. Between Indian and Australian managers, the biggest difference is in the low importance Australian managers attribute to organizational stability and growth.

Concept	Operative Value Score		
	India	United States	Australia
Organizational efficiency	69	65	64
High productivity	62	63	62
Organizational stability	*58**	41	41
Organizational growth	47	47	*29*
Employee welfare	44	*34*	45
Industry leadership	38	43	44
Profit maximization	36	*58*	38
Social welfare	18	*8*	25

Figure 6.9 Values relating to goals of business organizations.

Source: Reprinted with permission from *The Manager and the Man: A Cross-Cultural Study of Personal Values.* George W. England, O. P. Dhingra, and Naresh C. Agarwal, The Kent State University Press, 1974, p. 32.

Personal goals are another area of notable differences. They are of great importance to Indian managers. For Indian managers job satisfaction, dignity, prestige, security, and power are much more important than for Australians and Americans. England's findings also suggest that Indian managers more consistently emphasize obedience and conformity. Differences also exist in orientation toward change and caution. Indian managers assign greater importance to caution and less to change than American and Australian managers. The authors conclude that compared with the other nationalities studied, Indian managers were much less pragmatic—they tended, instead, to be moralistic.

Concept	Operative Value Score		
	India	United States	Australia
Job satisfaction	*67*	51	54
Achievement	64	63	55
Creativity	60	53	*44*
Success	57	52	*40*
Dignity	*48*	30	28
Prestige	*41*	11	10
Security	*40*	15	28
Individuality	38	33	33
Autonomy	24	*13*	16
Money	22	19	18
Power	*20*	6	6
Influence	19	12	12
Leisure	11	3	6

Figure 6.10 Values relating to personal goals of individuals.

Source: Reprinted with permission from *The Manager and the Man: A Cross-Cultural Study of Personal Values,* George W. England, O. P. Dhingra, and Naresh C. Agarwal, The Kent State University Press, 1974, p. 32.

However, this discussion has emphasized only one aspect of the value system—namely, a pragmatic–idealistic dimension. We should also look at values from a particularistic–universalistic perspective.

A particularistic orientation emphasizes obligations of friendship. A universalistic orientation stresses obligations to society as a whole. A particularistic orientation stresses interpersonal considerations, even if they may be detrimental to organizational effectiveness. In a country where particularism is important leaders would not maximize organizational efficiency; as suggested earlier, particularism might have a negative impact on effectiveness. Particularism tends to be important in developing countries. For instance, Zurcher's (1968) survey of Mexican, Mexican-American, and American bank officers and employees found that Mexicans were the most particularistic.

Closely associated with managerial values are managerial needs. Whereas managerial values directly affect an organization's performance, managerial needs do so indirectly by influencing managers' satisfaction with their existing jobs. To the extent that an organization is unable to satisfy the managers' needs, their satisfaction will be low. This, in turn, may affect aspects of behavior, which, in turn, may affect performance. The following section discusses how managerial needs differ across cultures and what these differences mean in relation to leadership style.

Need Strength   Need strength has been studied from the perspective of Maslow's need hierarchy, as well as from McClelland's perspective, which emphasizes the need for achievement, affiliation, and power. According to Maslow, individuals try to satisfy their needs in a particular order. They must satisfy the needs at one level before higher-level needs can motivate their behavior. Maslow defines lower order needs as primarily physiological (food, water, shelter). The need for self-realization is the highest in the hierarchy. Self-actualization occurs when one realizes one's potential to the fullest.

Figure 6.11 shows the nature of needs and what life goals are associated with them. [Alderfer's hierarchy (1972), which is a compression of Maslow's better-known hierarchy, appears next to Maslow's in the figure.]

According to Maslow, these needs are universal and constitute an ascending hierarchy. On the other hand, Maruyama (1974) has suggested that such a hierarchy is ethnocentric and has questioned its validity in Oriental cultures. Redding (1977) reports some results that seem to indicate the validity of such questioning.

A landmark study carried out by Haire, Ghiselli, and Porter (1966), for instance, found that higher-level needs such as self-actualization and self-esteem were of great importance to the entire set of managers, but the *degree* to which these needs were important failed to meet the researchers' expectations. Figure 6.12, taken from these authors' work, shows how the pattern of need fulfillment varies across cultures. As shown here, Japanese managers showed high need fulfillment across most of the five needs. Among the Anglo-American managers, the social needs were most fulfilled.

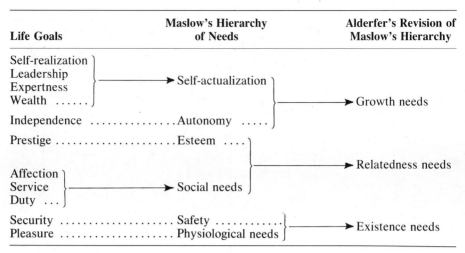

Figure 6.11   Relationship of life goals to need hierarchy.

Source: B. M. Bass and P. Burger. *Assessment of Managers: An International Comparison.* New York: Free Press, a Division of Macmillan, Inc. © 1979. P. 58.

Figure 6.13 shows how need satisfaction varies across cultures. It appears from the figure that members of developing countries are the least satisfied in this respect. (Note that high positive score denotes high dissatisfaction.)

Figure 6.14 shows that managers in developing countries perceive all the needs to be more important than managers from other countries. Managers in developing countries place the greatest importance on all the needs, and Nordic-European managers place the least. A major finding here is that the arena of self-actualization is where the greatest potential exists for increasing managers' satisfaction in all the countries.

More recently, in a survey of 3082 managers from twelve countries, Bass and Burger (1979) also found self-actualization to be the most sought-after managerial goal. This can be seen from Figure 6.15, which ranks the various goals. A score of 1.00 represents the most important goal, while a score of 11.0 represents the least important goal. The table shows that self-realization is the goal that receives the highest ranking across the various cultures.

In another study, Kanungo and Wright (1983) surveyed managers' attitudes in Canada, France, Japan, and the United Kingdom to determine the trends of job outcomes sought by managers from these countries. Differences in job outcomes would reflect the managers' varying level of needs. Contrasts between the British and the French managers were the most striking. The British had a strong need for self-actualization in their work, whereas the French had a stronger need for security and good working conditions.

McClelland and his colleagues' work resembles Maslow's in some ways but differs from it in others. McClelland's study has placed considerable emphasis on the notion of need for achievement. The original study (1961) found that in

Need fulfillment: by clusters of countries (standard scores).

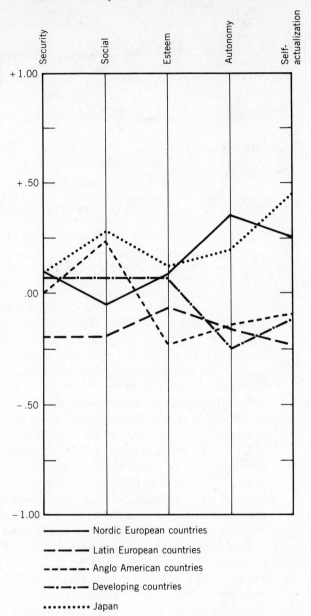

Figure 6.12 Need fulfillment: by clusters of countries (standard scores).

Source: M. Haire, E. E. Ghiselli, and L. W. Porter. *Managerial Thinking: An International Study.* New York: Wiley, 1966, p. 84.

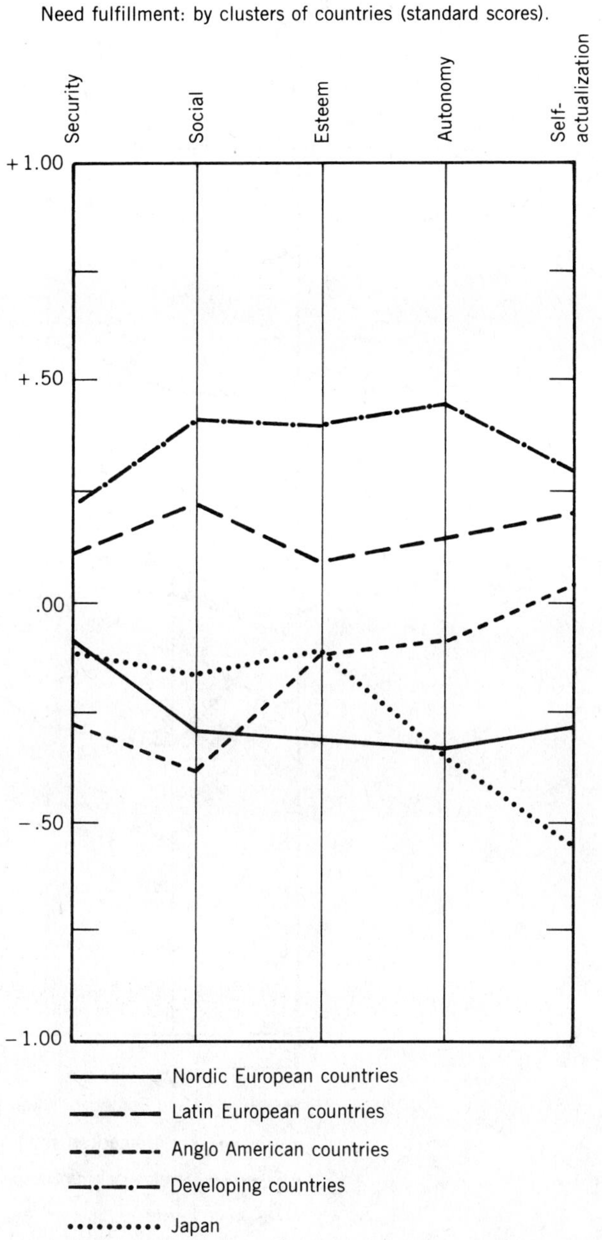

Need fulfillment: by clusters of countries (standard scores).

Figure 6.13 Need satisfaction: by clusters of countries (standard scores).

Source: M. Haire, E. E. Ghiselli, and L. W. Porter. *Managerial Thinking: An International Study.*
New York: Wiley, 1966, p. 92.

Need fulfillment: by clusters of countries (standard scores).

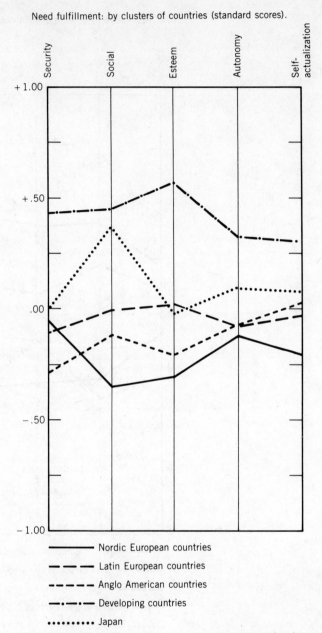

Figure 6.14 Need importance: by clusters of countries (standard scores).

Source: M. Haire, E. E. Ghiselli, and L. W. Porter. *Managerial Thinking: An International Study.* New York: Wiley, 1966, p. 103.

Country or National Grouping	N	Self-realization	Leadership	Expertness	Wealth	Independence	Prestige	Affection	Service	Duty	Security	Pleasure
Anglo-American												
United States	272	*3.33**	*4.33*	*6.00*	*7.33*	*5.13*	*7.42*	*5.38*	*6.32*	*7.66*	*6.35*	*6.26*
Britain	618	*4.14*	*5.18*	*5.73*	*7.93*	*5.36*	*8.01*	*4.98*	*5.88*	*8.33*	*4.95*	*5.54*
Low countries												
Netherlands	441	*6.08*	*6.02*	*4.40*	*8.90*	*4.82*	*7.72*	*5.70*	*5.80*	*5.16*	*5.15*	*6.30*
Belgium	248	*3.83*	*5.57*	*4.72*	*8.33*	*4.83*	*7.79*	*5.26*	*5.89*	*6.00*	*6.18*	*7.60*
Nordic												
Germany-Austria	284	*3.40*	*3.96*	*4.81*	*7.71*	*3.56*	*7.25*	*6.06*	*6.95*	*8.88*	*5.58*	*7.82*
Scandinavia	253	*3.95*	*5.90*	*5.18*	*8.49*	*5.07*	*8.43*	*4.91*	*5.44*	*7.85*	*4.67*	*6.14*
Latin												
France	154	*3.30*	*6.22*	*4.33*	*7.64*	*5.05*	*8.47*	*4.43*	*5.89*	*6.85*	*6.46*	*7.37*
Italy	368	*3.45*	*5.58*	*6.14*	*9.12*	*4.19*	*7.76*	*4.23*	*6.85*	*6.81*	*5.21*	*6.68*
Iberia	166	*3.02*	*5.64*	*4.44*	*8.96*	*6.07*	*7.38*	*5.31*	*4.79*	*6.38*	*5.58*	*8.44*
Latin America	142	*3.74*	*5.25*	*4.73*	*8.00*	*5.63*	*5.94*	*5.73*	*5.81*	*7.12*	*6.25*	*7.82*
Asiatic												
India	88	*4.95*	*5.65*	*4.40*	*7.57*	*5.24*	*6.23*	*5.89*	*5.46*	*5.17*	*6.57*	*8.85*
Japan	48	*2.79*	*3.96*	*4.13*	*8.84*	*3.83*	*8.44*	*5.69*	*7.19*	*5.32*	*6.39*	*8.59*
All	3082											
Higher *RoA*	1568	4.27	5.17	5.03	8.29	4.91	7.53	5.33	6.03	6.88	5.56	6.90
Lower *RoA*	1514	3.90	5.47	5.30	8.25	4.87	7.82	5.09	5.99	7.28	5.44	6.65
Both/Mean	3082	4.09	5.32	5.17	8.27	4.89	7.65	5.21	6.01	7.08	5.50	6.78
S.D.		3.0	3.0	3.1	2.8	2.9	2.9	2.6	2.8	3.1	3.3	3.0
%v(R^2)		9.5	5.6	4.6	4.6	4.8	4.1	4.4	4.4	15.6	3.4	10.5
F country		27.1	16.1	12.8	13.2	14.3	12.2	12.3	13.2	48.2	9.4	32.4
F RoA		0.2	18.2	0.1	0.7	0.3	3.4	1.6	1.5	1.2	0.5	1.0

*Values significant at the 1% level of confidence are in italics.

Figure 6.15 Mean rankings in importance of life goals, by nationality and rate of advancement (1.00 = most important; 11.00 = least important).

Source: B. M. Bass and P. C. Burger. *Assessment of Managers: An International Comparison.* New York: Free Press, a Division of Macmillan, Inc. © 1979, p. 62.

developed countries, individuals had a higher need for achievement; accordingly, it suggested that a positive relationship exists between the strength of achievement motivation and a country's level of economic development. Some variation can be found in developed countries as well, but the extent of variation in developed countries is far less than the variation in developing countries. Evidence of some variation even within developed countries comes from the work of Hines and Wellington (1974), who found that British managers had a higher need for achievement than managers in Australia or New Zealand. In a similar vein, England (1978) found that U.S. managers highly valued achievement and competence, whereas Australians placed a lower value on concepts such as achievement, success, and competition. Kanungo and Wright (1983) found that need for achievement was greater among British than among French managers.

As conceptualized by Maslow and McClelland, managers' and subordinates' differences in need strength should influence managerial styles. Because need strengths vary across cultures, managerial styles should also be expected to vary. Thus, in cultures in which safety and security needs dominate, cautious behavior will predominate. In cultures in which self-actualization is the dominant need, innovative behaviors are much more likely. Individuals who have high safety needs may need a protective superior; individuals with high esteem needs would respond more to praise; and individuals with high self-actualization needs would require more freedom and opportunity for participation.

This discussion has illustrated how differences in need may lead to differences in appropriate leadership styles. Another factor in which differences are important is beliefs.

Beliefs   Needs reflect what different cultures deem important. Values reflect individuals' normative orientation in different cultures. Beliefs, in contrast, reflect individuals' conceptions of what the world is like. Differences in beliefs reflect differences in how people construct social reality. Differences in perceptions of social reality lead, in turn, to different behaviors. As in other spheres (e.g., values and needs), there are similarities and differences in managerial beliefs across cultures.

The assumption that managers can determine the fruits of their labors, for instance, has had a profound effect on U.S. management concepts (Newman, 1970). Emphasis on precise, accurate data and a belief in the worth of planning is possible only when people believe in self-determination. In cultures in which fatalism is prevalent, emphasis on control may be diminished by the belief that external forces determine the resultant outcome. Management style would tend to be passive under these circumstances. Belief differences also exist concerning human nature. For example, Smith and Thomas (1972) found that Indian managers were cynical. Indian managers believed that businessmen were generally cold and calculating, that they must be willing to make decisions that hurt others, and that it is often necessary to compromise ethics and morals to accomplish a task.

An important aspect of managers' belief systems concerns the attitude toward participation. Although managers may have favorable beliefs concerning participative practices, they may also believe that the average worker prefers to be directed and to avoid responsibility. Originally emanating from the work of Haire, Ghiselli, and Porter (1966), this finding has been replicated by other studies in a variety of countries (Argyris, 1967; Roberts, 1970; Ajiferuke & Boddewyn, 1970; Clark & McCabe, 1970; Cummings & Schmidt, 1972; Barrett & Bass, 1976; Vardi, Shirom, & Jacobson, 1980).

Although there may be similarities in managers' attitudes toward participation—that is, managers may hold favorable beliefs about participative practices yet also believe that the average individual wishes to be directed—we can nevertheless discern some variations here. Such variations may be attributable to cultural differences. American managers, for example, believe more than managers in other countries that individuals have a capacity for exercising their initiative and displaying leadership behavior. We can explain this predisposition toward participative practices as a result of traditions persisting since the early days of American history.

Yet although tradition may account for this belief in America, contemporary approaches to participation have sought to establish a more general link between belief systems concerning the nature of the work and belief in participative practices. Dickson (1982) has carried out a study along this line. Studying top managers in Scotland, he found belief in participation to be linked with individuals' belief systems concerning the nature of work. He determined five belief systems about the nature of the work activity: (1) the work ethic, (2) the organizational belief system, (3) Marxist-related beliefs, (4) the humanistic belief system, and (5) the leisure ethic.

Individuals believing in the work ethic valued participation much less than others and saw few positive outcomes. Those who endorsed a humanistic belief system assigned greater importance to direct participation than did individuals who endorsed the work ethic. Individuals who held the organizational belief system viewed participation positively, because they did not consider it a threat to the managerial prerogative. People who believed in the leisure ethic saw little relation between it and participation inside organizations. Only those endorsing a Marxist belief system viewed participation in moral terms. (Beliefs, as emphasized earlier, are important because they reflect an individual's subjective conception of reality. It follows that employees' reward systems depend largely on the top managers' belief systems.)

This discussion has demonstrated how differences in beliefs, though closely associated with values, can have implications for management styles. Belief differences represent content differences, and in this way shape the reality for managers. Although beliefs do shape reality, cognitive processes can also affect how individuals view reality. The following discussion considers the influence of cognitive processes on the construction of reality. We will show that differences in such processes can have important implications for managerial functions—namely, choice of planning, organizing, staffing, leading, and control.

Cognitive Processes   As emphasized earlier, cultures differ in how they construct social reality. In constructing and trying to understand reality, individuals use a particular set of guidelines—a *paradigm*. Redding and Martyn-Johns (1979), accordingly, emphasize paradigms because they guide the process of cognition. To the extent that paradigms are influenced by culture, they are a form of social construct.

Redding and Martyn-Johns propose a three-stage model to account for how people develop paradigms. Figure 6.16 shows this process. The central notion here is that of perception. The perceptual process is inherently selective. Information extracted through perception is subject to cognitive processes of imagination, thinking, reasoning, and decision making. The result of this process is the emergence of a paradigm that tends to be relatively stable. Paradigms then constitute an important guide to behavior. In this model, paradigms (along with attitudes) affect motivation, which in turn affects behavior. The paradigms that these researchers consider important for the managerial process are those of causality, probability, time, self, and morality. These paradigms affect planning, organizing, staffing, directing and leading, and control—all identified earlier as traditional leadership functions.

Redding and Martyn-Johns (1979) follow Maruyama (1974) in distinguishing

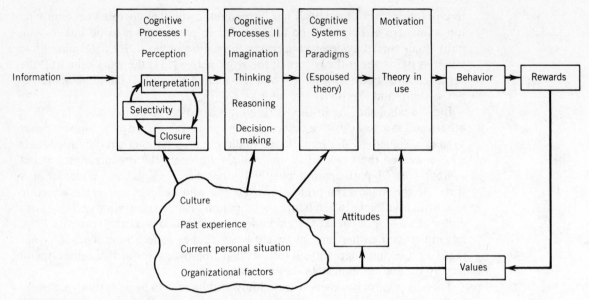

Figure 6.16 Development and effects of paradigms.

Source: S. G. Redding and T. A. Martyn-Johns. "Paradigm Differences and Their Relation to Management, with Reference to South-East Asia." Reprinted with permission from *Organizational Functioning in a Cross-Cultural Perspective* by George W. England, Ahant R. Negandhi, and B. Wilpert, eds., The Kent State University Press, 1979, p. 105.

between a unidirectional causal paradigm and a mutual causal paradigm. According to Maruyama, the former is typically found in Western societies; the latter is characteristic of Oriental society. The main differences between the two paradigms can be seen in Figure 6.17. An important difference between the two paradigms—one which has profound implications for management—follows from the assertion that Oriental cultures have a less-differentiated view of reality than Western culture. The conceptual categories do not have a high degree of abstraction. These authors suggest that as a managerial activity, organizing is difficult in Oriental cultures because abstract thinking is not very natural for people in the Orient. The authors buttress their point by suggesting that the scale of business in these countries is relatively small (with the exception of Japan).

These authors cite Lau (1977), who observes that most Chinese firms function without well-developed planning, without much formalized information, and without a clear demarcation of responsibilities. Historically, this aspect of the Chinese managerial system has been explained in sociological terms, but the authors suggest that an alternative explanation exists in terms of cognitive factors. To the extent that individuals in Oriental cultures cannot conceptualize the necessity of an organized planning system, formalized information, and clear allocation of responsibilities, their managers' behaviors may not enhance organizational effectiveness and efficiency.

	Unidirectional Causal Paradigm	Mutual Causal Paradigm
Science	Traditional "cause-and-effect" model	Post-Shannon information theory
Cosmology	Predetermined universe	Self-generating and self-organizing universe
Ideology	Authoritarian	Cooperative
Philosophy	Universalism	Network
Ethics	Competitive	Symbiotic
Religion	Monotheism	Polytheistic, harmonic
Decision process	Dictatorship, majority rule or consensus	Elimination of hardship on any single person
Logic	Deductive axiomatic	Complementary
Perception	Categorical	Contextual
Knowledge	Believe in one truth. If people are informed, they will agree	Polyocular. Must learn and consider different views
Analysis	Preset categories used for all situations	Changeable categories depending on the situations

Figure 6.17 Two ideal-type paradigms (after Maruyama).

Source: S. G. Redding and T. A. Martyn-Johns. "Paradigm Differences and Their Relations to Management, with Reference to South-East Asia." Reprinted with permission from *Organizational Functioning in Cross-Cultural Perspective,* George W. England, Ahant R. Negandhi, and B. Wilpert, eds., The Kent State University Press, 1979, p. 110.

Studies carried out by Brunel University's decision analysis unit (Wright et al., 1977) have shown that differences exist between Oriental and Western groups in assessing their accuracy of responses to straightforward questions. Differences did not exist between the proportion of items answered correctly by the two groups; however, there was a sharp difference in the estimates of the probability of being right between the two groups. The British students tended to be much more realistic than Oriental students in their assessments. From a comparative management perspective, this finding has interesting implications. To the extent that managers from Oriental countries are unrealistic in their assessment of situations, the various strategies they employ may lack maximal effectiveness from an organizational perspective.

Oriental and Western cultures also differ in how they conceptualize time. This difference in cognition is also likely to affect managerial behavior. Time and punctuality are of great importance to Westerners but not to Asians. Hall (1976) makes a distinction between monochronic and polychronic time. The former is associated with a system in which punctuality has high priority. Where there is a strong emphasis on punctuality, scheduling and keeping a date would have a high priority for coordinating various processes and facilitating a decentralized organizational system. A single time frame is absent in the polychronic time perception. This necessitates the existence of centralized control and smaller organizations; otherwise coordination is hindered.

We may also view differences between Oriental and Western cultures from the perspective of shame and guilt. Shame cultures (Oriental) produce restraint on interpersonal behavior: individuals accept the verdicts of others. A possible consequence is that autocratic behaviors may be more acceptable in these cultures. In a guilt culture (Western), the individual is largely accountable to himself or herself. Accordingly, the means of influencing subordinates must differ in these two types of culture.

Drawing on these distinctions, Redding and Martyn-Johns suggest several possible hypotheses. They suggest that Oriental firms are likely to use less formal planning systems and to have a less formal organizational structure. In addition, the leadership style that managers in these countries employ will not rely on interpersonal confrontation with subordinates; the control of performance will be less formal, and managers will show less precision and less urgency in various matters.

Although Redding and Martyn-Johns's notion of paradigms may be useful, we should keep in mind that these paradigms are not realities as such; rather, they are schematic perceptions. These perceptions serve to define a whole range of possibilities. As Redding and Martyn-Johns suggest, we should view them more as indicators of the poles of a continuum, not as discrete categories.

Apart from differences in the specific content of the cognitive process (as exemplified by paradigmatic differences), there are also differences in how people attend to tasks and to people. These differences may be captured best by a cognitive style variable called field dependence–independence. Gruenfeld (1973) suggests that this is a useful variable in studying task and human orientations in leadership behavior. The measure also clarifies people's ability to cope with complexity.

Field-independent people are considered analytical and differentiated rather than global and diffuse in their thinking. On the basis of their research, Witkin et al. (1962) have suggested that field-dependent people tend more often than field-independent people to conform to authority and to show little interest in achievement. At the same time, they are more personal and attentive, rather than impersonal, in their approach.

Witkin and his colleagues developed this concept, but more recent work stressing its application has been carried out by Gruenfeld and MacEachron (1975). In a study of 329 managers and technicians from 22 countries in South and Central America, Africa, Asia, and the Middle East, these authors found that managers from advanced, developed countries were more field independent than managers from developing countries.

Although this study has demonstrated the existence of variation in field independence across cultures, variation within cultures probably exists as well as a personality characteristic. One would suspect, however, that variance would be much higher across cultures than within cultures. There is evidence to suggest that education tends to increase field independence (McFie, 1961). We may therefore speculate that over the long term, even managers in less developed countries will become more field independent as educational opportunities increase. Growing similarities along this dimension may lead to a convergence in managerial style—a proposition consistent with Harbison and Myers's (1959) and Webber's (1969) notions of convergence.

This discussion has emphasized how cognitive factors can influence the process of management differently in different countries. More often than not, people pay greater attention to differences in values, beliefs, and needs. Although these factors are undoubtedly important, we must also acknowledge the importance to cognitive factors. They exert their influence in ways not immediately obvious—ways, however, that should not prevent us from exploring their ramifications.

We will now shift our discussion to examine cultural preferences in risk taking.

Differences in Risk Preferences   Bass (1981) suggest that individuals who are prepared to take risks are likely to be potential leaders. They cite the work of Wallach, Kogan, and Bem (1962) suggesting that high risk takers are more influential in discussions than low risk takers. Marquis (1962) and Collins and Guetzkow (1964) have reported results suggesting that high risk takers tend to be more persuasive than more cautious members of a group. According to Clausen (1965) and Burnstein (1969), high risk takers are characterized by high self-confidence. This motivates them to influence members of the group to follow their lead. Although the ability to take risks may guarantee that the managers will take decisive action, however, it does not mean they will reach an appropriate decision. The effect on one's influence in dealing with one's immediate group is one dimension of risk taking; from a managerial perspective, however, another important aspect of risk taking is its influence on one's decision in relation to the external environment. Farmer and Richman (1965) have given attention to this dimension by defining risk taking in terms of its degree of rationality and aggressiveness in relation to conservatism.

Although considered a personality characteristic, rational risk taking and its effectiveness are, according to these authors, also contingent on knowledge, use of strategic information, and one's level of expertise in applying scientific methods. The boundaries of rational risk taking may be enhanced through better education, more information, and creation of a more favorable attitude toward the scientific method. In countries where risk taking is irrational or where the boundaries of rationality are narrow, managerial effectiveness and efficiency would be correspondingly low.

Aggressiveness or conservatism in risk taking relates to the presence of achievement motivation. Just as achievement motivation varies cross-culturally, so does aggressiveness or conservatism in risk taking. According to Farmer and Richman, managers who have a relatively high achievement drive are the best risk takers. They are individuals who are neither conservative nor overly aggressive and speculative.

In terms of conservatism and aggressiveness, there appears to be a significant difference between American managers and their counterparts in Europe. American managers are the more aggressive risk takers. At the same time, it appears that in countries such as Indonesia, Burma, Turkey, and Egypt, management tends to be either conservative and speculative or irrational in its risk taking.

Cummings, Harnett, and Stevens (1971) undertook a study that dealt with (among other things) executives' attitudes toward risk. Figure 6.18 shows the results of this study. The authors characterized risk takers as being adventuresome and willing to expose themselves to hazardous risks, whether of a financial or a physical character. Risk avoiders possess different characteristics. Cummings, Harnett, and Stevens found that in terms of risk, Central Europe, Scandinavia, and Greece constitute one group, and Spain and the United States constitute two distinct groupings.

Bass and Burger (1979) more recently studied the risk preferences of managers from different countries. Figure 6.19 shows that tolerance for risk (or alternatively, risk preferences) seemed to be highest for American and Japanese managers and lowest for Belgian, German, and Austrian managers. Specifically, they found that in all the regions examined, managers preferred to take more risks under uncertainty than they felt they were actually taking. This is shown in Figure 6.20. For American managers, Bass and Burger found a significant difference between willingness to take risk and the actual risk taken. These findings are interesting and appear to have significant implications for managerial behavior.

We will now focus on the leaders' backgrounds, which may exert an independent influence on leadership behavior.

Leaders' Backgrounds   Several studies have indicated that leaders' backgrounds differ across cultures. Different backgrounds may lead to different value orientations and hence to the propensity for different behaviors. McClelland (1961) found that 54% of Turkey's leaders were from the upper classes, whereas in Poland 96% of the business leaders were from the lower middle classes, and in the United States business leaders were drawn equally from all classes. Granick (1972) reports that French managers are chosen from the graduates of the *grandes écoles*, whereas in England top managers often have limited formal education. British managers are selected and promoted on the basis of job performance, whereas in France eligibility for top executive positions is almost entirely a function of class rankings at the most prestigious schools.

American managers fall somewhere between these extremes. A college degree is almost a requirement for middle or top management, and a large proportion of top executives come from the better schools; nevertheless, so many junior managers have college degrees that selection to higher levels depends to a large degree on performance.

In other countries, still other patterns prevail. In India, for instance, the family head is also the business head (Chowdhry & Tarneja, 1961). In Southeast Asia, the Chinese generally run businesses, since they dominate the business world in general (Hagen, 1962). In Chile, the landed aristocracy are the business leaders. In Argentina and Peru, business leaders come from the middle classes (Harbron, 1965). And in the People's Republic of China, a high proportion of managers have manual or service backgrounds (Sheridan, 1976).

Bass (1981) classifies business leaders as originating from four different backgrounds, depending on cultural norms. In some countries, business leaders have been drawn primarily from dissenting minorities. During the Industrial Revolution, for instance, the majority of English business leaders came from the Methodist or other dissenting religious groups. In other countries, the major source of business leaders has been a meritocracy of one kind or another—in the Soviet Union, for example, where party officials, the military, and the technocrats are the upper classes, and where engineering or technical training is almost mandatory for career advancement in industry. Still another source of business leaders is large land-owning families, such as those found in many Latin American countries. Finally, the family unit dominates business in some countries—for example, India, where it is difficult for nonfamily members to advance into upper management positions.

These differences in managers' origins affect managerial style. Indian children learn obedience to their elders and a high degree of authority and obedience within the Indian family system; thus, in business there is generally little delegation, but instead an unquestioning acceptance of authoritarian leadership. In Latin America, the same person or family is often involved in a wide variety of enterprises. There is a consequent lack of specialization and little long-range planning; instead, immediate objectives dominate the decision-making process. In the United States, where managers come from all classes but are relatively well-educated, there is more of an emphasis on participatory decision making and delegation of authority.

In addition to background factors that affect leadership style, interpersonal issues warrant our attention. We will therefore examine these factors next.

Interpersonal Skills   Managers, being individuals, differ in their interpersonal behavior skills. Such differences may affect their performance as well as their leadership styles. Bass (1981) suggests that the social perceptual skills, interpersonal competence, effective intelligence, and efficient work habits associated with leadership tend to vary across cultures. Cultural variations in these skills reflect the variation in need for such skills across cultures. As far as social perceptual skills are concerned, managers everywhere appear to assume themselves to be more similar to their colleagues than they actually are. The greatest distortion was found for U.S. and Latin American managers. On the other hand, the Indian managers' projections were generally accurate.

Concerning interpersonal competence, Bass and Burger (1979) found that in a sample of 1000 managers, seven factors emerged that are linked with interpersonal competence:

1. Preferred awareness.
2. Actual awareness.
3. Submissiveness.
4. Reliance on others.
5. Favoring of group decision making.
6. Concern for human relations.
7. Cooperative peer relations.

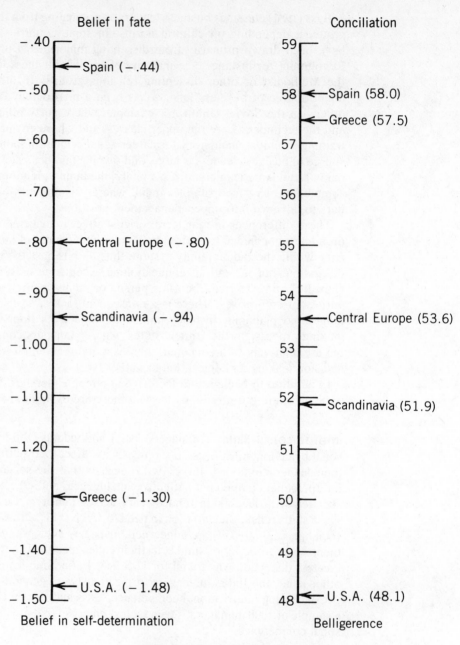

Figure 6.18 Managerial ranking: fate, conciliation, risk, and suspiciousness.

Source: L. L. Cummings, D. L. Harnett, and O. J. Stevens. "Risk, Fate, Conciliation and Trust: An International Study of Attitudinal Differences among Executives," *Academy of Management Journal*, 14:285–304, 1971. Reprinted with permission.

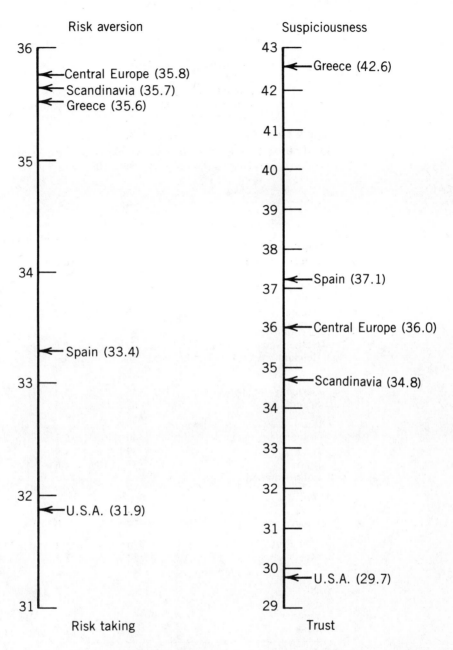

Figure 6.18 (continued)

United States	89%	Britain	50%
Japan	67	India	50
Netherlands	61	Italy	44
France	61	Iberia	44
Scandinavia	61	Belgium	39
Latin America	60	Germany–Austria	39

Figure 6.19 Average tolerance of risk.

Source: B. M. Bass and P. C. Burger. *Assessment of Managers: An International Comparison.* New York: Free Press, a Division of Macmillan, Inc. © 1979 p. 91.

Country or National Grouping	N	Risk taking under Uncertainty		
		Actual	Preferred	Dif.
Anglo-American				
United States	327	5.4	6.4*	*1.0*
Britain	109	5.2	*6.1*	*.9*
Low countries				
Netherlands	77	5.0	*5.3*	*.3*
Belgium	56	4.9	*5.0*	*.1*
Nordic				
Germany–Austria	156	5.4	*6.4*	*1.0*
Scandinavia	63	5.3	*5.6*	*.3*
Latin				
France	40	5.1	*5.7*	*.6*
Italy	39	4.9	*5.6*	*.7*
Iberia	35	4.6	*5.2*	*.6*
Latin America	2	—	—	—
Asiatic				
India	39	5.3	*5.8*	*.5*
Japan	72	5.0	*6.4*	*1.4*
Higher *RoA*	490	5.2	6.0	.8
Lower *RoA*	554	5.1	6.0	.9
Both/Mean	1044	5.2	6.0	.8
S.D.		1.8	1.6	
%v(*R²*)		1.7	8.8	
F country		1.3	*8.1*	
F RoA		3.2	0.8	

*Values significant at the 1% level of confidence are in italics.

Figure 6.20 Self-appraisals of actual and preferred risk-taking behavior.

Source: B. M. Bass and P. C. Burger. *Assessment of Managers: An International Comparison.* New York: Free Press, a Division of Macmillan, Inc. © 1979 p. 82.

(The countries constituting the sample were the United States, Britain, the Netherlands, Belgium, Germany–Austria, Scandinavia, France, Italy, Iberia, Latin America, India, and Japan.)

Preferred awareness is the managers' willingness to be aware of others' feelings, to be concerned with their subordinates' welfare, and to accept others' feedback. Actual awareness is the actual rather than the preferred dimension of understanding oneself and others. Submissiveness is the extent to which people submitted themselves to rules and authority. Reliance on others is the extent of dependence on other people in problem solving. Favoring of group decision making and concern for human relations and cooperative peer relations were the other factors that Bass and his colleagues related to interpersonal competence in a statistical analysis of the data. The factor that stood out in Bass's studies is preferred awareness—the factor with the highest common variance among the sixty self-appraisals.

These studies revealed that Spanish and Portuguese managers had the highest score on this dimension. The authors note that this reflects a cultural difference: individual dignity is given a high position in Iberia. In Germany and Austria, by contrast, the work ethic dominates. France was also low on this dimension. The remaining countries had moderate scores.

The study also reveals that while Indian managers were the most concerned about the rules, the Japanese were the least so. Indian managers viewed themselves as being very dependent on higher authority; German and Austrians viewed themselves as the least dependent. In cooperative peer relationships, French managers were the lowest, while the Dutch were the highest. (In other words, the Dutch were the most cooperative; the French were the least so.)

Other differences emerged as well. The Japanese were the highest in their desire to be objective rather than intuitive. These managers tended to be much more persistent that those of other nationalities. Moreover, their orientation was long term rather than short term, and they also viewed themselves as high in objectivity, persistence, proactivity, and long-term thinking. The French, on the other hand, were critical in their self-appraisals in these dimensions. It appears, in short, that they considered themselves to be less objective, persistent, and long term in their thinking.

Differences in interpersonal competence also emerge in an examination of how managers from different countries negotiate. The findings of Bass and Burger (1979) demonstrate that the Japanese and Dutch were the most locked in by group commitments—they were much less likely to deviate from their initial positions. Managers from the United States and Latin America, on the other hand, showed less commitment to their respective group positions. This was reflected in the fact that they were able to reach compromise faster and were deadlocked much less often. The Bass et al. study concludes by noting that U.S. and Latin American managers demonstrated much greater interpersonal competence than other managers. These findings are consistent with the prevailing importance of peer group judgment in Japanese decision making.

They also indicate the importance of interpersonal variables and their potential for influencing leadership behaviors.

DECISION-MAKING STYLES

An important facet of leadership behavior is style of decision making. How sound is a style? What kind of finality of judgment does it allow? Research emphasizing the importance of decision making shows up as early as studies by Cowley (1931) and Dunkerley (1940). Subsequent work has generally tended to confirm its importance. Apart from the judgment factor, Cowley found three other factors that seemed to represent the speed of decision making. Cowley's work may accurately characterize the decision-making process in the United States, but there are variations elsewhere.

Culture produces distinct decision-making styles. Europeans tend to base decisions on past experiences, with the emphasis on quality. U.S. managers are much more future oriented, emphasizing quantity over quality. Heller (1969) found that in Argentina, Chile, and Uruguay, authority is equated with rapid decision making, and the emphasis was therefore on speed rather than on seeking information or rationality. He found that boards of directors in Latin America generally were inefficient because they held meetings without precirculated minutes or an agenda to members. Similarly, McCann (1964) found a lack of conscious planning in Latin America, with decisions often relying on intuition or improvisations based on emotional arguments and justifications. In contrast, Harbron (1965) found that the Brazilians tended to put off decisions, adopting a ''wait and see'' attitude that resulted in avoiding big problems and emphasizing stop-gap solutions instead.

In the United States and Sweden, managers emphasized rationality. The Japanese desired to be objective in decision-making and stressed dependence on others in problem solving (Bass & Burger, 1979). Americans favor group decision making and participation (Bass & Burger, 1979; Kenis, 1977); in fact, Bass and Burger found the United States to be the country in which the most managers preferred group decision making—a perception that probably holds true for decisions of relatively minor significance. Spain and Portugal favored the group approach least.

Closely associated with a particular mode of decision making (individual versus group) is dependence on others in problem solving. We would anticipate that the greater the reliance on others in problem solving, the greater the likelihood of a group decision-making mode. The data cited in Figure 6.21 are somewhat consistent with this expectation. For instance, this figure shows that Italians are low in dependence on others in problem solving; at the same time, they are relatively less inclined toward a group decision-making mode.

The notion of relying on others as an aid in decision making is well-illustrated by Japanese managers. In Japan, the decision-making process works from the bottom up; all the members of the firm, however, share the responsibility for

Country or National Grouping	N	Dependence on Others		Individual vs. Group Decision Making	
		Act.	Prf.	Act.	Prf.
Anglo-American					
United States	327	*5.1**	*6.1*	*5.7*	*5.7*
Britain	109	*4.5*	*5.8*	*5.5*	*5.1*
Low countries					
Netherlands	77	*5.2*	*5.4*	*4.9*	*5.0*
Belgium	56	*4.5*	*5.2*	*4.9*	*4.2*
Nordic					
Germany–Austria	156	*4.7*	*6.3*	*4.7*	*4.0*
Scandinavia	63	*5.5*	*6.8*	*4.8*	*4.5*
Latin					
France	40	*4.2*	*5.4*	*4.5*	*4.2*
Italy	89	*4.2*	*4.8*	*4.0*	*3.4*
Iberia	35	*3.6*	*4.3*	*4.3*	*3.3*
Latin America	—	—	—	—	—
Asiatic					
India	39	*4.7*	*5.6*	*5.3*	*4.2*
Japan	72	*5.0*	*6.5*	*5.1*	*4.8*
Higher *RoA*	490	4.9	5.8	5.1	*4.7*
Lower *RoA*	554	4.8	5.9	5.2	*5.0*
Both/Mean	1044	4.8	5.9	5.2	*4.8*
S.D.		1.9	2.0	2.0	2.12
%v(R^2)		4.9	8.6	7.3	15.0
F country		4.3	8.0	6.5	14.0
F RoA		1.3	0.1	0.1	2.8

*Values significant at the 1% level of confidence are in italics.

Figure 6.21 Self-appraisals of reliance on others and favoring of group decision making, by nationality and rate of advancement (ROA).

Source: B. M. Bass and P. C. Burger. *Assessment of Managers: An International Comparison.* New York: Free Press, 1979, p. 131.

decisions. After reaching a consensus, the originating group sends its decision to other groups for approval. The more important the decision, the higher the decision will go for approval within the hierarchy. The Japanese reliance on others in making decisions has made the group rather than the individual the basic element of the firm. For this reason the leader in a Japanese system appears to have much less influence than an American manager in decision making. This is because decision making in the United States is more centralized; major decisions are made at a senior management level.

An apparent contradiction arises from the notion that Americans seem to prefer group decision making most. It should be emphasized that this preference is relevant primarily for lower-level decisions whose impact is not of major importance. In other words, group decision making is preferred in America for task-related issues rather than for major policy decisions. This appears to be the case in Japan also, but there is probably a difference of degree. The stress on bottom-up decision making, with its associated emphasis on harmony and smooth interpersonal relations, appears to be much more characteristic of the Japanese, and it appears at all levels of the organization.

Reliance on others and an individual rather than a group mode are important factors in decision making, yet the process is also affected by cognitive factors whose influence is probably important but perhaps relatively subtle.

Consequently, the following section discusses how differences in decision making may also emanate from how the respective groups view the process itself. Graves (1973) has documented this phenomenon by comparing British and French managers. The British mode of decision making does not seem to consider all the possible alternatives; at the same time, greater conflict arises regarding the value of various alternatives; finally, greater loyalty or commitment to the decision evolves. The French model, on the other hand, involves a process of giving alternative courses of action greater weight. Once the managers make their decision, however, lack of commitment may hamper its execution.

Graves proposes an alternative way of conceptualizing such differences by borrowing from a three-stage model first developed by Francis Bacon approximately 350 years ago. The first step in this process is conceptualization. This is how the parties perceive the problem in question. Following conceptualization is discussion, during which the parties review alternative solutions. Execution is the final step, involving implementation of the agreed-upon solution.

Aside from differences in how managers from different cultures view the decision-making process, differences in fundamental cognitive processes may also affect the nature of decision-making itself. We have referred to this point earlier. Managers from different cultures tend to perceive the same situation differently. Different perceptions will probably lead to different evaluations. This, in turn, means different strategies for coping with the situation.

Cummings, Harnett, and Stevens (1971) have identified other dimensions that can affect managerial decision making. They emphasize managerial attitudes toward fate, conciliation, and trust, each of which may affect managerial decision-making style. High scorers on the fate dimension believe that outside forces control events, whereas low scorers believe they can exercise some control over events. Highly conciliatory persons advocate understanding, help, and friendliness, guided by consideration of humanitarianism and cooperation. Finally, persons low in trust are selfish, hostile, excitable, and tense. Figure 6.18 summarizes the average scores on each dimension for the regions included in the study. On all four scales, the five regions are divided into sets of roughly comparable scores.

DEGREE OF DEMOCRACY

The literature on leadership has focused on what degree of democracy leaders exhibit and subordinates expect. Robinson's model, illustrated in Figure 6.22, shows how a given managerial style emerges from the interaction of culture with the nature of a task against the background of environmental constraints confronting the firm. The model postulates a feedback loop according to a given style's usefulness in realizing the firm's goals and to its capacity for enhancing or maintaining that style. The feedback loop also has implications for the company's environment. In Robinson's model, culture affects managerial perceptions of the firm's environment and of its managers' attributes. (We have referred earlier to how culture affects them.) This model seems to possess the characteristics of an open systems model—that is, it views the organization as being in a state of continuous interaction with its environment (in this case, culture) and as being modified by it in various ways. This is one of the model's strengths. Another useful feature is that the model is relatively specific. For example, it spells out the various facets of personal perceptions that are important from a managerial perspective.

Two important dimensions of leadership concern whether it is democratic or autocratic and participative or directive. The democratic–autocratic dimension deals primarily with how power is distributed. The participative–directive dichotomy, on the other hand, deals with how decisions are made. MacIver (1947) and Bass (1960) have noted that autocratic leaders may depend either on their power to coerce or their ability to persuade. A democratic leader may be one who strives for a majority decision or who adopts a trusting follower-oriented relationship (Bass, 1981). Lewin and Lippitt (1938) carried out the classic study demonstrating that democratic leadership may be superior to autocratic leadership. They found that members of a democratic group showed less tension and hostility and that their subgroups were more cohesive and enduring than those of the authoritarian groups. Since then, many other studies seem to support the Lewin and Lippitt study's conclusions.

Participation, on the other hand, has often been viewed as a continuum of decision making. That is, participation is the degree of subordinates' involvement in the decision-making process—whether the leader consults them individually or in a group before making the final decision. Alternatively, participation may involve the subordinates' sharing decision making with the leader. A third option involves the leader delegating responsibility to subordinates for making the decision.

Directiveness refers to two management styles: (1) the leader makes the decision without consulting subordinates; (2) instead of giving orders, the leader manipulates, sells, persuades, negotiates, or bargains with the subordinates. (This is essentially a decision-making continuum). Figure 6.23 illustrates the dimensions of this distinction.

Participative leadership has merited attention because of its association with several beneficial effects—at least in studies done in the United States. In a

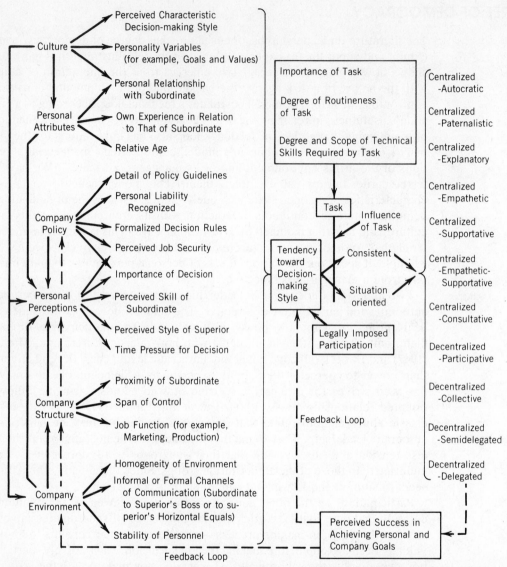

Figure 6.22 Development of decision-making style in relation to degree of participation.

Source: International Business Management, Second Edition by Richard D. Robinson. Copyright © 1978 by The Dryden Press. Reprinted by permission of The Dryden Press, CBS College Publishing.

Leader	Tannenbaum & Schmidt (1958)	Sadler & Hofstede (1972)	Heller & Yukl (1969)	Bass & Valenzi (1975)	Vroom & Yetton (1974)
Directive	Decides and announces decision	Tells	Own decision—no explanation	Directive	AI
	"Sells" decision	Sells	Own decision— with explanation	Persuasive– manipulative	
	Presents ideas and invites questions	Consults	Consultation	Consultative	AII, CI
Participative	Presents tentative decisions subject to modification	Consults	Consultative	Consultative	AII, CI
	Presents problems, gets suggestions, makes decisions	Consults	Consultation	Consultative	AII, CI
	Defines limits and asks group to make decision	Joins	Joint decision making	Participative	GII
	Permits followers to function within limits		Delegation	Delegative	

Figure 6.23 Conceptions of the dimension of participative versus directive leadership.

Source: B. M. Bass. *Stogdill's Handbook of Leadership.* New York: Free Press, a Division of Macmillan, Inc. © 1981, p. 311.

review of studies, Bass (1981) notes that participative leadership tends to promote acceptance of decisions and leads to much greater agreement than does directive leadership. It has also been linked with greater satisfaction among subordinates. Some studies (Katz, 1951) seem to suggest that workers enter or withdraw from groups as a function of their ability to make decisions in them. Overall, we find that participative leadership enhances decision quality and is intrinsically satisfying; on the other hand, this is more likely to be true in the long run than in the short run. Bass notes, for example, that participative leadership is not appropriate in situations in which the interaction is restricted by the task, emphasis is on maximum output, subordinates do not desire to participate, leaders are unready for participation, the nature of the task may limit interaction, and there are emergencies. These are essentially the boundary conditions determining the extent to which participative leadership is practicable without impairing an organization's effectiveness and efficiency.

Although studies in the United States have shown the importance of participatory practices, differences in preference for this mode exist in other countries. For example, Orpen (1978) studied fifteen American and twelve South African firms to determine the importance of participatory practices across cultures. The contingency theory predicted that under conditions of low competition, centralized firms would be more effective in both countries. In the United States, this was not so: decentralized firms were more successful than centralized ones. (In South Africa, most of the employees are black; given the South African government's apartheid racial policies, one would not expect blacks to be allowed participation in decision making to the same degree, if at all.) One of the study's conclusions is therefore that in cultures in which employees favor a democratic/participative style, they would respond in a manner detrimental to economic efficiency if they had to deal with a centralized system of decision making.

Evidence from other cultures also suggests that a participative leadership style is not necessarily the most appropriate one. In the Middle East, for example, business tends to be highly personalized. It is the top men who make the decisions (Badawy, 1980). Many Middle Easterners assume that to be successful, a company needs strong leaders who impose their wills on the organization. As a consequence, there is little delegation; decisions on even insignificant matters are made at the top (Pezeshkpur, 1978). Similarly, Turks were favorably inclined toward authoritarian and directive leadership when task oriented (Kenis, 1977). The Thais favored close supervision (Deyo, 1978). Managers in Malaysia, Indonesia, Thailand, and the Philippines favored an authoritarian style, whereas those in Singapore and Hong Kong were less authoritarian. Western countries favored the least authoritarian style (Redding & Casey, 1975).

The notion that there are systematic differences in participatory practices has been suggested by Bass (1968) in a preliminary study that considered both the attitudes of superiors to subordinates and of subordinates to superiors, under varying degrees of participation. The findings suggest a wide diversity among managers from different countries, as shown in Figures 6.24 and 6.25. Only 14.3% of the Anglo-American managers who played the part of the superior were most satisfied with an uninvolved subordinate, whereas 41.7% of the Greek managers and 53.3% of the Indian managers found this type of subordinate most satisfactory. From the other viewpoint, 62.5% of Dutch-Flemish managers playing the role of subordinate were most satisfied with a participative supervisor while only 22.2% of the Greeks were satisfied with this style. Between these extremes of preferences, Bass found an entire continuum of preferences, suggesting that varying degrees of participation are appropriate in different cultures.

Paternalism is another significant issue in this regard. As a form of leadership, paternalism implies a parent–child relationship between superior and subordinate. It shares some features with an autocratic style, but in addition implies mutual obligation and personal loyalties. Societies in which paternalism is normal prescribe social relationships both in terms of authority and of mutual obligations. Farmer and Richman (1965) rated a number of countries on paternalism, based on an extensive review of the literature as well as on reports from experts. They concluded that Japan was most strongly paternalistic—an attitude expressed through policies of lifetime employment, salary increases based on seniority, and provision of housing, recreation, and shrines for worship. Egypt was the next most paternalistic country. Chile, Germany, India, France, Mexico, and Saudi Arabia followed. At the other end of the continuum were the United States and the United Kingdom. The Soviet Union and Yugoslavia were only slightly more paternalistic.

The counterpart of paternalism for employees is respect and loyalty both to

Culture of Managers		Percent of Subordinates Most Satisfied in Decision-Making Meetings with Participative Supervisors	
40	*Dutch–Flemish*	62.5	
	19 Flemish		68.4
	21 Dutch		57.1
50	*Latin*	50.0	
	9 Colombian		55.6
	13 Italian		53.8
	14 French Swiss		50.0
	14 Spanish		42.9
72	*Anglo-American*	45.8	
	23 American		52.2
	49 British		42.9
36	*Indian*	41.7	
30	*Scandinavian*	36.7	
	18 Norwegian		38.9
	12 Danish		33.3
18	*Greek*	22.2	
246	Total	45.9	

Figure 6.24 Reported satisfaction of subordinates following meetings to make decision with participative and directive supervisors.

Source: B. M. Bass. "A Preliminary Report on Manifest Preferences in Six Cultures for Participative Management." Technical Report 21, Contract No. 00014-67(A), Management Research Center, University of Rochester, Rochester, NY 1968, p. 37.

the superior and to the company. This shows up in contrasting views of American and Japanese workers (Whitehill, 1968). Sixty-eight percent of Japanese workers felt that management should provide free or low-cost housing for employees, whereas only 10% of their American counterparts agreed. Sixty-six percent of the Japanese considered their company equal to if not more important than their personal life, while only 24% of the Americans held this view. Fifty-four percent of the Japanese would offer their seat to their supervisor in a crowded bus, but only 4% of the Americans would do the same.

Box 6.1

A U.S. firm in Spain had a different kind of "American" problem. The home office had a tradition of holding company picnics where management and workers mingled with ease in a comfortable environment. The firm tried to import its company picnic into Spain, and to highlight management's "democratic" belief, the U.S. executives dressed as chefs and served the food. However, the picnic failed to help elicit the desired rapport between the U.S. managers and the Spanish workers. In fact, it was a most awkward affair, as the lower level staff clung together and did not want to be served by their superiors. When an executive approached their table, everyone stood up. Spanish attitudes of class distinction and social groups prohibit casual mixing and socializing of workers with executives.

Source: David A. Ricks, M. Y. C. Fu, and S. Arpan, *International Business Blunders.* OH: Orid, 1974, p. 44.

Culture of Managers		Percent of Supervisors Most Satisfied in Decision-Making with Uninvolved Subordinates	
63	*Anglo-American*	14.3	
	44 British		13.6
	19 American		15.8
46	*Latin*	21.7	
	12 Spanish		16.7
	15 French Swiss		20.0
	8 Colombian		25.0
	11 Italian		27.3
39	*Dutch–Flemish*	28.2	
	21 Dutch		23.8
	18 Flemish		33.3
23	*Scandinavian*	34.8	
	15 Norwegian		33.3
	8 Danish		37.5
12	*Greek*	41.7	
30	*Indian*	53.3	
213	Total	27.7	

Figure 6.25 Reported satisfaction of superiors following meetings to make decisions with involved and uninvolved subordinates.

Source: B. M. Bass. "A Preliminary Report on Manifest Preference in Six Cultures for Participative Management." Technical Report 21, Contract No. 00014-67(A), Management Research Center, University of Rochester, Rochester, NY, 1068, p. 36.

Although it appears that Western countries generally favor a democratic style of leadership and that developing countries favor a more authoritarian style, there may be some exceptions to the rule. Studies by Meade (1967) and Sinha (1976) conclude that an authoritarian style is optimal in India, yet work by Kakar (1971) and Jaggi (1977) led to a different conclusion. For example, Kakar found that despite a national culture emphasizing a rigid hierarchy in relationships, Indian managers whom employees viewed as helpful and exerting low control could obtain better performance and satisfaction than the authoritarian managers. Kakar explains these findings through a notion of psychosocial identity. This notion suggests that behavior of individuals in organizations is influenced by the values and norms of the communities (i.e., affiliation groups) that are significant for the individual sense of identity. Such communities exist both within and outside of organizations, and, furthermore, may be mutually supportive or conflicting in their values and norms. In Kakar's study, the relevant groups consisted of first-level supervisors and the professional community of engineers. Kakar suggests that these employees' notions of an optimal authority relationship may be more relevant in explaining such findings than modal cultural norms. Some observers have noted that engineers have a higher need for autonomy than other groups. Kakar found that his data indeed suggested such an explanation. This may help resolve the apparent contradiction in the findings.

An important implication from Kakar's study is that although cultural differences are important, subcultural differences in the opposite direction may override them. Some support for Kakar's idea also comes from a study that Jaggi (1977) carried out—a study that seemed to indicate a strong consultative relationship between participative leadership and job satisfaction. Work done by Bass and Burger (1979) has more recently suggested that of the 1641 subordinates studied 51.7% chose to return to a participative supervisor. Only 33.3% would be expected to return on the basis of chance alone.

These findings still seem to document the importance of culture, though its significance may have declined somewhat in the intervening period. More specifically, Bass et al. found that these preferences ranged all the way from 40% for the Japanese participants to as high at 63% for the French. Support for this view also comes from the work of Inzerilli and Laurent (1983), who find that subordination has a much more negative connotation for the French (43%) than for American managers (31%).

These authors argue that the conception of organizational structure may be conceived in either instrumental or social terms and that this has implications for leadership behavior. An instrumental conception of structure is one in which the primary emphasis is on getting the job done. The relationship among various positions in the structure depends on the functional interdependency between them. By contrast, in a social conception of the structure, the various organizational positions are defined in terms of status. It follows that these positions would be organized hierarchically: individuals are either superior or subordinate to others. A directive leadership style tends to appear in those cultures that have a social conception of the structure. As the authors note, the French consider achieving organizational objectives to be less important than acquiring power. This tends to inhibit participatory practices because participation may diminish the manager's power. Figure 6.26 shows the dimensions in which the two structures differ. The key aspect of the distinction between them is that, in the United States, the superior–subordinate relationship is defined in impersonal terms, whereas in France it is defined in more personal terms. Accordingly, subordination may be more acceptable to American managers than to the French.

Child (1981) also reported some differences between West German and British firms. This study may reflect cultural differences in how authority relationships are conceptualized in different cultures. Based on studies of West German and British firms, the authors concluded that decisions made in West German firms often are more centralized than those made in British firms. Moreover, their findings led to the conclusion that West German managers tend to be less concerned about subordinates' personal development; they also care less for the expression of opinion by subordinates when this cuts across a formal status differentiation.

Other potentially important specific differences have been reported by Bass and Burger (1979). In analyzing communication patterns in different cultures, they found that American and Japanese managers stood out in viewing two-way communication as less frustrating than one-way communication. Japanese

	United States (N = 90)	France (N = 219)	P* Less Than
1. The main reason for having a hierarchical structure is so that everyone knows who has authority over whom	26	45	0.001
2. No organization could ever function without a hierarchy of authority	50	73	0.001
3. The notion of subordination always has a negative connotation	31	43	0.03
4. In order to maintain his authority, it is important for a manager to be able to keep a certain distance vis-à-vis his subordinates	50	28	0.001
5. Most managers seem to be motivated more by obtaining power than by achieving objectives	36	56	0.001
6. It is desirable that management authority be able to be questioned	80	69	0.03
7. One should submit to all of a superior's demands if he has legitimate authority	10	19	0.05
8. It is important for a manager to have at hand precise answers to most of the questions that his subordinates may raise about their work	23	53	0.001
9. An organizational structure in which certain subordinates have two direct bosses should be avoided at all costs	52	83	0.001
10. In order to have efficient work relationships, it is often necessary to by-pass the hierarchical line	68	53	0.01

*P estimated on the basis of Z scores.

Figure 6.26 Percentages of American and French managers who agree with statements related to structural issues.

Source: G. Inzerilli and A. Laurent. "Managerial Views of Organization Structure in France and USA," *International Studies of Management and Organization,* XIII: 104, 1983. This article is reprinted with the permission of the publisher, M. E. Sharpe, Inc., Armonk, New York 10504.

managers' preference for two-way communication is consistent with Ballon's view (1983) that Japanese groups expect the leader to be accessible. The leader should be receptive and should listen carefully to the subordinates' ideas and suggestions. This would occur with a two-way communication pattern. On the opposite end of the spectrum were countries like Germany, Austria, Belgium, and France, where managers tended to be easily frustrated by one-way communication.

Apart from differences in communication patterns, there is some evidence suggesting that variation in people's skills and abilities across cultures may also affect the nature of leadership styles. Findings to support this come from Heller and Wilpert (1979). They suggest that highly centralized decision making is closely related to low estimation of skills by subordinates. They sampled more than 1500 managers in 129 companies in approximately 8 countries. They found that British, Israeli, and German managers consistently described themselves as using the most centralized method. An important conclusion follows from the relationship between skill and participation. To the extent that participatory practices depend on the existence of appropriate skills, increasing skills may be a way of increasing participation.

This section has focused on how participative practices vary across cultures. Apart from the broad differences that exist between Western and developing countries, there are some differences that exist within these groups, to which we have referred. We have also focused attention on such factors as skill, which tend to modify relationships already expected solely on the basis of culture. We can sum up these considerations by suggesting that autocratic and democratic leadership styles represent two extremes of a continuum. Variations between these extremes are possible.

It is, in fact, unlikely that a country would lie at either extreme. Individual managers within any given country certainly exhibit a wide range of managerial styles. By describing a particular culture as either democratic or autocratic we mean simply that the majority of its managers adopt a style that is more democratic than autocratic or vice versa.

CONCLUSION

A review of the literature indicates that cultural differences affect behavior. Various studies (Haire, Ghiselli, & Porter, 1966; England, 1974; and Bass & Burger, 1979) attest to such differences. Whereas Haire et al. demonstrate the importance of needs, England and his colleagues (1974) explicitly concern themselves with the impact of values on behavior. Values may influence behavior either directly or by means of perceptual screening, or both. Managers whose primary value orientation is pragmatic are able to obtain better outcomes for their organizations and further their careers as well. Bass and Burger (1979) reached a similar conclusion.

It is clear from the material covered in this chapter that although leadership behavior may have similar functions across cultures, the nature of these behaviors is likely to vary as a function of differences in needs, values, beliefs, cognitive processes, risk preferences, leaders' backgrounds, and interpersonal skills. The various theories covered in this chapter illustrate the dynamics underlying leaders' behavior. The contingency approach to management is particularly well suited for understanding how behavior varies across cultures because it is concerned with appropriate leader behavior in different situations. As situations vary across cultures, a theory applicable in one may be irrelevant in another. For example, Bennett (1977) observed that high performing bank managers in the Philippines are low on Fiedler's LPC scale, whereas comparable managers in Hong Kong score high. Fiedler's contingency theory may be more explicit in delineating how leadershp behavior varies across cultures; however, we must not forget that the path-goal theory and Vroom's model implicitly say the same thing.

Cultural variability is not confined to the differences in needs, values, or beliefs to which we alluded earlier. In our discussion we also stressed cognitive processes because they influence how managers from different cultures construct social reality. Although its relative importance may be hard to assess, the work of Lau (1977), Wright et al. (1977), and Hall (1976) is certainly consistent with the concept of such differences and their significance. The cognitive construct of field independence, on the other hand, captures the notion of how analytical managers from different cultures can be.

Our review of cross-cultural differences has also examined differences in risk preference, managers' backgrounds, and interpersonal skills. We have noted that differences in these dimensions can also significantly affect leadership behavior.

This discussion has so far emphasized the determinants of differences in leadership behavior across cultures. These differences profoundly affect the nature of managers' decision-making styles across cultures, as well as the degree of democracy that the managers exhibit. Important issues in decision-making styles are its inherent soundness and the extent of finality of judgment that it allows. Participative leadership has attracted a lot of attention because it seems to promote acceptance of decisions and leads to greater satisfaction among subordinates.

Culture undoubtedly has an impact, but there are certain occasions when the predicted relationship does not hold. This is only an apparent contradiction, however; it may be reconciled by noting that cultural variability also exists within the nation. Triandis's notion of subjective culture (1972) is important in this context, for it emphasizes this concept of culture variability. More often than not, however, the cultural variability between countries is greater than that within a culture. These are also indications that certain countries tend to group together and that the difference between these clusters is greater than within a cluster. In this context, we should note that the focus of the literature has been on the United States, Western Europe, India, and the Middle East.

Other areas such as Latin America and the Far East have received some attention. Work on the Soviet-bloc countries, China, and Africa, among others, is conspicuously absent. Hofstede's (1983) warning that "all theories are culturally conditioned" is particularly appropriate because of this incomplete research. The concept of achievement common to many Western models of organizational behavior, for example, is difficult even to translate into other languages, and applying it to other cultures would be even more difficult. Redding (1977) questions the applicability of Western "ego-centered paradigms . . . to non-Western cultures where the focus is on relationships." Clearly, there is a risk of bias in much of this research.

These research findings are nevertheless important in emphasizing that culture affects leadership styles and thus contributes to a better understanding of leadership differences across cultures, though possibly from a predominantly Western viewpoint.

In this chapter we have also surveyed the various comparative management models. The importance of culture as a variable affecting leadership behavior has been emphasized. While concluding that culture is the primary variable, we noted that its significance may vary according to the fit between culture and the management philosophy.

The importance of leadership can perhaps be best summed up in the words of Jacques Maisonrouge, chairman of the board of IBM World Trade Corporation: ''It follows that the managers' quintessential responsibility is to help his people realize their own highest potential.'' How this task is accomplished varies across cultures.

CHAPTER 7
Country Convergence and Divergence

CONVERGENCE AND DIVERGENCE FORCES

Improbable as it seems, one-third of all employees assigned to overseas posts used to fail in their jobs (Henry, 1965). In certain MNCs, this ratio reaches forty percent (Tung, 1981). Those who "fail," however, do so not because of any lack of ability or talent, for their track records in the home offices are frequently impeccable. Instead, they fail because the cultural gap between them and their host country is simply too great to bridge.

Moreover, managerial policies that have been successfully implemented in one culture may fail in another. This problem is conceptually similar to what an individual faces in adapting to a different culture; the gap separating one culture from another, regardless of managerial policies, is simply too great to be bridged. What MNCs need to avoid these cultural mistakes is a map to the cultural work world, a guide to the chasm separating cultures.

These cultural maps are difficult to construct, however, and we must address certain fundamental questions about the cultural topography before we can map the terrain. Disagreement among observers of world culture further complicates the situation. Some researchers have argued that cultures are converging. According to this view, all cultures will ultimately form one gigantic international *work culture* devoid of any obstacles whatever. If this comes to pass, we will have little need for a cultural map of the world. The problems of cultural differences will simply resolve themselves. Other researchers, however, have argued that the forces of modernization are divergent: they are slowly driving apart (or keeping apart) individual cultures' identities. If this is so, a cultural map will be all the more important.

There is a third possibility—that both convergent and divergent processes are at work simultaneously. If this is so, what are the forces of convergence and divergence, and where do they operate?

Three notable forces are at work here. One is technology. Webber (1969) has speculated that cultural *convergence* will result from the homogenizing effect of universal technology. According to his theory, the universal industrialization process in the contemporary world will force the occupational structure of different cultures to become more similar. In each country, skilled technicians, machine repairmen, machine operators, and managers will perform virtually the same tasks. Webber also conjectured that as they become more skilled in using the new technology, workers in every country will become more indispensable to the organization, and therefore more indispensable to management as well. With increased power, workers would acquire increased status in their societies. Over a period of time work rather than class status would indicate one's social position. By gradually shaping a society's occupational structure, and consequently society itself, a universal technology could become a convergent force acting on disparate national cultures.

The second force that works toward convergence is education. As technology becomes more uniform throughout the world, it tends to foster increasingly similar forms of education, which, in turn, foster more uniform techniques and even values. Furthermore, according to Webber, the need for a highly trained working class leads to better-educated workers, which reduces social barriers and economic disparities.

Finally, the third force is the emancipation of workers from poverty and need. The new technology makes this more likely; it also encourages the emergence in all societies of pragmatic societal values that would replace the historically evolved values system idiosyncratic to each separate culture.

In general, this view of convergence argues that because managers the world over are involved in the same activity—namely, administration of industrial organizations—they have to respond in specific ways to be successful. They see the role of the manager as providing a central force that conditions organizational behavior, as opposed to the nationality and cultural background of the individual. These forces are based on the notion of the universality of managerial tasks. Any differences found between managers would be accounted for by individual, situational, and organizational differences rather than cultural variance (e.g., Eisenstadt, 1973; Kerr et al., 1960; Harbison & Myers, 1959; Mouton & Blake, 1970).

In contrast to this rational economic prediction, however, Webber also recognized forces of *divergence* throughout the world. He was concerned with the possible stresses in societies in the early stages of development—stresses that might result from the introduction of modern technology. His insight was prophetic. In their discussion of divergence forces, Vozikis and Mescon (1981) provide us with a good example of stress-induced reactions in a society. They assert that "the forced training, for instance, of Iranian pilots for the most sophisticated Tomcat aircraft, despite the elaborate and step-by-step training by American technicians, did not produce the productive results that the Shah expected; the reason is, of course, the cultural shock and stress that the poor pilots experienced by bypassing stages of development and technological generations. This disparity between stage of development and managerial expectations finally led to the Islamic revolution in Iran and a radical return to traditional values'' (p. 83). This example indicates the unpredictable and highly variable consequences of a backlash resulting from a high stress level.

Culture is susceptible to change, but it is also generally resilient. Culture can remain different from its surroundings. In our daily existence, we depend on and are supported by our culture. We can separate ourselves from it only with great difficulty. Webber (1969) has articulated this point himself:

Most of us act, think and dream in terms of the norms and standards we have absorbed from the culture in which we are reared. That which our culture values, we value; that which our culture abhors, we abhor. By education or experience, some of us become aware that there are other values and beliefs that make sense too—as much or more than our own. But we see them hazily and all too often, with age, the awareness slips away. A few, a very very few, are able to escape, overcome parochialism and see the world more objectively. But escape is by no means entirely desirable. We can feel alone and unsure when the comfortable values of our old culture fall away, become irrelevant and are replaced by nothing. (p. 80)

The resistance of cultures to change will probably slow down any existing forces of convergence. (This view is definitely consistent with our discussions in previous chapters.)

Finally, the availability of basic resources differ among countries. These differences can affect the speed and the direction of technological development; it can also affect the MNC's willingness to invest in these countries. Moreover, an international division of labor may be taking place, determined largely by the worldwide distribution of knowledge and human or natural resources. The more industrialized countries provide the knowledge and expertise to less developed nations in exchange for natural resources and labor. This scenario, if it continues, may counteract trends toward a world with homogeneous technology and occupational culture, at least for the near future.

Webber went one step beyond describing the forces of convergence and divergence—he also analyzed these forces by examining the different levels of their impact. Figure 7.1 shows this analysis (with some modification).

The first level is the interaction between work and workers. We have already described the convergent forces that technology exerts on culture. Webber believes that this convergent force operates at this level. He asserts that for workers across the world, equipment, task, job training, and expectations about performance on the job (not their own expectations, but that of their employers) will all become similar in the near future.

Population size and the availability of labor can also affect the direction of technological development. A densely populated country that produces a large cotton crop might be oriented toward labor-intensive textile production; a less densely populated country with large diamond deposits might develop a different kind of technology and, as a result, a vastly different occupational culture.

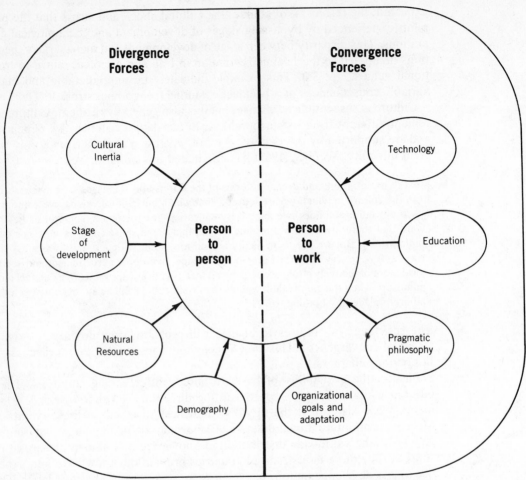

Figure 7.1 Forces influencing divergence and convergence among societies.

Webber also predicted convergence at another level: the firm in relation to its environment. He claimed that the same adaptive exigencies would operate for business organizations across the globe—namely, to serve quickly and efficiently the consumers utilizing their products.

It was in *person-to-person* relations that Webber anticipated the forces of divergence to be operating. The interaction between peers within the organization could help to reinforce existing cultural values and could provide a basis for resistance to change. However, He saw a preponderance of convergent forces even at this level. As technology became more complex and subordinates gained greater expertise, superiors throughout the world would become dependent on their subordinates, who would become more powerful in direct proportion. Moreover, as the new technology made consumer goods more plentiful and raised the general standard of living, subordinates would lobby to have their higher-order needs fulfilled in the work environment. Even at the level of personal relations, Webber expected convergent forces to predominate.

Other observers have criticized Webber for his optimism concerning prevalent forces of convergence. According to these criticisms, his analysis fails to examine cultural factors outside the work domain—for instance, the enduring forces of culture in the family (through child-raising) or in the community (through religious affiliation). Moreover, a country's natural resources and its demographic characteristics do not explicitly enter into Webber's consideration. His thesis omits these important sources of divergence at a societal level.

The debate over convergence versus divergence continues to rage. Ultimately, the issue will require empirical studies to reach a resolution. Webber's claim that this process of convergence is slow leaves the present grouping of countries open as a necessary challenge. "For a long time at the least," Webber himself has written, "cultural factors will exert a strong and differentiating influence upon managerial philosophy and practice: less on technological and production decisions, less on the relations of man and job, less on the firm's relationship to its customers and society; but more on the methods of motivation patterns of communication and styles of leadership" (p. 83). According to the specific characteristics that have been articulated, it would be possible to isolate cultures or clusters similar or dissimilar to each other to varying degrees. MNCs with overseas assignments or development programs can then verify that they are not asking employees to bridge a cultural gap that cannot be crossed.

How far has the research on cultural clusters progressed? The research has, to this point, dealt most conclusively with how nations cluster according to the values held by the workforce in each country. We should note, however, that these studies have been able only to isolate the clusters; *they have not yet been able to measure the distances between them.* Consequently, the empirical verification of the convergent or divergent movements separating or drawing together the culture work world remains to be accomplished.

CLUSTERING COUNTRIES ON ATTITUDINAL VARIABLES

Since comparative management involves the cross-cultural comparison of behavior in organizations, it attempts to establish whether cultural variables systematically influence the attitude and behavior of employees beyond the accepted, intracultural individual differences. An important task for researchers in this field is therefore to demonstrate that certain aspects of employee attitude and behavior can be generalized to a particular society and that these aspects vary and can be explained by cultural or national differences. This section reviews the organizational behavior literature that has described similarities and differences among various groups of countries using statistical techniques to "cluster" them according to their similarities. We then propose a cluster map of the countries included in the reviewed literature that would integrate and synthesize the current findings.

The variables forming the basis for the empirical grouping reviewed here relate to employee work attitudes. The comparisons are based primarily on general attitudes toward work (as reflected in the individual's work values or goals) rather than on more specific attitudes to the immediate job and its conditions. These variables will be used to group countries or nations (as opposed to cultures), as the unit of analysis.

By defining the country as the unit of analysis, the clustering of these countries provides important implications for managers and academicians. Managers in multinational corporations can better understand the basis for similarities and differences between countries. With this knowledge, they can more effectively place international assignees, establish compatible regional units, and predict the results of policies and practices across national boundaries. Clusters can help the academician by defining the extent to which data generalize to other countries. The results for a particular variable from one country can be generalized (with care) to an entire group of countries within a cluster. Clusters also aid the researcher in identifying the variables that explain the variance in work goals and managerial attitudes, such as language, religion, and level of industrialization.

The following analysis and results of country clustering draw heavily from the material of two papers by Ronen and Shenkar (1985) and Ronen and Kraut (1977), who have produced the most comprehensive review of the field. This chapter also emphasizes various aspects of research methodology that were introduced in Chapter 3.

DESCRIPTION OF REVIEWED STUDIES

Eight cluster studies emerged from the literature search. These are the studies by Haire, Ghiselli, and Porter (1966), Sirota and Greenwood (1971), Ronen and Kraut (1977), Hofstede (1976), Griffeth, Hom, DeNisi, and Kirchner (1980), Hofstede (1980), Redding (1976), and Badawy (1979).

Two of these studies examined one world region each. Redding (1976) studied eight countries in Southeast Asia, and Badawy (1979) studied six countries in the Middle East. Although these studies did not perform any clustering of countries, there are good reasons to include them in the review. The Arab group, surveyed by Badawy, did not appear in any other study, and its inclusion provided us with information on another world region with distinct work goals. Redding's study of Southeast Asia provides additional information on work values in countries not surveyed by any other study—namely, Indonesia, Malaysia, and South Vietnam—thus allowing a broader inspection of the variations within this region. Also, data from different organizations in Hong Kong, Japan, the Philippines, Singapore, and Thailand can be compared with data collected by Hofstede (1980) on subsidiaries of an MNC in those countries.

Two of the eight studies reviewed here are in book form rather than papers (Haire et al., 1966; Hofstede, 1980). The book format, needless to say, allowed for a more detailed report of both theory and methodology than would have been possible in a paper. Also, some studies used data collected by an MNC, while others collected data designed for the specific study (e.g., Haire et al., 1966).

This review will discuss (1) the variables used in the eight studies, (2) the sampling and questionnaire administration, and (3) the procedure for data analysis. The purpose is not only to evaluate the methodological rigor of these various studies, but also to establish a basis for comparison and synthesis. Finally, it will produce a world clustering map based on these studies. But first, let us review the variables, samples, and methodology used in these studies.

Variables

The studies reviewed several variables: work goal importance; need deficiency, fulfillment, and job satisfaction; managerial and organizational variables; and work role and interpersonal orientation. The variables used in each study, as well as the research instruments, appear in Table 7.1.

We will discuss each of these variables separately. Later, we will consider whether the diversity of the variables provides an adequate basis for comparison among the various studies.

Haire et al. (1966) surveyed work goal importance through an eleven item scale, later utilized by Redding (1976). Sirota and Greenwood (1971) listed fourteen work goals; Ronen and Kraut (1977) used a list of twenty-two work goals (for their own data); and Hofstede (1980) used several surveys, each with a different number of work goals. However, because all the scales use a modified list of Maslow's categories, there appears to be a solid basis for comparison. (The modified Maslow list omits biological needs while splitting the ego needs into autonomy and esteem.)

Haire et al. (1966) also examined need deficiency, fulfillment, and job satisfaction through eleven items depicting a modified Maslow list. The same instrument was used by Redding (1976). Badawy (1979) utilized a thirteen-item instrument based on Porter's derivation of Maslow's categories. Hofstede (1980) used more than one survey, and therefore a different number of items. Griffeth et al. (1980) used an attitude survey to measure satisfaction with nine job facets.

Need importance and need satisfaction are fundamentally different. Unlike need importance, need satisfaction is constrained by the individual's immediate job and is tied to the particular reward structure. Can studies that surveyed work goal importance be compared, then, to studies that surveyed aspects of satisfaction? The answer is yes. Haire et al. (1966) as well as Redding (1976) studied both importance and satisfaction variables, with similar results. We advise caution, however, in interpreting these results.

Four of the studies examined managerial or organizational variables. Two used eight items depicting classical versus democratic managerial attitudes toward workers' capacity for (1) leadership and initiative, (2) the sharing of information and objectives, and (3) participation and internal control (Haire et al., 1966; Badawy, 1979). Hofstede (1980), who also examined managerial styles, used a different instrument, asking respondents to choose among four types of managers, characterizing their actual and preferable supervisor. Griffeth et al. (1980) examined organizational variables: role overload, organizational commitment, organizational climate, and organizational structure.

Table 7.1 Variables Used in the Studies Reviewed

				Field Studies				
Variables	**Haire, Ghiselli, & Porter (1966)**	**Sirota & Greenwood (1971)**	**Hofstede (1976)**	**Redding (1976)**	**Ronen & Kraut (1977)**	**Badawy (1979)**	**Griffeth, Hom, DeNisi, & Kirchner (1980)**	**Hofstede (1980)**
Work goals importance	11 items based on modified Maslow's categories*	14 work goals	—	11 items as in Haire et al.	22 work goals†	—	—	Varying number of items from different surveys‡
Need deficiency, fulfillment, and job satisfaction	11 items based on modified Maslow's categories		—	11 items as in Haire et al.	—	13 items based on Maslow's categories (Porter's instrument)	65 items of satisfaction with 9 job facets	Varying number of items from different surveys
Managerial and organizational variables	8 items depicting classic or democratic managerial style		—	—	—	8 items depicting managerial style as in Haire et al.	Organizational variables, role overload, organizational commitment, organizational climate and structure	Manager's style: present and desired
Work role and interpersonal orientation	Cognitive descriptions of the managerial role	—	Survey of Personal Values (SPV) and Survey of Interpersonal Values (SIV)	Relations with subordinates	—	—	—	

Source: S. Ronen and O. Shenkar. Clustering countries on attitudinal dimensions: A review and synthesis. *Academy of Management Review,* 1985 (in press).
*The modified Maslow's hierarchy applied by Haire, Ghiselli, and Porter (1966) omits biological needs while adding the higher-level need of autonomy. The modified list thus contains the following needs: (1) security, (2) social, (3) esteem, (4) autonomy, (5) self-actualization.
†Ronen and Kraut (1977) also analyzed Haire et al.'s and Sirota and Greenwood's data.
‡The factors extracted were power distance, uncertainty avoidance, individualism, and masculinity.

Three studies surveyed work role and interpersonal orientation. Haire et al. (1966) researched cognitive descriptions of the managerial role using a semantic differential technique. Redding (1976) studied relations with subordinates. Hofstede (1976) used the Survey of Personal Values (Gordon, 1967; 1976) to measure practical-mindedness, achievement, variety, decisiveness, orderliness, and goal orientation; he also used the Survey of Interpersonal Values (Gordon, 1975), to measure support, conformity, recognition, independence, benevolence, and leadership.

A review of the variables raises the question of how comparable the data in these eight studies are. As we have seen, five of the studies referred to work goals importance; another five surveyed need deficiency, fulfillment, and job satisfaction; four of the studies included managerial or organizational variables; and three examined work role and interpersonal orientation. Furthermore, different researchers frequently measured the same variables using different instruments.

Nevertheless, there seem to be important reasons for comparing and synthesizing these various studies. First and foremost, the studies represent the most sophisticated efforts in clustering work attitude by nations, and they provide guidelines for future research. Second, there is a substantial overlap in variables examined in the studies, which increases the reliability of the comparison. We suggest, however, that work goals are preferable to other variables. Work goals are not constrained by the immediate job and environment, and they best represent the cultural milieu of individuals, thus allowing a more thorough cross-cultural research. Some researchers have suggested that one of the major links between the cultural milieu and individuals' job behavior is their work values (England, 1978; Haire et al., 1966; Hofstede, 1980). Still, the use of alternative measures to examine the stability of clusters is another possible strategy. It may be necessary, however, to use diverse measures in the same study to attribute clustering differences to the measures applied.

Sampling

The sampling method has important implications for how representative the studies are, how much one can generalize from them, and how easily they can be replicated. In this section, we discuss sampling in the various studies, seeking to evaluate methodological rigor, while calling attention to problems in cross-cultural sampling. Sample size, response rate, ethnic differences, and demographic and organizational variables are among the issues raised. Table 7.2 presents the sampling methods in the studies reviewed.

Sample Size   The samples reviewed vary from 248 employees in six Middle Eastern countries (Badawy, 1979) to 88,000 in 66 countries (Hofstede, 1980). Fiscal and technical considerations constrain the use of large samples, which are usually unavailable to the academic researcher. In some of the studies reviewed, however, the samples seem too small to represent the worker population in the countries surveyed.

Table 7.2 Research Procedure Describing Samples and Questionnaires

	Haire, Ghiselli, & Porter (1966)	Sirota & Greenwood (1971)	Hofstede (1976)	Redding (1976)	Ronen & Kraut (1977)*	Badawy (1979)	Griffeth, Hom, DeNisi, & Kirchner (1980)	Hofstede (1980)
Sample size	3,641	About 13,000	315	736	4,000	248	1,768	Total number of 88,000 respondents in two surveys
Number of countries	14	25	14	8 (Southeast Asia only)	15	6 in the Middle East	15 Western countries	65 (66 including U.S.)
Minimum sample size of each country	All samples are above 100	40 in each occupational group	7	Not reported	At least 40	Not reported	11	Varies, where fewer than 8 respondents on some items data omitted
Organization level/function	Various levels of management	• Sales personnel • Technical personnel • Service personnel	Middle-level managers	Middle-level managers	Technicians	Middle-management (exact definition given)	Managers	Various occupational levels
Control for ethnic/linguistic affiliation	Not reported	Not reported	Reported	Reported	Not reported	Not reported	Reported	Reported
Response rate	Not reported	Not reported	Not reported	Not reported	Not reported	85% (251, 248 usable out of 295)	Not reported	Not reported
Inclusion of only those born, reared, educated in same country	Not reported	Not reported	Not reported	Reported	Not reported	Not reported	Not reported	Not reported

Background information on employees	• Age • Education	Occupation	• Age • Occupation • Sex (3 females)	Not reported	Occupation (comparison to Haire et al.: Sirota & Greenwood)	• Age • Experience • Education • Occupation • Department	Not reported	• Occupation • Sex • Age
Organization size	Reported	Not reported	Not reported	Reported, just over half from organizations employing fewer than 100 people	Not reported (large size implicit from number of subsidiaries)	Reported	Reported as "large"	Implicit from number of subsidiaries
Industry	A variety of businesses & industries	Manufacturer of electrical equipment (one organization)	Not reported	Not reported	Multinational electronic company (one organization)	• Chemical • Petroleum • Transportation (no control)	International manufacturing corporation (one organization)	Manufacturer & seller of high technology products (one organization)
Headquarters location	Irrelevant	U.S.	Irrelevant	Irrelevant	U.S.	Irrelevant	U.S.	U.S.
Questionnaire translation	Yes, including back translation & checking by local social scientists & businesspersons	Yes, including back translation & pretesting	No questionnaire administered in English	Only for 3 countries. Face-to-face administration	Yes, including back translation	No translation. Respondents fluent in English	Yes	Yes. Check by in-company personnel. Back translating only exceptionally
Questionnaire administration	Through companies employers' associations, universities, training centers	Group session, on site, company time	A management program at IMEDE, Switzerland	Part-time training in various institutions of higher education & in-company	Company time	Training program's participants in Saudi Arabia	"On-location"	Company-administered

Source: S. Ronen and O. Shenkar, Clustering countries on attitudinal dimensions: A review and synthesis. *Academy of Management Review*, 1985 (in press).

*Ronen and Kraut (1977) have also reanalyzed the data from Haire, Ghiselli, and Porter (1966) and Sirota and Greenwood. The data presented in this column pertain only to Ronen and Kraut's own data.

Response Rate   With the exception of Badawy (1979), none of the reviewed studies reported the rate of response for their sample. The rate of response may, however, influence the representativeness of the sample, as a possible bias may be inherent in the process of self-selection. Haire et al. (1966) were aware of the response problem and suggested that people who were inclined to cooperate perhaps felt impressed by modern human-relations management.

Organizational Level   The eight studies surveyed different groups of employees. The middle management groups (used in three samples) were too vaguely defined in two studies (Redding, 1976; Hofstede, 1976). One study provided a detailed list of occupational titles included in the middle management sample (Badawy, 1979). In Griffeth et al. (1980), the group studied was even broader—namely, "managers"—with no specification of level. Haire et al. (1966) studied various levels of managers and noted the modest impact of managerial levels on their findings. Few of the studies, however, extended beyond the managerial layer. Hofstede (1980) studied various occupational groups.

Sirota and Greenwood (1971) surveyed three nonsupervisory groups: sales, technical, and service personnel. Ronen and Kraut (1977), in addition to reanalyzing the results of Haire et al. (1966) and Sirota and Greenwood (1971), studied technicians, thus adding to our relatively limited knowledge of nonmanagerial personnel. Sirota and Greenwood (1971) illustrated the problems involved in comparing data sets based on different types of workers. The authors reported substantial differences in the importance of work goals for the different kinds of workers studied. For instance, job security was ranked 2.5 by service personnel, but only 10 and 11 by sales personnel and technical personnel. Elsewhere, Kraut and Ronen (1975) have shown that both country and occupation contribute to differences in work attitude and behavior.

Organizational Size   The size of the employing organization was not always reported (e.g., Hofstede, 1976). In some studies, a large organization was implicit in the numerous subsidiaries reported (e.g., Ronen & Kraut, 1977). Redding (1976) noted that just over half of the respondents in his sample came from organizations employing fewer than 100 people, whereas Haire et al. (1966) reported the organizational size for all the respondents. The omission of organizational size by several authors may alert us to an additional constraint on the ability to generalize findings based on the samples reviewed. The impact of size on organizational structure as well as on job attitudes and behavior (Porter & Lawler, 1965) has already been established. Haire et al. (1966), for instance, found that managers from larger companies were more inclined toward a democratic–participative managerial attitude. Badawy (1979) found that those coming from smaller organizations were more democratic regarding subordinates' capacity for leadership and participation in goal setting. Workers in smaller organizations, however, held a classic attitude toward the sharing of information and the internal control of rewards. Organizational size was thus the major variable that could explain variation in internal control.

Industry   Some studies (Hofstede, 1976; Redding, 1976) did not specify in which industry respondents were employed. Badawy (1979) has specified the type of industry but has not broken the findings down by this variable. (For a few studies that researched the employees of one company each, the question, of course, was irrelevant.) If differences in departmental affiliation can explain some of the variance in employee work goals, we can assume that the type of industry will also affect these goals.

Headquarters Location   The studies involving one company (e.g., Sirota & Greenwood, 1971) were careful to note the location of the company head-quarters, a variable that seems to have considerable importance. For example, the extent to which an MNC tends to influence the values of its overseas workforce toward greater conformity with the values of its country of origin can be assessed.

Departmental Affiliation   Hofstede (1976) found that the function of em-ployees (e.g., finance, marketing, etc.) influenced (though not significantly) their work-related personal values. Badawy (1979) reported that marketing and general administration managers were most democratic toward leadership ca-pacity, whereas production executives held the most autocratic attitude. Pro-duction managers favored the sharing of objectives and information, but financial executives objected. Participation in goal setting was endorsed only by personnel managers.

Demographic Variables   Some studies did not report any demographic information on employees (Redding, 1976; Griffeth et al., 1980). Age was re-ported in four of the studies; occupation in five; sex and education in two; and experience and department in one (Badawy, 1979). The data already at hand, however, suggest that part of the variance in employee work goals can be explained by demographic variables rather than by country. Some of the evi-dence follows.

Education   Hofstede (1980) found that education correlated with both indi-vidualism and masculinity indexes (which he extracted from work goals), thus establishing a connection between educational level and work goals.

Age and Experience   Haire et al. (1966) reported that older managers showed greater fulfillment of needs but were more dissatisfied with this fulfill-ment. Hofstede (1976) reported that older managers described themselves as more ''conforming'' and more ''benevolent.'' Badawy found that managers in the thirty- to thirty-nine-year age group held a more democratic view of leader-ship than both younger and older managers, those between twenty-five and thirty-four had a more democratic attitude toward the sharing of information and objectives, and those between forty and forty-four favored participation in goal setting more than others. Badawy (1979) found that managers with less experience favored a classic autocratic attitude toward subordinates and the two middle groups held a classic view of participation in goal setting.

Sex   As Hofstede (1980, p. 261) summarized, the males in most of the studies rated advancement and earnings as more important, whereas the females rated interpersonal aspects, service, and physical conditions of the job higher.

Origin and Ethnic Affiliation   The studies provide almost no information about the origin of the respondents; only Redding (1976) emphasized that he included only those born, reared, and educated in the same country. Needless to say, a failure to account for those factors might be an enormous source of error in such studies.

Not all of the studies surveyed have taken account of the diversity within a country's borders. Haire et al. (1966), Sirota and Greenwood (1971), Ronen and Kraut (1977), and Badawy (1979) do not report whether they took note of this factor. In contrast, Redding (1976) included only designated ethnic and linguistic groups—for instance, the Chinese in Singapore. Similarly, both Hofstede (1976; 1980) and Griffeth et al. (1980) distinguished between the different linguistic segments of the Swiss population.

Reporting a country's internal diversity is important. Many countries are not homogeneous, but consist of distinct populations. These populations may differ in language (French and Flemish in Belgium; French, German, and Italian in Switzerland, etc.), climate and proximity to other countries (e.g., northern and southern Italy), or urban versus rural and other environmental elements. Such factors should affect the choice of the sample—or at least should be noted and accounted for.

There seems to be enough overlap in the samples chosen to justify a synthesis despite the differences in sampling methods. For instance, most studies included a managerial layer in their sample, and all four of the studies that examined one multinational company chose a U.S.-based corporation.

Procedure and Analysis

The six studies that performed worldwide clustering employed some type of multivariate procedure in their analysis. These multivariate procedures may be classified according to metric and nonmetric methods. Metric analysis was predominant, being used in five of the six studies.

Haire et al. (1966) used factor analysis to study cognitive descriptions of the managerial role through a semantic differential technique. Factor scores were calculated on the basis of the factor loadings of the nine scales constituting that part of the study. To create country clusters, the authors obtained a correlation matrix on the basis of all three parts of their study, each given an equal weight. Countries were grouped on the basis of similarity, each cluster consisting of countries similar to one another and dissimilar to countries in other clusters.

A Q (inverted) factor analysis was used by Sirota and Greenwood (1971) and by Hofstede (1976). In his 1980 study, Hofstede performed factor analysis within groups and between groups (ecological). Hofstede acknowledged trying smallest space analysis, with results very similar to those of factor analysis. He preferred factor analysis because he was most familiar with this method (1980, p. 9n).

Griffeth et al. (1980) use the generalized Pythagorean distance measure, D^2, to measure profile similarity. Cluster analysis was applied to the D^2 scores to create country clusters. The authors applied a one-way multivariate analysis of variance to determine the main effect of nationality. A multigroup discriminant analysis was performed to interpret the results of the analysis.

The only use of *nonmetric* multivariate analysis was by Ronen and Kraut (1977), who used the technique for their own data as well as for their reanalysis of the data in Haire et al. (1966) and Sirota and Greenwood (1971).

The consensus among the researchers that multivariate analysis is vital in the process of clustering raises the question of whether metric or nonmetric techniques are preferable. Although each method has advantages and disadvantages, we suggest that nonmetric techniques are generally better for the purpose of cross-cultural clustering (Ronen, 1982). In the next section, we will describe the nonmetric smallest space analysis and present the results of these analyses in detail. We do this for two reasons: first, this technique is innovative (particularly in its application to comparative management); second, these results were a major contribution to the subsequent synthesis of the clusters.

Various studies grouping countries according to their similarities in work attitudes and values were hampered by their analytical tools. They employed either factor analysis or simple observational analysis of the data. Because of their statistical assumptions and inability to portray the data directly, the techniques limit the conclusions we can draw from the results. More specifically, the methodology of these studies fails to consider three important issues:

1. What are the relative degrees of similarity among the different clusters of countries?
2. Are some countries within a cluster closer to other clusters than to their counterparts in the same cluster?
3. Where in the overall clustering are the "independent" countries located?

These limitations can be overcome by utilizing a multidimensional technique that enables the simultaneous consideration of diversity and uniformity. The analysis that Ronen and Kraut (1977) employed differs from its predecessors' in using a nonmetric multivariate analysis known as smallest space analysis (SSA), developed by Guttman (1968) and Lingoes (1965; 1977). By means of a computer program, this method maps the relationships among the analytical units being considered (in our case, countries). The greater the correlation between two variables, the smaller the distance between the corresponding two countries (points on our maps).

The results can often be presented in a two-dimensional map, reflecting the relationships among all possible pairs of countries. The process may be likened to cutting up a world globe and pressing it flat to get a two-dimensional picture of the earth. The description of the structure obtained is carried out first by interpreting the meaning of proximity between individual countries, and then partitioning the map into clusters that correspond to substantive concepts. We may next interpret the results on the basis of intercountry similarity within each cluster as well as distinctions between clusters.

The SSA results of Ronen and Kraut (1977) presented below are based on three sets of data. First, the study utilized a secondary analysis of data from the studies by Haire et al. (1966) and Sirota and Greenwood (1971). In addition, it used another body of data based on a study of 4000 technical employees working in fifteen countries for a European-based multinational electronic company. In these data, no country had fewer than 40 employees participating. Within a larger opinion survey questionnaire administered on company time, employees were asked to rate the importance of twenty-two work goals on a five-point Liker-type scale. The questionnaire was written in English, translated into the various languages used, and then independently translated back into English as a check on accuracy. The work goals, designed to tap a broad array of work-related expectations, appear in Table 7.3.

These data are displayed in the space diagram of Figure 7.2. The mapping represents the intercorrelations of ratings by the technical employees from fifteen countries, based on rank order correlations across the twenty-two work goals for each pair of countries.

Table 7.3 List of Work Goals Rated by Technicians

1. Opportunity for higher earnings
2. Security with company
3. Security in present position
4. Fringe benefits
5. Personal time
6. Co-workers
7. Autonomy
8. Effective department
9. Training opportunities
10. Contribution to company
11. Physical conditions
12. Recognition
13. Prestigious company
14. Company with advanced technology
15. Challenge
16. Organizational climate
17. Opportunity for promotion
18. Area
19. Supervisor
20. Keep (technologically) up-to-date
21. Use skills and abilities
22. Day-to-day learning

Source: S. Ronen and A. I. Kraut, Similarities among countries based on employee work values and attitudes. *Columbia Journal of World Business* 12(2):89–96 (1977).

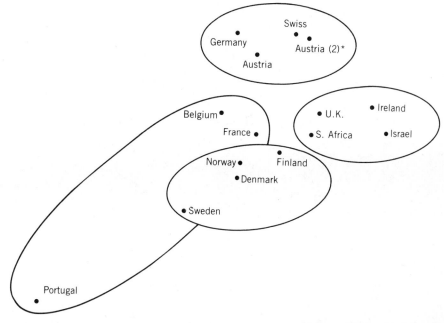

*Office serving communist countries

Figure 7.2 Smallest space analysis map of fifteen countries, based on technicians' ratings of twenty-two goals.

Source: S. Ronen and A. Kraut. "Similarities among Countries Based on Employee Work Values and Attitudes." *Columbia Journal of World Business* 12(2):89–96 (1977), p. 92.

Four clusters of countries can be observed from the space diagram: The Nordic cluster, including Norway, Finland, Denmark, and Sweden; the Latin European cluster, including France, Belgium, and Portugal; the Germanic cluster, consisting of Germany, Switzerland, Austria I, and Austria II (a separate subsidiary in Austria serving much of the Eastern European block); and last, the Anglo cluster, including the United Kingdom, South Africa, Ireland, and Israel (formerly a British mandate and strongly under the Anglo-American industrial influence).

The choice for clustering was consistent with popularly applied groupings based on language and cultural background, as well as on geographic proximity. From the resulting clusters, it appears that none of these attributes alone can account for the relatively clear clusters. For example, Germany, Austria, and Switzerland share the same language and are similar in cultural background and geographic proximity. The United Kingdom, Ireland, South Africa, and Israel are not in the same geographic area but share some cultural and linguistic background. France, which is similar to Belgium in location, language, and cultural background (at least for the French-speaking population), is close in our diagram to other highly industrialized countries in the Nordic cluster as well as the Anglo cluster. Portugal, which has been clustered with the Latin-European countries, seems to be quite dissimilar to its counterparts in the

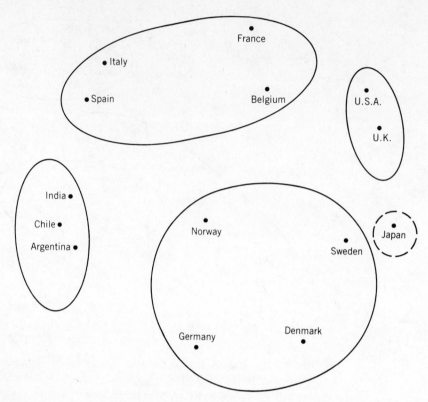

Figure 7.3 Smallest space analysis map of fourteen countries in the Haire et al. study.

Source: S. Ronen and A. Kraut. "Similarities among Countries Based on Employee Work Values and Attitudes." *Columbia Journal of World Business* 12(2):89–96 (1977), p. 92.

cluster, although it is even more dissimilar to the Germanic and Anglo countries.

Figure 7.3 depicts a space diagram of the intercorrelations based on the managerial attitudes reported by Haire et al. (1966). The clusters they found are clearly differentiated in the space diagram. These are the North European (Norway, Germany, Denmark, and Sweden), the Latin European (Belgium, France, Italy, and Spain), the Developing Countries (Argentina, Chile, and India), and the Anglo-American (United Kingdom and the United States). Japan was not included in any of these clusters and was labeled Independent.

From the SSA analysis, however, it is possible to observe both the interrelationship among the clusters and the relative positions of the individual countries within clusters and of the Independent country, Japan. The distribution of the countries from right to left seems to be based on their degree of industrialization. The Developing Countries (Argentina, Chile, and India) appear on the lefthand side. Near these are the two least developed countries of the four Latin-European nations, Spain and Italy. Moving to the right, we find the most highly industrialized countries—Japan, the United Kingdom, the United States, and Sweden.

Although Japan was identified by Haire et al. as an Independent country, and thus was not included in any of the other clusters, we can easily observe that Sweden and the Anglo-American countries are most similar to Japan in managerial attitudes. The Latin European countries have been identified in one cluster, as they were by Haire et al., but it is obvious that Belgium and France are more similar to one another (and closer to the Anglo-American countries) than they are to Italy and Spain.

An important difference between the results of the first data on technicians (shown in Figure 7.2) and those of the secondary analysis of the managerial data from Haire et al. is revealed in the positioning of Germany. In the Haire study, Germany appears in a North European cluster, probably because their sample lacked some of the neighboring countries. Figure 7.3 shows that Germany is distinctively part of a Germanic cluster, including Austria and Switzerland.

The data collected by Sirota and Greenwood (1971) were also reanalyzed using the SSA. Employees in twenty-five countries belonging to three different occupations were surveyed concerning their desired work goals. These work goals resembled those asked about in the first study of technicians, discussed above, and were cast in an identical format. The findings for their three occupation groups were very similar, and a good solution is provided by an SSA based on all three groups combined. The results are shown in Figure 7.4.

A broad Anglo-American cluster (the United States, the United Kingdom, New Zealand, Australia, Canada, South Africa, and India) appears to be clearly differentiated from the other clusters. The other clusters are the Nordic, including Norway, Finland, and Denmark (although Sweden seems to be independent of these); a broadly spread Latin American cluster (although Sirota and Greenwood distinguished a Northern group consisting of Mexico, Colombia, and Peru and a Southern cluster composed of Argentina and Chile); Latin European, including France and Belgium; and Central European comprising Germany, Austria, and Switzerland (a cluster not identified by Sirota and Greenwood).

The Independent countries seem to be Sweden, Japan, Brazil, and Israel. Venezuela, which Sirota and Greenwood label as an Independent, is included in the map within the Latin American cluster. Brazil, however, is outside this cluster and appears here, too, as an Independent country, closer to the Northern European countries (as does Argentina). Japan, as in the previous results, is an Independent country; it appears to be most similar to the Anglo-American and Nordic clusters.

In this space diagram (the most complex of the three presented), the more highly industrialized nations tend to fall in the center, while the developing countries are distributed on the upper and left borders. The clustering was directed largely by conventional wisdom—primarily, the knowledge of language similarities and, secondarily, geographical proximity. These factors also helped to identify Independents from among countries that appeared to be in

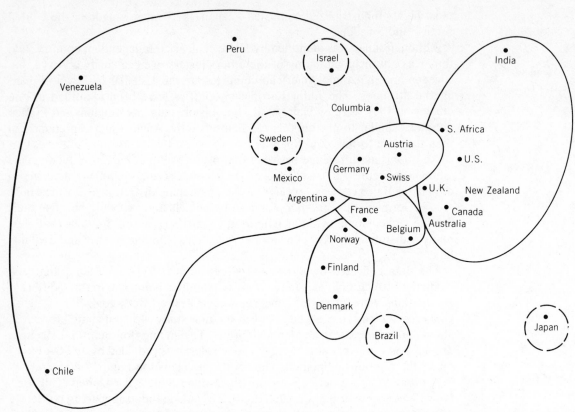

Figure 7.4 Smallest space analysis map of twenty-five countries in the Sirota and Greenwood study.

Source: S. Ronen and A. Kraut. *Business* 12(2):89–96 (1977), p. 93.

alien clusters. The resulting space diagram is relatively close to the Sirota and Greenwood clustering. There are two major exceptions, however: the map produces a distinct Germanic (or Central European) cluster and fails to support two Latin American clusters. In addition, the position of the Independent countries in relation to the various clusters shows up more clearly.

The analysis presented served to improve our ability to subdivide international populations of employees on the basis of their work values and attitudes, and to explore the forces underlying the various subgroups. In addition, it was intended to clarify the interrelationships between the country clusters and the relative position of the Independent countries with respect to the clusters.

Like geographical mapping techniques, the SSA provides a useful (if not totally precise) picture of the world we are exploring. The technique is flexible in permitting the analyst to partition the map into different regions, requiring only that one proceed according to substantive concepts and theoretical frameworks. This flexibility is a strength but also a major limitation of the method: it necessarily involves a dimension of subjectivity.

COUNTRY CLUSTERS AND THEIR UNDERLYING DIMENSIONS

Table 7.4 identifies the clusters of countries by the various studies summarized in the previous sections.

The use of national units for clustering is logical because national boundaries delineate the legal, political, and social environments within which organizations and workers function. Yet to understand why certain countries cluster, we should look across national boundaries for the dimensions underlying the clusters. Three such dimensions will be discussed: geography, language, and religion. The differentiation of these dimensions is mainly analytical, because geography, language, and religion are closely intertwined.

Examining Table 7.4, we can see that countries tend to group together geographically. Indeed, the names of the clusters describe geographic areas. One could argue that geography causally precedes other variables, such as language and religion, because a culture spreads first to those areas nearest its "birthplace." There is one striking exception, however, to geographical grouping: the Anglo-American cluster, which contains countries from all five continents. In this case, the spread of culture may be attributed to colonization and immigration. In addition, geography may also influence work goals in ways other than territorial proximity. Hofstede (1980), for instance, found that a country's climate correlated with its masculinity index, hence with its employees' work values.

Language is another dimension that underlies the clusters. A language contains meanings and values that are likely to influence individuals' work goals. For the most part, the countries in each cluster share a language or language group. For instance, people in the Anglo countries speak English; people in the Germanic countries speak German; and those in Nordic countries (with the exception of Finns) speak a variety of languages constituting a separate branch of the Germanic linguistic family. Language and geography are clearly interdependent: the spread of language and culture is associated primarily with physical (or, in the case of the Anglo-American cluster, with colonial) elements.

Religion, too, affects how the countries cluster. Religious beliefs are associated with certain values and norms. Some researchers have found support for the correlation of those norms with employee work goals (Ajiferuke & Boddewyn, 1970). An examination of the clusters indicates that most groupings have their religion in common. The Anglo, Germanic, and Nordic clusters, for example, are predominantly Protestant, whereas the Latin American and Latin European clusters are predominantly Catholic.

It is apparent that these three dimensions—geography, language, and religion—are not independent. In fact, it is likely (though not certain) that countries with one of these elements in common will share all three. Table 7.5 presents the distribution of these variables within clusters.

Another dimension that determines how countries cluster, though one less likely to correlate with the previous three, is technological development. According to Webber (1969), the level of technology and the corresponding level of development will affect managerial style and attitudes. We can discern some

Table 7.4 Country Clusters Suggested by the Reviewed Studies

Cluster	Haire, Ghiselli, & Porter (1966)	Sirota & Greenwood (1971)	Ronen & Kraut (1977) SSA of Sirota & Greenwood (1971)	Hofstede (1976)	Redding (1976)	Ronen & Kraut (1977)	Badawy (1979)	Griffeth, Hom, DeNisi, & Kirchner (1980)	Hofstede (1980)
Anglo	U.K. U.S.	U.K. U.S. Australia Canada India New Zealand South Africa Austria Switzerland	U.K. U.S. Australia Canada India New Zealand South Africa	U.K. U.S. Sweden		U.K. Ireland South Africa Israel		U.K. Canada	U.K. U.S. Australia Canada Ireland New Zealand South Africa
Germanic			Austria Germany Switzerland	Austria Germany Switzerland		Austria Germany Switzerland		Austria Denmark Finland Germany Norway Sweden Switzerland	Austria Germany Israel Switzerland
Nordic	Denmark Germany Norway Sweden	Denmark Finland Norway	Denmark Finland Norway	Denmark Norway		Denmark Finland Norway Sweden			Denmark Finland Netherlands Norway Sweden

Latin European	Belgium France Italy Spain	Belgium France	Belgium France	Brazil France Italy Switzerland	Belgium France	Belgium Greece Italy Netherlands Portugal Spain	Argentina Belgium Brazil France Italy Spain
Latin American	Argentina Chile India	Argentina Chile Colombia Mexico Peru	Argentina Chile Colombia Mexico Peru Venezuela				Chile Colombia Mexico Peru Portugal Venezuela
Near East							Greece Iran Turkey Yugoslavia
Far East				Hong Kong Indonesia Japan Malaysia Philippines Singapore S. Vietnam Thailand			Hong Kong India Pakistan Philippines Singapore Taiwan Thailand
Arabic					Abu-Dhabi Bahrain Kuwait Oman Saudi Arabia United Arab Emirates		
Independent	Japan	Brazil Germany Israel Japan Sweden Venezuela	Brazil Israel Japan Sweden	India Iran Japan		Japan	Japan

Source: S. Ronen and O. Shenkar, Clustering countries on attitudinal dimensions: A review and synthesis. *Academy of Management Review*, 1985 (in press).

Table 7.5 Distribution of Variables Across Clusters

Cluster	Religious	Languages	Levels of Industrialization	Geographic Areas
Nordic	1	2	2	1
Germanic	1	1(+)	2	1
Anglo	1	1	2	4
Latin European	1	1(+)	3	1
Latin American	1	1	2	1
Far Eastern	4	2	3	1
Arab	2	1	2	1
Near Eastern	3	3	2	1
Independent	4	4	4	4

indirect evidence of this effect in some of the clusters. Haire et al. (1966) show the three developing countries of Argentina, Chile, and India clustered together despite cultural differences. More direct evidence of this effect can be seen in the SSA plot of the Haire et al. data produced by Ronen and Kraut (1977), which shows, from left to right, a progression of increasing levels of development in countries. Hofstede (1980) presents additional evidence. He found that his individualism index (an underlying aspect explaining work values) was highly correlated ($r = 0.82$; $p < 0.01$) with per capita gross national product (GNP). Country scores on this index are the major difference between the Latin European countries and the Latin American countries, which Hofstede refers to, respectively, as more and less developed Latin countries.

Hofstede's cultural dimensions merit special attention because of his unusual methodology and his departure from more traditional dimensions. A short review of Hofstede's indexes follows. The first index, power distance, is a measure of the interpersonal power or influence between a boss and a subordinate, as perceived by the less powerful of the two. Uncertainty avoidance measures the degree to which a society deals with the uncertainty and risk present in everyday life. People with high uncertainty avoidance tend to worry more about the future, have higher job stress, tolerate less change, and stay with one employer for a longer length of time. The third factor, individualism, indicates level of dependence on or independence from the organization. It was positively related to such variables as personal time, freedom, challenge, and organization and negatively related to the use of skills, physical conditions, and training. Hofstede labeled the last dimension the masculinity index. Concepts such as manager, cooperation, desirable area, and employment security were negatively related to this factor; challenge, advancement, recognition, and earnings contributed positively.

Hofstede (1980) clustered the countries in his study according to their placement on the four indexes. The results of this cluster analysis appear in Table 7.4. We can now describe each cluster by its placement on the four continuums and by the attitudinal and work goal characteristics associated with that placement. Not only do we know which countries are most similar; we are also in a better position to predict the sources of similarities and differences. Hofstede thus provides us with four defining factors of culture (nationality) backed by both theory and empirical evidence. More important, these four defining factors are continuous variables, whereas culture and nationality are discrete variables.

PURPOSE AND IMPLICATIONS OF CLUSTERING

According to Hartigan (1975), the principal functions of clustering are (1) to name, (2) to display, (3) to summarize, (4) to predict, and (5) to require explanation. These functions may illustrate the implications of clustering countries according to their work values. The contributions appear to be both practical and theoretical.

1. Assigning one name (e.g., Nordic) to all the countries in a cluster makes it easy to identify the characteristic work values shared by this group. For example, the Latin European group is high on uncertainty avoidance, the Latin American group is low on individualism, and the Near Eastern group is high on power distance. This provides a preliminary information base on work values in countries where a corporation may consider operating.

2. For subtle differences to become more apparent, all the countries in the same cluster should be displayed on a map as physically adjoined to each other. This facilitates predicting the level of difficulty in changing managerial assignments between any two countries. It may also simplify the identification of areas where difficulties might arise. This information can help in making decisions on overseas assignments and in training personnel for them. The display may also assist in grouping business units or country organizations into international combinations (Kraut, 1975, p. 543; Ronen & Kraut, 1977, p. 95).

3. Data are summarized by referring to the properties of a cluster rather than to the properties of individual countries. The summary makes it easier to understand and manipulate the data. For instance, it becomes apparent that power distance and uncertainty avoidance tend to vary together (except in Far Eastern countries, where Western instruments may be inadequate). The summary of data enhances our understanding of the interactions among various work values.

4. If some countries in a cluster have a certain work values system, others probably have similar systems. Hartigan (1975) notes that we might make two kinds of predictions.

   a. When a new country is classified into a certain cluster on some other basis, the values of the cluster can be predicted for other variables. Thus, Honduras would be expected to be in the Latin American group and to have high power distance and uncertainty avoidance with low individualism. This may enable some prediction of work values in countries not yet studied.

   b. Members of a cluster should have similar measurements of new values. Thus, if Denmark is low on rules emphasis, we can predict that

Norway would also be low on this value. This enables better forecasting of problems associated with introducing organizational policies and practices, and it may also indicate whether the problems of certain groups of countries require different kinds of handling (Kraut, 1975, p. 544; Ronen & Kraut, 1977, p. 95).

5. The existence of clear-cut clusters requires an explanation and thus promotes the development of theories. Of special importance are those clusters that differ from geographic, linguistic, and religious classifications. For example, Brazil is not included in the Latin American cluster, which increases our awareness of nongeographic variables; it suggests that we should also consider factors such as economic development. In the long range, this phenomenon encourages the development of theories incorporating social, economic, and political phenomena as explanatory variables. Herein lies perhaps the greatest theoretical significance of cluster studies in different countries.

We can illustrate the practical implications of clustering through the following hypothetical case. An MNC is establishing a venture in Switzerland. The corporation's directors must determine if management skills will be imported from its subsidiaries in France, Germany, or Italy. (All three languages are spoken in Switzerland, albeit in different areas.) The country clustering suggests that managers be brought from Germany, since Switzerland and Germany belong to the same cluster of work values. German managers will consequently be more similar in attitudes to their Swiss colleagues and will be familiar with workers' attitudes in Switzerland.

CRITIQUES OF THE CLUSTER APPROACH

In all fairness, we should note that some researchers feel that cluster studies greatly exaggerate the differences between countries. These researchers conclude that the sources of different attitudes are primarily occupational and individual.

For example, England and Negandhi (1979) compared steel workers in India and the United States on their concern for societal issues and problems, their perceived job factor importance, and their preferred management style. They used a reference group of American auto workers to compare between- and within-country differences. As expected, large differences between countries were found in the workers' concern for societal issues and problems. Indian workers were highly concerned only with the economy and housing problems, whereas American workers were considerably more concerned about a variety of issues such as peace, health, crime, and pollution. These differences, however, did not transfer to other areas. In rating work factor importance, the Indian workers rated all factors as more important than both of the U.S. samples. The differences between the two American groups were as large as or larger than those between the United States and India groups on four of the eight job factors. The relative ranking of the eight items was also very similar for all three groups.

England and Negandhi (1979) thus concluded that there were few if any national differences in work values between the two countries. They went on to say that "in our judgment, the literature purporting to show real national and cultural differences in employee attitudes, behavior and commitment are highly exaggerated" (p. 180). Unfortunately, this study involved only two countries; although it was part of a larger nine-country study, the rest of the research is as yet unpublished. In addition, the statistical analysis presented was not sufficient to show where real national differences might exist.

A second study supporting this line of thought was an eight-country investigation by Schaupp and Kraut (1975). The workers were employed by subsidiaries of an American company. Schaupp and Kraut found no significant differences between countries in the ranking of attitudes by blue-collar workers. A Q-factor analysis showed that all of the countries loaded on one factor, indicating a high degree of similarity. Intercorrelations between countries were never lower than 0.69, with most above 0.85. To test whether or not the data might reflect company socialization, Schaupp and Kraut split their sample by the length of service with the organization. The Q-factor analysis of each group again resulted in only one factor, suggesting that company socialization was probably not the reason for the similarity among countries. Schaupp and Kraut leave open the possibility that this company may attract a particular type of worker because of its management style, which could account for the high degree of similarity.

The findings of these researchers support the importance of individual and occupational differences without negating the contribution of variance that can be explained by cultural differences. In their study, Haire et al. (1966) noted that ". . . it seems clear from the data reported here that there is a high degree of similarity among managers' attitudes in all the countries studied." They also state, however, that approximately one-third of the variance in work goals and managerial attitudes could be explained by country differences. This result is supported by England (1978) and by Griffeth et al. (1980), who found that approximately one-third and one-half the variance, respectively, can be explained by country differences. We should note, however, that the degree of similarity between countries is not determined on an absolute scale, but is relative to the level of dissimilarity with other countries, and therefore is influenced by the number of countries included in the clustering.

SYNTHESIZING THE CLUSTERS

Applying the dimensions discussed earlier to the different studies, and drawing from the similarities of results across the reviewed studies, we have created a synthesis of the eight studies' results in Table 7.4. This synthesis appears in Figure 7.5 as a map rather than a table, using per capita GNP as a general guideline for the concentric distances from the center of the map. That is, the nearer to the center a particular country is placed in comparison to other countries, the higher its GNP per capita is compared to those other countries. The most highly developed countries are close to the center, indicating the effect of the level of development on the countries' values and attitudes. How-

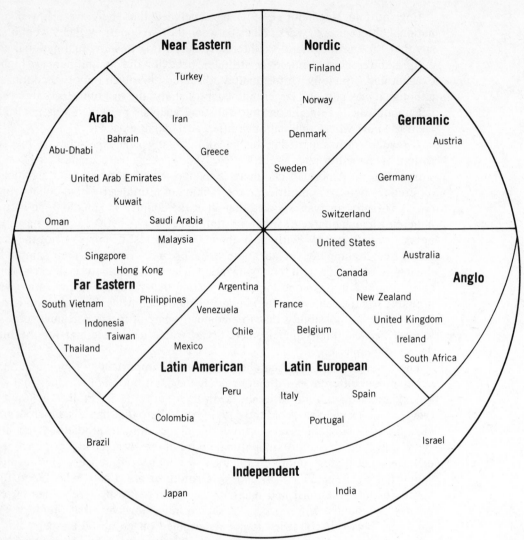

Figure 7.5 Country clusters based on employee attitude.

Source: S. Ronen and O. Shenkar. "Clustering Countries on Attitudinal Dimensions: A Review and Synthesis."
Academy of Management Review, 1985, in press.

ever, because of the limitation of a two-dimensional presentation, cluster arrangements (as well as proximity) do not always indicate intercluster similarity. In the following section, we will compare cluster membership across studies and explain the inclusion of countries in the synthesized clusters in Figure 7.5.

The Anglo Cluster

The Anglo cluster was found in all of the cluster studies. The only inconsistencies were in the work of Sirota and Greenwood (1971), who included Switzerland, Austria, and India in this cluster, and that of Hofstede (1976), who included Sweden. Ronen and Kraut's reanalysis of the Sirota and Greenwood data did not support the inclusion of Switzerland and Austria. A close observation of the Anglo clusters in Table 7.4 indicates that, with the noted exceptions, the countries in the Anglo clusters were former British colonies. This would also explain the inclusion of India (Sirota & Greenwood, 1971) and Israel (Ronen & Kraut, 1977). Both were at one time under British rule, although they are culturally diverse on other dimensions. Hofstede (1980) found that countries in the Anglo cluster generally have low-to-medium scores on the power distance index and uncertainty avoidance index and high scores on the individualism and masculinity indexes.

For the purpose of our synthesis, the countries characterized as former British colonies were included in the Anglo cluster. These include the United Kingdom, the United States, Canada, Australia, New Zealand, South Africa, and Ireland. India appears as Independent in Figure 7.1 because of the confusion of results over its placement. In Table 7.4, it falls variously into the Latin American cluster (Haire et al., 1966), the Independent category (Hofstede, 1976), and the Far East cluster (Hofstede, 1980).

The Germanic and Nordic Clusters

The Germanic and Nordic countries were differentiated in four studies (Hofstede, 1976; 1980; Ronen & Kraut, 1977; and Ronen & Kraut, 1977, reanalysis of Sirota & Greenwood, 1971). There appears to be some degree of reliability in the countries appearing in these clusters, depending on which countries were included in the study: Norway, Sweden, Denmark, and Finland consistently appear in the Nordic cluster, and Germany, Austria, and Switzerland compose the Germanic group. Two studies did not differentiate between the Nordic and the Germanic clusters (Haire et al., 1966; Griffeth et al., 1980). In both of these studies, the two clusters combined to form a Northern European cluster. The Haire results may be attributed to these researchers' more extensive study of Germanic countries. Griffeth et al. (1980), however, studied three Germanic and four Nordic countries, yet still found only one cluster. Sirota and Greenwood (1971) did not find a Germanic cluster in their analysis; however, Ronen and Kraut's SSA map of their data showed it clearly. Hofstede's (1980) data revealed that the two clusters were quite similar on three of the four indexes he defined; with the exception of the masculinity index, the clusters are very close and can be combined.

In the synthesis, the Nordic and Germanic clusters are separate but contiguous, reflecting the empirical results of Table 7.4. Austria, Germany, and Switzerland are included in the Germanic cluster, and Finland, Norway, Denmark, and Sweden in the Nordic group.

The Latin European Cluster

The last cluster commonly found was the Latin European cluster. Its most consistent members were France and Belgium. When Spain, Italy, and Portugal were included in a study, they also fell into this group. Although these countries differ in language, religion and geography are common dimensions of the cluster. There is some indication that this cluster may be subdivided into two groups: one containing Spain and Italy, the other France and Belgium.

The Latin American Cluster

A cluster that we might expect to resemble the Latin Europeans is the Latin American group. There is some indirect evidence to support this notion. The fact that Spain and Portugal colonized Latin America suggests strong cultural ties. One effect of colonization is similarity in religion and language—certainly evident in the Latin American group. Another cluster consists of Great Britain and its former colonies; thus, it is not unlikely that Spain and Portugal and their former colonies form one also. Hofstede's indexes (1980) provide further support for the combination of the Latin European and Latin American clusters. Both Latin clusters are characterized by a high power distance, high uncertainty avoidance, and high variance in masculinity. The major difference is on the individualism index, which is low for Latin American countries. As Hofstede has shown, the individualism index is highly correlated ($r = 0.82$; $p < 0.01$) with a country's per capita GNP. This observation implies that the major difference between the Latin European cluster and the Latin American cluster is their level of development; if this is true, then we may consider them a single cultural cluster. Spain—the least developed member of the Latin European cluster—also had the lowest score in that cluster on individualism. In addition, Ronen and Kraut's SSA map of the Haire et al. data shows Spain and Italy to be distinctly separate from the more developed France and Belgium and closer to the developing countries of Argentina and Chile.

Issues Regarding the Latin European and Latin American Clusters

These arguments for combining the Latin European and Latin American clusters assume that changes in the level of development cause changes in a country's individualism index. However, if one believes that cultural differences cause differences in the level of development or rate of development, these arguments are meaningless. Under this hypothesis, a less-developed country may never develop, or may develop at a much slower rate, because of the society's relatively unchanging values and goals. Following this argument, the Latin European and Latin American clusters may remain distinct clusters.

To resolve this apparent conflict of theory, however, we should observe values related to individualism over time for significant change. Hofstede (1980) attempted this by comparing the results from the 1968 and 1972 portions of his data set. He found that the individualism index for countries increased over the period from 1968 to 1972, although convergence did not take place. Hofstede speculates that the individualism index for a country will increase as its wealth increases. More evidence collected over a longer time period seems necessary, however, before we can draw this conclusion.

The clusters of Latin American and Latin European countries follow fairly closely the results of Hofstede (1980) and Sirota and Greenwood (1971). In keeping with the argument made concerning the similarities between these two clusters, they are contiguous on the map in Figure 7.1. These countries are not combined into one cluster because the evidence from the studies (Table 7.4) suggests stronger support for differentiating these clusters.

Other Studies—Other Issues

In six of the studies, results were limited to the clusters so far described. Hofstede (1980) investigated other countries in addition to those that fit into the previous five clusters. Not surprisingly, he found two new clusters, which we have included in our conceptualization. Other researchers seem to verify these findings.

The Near Eastern Cluster　The Near Eastern cluster contains Greece, Iran, Yugoslavia, and Turkey. This cluster is characterized by high power distance, high uncertainty avoidance, low individualism, and medium masculinity. Aside from Hofstede's dimensions, geography appears to be the main dimension these countries have in common. The variety of languages, religions, and histories makes it a particularly diverse grouping. It is difficult, however, to evaluate the validity of Hofstede's technique as reflected in this finding, because these countries were not included in any other study.

Griffeth et al. (1980) included Greece in the Latin European cluster. The differences in Hofstede's and Griffeth's methodologies, however, and their underlying dimensions for clustering, create difficulties in comparing their results. Because the other countries were not included in the Griffeth study, we can only guess whether or not a separate cluster of Near Eastern countries would have emerged had these countries been sampled. In our synthesis, the Near Eastern countries reflect Hofstede's grouping, forming a separate cluster (see Figure 7.5).

The Far Eastern Cluster　Hofstede (1980) also found a Far Eastern cluster, including Pakistan, India, Taiwan, Hong Kong, Thailand, Singapore, and the Philippines. These countries are characterized by high power distance, low-to-medium uncertainty avoidance, low individualism, and medium masculinity. Redding (1976) studied eight countries in the Far East using the Haire et al. questionnaire. We have considered these a Far East cluster (despite the unavailability of other countries to form a basis for comparison) on the grounds of results similar to those of Hofstede (1980) and in keeping with our own expectations. However, given the diversity of religion and language, and given the huge geographic area covered by these countries, one Far Eastern cluster may be a serious oversimplification. Furthermore, our Western instruments may be inadequate to measure validly the differences among Far Eastern countries' cultural dimensions. Because of these limitations, we have included a Far Eastern cluster in our synthesis, but with the reservation that more countries from the Orient must be included in future studies before we can draw reliable conclusions.

The Arab Cluster

Finally, one study defined an Arab cluster. Badawy (1979) used the Haire et al. questionnaire to examine Saudi Arabia, Kuwait, Abu-Dhabi, Bahrein, Oman, and the United Arab Emirates. As in the Redding study (1976), Badawy did not include countries representing other clusters, so comparisons are difficult. We propose, however, that this grouping represents a separate cluster of countries, distinct from the others described thus far.

Other Countries—Independents

Several countries that one or more researchers studied are noticeably absent from our clusters. They appear in different clusters in different studies or are classified as Independent. For example, Ronen and Kraut (1977) clustered Israel with the Anglo countries. This makes intuitive sense, because the British controlled Palestine for several decades, and many Israeli professionals are trained in the Anglo-American countries. On the other hand, Hofstede (1980), placed Israel in his Germanic cluster. This placement is also credible, given the large number of Western European Jews who immigrated to Israel in the 1930s and after World War II. These disparate findings suggest that differences in samples can have an important impact on cluster membership. The Sirota and Greenwood (1971) study and the Ronen and Kraut (1977) reanalysis found Israel to be an independent country. Clearly, we need more evidence before we can place Israel in a particular cluster. Until such evidence is available, we will consider it independent.

Japan has also posed problems for the clustering process. It has been included in six of the studies. Redding (1976) includes Japan in the Far East cluster, but as mentioned earlier, his study was limited to countries in the Far East; the other five classified it as an Independent. It therefore appears that Japan's combination of culture and development is not similar to any other country's. An alternative explanation is available for Japan's apparent uniqueness. With the exception of Hofstede and Redding, the studies including Japan do not include any other countries from the Far East. It seems likely that Japan would appear to be independent from the Germanic, Latin European, and Latin American countries studied in Haire et al. (1966). If researchers had included more countries—especially those with cultural dimensions in common with Japan—a cluster including Japan might have emerged. Given the present findings, however, it seems safest to consider Japan its own cluster, independent from other countries.

The countries classified as Independents allow us to hypothesize that economic development and technology override the traditional dimensions of language, geography, and religion as a basis for cluster membership. Countries higher on economic development tend to stand out from their geographic groupings (e.g., Israel, Sweden, Brazil, Japan). Countries listed as Independent are separate from other clusters, yet not necessarily similar to one another.

CONCLUSION

The clusters presented here include much of the non-Communist world. Many areas, such as Africa, have not been studied at all; other areas, such as the Middle East and the Far East, have not been studied sufficiently. These gaps in the research make it difficult to draw conclusions about cluster membership in these parts of the world. Major studies need to be undertaken that include countries from all areas of the world. Otherwise we will continue to confront the problems of countries such as Japan, where conclusions about cluster membership are limited by the countries included in the sample.

Despite these limitations, however, the results available thus far allow us to draw certain conclusions. First, it appears that we can cluster countries according to similarities on certain cultural dimensions. These dimensions typically measure work goals, values, needs, and job attitudes. The discriminant validity of these variables is supported by the fact that the resulting clusters consistently discriminate on the basis of language, religion, and geography. The support for the Anglo, Germanic, Nordic, Latin European, and Latin American clusters appears to be strong. Clusters describing the Far East and Arab countries are ill-defined and require further research, as do countries classified as Independents (e.g., Israel and Japan).

As multinational companies increase their direct investment overseas—especially in less-developed and consequently less-studied areas—they will require more information concerning their local employees, to implement effective interactions between the organization and the host country. The knowledge acquired thus far can help us to understand better the work values and attitudes of employees throughout the world. We have also learned which countries resemble each other and why. Our theories work well for Western countries, but are they equally applicable in non-Western countries? The answer to this question is uncertain. The theories show promise, however, now that they include countries from all parts of the globe.

What seems certain is that the cluster approach to mapping cultural differences provides an indispensable tool for international managers. In the past, managers could only follow their hunches about how to deal with complex issues in other cultures. Managers now have other means to help them in their efforts. Cluster studies are one of the most promising. Although hardly infallible—for no study, no matter how sophisticated, can identify or control every variable—cluster studies nevertheless offer a substantive method for assessing other cultures. This would have been helpful even during the relatively simple past. In today's complex world, it is crucial.

CASES FOR PART II

Case A: Showa–Packard, Ltd.

Part A

When Richard Johnson, president of the international division of Packard Foods, Inc., got on a JAL flight from Kennedy Airport to Tokyo, he was still undecided as to how best he could approach several delicate issues with the Japanese company in which was a joint-venture partner. He planned to make good use of the grueling eleven-hour flight to Tokyo to formulate his policy. In many ways, he considered this trip of vital importance. For one thing, the nature of the problems to be discussed was such that they were likely to affect the long-term relationship between the Packard Company and the Japanese partner in the management of their joint venture in Japan. Moreover, this was his first trip to Japan in the capacity of president of the international division and he was anxious to make a good impression and to begin to build a personal relationship with senior executives of the Japanese firm.

Mr. Johnson had assumed the position of president several months previously. He was forty-two years old and was considered to be one of the most promising senior executives in the company. He graduated from a well-known eastern business school in 1954. After two years of military service, he entered a prominent consulting firm. In 1959, he joined the marketing group of Packard Foods, Inc. Prior to his promotion to the presidency of the International Division, he had served as managing director of Packard's wholly owned subsidiary in Great Britain.

Source: Copyright © 1973 by the President and Fellows of Harvard College. This case was prepared by Michael Y. Yoshino as the basis for class discussion rather than to illustrate either effective or ineffective handling of an administrative situation. Reprinted by permission of the Harvard Business School.

Packard was a major manufacturer of breakfast cereals, canned products, instant coffee, frozen foods, and pet foods. The company's total sales for 1972 were roughly $1.5 billion and it had fifteen manufacturing subsidiaries and twenty sales subsidiaries throughout the world. International operations, including exporting, accounted for roughly 25 percent of the company's total sales. International sales had been growing at a rapid rate during the previous decade and the company's top management felt that this represented a major thrust for future growth.

The company, after about two years of difficult and often frustrating negotiations, was successful in establishing a joint venture in Japan with Showa Foods, a leading Japanese foods manufacturer. The arrangement was formalized in the summer of 1971 and the venture went into operation in the spring of the following year.

Prior to the establishment of this joint venture, Packard had had limited export operations in Japan through a major trading company, but the company's management recognized that in order to capitalize on the rapidly growing Japanese market for processed foods, the changing diet pattern, and the emerging mass market, more extensive local presence was essential. By the late 1960s, the company began to receive a number of inquiries from major Japanese corporations concerning licensing as well as the possibility of establishing a joint manufacturing venture.

Showa was one of the companies that approached Packard initially for licensing. It appeared to be an attractive potential partner. Showa Foods, Inc. had been a major producer of canned fish. In the early 1960s the company began an active program of diversification into new food products. The company successively entered into new product fields, including ketchup, mayonnaise, salad dressing, and a number of other lines. The company had established a reputation for high quality, and its brands were well established. Moreover, the company had built one of the most effective distribution systems in the industry, using a myriad of wholesalers and small retailers.

In the late 1960s, Showa began to seek still more new products. It was particularly interested in breakfast cereal, artificial coffee cream, canned soup, frozen foods, and pet foods. The company's management felt that these products would be a field for major growth. The management, after some investigation concluded that the quickest and most efficient way to achieve entry into these product lines was through either licensing or a joint venture with a leading American company. The Showa management felt that the timing was of particular importance, since its major competitors were also considering a similar move. Showa's expression of interest to Packard was indeed timely, since the latter company, having enjoyed considerable success in Europe, had become increasingly interested in Japan as the only untapped major market. Showa was at first interested in a licensing arrangement, but Packard, anxious to establish a permanent presence in Japan, wished to establish a joint manufacturing venture.

The negotiations concerning this joint venture were difficult in part because it was the first experience of the kind for both companies. Packard had had virtually no prior experience in Japan, and for Showa this was the first joint venture with a foreign company, although it had engaged in licensing agreements with several American and European firms.

The ownership of the joint venture was equally divided between the two companies. In addition to the predetermined level of cash contribution, the agreement stipulated that Packard was to provide technology and the Japanese partner was to make available part of the plant facilities. The joint venture was at first to produce and market breakfast cereal and instant coffee and later was to introduce pet foods and frozen foods. The products were to be marketed under the joint brands of Packard and Showa. The agreement also stipulated that both companies would have equal representation on the board of directors, with four persons each, and that Showa would provide the entire personnel for the joint venture from top management down to production workers. Such a practice is quite common among foreign joint ventures in Japan since, given the almost total lack of mobility among personnel in large corporations, recruiting would represent a major, often almost insurmountable, problem for foreign companies. The companies also agreed that the Japanese partner would nominate the president of the joint venture, subject to the approval of the board, and the American company would nominate a person for the position of executive vice-president. Packard agreed to supply, for the time being, a technical director on a full-time basis.

Representing Packard on the board were the executive vice-president of the joint venture, Mr. Johnson, as well as the president and executive vice-president of the parent corporation. Representing the Japanese company were the president and executive vice-president of Showa and two senior executives of the joint venture, namely, the president and vice-president for finance.

By the spring of 1973 the operations were well under way. Production began and a reasonably effective sales organization had been built. Although the operating plans were progressing reasonably well, Mr. Johnson had become quite concerned over several issues that had come to his attention during the previous two months. The first and perhaps the most urgent of these was the selection of a new president for the joint venture.

The first president had died suddenly about three months before at the age of 64. He had been managing director of the parent company and had been the chief representative in the

Showa's negotiations with Packard. When the joint venture was established it appeared only natural for him to assume the presidency; Packard management had no objection.

About a month after his death, Showa, in accordance with the agreement, nominated Mr. Kenzo Tanaka as the new president. Mr. Johnson, when he heard Mr. Tanaka's qualifications, concluded he was not suitable for the presidency of the joint venture. He became even more disturbed when he received further information about how he was selected from Jack Harper, the executive vice-president of the joint venture and one of Packard's representatives on the board. Mr. Tanaka had joined Showa forty years earlier upon graduating from Tokyo University. He had held a variety of positions in the Showa company, but during the previous fifteen years, he had served almost exclusively in staff functions. He had been manager of administrative services at the company's major plant, manager of the General Affairs Department at the corporate headquarters, and personnel director. When he was promoted to that position, he was admitted to the company's board of directors. When he later became managing director, his responsibility was expanded to include overseeing several service-oriented staff departments, including personnel, industrial relations, administrative services, and the legal department. Mr. Johnson was concerned that Mr. Tanaka had had virtually no line experience and could not understand why Showa would propose such a person for the presidency of the joint venture, particularly when it was at a critical stage of development.

Even more disturbing to Mr. Johnson was the manner in which Mr. Tanaka was selected. This first came to Mr. Johnson's attention when he received a letter from Mr. Harper, which included the following description.

By now you have undoubtedly examined the background information forwarded to you regarding Mr. Tanaka, nominated by our Japanese partner for the presidency of the joint venture.

I have subsequently learned the manner in which Mr. Tanaka was chosen for the position, which I am sure would be of great interest to you. I must point out at the outset that what I am going to describe, though shocking by our standard, is quite commonplace among Japanese corporations; in fact, it is well-accepted.

Before describing the specific practice, I must give you a brief background of the Japanese personnel system. As you know, the major companies follow the so-called lifetime employment where all managerial personnel are recruited directly from universities, and they remain with the company until they reach their compulsory retirement age which is typically around fifty-seven. Career advancement in the Japanese system comes slowly, primarily by seniority. Advancement to middle management is well paced, highly predictable and virtually assured for every college graduate. Competence and performance become important as they reach upper middle management and top management. Obviously, not everyone will be promoted automatically beyond middle management, but whatever the degree to which competence and qualifications are considered in career advancement, chronological age is the single most important factor.

A select few within the ranks of upper-middle management will be promoted to top management positions, that is, they will be given memberships in the board of directors. In large Japanese companies, the board typically consists exclusively of full-time operating executives. Showa's board is no exception. Moreover, there is a clear-cut hierarchy among the members. The Showa board consists of chairman of the board, president, executive vice-president, three managing directors, five ordinary directors, and two statutory auditors.

Typically, ordinary directors have specific operating responsibility such as head of a staff department, a plant, or a division. Managing directors are comparable to our group vice-presidents. Each will have two or three functional or staff groups or product divisions reporting to them. Japanese commercial law stipulates that the members are to be elected by stockholders for a two-year term. Obviously, under the system described, the members are designated by the chairman of the board or the president and serve at their pleasure. Stockholders have very little voice in the actual selection of the board members. Thus, in some cases it is quite conceivable that board membership is considered as a reward for many years of faithful and loyal service.

As you are well aware, a Japanese corporation is well known for its paternalistic practices in return for lifetime service, and they do assume obligation, particularly for those in middle management or above, even after they reach their compulsory retirement age, not just during their working careers. Appropriate positions are generally found for them in the company's subsidiaries, related firms, or major suppliers where they can occupy positions commensurate to their last position in the parent corporation for several more years.

A similar practice applies to the board members. Though there is no compulsory retirement age for board members, the average tenure for board membership is usually around six years. This is particularly true for those who are ordinary or managing directors. Directorships being highly coveted positions, there must be regular turnover to allow others to be promoted to board membership. As a result, all but a fortunate few who are earmarked as heir apparent to the chairmanship, presidency, or executive vice-presidency, must be "retired." Since most of these men are in their late fifties or early sixties, they do not yet wish to retire. Moreover, even among major Japanese corporations, the compensation for top management positions is quite low compared with the American standard and pension plans being still quite inadequate, they will need respectable positions with a reasonable income upon leaving the company. Thus, it is a common practice among Japanese corporations to transfer senior executives of the parent company to the chairmanship or presidency of the company's subsidiaries or affiliated companies. Typically, these men will serve in these positions for several years before they retire. Showa had a dozen subsidiaries and you might be interested in knowing that every top management position is held by those who have retired from the parent corporation. Such a system is well routinized.

Our friend, Mr. Tanaka, is clearly not the caliber that would qualify for further advancement in the parent company, and his position must be vacated for another person. Showa's top management must have decided that the presidency of the joint venture was the appropriate position for him to "retire" into. This is the circumstance under which Mr. Tanaka has been nominated for our consideration.

Mr. Harper's letter then went on to discuss other matters.

When he had read this letter, Mr. Johnson instructed Mr. Harper to indicate to the Showa management that Mr. Tanaka was not acceptable. Not only did Mr. Johnson feel that Mr. Tanaka lacked the qualifications and experience for the presidency, but he resented the fact that Showa was using the joint venture as a haven to accommodate a retired executive. It would be justifiable for Showa to use one of its wholly owned subsidiaries for that purpose, for understandably Mr. Tanaka had been a loyal, effective employee who had made significant contributions to Showa, but there was no reason why the joint venture should take him on. On the contrary, the joint venture needed dynamic leadership to establish a viable market position.

In his response to Mr. Harper, Mr. Johnson suggested as president another person, Mr. Shigeru Abe, marketing manager of the joint venture. Mr. Abe was fifty years old and had been transferred to the joint venture from Showa where he had held a number of key marketing positions, including regional sales manager, and assistant marketing director. Shortly after he was appointed to the latter position, Mr. Abe was sent to Packard headquarters to become acquainted with the company's marketing operations. He spent roughly three months in the United States, during which time Mr. Johnson met him. Though he had not gone beyond a casual acquaintance, Mr. Johnson was much impressed by Mr. Abe. He appeared to be dynamic, highly motivated, and pragmatic, qualities which Mr. Johnson admired. Moreover, Mr. Abe had a reasonable command of English. While communication was not easy, at least it was possible to have conversations on substantive matters. From what Mr. Johnson was able to gather, Mr. Abe impressed everyone he saw favorably and gained the confidence of not only the International Division staff, but those in the corporate marketing group as well as sales executives in the field.

Mr. Johnson was aware that Mr. Abe was a little too young to be acceptable to Showa, but he felt that it was critical to press for his appointment for two reasons. First, he was far from convinced of the wisdom of following Japanese managerial practices blindly in the joint venture. Some of the Japanese executives he met in New York had told him of the pitfalls and weaknesses of Japanese management practices. He was disturbed over the fact that, as he was becoming familiar with the joint venture, he was finding that in every critical aspect such as organization structure, personnel practices, and decision making, the company was managed as though it were a Japanese company. Mr. Harper had had little success in introducing American practices. Mr. Johnson had noticed in the past that the joint venture had been consistently slow in making decisions because it engaged in a typical Japanese group-oriented and consensus-based process. He also learned that a control and reporting system was virtually nonexistent and felt that Packard's sophisticated planning and control system should be introduced. It had proved successful in the company's wholly owned European subsidiaries, and there seemed to be no reason why such a system could not improve the operating efficiency of the joint venture. He recalled from his British experience that the American management practices, if judiciously applied, could give American subsidiaries abroad a significant competitive advantage over local firms.

Second, Mr. Johnson felt that the rejection of

Mr. Tanaka and appointment of Mr. Abe might be important as a demonstration to the Japanese partner that Showa-Packard, Ltd., was indeed a fifty–fifty joint venture and not a microcosm of the Japanese parent company. He was also concerned that Packard had lost the initiative in the management of the joint venture. This move would help Packard gain stronger influence over the management of the joint venture.

Showa's reaction to Mr. Johnson's proposal was swift; they rejected it totally. Showa management was polite, but made it clear that they considered Mr. Johnson unfair in judging Mr. Tanaka's suitability for the presidency without even having met him. They requested Mr. Harper to assure Mr. Johnson that their company, as half owner, indeed had an important stake in the joint venture and certainly would not have recommended Mr. Tanaka unless it had been convinced of his qualifications. Showa management also told Mr. Johnson, in no uncertain terms through Mr. Harper, that the selection of Mr. Abe was totally unacceptable because in the Japanese corporate system such a promotion was unheard of, and would be detrimental not only to the joint venture, but to Mr. Abe himself, who was believed to have a promising future in the company.

Another related issue which concerned Mr. Johnson was the effectiveness of Mr. Harper as executive vice-president. Mr. Johnson appreciated the difficulties, but began to question Mr. Harper's qualifications for his position and his ability to work with Japanese top management. Mr. Johnson had no concrete evidence but nevertheless had formed a definite impression of ineffectiveness in the last two or three months through correspondence and from two visits Mr. Harper made to the home office. During the last visit, for example, Mr. Harper had complained of his inability to integrate himself with the Japanese top management team. He indicated that he felt he was still very much an outsider to the company, not only because he was a foreigner, but also because the Japanese executives, having come from the parent company, had known each other and in many cases had worked together, for at least twenty years. He also indicated that none of the executives spoke English well enough to achieve effective communication beyond the most rudimentary level and that his Japanese was too limited to be of practical use. In fact, his secretary, hired specifically for him, was the only one with whom he could communicate easily. He also expressed frustration over the fact that his functions were very ill defined and his experience and competence were not really being well utilized by the Japanese.

Mr. Johnson discovered after he assumed the presidency that Mr. Harper had been chosen for this assignment ostensibly for his knowledge of Japan. Mr. Harper graduated from a small Midwestern college in 1943 and when he was inducted into the Army he was sent to the Japanese language school where he underwent a year's full-time, intensive language program. He was among the first language officers to go to Japan with the Occupation in the fall of 1945. He spent a year in the counterintelligence unit in Yokohama. Upon returning home, he joined Packard as a management trainee. Much of the ensuing years he spent in the field. In 1968 he became assistant district sales manager in three Western states—California, Oregon, and Washington. When the company began to search for a candidate for executive vice-president for the new joint venture, Mr. Harper's name came up quite accidentally. Reportedly, when Mr. Albert Gardner, Mr. Johnson's predecessor, mentioned the problem to Mr. George Vance, corporate vice-president for marketing, in a casual conversation, the latter recommended Mr. Harper. Mr. Harper had worked under Mr. Vance in the field in the early 1960s, and Mr. Vance had known his background. Mr. Gardner called Mr. Harper into New York to meet with him and explore the latter's interest in assuming the new position. Mr. Gardner felt that Mr. Harper would be an excellent choice because of his age (fifty-three

years), his experience in sales, and his previous language training. Mr. Harper, although somewhat ambivalent about the new opportunity at first, soon became persuaded that this would represent a major challenge and opportunity. He was sure that his advancement opportunity in the company was limited if he stayed on in his present position. Moreover, he thought it would be pleasant to get back to Japan after some twenty odd years. The fact that his children had all grown up made the move less complicated. He was still able to carry on a simple conversation in Japanese and believed that with some effort he might be able to regain his language competence.

Mr. Johnson was wondering by what means he could find out how effective Mr. Harper was in working with Japanese management and how the Japanese regarded him. Mr. Johnson was also considering, if Mr. Harper had to be replaced, what qualifications would be required for another person to be effective in this unfamiliar environment.

Part B

Toshio Honda, executive vice-president of the Showa Foods Company, Ltd., was reflecting on his way home from the office in his chauffeur-driven Toyota Century. Mr. Honda had been asked by the president of his company to represent Showa in dealing with Packard Foods Company, with which Showa had formed a joint venture, Showa–Packard, Ltd. The next day he was to meet with Mr. Johnson, president of the International Division of the Packard Foods Company. He recalled a pleasant visit he had had with Mr. Johnson a few months before when he visited Packard's headquarters in New York. Mr. Honda had been highly impressed by Mr. Johnson and thought he typified the bright, articulate, highly motivated, and pragmatic American business elite, but at the same time, Mr. Honda had some serious reservations about Mr. Johnson's, or for that matter the Packard company's, approach to Japan. This matter had been of concern to the Showa's top management for some time and Mr. Honda felt that this would be an appropriate opportunity to discuss a number of basic issues which would have lasting importance for the future of the joint venture. Of immediate urgency were the issues concerning the selection of a new president and the role of Mr. James Harper, executive vice-president of Showa–Packard, Ltd. These two factors would play a critical role in determining the type of management that the joint venture would evolve.

Showa's top management had selected Mr. Tanaka, managing director of Showa Foods, as the next president of Showa–Packard, Ltd., and it had no intention of withdrawing his name in the face of opposition from Packard. Mr. Tanaka had already been informed and he had indicated that he would gladly accept the new assignment. In the view of Showa's top management, there was no one else who was eligible for the presidency of the joint venture and, moreover, the position was appropriate for a man of Mr. Tanaka's status. When a man of Mr. Tanaka's rank, seniority, and status was to be retired from the parent company, he must according to the accepted Japanese practices, be given the presidency of a subsidiary or the executive vice-presidency of one of the largest and most imporant subsidiaries. Unfortunately, all such positions had been filled and there existed no other appropriate position for him. However, reappointment of Mr. Tanaka to another term as managing director of the parent company appeared to be exceedingly difficult because of his age as well as the fact that it was imperative to retire several directors at this time to make room for younger men.

Mr. Honda had known Mr. Tanaka for nearly forty years, ever since the latter joined the company as a young trainee. Mr. Honda had always liked him. Although he was not dynamic or imaginative, Mr. Tanaka had been tremendously loyal, hardworking, and committed. The company's senior top management felt strongly that Mr. Tanaka should be provided with a suitable postretirement position.

As far as Mr. Honda was concerned, Mr. Tanaka had been very much one of the company's own, and for his many years of faithful, and in many ways quite distinguished, service he indeed deserved the position in the joint venture.

Mr. Honda was concerned about what he considered to be harsh reactions by Mr. Johnson against the selection of Mr. Tanaka. True, Mr. Tanaka might not fit the mold which Americans would consider as desirable or even essential for a company president, but at least in the Japanese environment Mr. Tanaka in Mr. Honda's judgment had those personal qualities which made him an effective chief executive. In Mr. Honda's view, the Japanese management system stressed group and cooperative efforts. He believed that the primary function of a president was to facilitate group performance, that is, to maximize the output of the group by avoiding frictions within it and by developing a strong sense of group identity and solidity. He knew from his experience that, in Japanese corporate organizations, assignments and responsibilities were not determined on an individual basis, the leader must see to it that those who were capable, and did not have an appropriate status, were given the opportunity to demonstrate their full ability without disturbing group harmony. In the Japanese setting the effective leader was not necessarily a strong individual directing and inspiring the group to achieve the objectives that he himself had set for the group, but his main function was to encourage the group to set its own goals. Thus, interpersonal skills were essential. Mr. Honda felt that a man of Mr. Tanaka's talents would be particularly needed in the early stage of the joint venture's development because it would be critical to build a cohesive and smoothly functioning management team. Mr. Honda did not feel that Mr. Johnson was fair in judging Mr. Tanaka's potentials.

Furthermore, Mr. Honda felt that Mr. Johnson's countersuggestion of the appointment of Mr. Abe, a fifty-year-old marketing director, to the presidency was absurd and totally unacceptable. Showa's management had never seriously entertained the possibility. There were a half-dozen men in the joint venture alone who were senior to Mr. Abe, and obviously these men would be loath to accept his leadership. Moreover, it was totally unprecedented to promote a fifty-year-old executive, however capable, from the position of marketing manager directly to the presidency of a corporation. Certainly this would require a major overhauling of the organization and sweeping changes in personnel. Showa's top management, including Mr. Honda, saw no need for such drastic measures. Moreover, they were well aware that to promote Mr. Abe to the presidency of the joint venture would be the quickest way to ruin his bright future.

Going beyond the selection of a president, Mr. Honda had been concerned over the fact that Packard was becoming increasingly aggressive in attempting to introduce American management techniques into the joint venture, including such practices as budgeting, planning and control systems, personnel practices, and so on. Mr. Honda suspected that this was being done at the insistence of Mr. Johnson because these efforts had become particularly noticeable since the latter had assumed the presidency of the International Division. The past efforts to introduce American techniques had met serious resistance and there had been growing resentment among the Japanese management of the joint venture. In the system which had traditionally emphasized group efforts, shared responsibility, and consensus-based decision making, the ad hoc introduction of American techniques was beginning to cause serious strains.

These developments were making Mr. Honda increasingly doubtful of the wisdom of having entered a joint venture with Packard. Showa had initially preferred licensing to avoid such problems but in this case had had no choice other than accepting a joint venture in order to avail itself of the technology and the brand name of Packard. Moreover, Mr. Honda was puzzled by Packard's increasing intention of Americanizing the joint venture and its insistence on exercising active management control. Mr. Honda naturally understood that Packard's main motive for entering Japan was to establish a profitable base of operations. To Mr. Honda, it appeared that the best and quickest way to achieve such a goal was to leave the day-to-day management of the joint venture to the Japanese, who were familiar with the scene and that it would be mutually beneficial to do so, while the American company's forte lay in providing technical and production expertise as well as marketing assistance as required by the joint venture. Mr. Honda had become increasingly convinced of the difficulty of building a truly integrated management team to manage the joint venture. He came to recognize that the sooner the venture realized this, the better it would be for both parties. There were a number of quite successful American and Japanese joint ventures which were operating according to this philosophy.

Another question had been bothering Mr. Honda. This was the role and qualification of Mr. Harper, the executive vice-president of Showa–Packard. The function of this position had never been clearly defined. Mr. Honda understood initially that the role of executive vice-president was to serve as watchdog to protect Packard's interests, to offer a communication link between the joint venture and Packard, and to provide advice and assistance to the venture, particularly in the marketing area. From what Mr. Honda could see, Mr. Harper was fulfilling only the first function. As a communication link between the joint venture and the parent company, Mr. Harper had not proved effective in the eyes of the Japanese managers. Because he had spent almost all of his career with Packard in the field, Mr. Harper apparently knew only a few people at headquarters and was not knowledgeable about how and where to go to tap corporate resources. Replies to requests for advice and assistance routed through him appeared to take an inordinate amount of time and then, more often than not, the response appeared to be less than satisfactory. Mr. Honda was aware that Japanese management of the joint venture was becoming increasingly concerned over Mr. Harper's inability to provide the type of assistance that was most needed.

One major area in which Mr. Harper could have been truly helpful was in marketing. Showa's major marketing strengths had been with traditional wholesalers and retailers, but mass merchandising institutions had been growing rapidly during the past decade and they now accounted for roughly 15 percent of the total retail sales. For packaged convenience items, including processed foods, supermarkets had come to represent a much more important outlet than the aggregate average of 15 percent. In some products the supermarket accounted for over 50 percent of the total sales. Naturally, Showa had been making major efforts to shift its marketing emphasis to supermarkets, but it was confronted with the difficult task of achieving this goal without alienating the still predominant traditional wholesalers and retailers.

In this regard, the Showa management felt that Packard's experience in mass merchandising could be enormously helpful but it had been difficult to tap this resource. For one thing, the Japanese managers of the joint venture complained that Mr. Harper, despite many years of experience in the field sales organization, had proved disappointing. The Japanese managers found that Mr. Harper was excellent in describing his personal experience, but was rather inept in generalizing from his own experience and, particularly, in relating the American experience to the Japanese environment.

After several months of working with him,

the Japanese management of the joint venture had decided that Mr. Harper was not a fruitful source of marketing expertise and that the best way to learn from Packard was to send capable Japanese managers who were familiar with Japanese conditions to the American company for an extended period of training. Mr. Abe, marketing manager of the joint venture, had been the first to be selected for this purpose and Showa felt that his experience had been so satisfactory that it was going to send others for the same training. In the light of these circumstances, Showa management had all but concluded that Mr. Harper was of only marginal value to the joint venture.

Mr. Honda was wondering whether he should mention these facts to Mr. Johnson but found himself in a serious mental conflict. He liked Mr. Harper personally. It was clear to him that Mr. Harper meant well, and he appreciated the difficulty of having to work with Japanese executives. Mr. Harper appeared also to have been well liked by the company's distributors and wholesalers, at least in a social context. There were, however, some disagreements within the Showa management concerning Mr. Harper. Mr. Honda was aware that there was a group of executives who argued Mr. Harper should be replaced by another person more suitable for the position; another group advocated retaining Mr. Harper in the position inasmuch as they thought this would make it possible for Showa management to establish de facto control over the joint venture.

Mr. Honda had to make up his own mind on these issues, prior to meeting with Mr. Johnson the next day.

Case B: Canada Royal (International)

Settling Down to Business

With the difficult period of negotiations over, Carlos became enthusiastic about the new business and very obviously was interested in seeing it grow. He continually suggested potential projects and was also quite confident that the government would be a big customer.

There were other favorable signs; Carlos's son, a recent graduate in industrial engineering, was employed and began his training in Colombia. Under Floriano's guidance, sales were increasing. The year would end with sales of U.S. $17,932,000, up from $14,936,000, and income up from $220,000 to $1,630,000. Executives from Toronto visited with Miranda in Malindrania and Miranda was invited to Toronto. On a trip to Toronto, Carlos discussed the name of the new company with CanRoy officials and won the right to retain the name CanRom rather than CaRom as stipulated in the agreement.

One matter that was not completed, however, was the approval of the terms of reference for the general manager. Although Doug had left a draft proposal with Miranda to be discussed and accepted by the board of directors, no further action was taken and the matter was allowed to drop.

The Honeymoon Ends

The honeymoon did not last long. Within weeks of signing the agreement, Miranda called Strong to enquire about an appropriate fee for the new Chairman of the Board of Directors, Carlos's old friend Souza.[1] Doug realized Malindranians

received large fees for such positions, and suggested that $12,000 might be right. Carlos replied that the figure was too high and that he could negotiate with Souza for $5000. Strong agreed, and later found that Carlos was talking in monthly terms, not annual terms.

The $5000 per month Souza received during 1979 and 1980 was his primary source of income. Strong recalled:

> This was the first time I found out that Carlos was not just a quaint millionaire. When I discovered what he had done and complained he tried to put me in deep trouble with Souza.

Kim O'Leary, CanRoy S.A.'s planning officer, met Miranda shortly after the incident. Carlos's opening remark to Kim was: "Let me tell you the trouble your boss got me into." Kim commented:

> Not only did Carlos mousetrap Doug but he turned around and tried to blame any problems that arose from the deal on Doug. I told Doug that we have to be careful because this guy is out to get us at each other's throats.

Pedro Vargas provided a different perspective on the event. It easily could have been a misunderstanding:

> In Latin America we talk in terms of monthly salaries. It's a habit.

Miranda's son was also creating problems. Strong had tried unsuccessfully to convince the father and son that the best training spot would be in the large operating company in Venezuela. The son preferred Colombia and that is where he went. The son became disenchanted with his Colombian experience and started complaining to his father. Meanwhile his boss in Colombia was complaining that young Miranda never came to work on time, was undisciplined, and was wasting everybody's time. Rodrigues Floriano agreed to hire the son and he returned to Malindrania.

Source: This case was written by Professor Henry Lane and Bill Blake of the School of Business Administration, University of Western Ontario, as a basis for class discussion rather than to illustrate either effective or ineffective handling of an administrative situation. Names, places, and figures have been changed from the actual situation.
[1] Antonio Souza had previously been ambassador to Canada and had recommended Miranda to CanRoy.

These problems, however, were only the beginning in a series of incidents that threatened the stability of the new joint venture.

Employee Participation. Malindranian law stated that the transformation of a company should be an opportunity for the workers to participate as shareholders. During the transition period, INI approved the specific details of the plan to comply with the law's intent. The norm had been to sell the employees 10% of the shares and CanRom's transition plan was consistent with the norm. Both CanRoy and the Miranda group would offer 5% of CanRom's stock to the company's employees.

To achieve employee participation CanRom would, within six months, offer the shares to the Caja de Ahorro, the employees savings plan or credit union, which would arrange the financing of the shares for the workers. Miranda negotiated with INI that if the CanRom employees or the Caja de Ahorro, in their name, did not buy the shares they could be sold to employees of the Miranda group. Carlos was to oversee the sale of shares since he was the national partner.

The six-month period elapsed without an offer being made to the employees. The shares were first offered on October 19, 1979. On October 13, 1979, the employees replied they were unable to give an answer on their willingness to buy the shares since not enough information was provided and no offer of financing support was made. Miranda, however, took the response as a refusal. According to the INI resolution the shares should now be offered to employees of the Miranda group. Carlos took no action in this direction until ordered to do so by INI in March 1980.

Benjamin Almaro, CanRom's lawyer, commented that Miranda would never attend a board meeting where workers were present or let the operation in any way be determined by the workers. As Carlos's apparent delaying tactics emerged, CanRoy became concerned that CanRom might be in an illegal situation subject to legal or administrative actions.

Land Purchase. During 1979 Miranda and Strong agreed that the existing plant site was constrained. Strong wanted a new site in the same locale, preferably in the same industrial estate. Carlos informed Doug that a parcel of land, almost contiguous with the existing site, was available. A tentative agreement on a price of approximately $1,000,000 was made with the owner. Since Strong's spending limit was $500,000 he referred the request to Toronto where it was approved.

The deal fell through and CanRom did not purchase the land. Miranda blamed the failure on CanRoy, claiming it would not approve the price. Strong later learned that it was only an excuse. Carlos had continued negotiating with the land's owner to get the price down to $900,000 and, hopefully, to pocket the difference. He was, as Strong indicated, representing himself not CanRoy. The owner grew weary of the negotiations and ended them.

Building Modifications. CanRom solicited a bid to have the roof raised on its depot. Carlos thought the price quoted was absurd. One of his sons, who was in the construction business, produced a quote two-thirds less than the other—much to Carlos's delight. As it turned out, however, the price was only for project management and did not include labor or materials. When the differences in the two quotes were pointed out, Carlos went wild thinking CanRoy was trying to confuse the situation. Strong offered an explanation for Carlos's anger:

> He probably felt justified. He doesn't read anything and probably just looked at the two numbers. I've handed important documents to him personally and he has called his assistant in to read them.

Accounts Receivable. A common situation in Malindrania and Brazil is for customers to be months behind on payments. When placing a new order, they make a payment on their account. In effect the company is financing them, but it also helps to keep them locked-in as customers. If you sell only to those customers who pay on time, according to Vargas, you risk cutting sales substantially. As a result the required working capital may be three to four times higher than in other countries. Carlos put money into the business to see it grow, but a lot stayed in as working capital, which infuriated him.

Representing CanRoy. Carlos thought he would be representing CanRoy in Malindrania. When told he could not, he was extremely offended according to Vargas:

> Carlos got into the deal probably thinking he could become king of development in San Raphael. But we couldn't let him represent us. He built his empire on practices we can't follow. However, I don't think he realized this before the agreement.

A Strategy for CanRom

Throughout 1979 Floriano built up the sales force and sales. Despite his quick mind and natural ability, however, his independence and CanRoy's seeming disinclination to start new projects began to annoy Carlos. Miranda talked of many new projects during negotiations and expected a large part of his cash infusion to be used for growth. As the year rolled on and little new activity developed, he began to pressure CanRoy S.A. and Floriano. Carlos wanted the company to grow and was determined that there was some business into which CanRom could expand. He would make suggestions like, "Why don't we build a second plant?" or "Let's expand the product line!" Vargas provided Carlos's perspective, as well as CanRoy's:

> He probably began thinking that we sold him the business to get the money out of Malindrania and were no longer concerned about growth. He didn't believe we were trying to grow. We don't jump into markets haphazardly. When you start saying these things, Carlos starts complaining, "Why did I buy this company?"

Every CanRoy S.A. feasibility study further convinced Carlos that CanRoy did not know how to run a business.

By the spring of 1979 relationships were deteriorating all around. Carlos was intervening in CanRom's day-to-day operations and Floriano was complaining. For his part Carlos was increasingly annoyed by Floriano's relationship and allegiance to CanRoy.

A meeting of the Latin American Area CEOs and their wives, sponsored by CanRoy S.A., was held in Cancun, Mexico, in December 1979. Carlos was furious that Floriano was to attend. He called Strong demanding to know who was paying for Floriano's wife and to whom Floriano would be talking. During Floriano's week in Mexico, Miranda took over Floriano's office and started to change product prices, causing great difficulties for Jose Alves, the sales manager and Herme Valadares, the finance and administration manager.

Strong was also becoming concerned about Floriano's performance but for different reasons than Carlos. Although sales were good, Strong was upset that CanRom had not produced a strategic plan to follow. At the meeting in Cancun, Strong told Floriano that Randy Fretz, CanRoy S.A.'s new planning officer, would be visiting San Raphael to help with a strategic plan. Randy recalled that Floriano was content with his daily routine and was cynical about plans. Floriano was convinced that the plans were crazy and would not make a difference. Doug, however, had a different perspective. He told Floriano:

> Randy is coming to see you and you will produce a strategic plan. We won't put any money into Malindrania unless we have a plan, and we certainly won't invest in any of Carlos's crazy schemes without looking into them closely.

Randy went to Malindrania in November. It was the only Latin American country in which CanRoy operated where it was not dominant or at least on a par with its competition. Randy doubted if there were any big opportunities for

CanRoy in the country. He commented on the results of the study:

> The market survey of all possible products was not very positive. The idea of challenging American Industries was suicide. We didn't see anything big so we concentrated on finding some niches.

In May 1980 Floriano presented Randy's strategic plan to CanRom's board. Randy explained the results:

> We were trying to find the correct path for CanRom, but we hadn't found it. There were no clear opportunities. We recommended more market studies to discover some niches. Carlos was very annoyed.

Pedro Vargas provided Carlos's perception of the developing rift:

> Once Carlos realized that the growth was not there; that the money was used on working capital; and that he would not be able to represent CanRoy, he became very difficult to deal with. Investors in Malindrania and Brazil are used to getting fantastic returns. In Malindrania, if you make 20% ROI that's bad business. CanRom is less than 20%.
>
> The money CanRoy got from the transaction was excellent. Nobody in Malindrania would pay that price normally. Carlos was on a big ego trip—like marrying Miss Malindrania, for example. He just accepted CanRoy's statements and projections of profits. He never sent anyone to check the books. The market went down after the transaction and the projections had been optimistic.
>
> To be fair, Carlos's expectations of CanRoy may have been very high about growth. All he thought about was the benefit to him of being involved with a large MNC. It is very difficult for the head of a family concern to understand an MNC and vice versa. The head of a family company sees himself at the very top. He can talk with Doug Strong, but when he has problems, he would call the top people in Toronto. He puts himself at that level.

Shortly after the presentation to the board, Doug Strong sent a long letter to Ian Ferguson

discussing the situation in CanRom. The results of the market survey had led to a strategic plan that advocated holding market position through improved quality and service and by increasing productivity. No major expansions were recommended. This did not sit well with Carlos who was expecting expansion in a number of areas and who was also unhappy with the company's financial performance. Although profits were up, they were below budget. As a result dividends were not covering the interest payments on the money the Miranda group borrowed to buy their majority position in CanRom. Carlos's associates and family began to pressure him to do something about the financial squeeze.

To help alleviate the problem and reduce tension, Strong offered to vote in favor of paying 100% of profits in dividends that year rather than the normal 50%. Carlos agreed and the added payment was made.

Strong's main concern, however, was Carlos's increasingly uncooperative attitude. Doug now believed Carlos would not rest until he was managing the company. Doug recommended replacing Floriano with Vincente Lopez, CanRoy Brazil's chief planning officer. During the previous year Floriano had intervened on a number of occasions to prevent direct interference in CanRom's operations by Miranda, which had made Rodrigues increasingly unpopular (Exhibit 1).

Ian Ferguson's response to Strong's letter acknowledged the deteriorating situation and provided some suggestions:

> The content of your letter shows clearly that you are facing, in the not too distant future, a major showdown with Carlos Miranda, who obviously seems to behave rather erratically. I would like to make the following points for your consideration:
>
> **a.** A change of CEO is unlikely to help the situation over the longer term, if your belief is correct that Carlos Miranda wants to manage the Company.
>
> **b.** If your belief is correct, there is little

Exhibit 1

TO: Mr. I. M. Ferguson
            Canada Royal (International), Toronto

FROM: D. B. Strong

SUBJECT: CanRom and the Miranda group

Last week I spent two days in San Raphael, during which time we had a presentation of the CanRom strategic plan, the annual meeting of the company, and a board meeting.

The presentation, which I should like to review with you at some time, highlighted a few simple facts:

1. Our businesses face growing competition from a number of competitors and, in both, the national capacity is more than double the national consumption.

2. There are two identifiable business opportunities:

"product A"
"product B"

The capital cost of the first is prohibitive to a company the size of CanRom, unless some new production method is developed and made available; the second is possible but flies in the face of the Latin America Common Market which has allocated this product to Peru.

3. The immediate action indicated is essential and difficult, but probably rather pedestrian when viewed by Miranda. It is to hold our markets and our margins by improving quality and service, by improving productivity, and by administering the company more efficiently. In the midterm we seek added value.

Mr. I. M. Ferguson
c/o Canada Royal (International), Toronto

The annual meeting was pretty uneventful except for the dividend question which I describe below; R. Claston has left Carlos Miranda and was not reelected, his place being taken by someone we have not yet met.

The board meeting was the usual shambles we have come to expect. Carlos arrived one hour late and spent the meeting in a very negative posture. I had a number of private conversations with him and also with his son, who is much cooler and more logical, but it is clear that our relationship is on a knife edge.

He obtains the same information as CanRoy S.A. but does not believe this, as he finds it incredible that CanRoy does not require sales performance by product/salesman/area, overtime schedules, hirings and firings by department, etc. He has asked for the degree of information and we shall arrange for him to have it, within reason. There is no doubt that he will not rest until he is "managing" the company.

The results of the company for 1979 were below budget and this attracted a great deal of criticism. He has been aware of this for many months, of course, but has now come under pressure from the rest of the family because the dividend does not match the interest on the loan they raised to buy into Can-Rom. Identifying this as a major problem, and having sat through the strategic conclusions, I suggested he might like to propose a 100% dividend, particularly as the company has P 6.0 m on deposit. This helped a lot and we can expect a further dividend into CanRoy next week, making a total of P 2.9 m sent to Toronto in respect of 1979, before withholding tax.

(Continued)

Exhibit 1 (*Continued*)

The entire two days was dominated by a distasteful issue which he raised immediately on my arrival. He described a Saturday visit he made to the plant where he met (by chance) the personnel officer Barros. Barros invited him (and guests) to his office for a coffee where some photos of a barbecue were on display.

Carlos gave me, as an example of how he was being insulted and shut out, the story that Barros said how surprised he was that Carlos had not attended the barbecue, or the Christmas party, as invitations had been sent to both parties. Carlos then claimed he had asked and been told that the invitations had been sent to the San Raphael office of CanRom for onward transmission. The inference was that Floriano had suppressed the invitations.

3.
02 May 1980

I expressed my shock and asked for an investigation, which showed that it was all a dream. When Carlos raised the issue again at the board meeting I gave him the results of my investigation explaining that there must have been some misunderstanding between Barros and him.

At this he blew up and insisted that Barros be brought to the meeting along with the plant manager. This was done (we had to wait quite a long time) and we went through an embarrassing scene (with the full board present) of Barros trying to convince Carlos that a mistake had been made. Incidentally, the company did not hold a Christmas party at all, but gave hampers instead and the barbecue was for the sales force only and had no directors present.

I have put this down in detail because it may mark the beginning of the end of our relationship. He has also demanded that we bring in the internal audit team to investigate the sales manager whose father-in-law is a large purchaser of our products. I have agreed to do this.

There seems little common ground, other than a desire to make good profits, which is happening at present, and he is completely irritated by the planning process.

There is really no hope of having him sell part of his family's holding, and I doubt if another national group would be interested in buying part of our holding in the face of the majority Miranda position.

My tactics now are

a. To provide as much data as we can.

b. To have our CEO keep in contact with him.

c. To encourage the chairman to keep hold of the board meetings.

d. To change CEOs. Floriano is very unpopular as he stopped much of the early direct interference.

e. To press on with organizational development and the execution of the strategic plan.

DBS:BBL

chance for us to bring in another Malindranian group.

c. Under the circumstances, CanRom's state of affairs will be a constant irritating and time-consuming affair for CanRoy S.A.'s management, since the brunt of the shareholders' problems will have to be handled by CanRoy S.A. so as not to expose Can-Rom's CEO to unnecessary attacks by the majority group who could accuse him of managing CanRom solely for the benefit of CanRoy.

Miranda's Campaign Against CanRom Management

The greatest pressure on Floriano was created by Carlos's campaign against CanRom's sales and finance managers. Carlos claimed that Jose Alves, the sales manager, was acting improperly and that Herme Valadares, the finance manager, was incompetent.

Floriano was being squeezed. The majority partner wanted the two men fired and they were looking to Floriano and CanRoy for protection, and Floriano himself did not want to lose them.

The Sales Manager.   Jose Alves, a Malindranian citizen born in Spain, had been with Can-Roy since November 1973. He had a degree in commercial administration from the National University in San Raphael. Jose had been a salesman and manager of a regional office during the time Dalmau ran CanRom, but chose not to join Dalmau when he left the company. The period following Dalmau's departure had been a difficult one for CanRom. Sales declined precipitously and most of the company's salesforce quit. Finding competent salesmen to replace those departed was almost impossible and regaining lost sales was not easy.

Alves's high volume of sales to his father-in-law disturbed Miranda. Floriano, who knew of the sales, claimed that there was no problem or conflict of interest. Miranda alleged dishonesty. Another opinion expressed by one of the area officers at that time was:

The Malindranians probably saw Alves as a sharp guy they could use in their business; and his father-in-law may have been in competition with the partners.

The Finance Manager.   Herme Valadares, also a Malindranian, had a CPA and a degree from the National University in San Raphael. He had been with a ''Big 8'' public accounting firm for eight years prior to joining CanRoy in 1975. Carlos believed that Valadares was ineffective and maybe even incompetent. The complaints about Valadares's performance included excessive outstanding accounts receivable and discrepancies in expense account reporting and in inventory accounts.

A number of CanRoy officers thought there was another dimension to the problem. Carlos Miranda, it was rumored, had a reputation for bleeding companies dry. He was alleged to have set up downstream distribution companies which would buy from the manufacturing company at very favorable prices. The savings, however, were not passed on to the public, but rather, the excess was retained in the wholly owned distribution companies. Purchases from CanRom had been a point of contention during partnership negotiations. Carlos had wanted his companies to get a better price break than the competition. Strong refused and the partnership agreement stipulated that no company owned by Miranda could buy products at a price better than the best price offered to the trade. Carlos had an apparent modus operandi according to one CanRoy officer:

He wanted Alves and Valadares as shareholders in a company to front for him and to disguise the ownership. He had tried Floriano earlier. When the two refused he started a villification program against the Spanish born!

Doug was becoming more concerned about Floriano who clearly was caught between Can-Roy and Miranda. In June Doug wrote Carlos proposing a new CEO for CanRom—Vincente Lopez. Unfortunately, he would not be available until later that year. A further complication was created by Lopez's reaction. He was leery of working with Miranda and wanted an understanding that it would not be held against him if he could not cope with Miranda or remain in Malindrania very long.

The Audit

By August 1980 matters had deteriorated further. Miranda was sure that Alves, the sales manager, was defrauding CanRom and was pushing harder to have him fired. The report of the internal auditors did not satisfy Carlos and the regular auditors would not sign the company's accounts since the owners were accusing the management of irregularities. At a board meeting held on September 27, Carlos won grudging agreement from CanRoy to bring in another auditor under the guidance of a three-man committee; one member nominated by CanRoy, one by Miranda, and one to be mutually agreed upon. CanRoy's nominee for the committee was Gord Floe, CanRoy S.A.'s financial officer. After a short meeting on September 28, Floe asked for a list of twelve people acceptable to the Miranda group from which he would choose the third member for the committee. At 4:00 P.M. he left for business commitments in Toronto.

That evening a meeting of all the Malindranian shareholders was held. As Carlos explained:

> The Malindranian directors with all the Malindranian shareholders met on September 28 at 7:00 P.M. and agreed to name Cangallo Nelezy Associados,[2] and to send a telex to CanRoy S.A. informing them of the decision of the Malindranian Group which in view of the seriousness of the matters did not want to wait longer to make the audit since, considering the quality of the firm chosen, there would be no problem for CanRoy S.A.

On October 11 Floriano informed Strong that Miranda, not the audit committee, had telexed

[2] This firm was the local representative of an internationally known public accounting firm.

the new auditors requesting an audit of CanRom concentrating on accounts receivable, expense accounts, and inventories. The firm was instructed to report the results of the audit to Miranda and Souza.

On October 18 Floriano advised Strong that Miranda insisted on sending his own auditor, Pedro Sanez, into CanRom at the same time as the new audit team. Floriano again was caught in the middle. Miranda claimed that Sanez had nothing to do with the audit committee but as a vice-president and a shareholder he should be allowed to check anything he liked. Floriano realized the audit would not be external and impartial but was at a loss how to deal with the situation, especially since CanRoy auditors had been in the company repeatedly without board approval. Floriano believed that:

> Sanez is only interested in preparing a negative report as per Miranda's instructions.
>
> If we allow Miranda's plan to go through we will end up with a negative auditor's report, for he will never allow a positive report, and he will use that to attack our managing of the company and devalue CanRoy's position in any negotiations.

A Visit to Canada

In October, Carlos was invited to visit some of CanRoy's installations in Canada. Along with other CanRoy partners from Latin America, he visited plant sites, discussed business, and had the opportunity to relax at a company lodge. Carlos came prepared to have a run at Ian Ferguson with evidence he believed supported his case against CanRom. The evidence was the external auditor's report and documents from a construction company purporting to prove illegal payments by Alves. Strong could not believe Carlos's answer when asked how he had obtained the documents.

"We broke in," replied Carlos.

CanRoy executives had studied the auditor's report, which clearly indicated some administrative sloppiness that should have been caught by the regular auditors, but could find no reason to fire anyone. CanRoy took the position that it would not vote to replace Alves since there was no proof against him. Carlos was incredulous: "He's just a sales manager. He's much less important than your partner." Ferguson's reply: "We attach importance to the individual regardless of the position."

Continuing Problems with the Transformation

October brought more difficulties. A year earlier when the CanRom employees had refused in principle to subscribe to the stock because they were not provided enough information, Miranda had taken it as an outright refusal and eventually (after the date required by INI) placed the stock in trust for his employees. He was now offering it to them, but the trust had raised another disturbing conflict.

Floriano informed Strong that Belgrano (Miranda's company) was offering its employees 10% of the total Class A and B shares in CanRom. Strong telexed Floriano the same day:

> Regarding Belgrano share offer. Please ensure that no offer goes out on CanRom stationery. Would you please transmit the following message to Belgrano for Carlos Miranda:
>
> Am informed today that you are offering shares of CanRom for sale to employees of Belgrano. I should inform you that CanRoy will only contribute B shares in the case of sales to employees of CanRom unless we reach a prior agreement.

Miranda's response to the telex was acerbic. The main points were:

1. The CanRom employees had refused to subscribe to the stock and he was fulfilling the INI resolution through the trust, the establishment of which had been authorized by Strong and Vargas.
2. The problem of illegality had been caused by Floriano and Benjamin Almaro who had failed to establish the trust within the required time.
3. ÇanRom was paying dividends on the basis of mixed company status, which it legally was not

until the INI resolution was fully implemented. The company was subject to fines by INI.
4. Strong should stop intervening directly into CanRom matters as he had been doing for a long time.
5. Ian Ferguson should assess the conflicting viewpoints[3] and resolve the issue.

Almaro also had advised Strong of CanRom's illegal position. Strong, in turn, informed Ferguson by letter. Strong and Ferguson met in Toronto on November 13 to devise a strategy to resolve the irregularity. Strong later communicated CanRoy's official instructions to Almaro.

Almaro was to act on CanRoy's behalf and prepare a letter to INI recognizing the irregularity in the execution of the transformation agreement. The letter was to propose that CanRoy and the national shareholders would jointly offer employees 10% of the company's shares, which would be placed in a caja de ahorro financed by CanRom. CanRom would be reimbursed by dividends payable to the caja. Almaro was to get the union's approval prior to sending the letter. A week later, Almaro and a union representative were to visit INI to discuss the letter. CanRoy's reasoning was that Miranda could not refuse to go along with the plan and that its implementation would end his majority position and therefore his control of CanRom.

The Partners Meet in Toronto

On January 9 and 10, 1981, meetings were held in Toronto to discuss the INI situation, the audit report, and Alves and Valadares. Carlos was particularly adamant about firing Alves and insisted on CanRoy support. CanRoy participants thought they reached an understanding with Miranda:

1. At the next board meeting the powers of the CEO and the function of the board would be defined. The bylaws would also be revised.

---

[3] Carlos sent copies of memos, letters, telexes, and minutes of board meetings on the subject to Ferguson.

2. An audit committee would be formed with two members representing the national investors and one representing CanRoy.
3. Lopez would be sent to San Raphael to start working on the corrections recommended by the auditors.
4. The new general manager should have the right to decide on his management team and should have three months to evaluate Valadares and Alves.
5. Should the national investors decide to dismiss Alves (after Lopez takes over), CanRoy would not veto that decision or construe it as a confrontation.
6. These actions would be implemented by May 1981 and the partners would review progress by the end of August 1981. If either party felt progress was unsatisfactory CanRoy would fix a share price and the Miranda group would decide whether to buy or sell at that price.

The only condition Carlos attacked in the meeting was the firing of the sales manager. If he moved in the board meeting to fire Alves, CanRoy should support him:

> Nothing short of that will satisfy me. I'd rather terminate the partnership and sell my shares.

A week later Carlos wrote that the conditions were not satisfactory. While he was clear that he was not very interested in purchasing the stock, he was not clear on what he did want.

Carlos Visits CanRom's Plant

On January 20, Carlos visited the CanRom plant. The Union president informed Almaro and the plant manager confirmed to Floriano that Carlos had told the workers:

1. CanRoy was opposed to the creation of a caja de ahorro.
2. CanRoy was misusing the union to destroy Malindranian participation in the company.
3. CanRoy was pushing CanRom to bankruptcy. The company was not making enough money for Miranda to pay the interest on his loans.
4. Miranda was unable to contribute 10% of shares as he had already committed that amount to his own employees. All shares for the caja de ahorro would have to come from CanRoy.

Floriano also expressed concern that a strike could occur if action were not taken quickly to establish the caja. He also reported that everything at INI was at a standstill waiting for a new managing director and that little action could be expected for many months.

On February 3 Strong telexed his disappointment at Carlos's rejection of the Toronto agreement stating:

> In view of the obvious incompatibility of our relationship am coming to Malindrania with a financial offer to the national shareholders for the purchase of their shares.

CanRoy Negotiates to Buy Back CanRom

After much internal discussion on share valuation, Strong presented CanRoy's offer to buy Miranda's shares for P 195 per share or U.S. $7.4 million. Carlos rejected the offer on March 24, 1981, but requested that CanRoy's lawyers meet with his lawyer.

On March 27, the lawyers met in New York. Miranda had rejected the offer because it was not based on the same method as used for the acquisition in 1978. His lawyer contended that a factor of six times earnings plus unspecified adjustments yielded a price of P 261. Also the Miranda group would not approve the company's accounts until the management problems were corrected. Accord was required during the negotiations, however, and Miranda offered not to interfere in CanRom's management if Alves and Valadares were fired. Said Miranda's lawyer:

> It may be irrational but let him ask for one thing irrational and he won't do it again. The next time you can be angry.

The meeting ended with the lawyer agreeing that Miranda would provide a detailed counteroffer in fifteen days.

On April 23 Miranda offered to sell his shares at P 416 per share but gave no rationale for this price. However, it was believed to be a result of the high nuisance value that Miranda attached to his shares. The message was interpreted as:

It is going to cost you a lot to get out of this partnership.

The lawyers met again on April 29. It was clear that Miranda was not interested in selling and that he was planning to take over management of CanRom. A draft proposal for terms of reference for the general manager would put him on a "short leash" under the board and proposed amendments to the bylaws would reduce CanRoy's power by shifting decisions to the shareholders from the board of directors.

Options for resolving the situation included withdrawing management and technical assistance, offering to sell for less than P 195 a share and continuing the effort to try and get Can-Roy's job description for the general manager approved. Of paramount importance was the need to protect the CanRoy employees—Floriano, Valadares, and Villifane (plant manager). Miranda's lawyer mentioned the possibility that Floriano could be arrested. To ensure their safety, the three men would leave Malindrania prior to the forthcoming annual general meeting.

The Annual Meeting

CanRom's annual general meeting was scheduled for May 18, 1981. Doug prepared a detailed strategy for the meeting and sent it to Xavier Domtila who would represent CanRoy's interests. Domtila was to vote to approve the accounts of CanRom provided the Miranda group gave their approval without reservation. Particular emphasis was attached to the importance of obtaining full discharge for the company's management. At the subsequent board meeting Lopez's appointment as general manager was to be discussed but only approved if Miranda's group agreed to the job description proposed by CanRoy. Failing that, the Miranda group's appointment was to be accepted. Floriano, having delivered a letter of resignation to be held by

CanRoy's lawyer, was to be in Brazil prior to the meetings. Villifane's letter of resignation was to be left with Almaro as well.

Strong's plans were shattered by Floriano. A medical examination for his Brazilian visa showed that his diabetes and blood pressure were at unacceptably high levels. The combination of his medical condition and the stress of the situation were apparently too much for Floriano, who now took matters into his own hands and fired several key people to protect them from Carlos and others whom he claimed deserved firing (Exhibit 2). The result of his action was that CanRom was stripped of its management personnel. In addition, the sales manager, Alves, went immediately to work for American Industries taking one-third of Can-Rom's business.

The Miranda group expressed surprise at the firing (Exhibit 3) and called a meeting to be held prior to the board meeting to discuss the dismissals. Floriano was instructed to make a short appearance at the meeting, express the position that it was inappropriate for him to be the only representative of CanRoy present, and leave.

The Coup d'Etat

At a shareholders' meeting on May 24, Floriano resigned. The Miranda group quickly moved to appoint Pedro Sanez, Carlos's accountant, as general manager of CanRom. Despite CanRoy's protestations that this action was illegal there was little that could be done to prevent the takeover. In a telex to Xavier Domtila on April 8 Strong stated:

In these circumstances and in the terms of the technical agreement we now consider that CanRoy is entitled to terminate the agreement.

In his conclusion, Strong stated:

Our main purpose now is to extricate ourselves from the continual drain on our time, expeditiously and with minimum cost and publicity.

Exhibit 2
TELEX from Floriano to Strong

MAY 15, 1981
CANROY S.A. SAO PAULO
D. STRONG URGENT

THE MEDICAL EXAMINATION FOR MY BRAZILIAN VISA HAS SHOWN THAT MY DIABETES AND HYPERTENSION, WHICH I THOUGHT WERE UNDER CONTROL, ARE IN FACT AT UNACCEPTABLE LEVELS. APPARENTLY BOTH CONDITIONS ARE HIGHLY STRESS SENSITIVE AND THE LAST TWO WEEKS HERE HAVE BEEN SUPERLATIVE.

THEREFORE, AFTER MUCH DISCUSSION WITH KATHY I HAVE DECIDED TO GO TO CANADA AND TAKE TWO WEEKS HOLIDAY AND HAVE A THOROUGH CHECKUP THROUGH DR. ELLIS IN TORONTO.

ACCORDING TO THE RESULTS OF THE CHECKUP I WILL COME DOWN TO SAO PAULO ALONE OR IF THE RESULT IS NEGATIVE AND CANROY DOES NOT HAVE A ROUTINE LOW-STRESS JOB FOR ME I WILL TAKE RETIREMENT, WHICH I CAN ILL AFFORD BUT WHICH IS A CONDITION SET BY MY WIFE.

THE TIMETABLE IS AS FOLLOWS:

MAY 23	RESIGN AS VICE-PRESIDENT OF CANROM
JUNE 15	PACKING OF HOUSEHOLD GOODS (EARLIEST DATE AVAILABLE)
JUNE 21	KATHY FLIES TO CANADA
JUNE 26	SHIPMENT OF HOUSEHOLD GOODS
JUNE 28	I FLY TO CANADA
JULY 1–15	HOLIDAYS IN KINGSTON
JULY 15–26	MEDICAL CHECKUP, TORONTO

KATHY WILL NOT JOIN ME IN SAO PAULO. SHE IS MORE SENSITIVE THAN I TO THE CONSTANT CHANGES IN PLANS ABOUT MOVING AND IS NOT WILLING TO GO THROUGH ANOTHER PERIOD SUCH AS THE ONE SHE WENT THROUGH SINCE LAST JULY.

FLORIANO

STRONG URGENT

THE TIME TABLE IN THE PREVIOUS TELEX IMPLIES A REQUIREMENT FOR FUNDS FOR MYSELF AND FOR VILLIFANE IF YOU DECIDE HE SHOULD QUIT.

AS OF MAY 27 I WILL NO LONGER RECEIVE FUNDS FROM CANROM AND I WILL RETURN THE COMPANY CAR.

I HAVE DRAWN P 79000 AND CHARGED IT TO MY MOVING ACCOUNT WHICH WILL BE INVOICED TO CANROY S.A. TORONTO. HOWEVER, THIS SUM IS TOO LOW. THE QUOTATION FOR MOVING IS $186 PER 100 LB AND WE HAVE 13000 LB FOR A TOTAL OF $24180 OR P 82048 SO I NEED P 8000 MORE.

I NEED FUNDS FOR THE TICKETS	P	3400
MY LOCAL INCOME FOR MAY	P	12362
CAR RENTAL 33 DAYS	P	6930
HOTEL EXPENSES 16 DAYS	P	5500
TAX ON DIRECTORS FEES	P	9200
TOTAL JUNE	P	37392 OR US$10386 NET

IN JULY I SHALL BE IN TORONTO AND OTTAWA AND WILL NEED EITHER MY NEW SALARY OR AN ADVANCE AGAINST IT. ALSO I HAVE TO COLLECT MY BONUS FOR 1980 WHICH FOR OBVIOUS REASONS I HAVE NOT RECEIVED FROM CANROM.

FOR VILLIFANE IF YOU ASK HIM TO QUIT, THERE IS NEED OF P 18000 PER MONTH, PLUS MOVING, TICKET, AND HOTEL EXPENSES WHICH HE WILL HAVE TO SPECIFY.

WHEN PEDRO VARGAS WAS HERE ALMARO GAVE HIM A BANK ACCOUNT NUMBER THAT WOULD BE KEPT STRICTLY FOR FUNDS DESTINED TO ADVANCES TO VILLIFANE AND MYSELF. THIS BANK ACCOUNT WOULD HAVE TO RECEIVE US$13000 TO 18000 IN THE NEXT TEN DAYS AND THE BANKS HERE ALWAYS TAKE A WEEK OR TWO IN ACKNOWL-EDGING RECEIPT OF FUNDS SO SPEED IS OF THE ESSENCE. PUTTING FUNDS IN ALMARO'S NAME IS THE ONLY CERTAIN WAY OF PREVENTING THEIR EMBARGO BY CM, WHICH HE HAS THREATENED TO DO.

FLORIANO

Exhibit 2 *(Continued)*

STRONG

COMPANY SITUATION

THREE WEEKS AGO CM STARTED THE RUMOR THAT ALVES HAD TAKEN 25 CENTAVOS KICKBACK PER KILO ON THE PURCHASE OF 400 TON OF RAW MATERIAL. THIS WAS A BAREFACED LIE SINCE I DID THE PURCHASING. A FEW DAYS LATER HE STARTED THE RUMOR THAT ALVES HAD BENEFITED FROM THE SALE OF COMPANY CARS TO THE SALESMEN. ANOTHER BAREFACED LIE SINCE I PREPARED ALL THE CONTRACTS AND ALVES JUST SIGNED AS SALES MANAGER. AS A RESULT ALVES WAS PREPARED TO TAKE PHYSICAL ACTION AND I FIRED HIM TO AVOID A SCANDAL. THERE IS NOTHING THAT SAYS THAT AN EMPLOYEE HAS TO TAKE THIS SORT OF INDIGNITIES.

ALSO ABOUT THREE WEEKS AGO WE GOT TO SEE THE MINUTES BOOK AND IN IT WAS THE NOT VERY VEILED ACCUSATION THAT VALADARES HAD ABSCONDED WITH COMPANY FUNDS. VALADARES ALMOST HAD ANOTHER HEART ATTACK AND I FIRED HIM TO PREVENT FURTHER DAMAGE TO HIMSELF AND REPUTATION.

I ALSO FIRED MR. DIAS WHO HAD DEVELOPED A PECULIAR PATTERN OF GIVING CREDIT TO SPECIAL PERSONAL CUSTOMERS, WHO CHEATED OUTRAGEOUSLY ON HIS EXPENSE ACCOUNT, AND WHO SPENT THREE HOURS A DAY DRINKING IN THE CORNER BAR DURING WORKING HOURS.

ALVES IN FIVE DAYS HAS OPENED A WAREHOUSE TO DISTRIBUTE AMERICAN INDUSTRIES PRODUCTS. AMERICAN INDUSTRIES GAVE HIM IMMEDIATELY P 400000 CREDIT.

VALADARES HAS ALREADY A CHOICE OF THREE JOBS AT OVER P 260000 PER YEAR.

NEITHER WILL RETURN TO CANROY ALTHOUGH THEY FEEL VERY FRIENDLY TOWARD CANROY BUT BOTH FEEL THAT THEY WERE NOT DEFENDED AGAINST THAT AMORAL CROOK.

MARIA PALOMARES WHO HAD JUST BEEN HIRED AS VALADARE'S ASSISTANT IS QUITTING END OF THE MONTH. SHE IS AN AUDITOR AND WILL NOT WORK FOR CM AS SHE KNOWS FROM HER AUDITING THE FILTHY REPUTATION THAT CM HAS IN THE COMMUNITY.

LUIS, THE DRAFTSMAN, IS QUITTING THIS MONDAY BECAUSE ARTURO SPOKE TO HIM AS IF HE WERE A SLAVE. ISABELA REQUESTED THAT I FIRE HER AND I REFUSED SO SHE WILL QUIT AS MANAGEMENT'S SECRETARY END OF MONTH. PEDRO, SALES SUPERVISOR IS HOPING TO BE FIRED. IF NOT HE WILL QUIT SINCE HE ALSO WAS MISTREATED BY ARTURO. DAVID, THE SALES ADMINISTRATOR IS IN THE SAME BOAT. PHILIPE, THE WAREHOUSE MANAGER, DITTO. THE OTHER SALES SUPERVISOR ROBERTO CALDENA IS A HABITUAL ALCOHOLIC WHOM WE WERE ABOUT TO FIRE. HE WILL STAY. THE ACCOUNTANT, ANOTHER HABITUAL ALCOHOLIC, WHOM WE WERE IN THE PROCESS OF REPLACING. HE WILL STAY.

IN SUMMARY THE COMPANY AS OF THE 1 JUNE WILL HAVE NO CEO, NO SALES MANAGER, NO FINANCIAL OFFICER, NO SALES SUPERVISORS, NO SALES ADMINISTRATION, NO DRAFTSMAN, NO CREDIT AND COLLECTION HEAD, AND IN THE PLANT, IF SO DETERMINED, NO PLANT MANAGER.

PLEASE NOTE THAT MRS. VILLIFANE HAS BEEN VERY SICK IN MALINDRANIA AND VILLIFANE WOULD LIKE VERY MUCH A MOVE TO MONTEVIDEO OR BA WHERE SHE WOULD BE CLOSE TO ALL HER RELATIVES IN MONTEVIDEO.

AS A RESULT OF THE DEBACLE OF THE LAST TWO WEEKS THE COMPANY WILL:

A. LOSE 15 PERCENT OF EXTRUSION SALES DUE TO LOSS OF THE PUSH FROM ONE OF THE BEST SALES MANAGERS IN THE COUNTRY,

B. LOSE 50 PERCENT OF MOLDED SALES. THIS LOSS NOT RECOVERABLE,

C. LOSE MORE SALES SINCE CM HAS NOT SIGNED THE LETTER OF CREDIT FOR CANROY TO SHIP,

D. HAVE A PROFIT FOR 1981 OF LESS THAN P 2,700,000,

E. NOT BE ABLE TO RECOVER ITSELF FOR ONE AND A HALF YEARS IF CM LEFT TODAY AND CANROY STAYS, AND WE WILL NEVER RECOVER THE MOLDED MARKET, AND OF COURSE IF CANROY LEAVES AND CM STAYS THERE SHOULD BE LITTLE LEFT IN ONE YEAR.

I FORGOT ONE ITEM. THE UNION IS COMING TO THE TUESDAY BOARD MEETING TO FACE MIRANDA. IF HE CONTINUES BLOCKING THE SAVINGS ASSOCIATION WHICH IS IN THE LABOR CONTRACT THEY WILL HAVE GROUNDS FOR A FULLY LEGAL STRIKE.

FLORIANO

Exhibit 3
TELEX from Floriano to Jellinek

MAY 16, 1981
MR. MIKE JELLINEK[1]
CC: SR D. B. STRONG

YOU HAVE JUST RECEIVED A TELEX SIGNED BY SEVEN OF THE FOUR NATIONAL DIRECTORS ON THE CANROM BOARD.

THE CONTENTION THAT THEY ARE SURPRISED AT THE FIRING OF MR. ALVES AND VALADARES IS ONE ENORMOUS LIE. FOR ONE WHOLE YEAR MR. CARLOS MIRANDA AT EVERY BOARD MEETING AND IN CONVERSATIONS WITH D. STRONG HAS INSISTED THAT MR. ALVES BE FIRED. THERE ARE IN THE MINUTES OF THE BOARD SEVERAL MENTIONS BY MIRANDA OF MR. ALVES'S INCOMPETENCE. HE TRIED TO PRESENT SPURIOUS EVIDENCE THAT MR. ALVES WAS DISHONEST. HE PUT MR. ALVES'S FIRING AS CONDITION FOR NEGOTIATING IN NEW YORK AND MIAMI. AND IN THE LAST MONTH HE INTENSIFIED THE RUMOR CAMPAIGN AGAINST ALVES ACCUSING HIM OF DISHONESTY WITH FRIENDS AND CUSTOMERS. THE HARASSMENT THAT MIRANDA HAS PILED ON ALVES WOULD HAVE LANDED HIM IN COURT AND THE COMPANY IN TROUBLE IN ANY NORTHERN HEMISPHERE COUNTRY.

I FIRED ALVES AS A RESULT OF MIRANDA'S ONE YEAR OF PRESSURE AND HIS UNSPEAKABLE HARASSMENT OF AN EMPLOYEE.

THE SAME APPLIES TO MR. VALADARES EXCEPT THE PRESSURE TO FIRE HIM IS ONLY 6 MONTHS OLD. THE MINUTES OF THE BOARD HAVE AN ACCUSATION BY MIRANDA THAT VALADARES ABSCONDED WITH COMPANY FUNDS, A PREMEDITATED AND BAREFACED LIE. MR. VALADARES IS AN AUDITOR BY PROFESSION AND SUCH AN ACCUSATION COULD RUIN HIS CAREER. MR. VALADARES'S HEALTH HAD BEEN DETERIORATING AS A RESULT OF THIS HARASSMENT.

I FIRED VALADARES AS A RESULT OF MIRANDA'S 6 MONTHS OF PRESSURE AND THE DAMAGE THAT VALADARES WAS SUFFERING.

THE NEXT POINT IS THAT ALVES AND VALADARES BY LAW REQUIRED DOUBLE PAY ON FIRING SINCE THEY ARE NOT CONFIDENTIAL PERSONNEL UNDER ANY CIRCUMSTANCES. HOWEVER IF THERE WERE DOUBTS MIRANDA WROTE A LETTER TO INI TO JUSTIFY PUTTING MR. BALTES, A FOREIGNER, AS DIRECTOR IN WHICH HE SAYS HE NEEDS BALTES BECAUSE IN THE COMPANY HE HAS NO CONFIDENTIAL EMPLOYEES. THIS LETTER IS PART OF THE MINUTES OF THE BOARD.

ONE MORE POINT ABOUT MY AUTHORITY TO FIRE AND HIRE. I AM STILL OPERATING UNDER THE ORIGINAL GENTLEMAN'S AGREEMENT BETWEEN STRONG AND MIRANDA THAT I WOULD RUN THE COMPANY AS I HAD UNDER CANROY UNTIL CHANGED BY THE SHAREHOLDERS. SO FAR THE SHAREHOLDERS HAVE NOT CHANGED ANYTHING.

---

[1]President of Canada Royal (International).

This means selling out or eliminating Carlos from direct contact with the company.

Assumption of control by the Miranda group alarmed Citibank. Its loan of $4.7 million to the Miranda group to purchase the majority position had been conditional on CanRoy management of CanRom. The appointment of Sanez led the bank to recall the loan.

At the request of Sanez and with CanRoy's agreement Villifane returned to run the plant. This action demonstrated CanRoy's willingness to cooperate and negotiate, but it was stressed that cooperation would cease if a suitable agreement was not reached. Villifane was told that if he did not want to stay in Malindrania, a job would be found for him elsewhere in Latin America.

In the following weeks Carlos attempted to bypass Strong and communicate directly with Mike Jellinek in Toronto. Carlos claimed that CanRoy S.A. was blocking his communication with Toronto. Strong, learning of a widening gap between Henrique and Carlos, requested that Jellinek telex Henrique to confirm that Strong was the CanRoy representative responsible for dealing with CanRom. In the meantime Carlos requested technical assistance directly from Jellinek. Jellinek replied that he had sent Carlos's request to Strong and Strong telexed Carlos on July 5.

> You will have inevitable delays in our response if you continue to address CanRoy in Toronto. Since the events of May 24 when an illegal appointment of general manager was forced by the majority group of shareholders CanRoy no longer feels that a modus vivendi is achievable. Consequently, we see a lawyer's meeting to be useful only if the purpose is to find an acceptable way of terminating the relationship between CanRoy and the national group.

By August, Carlos was firmly in control of CanRom and had fired any remaining management personnel. Although Strong suspected sales were down drastically, no monthly reports were being forwarded to CanRoy S.A. so this was impossible to verify. Strong was particularly concerned about steps being taken by Carlos to reduce accounts receivable. He was pressuring customers to pay their debts or forcing them to refinance at interest rates of 21%. Eighteen percent was the legal maximum in Malindrania and CanRom was open to charges of usury. Almaro was pressing for cancellation of the technical cooperation agreement and reactivation of the claim to INI on behalf of CanRom workers. He also proposed bypassing Carlos and dealing only with his brother. Although Strong was upset by the

situation he was unwilling to get into a major dispute with Carlos, preferring to safeguard CanRoy's reputation as far as possible.

On August 5 Strong met with Henrique Miranda to try and resolve the CanRom situation. Henrique's suggestion that the Malindranian shareholders be allowed to manage the company for two years was ruled out by Strong who said it violated CanRoy's worldwide policy. It became apparent that Henrique was not interested in managing the company but was unhappy that Floriano had ignored some board resolutions. Strong stated that he would not place CanRoy personnel in any position where they could be harassed by Carlos again and that if things went wrong with the company under his management CanRoy's passiveness would change. At the conclusion of the meeting, the CanRoy representative agreed to prepare a new offer for the shares of the Miranda group for presentation the following day.

The following day Henrique refused the offer which represented repayment of the Miranda group's original investment (rights issue and contribution to capital) plus 51% of the retained earnings for 1979 and 1980. Both parties agreed, however, that something must be done to regularize the present company situation, and that evening Doug and Henrique met for private discussions. The meeting confirmed an earlier impression that Henrique was not likely to confront Carlos and split the family. Strong wrote Mike Jellinek:

> I had a drink with Henrique at his request. He told me that Carlos had been difficult all his life and was getting worse, that Carlos wanted to be president of the company and the family did not wish to stand in his way, and that Carlos insisted on the opportunity to manage the company. I pointed out that CanRoy understands this, but does not approve.
> Henrique said that we should keep in touch with each other and he gave me his private telephone number.

On August 6, Doug sent a letter to Henrique outlining the points he felt were essential to resolve the situation. Key recommendations included approval of the accounts for 1980, cessation of the practice of charging illegally high interest rates on accounts receivable, and the urgency of installing experienced management in CanRom.

Some Outcomes

Over the next few months the impasse continued. By December 1981 little had changed in CanRom's operations except that sales were steadily declining. Almaro analyzed developments since Carlos's takeover in a letter to Strong. Extrusion sales were down 18% over the same period the previous year and 28% behind forecast. At board meetings Miranda attributed the poor performance to the con-

traction in the economy, particularly in the construction industry. But American Industries figures for the same period showed extrusion sales rising (Exhibit 4). CanRom had moved from a 50% share of the market to a 20% share.

Miranda continued to use the name CanRom and a logo very similar to CanRoy's. CanRoy was continuing in its effort to stop this practice which it maintained misled consumers, was confusing, and weakened the company's Malindranian trademarks.

Villifane was at the center of a strange turn of events. When Floriano resigned from CanRom he told Villifane to return home to Argentina, and CanRoy S.A. offered Villifane a job there. However, Villifane argued he had been dismissed from CanRom and therefore from CanRoy, and he began legal action in the

Exhibit 4
CanRom Comparative Sales

1. Royex Sales (100s units)

	American Industries			CanRom		
Month	1980	1981	Diff.	1980	1981	Diff.
March	387	382	− 5	248	355	+107
April	391	390	− 1	253	333	+ 80
May	415	425	+10	359	309	− 50
June	365	414	+49	224	286	+ 62
July	403	425	+22	352	226	−126
August	397	463	+66	321	213	−108
September	374	391	+17	235	246	+ 11
October	395	409	+14	390	275	−115

2. Roymold Sales (100s units)

	CanRom		
Month	1980	1981	Diff.
March	99	114	+ 15
April	141	107	− 34
May	146	55	− 91
June	153	77	− 76
July	191	77	−114
August	173	88	− 85
September	171	43	−128
October	185	38	−147

Malindranian labor courts. CanRoy S.A. requested that Miranda not settle any claim with Villifane since he had been offered a job. Miranda ignored CanRoy S.A. and settled with Villifane out of court for $175,000. Miranda then reemployed Villifane in his old job and billed CanRoy for a share of the settlement costs.

Rodrigues Floriano returned to Canada needing urgent medical attention:

> He was not well when he left Malindrania. Doctors say he could work but not in a stressful situation and definitely not in Latin America. He's convinced he won't work again.

At fifty-two years of age Floriano retired from CanRoy.

INI had not issued a decision on the transformation process within its required time limit. In effect, this was a decision against CanRoy. CanRoy appealed to the Ministry of Finance. The minister found that the transformation was illegal and that Miranda's trust was not in compliance with INI conditions. CanRom had to reoffer the shares to the caja de ahorro. When Miranda responded that the shares had been sold to the trust, the minister replied that Carlos could sell his shares to whomever he wished (as long as they were nationals) but that he still had to offer 10% to the caja.

According to the minister, the transformation process should be repeated starting November 29, 1981, under INI's guidance. INI called Miranda and CanRoy together. At the meeting Miranda accused CanRoy of many illegalities, so INI decided to send its own audit team into the company to make a determination of the situation.

Miranda appealed to the Supreme Court at the end of 1981 to suspend the effects of the Minister of Finance's decision, while the court decides on the merits of the appeal, and to overturn the decision. Very significantly Carlos went to the court alone, without his brother—the first open indication of a family split.

On May 6, 1982, Doug Strong received a letter from the lawyer Almaro. The INI auditor's report was very damaging to Miranda and recommended annulling the transformation. If it was annulled, CanRoy would have to buy back Miranda's shares and would own 100% of CanRom again.

Doug laughed as he read the letter and began to recall the events of the past four years. Why, he wondered, had the partnership failed and what should be done differently the second time around?

Case C: International Bank of Malaysia Limited

Near the end of a four-week management development course in Hong Kong Mr. Ian Dankworth,[1] branch manager of the Kuala Lumpur

Source: Copyright 1974. The University of Western Ontario. This case was prepared by Associate Professor Joseph J. DiStefano for the sole purpose of providing material for class discussion at the School of Business Administration. Any use or duplication of the material in this case is prohibited without the written consent of the school.
[1] All names and locations have been disguised.

office of the International Bank of Malaysia, was reflecting on a serious personnel problem in his own office. Two of his department heads, Mr. Wong Chin Poh (Credit) and Mr. Zainuddin Bin Abdul Wahab (Administration), were causing serious disruptions to morale and performance through their efforts to discredit each other. Under ordinary circumstances Mr. Dankworth might have dealt with the situation as a "simple personality conflict between two managers.'' But in this case the problem was complicated by the fact that Wong was of Chinese ancestry while Zainuddin was Malay.[2]

This not only intensified their hostile feelings toward each other, but also constrained the options open to Ian for resolving the difficulties. He knew that any action he took would be subject to the scrutiny of the office employees and the federal government, both of whom were sensitive to the delicate relations between these two racial groups which accounted for the bulk of Malaysian citizenry. In fact, the government had recently moved toward increasing regulation of the racial mix within companies operating in Malaysia. As he considered these issues in light of the course he was just completing, Ian knew that he would soon be back in Kuala Lumpur and faced with resolving the problem.

Background

International was a worldwide commercial banking organization. Although the headquarters were located in the United States, foreign offices conducted their domestic affairs fairly autonomously within the limits of corporate policies. The Malaysia Operation was typical of the bank's organizational approach to international markets. Head Office was concerned with only those local branch activities which were necessary to their attaining certain objectives, which included the administration of truly ''international'' transactions (e.g., dealings of corporate customers with the foreign offices) and the handling of credit applications which were beyond the approval limit of local management.

The Kuala Lumpur branch had been in existence for many years and employed a total of fifty-nine employees. As general manager, Dankworth was responsible for the overall performance of International's Malaysian affairs. He gave direction to the various department

heads on corporate matters and when necessary saw to the integration of departmental activities. John White as senior representative coordinated International's ''major business developments,'' that is, those areas subject to the immediate interest of Head Office but ongoing in Malaysia. White also handled certain administrative services rendered to a few important clients. The local bank branches simply administered the details of any large deals prearranged by Dankworth or White.

Cheong Shul Lee as the regional manager for the domestic branch network had responsibility for all local operations and for the integration of International's requirements as dictated by Dankworth and White.

With the exception of Dankworth, White, and Wahab, all other managers were Chinese (an organization chart showing the reporting relationships and deployment of personnel is included in Exhibit 1.) Each maintained a staff relationship with the branch managers and provided functional assistance while monitoring branch activities to ensure adherence to precisely defined procedural rules and policies.

The normal work activities varied from department to department. The Credit Department was comprised of a small group of specialists who performed a critical function. All credit applications from the branches came to them for authorization. If the amount of the application was beyond their own approval limit (as set by their department head, Wong, and the regional manager), they nonetheless reviewed it and recommended the approval or refusal of the application before passing it on to the next approval level. Also within this department was the Credit Administration group who was in charge of policing all approved credits through the use of records and security documentation jointly required and coordinated by themselves and Administration. They inspected any existing credits issued by the branches, Dankworth, or White to check for any discrepancies from approved procedures.

Zainuddin Wahab headed the Administration

---

[2] Both men are Malaysian citizens. Throughout the case the use of ''Chinese'' and ''Malay'' will refer to ethnic origin not citizenship.

Exhibit 1
International Bank of Malaysia Limited
Organization Chart 1973

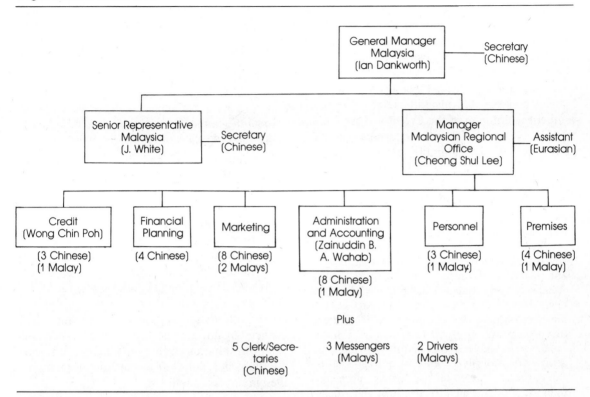

Plus

| 5 Clerk/Secretaries (Chinese) | 3 Messengers (Malays) | 2 Drivers (Malays) |

Department, which served two basic functions. It assumed responsibility for the internal accounting of the regional office itself and exercised central accounting control over all branch offices. This department accumulated and distributed pertinent figures to the other departments (e.g., loan records for credit) and prepared reports for Head Office. This department also served as the "foreign exchange center," reporting the consolidated branch position to the South East Asian foreign exchange control regarding the bank's position (their commitments of local currency for the prearranged future transactions of their clients). They also reviewed and authorized minor deviations from established procedures and/or rates when requested by the branches. Such exceptions were granted when the overall value of the business relationship with the customer warranted compromise on some minor issue.

The Accounting Department was the information center. This function required frequent interaction with and cooperation from the other department heads and personnel. For example, International was a commercial bank but certain clients pressured for personal loans for their VIPs. While approval in principle was granted by Dankworth, Zainuddin assessed the marginal cases and provided any nonstandard loan documentation such as information on the political or economic ramifications involved with any particular request. Many special applications which originated through White or the domestic branches, via the Credit Department, often required only administrative processing. They did, however, demand effort since approval of these applications was usually expected within a brief time after their submission. Zainuddin was quite capable of handling these procedures and had thus gradually gained some measure of control over all the largest domestic cases.

Since these activities, together with normal loan/accounting responsibilities, required the frequent interaction of the Credit and Administration Department heads, interpersonal difficulties caused considerable impact on the effectiveness and efficiency of the operation. Ian reviewed several examples of negative effects resulting from their squabbles.

- The Financial Planning group assessed the profitability of various customer deposit accounts which were required by the Credit Department as one of their many criteria for setting loan rates. Administration was required to provide several detailed reports concerning loan performance, deposit account balances, and so on. This meant that the Administration group had to deal with the branches in drawing the pertinent records together. Occasionally a competitive situation arose where Credit required precise costing information to assist in pricing an attractive loan opportunity. Administration might then hinder a rapid turnaround, citing branch tardiness as the cause.

- Personal loan applications were channeled into the regional office via the Credit Department to be endorsed by them. Since this was an exceptional service for a commercial bank, these applications might be blocked or delayed by Administration. Although the conflicts were based on a genuine difference of opinion regarding the anticipated cost-benefit trade-offs, Administration and Credit were both clearly unwilling to present and negotiate their respective positions in a conciliatory manner. The resulting delays hindered the business development efforts of the branch managers.

- "Even our office sports club has been affected," Ian complained. He explained that the club was partially sponsored by the company and that he encouraged participation by office personnel in its activities. Since Wong was on the committee

which operated the club, Zainuddin took every opportunity to criticize it. One example occurred when the committee decided to sell two of the carrom boards it owned.[3] They circulated a memo through the office requesting those interested in purchasing one to submit bids in writing by the following Saturday at noon (the end of the normal five-and-a-half-day working week). Zainuddin, who apparently didn't see the circular until 9:00 A.M. on the Saturday in question, stopped by the desk of the club secretary and said, "I just heard about the carrom boards and want to make a bid. But I have to leave for an appointment."

When noon arrived and the committee convened to open the bids, she told them of his comment. However, they decided to proceed as planned, opened the bids, and sold the boards. On Monday Zainuddin gave the secretary his bid (which turned out to be higher than any of those submitted on Saturday) and was furious when he discovered that the boards had already been sold. He exploded in full view of the office staff, yelling that it was obvious that Wong was at the bottom of the decision to deny him a fair chance. Again, Ian was forced to intervene and calm the situation even though he, as patron of the club, normally left the operating details to the employee committee.

About the Men Involved

Ian Dankworth, age forty, had joined International in 1956 in Australia where he had been born and raised. He had first moved to the Far Eastern operations in 1962 and had been in several locations. He had received no specific training for his present position, which he had occupied since 1971, other than the course he was just finishing. However, he had spent five years in Malaysia before becoming general manager and had previously served in the senior representative post. The terms of service for expatriates were geared to a higher cost of

---

[3] Carrom is a game roughly comparable to pool. The boards have four pockets and "seeds" about the size of checkers are used.

living and therefore allowed them and their families to enjoy a greater degree of luxury and comfort than their U.S. or European counterparts. Also the Malaysian organization was such that Ian was given greater responsibility than he could ever hope to have been given had he remained in Australia or gone to the U.S. operations.

Because of the time spent in Malaysia and because of his outgoing personality, Ian had frequent social contact with both Malays and Chinese (more with the latter). He learned to speak Malaysian and found himself a regular visitor to Malay and Chinese homes for festive occasions.

On the management course he was an active participant in both the classroom sessions and social gatherings. In the office he appeared totally in command. He managed the steady stream of people and problems that flowed to his desk with calm and decisive assurance.

As Ian thought about the two men whose behavior was concerning him, he recognized both surface similarities and marked differences in their backgrounds and experience. Zainuddin's history with International dated from his high school graduation in the mid-1960s and included two years at the U.S. home office. His Malay ancestry dated back several generations, and he was from a very "good" family in Kuala Lumpur where his father was a prominent lawyer. Zainuddin was a Muslim who appeared from his outward behavior (e.g., regular attendance at the Mosque each Friday and observance of all religious duties) to be devout.

Wong came from a fairly well-to-do family and was the son of a Chinese businessman. He was born in Malaysia, but his ancestors came from China. A university graduate in the late 1960s, he too had spent a training period in the United States in 1970 shortly after joining International. However, his time at the home office was only nine months. Wong was Buddhist, as were many of the Chinese in Malaysia. He did not appear to be as strict an observer of his faith as was Zainuddin.

Both men were married and lived in Petaling Jaya, a very large industrial and residential area approximately five miles outside Kuala Lumpur. They commuted each day by car from P.J., as it was commonly known. Their homes were of similar construction and size—brick with tile roofs—and were provided by the company.

In describing the men Ian characterized Zainuddin as a very nice person with a good sense of humor who often exercised it even at his own expense. "He's likeable, alright," said Ian, "but he's rather idle and is weak in technical areas." Ian went on, "He's liked by his staff, but is seen as a bit of a 'nit,' a joker, even by them."

Another problem existed which affected the normal office discipline of his staff. Zainuddin would turn up late for work, disappear for hours without an explanation or reason, take extended lunch hours, and this despite repeated requests, threats, and instructions from management to comply with standard office routine. Naturally, when senior management disciplined other staff on similar matters, they would invariably ask why Zainuddin could get away with it and not them.

Evaluating Zainuddin's effectiveness in the office, Ian said, "He's frankly useless, a conclusion shared by every senior representative I've ever had within one month of their arrival." "But," he added ruefully, "his presence is a political necessity."

Ian described Wong as "immature, with a childish sense of humor, more given to pranks. He's a hard worker and technically competent," Ian said, "but his staff senses his immaturity so he doesn't gain the respect that he should as an executive." Ian concluded, "He makes a contribution and has the potential to develop."

Social and Political Factors

Ian realized that the problem between his department heads was not just a personality clash concerning only himself and these two men.

More specifically, the government was trying hard to get more Malays into business and industry to improve their standard of living. But the Chinese had the reputation of being the real workers in the country. The commonly held stereotype viewed them as shrewd (sometimes bordering on dishonest) businessmen who would work eighteen hours a day if it were rewarding to them. In contrast, urban Malays were seen as living hand-to-mouth. Malay farmers were viewed as more hardworking but as being difficult to change and having a short-range perspective. For example, although technical developments made it possible to raise more than one rice crop a year, the paddy planter maintained the one-crop pattern since it was sufficient for his needs.

Conventional wisdom thus explained the steady progression of Chinese to high levels because of their ambition and willingness to work. But because of government action they were kept from the very top positions which political pressure reserved for Malays.

It was only a few months ago that a Ministry of Labour representative came into the International office and requested to inspect the salary book. From that data he extracted information on the percentage of Malays, Chinese, Indian, and others at each salary level. Later, Ian received a letter saying that the racial composition of the staff did not represent that of the country. It stated that the government objective was to achieve the following distribution at all levels in the organization.

Malays	30–40%
Chinese	20–30%
Others	Balance

The company was required to give written assurance that they were undertaking to meet these government aims.

Ian knew that when the Labour Ministry representative inspected their records next year he would expect an increase in the proportion of Malays. And he realized that the scrutiny would include the executive levels as well as the per-centage of total employees. This fact worried him as he thought about how to resolve the problems between Wong and Zainuddin. The situation was further complicated since he knew that Cheong, the regional office manager, would soon be replacing John White, who was being transferred to another post. Ian also knew that, although no serious sanctions had yet been exercised, the government could revoke International's charter in Malaysia if International did not comply with government policy. (See Exhibit 2 for a description of some of the motives and actions of S.E. Asian governments on related issues.)

Ian had observed the government stand on this issue toughen since the riots in Malaysia in 1969. Although these riots were rooted in communal divisions based on racial, economic, social, linguistic, religious, and rural/urban differences their immediate cause was the election results that year. During this election the Alliance Party, a coalition of United Malays National Organization (UMNO), Malayan Chinese Association (MCA), and Malayan Indian Congress which had ruled the country since independence from Britain in 1957, suffered unexpectedly heavy losses. Three opposition parties drawing support from Chinese urban electorates plus the militant champion of Malay rights (Pan-Malayan Islamic Party) combined to prevent the Alliance Party majority from reaching the two-thirds mark necessary to change the Constitution . . . a change the Alliance Party and Prime Minister Tungku Abdul Rahman had strongly promoted during the campaign.

Immediately after the results were announced, the MCA split from the Alliance announcing that it could no longer represent Chinese interests within the party. The three Chinese opposition parties responded with great excitement. The following day victory parades were organized and a mood of general celebration spread through the Chinese population. The following night, sparked by Malay activists in Rahman's UMNO, they were met with heckling by the opposition. Reportedly, pork

Exhibit 2
Some Second Thoughts about Foreign Investment*

During the past decade many billions of dollars have been poured into Southeast Asia by American, Japanese and Western European investors. In most cases, the host countries welcomed these investments in the belief that they would create new job opportunities for labor forces that were expanding at a frightening rate. Yet today in much of Southeast Asia there is a growing sense of frustration about foreign investment—and a growing dislike of it.

The reasons for this disillusionment are numerous. Often foreign investors prefer to cooperate in their joint ventures with members of the local power elite—or groups recognized as enjoying the protection of the power elite. And in a number of Southeast Asian countries, Chinese entrepreneurs have become the favorite partners of foreign investors; they are regarded as "natural" business partners partly because they can mobilize capital and partly because they are thought to have more business experience and acumen than the native entrepreneurs.

In Indonesia, as in some other countries, native entrepreneurs have already started to voice great worry over this pattern. They realize that it would be impossible for them to compete successfully against such a powerful combination of capital, business experience and political power. Meantime, the general public views with concern the way in which the nation's resources are falling more and more under the control of foreign capital without immediate or visible benefit to the populace at large.

Ignorance and Optimism

My own belief is that the disappointment with foreign investment in Southeast Asia has been caused both by foreign investors' ignorance of local needs and by overoptimistic expectations in the host countries about the contribution which foreign investment can be expected to make. Specifically, host countries have put too much faith in the ability and willingness of foreign investors to create the widest possible job opportunities. In fact, in many cases, economic realities lead a foreign investor to choose the most profitable technology without regard to the social needs of the host country.

*By Mochtar Lubis, Editor and Publisher, *Indonesia, Raja*.

A recent study conducted by Louis T. Wells, Jr. and published by the Southeast Asia Development Advisory Group of the Asia Society of New York gives a most illuminating insight into this problem. In his paper "Economic Man and Engineering Man" Wells reports, among other things, on his survey of eleven cigarette factories in Indonesia. Of the eleven, he found that three used capital-intensive technology, five used intermediate technology and three used labor-intensive technology.

To get a picture of what this means in terms of the use of labor, he reported that to produce a million cigarettes a month, the labor-intensive factories would need forty workers apiece, the intermediate factories would need six workers each and the capital-intensive factories only three workers.

Who Decides?

To make matters worse, Wells found that one of the two foreign investors who were using intermediate technology in their factories had decided to switch to capital-intensive technology, explaining that he had to modernize his plant in order to be competitive. This kind of behavior not only defeats the hopes of Southeast Asian governments that foreign investments will create large numbers of jobs, but it actually compounds the problem by inducing domestic capitalists to adopt sophisticated technology, too. One can already see the results of such competition in the Indonesian textile industry. This was a business which the government had once hoped would use labor-intensive technology and so absorb large numbers of workers. Instead, new investors have put in more capital-intensive technology.

In short, the experience of the last decade in Southeast Asia has shown how governments lose the ability to direct the flow of foreign capital into the various sectors of their economy and also to plan the kind of technology foreign investors should introduce. Obviously, the governments themselves are at fault when their foreign-investment bureaus or committees become merely license processing offices, and the foreign investor is left to decide for himself in which sector of the economy he will invest and to make his own decisions about production targets, marketing policies, etc.

(*Continued*)

Exhibit 2   (*Continued*)

To take Indonesia as an example once again, bitter protests have been voiced there against foreign investment in the bottling of soft drinks, the manufacture of ice blocks and ice cream, accounting services, insurance and building. In these fields, the more efficient, foreign-capitalized companies are driving the small domestic firms out of the market. (By contrast, the Malaysian government now aims at allocating at least 30% of all contracting business in Malaysia to Malaysian entrepreneurs.)

None Too Soon

One can easily foresee serious tensions developing in the near future between the peoples of Southeast Asia and foreign investors there. It would be prudent and wise for both governments and foreign investors to take a long, hard look into the causes of such tensions and to make the necessary adjustments. To begin with, I believe that every host country should reestablish full control over the technology introduced by foreign investors. Beyond that, it should direct foreign investors into the economic sectors where their presence is needed and will contribute most effectively to economic development in coordination with the overall national plan. Finally, the host country and the foreign investor should jointly regulate prices, establish a fair profit margin for the investor, insure an equitable division of jobs between expatriate and domestic personnel—and, of course, prevent any unfair disparity of income between expatriate and domestic personnel.

All of this, naturally, implies the development of a new business philosophy by many foreign investors. They must be keenly aware that while they are welcome in most Southeast Asian countries and allowed to earn fair profits there, the people of Southeast Asia expect from foreign investment a meaningful contribution to their own welfare and progress. It is not yet too late to establish a constructive new approach by both foreign capital and the governments of Southeast Asia—but it is none too soon either.

---

was thrown at some participants, a grave offense to the Muslims who view it as unclean.

Whatever the immediate cause, serious rioting followed, and the opportunity to vent the racial enmity which had been smoldering for many years was quickly seized by both sides. Conservative government estimates gave 200 killed and blamed the rioting on the Communists.[4] Chinese suffered disproportionate casualties, a fact many attributed to the total domination of the police and armed forces by Malays. In the aftermath of the riots the Constitution was suspended and a power struggle continued from May to September. Rahman was accused of being soft on the Chinese, and he counterattacked by ousting two of his critics from the Alliance. Finally, his resignation was forced (with an appropriately face-saving story) and the legislature was reconvened in February 1970.

[4] *Far Eastern Economic Review*, June 12, 1969, p. 698, reported 400 dead and thousands homeless.

The residue of bitterness about these events, which in themselves originated in historical racial friction, could still be seen four years later. Ian knew that this bitterness was a force he must consider in deciding what to do about Wong and Zainuddin.

Long- and Short-Range Problems

Ian realized that he had to deal with the short-run problem of what to do about the two men. But he also knew that how he dealt with them would affect his options on handling the quotas established by the Ministry of Labour. Several alternatives were open to him. He could duplicate positions, pairing a figurehead Malay with a Chinese who would perform most of the tasks. Or he could simply stall and continue with his present staffing arrangements. Another route would be to attempt to comply with the government requirement as quickly and fully as possible. Additionally, he might plan a judicious mix of these approaches.

Exhibit 3

Attendance of Racial Groups by School Year, 1953

School Year	Malay		Chinese*		Indian	
	Number	**%**	**Number**	**%**	**Number**	**%**
1	106,597	31.4	64,949	29.6	18,313	42.9
2	73,971	22.0	51,732	23.6	8,360	19.6
3	63,539	18.8	41,126	18.8	5,925	13.9
4	46,872	13.8	28,622	13.1	5,005	11.8
5	32,191	9.4	20,620	9.4	3,113	7.3
6	14,847	4.6	12,244	5.5	1,914	4.5
Total	338,017	100.0	219,293	100.0	42,630	100.0

Source: The Economic Development of Malays. Baltimore: The Johns Hopkins Press, 1955.
*Secondary school enrollment drops from 6765 in grade 7 to 166 in grade 12.

As he considered these options, he started to lay out the facts he would need to make a decision. For example, there were financial implications. The total bank income in 1971 was M$12,400,000 and by 1972 had jumped to M$15,800,000. Overhead expenses as a percentage of gross income (total revenue less deposit interest) were about 72% (M$9,100,000) in 1971 and up to about 76% (M$12,008,000) in 1972. About 50% of overhead was taken up by salaries. The executive staff earned between M$1000 and M$2000/month (Zainuddin and

Wong were both below M$1500/month). Executive trainees started between M$500 and M$550/month and were increased to M$1000/month upon completion of the training program, which usually ran from eighteen months to two years.

But financial concerns were not the only factors influencing his decision. Ian worried about the availability of competent Malays who he knew constituted a much lower proportion of the high school and university graduates relative to the Chinese. Although, primary educa-

Exhibit 4

Estimated Percentage of Enrollment by Level of Education

Level	1965			1972		
	Total No.	**Enrollment**	**%**	**Total No.**	**Enrollment**	**%**
Primary	1,394,643	1,217,309	87	1,629,502	1,530,000	94
Lower secondary	608,068	231,555	38	713,271	625,486	88
Upper secondary*	361,748	41,753	12	463,283	101,013	22
Post secondary†	324,831	14,482	4	446,202	24,798	6
University	792,769	2,835	0.4	1,135,942	9,439	0.8

Source: V. Kanapathy. *The Malaysian Economy: Problems and Prospects.* Singapore: Asia Pacific Press, 1970.
*Includes general, vocational, technical, and agricultural schools.
†Includes technical and agricultural colleges and all teacher training institutions.

Exhibit 5
Selective Census Data

% Malay by Census Year

	1921	1931	1947	1957	1964
Malays	54	49.2	49.5	49.8	50
Non-Malays	46	50.8	50.5	50.5	50

Distribution of Population, 1964

Total number	6,916,000
Malays (including indigenous tribes)	50%
Chinese	37%
Others (mainly Indians, Pakistanis, and Ceylonese and 16,000 Europeans)	13%

Shift in Rural Population Makeup (in thousands)

	1947	1957
Total	3607	3611
Malay rural	2153	2521
Non-Malay rural	1454	1090

Source: Chak-Yan Chang. Political Violence in Malaysia and Singapore. Unpublished M.A. thesis, University of Western Ontario, Canada, 1971.

Exhibit 6
Educated Manpower 1965–1980 (Estimated Stock and Requirements)*

Occupational Level (1)	1965 Stock (2)	Manpower Needed, 1965–1970					1970 Stock (8)	Additional Requirements 1970–1980 (9)‡	1980 Stock (10)	Additional Requirements 1965–1980 (11)
		To Fill Vacancies (3)	To Replace Expatriates (4)	To Replace Retirement, Deaths, etc. (5)†	To Fill New Jobs (6)	Total (7)				
Total	128,380	5,581	2,552	19,255	32,122	59,510	187,890	85,350	273,240	144,860
Professional	7,938	742	1,828	1,190	2,876	6,636	14,574	10,887	25,461	17,523
Subprofessional	12,487	1,219	698	1,872	3,902	7,691	20,178	15,658	35,836	23,349
Skilled	107,955	3,620	26	16,193	25,344	45,183	153,138	58,805	211,943	103,988
Agriculture	7,816	571	60	1,172	7,028	8,831	16,647	7,879	24,526	16,710
Professional	275	75	58	41	438	612	887	663	1,550	1,275
Subprofessional	1,035	101	2	155	1,676	1,934	2,969	2,304	5,273	4,238
Skilled	6,506	395	—	976	4,914	6,285	12,791	4,912	17,703	11,197
Technical	66,906	1,995	701	10,035	14,033	26,764	93,670	39,616	133,286	66,380
Professional	1,300	148	470	195	481	1,294	2,594	1,938	4,532	3,232
Subprofessional	4,538	648	231	680	803	2,362	6,900	5,354	12,254	7,716
Skilled	61,068	1,199	—	9,160	12,749	23,108	84,176	32,324	116,500	55,432
White collar	53,658	3,015	1,791	8,048	11,061	23,915	77,573	37,856	115,429	61,771
Professional	6,363	519	1,300	954	1,957	4,730	11,093	8,286	19,379	13,016
Subprofessional	6,914	470	465	1,037	1,422	3,395	10,809	8,000	18,309	11,395
Skilled	40,381	2,026	26	6,057	7,681	15,790	56,171	21,570	77,741	37,360

Source: Educational Planning and Research Division, Ministry of Education, Malaysia.

*These figures do not include the number of teachers, health service personnel, and scientists.

†Based on 3% of annual replacement rate.

‡Based on 74.7% of 1970 stock at professional level, 77.6% at subprofessional level, and 38.4% at skilled level.

Exhibit 7
Banks in Malaysia

	Number of Firms by Year			
Ownership	**1965**	**1966**	**1967**	**1968**
Indigenous	6	7	7	7
Foreign	15	14	13	11

tion was given in Malay, Chinese, and English, it was voluntary and the dropout rate was high (see Exhibit 3). Furthermore, as late as 1955 there were no secondary schools giving instruction in Malay. The 1971 data showed 1,464,000 in primary schools, 539,700 in secondary schools, and 35,900 attending university or other institutions of higher education.[5]

Figures showing the estimated percentages of enrollment by level of education for 1965 and 1972 are given in Exhibit 4.

Because the pressure to lure the few Malay graduates available was exerted on all firms, the salary offers were increasing rapidly. Ian knew of two American oil firms who were paying new trainees (some of whom had not graduated from university) as high as M$750/month. And he expected the competitive "bidding" to get worse until the supply of graduates increased significantly. Because of the limited supply of teachers, this was unlikely to occur in the near future despite the increasing enrollments in primary schools and heavy government spending on education (about one-fifth the budget).

Ian also examined other demographic data for any significant trends which might affect manpower planning. These are presented in Exhibits 5 and 6.

Enjoying the opportunity to consider these

[5] *Far Eastern Economic Review*, 1973, Asian Yearbook, p. 215.

issues away from the day-to-day pressures of the office, he realized that whatever decisions he made had to be put in the context of an increasingly antiwhite climate.

A hedge against the future might be to advise Head Office to sell to or merge with a local banking network through which International's services could be maintained within the local domestic market in an "undisturbed" operating manner. As he looked at the data shown in Exhibit 7, he realized that the Malaysian government might force such a change in the future.

Conclusion

Considering the problems he faced when he returned home next week, Ian summarized the decisions he needed to make. In the short run he had to resolve the difficulties between Wong and Zainuddin or suffer the consequences of decreasing office morale and efficiency. In the longer run he had to deal with the government pressures to increase the percentage of Malays throughout the K.L. office of International . . . and he knew that visible progress had to be made in a reasonable period. As he finished his preparation for the next day's classes and thought about his fellow managers who were already enjoying a cool beer downstairs, he wondered what he should do about these problems that were so closely related to each other.

PART III
Managing the MNC

There are similarities in the ways that organizations manage their foreign business activities and their subsequent corporationwide structural modifications—similarities that often result from contextual factors, whether political, economic, or cultural. Likewise, there are differences that we can attribute to historical development, to the nature of the involvement abroad, to the requirements of the host country, and to cultural differences in general. An examination of both these similarities and differences is crucial to understanding the structure of international business.

To a large degree, structure is what determines an organization's ability to deal with its environment. This is particularly true of the multinational organization, which operates simultaneously in several different environments. In the following chapters, we will discuss the impact of the internal as well as external environments on the multinational corporation's structure and process. Structure affects organizational climate, innovative capacity, decision making, and control process. Keep in mind that no one structure is *ideal*. However, whatever structure is chosen as most appropriate must remain flexible in order to be proactive, responsive, and adaptable.

Because of the growing complexity of organizational design, effective management requires extensive coordination cutting across direct hierarchical lines of organizational structure. Accordingly, Part III will first examine the development of international business, the rise of the MNC, the structural similarities and differences in operations at the international level, the changing environmental forces, and the structural modifications that MNCs have adopted in dealing with these variables. We will briefly review the major determinants of structure—both the internal and external environments. Next, we will discuss

Factors affecting multinational structure.

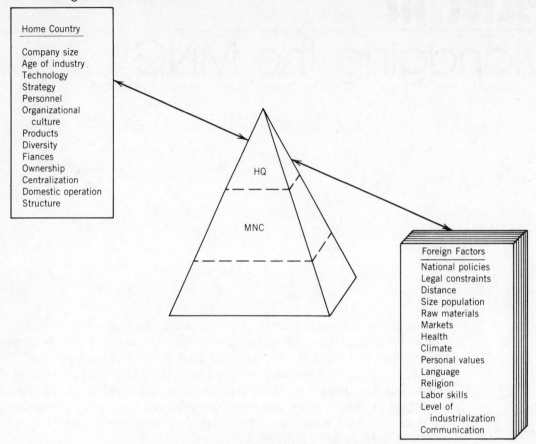

Home Country

Company size
Age of industry
Technology
Strategy
Personnel
Organizational
  culture
Products
Diversity
Fiances
Ownership
Centralization
Domestic operation
Structure

HQ

MNC

Foreign Factors

National policies
Legal constraints
Distance
Size population
Raw materials
Markets
Health
Climate
Personal values
Language
Religion
Labor skills
Level of
  industrialization
Communication

the problems and criteria for designing the appropriate structure and choosing the most appropriate formats. We will also consider organizational processes, because they are usually sensitive to cultural impact. Finally, we will highlight the issue of organizational change. This is an important consideration because managers must be alert to the pressures for change, sensitive to cultural difference in attitudes toward change, and able to proact for changes in design rather than react haphazardly as changes occur.

The material will be covered in the following sequence:

Chapter 8 discusses internal organizational processes, components of structure, and the variations in MNCs' organizational structure.

Chapter 9 reviews the MNCs' environmental characteristics.

Chapter 10 integrates the internal and external views of the MNCs.

Chapter 11 then concentrates on the relationship between subsidiaries and host countries.

Chapter 12 highlights selection and training of international managers.

We shall begin Part 3 by reviewing the major concepts of organizational structure and then proceed to review the basic variations in MNCs' structure.

CHAPTER 8
Variations in the Organizational Structure of MNCs

THE PURPOSE OF STRUCTURE

Every organization must arrange its activities to accomplish its tasks and goals—that is, to be effective. If an organization is created to make profits or to provide services, or both, it must make the most efficient use of its resources to accomplish those goals. An organization is a coalition of interest groups sharing a common resource base, paying homage to a common mission, and depending on a larger context for its legitimacy and development (Miles, 1980; Cyert & March, 1963). Yet, however strong the common interests within an organization, the groups involved must work together in some way to be effective. This need for collaboration is the purpose of structure.

Organizational structure (or chart) provides the blueprint for this arrangement. Structure determines the relationships among organizational parts, between the parts and the whole, and between the organization and its environment. This blueprint contributes to the processes by which the separate pieces fit together to serve a common purpose. As such, patterns of interlocked behaviors emerge as a result of "assembling ongoing interdependent actions into sensible sequences that generate sensible outcomes" (Weick, 1979, p. 30).

Therefore, effective organizational design requires the skillful application of internal division of work, internal control and coordination, and the management of relations with the external environment. Effectiveness depends on the *fit* between the organization's parts and processes that structural design determines. What needs to be done (the task) and how it gets done (the process) can be either facilitated or hindered, depending on the structure of this interaction. Organizational structure differentiates and integrates components of complex

307

organizations both formally (through rules, procedures, and hierarchies) and informally (through organizational culture, social pressures, and informal patterns of communication).

To better understand structure and its purposes, we should look at the organization's parts, processes, and interactions. This will provide us with an understanding of how organizations can be designed to optimize their performance; it will also provide an understanding of how problems can arise when structures do not correspond to various demands—both internal and external—that face the organization.

First, we should consider the major dilemma of structure. This can be conceptualized in terms of differentiation and integration.

Differentiation

Structure is generally expressed in terms of the *division of work* and the methods of *control* and *coordination*. The division of work among task-specialized units reflects the internal complexity within the organization, which in turn determines the range of each unit's task and its employees' qualifications.

The differentiation in organizational structure is two-dimensional: horizontal and vertical. The differences among units at the same level reflect the degree of horizontal differentiation. As we will see later, horizontal differentiation also enables the organization to deal with environmental complexity by creating numerous departments responsible for different aspects, such as public relations, social responsibility, and so on (Lawrence & Lorsch, 1967). Vertically, organizations divide responsibility and decision-making tasks by level of authority. The number of layers of management reflects the different levels of responsibility and authority. These differences result in the degree of vertical differentiation.

Integration and Coordination

As organizations grow, they tend to become more structurally complex. Coordination and control become increasingly important. To create a unity of purpose, management must integrate separate organizational units. This is accomplished through several mechanisms that can be hierarchically arranged in terms of cost and involvement (Lawrence & Lorsch, 1967; Mintzberg, 1979; Thompson, 1967; Galbraith, 1974; March & Simon, 1958). When differentiation is minimal (i.e., when uncertainty, interdependence, or both are minimal), simple methods such as rules, standard operating procedures, and written policy statements can be used. As differentiation increases (i.e., as uncertainty and interdependence increase), so does the need to process information. This can be accomplished, for example, by referring problems to one's superior and by advanced planning to establish targets and goals.

Other mechanisms used to implement this process are committees (standing or ad hoc), whether in the form of task forces, meetings, reporting systems, or performance appraisal. Meetings serve the function of sharing information,

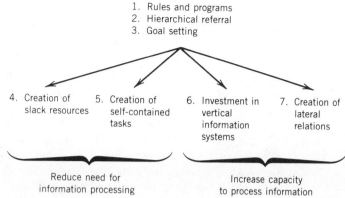

Figure 8.1 Organizational design strategies.

Source: J. R. Galbraith. ''Organization Design: An Information Processing View,'' *Interfaces* 4:29, May 1974. Reprinted with permission.

making and reviewing policy decisions, spelling out rules, dividing and coordinating work and responsibilities. Reports and reporting systems are the effective tools of control. Performance reviews and appraisals serve to motivate and guide managers toward corporate goals, help set and monitor priorities, organize work, and guide managers' career paths. (For examples of the creative use of committees, see the Appendixes regarding Exxon, ITT, Dow Chemical, and General Mills.)

Used in these ways, committees tend to serve primarily a planning function: devising and coordinating planning systems throughout the company. While these mechanisms coordinate, plan, and control—and thus represent a centralizing or centripetal force—the diversity and complexity of operations represent decentralization, thus serving as a centrifugal force.

When these methods are no longer adequate, however, managers may become overloaded with information. Organizations can choose to handle the overload by creating slack resources, or they can reduce interdependence by creating self-contained units. They may also increase the organization's information processing capacity through the use of vertical information systems (such as MIS) or by promoting lateral relations. The simplest form of lateral relations is direct contact between managers and employees around a particular problem to achieve ''mutual adjustment'' (Mintzberg, 1979). As these methods become inadequate, organizations can opt for other mechanisms, such as creating liaison roles between departments, task forces, and teams. In the most extreme cases of interdependence and uncertainty, organizations can change their structure to a matrix format wherein managers function as partners on particular projects. In this manner, lateral relations permit joint decision making at the lowest possible level of competence, that is, where the information and expertise to interpret and act are available (Galbraith, 1974) (see Figure 8.1).

Given a choice of available integrating mechanisms, different styles of coordinating and resolving conflict emerge. Thus, integration can be defined by the quality of the interaction, which can range from forcing (giving orders), to smoothing (avoiding issues), to confrontation (directly stating the issues) (Lawrence & Lorsch, 1967). The type and nature of integration depend once again on the amount of uncertainty and the nature of the interdependence of the task units. Without integrating their components, organizations can become chaotic and internally competitive; they can suffer an increase in conflict levels and lose sight of overall organizational objectives.

The approach to defining and coordinating can be routine: establishing rigid roles, specialized functions, precisely defined duties, and an explicit command hierarchy. These are the characteristics of a "mechanistic" organization structure, which has been shown to be most effective in stable environments. Another approach is more flexible and dynamic (i.e., nonroutine). Roles, duties, and functions in this approach are much less formal and less rigidly defined; communications flow in all directions. This approach characterizes the "organic" organization structure found to be more effective in dealing with unstable environments (Burns & Stalker, 1961).

The relationship between differentiation and coordination is unidirectional: the more differentiation and specialization that exist, the more effort to be invested in integration and coordination is necessary. Solving this dilemma requires a decision by management that is based on various conditions including such variables as technology, organizational size, product, and environmental conditions.

STRUCTURAL CHARACTERISTICS OF ORGANIZATIONS

So far, we have described structure in terms of the different task units or departments within the organization, or its complexity, that result in the extent of differentiation, that is, the differences between units. We also have characterized structure by how explicitly the means and ends of work are stated through written policies, procedures, operating manuals, job descriptions, and goal statements (e.g., annual reports). In this way, roles and tasks are clearly specified. The extent to which this specification occurs reflects the degree of formalization.

We can also describe organizational structures in terms of the amount of control exercised at each level. The degree of an organization's centralization reflects the extent to which directives are passed down as decisions are made at the top. On the other hand, decentralized structures reflect participation in planning and decision making at lower organizational levels. The distribution of control reflects the number of levels of management (defined as vertical differentiation) and the number of subordinates reporting to an immediate supervisor at a particular level (defined as span of control). The first variable gives the organization its "height"; the second determines its "width." Together, these two variables determine the organization's shape or configuration. For example, a "flat" organization has fewer levels of management and a greater number of employees reporting to one supervisor. Webber's (1947) model of

Required Structural Flexibility

		High (Organic)	Low (Mechanistic)
Required Structural Differentiation	**High**	High complexity Low formalization Low centralization 1	High complexity High formalization High centralization 2
	Low	3 Low complexity Low formalization Low centralization	4 Low complexity High formalization High centralization

Figure 8.2 Organizational structure profiles.

Source: R. H. Miles. *Macro Organizational Behavior.* Santa Monica, CA: Goodyear, 1980, p. 26.

bureaucracy evolved from the organizational need to pursue coherent purposes.

Hall (1962) has delineated the main dimensions of the bureaucratic model of organizational structure:

- Hierarchy of authority
- Division of labor
- Rules
- Procedures
- Impersonality
- Technical qualification

Although various theorists and researchers have claimed that the bureaucratic approach represents an ''ideal'' model that is not applicable to many organizations, the dimensions are definitely helpful in providing a yardstick against which to measure and examine various organizational structures. Moreover, the model is a classic framework for relating the individual to structural dimensions. According to this model, organizations can achieve this goal by centralizing authority, specializing functions, standardizing procedures, formalizing policies, and increasing the levels of management. Successful companies varied in these dimensions in response to external and internal demands (Woodward, 1965; Lawrence & Lorsch, 1967; Pugh et al., 1968).

Figure 8.2 demonstrates how the degree of required structural differentiation and flexibility determines the extent of an organization's characterization along these dimensions.

Given these characteristics of organization—complexity, formalization, centralization, and configuration—different structural profiles emerge even within the same industry. Figure 8.3 shows the differences in profiles between two manufacturing firms in England (Pugh et al., 1968). Different profiles have

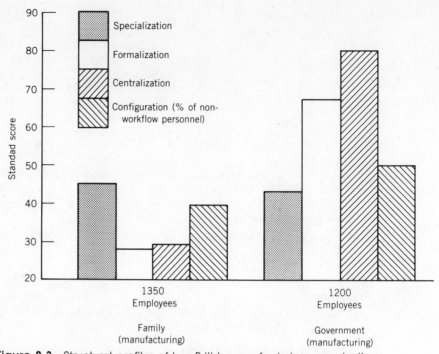

Figure 8.3 Structural profiles of two British manufacturing organizations.
Source: D. S. Pugh, D. J. Hickson, C. R. Hinings, and C. Turner. "Dimensions of Organizational Structure," *Administrative Science Quarterly* 13:80, 1968.

different implications for organizational processes, such as leadership, communications, decision making, goal setting, control, motivation, and interpersonal relations (Likert, 1961). In highly centralized organizations, for example, top management provides an autocratic style of leadership: it makes the decisions, communicates from the top down, plans and sets goals at the highest levels, and exercises control (e.g., of budgets, performance, etc.).

Structural profiles also influence an organization's capacity and ability to innovate. For example, centralization may reduce the number of new ideas generated because communication cannot flow upward, but it may facilitate implementation of those ideas by giving orders (although resistance and noncompliance can occur as a result of "forcing"). Complex organizational structures, on the other hand, tend to generate more ideas, yet their diversity and difficulties in integration can impede their implementation. Formalization also tends to reduce the number of ideas by restricting information flow; like centralization, however, it facilitates implementation by specifying what is to be done and how to do it (Zaltman, Duncan, & Holbek, 1973). Organizational climate and style of conflict management can also affect the generation of ideas and the facility of implementation. The more open and trusting the climate and the greater the use of problem-solving approaches to conflict management, the more willing the members generally are to contribute ideas and efforts to bringing about change (Argyris & Schon, 1978).

The degree of centralization and decentralization required in an organization is a function of the dynamic balance of controlling forces on one side and diversity and complexity on the other. The primary concern is how to maintain responsiveness yet also provide coordination and control.

The locus of decision making at the unit level represents decentralization; at the corporate level, it represents centralization. The advantages of decentralization are that decision making occurs closest to the operation and environment, thus enhancing flexibility, adaptability, and timely decisions; it also prevents information overload at top management levels. Moreover, it serves as a way to motivate, train, and develop managers and to stimulate initiative and creativity. Granting more autonomy to area managers not only enhances a positive company image in that region but is often required by local governments as well.

The disadvantage of decentralization is the difficulty of maintaining a unified corporate strategy and uniform policies and procedures; realizing economic benefits through rationalization also becomes problematic. In addition, decentralization requires a large amount of managerial resources and competence.

The decision to centralize or decentralize operations relies on several criteria related to characteristics of the industry, the company, the environment, the decision, and the information available (see Table 8.1). Company characteristics include the size of the firm, the nature of the business, the profitability of the subsidiary, the degree of integration and interdependence in multinational

Table 8.1   Centralization or Decentralization?

One way to approach the subject of control of international business is to consider it to be largely a choice between centralization of decision-making at the senior corporate level and decentralization, in which many decisions are delegated to the country or regional level. The pro-centralization arguments stress that it leads to

- Greater conformance to corporate goals and policies;
- More careful nurturing and utilization of corporate resources;
- Greater cost-effectiveness, since duplication of activities and resources can be controlled; and
- Better handling of crises or emergencies, since power and authority are already centered where crucial decisions can be made and follow-through can be monitored.

The arguments for decentralization are based on the premise that local business managers frequently know the conditions in their countries better than anyone on the corporate or even regional level. Thus, decentralization means

- Some of the decision-making burdens on a few senior managers can be lightened, and, thus freed, they can spend more time charting corporate strategy;
- Instead of having to refer many matters up the hierarchy, individual businesses or units can operate with greater flexibility and speed;
- Delegation of responsibility can develop experienced managers at lower levels that form a talent pool for general executive positions; and
- A unit's success or failure is a function primarily of its *own* management, and therefore performance may be clearly measured.

Source: Reprinted from *Business International*, p. 90, with the permission of the publisher, Business International Corporation, New York.

operations, the technology used, the markets, strategies and objectives, the organizational structure and communication systems, the senior management's interests, and the availability of managerial talent and competence (Prasad & Krishna Shetty, 1976; *Business International,* 1981; Stieglitz, 1965; Alpander, 1978).

Another factor to consider is the degree to which operations are interrelated. Conglomerates tend to have fewer central controls, while firms with a smaller number of foreign operations tend to have more centralized authority. The firm's size is related to the number of operations: the larger the firm, the greater the amount of information needed to process for decision making. Also, the level of environmental complexity or its high rate of change will have similar effects. Without decentralization, this can result in information overload at the top or in a lack of crucial information due to a breakdown in communications. Decentralization is also related to the degree of geographic dispersion of operations—the greater the scatter, the less the control. The nature of the business is also important. For example, if foreign operations are sales subsidiaries, this allows for greater decentralization than heavy manufacturing, which requires economics of scale and rationalization.

However, where local conditions require modifications in product or process, or where local governments require technological transfer, research and development (R&D) functions tend to be decentralized. Rapidly changing or shifting markets also require greater decentralization of decision making to ensure timely responses to threats and opportunities (i.e., a competitor's entry into the market or new market potentials). Different strategies or patterns of growth affect the decision because firms that have developed through acquisitions tend to allow greater autonomy (often determined by legal charter), whereas strategies of internal development result in greater centralized control. Organizational structure is a major determinant in achieving these goals. For example, worldwide product or regional formats are difficult to control; matrix structure is even more so. Decisions take longer, tend to be of poorer quality, and lose power because of geographic separation. Communications systems facilitated by technological advances can result in greater central control. The degree of internal management consistency refers to the interrelation and reinforcement of the companies' management philosophies, reward systems, span of control, CEO interest, and style. This will affect the degree to which decentralization is allowable (*Business International,* 1981).

Environmental characteristics related to the choice of decentralizing are the need for knowledge of local conditions and customs, the rise in nationalism, and the levels of local instability and complexity.

The nature of the decision to be made affects the level at which it is made. Decisions related to the overall strategy, allocation of financial resources, staffing, and control tend to be made at the top as operating decisions are not subject to national variance (R&D, engineering, quality control). Product adaptations and marketing strategies tend to be decentralized. The amount and quality or availability of information will also determine the level at which decisions are made.

National differences also affect the degree of decentralization. European MNCs seem more willing to permit greater local control, whereas Americans lean toward strong centralized management. This may reflect cultural differences in attitude toward obedience and authority (Budde et al., 1982) as well as the previous colonial history of European countries (Daniels & Arpan, 1972). An exception to the European corporate trend of delegating decision making is that a number of firms have begun to centralize for cost-saving purposes under well-specified conditions, such as a sufficient volume of material available from a few sources. However, where production processes larger amounts of commodity-type material (e.g., food industry), it may be most cost-effective to purchase locally (*Business International,* 1981).

The formal organizational structure, which is usually represented by the organizational chart, should be perceived as providing a framework for the dynamic ongoing processes within the organization. Indeed, various theorists describe organizations in terms of the decision-making process (Simon, 1961) and information processing systems (Galbraith, 1974). These models stress the importance of individuals' positions in various junctures of communication and decision making, their ability to act rationally, and their capacity for processing information and, finally, provide for systematic patterns of interrelationships. The design elements involved are authority and responsibility of each executive, kinds of information flow along lines of communication, and procedures for channeling and processing information (Stopford & Wells, 1972).

Organizational processes define the relationships between people, the means for arriving at and coordinating decisions, and executive communication. They also define the indirect reporting relationship, as well as the relationship between *line* and *staff* functions. Moreover, organizational processes provide a time dimension in which these activities occur. They provide an "overall results" orientation and allow for flexible and speedy responses. Designing and implementing organizational process, therefore, places decision making in the context of systematic evaluation of planning alternatives.

Before proceeding to describe the variations in MNC structure, it is necessary to view them not only from a functional viewpoint, but also in historical perspective. The reason for such a review is the influence historical antecedents have on the evolving structural forms as well as their rate of transformation.

HISTORICAL PERSPECTIVE

First, we should recapitulate the evolution of business abroad in an historical perspective. The Industrial Revolution (1830–1900) was a period marked by great technological innovation. Entrepreneurs seized upon opportunities that new technologies created. Industrial centers emerged in every country as rural farmers became urban workers.

The subsequent era of mass production (1900–1960) emphasized efficiency in production, economies of scale, and the development of marketing approaches. The search for markets gave rise to the export trade. The postindustrial era

(1960–present) has witnessed an increase in service industries, multi-industries, and trends of internationalization. Companies, including the industrial giants, began seeking ways to minimize the cost of goods, labor, and transportation and to increase the benefits of new markets abroad.

However, recent trends in the international arena (e.g., nationalism, political instability, and economic decline) have served to curtail the MNCs' previous freedom to operate as they desired. Foreign governments have begun to place more regulations and restrictions on business to better control local economic development. The international climate is currently less receptive to business than before. It stresses social responsibility not only in business ethics but also in contributing to the quality of life and of the work life (*Business International,* 1976; Franko, 1978; Rose, 1977).

The 1960s and 1970s have been called "the age of the MNCs." In the 1960s, American MNCs emerged to dominate the international scene. U.S. dominance peaked in the mid-1960s as a result of the advanced technology, greater risk-taking propensity, and higher tolerance for ambiguity of American firms. Going multinational was considered "fashionable"; as a result, many firms entered the international scene—often without adequately assessing the consequences. In the early 1950s, they had pursued aggressive strategies by taking advantage of cheap labor. But by the late 1960s, the dollar had once again become overvalued, and exporting had become difficult. American involvement abroad was once again defensive. As a result, American MNCs developed Third-World manufacturing capabilities, since Third-World exporting was more profitable (Rose, 1977).

The 1970s, however, brought disenchantment. American MNCs faced pressures from local governments and from labor and liberal groups whose attacks stemmed from host-country economic malaise. Local competition and competition from the Third-World, Japanese, and European MNCs increased, resulting in a loss of the American MNC market share. In addition, market needs had changed. The marketing of labor-saving devices and luxury items came under criticism as inappropriate and wasteful, and efforts to reach the middle class abroad through advertising were limited. Respect for American brand names declined. American MNCs also failed to adapt their technology to the smaller scale required in developing countries. And because the United States was better at innovation than at preserving its market share, MNC activity declined even further (Rose, 1977; Franko, 1978).

As host countries began to develop economically, technological and managerial knowledge spread. Host-country governments began to insist that American firms "unbundle" technology. The result was that in some observers' eyes, the MNC eventually had "nothing new to offer." Moreover, host governments' ability to locate sources of capital in world banks and development funds further restricted the MNCs' power.

The American MNCs experienced other disadvantages as well. The companies' foreign status seemed increasingly obstructive to their activities. Some MNCs kept low profiles abroad, to make themselves less obvious targets for host-country hostilities. They also behaved in a more collegial, less adversarial manner. Non-American MNCs, however, seemed better able to work collectively with governments, unions, and competitors (Franko, 1978).

Between 1971 and 1975, American MNCs sold 10% of their subsidiaries (only one-third of them voluntarily) as a result of inadequate earnings in low-technology, high-competition industries (Rose, 1977). Exceptions to this trend were the critically integrated MNCs (e.g., oil MNCs) had a unique advantage—a worldwide system of marketing contacts—so that when the OPEC nations formed their cartel, they could not sell their products effectively without the MNCs' experience and distribution channels. But even in this area, more and more crude oil (some estimate it at 40%) has recently been traded directly by the producer governments. During the early 1970s the formation of new subsidiaries also declined significantly. Still, the threat of American dominance was felt, and the non-American MNCs' expansion rate has surpassed that of the U.S. MNCs (Franko, 1978).

The multinational company is not threatened by extinction, however, as long as host governments can control access to markets and local financing and as long as MNCs still have technology, management techniques, and a worldwide marketing network. This condition of mutual need and complementary capabilities provides the basis for cooperation. It also indicates the need for companies to be more sensitive and responsive to the local environment (Janger, 1980; Heenan & Keegan, 1979; Jain & Puri, 1980). We should consider these factors along with those reviewed in previous sections to understand and evaluate the implications of the MNCs' various structural forms.

STRUCTURAL FORMATS
National Subsidiary Structures

European companies tend to use a national subsidiary structure rather than a system of international divisions. In this case, national subsidiaries report directly to the top without intermediate or intervening levels of management, such as international or regional divisions. Each subsidiary is treated separately and has high visibility, having what is often referred to as a mother–daughter relationship (see Figure 8.4). Reporting is not as formalized (Duerr & Roach, 1979) as in the international division format.

A national subsidiary structure helps to grant autonomy to affiliates—something that is of increasing importance in a nationalistic world. It promotes strong ties with the host country, enhancing sensitivity to change and fostering long-term responsiveness. Granting autonomy also promotes the development of career expatriates. Another key advantage of this structure is that top management and board members are directly involved: problems are handled at the top in such a way that responses are most in keeping with overall and long-term corporate interests. This structure is most responsive in terms of strategy and planning and in the face of crisis. The stature of the top office is particularly

Table 8.2 Executive Epigrams

This month's epigram column is devoted to a contribution from Robert M. Worcester, managing director of Market & Opinion Research International (MORI) a UK-based survey firm. "During the attitude research surveys that we do for companies," says Worcester, "we have found that often employee perceptions are fostered by the organizations in which they work. So we decided to have a little fun and draw up charts based on some of the organizational cultural differences that our researchers have come across. Not all of the charts are original but there is more than a germ of truth in some of them.

"Arab organizations have no communication, Italian organizations have bad lateral communication, while British organizations have good lateral communication but precious little upward communication. In U.S. organizations, everyone thinks that he has a pipeline to the boss."

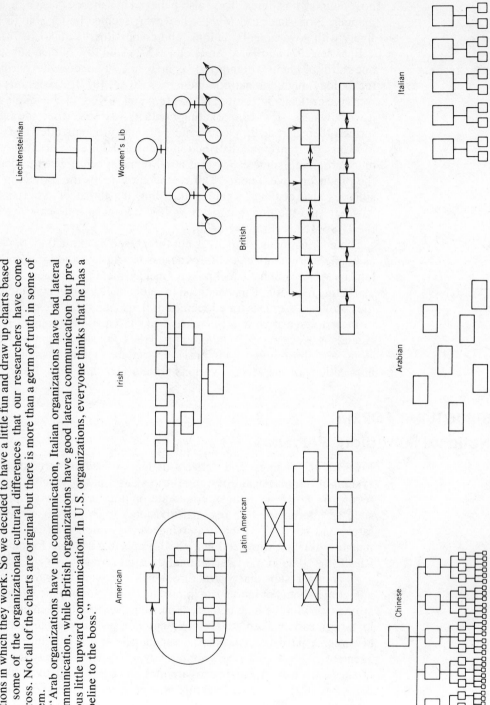

Recently, the entire epigram column was devoted to a light-hearted feature on organizational diagrams contributed by a UK reader. It prompted other readers to devise their own charts, based on national cultural differences, which are illustrated below.

The Yugoslav chart is contributed by an anonymous Yugoslav manager, who says "it is typical of the inefficiency and rigid-ity to change found in organizations in this country."

Ole Jacob Raad of PM Systems Consult AS of Trondheim contributed what he calls "the Norwegian chart or the democratic model of the future. Under this system, front-line supervisors live in an increasing information vacuum with regard to what is said and done at higher levels. What they eventually learn about these things they hear from subordinates who represent the employees on the board of directors."

The French, United Nations, Soviet Union, Vatican, and Albanian organizational charts are attributed to U.S. quality control consultant Dr. J. M. Juran. They were contributed by Gilles C. Nullens, division head of finance and contracts for CCR Euratom of Italy.

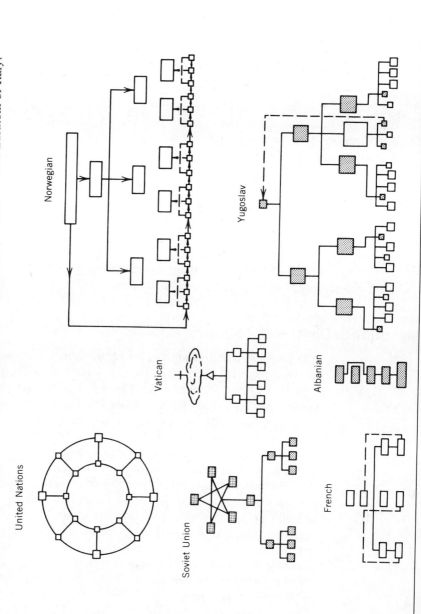

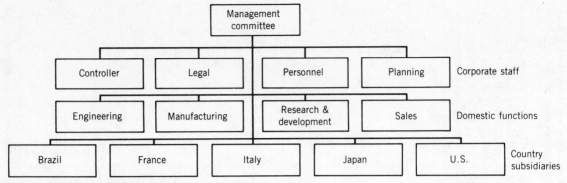

Figure 8.4 European MNC (mother–daughter) structure.

Source: Reprinted from *New Directions in Multinational Corporate Organization*, p. 21, with the permission of the publisher, Business International Corporation, New York.

significant and useful in negotiating with senior government officials (e.g., in Latin America). Moreover, fewer levels of management produce less distortion in communication.

The structure is limited, however, especially in handling global issues. To whom should management report? Uncertainties result in an inefficient use of top management time. Since the early 1970s, the use of this format has declined; most firms have moved toward multidivisional structures.

International Divisional Formats

The international division is part of the domestic structure and it groups all international activities in one division organized by function, product, or geography, as shown in Figure 8.5. Managers of foreign subsidiaries report to a general manager or division vice-president, who coordinates and controls the activities of the subsidiaries and acts as a champion for upper management. In doing so, he or she commands enough attention to get needed support and resources (especially capital and personnel), thereby working actively to globalize staff functions. This executive has complete and exclusive authority, thus centralizing responsibility for all outside operations. Such authority encourages a companywide view for foreign operations, creating an impartial position in dealing with the various subsidiaries.

An international division has several clear advantages. It provides the international group with cohesion and unity and it concentrates resources. This structure also develops the organization's capability to respond to multinational markets and opportunities. It also further promotes the development of an international strategy.

Such a structure is not without its disadvantages, however. The international division generally has low priority compared with better-established domestic divisions; and problems often arise in coordinating international and domestic activities. Technical or product expertise is not easily passed on. The use and allocation of resources on a global scale is difficult to mastermind effectively.

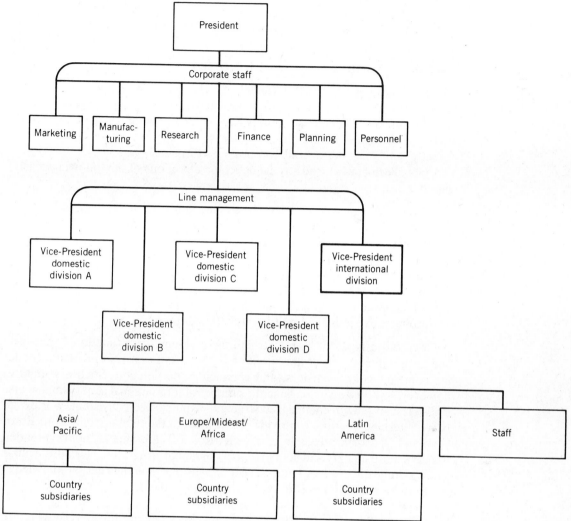

Figure 8.5 International division structure.

Conflicting priorities, overlapping and conflicting profit objectives, and re-source rivalry often result in poor cooperation among domestic divisions. These divisions are not usually accountable or responsible for profits and losses in the international division. As a result, they give low priority to export orders. Domestic and international divisions compete for single profit margins on ex-port sales, creating problems in transfer pricing. This we–they syndrome is exacerbated as the international division grows and becomes more profitable (Prasad & Krishna Shetty, 1976; Davis, 1979; *Business International,* 1981).

Although international divisions have predominated in American MNCs, they have tended to be transitional structures preceding the development of a more integrated global structure. However, the international division structure is often useful in managing emerging countries or responding to specialized and newer markets (Fouraker & Stopford, 1968; Davis, 1979; Robock et al., 1977).

Global Format (Worldwide Integrated Structures)

As companies have pursued strategies of increased product diversification and have attempted to maximize gains from both domestic and international activities, worldwide (or global) structures have emerged to replace the international divisions. Global structures have equalized foreign and domestic operations, thereby improving the overall corporate performance.

A global orientation leads to the development of one of the following organizational forms:

1. Global functional divisions such as manufacturing, marketing, and finance, responsible for worldwide operations in their own functional areas.
2. Global geographic divisions, each responsible for all the products manufactured and marketed within a given geographical area.
3. Global product divisions responsible for producing and marketing a product or a group of products worldwide.
4. Mixed structures with a combination of geographic operations, worldwide product divisions, and multiple functional links.

Three basic types of global structures have emerged: functional, product, and geographic. All three are based on principles of unity of command, reducing communications barriers, and enhancing coordination. Such a structure, however, required an increase in the number of international general managers. This phase of growth emphasized strategic planning on a consistent, worldwide basis, altering structure to provide closer links to the total organization. European and Canadian MNCs (e.g., Nestle, Royal Dutch Shell, Unilever) tended to move more quickly and spontaneously to global structures, perhaps because smaller domestic markets led to earlier expansions, and thus earlier knowledge of international business (Fouraker & Stopford, 1968).

Worldwide Functional Format At the international level, this structure (see Figure 8.6) is rarely used, because it is most suitable for firms with narrow, highly integrated product lines (e.g., Caterpillar, automobile industry).

The division of responsibility is assigned according to function on a global basis. This allows for increased specialization and more central control. Knowledge and expertise are concentrated; work is clearly delineated and defined by tasks. Thus, structure allows for a small top management staff with primary authority and a high level of profit and cost responsibility. It focuses on the profitability of the total organization. Worldwide functional structures attempt primarily to avoid duplication and dilution of specialists and to streamline operations. Although functional structures integrate (on a worldwide basis) marketing, finance, and production, this format exacts the price of sensitivity to geographic needs, thus making regional coordination difficult.

Because so much decision making occurs high in the hierarchy, top manage-

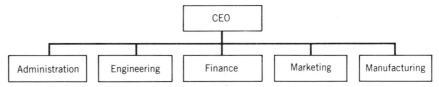

Figure 8.6 The worldwide functional structure.

Source: Business International Corporation. *New Directions in Multinational Corporate Organization.* New York: Business International Corporation, 1981, p. 19.

ment often loses touch with daily operations and local conditions. Such a structure restricts the transfer of products and technical expertise at many levels. This structure is more prevalent in Europe than in the United States.

Ansoff and Brandenburg (1971) describe the centralized functional format as one of several basic organization forms. It was prevalent in American industry in the 1920s. In this format, similar logistical activities are grouped under major functional managers who report to central headquarters. The functional format is characterized by increased differentiation due to a high degree of professionalism, such as technical expertise, ease of recruitment, and career path development. Its advantages are steady-state efficiency, economies of scale, and synergy. Simple communications and decision-making networks are adequate until the organization becomes too large.

The major disadvantage of the functional format is that operating concerns tend to preempt strategic concerns. This format does not develop general managers; therefore, it is best suited to a firm with a limited number of similar product lines operating within a stable environment, or one in which the production process is highly related or integrated (as is true of the automotive, steel, and petroleum industries).

Worldwide Geographic/Regional/Area Format In attempting to correct for lack of regional coordination of local knowledge, some organizations have adopted worldwide regional or geographic structures (e.g., ITT, IBM, automobile industry, oil firms). In this format, activities are grouped by geographic areas with regional managers, who have full responsibility for their area, reporting directly to the president (see Figure 8.7).

The advantages of grouping activities into divisions according to geographic region are that products and services can be adapted to the particular needs of a region and, because they are closer to the market, can respond more readily to consumer demands. Although this format promotes economies of scale within a region (e.g., manufacturing and distribution) by integrating regional activities, it tends to inhibit product coordination and produces duplication of functional efforts across different regions. Communication between a firm and a region is improved, however, communication between regions is often difficult. A regional organization is used when production can be duplicated in different regions to meet foreign national requirements—to respond to different customs that affect work and sales patterns and different monetary systems, rate of

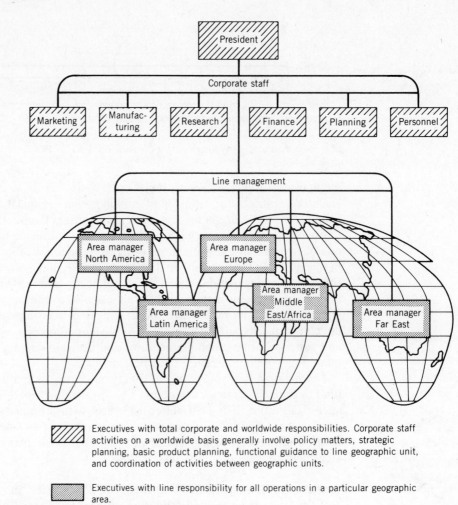

Executives with total corporate and worldwide responsibilities. Corporate staff activities on a worldwide basis generally involve policy matters, strategic planning, basic product planning, functional guidance to line geographic unit, and coordination of activities between geographic units.

Executives with line responsibility for all operations in a particular geographic area.

Figure 8.7 Geographic structure.

Source: G. H. Clee and W. M. Sachtjen. "Organizing a Worldwide Business," *Harvard Business Review,* November–December 1964, p. 60.

exchange, and tariffs, that is, different legal, economic, and social constraints (Stieglitz, 1965). This format is typical of service organization (e.g., Banks), although it also occurs with manufacturing and sales concerns (*Business International,* 1981).

Corporate headquarters retains responsibility for worldwide planning and control, with a central staff serving as the main coordinating force. This format is particularly useful when products are fairly standard and require low level technology. It is also most useful when the company is highly marketing-oriented, when sales revenues derive from standard end-use markets, and when a chief goal is meeting local market requirements.

A regional global format is more flexible in response to local conditions, because it is more sensitive to the differences in national and regional market characteristics, as well as in local government requirements and constraints. Responsibility resides with an executive familiar with the region, thereby consolidating regional know-how. This simplifies regional planning and strategy, better defines accountability, and therefore facilitates evaluating managers. Lines of authority are thus more logical and provide easier channels for communication. This structure also facilitates coordination of technical and functional capability within a region and provides a broad management training experience.

The major disadvantage of this structure is that it creates operating problems when faced with diverse product lines and marketing characteristics. Product emphasis is weakened. Division by region can interfere with the flow of products between manufacturing and marketing. It is also difficult to transfer technology as well as new ideas and experience between regions in such a format. Problems arise regarding transfer pricing. Company systems and policies tend to diverge and become inconsistent among regions, and costly duplication of functional and product specialists occurs.

Worldwide Product Format   As product diversification and market expansion has moved management structures toward a more global approach (e.g., Bell & Howell), product divisions have gained worldwide responsibility for sales and profits. With a worldwide product divisional format (Figure 8.8), it becomes easier to achieve product and marketing integration and more useful integration given a diversified range of products, a variety of end-use markets, and differences in technology. Each product division generally has its own international vice-president, export department, manufacturing plants, and sales and marketing forces. This format is particularly useful in companies experiencing rapid growth; it allows for flexibility in adding product lines and capitalizing on new market opportunities.

Such a format, however, cannot always adequately coordinate product divisions abroad. International and regional knowledge may be lacking or inadequate as international expertise becomes fragmented and dispersed. Multiple product plants sometimes create problems in reporting relationships, resource allocations, and profit accountability. Coordinating different product activities in a single country may also result in local coordination problems, such as failing to provide a uniform company effort, particularly at the staff (functional) level (Davis, 1979; *Business International,* 1981; Prasad & Krishna Shetty, 1976; Fouraker & Stopford, 1968).

Mixed Structure Format   Given the advantages and limitations of each format, MNCs must assess their needs and organizational characteristics in order to choose the most appropriate structure. Sometimes that structure is a hybrid of many different formats.

The purpose of combined forms is to deal with the increasing interdepen-

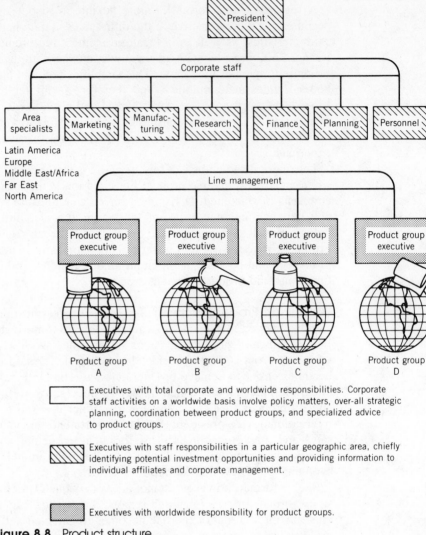

Figure 8.8 Product structure.

Source: G. H. Clee and W. M. Sachtjen. "Organizing a Worldwide Business," *Harvard Business Review,* November–December 1964, p. 63.

dence between function, regional area, and product. This maintains internal cohesion while meeting market opportunities, surviving local regulations and constraints, and coordinating and controlling the multiple sources of diversity.

A single division within a company can have its own particular structure. At Caterpillar, for example, there is one product division set apart from the rest of the organization that is structured on a function-by-region format. In another case, a company can opt for several formats at the same level. Union Carbide is structured by product divisions at home and by regional divisions abroad. GTE's international division is subdivided by product division. Figure 8.9

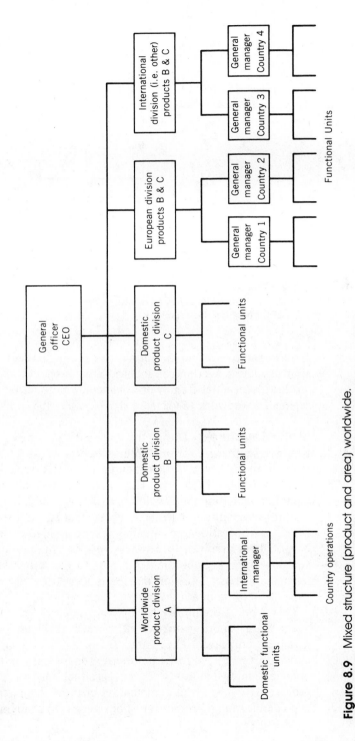

Figure 8.9 Mixed structure (product and area) worldwide.

Source: S. M. Davis. "Basic Structure of Multinational Corporations," in S. M. Davis, ed. *Managing and Organizing Multinational Corporations.* Elmsford, NY: Pergamon, 1979, p. 208.

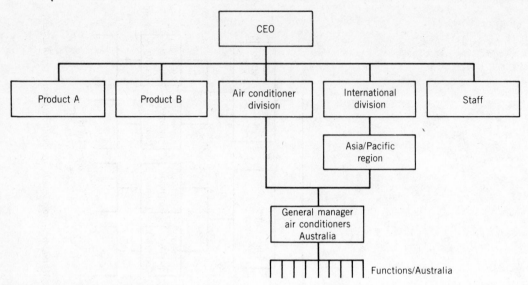

Figure 8.10 A matrix structure.

Source: Reprinted from *New Directions in Multinational Corporate Organization*, pp. 81, 82, with the permission of the publisher, Business International Corporation, New York.

shows examples of mixed formats by product, region, and international division. A matrix overlap can incorporate geographic and functional input into a worldwide product framework or include product or function in a worldwide regional framework (*Business International,* 1981).

Matrix Structures   During the 1970s the "new wave" of organizational structure was the matrix format—otherwise known as adaptive or project management format (Ansoff & Brandenburg, 1971; Davis, 1978; Janger, 1979) (see Figure 8.10 and Table 8.3). Here activities fall into two groups: (1) strategic planning, including the development of resources and skills, and (2) operations and implementation of strategic plans, that is, the project group.

Primary operational responsibilities are divided between two peer managers, one of them assigned to business results—operations—and the other to resources-support. Subordinates report to the latter while often taking orders from the former. Decision making is shared by the manager and a common superior serving in a judicial role (Janger, 1979).

This type of organization employs a multiple command system with managers often reporting to two or more bosses: project managers, functional manager, corporate office, and so on, as shown in Figure 8.11. This form evolved from a need for structural responsiveness in industries with high technological intensiveness, frequent product mix changes, or short product/project life cycles, or a combination of these. This structure is the most fluid and flexible, and it promotes responsiveness to changing market and technolog-

Table 8.3   What Is a Matrix?

The identifying feature of a matrix organization is that some managers report to two bosses rather than to the traditional single boss; there is a dual rather than a single chain of command.

Companies tend to turn to matrix forms

1. When it is absolutely essential that they be highly responsive to two sectors simultaneously, such as markets and technology;
2. When they face uncertainties that generate very high information processing requirements; and
3. When they must deal with strong constraints on financial and/or human resources.

Matrix structures can help provide both flexibility and balanced decision making, but at the price of complexity.

Matrix organization is more than a matrix structure. It must be reinforced by matrix systems such as dual control and evaluation systems, by leaders who operate comfortably with lateral decision making, and by a culture that can negotiate open conflict and a balance of power.

In most matrix organizations there are dual command responsibilities assigned to functional departments (marketing, production, engineering, and so forth) and to product or market departments. The former are oriented to specialized in-house resources while the latter focus on outputs. Other matrices are split between area-based departments and either products or functions.

Every matrix contains three unique and critical roles; the top manager who heads up and balances the dual chains of command, the matrix bosses (functional, product, or area) who share subordinates, and the managers who report to two different matrix bosses. Each of these roles has its special requirements.

Aerospace companies were the first to adopt the matrix form, but now companies in many industries (chemical, banking, insurance, packaged goods, electronics, computer, and so forth) and in different fields (hospitals, government agencies, and professional organizations) are adapting different forms of the matrix.

Source: S. M. Davis and P. R. Lawrence, "Problems of Matrix Organizations." *Harvard Business Review,* May–June 1978, p. 232. Reprinted with permission.

ical requirements. It generally favors a more general management perspective. Examples of matrix organizations are Citicorp, Shell Oil, TRW, and Texas Instruments (all MNCs).

Combining functional divisions with either product or geographic divisions attempts to improve coordination and control, given a large number of foreign subsidiaries and acquisitions. These forms, however, were found to be limited in their usefulness and may serve best as transitional structures. It should be noted that some companies are reconsidering this structure and are searching for alternatives (e.g., General Electric and Dow Chemical).

There are, as usual, disadvantages as well as advantages to this format. Matrices often lead to duplication of capacities and capabilities, resulting in a loss of economy of scale and synergy. The need for cross-function communication and integrating mechanisms increases as ambiguity and stress increase. Other problems include "groupitis" (every decision has to be made by the group), power struggles, confusion about pecking order, excessive overhead,

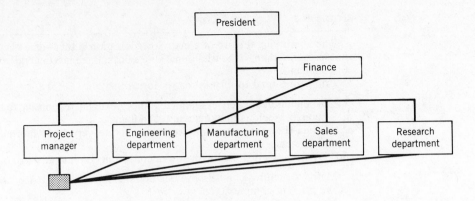

Note: Team members are drawn from various departments as needed, and report to *both* the project manager and their home department head.

Figure 8.11 Matrix organization in manufacturing.

Source: M. Jelinek. "Organizational Structure: The Basic Conformations," in M. Jelinek, J. A. Litterer, and R. A. Miles, eds. *Organizations by Design: Theory and Practice.* Plano, TX: Business Publications, 1981, p. 263.

delays in decision making, and preoccupation with internal operations (Davis & Lawrence, 1978). Therefore, the choice of matrix needs to be made so that the fit between structure and strategy is significantly improved (Egelhoff, 1982).

The matrix approach offers a compromise: a structure less decentralized than full-scale divisionalization but considerably more decentralized than the functional structure. Companies have developed three matrix designs:

1. The product-function matrix, which has a functional "resource" manager with a number of product managers charged with achieving "business results" and responsibilities that cut across functional lines.
2. The product-region matrix, which overlays a regionally divisionalized structure with a number of product managers charged with achieving "business results" and with responsibilities that cut across regional lines (see Figure 8.12 for an example).
3. The multidimensional matrix, whose divisions are organized into product-functional matrices and are, in turn, part of a product-regional matrix.

For the matrix organization to function satisfactorily, management must take particular care in staffing the organization. It requires managers who know the business in general, who have good interpersonal skills, and who can deal with the ambiguities of responsibility and authority inherent in the matrix system. Training in such skills as planning procedures, the kinds of interpersonal skills necessary for the matrix, and the kind of analysis and orderly presentation of ideas essential to planning within a group is most important for supporting the matrix approach. Moreover, management development and human resource

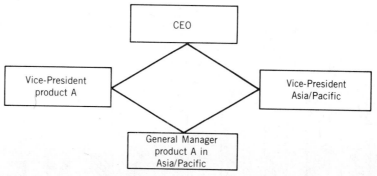

Figure 8.12 *The matric structure.*

Source: Reprinted from *New Directions in Multinational Corporate Organization,* p. 21, with the permission of the publisher, Business International Corporation, New York.

planning are even more necessary in the volatile environment of the matrix than in the traditional organizations.

Innovative Forms

Concentrating Attention   An innovative format is often used in large manufacturing firms in which economies of scale are necessary, assets and competencies are relatively inflexible, and products have long lives. Activities are grouped into a current business group and an innovative group. The current business group consists of businesses that are currently profitable and have established product markets. Strategic activity in this group involves exploitation of current position and expansion planning. The innovative group, in contrast, is responsible for the development of new product-market positions and diversification opportunities. A new product is conceived, planned, and implemented by this group on a project basis, and, upon establishing its commercial feasibility, it is then transferred to the current business group. The latter group can be structured on a functional or divisional basis. The advantage of this approach is the high degree of responsiveness on all organizational performance criteria, although some economy of scale is sacrificed by duplication of resources. Problems arising in the communication between groups concern new needs, opportunities, and trends that frontline people (e.g., salespeople) perceive; other problems involve a tendency to neglect opportunities for expansion in favor of diversification.

General Electric pioneered this form under the term strategic business units (SBUs) (Ansoff & Brandenburg, 1971). Product divisions are redefined as independent business units and planning entities. This format is highly market oriented. It encourages the roles of entrepreneurship and stresses the importance of strategic planning. An organization may apply an adaptive mechanism for some isolated parts of the organization or in particular subsidiaries. For example, GE light products (lamps) in Brazil report directly to the headquarters

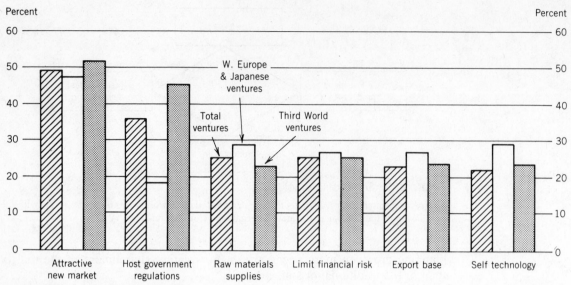

Figure 8.13 Why joint ventures?

Source: A. R. Janger. *Organization of International Joint Ventures.* New York: Conference Board, Report No. 787, 1980, p. 3. Reprinted with permission.

product division in Cleveland, while other products in Brazil report to the international divisions. Five factors, however, inhibit the use of this form abroad (*Business Week,* 1976):

1. It is relatively new and untested.
2. It creates problems between markets and country as a unit of planning.
3. Country boundaries impose limits.
4. It is difficult to integrate with other units.
5. It is difficult to draw on centralized support services.

Joint Ventures   Although executives often choose matrix structures because they respond best to product, function, and regional needs while optimizing coordination and control (i.e., internal demands), joint ventures respond best to increasing pressure from economic, social, and political conditions (i.e., external demands) (Friedmann & Benguin, 1971; Franko, 1971; Pfeffer & Nowak, 1976). The advantages and disadvantages of joint ventures have been delineated by Janger (1980) and will be summarized in the following paragraphs (see Figures 8.13 and 8.14).

Over 40% of Fortune 500 companies with over $100 million in sales are engaged in joint ventures. The reasons for the increasing interest are as follows:

1. The potentially attractive new market for companies in mature markets.
2. They address the need to deal with rising economic nationalism.
3. They find sources of raw materials.
4. They share economic risks and reduce the amount of capital needed.

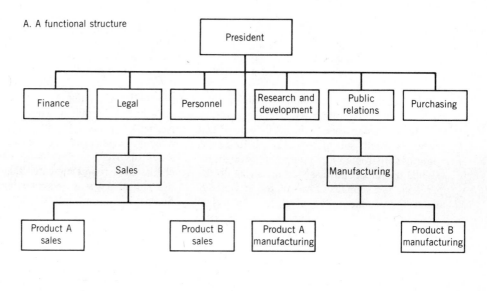

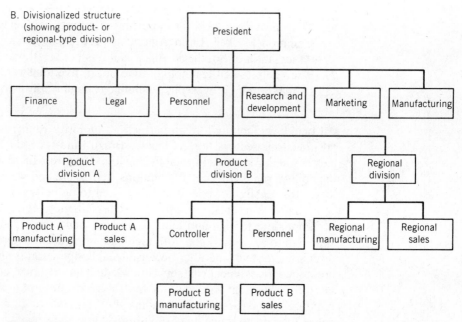

Figure 8.14 Schematic organization structures of functionally organized and divisionalized joint ventures.

Source: A. R. Janger. *Organization of International Joint Ventures.* New York: Conference Board, Report No. 787, 1980, p. 7. Reprinted with permission.

Box 8.1

A major U.S. manufacturer of mixed feed and poultry was interested in establishing a market in Spain, and preliminary market studies corroborated the existence of sufficient demand for the firm's products. Despite advice to the contrary from local businessmen, the firm established a wholly-owned subsidiary. The factory was promptly constructed and equipment brought in; a skilled technical staff assisted in setting up the operation, and supplies of raw materials were arranged. The product rolled off the line, but as had been warned, the firm was unable to sell its products. Only then did the parent firm fully understand the situation in Spain: The poultry growers and feed producers had had generations of business relations and were like a closely knit family; newcomers were effectively barred from entering the market. Had the company made a joint venture with an existing local firm, they would not have had the problem. To solve this problem of having no market for the feed, the subsidiary bought a series of chicken farms, only to face another disaster: They had no one to buy their chickens! A report indicated that at last contact, the subsidiary was busy buying restaurants in Spain.

Source: David A. Ricks, M. Y. C. Fu, and S. Arpan. *International Business Blunders.* OH: Grid, 1974, p. 24.

5. They help identify local expertise, both political and cultural.
6. They provide a base for exporting in a particular region (e.g., European Common Market, Latin American Free Trade Area (LAFTA), and the Association of Southeast Asian Nations).
7. They help to sell technology (one out of five joint ventures are organized to make money by selling technology mainly through licensing arrangements).

Local laws limiting foreign partners to minority equity positions in some or all industrial sectors (e.g., Canada, Brazil, and recently France) have been another major impetus in establishing joint ventures. Increasing environmental instability, rapid currency fluctuations, terrorism, and weak infrastructures all affect the viability of operations that need to be buffered from these forces.

With joint ventures, these forces are less disruptive; it is easier and faster to accommodate foreign and local differences, and the organization is more responsive to local markets. Although planning takes longer, implementation is often quicker and smoother because local cooperation is enhanced by government incentives, local partners' knowledge, and political contacts. Thus, joint ventures represent the wave of the future by promoting cooperation across national boundaries, thus extending the "family" (e.g., Japanese style). Because there is no single highest authority, however, reaching consensus on any one issue is difficult.

There are alternatives to joint ventures:

1. Export or supplier agreements (i.e., exclusive rights to distribute or supply).
2. Trademark agreements (i.e., use of trademark in return for royalties).
3. Licensing agreements (i.e., use of technology in return for royalties).

4. Combinations of the above to form manufacturing associations or franchising.
5. Minority holding—the so-called silent partner approach.

We must note the drawbacks involved here, however. Although the purpose of these alternatives is to make money and reduce risk, problems arise from loss of control over technology, product quality, and local reputation, as well as from loss of profit or capital gain when new and growing markets emerge.

Successful joint ventures require (1) acknowledged intent by partners to share management and control, (2) the agreement that partnerships are mostly between legally incorporated entities, not individuals, and (3) the agreements that equity positions are held by both. The existence and size of equity reflect the character and relative strength of each partner's management role, although absolute size is less important than contractual protections. Partnerships in First-World countries are often formed with a group or private corporation, in the Second-World countries with the central government, and in Third-World countries with public corporations or government agencies. The bulk of joint ventures are formed between American and local companies, except in extractive industries.

Some joint ventures are formed to combine technological and marketing knowledge; however, some firms (e.g., Dow-Corning and General Electric) have combined technological capabilities. Most joint ventures operate in a single business area and therefore use functional structures (see Figure 8.15). Joint ventures can be formed on a short-term as well as a long-term basis.

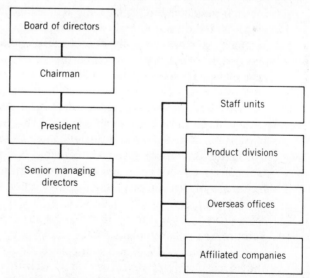

Figure 8.15 Structural depiction of the General Trading Company.

Source: Reprinted from *New Directions in Multinational Corporate Organization*, p. 10, with the permission of the publisher, Business International Corporation, New York.

Prior to the 1970s, joint ventures occurred because of an opportunistic planning attitude. More recently, they have been formed as part of a strategic plan initiated by fewer entrepreneurial individuals, and more often from regional or international division recommendations. Joint ventures with trading companies, common in Japan, are formed by multibusiness companies that do not have international divisions but want to manufacture or sell abroad from product divisions. This partnership provides export channels for smaller firms that cannot sustain their own foreign organizations (e.g., ALCOA).

Joint ventures present problems as well as opportunities, however. The most obvious is possible curtailment of independent action or freedom. Other problems emerge as firms add another layer of planning, and as cultural diversity results in different systems, ways of negotiating, and business norms (e.g., the Japanese versus the Korean approach to confrontation: the Japanese avoid; Koreans seek). Different criteria of performance indicators may also complicate the situation: for example, return on investment (ROI) used by the United States versus return on equity (ROE) used by Japan; volume and market share versus productivity and efficiency; long-term stability versus short-term high-level payouts. Government objectives differ in terms of providing jobs, training, and social benefits. MNCs must also consider the government's personnel and political agendas. Because of these differences, it is often difficult to resolve conflicts, to arrive at decisions, and to implement them. Shared management is less conducive to rapid unified response to change and can split into factions in the face of adversity.

How are joint ventures organized? A board of directors serves as the highest policy maker, its primary responsibility being to identify and resolve conflicts. Internal management, led by the managing director, runs the business, provides unified direction and control, and integrates objectives and agenda. The managing partner—usually one of the owners—is responsible for leadership and ongoing linkages between partners and internal managers. However, it is difficult to provide unified management direction without managing partners, although they may vary in terms of involvement.

The system of management control is chosen in terms of performance measurement. Culture is a strong influence in this regard. American and German parties are statistically and analytically minded. The American firms tend to use figures to support product planning, business, and strategy, whereas the Germans use production and sales figures more often. Moreover, methods and frequency of control vary from financial reports (82%), informal visits by owner company executives (78%), financial audits (60%), and formal planning systems (55%) (favored by the United States), to evaluation of performance against venture and market plans (48%), monitoring sales and project reports on a continuing basis (40%), and staff performance reviews (22%). What determines the success of joint ventures is how well their structure fits the strategy and power situations as well as the environment.

A study by Daniels and Arpan (1972) shows differences between countries in *equity preferences*. The degree of ownership (actual control) desired was substantially different across nations in equity preference and in the implementation of preference into rigid policy. The Canadians (who want 100% control) and the French (who want minority interest) are more rigid—they are willing to forgo investments if preferences are not met. The Germans prefer fifty–fifty joint ventures but are more willing to adjust. The British and Dutch view equity arrangement on the merits of each investment, thus showing the greatest flexibility.

Reasons for preferences in degree of equity and flexibility differ. The French prefer a minority interest because of the belief that the national environment is so diverse that local management ensures better control. Feelings of inferiority about their own management methods and the experience of other countries failing in France create an unwillingness to take on more control. The Germans, who desire maximum returns and need to maintain a low profile (given anti-German sentiment following World War II), are more willing to be flexible. To gain community acceptance, they often Anglicize their names in the United States. The Dutch and British tend to be more flexible as a consequence of long and varied colonial experiences. Canadians are more rigid in wanting total control because of the nature of industry expansion (generally through vertical integration), their desire to protect minority stockholders, and their experience of how foreign investors operate in Canada. Other reasons for differences in equity preference are home-country influences, the number of different environments and extent of foreign operations, size, diversity, and degree of competition.

GROWTH AND DEVELOPMENT

Organizations develop in a series of stages that reflect the strategies they pursue and the subsequent structural modifications they require (Scott, 1973). In Scott's three stages of organizational development, the firm progressed from *small* to *integrated* to *diversified* business (see Table 8.4). These stages require adaptations in structure, strategic choice, and systems of performance measurement, reward, and control. The stage of development, in turn, will affect the further strategic formulations of the firm. For example, strategies of diversification are most often pursued in the third stage of development. The diversified stage (characterized by multiple product lines) is further divided into dominant, related, and unrelated subdivisions, according to how much and in what way the company has diversified. Dominant business companies derive 70 to 95% of sales from a single business or a vertically integrated chain (e.g., GM, IBM, U.S. Steel, Texaco). Related business companies are diversified into related businesses in which no single business accounts for more than 70% of sales (General Foods, Kodak, DuPont, GE). Unrelated businesses have diversified into unrelated businesses in which no single business accounts for as much as 70% sales (Litton, Olin, Textron). The latter two subdivisions tend to be managed by divisional structures; the first tends to be functionally managed (Wrigley, 1970).

The relationship of strategy and structure in firms across nations can be seen in Table 8.5.

Table 8.4 The Three Stages of Organizational Development

Company Characteristics	Stage I	Stage II	Stage III
Product line	Single product or single line	Single product line	Multiple product lines
Distribution	One channel or set of channels	One set of channels	Multiple channels
Organization structure	Little or no formal structure; "one-man show"	Specialization based on function	Specialization based on product–market relationships
Product–service transactions	Not applicable	Integrated pattern of transactions: $A \rightarrow B \rightarrow C \rightarrow$ Markets	Nonintegrated pattern of transactions: A $B \rightarrow$ Markets C
R&D organization	Not institutionalized, guided by owner-manager	Increasingly institutionalized search for product or process improvements	Institutionalized search for *new* products as well as for improvements
Performance measurement	By personal contact and subjective criteria	Increasingly impersonal, using technical and/or cost criteria	Increasingly impersonal, using *market* criteria (return on investment and market share)
Rewards	Unsystematic and often paternalistic	Increasingly systematic, with emphasis on stability and service	Increasingly systematic, with variability related to performance
Control system	Personal control of both strategic and operating decisions	Personal control of strategic decisions, with increasing delegation of operating decisions through policy	Delegation of product–market decisions within existing businesses, with indirect control based on analysis of "results"
Strategic choices	Needs of owner versus needs of company	Degree of integration; market-share objective; breadth of product line	Entry and exit from industries; allocation of resources by industry; rate of growth

Source: B. R. Scott, "The Industrial State: Old Myths and New Realities." *Harvard Business Review,* March–April 1973, pp. 133–148; B. R. Scott, *Stages of Corporate Development* (Case Clearing House, Harvard Business School). Copyright 1971 by the President and Fellows of Harvard College.

The three stages of development suggested by Scott highlight these structural changes at the international level. In the initial period (Stage I), foreign subsidiaries were tied to the company with loose financial links similar to those in a holding company. Foreign activities (developed out of the entrepreneurial mode) were often unplanned, because they were not considered to be critical to overall company objectives; instead, they reflected an effort to protect an interest or gamble. This transitory autonomy, however, gave way to a second stage of organizational consolidation as a result of increased organizational interest—in turn, the result of significant profit contributions or an increasing number of activities. In this stage, the international division was developed

Table 8.5 Strategic and Structural Choices of Leading Nonfinancial Companies in Five Industrial Countries, 1950–1970

Country	Year	No. of Companies*		Single	Strategic Classification		
					Dominant	Related	Unrelated
United States	1949	500	% dist.	34	35	27	3
			% MD	5	20	44	100
	1969	500	% dist.	6	29	45	19
			% MD	24	62	90	98
United Kingdom	1950	92	% dist.	34	40	24	2
			% MD	6	11	32	0
	1970	100	% dist.	6	34	54	6
			% MD	17	73	79	50
France	1950	100	% dist.	42	21	33	4
			% MD	5	0	12	0
	1970	100	% dist.	16	32	42	10
			% MD	19	59	64	50
Germany	1950–1955	99	% dist.	34	26	32	7
			% MD	0	8	9	0
	1970	100	% dist.	22	22	38	18
			% MD	9	45	88	56
Italy	1950	84	% dist.	30	24	43	4
			% MD	0	0	14	33
	1970	100	% dist.	10	33	52	5
			% MD	0	45	58	60

Source: R. E. Caves, "Industrial Organization, Corporate Strategy and Structure." *Journal of Economic Literature,* XVIII:72, March 1980.
* The lines labeled "% dist." indicate the percentage distrubution of companies among the four strategic categories. The line labeled "% MD" indicate the proportion of companies in each category that are multidivisional.

mostly in the United States (as opposed to European firms, which often by-passed this stage). In the third stage, the organizational structure is altered through global formats to provide closer links with the rest of the organization, so that strategic planning is emphasized on a more consistent, worldwide basis (Fouraker & Stopford, 1968; Davis, 1979; Scott, 1973).

There are several different strategies or growth patterns that can lead to the multinational level. Paralleling Scott's (1973) study, they have been delineated by Kuhn (1982) at a lecture delivered at N.Y.U. and appear in Figure 8.16.

Organizations with a single or a few related product lines and a high degree of vertical integration (Type II) tend to be capital-intensive and organized in a centralized, functional structure. They usually concentrate on domestic markets. Foreign operations can be integrated into functional units. This is the case when foreign operations are few or are limited to export sales, or both.

The involvement of American multinational firms was initially through exports. As those involvements grew in number and size, international divisions were created to coordinate and centralize these activities. Although the international division can itself be in a miniversion of a Stage III structure, it can be

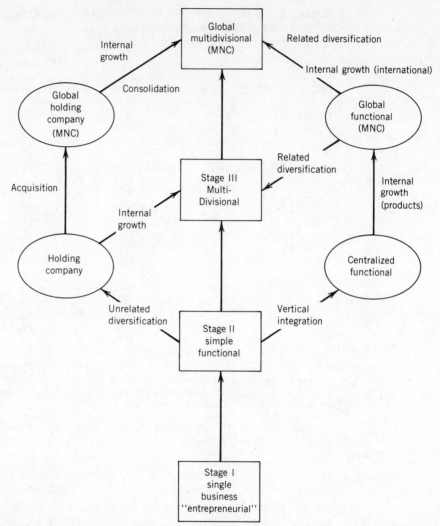

Figure 8.16 Stages of development of organizations—growth and strategies of the MNC.

attached to a Stage II (functional division) or Stage III (product division) structure.

A Stage II simple (function) company can grow through vertical integration strategies to a centralized functional company. Through internal growth and overseas opportunities, the firm can expand to the global or worldwide level while retaining its functional format. For example, manufacturing abroad becomes a desirable opportunity because the costs of labor and supplies may be less. Thus, the marketing function moves abroad to capitalize on and be more responsive to growing forcing markets. Such flexibility helps the company retain its functional forms; however, this structure soon becomes inadequate to handle the increasing complexity and diversity of the global environment.

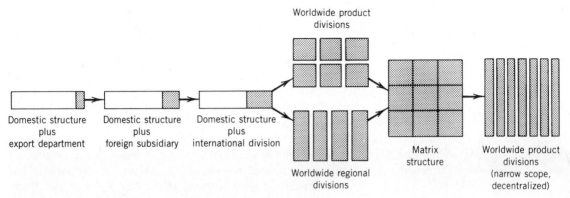

Worldwide product divisions

Domestic structure plus export department → Domestic structure plus foreign subsidiary → Domestic structure plus international division

Worldwide regional divisions

Matrix structure

Worldwide product divisions (narrow scope, decentralized)

Figure 8.17 Structural evolution of multinational corporations.

Source: Reprinted from *New Directions in Multinational Corporate Organization,* p. 22, with the permission of the publishers, Business International Corporation, New York.

Functional structures are the dominant form of European firms. European MNCs tend to maintain their functional formats longer than American MNCs. The European firms first combined functional structures for domestic operations and maintained highly decentralized holding company organizations for international operations. By the late 1960s and early 1970s, these firms moved toward a worldwide product format, bypassing the international division structure used by the United States (Robock et al., 1977).

As the firm grows internally and through related diversification strategies, it adopts a more flexible structure. It moves from a Stage II (a simple functional format) to a Stage III (multidivisional) structure. Those organizations with more highly diversified product lines tend to be organized in a decentralized divisional structure. However, because firms develop a Stage III structure for domestic activities, they are more likely to enter new overseas business (Stopford & Wells, 1972).

The initial structural response to diversification of direct investment is to establish an international division in a Stage III organization. This division is at the same organizational level as other domestic product divisions, although it is the sole profit center for all foreign operations. As the international divisions in American firms grew more profitable, for instance, they developed global structures in order to be more responsive to product and regional needs. Firms can reach the multinational level through alternative routes and in alternative forms. Through continued unrelated diversification abroad (e.g., by acquisitions) a firm can evolve into a global holding company. As it grows internally and improves its coordination and control, it evolves into a global multidivisional structure. Figure 8.17 shows the structural formats that have evolved as foreign activity increased.

American firms have tended to lag behind the European ones in "going multinational" because they found greater market opportunities at home. European MNCs, however, exported more, and as a result had more foreign market experience. As the American markets began to shrink, American firms looked abroad. Wilkins (1970) discusses the reasons for the development of the

MNC. Among them are the importance of direct foreign investment and the decision to produce abroad—both of which improved sales marketing (since foreign agents handling export sales failed to provide adequate servicing or product differentiation). Additionally, foreign tariffs and patent laws made exporting less profitable. Foreign acquisitions help eliminate price wars and result in certain firms joining forces with a foreign-based competitor. "Overall, the forces that caused or facilitated multinational status correspond well to those uncovered by Chandler" (Caves, 1980, p. 69).

Patterns of growth abroad often reflect the patterns of growth at home. Chandler's four phases of industry growth are (1) expansion and accumulation of resources, (2) rationalization of resources, (3) expansion of markets and product lines, and (4) structural modifications (Fouraker & Stopford, 1968). The American firms, for example, began to export products developed for the American markets that were not available abroad. This resulted in a monopoly in world markets that offset high labor costs in the American companies; the companies then began to invest in plant and equipment abroad to protect their export market while realizing increasing profitability through cheaper local resources—people and material. Profitability continues to increase as these resources are rationalized and as new market opportunities develop. Companies already operating in the area are thus in a much better position to see these opportunities and respond quickly to them. However, growth and expansion begin to put pressure (i.e., the need for increasing information processing capacity and better control and planning) on existing organization structures, which may mean that the organization needs to make structural changes.

CONCLUSION

It should come as no surprise that MNCs assume a great variety of structures in a great variety of environments. The most common of these structures are national subsidiary, international division, and global format structures. Each of these has its own advantages and disadvantages. Moreover, each meets the managerial biases of certain cultures or countries. However, more recent developments have prompted managers to organize their corporations according to innovative or flexible structures—among them mixed structures, matrix structures, "concentrating attention" structures, and joint ventures. All of these structures are essentially responses to external and internal pressures facing the MNC.

We should keep in mind, however, that structure—whether traditional or innovative, formal or informal, complex or simple—is not a static thing. It changes and evolves. The processes that induce change may be the result of managerial policy or the consequence of forces beyond the control of managers. But change itself is inevitable. Managers must therefore acknowledge and understand the processes of change as fully as possible. To the degree that they do so, managers retain the possibility of influencing change and not simply being influenced by it.

Although the environment greatly influences an organization's structure, the structure in turn provides the organization with an effective means for dealing with its environment. Structure provides a means for accomplishing tasks and reaching goals, whatever those tasks and goals may be. The complexity of the MNC's environment does not overrule the truth of this statement.

Like any other organization, the MNC must use structure to serve the purposes of differentiation, integration, and coordination that it serves elsewhere. MNCs differ in that they must differentiate, integrate, and coordinate their functions to meet unusually complex circumstances. The result is generally a more complex organizational structure.

Having considered the major determinants of organizational structure, we should now move on to examine the MNCs' intricate cultural, political, and economic environments that may result in variations in structural formats.

CHAPTER 9
Environmental Considerations

Organizations of any sort exist and conduct business within the context of a complex, multifaceted environment. They influence the environment and are themselves influenced by it; thus, they become part of the very environment they inhabit. Managers and organizations must continually confront and evaluate the impact of this vital and unavoidable synergy.

Environmental influences can be either positive or negative. Environments are the context for organizational operations—a backdrop of risks and opportunities. They can impede operations through governmental or economic regulation—for example, through taxation—or enhance operations through policies of noninterference and subsidy. Environments can also provide resources for the organization to draw on, resources from which they can receive products or services. For instance, changes in environmental resources (such as availability of raw materials) can mean changes in the organization's production methods, quotas, or products. Changes in the marketplace can also bear directly on market research and product-development strategies.

Organizations must, therefore, be adaptable. To be adaptable, however, they must be sensitive to the environment and prepared to change in ways that reflect environmental circumstances. Managers must scan and probe the environment to understand its impact on the organization. This is no easy task, however, because individual managers may perceive and interpret environments differently. Variables include the managers' own willingness to explore the environment, their breadth of exploration, their sensitivity to change, and, above all, their mode of interpretation or analysis in using collected data.

All of these factors create powerful uncertainties for managers—uncertainties that they must cope with in making decisions. Many managers rely on sources both within and outside the organization to help them read and interpret the environment. In addition, differences in interpretive styles might be compared to the difference between astronomers and astrologers.

Academics, textbook writers, and other theoreticians are the organization's astronomers. They study various aspects of the environment to describe their impact on organizational functioning. In contrast, boundary spanners are the organization's astrologers. These are individuals or groups that monitor the environment for change and serve as an interface between the organization and environment. For example, purchasing departments obtain raw materials; they can also alert the organization to scarcity or abundance of resources. Similarly, sales and marketing departments scan the environment to assess changes in customer's needs or demands.

But unfortunately, managers are too often cast in the role of the organization's sorcerers. They are expected to perform miracles, both organizationally and financially, and their methods are often just as arbitrary and undefinable as magic. In analyzing the information they receive from internal and external sources, managers may focus on (1) the input–output exchange between organization and environment (E-O-E), (2) contingencies, such as the impact of environmental events on organizational structure (E-O), or (3) the processes of adaptation—for example, the impact of organizational decisions on the environment (O-E).

The manager's method of analysis reflects a theoretical model that may or may not be consciously perceived. Likely as not, the manager has simply adopted an approach that worked in the past. Yet the method of analysis will determine the organizational strategy—hence the importance of developing sound models for the organization's relationship to the environment. Models provide a framework, a means of conceptualizing organizational–environmental interaction and then synthesizing the data generated by studying this interaction. Models direct the manager's focus to what is relevant, both now and in the future, for the organization's operations. Consequently, they provide strategies for improving organizational effectiveness; in doing this, they determine not only the manager's role within the organization but also the organization's role within the environment.

ENVIRONMENTAL COMPONENTS

The "causal texture" of any given environment is the combination of all the forces, general and specific, that influence the organization's operations (Emery & Trist, 1965). In the case of the MNC, the environment is international. It includes the economic, technological, political, physical, and cultural context of operations. It is the various combinations of these components that constitute the particular organization's unique environment. We should explore and evaluate each component, although some will have greater impact than others, and will thus require a more extensive analysis (Sethi, 1970; Kast & Rosenzweig, 1979, p. 131).

The MNC's *economic environment,* for example, reflects the employment picture, per capita income levels, GNP, foreign exchange risk, balance of payments, and commodity and trade agreements. Because of their impact on the profit picture, these factors are vital to the MNC when considering investment potential and the cost–benefit of setting up operations in a particular region overseas.

The *technological environment* reflects the state of the art in production and information processes and directly influences the market share or growth potential of any given firm. It also raises issues regarding the transfer of technology and the subsequent positioning of the MNC in a particular marketplace. If, for example, MNCs are operating in an underdeveloped country, that country's level of technology is more than likely underdeveloped as well. One reason for host countries to accept MNC operations is to benefit from the MNC's technology, to improve economic conditions, and to promote economic development. In technology transfer, the host country comes to ''own'' the technology, and thus becomes less dependent on the MNC for its development. The host country then has more autonomy and is better able to protect its sovereignty. More countries are now demanding technology transfer through the establishment of local R&D. This development presents problems to the MNC: R&D is costly, and it undermines both the proprietary nature of the MNC and its competitive edge, thus decreasing the MNC's leverage in the marketplace generally as well as in the country. The host countries, however, argue that the MNCs exploit their resources and labor and perpetuate the countries' subservient position and underdeveloped status by keeping them in the dark. For example, Coca-Cola and IBM left India because of that country's demand for technical secrets through the requirement of local ownership of 51% of the subsidiary.

The *political environment* includes factors such as the role of government in business; the degree of instability and subsequent threats to MNCs through expropriation, terrorism, and strikes; and the ideological stance toward capitalism, the MNC's life blood.

The *physical environment* includes the impact of population, climate, natural resources, geography, and ecology. Population is a possible resource for labor as well as a market indicator. Differences in climate result in different market potentials (e.g., selling ski wear in France instead of Thailand). Inclement weather may affect MNC operations (factories in tropical climates may close because of monsoon rains, tsunamis, etc.). Geographic location and accessibility to transportation and resources also warrant consideration. The balance of natural resources has become more of a concern recently, too, particularly in view of the disastrous effect Japan's rapid industrial economic development has had on its ecological environment. Worldwide organizations have pressured MNCs to include these concerns in their planning and operations.

Another constellation of variables is the *social/cultural environment,* composed of values and customs (e.g., religion and language) discussed in earlier chapters and reflected in Figure 9.1. Understanding these variables is important

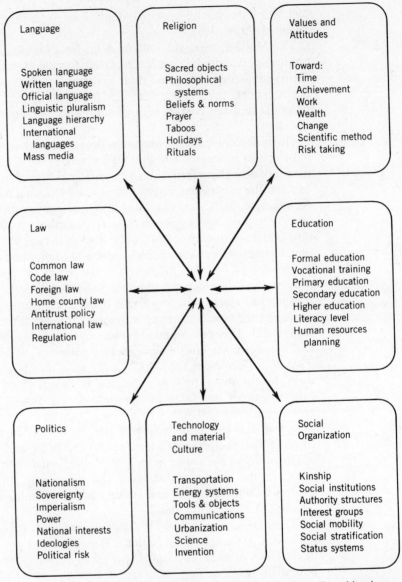

Figure 9.1 Composition of the cultural environment of international business.

Source: T. N. Gladwin and V. Terpstra, Introduction, in V. Terpstra, ed. *The Cultural Environment of International Business*. Cincinnati: Southwestern, 1978, p. xiv. Reprinted with permission.

in negotiations and labor relations, as well as in the training and development of indigenous managers and workers. Differences in decision making, leadership style, and communication patterns (particularly nonverbal) can seriously interfere with the success of operations.

In the following sections we shall examine specific conditions in the international environment that may affect any organization.

CULTURAL CONTEXT

Organizational–environmental interaction—the input–throughput–output cycle—is influenced by cultural phenomena. Cultural variables such as values and beliefs will affect the input side in determining the extent to which natural resources can be harnessed to serve the organization, as we discussed in Chapters 5 and 6. These variables will also determine the nature of the workforce: employees' willingness to work (motivation), the relationship between superiors and subordinates, levels of productivity and quality, the level of skills, the extent to which employees are trainable, and the level of compensation expected. For example, biases in Arabic countries against manual labor will have a direct impact on an operation's need for labor; in these countries, foreign labor may have to be brought in, even though unemployment in the host country is high. Another example is the difference in attitudes of Japanese and American firms toward productivity and quality; organizations may need to take such differences into account.

Cultural variables will also affect organization processes such as managerial styles, decision making, and strategy formulation. For instance, different management styles will be necessary in Latin America and Scandinavia, because the boss–worker relationship differs greatly. Latin American workers expect the boss to be authoritarian; Scandinavian workers expect him or her to be more participative. Similarly, Japanese firms encourage decision making in a group, with input from all levels within the organization; in France, however, decisions tend to come from the top and then pass down through the organization.

Finally, because market receptivity for various products and services is, in part, culturally determined, cultural variables affect the organizational outputs. Spiritual rather than material values have implications regarding potential consumers and patterns of consumption. Designer jeans for women, for instance, will not be well-received in traditional Islamic countries. Mental health services may not be used in countries where strong religious beliefs dictate that the mind is God's domain, not the doctor's.

Social scientists have long studied different cultures to identify the forces that characterize and distinguish them. In Chapter 5 of this book, we examined Hofstede's (1980) four basic indexes for differentiating cultures: (1) power, (2) uncertainty avoidance (the extent to which a society feels threatened by uncertainty or ambiguity), (3) individualism–collectivism (the extent to which people take care of themselves or exhibit loyalty to a social group), and (4) masculinity–femininity (the extent to which dominant values, such as assertiveness, are either masculine or feminine traits). The index most relevant to this chapter is uncertainty avoidance. Countries that score high in this category are characterized by a low tolerance for ambiguity, a high need for security, a high resistance to change, a low risk-taking propensity, high anxiety levels, and low levels of decision making. These countries tend to need formal structures and are highly rule oriented. Such characteristics will obviously influence an organization's structure, managerial style, and strategy.

For example, consider the issue of local (host) versus parent (headquarters) managers. The local manager's willingness to scan the environment, and their openness to cues and indicators, depend on their ability to tolerate uncertainty but also on the culture's ability in general. High needs for security will interfere with managers' ability to perceive threats or opportunities, to take risks, and to make necessary decisions and changes. Their focus may be on survival through structural rigidity instead of on adaptation through structural flexibility. The changes for innovative management are thus reduced. Certain structures may be less tolerated (e.g., matrix structures require an ability to tolerate ambiguity) and therefore will not be adopted even though they are best suited to a particular industry. Changes in the environment create uncertainty; the ability to respond to change is what ensures corporate viability. It is clear that the differences in culture will affect the subsidiaries' reactions to the MNC's policies and styles.

The cultural context thus becomes an environment of its own—an environment that can have great impact on the organization's performance. Because of its importance, the cultural context has been studied in terms of its variability, complexity, hostility, heterogeneity, and interdependence (Gladwin & Terpstra, 1978). We should consider each of these aspects briefly (see Table 9.1).

Variability is the degree to which conditions within a culture are stable or unstable; it is also the rate at which they change. This flux can create uncertainty; it requires MNCs to be flexible and adaptable. Consequently, organizations must rely on local experts to keep them informed.

Cultural complexity reflects the extent to which the rules of human behavior are implicit or explicit—"high or low context," in Gladwin and Terpstra's terms. In most Western countries, human interactions are direct and explicit, whereas in Eastern countries, such as Japan, much is communicated "between the lines" through nonverbal cues and particular uses of language. Negotiations in these countries are difficult, and require training and preparation.

Cultural hostility refers to the host country's negative reactions to the operations of the MNC and, by implication, to its organizational goals. Needless to say, the legitimacy and acceptability of the firm (as perceived by its host country) will affect the MNC's ability to obtain resources and dispose of goods.

Cultural heterogeneity is the degree to which cultures are similar or dissimi-

Table 9.1 Dimensions of the Cultural Environment of International Business

Dimension		Continuum	
		(Low)	**(High)**
Within cultures	Cultural variability	Low & stable change rate	High & unstable change rate
	Cultural complexity	Simple (low context)	Complex (high context)
	Cultural hostility	Munificent (benign)	Malevolent (illiberal)
Among cultures	Cultural heterogeneity	Homogeneous	Heterogeneous
	Cultural interdependence	Independent	Interdependent

Source: T. N. Gladwin and V. Terpstra, Introduction. In V. Terpstra, ed., *The Cultural Environment of International Business*. Cincinnati: Southwestern, 1978, p. xviii. Reprinted with permission.

lar. MNCs need to be aware of these differences, as they require different responses or methods of management.

Cultural interdependence is the degree to which developments in one culture are related to developments in others. For example, events in Iran will certainly affect dealings with the other Islamic countries. Interdependence can be experienced as a threat to national sovereignty, particularly when this interdependence is unbalanced. This may have resulted in the Canadian nationalization of energy resources (Holsti, 1980). Understanding these variables will help to define the role of the manager and the MNC in foreign countries.

Now let us examine more closely how cultural context variables affect practicing executives in foreign territories.

ROLE OF THE MANAGER OVERSEAS

The manager is, first of all, a translator of company policy. The overseas manager is involved in making decisions about the subsidiary's operations. He or she performs this function by transforming the headquarters' policies and strategies into locally relevant procedures. The manager of a local subsidiary needs to watch for changes in the surroundings and to know enough about local customs to interpret the significance of these events. For this reason, indigenous managers can be extremely useful, particularly in a turbulent environment. However, MNCs often prefer to use expatriates, who are more familiar with and loyal to company policy and procedures.

The manager is also a translator of managerial style. In some countries, the host government requires the use of a local manager in subsidiaries from the start of operations, or at a specified time thereafter. Host countries apply pressure to employ nationals in high-level managerial positions to increase domestic control over foreign subsidiaries and to foster the development of trained national managers. External pressures by these countries can take the form of direct regulation, quota requirements, and bureaucratic impediments.

The process of management indigenization, that is, the use of foreign nationals in management positions, creates the potential for conflict between managerial practices and attitudes, because these are rooted in different value systems. Environmental factors—whether educational, social, cultural, economic, political—all influence managerial behavior. Hence MNCs are concerned with the extent to which subsidiaries will modify parent policies and procedures to satisfy local objectives, goals, and environments, and to what extent the MNC must adapt its managerial style to the parent company (De la Torre & Toyne, 1978). Figure 9.2 indicates the interrelatedness of these interactive variables.

In addition, if the MNC takes on the task of training local managers, the expatriate manager must be a translator of culture as well. She or he will need a knowledge of local social and business customs and negotiation skills. Managers must understand different levels of culture—formal, informal, and culturally determined communication patterns such as attitudes, social organization, thought patterns, forms of reasoning, roles, and so forth (Hall, 1960).

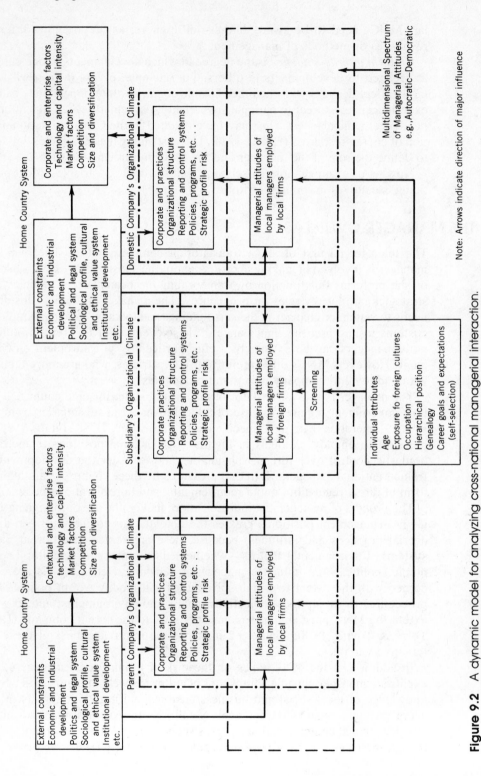

Figure 9.2 A dynamic model for analyzing cross-national managerial interaction.

Source: J. De la Torre and B. Toyne. "Cross National Managerial Interaction: A Conceptual Model," *Academy of Management Review* 3(3):469 July 1978. Reprinted with permission.

Consider, for example, Reischauer's detailed review of Japanese culture (1977). In Japan, one needs to understand the subtleties and nuances of the communication process. This requires a sensitivity to nonverbal cues and the use of language. The spoken word does not carry the same impact here as it does in Western culture. In saying "yes," for instance, the Japanese indicate that they understand your communication although they may not necessarily agree with it. In the word *yes*, the listener accords respect to the communicator who, mistaking it for agreement, can become confused by what appears to be illogical and inconsistent responses.

American: Operations will begin on June 15.
Japanese: Yes.
American: But the necessary material will not be available by June 15.
Japanese: Yes.
American: Then there is no possible way for operations to begin June 15.
Japanese: Yes.

Another critical aspect of communication is that in the Far East, saving face is as important as being logical and consistent. The need to save face may prompt statements for which the chief purpose is not accuracy, but honor.

Westerners must also understand the nature of Japanese business communications. In Japan, business decisions emerge through group consensus—the "Ringi" system by which all company members affix their sign of approval to widely circulated proposals. This decision-making process takes longer than for Westerners, whose decisions are frequently arrived at unilaterally by the "Boss." Once it reaches decisions, however, Japanese management acts more quickly than its Western counterparts, who are often bogged down in winning support for a certain procedure.

Another example can be found in Latin America, where business ventures do not proceed in accordance with North American notions of time. Few businesspersons are punctual by U.S. standards. Work often proceeds at a leisurely pace. Consequently, the Latin sense of time can be a source of frustration for American businesspersons, who interpret a quick response as indicating business interest. There is no such correlation in Latin America; as a result, business takes longer.

These examples should suggest that in serving as intercultural translators, managers need to understand the influences of prejudice and stereotyping that have been highlighted in Chapter 4. They should also be willing to tolerate ambiguity and to be receptive to alternative ways of doing business. Such flexibility requires the ability to show respect, empathy, and persistence (Harris & Moran, 1979). Chapter 12, which is devoted to the selection and training of international assignees, will address these issues in greater detail.

ROLE OF THE MULTINATIONAL COMPANY

When the MNC begins to operate abroad and takes on the task of training local managers and employees, it becomes involved in the transfer of technology as well as culture. In this respect, the manager becomes an intercultural communicator transmitting the parent company's culture. He or she is also an agent of change. As a result, the MNC affects the entrepreneurial and working classes by providing them with opportunities. These opportunities may favor certain groups, thus influencing the host country's ethnic stratification. The impact of consumerism, too, may foster economic inequality. Thus, the MNC's role as an agent of change may result in increased tensions or conflict within the host country (Kumar, 1980).

Such conflict, whether technological or cultural, is often referred to as a conflict of interest: "The MNC, as an institutional citizen of several countries, must resolve the conflict between corporate objectives and national policies and divergent socioeconomic structures and values" (Sethi & Sheth, 1973, p. xvi). Critics often attack MNCs for their use of the home government's power to make profits; some observers have even charged that certain companies' economic interests actually determine the parent countries' governmental policies. For example, the United Fruit Company influenced the politics of Guatemala, Nicaragua, and other Central American nations for decades. Corporate interests often clash with the host nation's goals, thus interfering with the individual governments' ability to protect their own national interests and to harmonize domestic policies (Sethi & Sheth, 1973). Host nations may feel that their sovereignty is being threatened.

Managers should consider the importance of MNC–host-country relations. A nation exists as a discrete entity to provide general governance, resolve conflicts, allocate resources, control the monetary system, provide physical security, and usually maximize economic benefits in international trade. The nation also provides an identity for its members and a sense of group-relatedness, thus serving their psychological needs. According to Fayerweather (1975), an MNC can assume four possible roles in the host country: contributory, reinforcing, frustrating, or undermining. If sufficiently threatened, the host country may react by nationalizing MNC operations. The MNCs will be accepted in the host country only to the extent that its operations do not usurp the country's authority in providing for its people.

Some changes now underway, however, further complicate the manager's perceptions of MNC–host-country relations. The increasing interaction between countries through advances in communications, technology, and travel creates a process of internationalization, a growing cultural similarity that cuts across national boundaries—in effect, an evolving world culture. The flow of material, people, and information between countries creates more permeable boundaries and a greater common pool of resources, markets, and products. Counterreactions exist as well. The trend toward internationalization has met with resistance. Greater interdependence does not necessarily result in international consensus; it can, in fact, result in greater fragmentation (Holsti, 1980). Resistance to internationalization arises from a desire and need to reassert control and self-determination and to preserve a national identity despite potential economic gains possible from market interdependence.

In an effort to proclaim self-sufficiency, to foster group cohesiveness, and to preserve cultural values, nations are redefining their boundaries to reduce external penetration. These efforts constitute the "centrifugal force of national aspirations" and serve to counteract the "centripetal forces of transnationalism" (Holsti, 1980). Host-country governments may exert greater controls on organizations (e.g., by reducing joint policy making and monitoring the flow of goods). Governments may adopt policies of isolationism to resist integration and may nationalize industries strategic to their national goals. Reasserting government control not only protects the nation from external threats but also counteracts internal threats (e.g., secessionist movements that threaten national unity).

In Canada, policies to nationalize the energy industry resulted from a perceived asymmetry in the relationship with the United States and from growing separatist forces within Canada. The great cultural similarity between the United States and Canada and the high degree of interconnectedness resulted in a fear of absorption by the United States or loss of Canada's identity to its dominant partner. The move to nationalize the industry therefore served to redefine the United States–Canada boundary and to reassert the Canadian federal government's control of both its external and internal relationships. Because of the increased awareness of corporate social responsibility and business ethics, Chapter 11 will be devoted to the subsidiary-host country relationship.

ROLE OF GOVERNMENT
Industrial Policy

In their growing concern over national identity and welfare, governments have adopted policies that reflect different degrees of control over the business sector. Industrial policies also reflect the degrees of government influence, ranging from regulation to ownership. These policies can affect the countries' microeconomic structure, efficiency of business operations, and international competition.

For instance, governments seek to control the regional impact of industry by promoting certain geographic locations that need industrial development and employment opportunities. They also bail out declining industries. Governments intervene to avoid layoffs and the subsequent economic and political repercussions of unemployment. They institute policies to control inflation, to maintain stability of local currency, and to reduce uncertainties in the supply and price of resources. In Europe, the OPEC "oil shock" of 1973 prompted industrial policies to protect national industries from such unilateral decisions (Mills, 1978). Japan, a country with close government–business relations, suffered far less from the OPEC activities than some other countries.

Countries use industrial policy to establish national economic guidelines and to influence the economy for political purposes. The profit motive is often secondary. In Japan, for example, government subsidies made economic growth feasible. The government considers such growth more important than profit making. The ruling religious factions in Iran felt that preserving cultural values mattered more than stimulating economic growth. In keeping with national economic planning goals, government involvement in business can serve to boost exports, cut imports, or push industrialization—particularly in the less developed countries (LDCs). China provides a good example of such priorities.

Government involvement can also create or preserve a strategic industry deemed essential to national security, independence, or growth. Canada nationalized its energy industry to assert independence. The Japanese government's financing of the electronics industry sought to promote growth and establish the market share abroad. In short, governments intercede to cope with the financial needs or investment problems of new industries or those that require large technological changes. France and Germany are two nations that provide capital for unusually large R&D expenditures. The production of the Airbus, for example, was largely supported and encouraged by a mutual interest and the cooperation of the governments.

Controls can assume the form of taxation, subsidy, licensing, regulations, and ownership. The United States relies mostly on taxation and regulation. Controls by governmental agencies, however, such as the Civil Aeronautics Boards, the Interstate Commerce Commission, and the Federal Communications Commission, often serve certain interest groups more than they regulate operations. Although some factions would prefer to let competition serve as a regulator, those concerned with antitrust activities advocate a more active approach. Taxation functions drain excess profits from the exploitation of scarce resources (e.g., oil) or commodities made artificially scarce (e.g., alcohol or tobacco) through a windfall profits tax. Concerns for the public good often outweigh concern for high profit and industrial growth; however, some observers see the Occupational Safety and Health Association (OSHA), Consumer Protection Agency (CPA), Environmental Protection Agency (EPA), the Equal Employment Opportunity Commission (EEOC), and other agencies as hampering economic potential. The Reagan Administration's regulatory (or deregulatory) policies seem to promote business interests more than those of the Carter Administration.

The American system of "regulated free enterprise" differs from the Japanese system of "guided free enterprise." In the United States the government's relationship with business is considered adversarial; by contrast, the Japanese government assumes a paternal, protective stance. Cooperation between business and government is based on mutual concern for the common economic good. Although the lack of distinction between business and government is viewed skeptically by some (critics in the United States refer to it as Japan, Inc.), no one can discount the success of the Japanese economy, which is a result (at least in part) of this relationship. The Japanese government's role in business has encouraged modernization, accelerated market strength, and reduced disruptions caused by declining industries. The objective is to stimulate the economy rather than to control it.

The Japanese government's role in business is also made easier by the much greater flexibility of the distance between public and private sector than in the

United States. In Japan several types of companies are subject to public policy: (1) direct government enterprise, (2) public corporations, (3) auxiliary foundations (private in name only), and (4) national companies given financial or administrative guidance. Thus, the direct influence of government can vary as necessary or desirable (Vogel, 1978).

State Ownership

State ownership, the most extreme form of influence, can come about through the accident of history, tradition, or economic necessity (see Figure 9.3). In any case, the relevant maxim here is "the government knows best." State control is often a result of postwar confiscation or of efforts to rebuild the economy or to break up monopolies (e.g., salt or tobacco) that threaten the economy. France, for example, is a leader in industrial policy, partly because of its postwar sense of vulnerability and national insecurity. France turned to its leader (the state) to provide direction and initiative. This move was reinforced by a cultural system that values authority and stability. Currently, the socialist government of François Mitterand has returned to a policy of nationalization.

Government ownership (see Tables 9.2 and 9.3) follows three patterns: (1) rescues, (2) diversifications, and (3) high-risk ventures (Walters & Monsen, 1979). Rescue takeovers serve to fight unemployment or declining industries (e.g., steel and textiles) and to resolve financial problems in growing industries (e.g., the auto industry—Alfa Romeo in Italy, Volvo in Sweden, Lyland in Britain, Chrysler in the United States, etc.). Although rescues are initially viewed as temporary, they tend to become permanent, since takeovers result in competitive advantages worth protecting. There is no need to earn profits (British steel), no fear of loss or bankruptcy, and no need to pay dividends to stockholders. These businesses gain preferential access to state financing, built-in markets, and preference in purchasing from domestic sources. The state can develop monopoly power by placing competing business under single state ownership and by controlling purchase and sales decisions. Incentives for industry to regain control are thus reduced.

State ownership can take other forms. State-owned companies can expand through diversification or consolidation. For example, while the number of state-owned companies in France has declined over the past twenty years (from 170 to 30), the number of subsidiaries of state-owned companies has increased from 266 to 650. Moreover, government establishment or takeover of companies considered high-risk ventures or requiring heavy R&D expenditures is yet another form of government ownership. Britain's National Enterprise Board, for example, determines allocations for such ventures.

Arguments challenging the wisdom of government involvement in industrial policy focus primarily on its impact on efficiency, innovation, growth, and global competition. With government protection, there is little impetus for growth or efficiency. It is difficult to measure performance and productivity as well as monitor accounting practices. Hidden subsidies in the form of tariffs or quotas result in a lack of transparency in dealing with these firms. U.S. govern-

Who owns how much?

Privately owned: ○ all or nearly all
Publicly owned: ◔ 25% ◑ 50% ◕ 75% ● all or nearly all

	Ports	Tele-communications	Electricity	Gas	All productions	Coal	Railways	Airlines	Meter industry	Steel	Shipbuilding	
Australia	●	●	●	●	○	○	●	◕	○	○	na	Australia
Austria	●	●	●	●	●	●	●	●	●	●	na	Austria
Belgium	●	●	◔	◔	na	○	●	●	○	◑	○	Belgium
Brazil	●	●	●	●	●	●	●	◔	○	◕	○	Brazil
Britain	●	●	●	●	◔	●	●	◕	◑	◕	●	Britain
Canada	●	◔	●	○	○	○	◕	◕	○	○	○	Canada
France	●	●	●	●	na	●	●	◕	◑	◕	○	France
West Germany	●	●	◕	◑	◔	◑	●	●	◔	○	◔	West Germany
Holland	●	●	◕	◕	na	na	●	◕	◑	◔	○	Holland
India	●	●	●	●	●	●	●	●	○	◕	●	India
Italy	●	●	◕	●	na	na	●	●	◔	◕	◕	Italy
Japan	●	●	○	○	na	○	◕	◔	○	○	○	Japan
Mexico	●	●	●	●	●	●	●	◑	◔	◕	●	Mexico
South Korea	●	●	◕	○	na	◔	●	○	○	◕	○	South Korea
Spain	●	◑	○	◕	na	◑	●	●	○	◑	◕	Spain
Sweden	●	●	◑	●	na	na	●	◑	○	◕	◕	Sweden
Switzerland	●	●	●	●	na	na	●	◔	○	○		Switzerland
United States	●	○	◔	○	○	○	◔	○	○	○	○	United States

na = not applicable or recognizable production • excluding Country

Figure 9.3 Who owns how much?

Source: "Public Sector Enterprise," *The Economist,* December 30, 1978, p. 39.

ment involvement in the mid-1970s contributed to disastrous mismanagement, corruption, price freezing, and expanded losses. Industries are kept alive at the taxpayers' expense and protected at the consumers' expense. As *The Economist* stated, "While a good public enterprise achieves maximum benefit for the minimum of public effort and money, most public sectors do the reverse" (December 30, 1978). Here again, the value system and ideology are the main ingredients in the government's policy.

Government involvement may promote competition (e.g., the U.S. divestment of AT&T) or, conversely, it may create unfair competition. National procurement preferences, merger promotion, nationalization, and cartels (or orderly marketing agreements) contradict notions of free trade. Government industries prefer (or are directed to use) other state-controlled industries for obtaining inputs or disposing of outputs. Often, the host government itself serves as a lucrative market, inaccessible to foreign industry—a market challenging the profitability of competition with government-backed industries that place the United States at a disadvantage. The American balance of trade suffers as fair competition is undermined. No doubt, particular governments decide to what extent a protectionist policy is advantageous at a particular time for particular products.

POLITICAL CLIMATE

The impact on a particular company of political change is not immediately evident or predictable, but it is safe to say that political climate plays a crucial role in MNC activity. The political upheavals in Iran during the late 1970s resulted in huge financial losses for American-owned industries. The impact of political conflict on a company can take many forms: damage to property; loss of labor through strikes (e.g., Italy) or through dangerous conditions (e.g., civil war in Lebanon); or loss of control of ownership (as with the Peron regime in Argentina). Given the relative frequency of political change and its potential impact on a firm, it seems surprising that large MNCs do not have sophisticated models and methods of assessing political risk. Most approaches to date have been intuitive, subjective, and vague rather than based on a conceptual model of the relationships between these events and the industry's functioning.

Political Risk

We should differentiate political risk from political change or uncertainty (Kobrin, 1979; Rummel & Heenan, 1978). Political uncertainty refers to unmeasured subjective doubt, whereas political risk is considered an objective measurement that estimates the impact of a given event on a given firm. Although political change may be fast and furious, the impact of these changes on the firm is not necessarily known or easily predictable. A dramatic change in regime (e.g., from social democracy to military dictatorship), for example, does not necessarily mean that expropriation is inevitable (as in Nicaragua) or irreversible (in Chile, the Allende regime's policies were, in fact, reversed). Kobrin

Table 9.2 Major State-Owned Industrial Companies in Western Europe

Aerospace	Aluminum	Automobiles	Chemicals	Computers and electronics	Mining (coal and metals)	Paper and wood products	Petroleum	Steel
Aerospatiale *France*	Ardal og Sunndal Verk *Norway*[4]	Alfa Romeo *Italy*	ANIC *Italy*	CII-Honeywell Bull *France*[13]	Charbonnages de France *France*	Enso-Gutzeit *Finland*	British National Oil Corporation *Britain*	British Steel *Britain*
Alitalia *Italy*	VIAG *Germany*	BL Ltd. *Britain*	BP Chemicals *Britain*[7]	Inmos Limited *Britain*[14]	Entreprise Miniere et Chimique *France*	Stätsforetag *Sweden*	British Petroleum *Britain*[16]	Cockerill *Belgium*[19]
British Aerospace *Britain*	Vereinigte Metallwerke *Austria*	Renault *France*	Charbonnages de France-Chimie *France*[8]	International Computers Ltd. *Britain*[15]	National Coal Board *Britain*		CFP-Total *France*[17]	Italsider *Italy*
Dassault *France*[1]		Volkswagen *Germany*[5]	DSM *Netherlands*		Saarbergwerke *Germany*		ELF-Aquitaine *France*	Norsk Jernverk *Norway*
Messerschmitt-Boelkow-Blohm (MBB) *Germany*[2]		Volvo *Sweden-Norway*[6]	ELF-Aquitaine *France*[9]		Stätsforetag *Sweden*		ENI *Italy*	NJA *Sweden*
VFW-Fokker *Germany*[3]			Entreprise Miniere et Chimique *France*				Neste *Finland*	Swedish Steel *Sweden*[20]
Rolls-Royce *Britain*			Montedison *Italy*[10]				OMV *Austria*	Saarbergwerke *Germany*
SNECMA *France*			Neste *Finland*				Saarbergwerke *Germany*	Salzgitter *Germany*
			Norsk Hydro *Norway*[11]				Statoil *Norway*	VÖEST-Alpine *Austria*
			OMV *Austria*				Swedish Petroleum *Sweden*[18]	
			Saarbergwerke *Germany*				VEBA *Germany*	
			VEBA *Germany*[12]					

Source: K. D. Walters and R. J. Monsen, "State-Owned Business Abroad." *Harvard Business Review*, March–April 1979, p. 163.

[1] French government to have a 21% stake in capital and double voting rights.

[2] 43% owned by German states of Bavaria and Hamburg.

[3] 26.4% owned by German state of Bremen.

[4] 75% state owned.

[5] 40% state owned.

[6] Proposed recapitalization giving Norwegian government up to 40% stake was recently rejected by stockholders; Volvo's Dutch subsidiary, Volvo Car, 45% owned by Dutch government since January 1978.

[7] Subsidiary of British Petroleum.

[8] Subsidiary of Charbonnages de France.

[9] 70% state owned.

[10] State has 50% interest in company's controlling syndicate.

[11] 51% state owned.

[12] 43.7% state owned.

[13] Honeywell owns 47%, and Machines Bull (in which CGE and French state are shareholders) 53%.

[14] Proposed microprocessor to be controlled by National Enterprise Board.

[15] National Enterprise Board owns 24%.

[16] 51% state owned.

[17] 40% state owned.

[18] 50% state owned.

[19] State has announced an intention to take a 60% stake in this, the largest of Belgium steel producers, and a lower share of other steel companies.

[20] 50% state owned.

Table 9.3 Who Owns the Big Boys*

Name	Country of Ownership*	No. of Employees, in thousands	Net Profit, in millions of dollars	Public Ownership
Royal Dutch/Shell	Britain/Holland	155	2,554	1
Brit. Petroleum	Britain	81	580	4
Unilever	Britain/Holland	327	500	1
Iri	Italy	524	—	5
Philips	Holland	384	278	1
Veba	W. Germany	68	33	3
Eni	Italy	103	− 167	5
Fiat	Italy	342	69	1
Slemens	W. Germany	319	307	1
Daimlier-Benz	W. Germany	169	233	1
Volkswagen	W. Germany	192	198	3
Com. Francaise des Petroles	France	45	29	3
Hoechst	W. Germany	181	103	1
BASF	W. Germany	126	185	1
Renault	France	243	2	5
Bayer	W. Germany	170	150	1
Nestle	Switzerland	140	413	1
Thyssen	W. Germany	134	74	1
Electricity Council	Britain	159	253	5
Peugeot-Citroen	France	185	249	1
ICI	Britain	154	431	1
Elf-Aquitaine	France	37	375	4
Ini	Spain	225	− 158	5
Electricite de France	France	101	144	5
BAT Industries	Britain	152	400	1
ITT Europe	US	204	—	1
Cie Generale d' Electricite (CGE)	France	170	58	1
AEG-Telefunken	W. Germany	158	− 5	1
St Gobain-Pont- a-Mousson	France	159	137	1
Montedison	Italy	135	− 501	3
British Steel	Britain	197	− 857	5
Gutehoffnungshutte	W. Germany	84	45	1
RWE	W. Germany	58	190	3
Empain-Schneider	France	134	—	1
Mannesmann	W. Germany	106	102	1
Pechiney-Uçine- Kuhlmann	France	97	80	1
Fried. Krupp	W. Germany	87	6	1
Ruhrkohie	W. Germany	143	½	2
Nat. Coal Board	Britain	303	39	5
Rhone-Poulenc	France	111	18	1
British Leyland	Britain	195	− 99	5
Ciba-Geigy	Switzerland	74	209	1
Petrofina	Belgium	23	153	1
Ford-Werke	US	56	275	1
Dunlop-Pirelli	Britain/Italy	169	—	1
Akzo	Holland	84	− 73	1
GEC	Britain	191	185	1
Estel	W. Germany/Holland	78	− 183	2
DSM	Holland	33	48	5
Imperial Group	Britain	96	204	1

Source: ''The State in the Market.'' *The Economist,* December 30, 1978, p. 51.
*Europe's fifty largest industrial companies (1977 figures).
Key to public ownership: 1—none, 2—up to 25%, 3—26–50%, 4—51–75%, 5—wholly owned (1978 figures).

et al. (1980) suggests that political risk should be redefined as the impact of political change on operations and on the decision-making processes. Kobrin et al. (1980) describe how firms have assessed the noneconomic environment, how those evaluations have been integrated into decision making, and how the results have affected managerial strategy. Their findings indicate that assessments tend to be reactive, not proactive, that sources of information are usually within the firm, and that assessments not made independently of investment planning serve primarily as background for making decisions not as input. In other words, assessment is not integrated into company policies.

Political risk is determined differently for different companies. Not all companies will be equally affected by political changes. For example, industries requiring heavy capital investments are considered more vulnerable to political risk (Alsop, 1981) than those requiring less. Vulnerability depends on the nature of the business: product and service businesses (e.g., extracting or energy-related industries) are more vulnerable than manufacturing. Kobrin (1981) states that vulnerability is a function of the type of industrial sector, level of technology, ownership structure, and managerial style. Assessment of national political risk (called macrorisk) may be less useful than industry or project-specific assessments (called microrisks). The scope and assessment will depend on the needs of the firm.

Naturally, obtaining information is essential to assessing political risk. However, much information tends to be general, overly subjective, and derived from biased (if not necessarily inaccurate) sources. Farmer (1979) discusses the need to corroborate information by tracing its source, talking to locals, identifying key people, asking the right questions, and spotting inconsistencies or errors. He discusses two types of information networks: imploding and exploding. In the first type, one person (who may or may not have correct information) passes it on to others, who do the same. In the second, a greater number of informants generate the information, which then can be corroborated.

Although Farmer stresses the use of locals from all levels, other sources of information exist. Many companies (e.g., Gulf Oil) have hired outside consultants (e.g., former politicians or foreign service officers) as political analysts, or they have assigned internal departments to this function. Still others rely on the local manager, who may be unfortunately ill-equipped and ill-prepared to function as a political analyst. Karr (1980) describes several useful sources: advisory councils of foreign businesspersons and retired government officials (as formed by General Motors and Caterpillar); academics and former political figures (Henry Kissinger, for example, is a consultant for Merck, Sharp & Dohme, and for Chase Manhattan); private intelligence systems (ITT); joint ventures (e.g., what the Cabot Corporation has established); and well-placed groups of local managers (used by Xerox). Other organizations have developed computer program analysis: American Can Corporation uses PRISM (Primary Risk Investment Screening Matrix) to assess economic desirability and risk payback. Other sources of information are project finance officers, banks, and the media.

Given the numerous possible sources, the information received can be conflicting; so can the interpretations. Line and staff personnel's perceptions of risk can vary dramatically—particularly since their views reflect different vested interests. Line managers, for example, have much at stake in getting a project through, and might thereby minimize the degrees of risk. Staff managers, on the other hand, might overreact, thereby exaggerating the degree of risk. One must always take human subjectivity and bias into account.

Assessment of Risk

Once the information is gathered, how do MNCs assess risk? Most corporations spend their energies analyzing response rather than attempting predictions—in other words, they assess risk reactively rather than invest in predictions. Moreover, risk can be analyzed either subjectively or objectively. Rummel and Heenan (1978) describe techniques such as "grand tours," "old hands," and "Delphic oracles," as well as quantifiable methods. Grand tours usually involve dispatching a company delegation to inspect the local surroundings and meet with local officials. However, the delegates often receive only selective information and miss the whole picture. The old hands method involves the judgments of "experts"—educators, diplomats, and other businesspersons—and relies on external sources of information. Delphic techniques, using internal and external sources (or a combination of both), identify selective elements of the political environment and judge their importance. This approach requires accuracy and comprehensiveness, well-reasoned and timely opinions, and sound judgment. Quantifiable methods predict trends, describe relationships, identify indicators, develop typologies, and analyze events.

Rummel and Heenan (1978) suggest a combined approach and emphasize the importance of intuition and sensitivity. They propose four criteria for analyzing risk: (1) domestic instability (amount of turmoil, rebellion), (2) foreign climate (measured by events such as diplomatic expulsion), (3) political climate (reflected in swings from left-wing to right-wing regimes), and (4) economic climate (the degree of government intervention, GNP, inflation, and external debt levels).

Kobrin (1981) proposes a typology of assessment techniques based on structure (explicitness or implicitness of model) and systemization (formalization of methodology) (see Table 9.4). In his view, the problem of assessment is operational. Criteria such as accuracy, validity, comparability, and means of communicating expert judgments to managers all need to be spelled out. He describes two sources of data, observational and expert, which can be further broken down based on degree of structure or systemization. Subjective (implicit) models of political risk are unstructured, whereas objective (explicit) models are considered structured. Systemization can mean anything from general impressions to sophisticated complete analyses; an unstructured, unsystematized approach would be based on intuition and implicit assumptions regarding an event's impact on operations or managerial contingencies. An example of a systemized, unstructured approach is BERI (Business Environ-

Table 9.4 Attributes of Assessment Methodologies

	Data Source	Coverage	Explicit Model of Process	Relatively Explicit Methodology
Rummell and Heenan	Observational	Cross-national scan	Yes	Yes
Arthur D. Little	Observational	Cross-national scan	Yes	Yes
The Futures Group	Observational and expert gen.	Cross-national scan	Yes	Yes
Industrial Firm "A"	Experts	In-depth coverage/ selected countries	No	No
Industrial Firm "B"	Experts	In-depth coverage/ selected countries	No	Yes
BERI	Experts	Cross-national scan	No	Yes
ESP	Experts	In-depth coverage/ selected countries	No	Yes
Frost and Sullivan	Experts	Cross-national scan	Yes	Yes
Shell/ASPRO-SPAIR	Experts	In-depth coverage/ selected countries	Yes	Yes

Source: S. J. Kobrin, "Political Assessment by International Firms: Models or Methodologies?" *Journal of Policy Modeling,* 3: 2:256, 1980.

mental Risk Index), a computer program combining a highly general regular scan of information, and Economic, Social, and Political Analysis (ESP), used in Latin America, as developed by the chemical industry.

In both, the methodologies are formalized but the models are implicit, that is, not conceptually derived in terms of the predicted impact of events. Examples of systematized-structured approaches are the World Political Risk Forecast (published by Frost & Sullivan, Inc.), a systematized-structured approach based on a deductive model. It takes elements or issues considered relevant to particular "actors" (people) and then measures their impact in terms of position, power, and salience. Another method, ASPRO/SPAIR (developed by Shell Oil), uses an inductive model in which experts estimate the values of variable factors affecting the business climate. This method, however, is particularly costly and time-consuming. The BERI method is useful for a general, preliminary scan (to assess macrorisk), whereas ASPRO/SPAIR should be used for microrisk assessment (i.e., industry specific). Kobrin (1981) concludes that "effective political assessment is more likely to result from explicit specification of casual relationships and implementation of systematic analytic procedures than development of increased methodological sophistication or elegance" (p. 251). He argues that it is important to assess political risk in terms of managerial contingencies in order to adapt appropriate strategies.

Variables are, of course, related instability and economic deprivation—the final modifying variable. Johnson (1980) states that risks are locationally determined (macro-level risks), and are related to the unevenness of the development process and the strength of the country in terms of national power. From these assumptions, he constructed a four-cell typology.

What are the strategies for risk reduction? Alsop (1981) proposes the following:

- Ingratiating the company with the host government by contributing to the regime's economic and political goals (e.g., by training workers, providing technology, increasing the amount of exports, and thereby improving the nation's balance of payments).

- Creating a "good citizenship image" to accommodate the country by locating the firm in an area designated for development by the country planning agencies.

- Establishing joint ventures with local firms.

- Working with several investors and banks in order to spread the risk.

- Taking out insurance—both government (OPIC) and commercial (e.g., Lloyds of London).

- Selling technology rather than large capital investments.

Other suggestions—sometimes called "loss control" measures—maintain host-country dependency on technology through brand names and centralized research: keep a low profile (e.g., Good Humor, a well-established brand of ice cream in the United States, is foreign owned); install an ongoing system to monitor the environment; develop contingency plans.

As the world becomes increasingly internationalized, MNCs will try to capitalize on foreign markets and resources. They will need to be more sensitive to political change and to understand how these changes will affect their operations. With this understanding, they will also need to make decisions and formulate strategies to increase profit and minimize loss. Even large, active MNCs do not analyze political risk with proper care and sophistication; their typical response to political risk is to avoid it. In doing so, they may miss valuable opportunities.

ROLE OF LABOR

Differences in the Workforce

In planning for its operations abroad, the MNC needs to take into account the role of the labor force. Labor supply and skills vary dramatically from country to country. Government regulations about quotas and local versus expatriate employers may also vary, reflecting the prevailing cultural attitudes. The Malaysian government, for example, closely regulates the proportion of Malay and Chinese workers. Local customs such as rituals and national holidays may affect productivity goals. Discrimination or antidiscrimination policies, both racial and sexual, also need to be considered. For instance, affirmative action guidelines in the United States restrict the MNCs' hiring activities. Companies with women, blacks, or Jews in top management positions should be careful when sending representatives from these groups abroad to Arabic or South African settings.

Education and skill levels will determine the amount and kind of training programs needed. Job design can also be affected; skilled workers may require greater variety and autonomy. For example, the labor force in Sweden tends to be well-educated, fairly affluent, and socially aware. These workers found assembly-line jobs unfulfilling; as job satisfaction declined, so did productivity. In response, Volvo designed a plant in Kalmar with job functions that would better match workers' needs for autonomy, variety, and meaningful tasks. Although creating such an environment was more costly, improved productivity compensated for these costs (Tichy, 1974). In other countries, workers may prefer routinized jobs because they are less demanding or may provide more opportunities for socializing.

Policies concerning labor practices may also determine the cost of labor. In Japan, for example, labor is considered a fixed cost, because guaranteed lifetime employment (mainly in large companies) precludes using layoffs as cost controls. It also provides an atmosphere more conducive to automation, since workers do not see their jobs as threatened.

Depending on which unions are present, how well they are organized, and what their stances may be toward management, union activity will also have differential impact, both across countries and across industries. Unions are less prevalent in LDCs, and their activity is strongly watched by the political regime. In Poland, for instance, union activities are restricted by Communist government controls. In Japan, unions are organized by company, not by industry. The Japanese relationship is cooperative: what is good for the company is considered good for the workers, and unions are more willing to forgo wage benefits when company profits falter than unions in the United States are. Under these circumstances, inflation is easier to control.

In countries where unions take on an adversarial role, company profits are vulnerable to union strikes and sabotage. Countries with the worst management–labor relations (measured by the frequency of strikes) are Canada, Italy, the United States, Ireland, France, and Britain.

Industrial Democracy

In some countries, there is a social movement promoting greater worker influence. This movement, often called industrial democracy, is "the outcome of a political thrust toward greater guarantees provided by law of social and economic entitlements" (Mills, 1978). Rising levels of education and affluence and social awareness have propelled this movement. Industrial democracy (see Table 9.5) evolves for different reasons in different places and at different times. Tradition, board structures, and labor strife are institutional factors. For instance, codetermination—worker representation on company boards—has been common in Germany since 1947, and is now required by law (at a rate of 50%). In other countries (Austria, Denmark, Sweden, Holland) the percentage (usually 33%) varies. Industrial democracy arose elsewhere from labor–management conflict. The greater the extent of industrial democracy, the lower the rate of strikes.

Table 9.5 Countries Ranked by Degree of Industrial Democracy

Ranking	Country
High	Yugoslavia
	West Germany
	Austria
	Norway
	Sweden
	Denmark
Medium	Netherlands
	France
	Belgium
	Switzerland
Low	Italy
	United Kingdom
	Ireland
	Spain
	Greece
	Portugal
	United States

Politics, too, has played a role in the emergence of industrial democracy. The countries in which industrial democracy is most prevalent tend to be socialist. Industrial democracy appears to be inversely related to Communism and capitalism. Additional factors include the degree of stability, demands for nationalization, and counterunion movements; in addition, social factors such as employee opposition, educational levels, and worker and manager ideology all constitute forces that shape the nature of these policies.

Mills (1978) describes five shapes or "faces" of European industrial policy. These are (1) codetermination, (2) work councils, (3) shop-floor participation, (4) financial participation, and (5) collective bargaining (Table 9.6).

Table 9.6 The Five Faces of European Industrial Democracy

1. Codetermination: workers on boards

First instance: 1947 in German coal and steel industries as anti-Nazi device (50% workers).

By 1974, minority representatives on boards (usually 33%) required by law in Germany, Austria, Denmark, Sweden, Holland. Upped to 50% in Germany, 1977 (private companies with 2,000+ employees). German formula, roughly, proposed for Britain by Bullock Committee, 1977, but no legislation in sight.

Worker polls (1976) in Britain, Denmark, France showed workers do not feel it very important. Not much interest in form in Scandinavia. Many people everywhere feel it is essentially cosmetic.

EEC proposes two-tier structure: (1) 50% owners-50% workers, (2) 100% management, latter reporting to former, for all Eurocompanies in future.

Generally conceived/perceived as "communications" structure against worker "control" device; no known instance in Europe (yet) of workers on boards blocking management decisions, or seeking to.

In Britain, Germany, much publicized by press (in Britain as industrial democracy").

Wherever present, achieved by legislative process, or national law. Opposed by Communists.

2. Works councils

Since World War II, either through legislation or collective bargaining, works councils mandatory in all

Table 9.6 (*Continued*)

European countries in varying degrees and strengths. Stated functions: to improve company performance, working conditions, security.

In some companies, worker/union-run; in some, management chairs. Usually mostly workers, some stewards; usually members elected democratically from workplace.

In France, where legally mandated, weak discussion groups without power. In Britain, nonmandated wide variance between weakness and strength. In Holland and Germany, where mandated, powerful and legally protected. In Scandinavia, where mandated, not considered important structures. In Italy, where not mandated, extremely powerful.

Generally, particularly Holland and Germany, growing in influence (and achievements) over factory-level management decision making, performance, and productivity.

Usually achieved, in most countries, through legislative process, or national law.

3. Shop-floor participation

Other names: work place democracy, quality of work life, job enrichment.

Seminal efforts: Britain's Tavistock Institute, Norway's Work Research Institute, notably latter.

Various notions/restructuring processes designed to provide workers with greater participation in decisions affecting day-to-day performance of work.

British Work Research Unit (1974), A.N.A.C.T. in France (1974), Work Research Unit in Sweden (1977).

Unilateral (management only) "job enrichment" activities increasingly unpopular with unions, particularly in Sweden and Holland, as "union-busting"; bilateral, joint union-management participative activities, particularly in Germany, increasingly popular with both unions and managements.

German Humanization of Work Act (1974): $109,000,000 over five years for experimentation in this area. Almost no legislative mandates; almost wholly private/voluntary, wherever found.

4. Financial participation

Other names: profit sharing with unions/workers.

Except for scarce voluntary plans, nonexistent in Europe outside France, although much discussed/advocated by unions, notably in Sweden.

Under French law (1973), most workers get nothing, the few get pittances; considered a farce.

Swedish Meidner Plan (1976) proposed giving 20% of all private profits to unions; considered a key reason for voters' ouster (1976) of Social Democrats who endorsed it.

Most proposed financial participation plans suggest laws mandating percentages of all profits going into centrally administered fund, dominated or controlled by union confederation (e.g., Meidner Plan: Sweden). Most seen as union ploy to dominate economy over long run as profits accrue; in most, payouts to workers small or even nonexistent.

Union advocates call such plans "capitalist alternative to socialism," but voters are not buying, hence absence of legal achievements in this face.

Opposed by Communists.

5. Collective bargaining

Still number one mainstay of industrial democracy in Europe in all countries; notably weak in France and Britain; notably strong in Germany, Holland, Italy, Belgium, and Sweden.

Worth noting: "faces" above, and laws creating same, carefully avoid any intrusion on rights of collective bargaining, or relationship thereto. Such laws, as noted, tend to provide new "social" rights; collective bargaining is (except in Italy and Sweden) economic.

In Italy, where no industrial democracy legislation exists, unions (notably powerful metal workers) have used bargaining to achieve industrial democracy gains won politically elsewhere.

In Sweden, new 1977 Democracy At Work law radically opens collective bargaining to matters traditionally considered management prerogative for first time, down to local union levels.

Source: T. Mills, "Europe's Industrial Democracy: An American Response." *Harvard Business Review,* November–December 1978, p. 149.

Codetermination in Germany means a two-tiered board, half of whose members are labor union representatives. The European Economic Community (EEC) is proposing this system for all Euro-companies in the future. In another form of "power sharing," Swedish labor representatives serve a monitoring function by inspecting company books.

Work councils, mandated in most European countries, serve to improve company performance, working conditions, and security. They are run by unions or management and have varying degrees of power. The degree of power is not necessarily a function of being mandated. In Holland, Germany, and Italy, these councils are powerful; and in the latter, they are not mandated.

Shop-floor participation—also known as workplace democracy, quality of work life, and job enrichment—is becoming more and more popular in the United States (particularly in the form of quality circles, a Japanese participatory technique). Participative management—worker involvement in decision making—apparently improves productivity and quality of work by increasing worker commitment. Greater concern for workers' welfare has resulted in other efforts at humanizing the job; alternative work schedules, such as flextime, the compressed work week, and job sharing, provide workers with greater control to match their life needs with their work needs. By arranging one's working hours or days, or even sharing one's job, workers can enrich their lives with better opportunities for education, raising families, or leisure activities. These efforts have resulted in greater job satisfaction, improved quality of work, and reduced absenteeism and turnover (Ronen, 1981; 1984).

In *financial participation*, or profit sharing, workers share the corporation's wealth. This form of industrial democracy is rare, and is mandated only in France. In Sweden, the 1976 Meidner Plan proposed giving 20% of all private profits to unions, but the plan's advocates were voted out of office in the next election. In the United States, profit sharing usually means giving workers stock in the company as bonuses or benefits. In Canada, worker-owned collectives are being formed to bolster dying industries that threaten loss of employment (Bhere & Tixiec, 1981).

Collective bargaining is traditionally the mainstay of most labor power, and is also the force behind new forms of industrial democracy. This is particularly true where such forms are not legislated, as in Italy. The domain of collective bargaining is being expanded in Sweden by the Democracy at Work Law of 1977, in which unions acquire greater influence in dealing with management (see Table 9.7).

The EEC is interested in standardizing laws for labor participation to preserve industrial peace through increased job satisfaction, better communications, and earlier conflict resolution. By increasing worker commitment to corporate success, the EEC hopes to moderate wage demands, reduce turnover, and facilitate innovation and change through cooperation.

Cooperation between labor and management is not, however, readily accepted by the countries in which it is mandated. Unions view it with suspicion, believing that it undermines their influence over workers. Workers, in turn, are wary of increased demands on them, and often take the stance that "it's not my

Table 9.7 Significant European "Industrial Democracy" Legislation

Date	Country	Law Activity
1945	France	Works councils mandatory
1946	Sweden	Works councils mandatory
1947	Germany	Codetermination (iron and steel 33%)
1951	Belgium	Works councils mandatory
1951	Germany	Parity codetermination (iron and steel 58%)
1952	Germany	First works constitution act
1967	France	Financial participation (profit sharing) act
1970	Italy	Worker's charter act
1971	Norway	Codetermination law (33%)
1971	Holland	First works council act
1972	Sweden	First codetermination act (33%)
1972	European Economic Community	Fifth directive (two-tier boards in Eurocompanies)
1972	Germany	Second works constitution act
1973	Austria	Labor constitution act (councils, codetermination)
1973	Norway	Codetermination act (33%)
1973	Holland	Two-tier board act
1973	Sweden	Worker dismissal protection act
1973	Germany	Metalworker "Humanization of Work" strike
1974	United Kingdom	Bullock Commission authorized
1974	United Kingdom	British Work Research Unit established
1974	France	Sudreau Commission report
1974	France	A.N.A.C.T. established
1974	Denmark	Codetermination act (33%)
1975	European Economic Community	"Gundelach Report" (two-tier boards)
1975	France	Cosurveillance proposed
1975	Sweden	Meidner (financial profit-sharing proposed)
1976	Germany	Parity codetermination act (50%)
1976	United Kingdom	Employment protection act
1976	Sweden	"Democracy at Work" act (unrestricted bargaining)
1976	Denmark	Work environment act (psychological welfare)
1976	Norway	Work environment act (psychological welfare)
1976	Holland	Second works council act (tougher)
1976	France	Manual worker protection act
1976	Italy	FLM/Fiat contract (union rights in management)
1977	United Kingdom	Bullock Commission report

Source: T. Mills, "Europe's Industrial Democracy: An American Response." *Harvard Business Review,* November–December 1978, p. 145.

job." For example, in Italy, with its unions' Marxist leanings, cooperation is seen as "selling out" to management. The corporation believes that cooperation slows down the decision-making process and interferes with its managers' freedom and control. Top managers tend to feel that economies of scale will diminish as industrial democracy complicates efficient functioning. Middle management tends to feel left out and worries about loss of power.

There is little doubt, however, that industrial democracy is gaining momentum in the United States. Witness, for example, the recent union–management agreements in the auto industry. Whether greater labor participation will remain voluntary or be mandated as abroad is uncertain. The durability of the movement is also unclear.

The impact of industrial democracy on the multinational company will depend in part on how extensively its measures become institutionalized. For example, the EEC Vredeling proposal would require companies to present extensive information to labor groups before certain business decisions are made. The International Confederation of Free Trade Unions is currently lobbying in the United Nations for codes of conduct governing employers. The International Labor Organization is drafting health and safety guidelines for workers. The power of unions is increasing on an international level. Corporations express concern that existing and proposed codes will establish an effective international labor movement capable of negotiating across national boundaries. Viggo's, the Swedish subsidiary of BOC International (London), threatened to reduce jobs in Sweden, prompting a labor union appeal to the Organization of Economic Cooperation and Development (OECD), which ruled in favor of "meaningful negotiations" with local unions (*Chemical Week*, 1981).

MNCs need to monitor these trends. If well-informed, they can respond with lobbying participation in forming the codes and by writing their own codes to anticipate those forthcoming. How extensively codes will be mandated or enforced may be mitigating factors.

ROLE OF THE ECONOMY
Indicators

When an MNC decides to "set up shop" in a particular country, its managers look at that country's economic indicators, because investment strategies rely in part on the economic health of a country. Indicators of economic health include GNP, balance of payments, inflation rates, stability of local currency, government spending and resource management policies, levels of unemployment, and per capita income and spending. For example, government spending policies may restrict operations to particular projects that interest the government. A country's balance of payments might determine the amount of exports or imports allowed. Inflation rates and currency stability might affect the profit picture by inflating costs. Brazil's currency devaluation, resulting from an inflation rate of over 100%, means that production costs increase with the cost of supplies (*Chemical Week*, 1981). Per capita income and spending indicates market potential of certain consumer goods.

Although a sounder economy may imply a lower risk, a floundering economy may provide opportunities as well as dangers. Under these conditions, local governments may be more receptive to the MNC, viewing it as a source of economic stimulation, a means of developing resources (natural and human), and a source of advanced technology. Agreements between the local government and the MNC can be economically beneficial to both. High levels of unemployment may indicate the possibility of cheap labor for the MNC, which in turn improves the local standard of living and develops a skilled labor force by providing employment. These changes may enhance political support of the current regime. However, host countries may also view MNCs as exploiting their resources without contributing to the common economic development. As a result, some governments have instituted policies restricting operations or requiring additional services.

MNCs need to consider the host government's policies regarding local ownership, price controls, repatriation profits, and currency devaluation. For example, profit controls created by the Andean Pact nations restrict the amount of profit that can be exported (no more than 20% of registered capital) or reinvested locally (no more than 14%). In Turkey, an MNC cannot transfer earnings abroad (*Chemical Week,* 1981). A few examples of such policies are shown in Table 9.8.

MNCs should also consider the influence of national economic planning agencies. International enterprises need to accommodate plans developed by the government-established priority sectors or by specific targets within those sectors. An MNC may find itself constrained by the geographical distributions, location of operations, employment policies, and specific technologies of these agencies, and it should therefore make every attempt to participate in local planning. Countries differ in the extent to which they make conscious efforts at planning. The United States, for example, does very little planning. In France, planning is managed by indirect controls; discriminatory taxation and financing facilities are used to persuade companies to follow a particular direction or course of action. India's national plans limit the total participation of foreign enterprise and delineate which specific areas are open to foreign investment (Robock et al., 1977).

Assessment

Assessment of economic indicators can vary depending on the MNC's interest. The criteria for evaluating economic conditions vary as a function of decision-making processes and objectives; in turn, these criteria will suggest what operations to undertake. Variables that serve as criteria can also vary depending on the country, the project, the type of involvement considered, and the economic profile. We can evaluate a country by comparing it with other countries, other regions within the country, its own past performance, its level or stage of economic development, the investment climate specific to a planned project, the debt and reserve capacity, or a general notion of economic health.

Assessment of national economic environments is not necessarily straightforward. Traditional estimates of purchasing power—the ratio of GNP to population—do not allow for differences in distribution patterns and growth rates, particularly in the LDCs. We might obtain a partially better measure of pur-

Table 9.8 Changing Rules of Foreign Investments

ARGENTINA

Taxes have been reduced, but the currency-exchange rate is putting a crimp in corporate profits.

BELGIUM

A new economic program, intended to create jobs, requires each company to deposit in a special account all salary payments exceeding a certain amount, and the biggest wage-earners must invest 10% of their income in Belgian companies or government bonds.

BRAZIL

The government is expected to experiment with further short-term economic measures to reduce the high inflation rate and the serious balance-of-payments deficit. The authorities have already imposed a steep currency-devaluation measure, price controls, and restrictions on borrowing from Brazilian banks. Next, the government may prod companies to step up their borrowing from outside the country and to invest the proceeds in Brazil.

BRITAIN

Taxes on North Sea oil and gas have been increased seven times in the past eighteen months, and a new "supplementary tax" will be detailed in March. Chemical companies complain that their energy costs are significantly greater than those paid by their competitors on the Continent.

CANADA

The National Energy Policy requires oil and gas companies to be at least 50% Canadian-owned by 1990. There will be an 8% tax on their gross production and a 30¢/Mcf. tax on natural gas sales. Companies that are at least 75% Canadian-owned can earn grants for exploration and development.

EGYPT

Foreign investment has been impeded by bureaucratic red tape and inadequate laws. Now Abdel Razak Meguid, minister for economics and finance, plans to present to the parliament sixteen bills designed to encourage and facilitate foreign investments.

FRANCE

President Giscard d'Estaing is expected to win the April 26 election, but Socialist François Mitterrand is accorded a slight chance for an upset victory. If incumbent Industry Minister Andre Giraud becomes prime minister, French oil companies—and their chemical branches—are expected to function to a greater degree than now as instruments of the state.

France protects certain industrial sectors such as fertilizers, keeping out foreign investors.

GREECE

The present government has drawn up a new, yet-unpublished law providing increased incentives for investments in petrochemicals and fertilizers. In some cases, investors could receive industrial-development grants. However, the November election could bring in a Socialist government unfriendly to foreign investors.

IRELAND

The corporate income tax, formerly 45%, has been reduced to 10%. However, for companies established before 1981, the tax will not apply until 1990 to profits on exports.

ISRAEL

To attract foreign capital into chemicals and other exporting industries, the government has extended to twelve years the period of eligibility for certain tax benefits, previously available for only five years. Also, the government has been divesting its holding in companies, such as Haifa Chemicals.

ITALY

The government is prescribing new measures for the chemical industry. In one program, state-owned ENI is taking over certain private companies with financial difficulties. Under a law not yet enacted, state-owned and private companies are to be restructured, and there will be more emphasis on cooperation, less on profit-seeking. Also, $700 million in government funds will be pumped into the industry.

JAPAN

All companies face higher taxes. Effective April 1, the corporate income tax rate, now 40%, will go up to 42%. And several years from now, in the face of stiff opposition from the business community, the Finance Ministry will seek to impose an industrywide value-added tax.

MEXICO

Foreign investors that build chemical plants in certain areas can get tax benefits and energy and feedstock discounts, sometimes up to 30%. Foreign ownership is generally limited to 49%, but the formula permits some flexibility. The state-owned oil company has priority for the production of petrochemicals. Civil disturbances remain a threat.

MOROCCO

A small percentage of profits must be invested within the country. In general, a company's board chairman

Table 9.8 (*Continued*)

and a majority of its directors must be Moroccans; but special arrangements can be negotiated if a company has invested more than $5 million.

PAKISTAN

Most segments of the chemical industry, but not petrochemicals, are open to foreign investors. The government sets the prices on most commodities, but permits price increases based on increases in production costs.

PHILIPPINES

The government has abolished price controls except for those on goods in short supply, such as petroleum. Chemical investments have been exempted from the 40% limit on foreign ownership. At least 95% of a company's employees must be Filipinos and local raw materials must be given preference over imports, but officials show some flexibility on those provisions. Taxes have increased rapidly.

PORTUGAL

New laws are expected to facilitate private investments. Recently adopted incentives include tax exemptions and special tax allowances on investments deemed helpful to the nation. But there are complaints about a slow-acting bureaucracy and excessive absenteeism and strikes.

SAUDI ARABIA

Investors in the petrochemical industry can count on a secure supply of feedstocks at a fraction of their market value, low-interest loans with a five-year grace period, and a government committed to free enterprise. But the trained workforce is relatively small, making it difficult for a company to attain the required 75% Saudi employment quota within five years.

SOUTH AFRICA

There is a continuing risk of racial conflict. Fertilizer price ceilings are intended to keep food prices down. Import controls are being relaxed, and there are no restrictions on exports or use of feedstocks. Foreign investors are allowed to buy local currency at a 30% discount for certain purposes.

SOUTH KOREA

The government has ended its restrictions on repatriation of profits, and has modified the law that limited foreign ownership to 50%. Now foreign ownership can be as much as 100% in certain cases, such as ventures bringing new technology or diversification. But political unrest continues.

SPAIN

The moderate Socialists, regarded as the probable winners in the 1983 elections, are expected to be even more aggressive than before in encouraging foreign investment. Incentives already include plant-site procurement, tax allowances and government loans. Foreign ownership can range up to 100%.

SWEDEN

Some political parties and trade unions are advocating a law requiring companies to use a portion of their profits to buy stock for the unions. That law, which may be years away, could give the unions greater influence on corporate managements. An existing law allows workers to negotiate on any company decision that affects them.

TAIWAN

New efforts are being made to attract foreign investments. Recently enacted laws provide additional advantages for technology-oriented companies whose research-and-development expenditures exceed a certain minimum. Producers of petrochemical intermediates complain that the government has not protected them against low-priced imports from the United States.

THAILAND

The government offers incentives for foreign capital, but there is a trend toward more domestic ownership in new and existing companies. With the country's own natural-gas production beginning this year, the Petroleum Authority of Thailand will be the only source of petrochemical feedstocks, and customer companies will have to abide by its rules.

TURKEY

Chemicals are one industry in which foreign investments are permitted under recently adopted rules. Foreigners can invest not less than $1 million or more than $50 million in a single venture, and their ownership must not exceed 49%. Because of currency problems, foreign investors have been unable to repatriate their earnings.

VENEZUELA

The new development plan puts increased emphasis on foreign capital in petrochemicals and pharmaceuticals. Some of the Andean Pact's rules are being bent to allow, for example, companies to deposit their excess profits in special accounts. Within fifteen years after a company is established, its foreign ownership must be reduced to no more than 49%. Price controls remain in effect on pharmaceuticals.

Source: "New CPI Tactics Reduce the Risk of Investing Abroad." *Chemical Week*, February 25, 1981, p. 42.

chasing power by converting local currencies to a common unit through the current exchange rate. What complicates matters further is variation in the concept, coverage, quality of national statistics, and statistical biases.

Sources of information regarding the economic environment are available from the United Nations, World Bank International Monetary Fund (IMF), and OECD. These are often combined with scanning techniques from forecasting tools. For example, a macroeconomic approach would include price level forecasts from inflation trends, wage/productivity ratios, and balance of payments from foreign exchange earnings prospects, as well as from anticipated foreign exchange needs. An exchange rate forecast is determined by many factors. Another consideration is the stage of economic development and the concomitant strategies stressing capital inflow versus industrialization, for example, capital-intensive versus labor-intensive industries.

In addition, we must consider the factor of external dependence. External dependence refers to the national economy's vulnerability to fluctuations in international trade, as measured by the ratio of foreign trade to GNP. Countries low on external dependence include the United States, the USSR, and China. A country's obligation to service and repay foreign loans also indicates the degree of dependence. A measure of the capacity to repay would be the comparison of external debt and interest obligations with foreign exchange earnings. Economic integration refers to the participation in regional coordination, as in the EEC. This might impose limitations or barriers on the MNC.

ROLE OF THE MARKETPLACE

What is the marketplace of the international environment like? It is as varied as the countries and cultures that compose it. One area in which the MNCs impact on the LDCs is consumer spending patterns. In this respect, MNCs are agents of cultural change, which can sometimes be antagonistic to the host-country's cultural belief systems. In extreme cases, the marketing of certain products in LDCs can harm the health of that country's population. For example, Nestle's introduction of infant formulas in parts of the Third World resulted in a decline of breast-feeding, which in turn increased the incidence of malnutrition. This created a worldwide uproar and censure of Nestle's policies. Coca-Cola, whose marketing of soft drink products has also contributed to malnutrition in impoverished countries, is attempting to correct the problem by adding nutritional supplements to its formula in some areas. Increasingly, MNCs are having to consider their social responsibility in marketing their wares.

Culture may therefore serve as a general context for marketing strategies; however, managers need other information to assess the market potential of countries.

Indicators

Indicators of market potential are derived from many variables: GNP, population, and degree of industrialization. For example, to survey countries for the possible marketing of designer jeans, several steps are necessary. First, one needs to explore the demand for the product by considering the product's purpose or function (to provide fashionable leisure wear) and customer needs (to be fashionable). Then certain gross indicators can be chosen, based on their relevance to the product or need. The market for designer jeans would depend on the consumers' purchasing power, how much is spent, accessibility to distribution channels, advertising, and production or import of similar goods. Marketing personnel must assign values to these indicators from available data and weigh them in terms of their scores. This procedure provides a general overview; it is a first step.

Assessment

These general economic data are used to assess the climate for market entry through classification schemes, multiple factor analysis, or authorized customized models. Classification schemes are based on outlining similar business environments that would create similar investment potentials. These schemes rely on financial, sociocultural, and socioeconomic characteristics, transportation, and communication variables. Multiple factors are derived from combining some of these variables, many of which have been differentially weighted: market growth, market intensity (degrees of purchasing power), and market size (relative size/percentage of region total) (see Table 9.9). In customized models, secondary data are applied to specific objectives and industry characteristics. Extrapolation techniques, surrogate indicators, barometric analysis, and econometric forecasting models all help in estimating the demand for a given product. Secondary data can also monitor environmental change as an indicator of general health and growth (Douglas & Crain, 1983, p. 1).

Strategies

Ayal and Zif (1979) provide a framework for planning and evaluating multinational expansion strategies, focusing on the rate of entry into new markets. They discuss two major and opposing strategies: market diversification and market concentration. Market diversification implies a fast penetration into a large number of markets and a diffusion of efforts among them. Market concentration involves concentrating resources in a few markets and gradually expanding into new territories. Each strategy will result in different consequences for sales, market shares, and profits over time.

After identifying potential markets, managers then choose a strategy, determine the priorities for entry, and decide on the overall level of the marketing effort. The chosen strategy should help to clarify these steps. Market concentration is characterized by slow and gradual rates of growth in the markets served. Market diversification is characterized by a fast rate of growth. Different patterns result in the development of different competitive conditions and different levels of allocated resources, marketing effort, and marketing mixes.

Diversification leads to lower market efforts—few promotional expenditures, more reliance on commission agents, and a stronger tendency toward a

Table 9.9 Eighteen West European Markets and How They Compare

BE's annual statistical survey of Western Europe . . . presents in highly compact form the most important indicators of market size and growth for nineteen countries. Further issues will provide broadly comparable data on Africa and the Middle East and on Eastern Europe.

These market indicators provide a useful and flexible tool for evaluating a company's sales performance or planning future marketing and investment priorities. Among the uses to which *BE* readers have put them:

- Setting sales targets. Growth figures identify the prime areas.
- Redesigning sales incentive programs. By highlighting areas of probable growth, the tables should help to formulate compensation schemes.
- Reporting. The indicators have proved invaluable to executives called upon to make an on-the-spot report.
- Evaluating advertising. Where should advertising be directed? To whom? These questions can be partly answered by checking *BE*'s assessment against your own figures for market penetration, size, and level.
- Gauging sales performance. How well do growth records in sales of basic items compare with those of your product against GDP, per capita income or passenger car use?

Different companies will give greater or lesser emphasis to each indicator, in accordance with their particular industries. However, in an effort to arrive at some common denominator for comparing the national markets, *BE* has computed three composite indices. Each of these indices (shown in the table below) distills a different aspect of the complex reality.

In Europe, all or most of the following ten indicators are used in varying combinations in our equations: population, GDP, national income, private consumption, passenger cars, telephones, television sets, steel consumption, cement production, and electricity production. For Africa and the Middle East, as well as for Eastern Europe, some small changes in this data base have been made necessary to make up for lack of information.

- Market size. This column shows the relative size of each national or subregional market, as a percentage of the total West European market. The indices represent an averaging of the corresponding ratios of nine indicators, giving double weight to population figures.
- Market intensity. This measures the "richness" of the market, or the degree of concentrated purchasing power it represents. In this column the European average is taken as 1.00, and each country is measured against this yardstick. The figure for each country is derived from its various per capita consumption and ownership levels, with double weighting for overall private consumption expenditure and for ownership of passenger cars.
- Market growth. This is essentially an average of the real percentage growth of ten different indicators over the past five years.

THE COMPOSITE INDICES

	Market Size (%)	Market Intensity	Market Growth (%)
Belgium–Luxembourg	3.2	1.29	12
Denmark	1.7	1.32	11
France	15.6	1.20	15
Germany	20.4	1.36	8
Ireland	0.6	0.69	17
Italy	13.6	0.96	12
Netherlands	4.0	1.17	15
United Kingdom	14.7	1.03	3
EEC total	73.9*	1.15	10
Austria	2.3	1.28	13
Finland	1.3	1.10	9
Greece	2.0	0.72	39
Iceland	0.1	1.62	21
Norway	1.6	1.57	14
Portugal	1.3	0.40	33
Spain	8.1	0.82	29
Sweden	3.1	1.53	3
Switzerland	2.3	1.55	−1
Turkey	4.3	0.23	68
Non-EEC total	26.1*	0.70	22
Europe total	100.0	1.00	13

*May not add due to rounding.

Table 9.9 (*Continued*)

The composite indicators reveal several interesting trends. To mention only the most obvious:

In terms of market size, the EEC's share of the total West European market has been steadily eroded over the past five years, from 76.1% to 73.9%. Italy dropped back this year compared with the 1979 indicators, with Denmark, France and the UK edging forward and other EEC countries holding their own. In the non-EEC area, only Portugal and Sweden lost ground, while all others matched or improved their positions over the previous year. Germany, France, the UK and Italy together make up 64.3% of the West European market, while outside the EEC Spain leads with 8.1%.

Market intensity went up from 1.14 to 1.15 in the EEC markets, while in the non-EEC markets it dropped from 0.72 to 0.70. In the EEC area, only Italy and Ireland lie below the European average of 1.00, while West Germany maintains its EEC lead at 1.36 and all countries have moved up except Italy. Four countries, all outside the EEC, dominate the West European pecking order: Iceland with 1.62, Norway with 1.57, Switzerland with 1.55, and Sweden with 1.53. At the other end of the scale comes Turkey with only 0.23.

Market growth for 1973–78 has dropped compared with 1972–77, with the EEC area recording 10% against 12% and the non-EEC area 22% against 25%. Only Turkey managed to improve slightly its position, registering 68% compared with 67%. The West European Mediterranean countries again did best, with Turkey followed by Greece at 39%, Portugal 33%, and Spain 29%. Portugal's market-growth rate has dropped by about a third of the previous level, however. The slowest growth countries over 1973–78 were Switzerland, Sweden, Finland, Germany, and the UK, all with rates below 10%. All other countries recorded double-digit growth.

Source: "18 West European Markets and How They Compare." *Business Europe,* published by Business International SA. January 25, 1980, p. 27.

skimming approach to pricing. Concentration leads to large investment in market share: heavy promotional outlays, stronger control of distribution channels, and penetration pricing.

Entry strategies are characterized not only by the rate of entry but also by market segments. Some of the alternatives are listed here:

1. Concentrate on a specific segment and gradually increase the number of markets. This strategy appeals to distinct groups of similar customers; when the cost is high, penetration segments need to be large and stable.
2. Focus on market concentration and segment diversification through a product line that appeals to many. This strategy involves considerable promotion and distribution; the sales potential, however, is large.
3. Focus on diversification and segment concentration through a specialized product line; this strategy depends on the potential of customers in many countries and a low cost of entry.
4. Focus on dual diversification (in both segments and markets) through an aggressive product line that appeals to many segments. This strategy requires sufficient resources (e.g., large firms, with many sales offices) to accomplish fast entry.

The allocation of effort progresses from export by independent agents and sales subsidiaries to manufacturing subsidiaries. The Volvo company's expansion into twenty countries is a case in point. Selection of market expansion strategy depends on the product, the market, and the criteria of the firm (see Table 9.10).

MNCs need to assess the market potential, decide which markets look at-

Table 9.10 Product/Market Factors That Affect the Choice Between Diversification and Concentration Strategies

Product/Market Factor	Prefer Diversification If	Prefer Concentration If
Sales response function	Concave	S-curve
Growth rate of each market	Low	High
Sales stability in each market	Low	High
Competitive lead time	Short	Long
Spillover effects	High	Low
Need for product adaptation	Low	High
Need for communication adaptation	Low	High
Economies of scale in distribution	Low	High
Program control requirements	Low	High
Extent of constraints	Low	High

Source: I. Ayal and J. Zif, "Market Expansion Strategies in Multinational Marketing." *Journal of Marketing* 43:89, Spring 1979. Reprinted with permission.

tractive, determine a marketing strategy, and evaluate it in light of corporate objectives and available resources. Other considerations include the existence of protective trade barriers tariffs, and competition, the cost of goods and labor, the ability to generate high demand, and the availability of media and distribution channels.

ROLE OF GLOBAL COMPETITION

The survival of any company depends directly on the nature and scope of the competition it faces. Competitors form one element of the environment that MNCs need to explore, assess, and respond to. Strategic decisions regarding the MNC operations—what, where, and how—must derive at least in part from the evaluation of competitive forces. For example, IBM, the world leader in the computer business, now faces serious competitive threats on several fronts: the Japanese, a number of joint ventures recently formed, and other industries, such as telecommunications and office equipment, which are expanding horizontally.

Porter (1979) describes five forces that shape the nature and degree of competition:

1. New entrants into the market bring new capacity, new resources, and a desire to gain a market share. How much of a threat they pose depends on the barriers present and on the reactions (possibly retaliations) of those companies already occupying positions in the arena. Barriers to entry can be the required economics of scale, the degree of product differentiation, the amount of capital required, the disadvantages of cost, access to distribution channels, and government policies. In the computer market, for example, potential contenders must take into account the large economics

of scale and large capital requirements, as well as IBM's ability to retaliate through price cuts.

2. The power of suppliers is another force that shapes competition. Suppliers can raise prices, reduce quality, or restrict access (in the case of oil, e.g.), thereby squeezing profitability. Suppliers are powerful to the extent to which (a) they dominate the market, (b) their supplies are unique, (c) they do not have to contend with other products for sale to the industry, (d) they threaten to integrate forward, and (e) they are important to the customer.

3. Buyers, on the other hand, are able to affect competition levels if (a) they are concentrated, (b) they buy in volume, (c) the products purchased are standard or undifferentiated, (d) the products form components that represent a significant fraction of cost, (e) product quality is important, and (f) the buyer can integrate backwards.

4. Substitution also affects competition. A product that could be substituted with a cheaper one might thereby be subjected to trends that improve price performance trade-offs; other companies might imitate it, thereby becoming part of the competition. In the case of IBM, several companies were able to gain market share by manufacturing compatible machines that could be substituted for IBM mainframes.

5. Finally, competition is shaped by competitive positioning (''jockeying for position''), depending on the number and size of competitors, the rate of industry growth, the extent of product differentiation, the size of fixed costs, irregularities in supply and demand, and the existence of exit barriers. In the computer industry, competitive positioning is intense because the products are not always differentiated, fixed costs are high, and governments (having identified computers as essential to economic development) impose exit barriers. Japan is a case in point.

Strategies

Firms participate in international activities through three basic mechanisms: licensing, export, and foreign direct investment. The differences in competing internationally emphasize the need to develop an international competitive strategy. These differences include cost factors, market circumstances, government roles, resources, goals, and ability to monitor competition. What strategies are effective in managing global competition? Porter (1980) suggests the following:

1. Choose suppliers and buyers.
2. Influence balance of forces.
3. Anticipate shifts and changes in industry.
4. Differentiate product.
5. Solidify position with a few customers.
6. Establish technical leadership.
7. Integrate vertically—forward or backward.
8. Raise economics of scale or the amount of capital needed to enter.
9. Be innovative in marketing approach.

Advantages and Disadvantages

There are several benefits to having a global competitive advantage: production economics of scale, product differentiation, proprietary product technology, mobility of production, and favorable ("in the public good") corporate image. But such a position has disadvantages, too: managerial task complexity, institutional restraints, and resource limitations. Globalization can be triggered by environmental factors such as relative cost factors, income levels, the state of economic development, the nature of distribution channels, and the availability of marketing media. It can also, of course, be triggered by strategic innovations such as product redefinition, identification of market segments, reduction in the cost of product adaptation, standardization of product design, and central production for local assembly.

What trends affect global competition? Greater homogeneity among countries, aggressive industrial policies (as in Japan), national recognition and protection of distinctive assets (as in Africa and South America), the free flow of technology, the gradual emergence of new large-scale markets (China, e.g.), and competition from newly developing countries (as in Southeast Asia) are some of them.

Global industries have several alternatives:

1. Broad-line (or full-line) competition.
2. A global focus, in which the target is a particular market segment.
3. A national focus, in which the target is a particular market.
4. A protected niche, in which protection is ensured, for example, by the government.

Competition is a key factor in profitability. The more competition an MNC faces, the more jeopardized its profits are. Not even IBM can afford to ignore its rivals.

ROLE OF ECOLOGY

What is the impact of worldwide industrialization on the natural environment? Increasingly, business and government are called on to demonstrate ecological responsibility. MNCs can no longer ignore the implications of their activity in any sphere.

Ecological concerns can become the domain of powerful influence groups and of government regulation. For instance, the American antinuclear movement has been powerful enough and vocal enough to interfere with the opening of nuclear power plants. And at the government level, the EPA has had a significant impact on the nuclear industry. However, power can vary as the administration changes. Under former President Carter, the EPA had far greater impact that it does under the Reagan Administration. Few companies can ignore the impact even of individuals. Ralph Nader, for example, has repeatedly criticized and legally confronted the automobile industry; Rachel Carson attacked the pesticide industry with her book *Silent Spring*.

MNCs need to incorporate ecological concerns into their strategies, because they must frequently justify their actions. Table 9.11 offers a list of several groups concerned with environmental issues.

Multinationals operate in a heterogeneous world of environmental problems and policies. Sovereign nations are going about the business of environmental and health protection at different paces and are using different techniques. Variations in environmental policy "climates" reflect differences in levels of industrialization, living standards, government–business relations, philosophies of collective intervention, patterns of industry competition, and degrees of sophistication in public policy. According to Gladwin (1977), MNCs will be held accountable for their roles in jeopardizing the natural environment. MNCs need to integrate ecological considerations with strategy; in "ecological incorporations," environmental impact assessment will coexist with the process of project appraisal. A model indicating the environmental problem–policy cycle is offered in Figure 9.4.

Let us take a closer look. Kelley et al. (1976) compared environmental concerns in the United States, the USSR, and Japan. Differences in political needs, attitudes toward nature, and ideologies were expected to have differential effects on handling environmental problems. In the United States, some people view government regulation as unjustifiable interference with property rights. Only in the 1950s did environmental action groups begin to alert the country to the profound ecological consequences of technologically and industrially based economic power. The government, however, continued to emphasize economic growth, and federal and state officials tended to regard its importance as primary.

In the Soviet Union, rapid industrial growth, urbanization, and the desire to develop heavy industry were all tied to political concerns for industrialization. The results, however, were depletion of resources, inadequate systems of waste disposal, and pollution. In the last few decades, Soviet policy makers have struggled to manage the environmental impact of industry. Problems of enforcement apparently remain.

In Japan, rapid industrialization, population growth, and urbanization have seriously strained the ecological balance. Here, too, the government considered environmental issues secondary to the need for industrialization and urbanization, both before and after World War II. Environmental horrors, or "Kogai," were the price paid for becoming an "economic superpower"; Kogai upset the Japanese ideal of human beings living in harmony with nature. The Japanese do not share the common Soviet and American views that environmental resources are limitless and that problems can be solved through advanced technology rather than through conservation.

The different economic systems of these three countries have made little difference in the size and existence of environmental problems. "Whether capitalist, communist, or on the middle ground of a guided or regulated economy, each of the three nations has experienced a similar pattern of environmental deterioration . . . the questions of capital ownership and industrial control are related only peripherally to issues of effective environmental preservation" (Kelley et al., 1976, p. 28).

In addition, assessing the physical environment is important to the MNC.

Table 9.11 Selected Governmental and Industry Groups That Deal with Environmental Issues

International Governmental Organizations

Commission of the European Communities
Council of Europe
Food and Agricultural Organization (via Industry Cooperative Program)
General Agreement on Tariffs and Trade
Inter-American Development Bank
Inter-American Economic and Social Council
Inter-Governmental Maritime Consultative Organization
International Bank for Reconstruction and Development
International Civil Aviation Organization
International Council of Scientific Unions
International Joint Commission
International Labor Organization
International Organization for Standardization
North Atlantic Treaty Organization (Committee on the Challenges of Modern Society)
Organization of American States
Organization of Economic Cooperation and Development (via Business and Industry Advisory Committee)
United Nations Development Program
United Nations Education, Scientific, and Cultural Organization
United Nations Environment Program
United Nations Economic Commission for Europe
United Nations Economic Commission for Latin America
United States Agency for International Development
World Health Organization
World Meteorological Organization

Chemicals Industry

American Chemical Society
The Ecological and Toxicological Association of the Dyestuffs Manufacturing Industry
European Council of Chemical Manufacturers' Federations
Institute for Chemical Toxicology
Manufacturing Chemists Association
Synthetic Organic Chemical Manufacturers' Association
The Swiss Society of Chemical Industries

Metal Industry

American Institute of Mining Engineers
American Iron and Steel Institute
American Mining Congress
European Primary Aluminum Association
German Steel Industries Association
International Iron and Steel Institute
International Primary Aluminum Institute

Petroleum Industry

American Petroleum Institute
Inter-Industry Emission Control Program
International Petroleum Industry Environmental Conservation Association
International Tanker Owners Pollution Federation
North Sea Operators Committee
Oil Companies International Marine Forum
Petroleum Association for Conservation of the Canadian Environment
The Petroleum Association of Japan
Petroleum Industry Environment Executive (Australia)
Stichting CONCAWE
U.K. Institute of Petroleum

General Industry

American Institute of Merchant Shipping
Chamber of Commerce of the U.S.A.
Committee for Economic Development
Conference Board
Confederation of British Industry
Council of European Industrial Federations
Council of Netherlands Economic Organization
Federation of Belgian Industries
Federation of German Industries
Federation of Swedish Industries
International Center for Industry and the Environment
International Chamber of Commerce
International Organization of Employers
Japanese National Committee of the ICC
National Industrial Pollution Control Council
National Academy of Engineering
National Academy of Sciences
National Association of Manufacturers
Union of Industries of the European Community
U.S. Council of the ICC

Source: T. N. Gladwin, *Environment, Planning and the Multinational Corporation.* Greenwich, CT: JAI Press, 1977, pp. 166–167. Reprinted with permission.

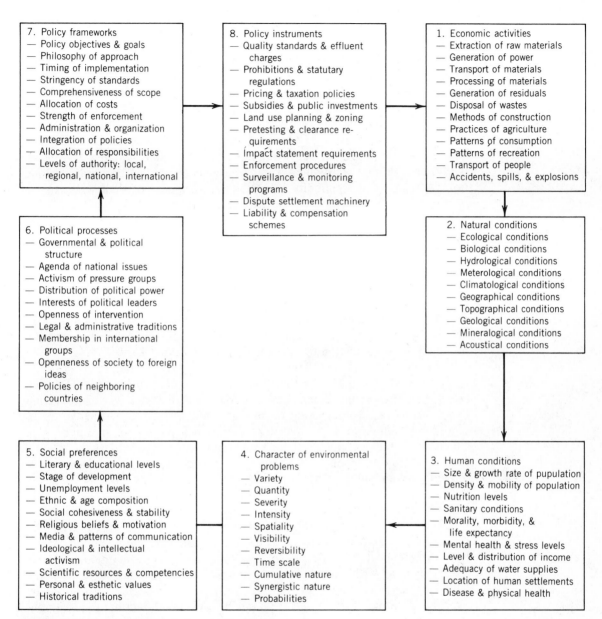

Figure 9.4 The environmental problem–policy cycle.

Source: T. N. Gladwin and I. Walter. *Multinationals Under Fire.* New York: Wiley, 1980, pp. 426–427. Copyright © 1980. Reprinted with permission.

Although natural resources may be abundant, they could be difficult to extract. Lack of transportation routes or facilities can seriously impede operations; MNCs may have to consider investing large amounts of capital to develop transportation networks before they can benefit from the abundance of resources. Several South American countries are trying to develop a joint transportation system that will utilize the extensive waterways within the continent. Government policies may also regulate how much natural resources can be extracted by any company (*World Business Weekly,* 1980). Regional climates also must be considered: heavy rainfall and subsequent flooding or, alternatively, drought and consequent water shortages may affect corporate production. A region's susceptibility to earthquakes, floods, or tidal waves is yet another factor that deserves close attention.

ROLE OF TECHNOLOGY

An organization may have state-of-the-art technology, as well as the methods and materials used in production. The choice of routine versus nonroutine methods of production or activity describes technology in terms of the number of exceptions encountered in daily operations and the nature of the process needed for finding solutions. These variables determine the level of uncertainty to which the organization must respond (Perrow, 1967; 1970).

The state of the art may change rapidly (as in the information industry—e.g., computers) or be stable (as in the manufacturing of consumer goods). To maintain a competitive edge, companies need to keep abreast of the relevant technological changes. In nonroutine technology, active R&D departments are required and may, in fact, overshadow other departments in importance. Changes in the technological environment—external or internal—affect a product's life cycles, marketing strategies, and manufacturing processes.

The development of technology gives the MNC a competitive advantage and is often proprietary in nature. Many pharmaceutical companies, for example, enjoy profits from exclusive drug patents and discontinue manufacturing of the drugs when these patents expire. In other words, the manufacture of a particular product is no longer profitable when the technology goes public. MNCs have often chosen underdeveloped countries as sites for operations, bringing their technology with them, because of resource availability (raw materials, labor) and less extensive regulation. As these countries begin to develop, however, regulations are increased in an effort to maintain national sovereignty.

Transfer of Technology

More and more countries are demanding transfer of technology—that is, a system in which the MNC gives up its proprietary rights, stimulates R&D through local departments, and thus trains locals. Obviously, such demands are costly for the MNC. Some of the many issues involved in this regard have to do with technology, the extent to which it is understood, the level of its sophistication, the mode of transfer, and concerns of human rights.

For example, labor-saving technology may not be appropriate in countries where overpopulation provides an extensive workforce. Labor-intensive rather than capital-intensive industries are more suitable in this case. Another issue, the "black-box" phenomenon, concerns the degree to which the technology is known or understood or, if excessively esoteric, is perceived as guarded. Modes of transfer include direct sale of technology for profit, release of proprietary information to ease capital shortages in R&D and to evade nontariff barriers (e.g., Honeywell), "measured release" of technology (i.e., withholding key pieces of information if a monopolistic position will allow it), and jettisoning of unneeded technology (Motorola to Mitshushita). The level of sophistication is also of concern. Is it appropriate to send or transfer the most sophisticated technology if it is not the most useful? Or is it better to transfer less sophisticated but adequate technology, given the country's level of development, at the risk of being accused of "dumping"? Sethi and Sheth (1973) outlined two approaches:

1. Transfer only the most modern and sophisticated technology. This limits spillover to other economic sectors (thwarting economic development) and requires highly trained workers and extensive training for a narrow segment of the labor force.
2. Transfer technology whose cost of development is totally handled by the corporation. This allows pricing of goods according to production costs without assuming R&D costs, since R&D leads to development through spillover into other sectors and reduces requirements for skilled labor and intensive capital.

Concerns about rights become important when countries have policies that restrict the skill development of certain groups within the labor force, as in South Africa. Political revolutions, too, take their toll. They can result in "brain drains," as in Angola, when the Portuguese left following their defeat. These issues are addressed specifically by United Nations Resolution 1904, entitled *Brain Drain Resolution*, proposed on July 5, 1974. Since 1970, the United Nations General Assembly has been working on Resolution 2626—*The International Development Strategy for the Second U.N. Development Decade*—which addresses specific rates of growth (GNP) for developing countries, output targets, and the average increases in annual gross domestic savings and exports. In 1974, Resolution 3201—*The New International Economic Order*—addressed commodity agreements to stabilize exports, linking aid to special drawing rights, setting aid targets, tariff preferences, and debt refinancing, stipulating the right to nationalize assets, and advocating the transfer of technology. Other activities throughout the decade 1970–1980 are listed in Table 9.12.

Technology, the major input requirement for economic development and growth, is not value-free. The degree of dependence it nurtures, the terms of acquisition, the nature of the transfer process, and the cost and appropriateness of technology to the LDC are all dimensions that have prompted greater involvement through government and international policy. Technology suppliers

Table 9.12 United Nations Resolutions

Date	Resolution	Issue
1970	2626	International Development Strategy for the 2nd UN Development Decade
May 1, 1974	3201	New International Economic Order Implementation
	3202	
Dec., 1974	3281	Charter of Economic Rights—right to expropriate
July 5, 1974	1902	Creation of International Technical Information System
	1903	Committee on Science and Technology (Computer Technology)
	1904	Brain Drain
	1905	Coordination of UN effort in technology
Sept. 16, 1975	3362	Patents and trademarks revised
Dec. 15, 1976	3507	Establishment of regional centers for technical transfer in developing countries
May 1976	87	UN committee on technology and development
Aug. 4, 1976	2034	
Dec., 1977	31/188	Code of conduct on transfer of technology
	32/192	Brain Drain study
	32/184	Meeting for UNCTAD
1978	33/157	Progress on conduct code

are undergoing increasing regulatory scrutiny involving antitrust or tax concerns. This raises issues of national security (for both home and host countries) and of MNC revenues; it also requires the assessment of the risks of inadequate compensation, loss of international competitiveness, and R&D overhead cost (e.g., CDCs' sales of sophisticated technology to the Soviet Union).

Even a single technology transfer involves a tangle of information: rights and services, product design, production techniques, and managerial functions (product, person, and process). The nature of the transfer affects the user and the host country's capacity for acquiring new technology. Who controls the technology, and to what degree? The transfer involves a relationship between firms over time involving type of technology, supplier commitment, and duration of management. The ingredients of the technological package will vary, as will industry type, recipient firms' abilities, the organization's life cycle, and its stage of technological development. International patent and trademark systems perpetuate oligopoly and encourage economic dominance. While MNCs need to cover their R&D costs, LDCs complain that it is unfair to do so at their expense because R&D efforts are not geared to their needs. This highlights the question of the value of the transfer and the degree of foreign control over the user firm. There has been a shift lately from direct investment and ownership to licensing due to regional restrictions, standardization of products, maturity of industry, improved technological sophistication, and improved bargaining skills. Licensing is the only mode of transfer in socialist countries.

Is the Western process of industrialization the quickest or the most appropriate path to development? Is it suitable for all societies? Rapid capital-intensive industrialization results in the trickling down of skills to the labor force, interdependence with technology, appropriateness of products and labor, rural underemployment, and income maldistribution. Consequently, recipient countries often develop policies to monitor the inflow of technology and balance of payment costs. Their goal is to promote indigenous scientific and technological development through laws, registries, review boards, tax incentives, or taxation of excess technological payments. Supplier firms have also developed policies as a function of their technology, size, product maturity, and extent of international experience. Some have adopted the strategy of licensing off-the-shelf technology while retaining the monopoly on more sophisticated technology. These strategies are based on expected returns from direct cost and indirect opportunity cost, and the optimum foreign market entry mode. These supplier firms are constrained by their own country's government policies. However, these tend to be vague and based on conflicting interests: employment, national security, international competitiveness, revenue loss, and balance of payments. The American policy supports a free flow of technology.

Regional policies have been developed by the United Nations and regional coalitions. The United Nations' aims are to strengthen the bargaining power of the recipient countries, control suppliers, strengthen indigenous science and technology capacity, and increase the LDCs' share of manufacturing exports and international competition. The issues of international technology transfer, however, still need to be developed through theory building, measurement, and policy research (Contractor & Sagafi-Nejad, 1981).

CONCLUSION

This chapter has examined the many dimensions of the external environments that influence MNCs. These dimensions include culture, government, political climate, the labor force, the marketplace, and technology.

In evaluating and comparing the properties of the environment for organizational considerations two main approaches have been developed in the field. The first divides the environment into meaningful *components* (e.g., Kast & Rosenzweig, 1979) and has been discussed in the chapter's introduction and developed in various forms throughout the preceding sections. The other approach introduces various *dimensions* or characteristics of the environment, which enables us to evaluate the environment and its components on a continuum. The first conceptual framework was developed by Aldrich (1979), and suggests six dimensions along which organizationally relevant environmental conditions may vary. These are described in Table 9.13.

The second useful framework for analyzing environmental uncertainty was developed by Duncan (1979) and is presented in Table 9.14. Duncan has based his conceptual analysis on two characteristics along *simple–complex* and *static–dynamic* dimensions. As Bedeian notes (1984, p. 186) the simple–complex characteristic refers to the degree to which a decision unit (an individual or organization) must deal with few or many elements that are similar or dissimilar to one another. Static–dynamic refers to the degree to which ele-

Table 9.13 Dimensions of Organization Environments

Environmental capacity: The relative level of resources available to an organization within its environment, varying from lean or low capacity to rich or high capacity environments

Environmental homogeneity–heterogeneity: The degree of similarity between the elements of the domain population, including individuals and organizations. Varies from undifferentiated or homogeneous to highly differentiated or heterogeneous environments

Environmental stability–instability: The degree of turnover in environmental elements. (Note that high turnover may still be patterned and is thus predictable.)

Environmental concentration–dispersion: The degree to which resources, including the domain population and other elements, are evenly distributed over the range of the environment. Varies from random dispersion to high concentration in specific locations

Domain consensus–dissensus: The degree to which an organization's claim to a specific domain is disputed or recognized by other organizations

Turbulence: The extent to which environments are characterized by an increasing interconnection between elements and trends, and by an increasing *rate* of interconnection

Source: H. E. Aldrich, *Organizations and Environments,* © 1979, p. 74. Reprinted by permission of Prentice-Hall, Inc., Englewood Cliffs, NJ.

Table 9.14 Environmental Dimensions

Degree of Complexity	Degree of Change	
	Stable	Dynamic
Simple	Low uncertainty Stable, predictable environment Few products and services Limited number of customers, suppliers, and competitors Minimal need for sophisticated knowledge Example: Container industry	Moderately high uncertainty Dynamic, unpredictable environment Few products and services Limited number of customers, suppliers, and competitors Minimal need for sophisticated knowledge Example: Fast food industry
Complex	Moderately low uncertainty Stable, predictable environment Many products and services Many customers, suppliers, and competitors High need for sophisticated knowledge Example: Food products	High uncertainty Dynamic, unpredictable environment Many products and services Many customers, suppliers, and competitors High need for sophisticated knowledge Example: Computer industry

Source: Adapted by permission of the publisher, from "What Is the Right Organization Structure? Decision Tree Analysis Provides the Answer," by Robert Duncan, *Organizational Dynamics,* Winter 1977, p. 63 © 1977 AMACOM, a division of American Management Associations, New York. All rights reserved.

ments of a decision unit's surrounding environment remain the same or are marked by change. *Perceived uncertainty* is seen as resulting from an interaction of the simple–complex and static–dynamic components and is composed of (1) a lack of information concerning environmental factors, (2) an inability to accurately assess environmental probabilities, and (3) a lack of knowledge regarding the costs associated with an incorrect decision. In order to examine the integration of the internal and external aspects of the MNC, we shall now proceed to review the models that are based on the systems approach. It will provide us with the tools necessary to compare MNCs' structures and processes across various environmental and cultural combinations.

CHAPTER 10
MNCs' Design and Process

We have seen in Chapter 8 that there are various ways to design the organizational structure of MNCs and various ways to manage them. In Chapter 9, we reviewed the major environmental elements with which a company interacts. Our task now is to integrate the characteristics—both internal and external—that are used to analyze and evaluate a suitable structure and review process for choosing an effective organization.

The task is challenging. Its complexity is evident in the numerous variables that must be considered in such a process. In addition, management is usually limited objectively in its capacity to scan all the relevant variables, as well as limited subjectively by its members' beliefs and values to a given selective process. Such perceptual biases invariably stress certain considerations while underestimating others. However, the field of organizational analysis and design provides us with several conceptual models that help both students and practitioners to approach the structure of organization from a variety of perspectives, each according to the goals of the intended analysis.

SYSTEMS APPROACH TO ORGANIZATIONS

If we choose to study organizations as being independent of situational and environmental variables, we are using a *closed system model*. In this view, we see the organization as self-contained and focus our attention on internal processes. We explore planning and control functions in terms of economic efficiency and goal achievement. The organization adopts a rational stance and attempts to eliminate uncertainty. This model is congruent with theories of scientific and administrative management and with Weber's (1947) depiction of bureaucracy.

Although this approach is useful for certain purposes, it does not fully take into consideration the environment's impact on the organization. Nor does it take into account the organization's need to manage uncertainty rather than try unsuccessfully to eliminate it. This approach can be useful at the operations or technical level, but it does not consider the emergent complexity of the ongoing interaction with the environment and its influence on the relationships between different levels and units within the organization (Thompson, 1967). Even so, if the relevant unit of analysis (department, division, or the whole organization) is recognized and the approach is applied to a well-defined purpose (e.g., appraising departmental efficiency), then the model can be suitable and useful.

This approach is also consistent with certain theories of management to which organizations and managers ascribe. (In this case the term *theory* should be interpreted as designating philosophy, beliefs, convictions, and values). For example, if management espouses one of the traditional theories of management (Taylor's scientific management theory, Fayol's administrative theory, or Weber's bureaucratic model), then the focus of attention will most likely be internal at the shop or technical level. Management will specify the relationship between the worker and the task technology by designing a task structure that includes fractionating the job (breaking down the task to its simplest component) and specializing role functions (assigning each component to a particular worker). This is done in the interest of greater efficiency and productivity; planning and control play an important role and are the task of management only. In keeping with Thompson's discussion of closed systems at the technical level (1967), this approach assumes perfect knowledge, that is, rationality.

Reality, however, is much more complex. An effective structure requires a more comprehensive model. One of the most useful is the *open systems model*. The open systems model considers more fully the situational variables—the interaction between various units and between units and the environment. It also considers the impact of the informal aspects of the organization—informal social groups, for instance, and various sources of information—as they relate to more formal aspects, such as communications channels and leadership styles. In this model, the organization's goal is survival and adaptation, achieved through evolution and self-stabilization. This model is most relevant in cases when uncertainty is the greatest, at the level where the organization interacts with the environment. One of management's important tasks is to mediate between the operations level, which demands rationality and certainty, and the institutional level, which faces uncertainty and has only a limited ability to consider all possible events ("bounded rationality").

Within this approach there are a variety of models that emphasize different perspectives to understanding and responding to the environment. For example, one approach—the contingency approach—recommends that organizations respond to the environment by modifying their structure; another approach—the resource dependency approach—recommends, instead, that organizations respond to the environment by maximizing their control over crucial resources. We shall briefly discuss these models, keeping in mind that their different approaches make them effective tools for understanding and analyzing the various structural forms. (The models will also allow analysis of actual cases, to be discussed later.)

First, however, we should view the organization from a historical (ecological) perspective by considering the *natural selection model*. This model depicts organizations as adopting a passive, reactive posture to environmental events.

The natural selection model (Hannan & Freeman, 1974; Aldrich, 1971) supports the notion that the environment determines organizational structure. According to this model, environments differentially "select" organizations for survival on the basis of the fit between organizational structure (and activities) and environmental characteristics. Thus, the organization that "survives" is the one that best suits the environment. The natural selection model views the match between organizations and environment from a long-term perspective. It describes three stages in the selection process (Campbell, 1969). In the first stage, variations occur in organizational structure, whether planned or unplanned. In the second, the environment selects those variations that best suit it. In the third and final stage, the organization creates retention mechanisms (e.g., standard operating procedures) to ensure continuation of the variations selected, regardless of their sources. In this model, death and survival, not adaptation, is the mechanism of change. This model neglects the intraorganizational managerial process (i.e., decision making) and the potential impact of the organization on its environment. It fails to consider the overall process or system but reaffirms the predominance of environmental conditions.

The following discussion offers a suitable comprehensive conceptualization for organizational analysis.

OPEN SYSTEMS APPROACH

Because of time and energy constraints, and the immediacy of organizational operations, managers tend to focus on internal events. Although they direct some attention to resource availability and utilization of output, there is a danger that managers will deal mainly with internal processes, thus neglecting the larger context of organization and environment. The open systems model helps managers by redirecting their attention to include external processes and reminding them of the organization's continuous interaction with the environment. This model describes the processes both within the organization and between the organization and its environment—their character, sequence, and cyclical nature (see Figure 10.1).

In this model, information, material, and energy flow from the environment to the organization. Sometimes this flow returns to the environment as well. The boundary separating the organization and the environment is thus perme-

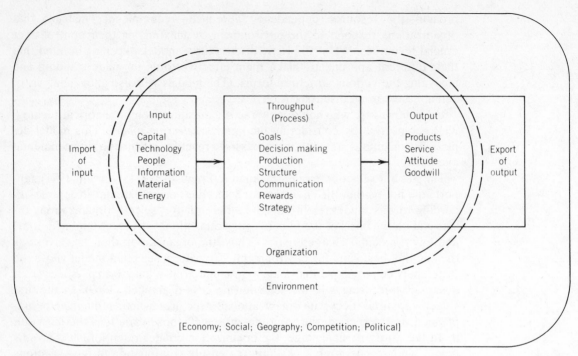

Figure 10.1 The organization as an open system.

able. Katz and Kahn (1978) describe nine characteristics common to open systems:

1. They import energy, for example, resources.
2. They transform energy through internal processes.
3. They export products into the environment.
4. They can exhibit cyclical patterns of activity, that is, outputs can become inputs.
5. They can store energy and increase internal organization to avoid chaos, disorderly feedback, and negative entropy.
6. They select and code relevant information and use information to correct functioning, that is, they provide feedback.
7. They demonstrate a continuous exchange of energy between organization and environment—an exchange that balances and preserves the system.
8. As they grow, they become more differentiated—more specialized in their role and function.
9. They can achieve the same end through various means (equifinality).

The open systems approach thus allows us to comprehend the total picture of the organization and its environment. It emphasizes the feedback functions that provide the organization with a means of evaluating and correcting its performance. The approach includes external influences as well as principles of internal functioning. It demonstrates that systems cannot be understood without studying the forces that impinge on them.

Note that within this framework there are few models that portray organizations as proactive and capable of changing as well as responding to the environment. These models vary in their emphasis: the *resource dependency model* views organizations as employing a strategy to "engineer" their relationship to the environment. This process is at the root of the political economy model or resource dependence model (Aldrich & Pfeffer, 1976; Pfeffer & Salancik, 1978; Yuchtman-Yaar & Seashore, 1967), which states that when obtaining resources organizations must transact with the environment. Although it considers the importance of environmental contingencies and constraints, the model also stresses that variations in organizational characteristics are conscious, planned responses to environmental contingencies. The environment is seen as either the flow of information perceived by the organization's members or the availability of resources (Aldrich & Pfeffer, 1976). In the first view, the environment is characterized by the amount of uncertainty. In the second view, the nature of the exchange or transaction with the organization defines the environment. The environment affects the distribution of influence because certain members have information and can thus reduce uncertainty. It also creates power issues between the organization and environment because of the organization's power to create demand, control competition, and alter the market, that is, its bargaining position. This model argues for greater attention to internal *political* decision-making processes within the organization and to choice of strategies. Organizations depend on the environment, particularly for resources.

To survive and to be effective, organizations must mobilize from the environment scarce and valued resources. These are critical for their operations and make organizational effectiveness possible. This continuous bargaining relationship emphasizes the notion that organizations are most effective when they maximize their bargaining position and optimize their resource procurement (Yuchtman-Yaar & Seashore, 1967, p. 898).

Another model that emphasizes aspects of the environment is the *enacted environment model*. The stress in this model is that managerial decisions define the environment to meet organizational needs. The organization's structure and strategy define risks and identify opportunities. The organization focuses selectively on specific environmental characteristics, in effect constructing an environment from the perceptions attained. Environments are thus "invented" by the organizations themselves. This "perceived" (invented) environment is known as the "enacted environment" (Weick, 1969). Organizations reshape the environment through strategies that maximize the use of resources or reduce uncertainty. "Organizing is directed towards resolving the equivocality that exists in informational inputs judged to be relevant" (Weick, 1969, p. 29). Thus, organizations are proactive; they select aspects of the environment to which they then respond. They select their environments from a range of alternatives. Because all judgments originate in human perceptions—which are by definition subjective—this selection can be arbitrary, disorderly, incremental, and strongly influenced by social norms and customs (Starbuck, 1976). Perceptions differ, and thus, so do strategies.

We have seen that there are choices in creating various organizational structures and instituting methods of managing them. Various notions of structure have traditionally stressed that organizational structure is predetermined by the environment. We can modify these views based on our knowledge that effective organizations adopt structures that are responsive to the situation's demands, both internal and external. This so-called *contingency theory* states that the choice of structure hinges on the given organizational and environmental characteristics (Lawrence & Lorsch, 1967).

As we have just seen, however, other arguments suggest the reverse: namely, that the choice of structure determines these organizational characteristics and defines the environmental domain in which the organization then operates (Child, 1972; Thompson, 1967; Aldrich & Pfeffer, 1976).

Let us now consider how the organization and its environment interact according to the contingency model. This model states that there is no single best way to design an organization. Instead, the specific design of an organization or a subsystem must match (fit) its environment (Lawrence & Lorsch, 1967). "Successful organizations are those which are able to diagnose and meet environmental requirements for differentiation and integration. Thus, appropriate patterns of structure vary and are contingent upon the conditional relationship between an organization and its environment" (Bedeian, 1984, p. 197).

CONTINGENCY MODEL

Environmental characteristics influence organizational structure. The more complex the environment, the more complex the organization, because the organization's response to the environment may mean greater diversity, not only structurally (by adding subunits, e.g.) but functionally as well. As we have seen, Lawrence and Lorsch (1967) defined this response as *differentiation*. Their research showed that in firms considered more successful, the level of organizational differentiation matched the level of environmental complexity. In other words, these firms had a higher degree of differentiation. The greater the degree of differentiation is, however, the more attention is necessary to coordinate and integrate the organizational components. Different integrating mechanisms are required depending on the nature of the environment and its information-processing demands. Coordinating mechanisms include rules and policies, direct contact, mutual adjustment, liaison role teams, and matrix designs. The choice of mechanism reflects the amount of information that needs to be processed. Uncertainty creates greater information requirements and the need for flexibility and responsive decision making. In sum, the more uncertain and unpredictable the environment is, the more differentiation and integration are required in an organizational structure. This notion is presented in Figure 10.2.

Organizational structures or managerial systems are influenced by the envi-

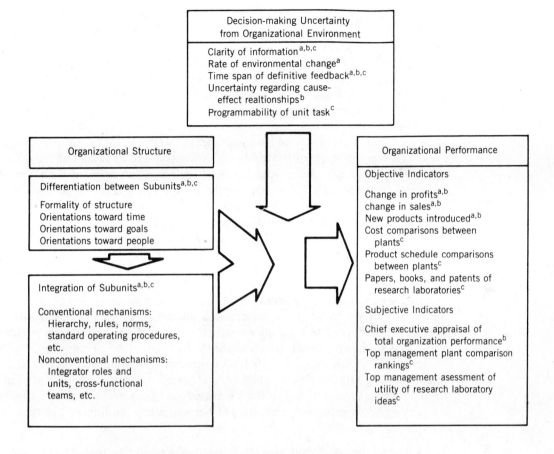

a. Lawrence and Lorsch, "Differentiation and Integration in Complex Organizations," 1967: Chemical-processing organizations.
b. Lawrence and Lorsch, Organization and Environment, 1969: Plastics, food-processing, and standardized container organizations.
c. Lorsch and Morse, Organizations and Their Members, 1974: Manufacturing and research organizations.

Figure 10.2   An overview of the contingency studies of the Harvard Group.

Source: R. H. Miles. *Macro Organizational Behavior.* Santa Monica, CA: Goodyear, 1980, p. 256.

ronment in still another way—by differences in environmental rates of change or in environmental dynamic variability. The higher the rate of variability, the more flexible and adaptable an organization must be. Flexibility often requires a less formal organizational structure, more decentralized decision making, and more informal communication. Such flexibility is characteristic of an "organic" management system. More stable environments (those with lower variability) are best managed by a more bureaucratic, formal structure with centralized decision making and far more rules, policies, and procedures. This rigidity is characteristic of the "mechanistic" system. The more dynamic environment is best matched with an organic structure, whereas the more stable environment is best matched with a mechanistic structure (Burns & Stalker, 1961). This contingency approach focuses on the impact of environmental forces. Characteristics will determine organizational structure, and fitting organizational design to the environmental requirements will maximize effectiveness. Environmental limitations or constraints will require changes in structure.

Managerial behavior and organizational design need to account for situational differences, that is, they must maintain a "situational perspective" of such elements as rewards and measurements, strategy, tasks, organizational members, top management style, the environment, and existing culture (Duncan, 1979; Lawrence & Lorsch, 1967). Effective organizational structure is therefore contingent on the various forces with which it can best be matched. This is the contingency theory of organizations (Miles, 1980).

To better understand the contingency approach, we shall review two key elements on which design is contingent: technology and the environment.

Technology

Technology can be broadly defined as the techniques and processes of changing inputs (resources) to outputs (products and services). Although some theorists consider the effect of technology on structure to be of secondary importance, many key studies highlight its relevance (Woodward, 1965; Thompson, 1967; Perrow, 1967; Hickson et al., 1969). Woodward (1965) studied fifty to sixty manufacturing firms in Essex, England, and tested the classic theories of management to evaluate whether or not a certain type of organizational structure is universally most effective. She divided her sample according to the type of technology employed:

1. *Unit* includes both unit and small-batch production system. Production is designed to meet unique customer requirements (e.g., made-to-order products such as custom-tailored suits, prototype electronic equipment). Control over the production process and predictability of production are low.
2. *Mass* includes both large-batch and mass-production systems. Production is standardized on an intermittent basis with moderate control and predictability (e.g., automobile assembly lines and large bakeries).
3. *Process* includes batch processing and continuous processing (e.g., manufacture of chemicals and pharmaceuticals; oil refining). Production is standardized on a continuous basis, permitting high control over processes and predictability of outcomes.

Woodward (1965) found that successful organizations had different structures, resulting from differences in technological process—particularly the span of control, level of decision making, and degree of formalization. For example, unit and process technologies had a smaller, narrower span of control and "more organic" management systems (e.g., less centralized and less formalized). Her conclusion was that different technologies imposed different kinds of demands on individuals and organizations, and these demands had to be met through an appropriate structure (p. vi) (see Figure 10.3). In attempting

Structural Characteristics	Technology-Structure Relationship
Number of levels of management Span of control of chief executive Ratio of managers to total personnel	
Ratio of direct to indirect labor Ratio of manual workers to clerical and administrative staff Ratio of wages and salaries to total costs Labor costs	
Span of control of first-level production supervisor Separation of production administration from actual supervision of production operations Amount of written communications Use of control and sanction procedures Specializations between line and staff functions	
Amount of verbal communications Role ambiguity concerning duties and responsibilities (and index of organizational flexibility) Number of skilled workers	

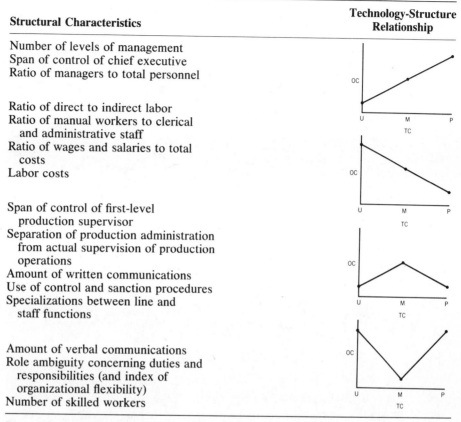

Note: OC = organizational structure characteristic; *TC* = technical complexity; *U* = unit-production system; *M* = mass-production system; *P* = process-production system.

Figure 10.3   Relationships between technical complexity and structural characteristics to effective firms.

Source: R. H. Miles. *Macro Organizational Behavior.* Santa Monica, CA: Goodyear, 1981, p. 58; from Woodward. *Industrial Organization,* pp. 50–80.

to generalize across manufacturing firms, Woodward's study discovered underlying differences in technologies that subsequently produced differences in structure.

A wider conceptualization of technology includes all the processes involved in the transformation (throughput) of information, services, production, and any other element involved in the organizational processing of input to produce an output. Perrow (1967, 1970) developed a typology of technology that is based on two dimensions: the number or variety of exceptional cases that occur during a technological process and the extent to which these exceptions are analyzable. In other words, if there are exceptions, how do we search for the information necessary to make a decision? He found that technology (the independent variable) defines organizational characteristics, for example, structure and goals (the dependent variables). Perrow defined technology as the *ac-*

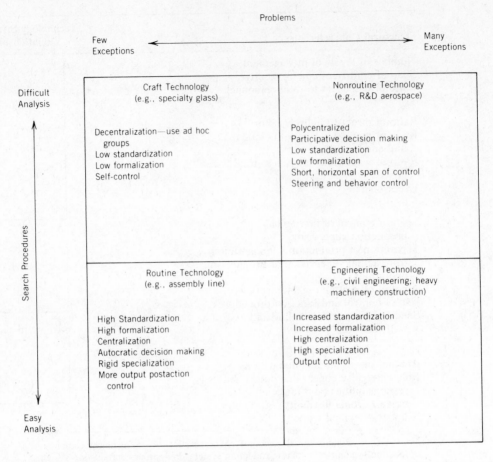

Figure 10.4 Perrow's technological typology.

Source: Adapted from Charles Perrow. ''A Framework for the Comparative Analysis of Organizations.'' *American Sociological Review* 32:194–208, 1967.

tions performed to change the object, and the *form* of the individual's interaction with the process of transformation. In other words, technology was operationalized as the number of exceptional cases encountered (e.g., uncertainty) and the nature of the search process needed when exceptions occur (e.g., logical versus intuitive). He designed a 2-by-2 matrix of these dimensions with which he identified four technological types: craft, routine, nonroutine, and engineering, as illustrated in Figure 10.4. He then described organizational characteristics, that is, structure, that were required by these types. Some of the structural variables were degree of centralization, formalization, configuration, and forms of control and coordination.

The Aston group (Hickson et al., 1969) was less interested in exploring the effect on structure of modal (overall) technology than in the technology used by different units. The central technological concept used was work flow integration—the degree of automated, continuous, fixed sequence of operations technology (as distinct from material technology and knowledge technology). This measure of technology was varied over industry types and related to an organization's structural dimensions such as degree of formalization, centralization, and line versus staff control mechanisms. These authors replicated Woodward's technology–structure contingency relationship and found that the more technology was automated, continuous, and fixed-sequenced, the more highly structured it was (i.e., specialized, formalized, and standardized) and the larger its span of control became. They also found the organization's size to be a better predictor of structure than modal technology, because the subunits in smaller organizations are more directly involved (or impinged upon) by the modal technology. Organization designers thus need to be aware of how the differences in subunit technologies affect organization structure.

Not only is the work flow integration within a unit important, but the integration of tasks *between* units has a significant impact on design as well. Thompson (1967) described technological differences in terms of the task interdependence, that is, the extent to which change in one unit will create change in the other. He defined three types, ranked in order of increasing interdependence: pooled, sequential, and reciprocal. In pooled interdependence, each subunit's output contributes to and is supported by the whole organization (e.g., branch operations). Sequential interdependence incorporates pooled interdependence, but the input of one subunit is dependent on the output of another. In reciprocal interdependence (which includes the previous two) each subunit's inputs and outputs depend on the other's inputs and outputs. These forms of interdependence correspond, respectively, to mediating, long-linked, and intensive technologies (see Figure 10.5).

Different patterns of interdependence require different kinds of management and structure. Methods of coordination and control—standardization, planning, and mutual adjustment—can be rank-ordered in terms of increasing cost

Technology Type	Dominant Form of Task Interdependence	Management and Design Requirements			
		Demands Placed on Decision Making and Communications	Extent of Organizational Complexity	Type of Coordination Required	Organizational Example
Mediating	Pooled (O → X, Y, Z)	Low	Low	Standardization and categorization	Commercial bank
Long-linked	Sequential (X → Y → Z)	Medium	Medium	Plan	Assembly line
Intensive	Reciprocal (X ⇄ Y ⇄ Z)	High	High	Mutual adjustment	General hospital

Figure 10.5 Thompson's classification of organizations by task interdependence.

Source: R. H. Miles. *Macro Organizational Behavior.* Santa Monica, CA: Goodyear, 1981, p. 66; from J. D. Thompson, *Organizations in Action.*

and effort, thus increasing demands on communication and decision making. Each method is most effective for a particular type: pooled, sequential, and reciprocal, respectively. To appreciate the impact of interdependence on organization design, one needs to know both the magnitude and the distribution of its effect—how great and how widespread it is. This method appears to provide better predictive value, and thereby aids in the design process (particularly in terms of interdependence between individuals, groups, and suborganizations).

In sum, technology—the way in which tasks are accomplished within units, between units, and between organizations—is thought to affect significantly how organizations are structured and controlled. A design that fails to account for the nature of the industry and of the tasks at hand cannot be expected to facilitate the achievement of organizational goals. By organizing tasks and units coherently according to the demands of material, human and information resources, and transformation processes, the organization not only can be effective but can maximize efficiency as well.

Environment

In the previous chapter, we discussed the potential role of the environment in determining organizational structure. To summarize briefly: the most effective organizations have developed organizational structures that match or correspond to differences in their environments (Lawrence & Lorsch, 1967; Burns & Stalker, 1961; Emery & Trist, 1965; Mintzberg, 1979; Thompson, 1967). According to Thompson (1967), the central problem facing an organization is coping with uncertainty. Uncertainty arises from environmental conditions such as the rate of change, the degree of complexity, and the extent of interconnectedness (causal relations) among the elements. Increased uncertainty can be dealt with by adapting organization structures, that is, by creating specialized units (increasing differentiation) (Lawrence & Lorsch, 1967), allowing more flexible management systems (organic types) (Burns & Stalker, 1961), increasing organization capacity to process greater amounts of information (Galbraith, 1974), and providing appropriate mechanisms of coordination and control (Thompson, 1967). These changes improve the organization's responsiveness to environmental change and demand. Through their designs, organizations can also reduce environmental contingencies by buffering their core technology and defining their domain, that is, areas of interaction with the environment (Thompson, 1967; Child, 1973). Boundary-spanning roles are created within organizations and function as mediators between the organization and the environment (Aldrich & Herker, 1977).

Conditions within the environment can have an impact on organizational functioning. These conditions, both general and specific, make up the "causal texture" of the organization (Emery & Trist, 1965). Organizations can better understand and predict the impact of these conditions through causal "mapping"—pictorial representation of the impact of the interactions and interconnectedness of these events. To be most effective, organizations need to be designed to manage their relations with their environments.

Culture

The impact of culture on organizational design is a hotly debated issue. Uncertain definitional and theoretical aspects of culture have impeded cross-cultural research efforts. Without an adequate definition and theoretical basis, "culture" often becomes a residual variable, that is, one that explains whatever is left over or the unexplained variance in a given situation. Many theorists argue for a universalist (or culture-free) approach (Weber, 1947; Hickson et al., 1974, 1979). Others maintain the importance of culture in explaining national differences (Budde et al., 1982; Child, 1981; Crozier, 1964; Hofstede, 1980). Either way, the importance of culture remains controversial.

Some partisans of the culture-free camp advocate a contingency approach— one in which technological imperatives, organizational size, environmental stability, and strategic development determine structure. Another noncultural approach is the political–economic model, in which differences in an organization's characteristics result from differences in ownership and market mechanisms, which, in turn, result from the capitalist and socialist systems. In this model, the key issues are the effects of private versus public ownership, the role of the state, and the nature of power sharing on structure.

The culture-free thesis assumes that relationships between context and structure are stable across cultures (Welge, 1981). However, studies have also shown that while contexts are kept as similar as possible, organizational differences between nations still exist that are attributable to culture (Child, 1981; Budde et al., 1982; Gallie, 1978; Maurice et al., 1980). Thus, contingency and capitalism arguments are not sufficient to explain national differences. "The economic system always exists inside a socioculture system and both systems are historical products" (Jamieson, 1980, p. 238). Culture modifies the impact of capitalism (Budde et al., 1982). In short, we can make a distinction between values and norms already embedded in a nation's social and institutional development, that is, the "civic culture" (Almond & Verba, 1963), and the intrinsic culture (Goodman & Moore, 1972). The patterns of political and social attitudes that reflect institutional development and modernization often conflict with the more intrinsic or traditional culture. This clash often creates political instability for which the MNC may become the target: the corporation ends up being blamed for upsetting the old ways.

Despite considerable difficulties, some researchers have undertaken studies of cross-national differences in organizational design. These difficulties include the impact of contextual factors—an impact that is weaker and less consistent when the unit of analysis moves from structure to roles and behavior. The effects of culture are less powerful on formal structure and overall strategy; most differences attributable to culture show up in organizational processes, such as authority, style, conduct, participation, and attitudes. Nevertheless, differences in culture can result in structural differences (Child, 1981; Hofstede, 1980; Welge, 1981) (see Figure 10.6).

Crozier's (1964) study of French bureaucracy as a reflection of French culture is a classic example of culture's impact on structure. This study showed that isolation of the individual, rigidity between levels, and hierarchic differ-

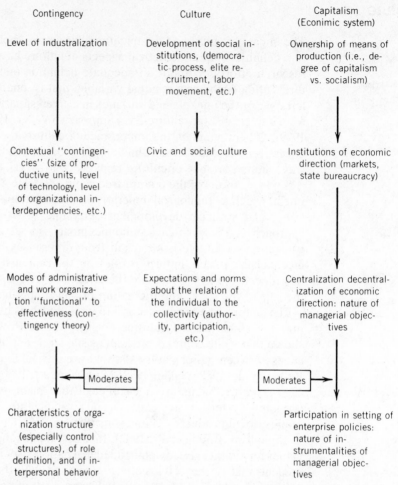

Figure 10.6 Arguments from contingency, culture, and capitalism viewpoints.

Source: J. Child. "The Cross National Study of Organizations." In L. L. Cummings and B. M. Straw, eds. *Research in Organizational Behavior,* Vol. 3. Greenwich, CT: JAI Press, 1981, p. 348.

entiation by status and privilege, all hallmarks of bureaucratic systems, are reinforced by cultural patterns.

Hofstede's cultural clusters (power distance, uncertainty avoidance, masculine–feminine, and individualism–collectivism) also have implications for structure (1980). For example, people in countries scoring higher on power distance (the acceptance of unequal distribution of power within an organization) prefer structures that resemble tall pyramids, with a narrow span of control (a high percentage of supervisory personnel) and a large degree of centralization. Countries scoring high on uncertainty avoidance prefer structures characterized by high formalization, standardization, specialization, and a rigid hierarchical structuring of activities. The masculinity–femininity and the individualism–collectivism clusters have implications for job design and participation. Sociological variables (e.g., views on elitism, scientific method, wealth and material gain, risk taking, achievement, and class flexibility) will also affect structure (Hays et al., 1972). Relationships between cultural value orientations (Kluckholn & Strodtbeck, 1961) and organization characteristics have also been postulated (Child, 1981; Brown & Schneck, 1979) (see Table 10.1).

Researchers have found cross-national differences in studies attempting to control for contextual factors by matching industry, organization size, and technology. The identified differences include (1) employee attitudes and relations with management (Gallie, 1978), (2) hierarchical and lateral divisions of functions, (3) status of departments and careers, (4) perceptions of work roles (Maurice et al., 1976, 1980), (5) role definition, job descriptions, promotions, and delegation (Child & Kieser, 1979), and (6) the impact of strategy and managerial practices on employee morale and interpersonal relations (Negandhi, 1979). Several studies have demonstrated culturally based preferences for centralization, as this characteristic is most likely to reflect differences in philosophies of control, norms on authority relationships, and managerial attitudes (Child, 1981).

The culture versus contingency debate continues (see Figure 10.7). Perhaps it is most useful to understand culture as another contingency variable whose relationship with structure is interactive, as was shown to be the case with strategy and technology.

A study by Budde et al. (1982) explored the similarities and differences in management and organization across two countries, England and Germany, as a function of contextual contingencies, the economic and political systems, and culture. The researchers compared corporate goals, managerial objectives, and modes of organizational structuring (decision making). They chose England and Germany because of their similar economic-political systems (capitalism), levels of industrialization, and industries (this allowed control for context). Both countries had similar goals: high profitability and growth (due to capitalism) and similar structures as determined by context. The differences in managerial objectives and decision-making styles were cultural. National and cultural differences emerged in the delegation of decisions, the means of control, and structuring of decision making. This study also revealed the impact of culture on the importance attached to different organizational policies and personal satisfactions.

While Britain and Germany both subscribe to capitalism, each government has its own unique relationship to industrial and financial institutions. Britain's industries are more often state owned, which has led to a greater acceptance of government involvement (though also to a greater criticism). Germany's economic system is described as more of a *laissez-faire* capitalism. German industries have closer ties to financial institutions and are more concerned with satisfying stockholders. Each country's industry displays different growth patterns. Britain's industries have grown through merger and acquisition, which has resulted in large firms with smaller, not fully rationalized subsidiaries. German industry, on the other hand, has grown through direct investments

Table 10.1 Examples of Relationships Postulated Between Cultural Value
Orientations and Organizational Characteristics

Value Orientation*	General Organizational Characteristics	Examples of Specific Practices
Human nature: good > evil	Emphasis on subordinate autonomy and intrinsic motivation	Subordinate goal setting: job enrichment
Man to nature: mastery > subjugation	Policies of innovation, and of developing individual expertise	Support for venture management: positive exercise of strategic choice including active negotiation of boundary conditions with external groups
Time orientation: future > past	Strategic emphasis and long-term planning: formal schemes for thorough organizational socialization and career planning	MBO approach rather than budgetary control: use of workforce planning and assessment centers
Orientation toward activity: being > doing	Human relations philosophy: emphasis on interpersonal sensitivity; interest in social as well as economic and technological criteria in work organization	Management style high on consideration relative to initiating structure: organizational morale and climate included in performance monitoring
Relationships: individual > hierarchical	Minimization of hierarchy: emphasis on delegation and participation; control through assessment of achievement rather than through insistence on conformity to rules	Amenities and fringe benefits not differentiated by status: employees deal directly with members of public (where relevant) without referral upwards

Source: J. Child, "Cross National Study of Organizations." In L. L. Cummings and B. M. Straw,
Research in Organizational Behavior, Vol. 3. Greenwich, CT: JAI Press, 1981, p. 326.
*> = stronger than, or preferred.

(particularly capital equipment), which has resulted in smaller firms and larger
plants. Such industry profiles seriously affect managerial structure, organization, and opinion.

In determining organizational structure, managerial values also have a great
impact, as has already been shown in Parts I and II of this book. Higher degrees
of authoritarianism and uncertainty avoidance result in greater hierarchical
differences, hard work, and low risk taking. Thus, one finds more centralization in decision making, a greater use of procedures to increase control, and
more importance attached to company prestige. There is less delegation, more
standardization and formalization, and greater emphasis on the specialist function as a source of control.

The arguments from contingency and culture are today regarded as opposed standpoints in organizational analysis. The former tends toward an emphasis upon cross-national similarities which are thought to be "culture-free"; the latter tends toward an emphasis upon dissimilarities which are thought to be "culture-bound." Their implicit theories of behavior within organizations are also almost diametrically opposed. Contingency theorists tend to view organizational behavior as externally constrained through the medium of structure, as follows:

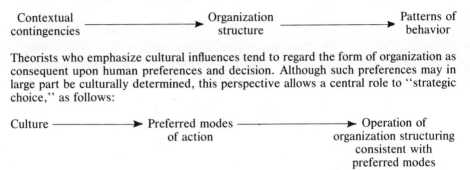

Theorists who emphasize cultural influences tend to regard the form of organization as consequent upon human preferences and decision. Although such preferences may in large part be culturally determined, this perspective allows a central role to "strategic choice," as follows:

Figure 10.7 Contingency versus culture debate.

Source: J. Child. "Cross National Study of Organizations." In L. L. Cummings and B. M. Straw, *Research in Organizational Behavior*, Vol. 3. Greenwich, CT: JAI Press, 1981, p. 349.

English culture emphasizes individual rights over collective rights. Consequently English managers tend to show a greater concern for human relations; they focus on their subordinates' well-being and development. In practice, delegation and participation are greater and emphasis on hierarchical distance and control is less. Profitability is valued because it attracts good managers, provides employees with benefits, keeps morale high, and provides a good yardstick of efficiency. Growth is valued because it provides opportunities for personal development and personal benefits. Thus, security and personal growth serve as major sources of job satisfaction.

In Germany, although organizational goals of growth and profit are the same, the reasons for valuing them are different. Growth and profitability are valued because they are good for the company; they also improve corporate prestige. Earning more money and gaining greater authority directly influence employee job satisfaction. In England, influence can be achieved regardless of formal position, whereas in Germany, promotions tend to be slower, with top managers chosen from outside. Differences in institutional arrangements result in different pressures and subsequent differences in managerial objectives. In Germany, the closer relationship with financial companies leads to pursuit of market-oriented objectives, that is, product–market position. In England, government intervention is allowed, though many observers consider it misguided and misinformed. There is, therefore, less pressure in terms of product–market growth, which allows more time for attracting and developing young talent.

The developing world must learn to assess the ways in which its traditional cultures may constrain managerial options. Budde et al. (1982) concludes, "There is little doubt that cross national differences do persist and only further research will indicate how much these are due to environmental factors not previously considered by the contingency theory, such as the country's educational structure, the role of financial institutions, and aspects of product and labor market structures, or to more general cultural values in the region or country, or simply to strategic choice" (p. 28). Or as Jamieson (1980) puts it: "The economic system always exists inside a sociocultural system and both systems are historical products" (p. 238).

A study by Daniels and Arpan (1972) compared management practices and policies of expatriate firms of various nationalities operating between 1957 and 1967 in the same national environment. The authors were interested in which environmental conditions would affect divergences in operations and flexibility in practices and in differences of national adaptiveness to foreign operations. They found differences of national adaptiveness to foreign operations. Differences in managerial attitudes were found to be influenced by foreign operations' environmental (ownership policies), internal, and cultural factors. Differences in internal control mechanisms were found between countries. Cross-cultural homogeneity was found in financial control, in that virtually no autonomy was granted on financial matters. Heterogeneity was also found in other operating areas. American subsidiaries of Italian and Scandinavian firms were independent in marketing, production, and R&D functions. Subsidiaries of German and British firms were given limited freedom. Characteristics of the external environment and internal parameters were differentially ranked as important factors in the degree to which internal control was granted. For example, tax structures (external factors) were ranked as most important by Canada, France, and Italy. Scandinavian firms considered internal factors more important.

Different goals and measures of success between countries also resulted in different methods of control. For example, in the United Kingdom, ROI was the major consideration and was accomplished through intracompany transfer pricing practices, over which they assumed considerable control. Canada's use of market-oriented transfer pricing (as opposed to cost-oriented systems) was based on the similarity of American management techniques and the desire to avoid hostility from U.S. subsidiaries. In France, where the dominant goal was income tax maximization, transfer pricing was used to obtain desired results even at the expense of good host-country relations. In Germany, corporate concern for financial stability resulted in prudent plant expansion and emphasis on fixed-asset positions and production efficiency. Concern for yearly profit (ROI), transfer pricing, and income arranging is lower, because of past experiences with inflation and wars. American firms, on the other hand, exert closer controls over short- and long-run subsidiary operations. This, in turn, contrasts with the policies of Scandinavian and Italian firms.

In Italy, the major goal of tax minimization to maximize parent-country profits results in less concern for subsidiary profits in high-tax countries. In Scandinavia, the major concern for long-term performance relies on host-government acceptance and large size—the proportion and importance of foreign to domestic operations to maintain market position.

PROCESS MODELS

In looking at the final segment of the organization–environment fit, the output side, we are concerned with the potential impact of the organization on the environment; we view the organization as more active than reactive. Strategic planning must manage the environmental components such as markets, competition, and resources. The organization is seen as (1) adaptive (i.e., able, given environmental conditions, to use feedback to evaluate and correct performance), and (2) proactive (i.e., able to anticipate and plan for environmental change). This perspective is characterized by the process model, which stresses the organization's ability to change the environment through a strategic choice and adaptation. Figure 10.8 illustrates this process.

Strategic Adaptation

This model stresses the importance of strategy and long-range planning. Thompson (1967) defines the points at which the organization depends on inputs from the environment. These points create a network of interdependencies marked by varying degrees of power and dependence. Organizations can manage the dependence through strategies such as contracting, coopting, and coalescing, as well as by considering other planning alternatives (see Table 10.2). A comprehensive list of coping strategies appears in Table 10.3. It emphasizes the complexity and the many alternatives associated with strategic choices.

Great dependencies threaten organizational survival and autonomy. Organizations need to reduce dependency by managing their external dependence. Kotter (1979) suggests several strategic approaches: (1) reducing demands by reducing dependence, that is, by selecting the domain (field of activity), (2) gaining countervailing power (either by establishing favorable relations or controlling who operates and how), and (3) minimizing the cost of compliance through organizational design. Let us look at each of these approaches.

The selection of domain depends on resources and legal charters. By seeking environmental niches, one can reduce the domain, thereby reducing competition or regulation and increasing suppliers and customers. The domain, on the other hand, can be expanded through diversification, vertical integration, geographic expansion, developing of new product lines, merger, acquisition, or internal development.

Favorable relations can be established through public relations and advertising, the creation of a large number of boundary-spanning roles, recruitment of outsiders, negotiation of contracts to gain greater legal power, cooptation of key numbers of directorships, and establishment of joint ventures or coalitions with others (Pfeffer & Nowak, 1976).

Controlling *who* operates and *how* may mean forcing out competition and joining trade associations and other coordinating councils that influence indus-

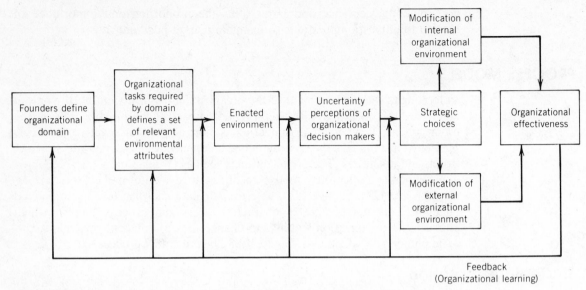

Figure 10.8 A conceptual model of the organizational choice and adaptation process.

Source: R. H. Miles. *Macro Organizational Behavior*. Santa Monica, CA: Goodyear, 1980, p. 280.

try through informed channels. These activities, however, may be limited by antitrust laws and contemporary social norms and values. In managing external dependence through organizational design, the goal is to adapt to the environment rather than to change it. This can be done by creating separate subunits to deal with different sources of external dependence, that is, purchasing, marketing, labor relations, and public relations.

Focusing on the different process segments provides us with rich information and a variety of alternatives. However, using the open system model (E-O-E, which includes all segments of the input, throughput, and output process) gives us by far the most comprehensive picture. It enables us to identify all the known processes and to categorize all the known variables, and thus to adapt to them better. The manager's focus on a particular segment is, however, an important factor in analyzing the ability to adapt. The best approach is to mix focuses and strategies to gain the greatest amount of information and the widest possible range of alternatives. Unfortunately, different organizations adopt different and sometimes inflexible strategies. Miles et al. (1978) describe three roles that organizations seem to adopt in relation to the environment: the entrepreneur, who defines the domain; the engineer, who operationalizes the technology; and the administrator, who reduces uncertainty and monitors the environment for change. These roles correspond to the focus on particular process segments. The entrepreneur focuses on the O-E, or the organization's impact on the environment. The engineer focuses on the internal processes. The administrator focuses on the input or E-O side.

Table 10.2 Thompson's Coping Strategies for Reducing Uncertainty in the Environment

Type of Organizational Strategy	Examples
Intraorganizational Strategies Designed primarily to shield the organizational core from disturbing environmental events rather than to change the events themselves	Buffering, leveling, forecasting, rationing
Domain Choice Strategies Designed to cause a shift in domain or environment from one to another rather than to cause a change in either existing organizational structures or environmental attributes	Choosing another domain; adding to or subtracting from an existing domain (as in diversification and divestiture)
Interorganizational Strategies Designed primarily to alter the state of existing environmental affairs. Two types may be distinguished: a. Cooperative strategies b. Competitive strategies	 Contracting, coopting, and coalescing strategies Maintenance of alternatives, institutionalization, and prestige enhancement

Source: R. H. Miles, *Macro Organizational Behavior.* Santa Monica, CA: Goodyear, 1980, p. 295.

Management systems play different roles at different times. In organizations that adopt the "defender" position, top management seeks to provide organizational stability by serving a control function. "Analyzers" are organizations whose management seeks a balance between the organization and the environment that will minimize risk and maximize profit. "Prospectors" serve to find and exploit new opportunities by surveying the environment and changing it. "Reactors" attempt to adjust to the environment, but their behavior is inconsistent, unstable, and usually unsuccessful. According to Miles et al. (1978), "Most organizations engage in an ongoing process of evaluating their purpose—questioning, verifying and redefining the manner of interaction with their environment" (p. 546).

Planning and Strategy

Planning at the multinational level is complex, given the complexity of profit optimization. The instability of the economic, financial, and political environment increases both uncertainty and the pressures for social responsibility that host governments exert on the corporation. Differences exist in the time horizons, nature of planning targets, roles of line and staff in developing plans, and roles of local governments and central planning agencies (Hawkins & Walter, 1981). American corporations reduce planning cycles to keep in line with the

Table 10.3 Organizational Strategies for Coping with the External Environment

Organizational Theorist	Organizational Strategies
Selznick (1949)	Cooptation
Litwak and Hylton (1962); Zald (1970)	Institutionalization
McCaulay (1963)	Long-term contracts
Thompson (1967)	Intraorganizational strategies:
	Buffering
	Smoothing
	Forecasting
	Rationing
	Boundary spanning
	Growth and encapsulation
	Interorganizational strategies:
	Contracting
	Coopting
	Coalescing
	Competing
Evan (1966)	Interorganizational flow of personnel
	Public relations
	Cooptation
	Acquisition and merger
	Espionage
	Litigation
	Arbitration
	Mediation
	Noncontractual agreements
Perrow (1970)	Voluntary restriction of competition
	Mergers
	Administered prices
	Price fixing
	Cost-plus contracts
	Forward and backward integration
	Reciprocity agreements and norms
	Cooptation
Aiken and Hage (1971)	Temporary coalitions
	Joint ventures
Pfeffer (1976)	Interorganizational mergers
	Appointments of members to board of directors
Child (1972)	Strategic choices of:
	Domain
	Organizational boundaries
	Enterprise location
	Material and personnel
	Performance standards
	Basic operating mechanisms
	Operating technology
	Structural configuration
Galbraith (1973)	Structural modifications:
	Creation of slack resources
	Creation of self-contained units

Table 10.3 (Continued)

Organizational Theorist	Organizational Strategies
	Investment in vertical information systems
	Creation of lateral relations
Miles, Snow, and Pfeffer (1974)	Long-term contracts
	Joint ventures
	Cooptation
	Merger
	Third parties (trade associations, coordination groups, government agencies)
	Market forms (oligopoly, monopoly, monopsony)
	Suspended competition
	Domain choice
	Diversification
Staw and Szwajkowski (1975)	Commission of illegal corporate acts:
	Price discrimination
	Tying arrangements
	Refusal to deal and exclusive dealing
	Franchise violation
	Foreclosure of entry
	Reciprocity
	Allocation of markets
	Monopoly
	Conspiracy
	Illegal mergers and acquisitions
Hirsch (1975)	Cooptation of institutional gatekeepers
	Patents, copyrights, and trademarks
	Price and distribution-channel control

Source: R. H. Miles, *Macro Organizational Behavior*. Santa Monica, CA: Goodyear, 1980, pp. 293–294.

budget, whereas European MNCs tend to lengthen these cycles five to ten years (Duerr & Roach, 1979; Basche, 1976; Doz, 1980a, 1980b).

Strategy, in contrast, is the blueprint that indicates "how the organization intends to get where it wants to go" (Thompson & Strickland, 1980, p. 20). Stated in another way, and in keeping with a less static model, strategy is a pattern in a stream of significant decisions (Mintzberg, 1979). Strategy determines what business to be in (corporate level) and how to do business (business level). Corporate strategy departments, staff departments, and chief executive officers thus need to monitor the environment to assess threats and opportunities, while evaluating company strengths and weaknesses.

In this regard, Chandler's study (1962) of development at DuPont, General Motors, Sears Roebuck, and Exxon provides a useful historical perspective on the relationship of strategy with structure. Changes in structure evolved as environments (e.g., markets) changed and as different strategies were subsequently chosen. The original organizational structure also affects strategy in that a single, large, centralized business (Ford) might choose to expand operations through vertical integration, whereas a company (General Motors, e.g.) that was created by combining several smaller firms might continue to expand through acquisitions. Chandler's study provided a format that later studies used in examining organizational structure in other countries. Harvard produced studies of the United Kingdom (Channon, 1973), Italy (Paven, 1973), and France and Germany (Dyaz & Thanheiser, 1976) that confirm Chandler's beliefs that new structures emerge from the pursuit of different strategies. These studies have demonstrated that as diversification increases, firms adopt divisionalized structures.

A study by Egelhoff (1982) used several variables to measure strategy elements that included extent of foreign product diversity, extent of product modification differences among foreign subsidiaries, rate of product change in company, size of foreign operations (percentage of sales from the total sales), size of foreign manufacturing (percentage of foreign sales from foreign manufacturing), number of foreign subsidiaries, extent of outside ownership of foreign subsidiaries, and extent to which growth was achieved through foreign acquisition. These variables or strategic conditions, shown in Table 10.4, fit different structures.

Research suggests that effective organizations tend to implement certain strategies with particular organizational structures. The link between structure and strategy in the MNCs has been described in the literature (Brooke & Remmers, 1970; Stopford & Wells, 1972; Franko, 1978; Brandt 1978). The crucial question of which structures are appropriate for implementing which strategies remains.

Diversification

Diversification strategies result from external pressures or internal characteristics; they produce different ways of controlling operations. Slower market growth rates, increased R&D expenditures, and increased consumer spending have resulted in pressures to develop new products and markets. Firms therefore must diversify to sustain growth. Both the increased diversity and increased competitive pressures have led many firms to adopt a divisional format.

Diversification affects structure in several ways. Strategies in diversifying abroad include the transfer of the manufacture of added product lines to foreign locations, and then the building of a structure to manage the diversification. However, American MNCs have typically diversified into areas of new (rather than existing) technology, and therefore are not under pressure to transfer abroad. Diversification can be based on technology (as at General Electric) or by vertically integrated products (as at Texton). Diversification of related business results in increasing central control, whereas unrelated diversification results in increased divisional autonomy. Extensive diversification leads to innovation in new products and in transferring new products to foreign markets.

Table 10.4 Summary of the Important Fits Between the Elements of Strategy and Types of Structures

Elements of Strategy	Types of Structure			
	Functional Divisions	**International Divisions**	**Geographical Regions**	**Product Divisions**
Foreign product diversity	Low foreign product diversity			High foreign product diversity
Product modification differences between subsidiaries	Low product modification differences between subsidiaries			
Product change				High rate of product change
Size of foreign operations		Relatively small foreign operations	Relatively large foreign operations	Relatively large foreign operations
Size of foreign manufacturing			High level of foreign manufacturing	
Number of foreign subsidiaries	Few foreign subsidiaries	Low to moderate number of foreign subsidiaries	Large number of foreign subsidiaries	Large number of foreign subsidiaries
Extent of outside ownership in foreign subsidiaries	Low level of outside ownership in foreign subsidiaries			
Extent of foreign acquisitions	Few foreign acquisitions			

Source: W. Egelhoff, "Strategies and Structures in the MNC: An Information-Processing Approach." *Administrative Science Quarterly* 27:435–458 (1982).

Regional diversification depends on the degree to which geographic dispersion places stress on the international division. Firms with a high marketing orientation, mature product lines, low R&D, and pressure to standardize and rationalize tend to choose structures that centralize production and decentralize marketing decisions (Stopford & Wells, 1972).

Another approach is to view strategic choice and structural adaptation as a consequence of market structure (Caves, 1980). Market structure refers to elements of the market such as the number, size, and distribution of sellers and buyers, barriers to entrance and exit, extent and character of product differentiation and global competition, and demand parameters (e.g., elasticity and growth rate). By correctly matching strategy to both market opportunities and organizational structure, a firm can increase its profits and the efficiency of resource use—that is, it can maximize value and minimize cost. High competitiveness, for example, requires tight coordination through control of resources, higher vertical hierarchy, and increased reporting; yet it also requires increased decentralization of decision making (Pfeffer & Leblebici, 1973).

One issue of growing international concern is the degree to which corporations control the market or are controlled by it. This issue has even triggered debates about the need for government or United Nations regulation (Scott, 1973). Galbraith (1967) favors regulation because he believes that corporations have adopted strategies of market dominance rather than profit maximization. He argues that corporations have built up structures and strategies that insulate them from competitive market pressures. In contrast, Scott (1973) argues that competitive pressures have shaped corporate structure and that the market can control corporations more effectively than regulation. He describes the evolution of corporate structure as a consequence of strategies adopted in response to market change and then makes comparisons between the United States and Europe.

American companies, for instance, diversified before their European counterparts for two reasons: the threat of antitrust suits in horizontal mergers in the United States and a lag in long-range planning in Europe. Contributing to this lag were efforts at reconstruction following World War II, a bureaucratic style of management, and family ownership (particularly in the United Kingdom and Italy). Those European MNCs that diversified quickly tended to have American-based firms (Caves, 1980). Competition increased the pressure to divisionalize (though more keenly in the United States than in Europe because of the threat of antitrust suits and supply/demand contingencies). Europe later felt the effects of increasing competition with the advent of the European Common Market (Scott, 1973).

By 1967, more than 90% of the Fortune 500 firms had diversified; more than 80% were multidivisional (Scott, 1973). Diversification has brought a decline of functional structures and a rise in product division structures (see Figure 10.9)—''Functional/subs, a hybrid wherein the principal business is directly managed by top management in the traditional functional form and the other, smaller diversified businesses are managed as product divisions or subsidiaries'' (p. 138). Only about half the Fortune 500 are pure functional forms (most prevalent in dominant single-business types) and their numbers are declining (Rumelt, 1974). In European firms, we can see the same trend toward diversification, rapid increase in companies using product division, and a decline in single businesses (see Figure 10.10).

As companies grow, they expand not only into other business areas but also into other geographic areas, often outside their domestic borders. Strategies of diversification often push companies into the international arena. Product diversification at home is a necessary condition for product diversity abroad. Conversely, entry into foreign markets as such does not necessarily result in a divisionalized structure. Thus, diversification alone does not result in adoption of divisional forms. Often there is a twenty- to thirty-year time-lag between a change in strategy and a change in structure (Scott, 1973).

The evolutionary structures that American firms have developed for expansion abroad parallel those accompanying growth and diversification at home (Stopford & Wells, 1972). Scott describes firms as developing in a series of

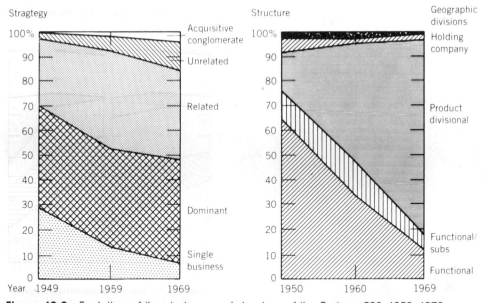

Figure 10.9 Evolution of the strategy and structure of the Fortune 500, 1950–1970.

Source: B. R. Scott, ''The Industrial State: Old Myths and New Realities.'' *Harvard Business Review,* March–April 1973, p. 139; from R. Rumelt. ''Strategy, Structure and Financial Performance of the Fortune '500' 1950–1970.'' Unpublished DBA dissertation, Harvard Business School, 1972.

stages—from the entrepreneurial stage through the transitional (product divisions) to a functional multidivisional stage (Scott, 1973)—however, they become multinational when they expand abroad. MNCs are usually in the third stage of development—the multidivisional stage. Most multinationals evolve from a stage-III or multidivisional structure (Prasad & Krishna Shetty, 1976). These firms account for most foreign direct investment (Fouraker & Stopford, 1968), are a primary source of American export strength, and lead in R&D, because innovative capacity is one of the primary sources of competitive advantage in foreign markets.

The relationship between strategy and structure is interactive. Although strategy change requires change in structures, current structures can also shape the strategies that organizations pursue. Small integrated firms with functional formats often pursue acquisition strategies, whereas they may prefer to grow through internal development. Other differences in corporate characteristics can also result in differences in venture behavior (Burgelman, 1983). As mentioned earlier, for example, the nature of the technology can determine a firm's strategy preferences: firms with long-linked technologies often prefer to pursue vertical integration; firms with mediating technologies pursue horizontal integration by expanding the population served; and firms with intensive technologies incorporate their clients (Thompson, 1967).

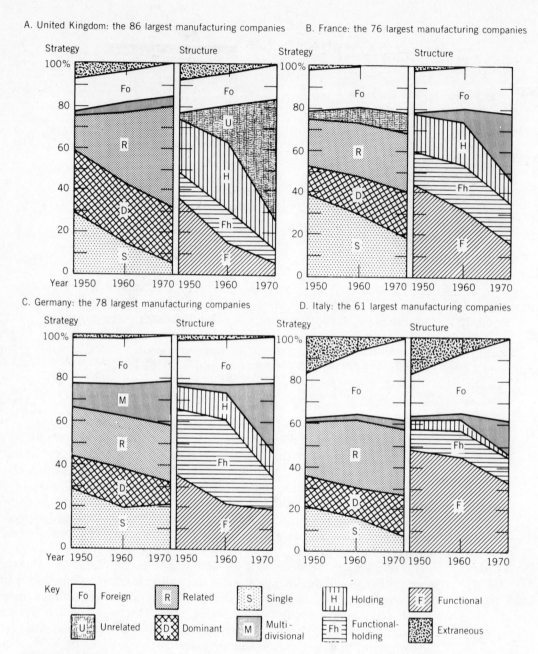

A. United Kingdom: the 86 largest manufacturing companies   B. France: the 76 largest manufacturing companies

C. Germany: the 78 largest manufacturing companies   D. Italy: the 61 largest manufacturing companies

Key: Fo Foreign; R Related; S Single; H Holding; F Functional; U Unrelated; D Dominant; M Multi-divisional; Fh Functional-holding; Extraneous

Figure 10.10 Evolution of the strategy and structure in the four major Western European countries, 1950–1970.

Source: B. R. Scott, ''The Industrial State: Old Myths and New Realities.'' *Harvard Business Review*, March–April 1973, p. 140.

BOUNDARY SPANNING ROLES: CREATION AND FUNCTIONS

The boundary roles of a multinational corporation critically link environmental characteristics with the MNC structure. These roles play a necessary and vital part in the MNC's adaptation to, and ultimate survival in, its environment. All MNCs have some boundary roles; however, organizations vary as to whether these roles are formal or informal, full or part time, elaborate or simple.

Functions of Boundary Roles

Information Processing   Those who perform boundary roles are exposed to large amounts of information, some of which is important to the MNC. These boundary spanners (or gatekeepers as they are often labeled) are important because they mediate the flow of information between the organization in its environment. Personnel in boundary roles thus process information for the MNC, selectively transmitting the information that is significant to the organization. Clearly, not all information from the environment is equally important; without such a screening process the MNC's communication channels would be overloaded. Moreover, boundary role personnel must summarize data and organize them into usable form, showing the interrelationships and the implications of the raw data. Furthermore, boundary role personnel often must use their expertise to draw inferences or extrapolate from the information gathered.

Thus, informational boundary spanning is a two-part process that consists of (1) obtaining information from external areas and (2) disseminating that information to internal users (Tushman & Scanlan, 1981). Boundary role personnel must be able to translate across communication boundaries and be aware of contextual information on both sides of the boundary. The individual's ability to span a boundary is predicated on his or her having the work-related expertise required to communicate effectively on both sides of the communication boundary.

In turn, the MNC's capacity to adapt to varying environmental conditions is dependent on the ability of the boundary role personnel to select, interpret, and transmit information from the environment to the MNC.

External Representation   Unlike informational boundary role personnel, who acquire information from external areas and transmit it internally, representational role personnel perform a more routine transacting/representation role. These personnel are involved in a one-step information flow of transmitting substantial information to the external environment (Tuschman & Scanlan, 1981). Thus, although individuals in representational roles engage in substantial external communication, they do not link information between areas within the organization. Unlike informational boundary role spanners, they do not usually mediate critical resources for the organization and therefore do not possess as much power within the organization as informational boundary spanners.

The external representation functions include the following:

1. The acquisition and disposal of resources—marketing and sales representatives, personal recruiters, and buyers. Personnel in these positions represent the organization to the environment, reflecting the policy decisions of management.

2. Political legitimacy and hegemony. Such personnel serve not only a representative but also a negotiating function. An example is the corporate lawyer, who ultimately affects the MNC's power with other entities. Kochan (1975) notes that in response to threats to its control over employees, city governments have created collective bargaining units—an illustration of boundary spanners whose function is to maintain political legitimacy and power.

3. Maintaining the organizational image and enhancing social legitimacy. Those involved with enhancing the organization's social legitimacy do not bargain or negotiate with various target groups but they unilaterally disseminate information in an effort to influence others. Advertising and public relations personnel, for example, not only keep the organization visible, but strive to influence the behavior of targeted groups (Aldrich & Herker, 1977).

Establishment of Boundary Roles

Thompson (1967) has suggested that organizations establish boundary spanning units in order to deal with environmental pressures and buffer their impact on the rest of the organization. By doing so, Thompson argued, the organization wishes to absorb environmental uncertainties and increase its power over environmental forces.

MNCs do not operate in a vacuum. Thus, all MNCs have some boundary spanning roles, even if only at the level of the CEO. However, although MNCs have formalized, full-time boundary role positions, others have only part-time and less elaborate positions. The number of formally established boundary spanning roles within an MNC is dependent on many factors, one being organizational size. The smaller an MNC, the easier it is for it to survive with a fairly simple organizational structure and few differentiated boundary roles and functions (Child, 1973). In addition, environmental complexities will determine the need for differentiated boundary role positions. As organizational and environmental complexities increase, MNCs require more formalized and differentiated boundary spanning activities.

Moreover, as a response both to the interaction of technology and the environment and to environmental pressures, MNCs can be expected to increase the number of boundary spanning roles (Aldrich & Herker, 1977). MNCs that are service-oriented, linking clients with each other (e.g., banks, insurance companies), can be expected to have the highest proportion of boundary roles, because their main function is direct client interaction (Hasenfeld, 1972). Conversely, MNCs using an intensive technology have fewer boundary spanning units and buffer most of them from the environment by temporarily drawing the client into the organization, temporarily assigning the client an organizational role, and forcing the client to change his or her behavior to suit organizational norms. On the other hand, organizational professionals, who need to maintain contact with a professional reference group and keep abreast of changes (technological or otherwise) in their field, may engage in a great deal of boundary spanning contact (Aiken & Hage, 1968).

In addition to technology, much of the role and structure differentiation in MNCs is attributable to environmental pressures. For example, the growth of pressure groups with vested interests, such as those spawned by the consumer and ecology movements, have brought pressure on MNCs. These corporations have responded by establishing public relations and social responsibility departments (both examples of boundary spanning roles) to meet these demands. Also, an MNC can be expected to have a higher proportion of boundary spanning units in an environment in which the important elements are concentrated rather than dispersed. In addition, MNCs facing heterogeneous environments will have more boundary role positions than those facing a relatively homogeneous environment and stable environments, which require less monitoring than rapidly changing environments.

Formalization, Routinization, and Power in Boundary Roles

Whether or not boundary roles will be formalized into full-time positions depends on the MNC's recognition of the potential costs (economic, political, or social) arising from its failure to maintain effective links with elements in the environment. The more critical these potential costs, the more effort will be directed toward explicitly formalizing the role and selecting a qualified candidate. Boards of directors serve important boundary spanning roles, and they often act as a buffer group between the full-time employees and the public, promoting and representing the MNC to other groups such as customers, stockholders, suppliers, and so on (Zald, 1967).

Boundary roles may vary considerably depending on how routinized they are. Environmental as well as internal elements will dictate how routine a boundary spanning position will be. If there is a high frequency of interaction and the elements at the boundary are homogeneous, this may allow highly routinized behavior (e.g., purchase requisitions used by purchasing agents) (Aldrich & Herker, 1977).

Thompson (1962, 1967) identified three environmental conditions that may lead to routinization of boundary spanning roles:

1. If the organization provides many services for a large number of people, it must either increase the number of personnel in boundary positions or else routinize the tasks of existing boundary spanning personnel so they can handle a greater volume of work.
2. If the organization uses a mechanized production technology, characterized by large runs or standardized products, it may in turn depend on a high volume of standardized transactions for each boundary role employee.

3. Stable environments will be more likely to produce highly routinized boundary roles than unstable environments, which will require more flexibility in dealing with its frequent changes.

Additionally, internal organizational structure may demand routine behavior as a social control mechanism. Because the boundary roles will be programmed with clearly defined operating procedures, MNC employees will be forced to follow organizational norms and procedures. Hence, routinization of roles not only increases efficiency, but also helps the MNC control its employees' behavior by ensuring that a boundary role staff member will act consistently with the organization's goals and procedures. Conversely, boundary roles that deal with heterogeneous elements must have minimal routinization to allow for maximum flexibility in adapting to idiosyncratic circumstances. In sum, routinization depends on (1) the volume of repetitive work, (2) the predictability of outcomes from interaction with the environment, (3) the homogeneity and stability of the environment, and (4) the need or desire to control the employee's behavior.

When boundary role personnel face a heterogeneous, dynamic environment, they are expected to exercise discretion and develop expertise. The extent to which they are successful in recognizing contingencies will dictate how much power they can obtain within the organization. Thus, boundary role incumbents possess a gatekeeper's power, filtering information into the organization, which they then interpret and analyze. If the employee's interpretations and analyses turn out to be correct, and if the information is vital for organizational survival, the employee's power will be enhanced (March & Simon, 1958). This power is further enhanced by the extent to which the environment the boundary role incumbent faces makes routinization difficult, if not impossible.

QUESTIONS FOR ORGANIZATIONAL DESIGNERS

Several problems in developing designs confront the MNC. Formal guidelines defining relationships among superiors and subordinates, profit centers, and line and staff functions are inadequate, as these relationships are no longer clear-cut. The old "one man–one boss" adage must be reexamined in light of the organizational realities of dotted-line reporting relationships. Profit centers are no longer autonomous, but are in fact becoming very interdependent. Staff roles have taken on greater control functions.

The major questions that designers of international organizations must answer are as follows:

1. How should operations (principally production and sales activities) be grouped or coordinated worldwide?
2. To what extent should management decentralize responsibility and authority?
3. How can management provide overall coordination and retain overall control while responding effectively at the corporate as well as the local level?

Among the major criteria for design that need to be considered are the following:

1. The economics of business, that is, how to achieve the most economical use of resources with the least duplication of functions and facilities.
2. The anticipated results, that is, how to achieve the best results in highly competitive markets that provide the greatest flexibility, maneuverability, and viability.
3. The competence of available personnel.
4. Degree of foreign involvement, that is, export sales, licensing agreements, assembly, and production through built or bought unit subsidiaries.

Given the organization's objectives and strategy, the designer needs to decide what structure will offer the maximum performance potential for achieving those objectives. The designer must consider a number of structural variables:

1. Level of management responsibility.
2. The types of decisions assigned at each level (e.g., strategic, administrative, and operations).
3. The subdivision of responsibility for those decisions (e.g., planning, controlling, and implementing).
4. The types of logistic function.
5. The manner of grouping management and logistic functions (e.g., by function, product, market, or geographic area).

Different structures (or combination of structures) will emerge as a result of these considerations and will determine organizational effectiveness or maximum performance potential. Ansoff and Brandenburg (1971) offer one of the comprehensive process-oriented criteria for organizational effectiveness associated with its design. They developed a conceptualization integrating physical, informational, behavioral, and economic variables needed to aid managers in selecting effective organizational structure, with the full recognition that some of these variables may lead to conflicting conclusions. These variables are suitable for organizations that have an identifiable output that the organization seeks to produce efficiently, given the organizational objectives and its strategy.

The main categories represent the following concepts:

1. Steady-state efficiency. Measures the efficiency when the levels of throughput (process) and its nature remain relatively stable over time.
2. Operating responsiveness. Measures the ability of an organization to make quick and efficient changes in the levels of throughput.
3. Strategic responsiveness. Measures the firm's ability to respond to changes in the nature (rather than form) of its throughput.
4. Structural responsiveness. Measures the capability of an organization to change itself.
5. Decision and information quality. Concerns the quality and timeliness of information inputs, the timely recognition of decision needs, the quality of

decision analysis, and the effectiveness of leadership in gaining decision acceptance.

6. Economic feasibility. Is measured by the availability of money and fiscal resources necessary to build and maintain the organization.
7. Human resource feasibility. Measures the match between available human resources and the requirement of the organization.

Different organizational forms develop as a result of the designer's decisions. The grouping of managerial and logistical systems can occur on the basis of function (e.g., finance, marketing, production), products, geographic regions, or project (matrix structure).

The most effective design integrates simultaneously five elements: product, function, market/customer, geography, and technology. The choice of structure is determined in part by the conflict of functional, geographic, and product needs. Technical and product needs include specialized knowledge and experience as provided by R&D, manufacturing, and engineering and servicing departments. Functional or specialized business needs involve departmental knowledge in finance, legal, planning, and personnel matters. Regional or environmental needs involve knowledge about and experience in the area's political, economic, and social trends and forces such as host government expectations (Jain & Puri, 1981), labor, and consumers affairs (*Business International,* 1981).

The basic challenge in an international structure is how best to coordinate these elements and departments at each level and for the organization as a whole. In choosing the most appropriate design (given the company's needs and concerns) the designer must therefore address the questions listed in Box 10.1.

Hutchinson (1976) has offered a summary of corporations' concerns and the suitability of various structures in meeting these concerns, which are presented in Table 10.5.

An example of Unilever's criteria for design is shown in Table 10.6, which relates the degree of diversification, the strategies of maintenance versus expansion, and the degree of centralization of resource allocation with the appropriate organizational structure.

CHANGE PROCESS
Recognizing the Need for Change

Given the growing complexity and the increasing rates of change within both the organization and the environment, MNCs are under constantly increasing pressure to evaluate their organizational structures in view of their strategies and goals. The decision to change the organizational structure toward greater responsiveness to these pressures and demands cannot be taken lightly. Changing an organization requires careful consideration of what problems the change seeks to correct as well as the possible outcomes. The extent of change must be proportionate to the nature of the problem or existing dysfunction. Employees

Box 10.1

Essential Questions of Organizational Design

- What is the nature of the problem? What is its scope: broad, covering many business issues; or very specific? What is its source: structure, management policies, personalities, etc.? Is it temporary or permanent? At what organizational level does it occur? (Note that a problem that appears at a low level often stems from a higher one.)

- What does management want the company or unit to do? (What might it do? What can it do? What should it do?)

- What internal and external resources are available to accomplish the above mandate?

- What must be done to transform the resources into finished products or services?

- Which resources will be contained in which units?

- What are the critical tasks that the organization must do well in order to survive and prosper (e.g., high-quality manufacturing, sales, or technological development)?

- What kinds of management decisions are crucial to the success of the enterprise? How often must they be made, and at what organizational level?

- In what ways do the company's structure, policies, and regulations enhance or impede the pursuit of its strategy as well as the work environment of individuals and groups?

- How does work move through the organization? As it flows through, who initiates a piece of work? Who does the studies? Who needs to be informed? Who needs to be consulted? Who is the decision maker? What are the critical interactions that occur between individuals and work units? How much uncertainty is associated with the work at different points? Where do problems such as breakdowns in communications, missed targets, or delays occur?

- To what extent can work, information flows, coordination, and control systems, etc. be standardized?

- To what degree should the firm attempt to specialize?

- How adaptable can and should the organization be to the external environment?

- To what extent should operating units be "self-contained," with their own complete line and staff operations?

- What degree of decentralization is best?

- How much accountability for results is given to the managers of each unit?

- What is the role of staff (to advise, audit, coordinate, troubleshoot, direct, etc.)? Also, which staff functions (advertising, auditing, legal, planning, etc.) should be performed internally and which should be handled by outsiders—and to what extent?

- What horizontal linkages between individuals and units are required? Why should each linkage exist? What transactions take place at the linkage points and what is the best way to handle them?

- Which executives should be close to headquarters rather than scattered about in various regions or countries?

- What formal and informal mechanisms should be created for the purpose of feedforward control? (Examples include budgets, forecasts, plans, and projections.)

- What formal and informal mechanisms should be created for the purpose of feedback control? (Examples include written reports, periodic meetings with senior management, and special audits.)

- How should managers be motivated to work toward common objectives? What reward systems—such as compensation, promotion, and commendation—are appropriate?

- What are the strengths/weaknesses of the key managers and what are their career goals? How will each fit into a new organization?

- What are the CEO's personal interests? What are his goals? Which functions does he want to

(Continued)

supervise directly? How wide a span of control suits him? With how much organizational flexibility is he comfortable? What does he perceive to be the role of staff units?

- What are the estimated costs of implementing and living with a new structure?

- What specific organizational alternatives can be developed from the foregoing analyses? Which of these should be adopted? Why?

Source: Business International Corporation. Used with permission.

who will be affected by the change should be involved in the planning to reduce their resistance to implementation. Such involvement may also help managers to foresee and plan for unanticipated consequences.

In considering the need for change, we can look for symptoms or signs, some of which are delineated in Box 10.2.

Some of the final guidelines necessary in planning for change are suggested in Box 10.3.

Managing the Process

People often experience change as disruptive and stressful. Organizations and their employees tend to prefer the status quo, relying on the old ways of doing

Table 10.5   Suitability of Basic MNC Organizational Structures to Corporate Concerns

Area of Corporate Concern	International Division	Worldwide Product Division	Area Division	Matrix	Focused Market Units
		Level of Suitability*			
Rapid growth	M	H	M	H	H
Diversity of products	L	H	L	H	H
High technology	M	H	L	H	H
Few experienced managers	H	M	L	L	L
Close corporate control	M	H	L	H	H
Close government relations	M	L	H	M	M
Resource allocation:					
Product considerations should dominate	L	H	L	M	M
Geographic considerations should dominate	M	L	H	M	M
Functional considerations should dominate	L	M	L	H	M
Relative cost	M	M	L	H	M

Source: J. Hutchinson, "Evolving Organizational Forms." *Columbia Journal of World Business.*
11(2):51 (Summer 1976).
*H = high; M = medium; L = low.

Table 10.6 Unilever's Criteria for Selecting Organization Structures

Degree of Diversification	Emphasis of Company Objectives and Plans	Allocation of Resources	Appropriate Organization Structure
1. Homogeneous in terms of product technology, trade and distribution channels, consumer or user needs	Either maintenance and efficiency of operations or effective expansion	Centralized	Functional
2. Diverse or partly diverse product technology and/or trade and distribution channels and/or consumer or user needs	Maintenance and efficiency of operations	Centralized	Functional with some special devices (e.g., operational committees)
3. Same as 2	Effective expansion	Partly centralized, partly decentralized: similar resources for different activities are centralized and different resources decentralized	Two-dimensional structure*
4. Diverse product technology, trade and distribution channels, consumer or user needs, with some binding elements (e.g., same raw materials, labor force under the same collective agreement)	Maintenance and efficiency of operations	Partly centralized, partly decentralized	Two-dimensional structure
5. Same as 4.	Effective expansion	Decentralized, with corporate services determined by efficiency, practicability, and uniqueness	Divisional (geographic or by product)
6. Diverse in almost all aspects, with hardly any binding factors	Maintenance and efficiency of operations	Decentralized, with some common services, based on minimizing costs	Divisional (geographic or by product)
7. Same as 6.	Effective expansion	Separate	Separate operating companies

Source: A. R. Janger, *Matrix Organization of Complex Businesses.* New York: The Conference Board. Report No. 763, 1979, p. 14.
*Two-dimensional structure is Unilever's term for matrix structure.
Note: Availability of raw materials, the transport costs, or the distribution of finished products could be decisive in selecting a geographic divisional structure.

Box 10.2

When Is Change Needed?

- A change in the size of the corporation—due to growth, consolidation, or reduction;
- A change in key individuals—which may alter management objectives, interests, and abilities;
- A failure to meet goals, capitalize on opportunities, or be innovative;
- An inability to get things done on time;
- A consistently overworked top management that spends excessive hours on the job;
- A belief that costs are extravagant and/or that budgets are not being met;
- Morale problems;
- Lengthy hierarchies that inhibit the exercise of strategic control;
- Planning that has become increasingly staff-driven and is thus divorced from line management;
- Innovation that is stifled by too much administration and monitoring of details; and
- Uniform solutions that are applied to nonuniform situations. The extreme opposite of this condition—when things that should or could function in a routine manner do not—should also be heeded as a warning. In other words, management by exception has replaced standard operating procedures.

  The following are a few specific indicators of *international* organizational malaise:

- A shift in the operational scope—perhaps from directing export activities to controlling overseas manufacturing and marketing units, a change in the size of operations on a country, regional or worldwide basis, or failure of foreign operations to grow in accordance with plans and expectations;
- Clashes among divisions, subsidiaries, or individuals over territories or customers in the field;
- Divisive conflicts between overseas units and domestic division staff or corporate staff;
- Instances wherein centralization leads to a flood of detailed data that are not fully understood or properly used by headquarters;
- Duplication of administrative personnel and services;
- Underutilization of overseas manufacturing or distribution facilities;
- Duplication of sales offices and specialized sales account executives;
- Proliferation of relatively small legal entities and/or operating units within a country or geographic area;
- An increase in overseas customer service complaints;
- Breakdowns in communications within and between organizations; and
- Unclear lines of reporting and dotted-line relationships, and ill-defined executive responsibilities.

Source: Business International Corporation. Used with permission.

things. Rather than confronting problems, people tend to ignore them, wish them away, or else accept them as unsolvable. Coping with problems through change requires a great amount of time, energy, and money; it also requires the ability to tolerate uncertainty and ambiguity. Managers need to commit the necessary resources and to maintain realistic time perspectives by remembering the long-range goals rather than succumbing to short-term pressures. They

Box 10.3

Some Final Organizational Guidelines

● *The need to ensure internal consistency among structural elements is of great importance to a firm's organizational viability.* Thus, management philosophy, the degree of decentralization, the CEO's span of control, how decisions are made, reward systems, and the like should be mutually consistent and reinforcing. Success in achieving this condition frequently explains why two companies in the same industry can be organized differently and yet be equally prosperous.

● *Nothing is permanent.* As one sage once remarked, "At some time in the life cycle of virtually every organization, its ability to succeed in spite of itself runs out."

● *If things are working, do not reorganize.* An organization is like a mosaic: change one piece and the whole design may change. Every "solution" breeds new problems.

● *If you have a business problem, make certain it is due to the organization before you rush to reorganize.* If it is an organizational dilemma, is it related to structure, people, or business systems? When you have discovered what the trouble is, concentrate on solving that specifically—do not try to deal with all three at once. This will help mobilize resources and give people a sense of purpose, since they will perceive that the main problem area is being addressed.

● *When working on an organization problem, do not be tempted by complex solutions.* Try the simple ones first.

● *It may not be appropriate to organize every business or division within the company the same way.* Analyze the objectives and the circumstances of each and organize them so that they can best meet their particular goals.

● *Organizations must be designed around their own unique features*—such as location, employees, products/services, and the real, de facto organization and reporting relationships (which may differ from those displayed on formal charts).

● *Emphasis should be placed on clear-cut delegation of authority and execution of responsibility.* This involves setting performance criteria and rating individuals and the structure according to these criteria.

● *In general, organizational formats are not "pure."* There is no single, universal definition of matrix, for example. Many varieties are practiced.

● *Executives should not overemphasize the search for one clear, optimal solution.* There is no one best way to organize; often, several useful alternatives exist. Most companies tend to have a "mixed" organizational setup that combines two or even more approaches (e.g., worldwide product and international division). Those charged with the task of reorganizing must therefore decide on those designs most appropriate under the circumstances—given the cost of changing the structure, the individual and group issues involved, the relevant political factors present in the informal organization, and so on.

● *Organizational planning should be done as frequently as company planning and budgeting.* The organization requires constant monitoring. The key question is, Does your organization help you meet your goals?

Source: Business International Corporation. Used with permission.

also need to be sensitive to the demands that change places on its employees to facilitate the process and the implementation.

Perhaps the best way to approach changing the organizational structure is to view change as a continuous, dynamic process rather than as a "one-shot deal." Therefore, the most appropriate organizational structure is one that is organic—that is, one that is purposely designed to respond to change in a flexible manner. Organizational structures of this sort will be less disruptive than more rigid formats. In this way, the organization can best survive and remain viable and profitable in a world of increasing complexity and rapid change (Whitsett, 1976; Bourgeois, 1981; Perlmutter & Heenan, 1979). It should be stressed, however, that even in an organic organization, employees may have internalized other methods and policies, so that change may require a resocialization process. The problems of implementing change are manifold under any circumstances and are even more complex in a cross-cultural setting. Issues such as communication, conceptual ability, source of change, amount of workers' participation in the planning, and the levels of managers' commitment and involvement all can differ from country to country. Methodological problems arise in regard to the reliability and validity of measurement and evaluations across cultures. Other problems include union resistance, training difficulties, and stability over time (Whitsett, 1976).

We can highlight the difficulties of applied organizational development in foreign countries by considering Latin America. Even given similarities in capitalist ideology, business practices, entrepreneurial models, and desire for progress, problems nonetheless arise for psychosocial, cultural, and politico/economic reasons. Among the psychosocial factors is the more defined Latin American social system, which conflicts with the egalitarian values of organizational development in the United States. For example, the notion of participative management is bewildering to Latin Americans; both superiors and subordinates generally prefer authoritarian management styles.

Moreover, limited social mobility reinforces strong clan distinctions, which in turn are strengthened by the fatalistic philosophy of keeping one's place. Maintaining hierarchic formality and social distance contraindicates the use of sensitivity training groups in these countries. Organizational development stress on informality and intimacy are foreign values in this culture. Other cultural factors include the use of smoothing instead of confrontation in conflict resolution. Emerging nationalism for political and economic reasons has increased xenophobia; therefore, new techniques brought in by the United States seem manipulative, often resulting in a distrust of American social technology. The entrepreneurial model of economic development is also not conducive to organizational development techniques. Given these obstacles, organizational designers need to adopt attitudes and techniques appropriate to other cultures (Bourgeois & Boltvinik, 1981). These were highlighted in Part II of this book.

We should now examine the resulting differences in MNCs structure and processes across three distinct cultural and economical environments: the American, European, and Japanese organizations.

COMPARISONS OF AMERICAN, EUROPEAN, AND JAPANESE MNCS

American MNCs

In American firms, the initial foreign involvement through export led to developing independent trading companies or to internal export departments. Most activities involved licensing or direct investment. International divisions were formed to consolidate these activities under one division. The more heterogeneous these activities, the greater the need for consolidation and further strategic planning. A Harvard Business School study showed that only 14% of American firms skipped the stage of establishing international divisions. Corporations tended to use worldwide product formats in which the firms were more diversified. Worldwide regional formats tended to be used (1) where diversification of product lines was low, (2) where the product line was mature and served a common-end market, (3) where manufacturing costs are low because of stable technologies, (4) where the foreign growth potential was high, and (5) where the percentage of sales (compared to other divisions) was high. A worldwide functional format is most commonly used in extractive and service industries with a highly integrated product line. This form is used in firms with a small degree of international operations and in some European companies.

While pure forms are uncommon, hybrids or mixed structures have evolved to create more synergy between product, region, and function and to account for their needs. Some worldwide product divisions, for example, include one or more area divisions. Others include international divisions, which in turn encompass a few worldwide product subdivisions. What accounts for these mixes is the history of the company's mergers and acquisitions, the attempt to manage the impact of product life cycles, and the transitional stage represented in the organization's evolution (*Business International*, 1981).

American multinational companies tend to use geographic divisional structures more frequently than European MNCs, which use a product division structure. This is a result of the European companies having limited domestic markets—they export more frequently, keeping the control home based.

Americans prefer geographic divisions because product and market opportunities are closer; therefore, organizations can be more adaptive to regional changes and needs. For example, products can be refined based on local needs. The decision-making authority is delegated to the geographic division heads in the interest of effectiveness and efficiency. Products can be changed more rapidly in response to changing needs and demands.

European MNCs

Until the late 1960s, the European MNCs tended to be organized as international holding companies. In this format, corporate functions were kept at company headquarters, with heads of the subsidiaries reporting directly to the president or board. As previously indicated, this is known as the mother–daughter structure. Subsidiary managers established coordination and control, in part because colleagues had close personal interrelationships with people of similar nationality, class status, and experience in absorbing the company culture. This is in stark contrast with the American system of control—one marked by more impersonal, mechanistic management methods such as rules, job descriptions, financial and other formal documents, and standardized reporting systems.

European firms' tendency to delegate more power to local managers also emerged from the marketing of well-known products with high price elasticity, circumstances in which the key element in managerial decision making was knowledge of local price and market. Local market competition was often eliminated by tariff barriers and the tendency to form cartels. These firms often had close connections with local governments, because subsidiaries were often created during colonial control by the parent company's country. By 1971, however, these mother–daughter relationships had declined (from sixty-one to twenty-five out of a sample of seventy firms). Forty-four had moved to multidivisional structures by this time. This change resulted from several factors. First, external competition increased as a consequence of the gradual elimination of tariff barriers in the Common Market. Second, there was a trend by the European Economic Council and individual countries to create and enforce antitrust legislation, which served to destroy cartels. Finally, Japan and the United States had penetrated European and world markets, thus increasing their market share (*Business International,* 1981).

European firms grew as a result of foreign involvement, in contrast with the American tendency to grow in the domestic arena first. The European approach was to consider the continental market nation by nation, whereas the American firms tended to organize European operations on a continentwide basis, thus enhancing coordination and control. Since the mid-1960s, these approaches have converged, with the American MNCs having greater appreciation of national differences while the Europeans have gained greater appreciation for the need to coordinate. Although there is a growing prevalence of mixed structures in both European and American MNCs, the former tend to organize along product lines, with less inclination to regionalize or use international divisions. Only two European MNCs use regional divisions—both Swiss (e.g., Nestle). Few European firms use global product formats, instead preferring to integrate European operations with domestic ones (Duerr & Roach, 1979).

In the United Kingdom, firms shifted to worldwide product divisions with little government planning, in the face of strong antitrust enforcement and extensive foreign penetration. Countries with strong central planning and low penetration (e.g., France) adopted multidivisional structures. Firms most susceptible to foreign competition adopted worldwide product structures, bypassing the intermediate stage of international divisions (used by 90% of American MNCs), although some continental firms did establish these divisions (e.g., French and German companies in countries with larger domestic markets). European MNCs changed to global structures at the same time, creating domestic divisions, while American firms shifted their domestic setups from functional to divisional before they went global (*Business International,* 1981).

In a study done by Daniels and Arpan (1972), firms were initially reluctant about their involvement abroad. They based first moves on risk minimization. Similarities of language, geography, and custom were important motivating factors. For instance, Canadian industries expanded into the United States in fourteen out of sixteen cases. The United States expanded into Commonwealth countries in eight out of nine cases. In five out of six cases, the French expanded into neighboring countries or former colonies. Contiguous countries were most often chosen because of a greater awareness of nearby opportunities, a desire to integrate foreign and domestic operations by minimizing distance, and common language, customs, and business practices. However, once firms gained more experience in international business, these bases of preference became less salient.

Japanese MNCs

In the past, the Japanese developed general trading companies (*sogo shosha*), which we can consider the first truly transnational organizations. These companies offered an extensive number of products and services using sophisticated communications systems. Another widely known form was the manufacturing firm (*kaigai jigyobu*), which developed international overseas divisions. Currently, pressure to increase foreign direct investments (which have been negligible up to the present) is growing. This pressure results from import substitution programs of host countries, rising domestic wage levels, and a high dependence on foreign suppliers for raw materials (also of foreign criticism—mainly from the United States).

The evolution of Japanese firms into multinational status is now progressing. Their foreign direct investment is below $3.5 billion—less than that of the United States (Yoshino, 1979). Previously, smaller manufacturing firms used export strategies to create export departments and to organize imports in purchasing departments. Trading companies were used as partners to assist in marketing, distribution, and financing and to monitor new markets and technological developments. These smaller firms are more involved in overseas markets than their American counterparts. American firms with less than $200 million in sales tend not to operate abroad. The difference is a result of strong competition in Japan for the limited domestic market as well as the support of the Japanese government for expanding international trade (*Business International,* 1981).

By the 1970s, these manufacturing firms sought to invest overseas as a result of both import restrictions and host countries' concessions to attract foreign investors. What further enhanced this trend was the desire not to lose out on foreign markets, to capitalize on economic benefits of manufacturing abroad (including cheap labor and available raw materials), and to compete more effectively by improving efficiency and integrating holdings.

This move to invest abroad has resulted in pressures for changes and adaptations of organizational structure and decision-making styles. The evolution of the structure of Japanese MNCs has followed Stopford's three phases: initial autonomy consolidation, creation of a specialized international division, and integration into the mainstream. Japanese MNCs have not arrived at the final stage, however (Yoshino, 1979). Export divisions have become overseas (international) divisions (*kaigai jigyobu*) with two or more product lines whose activities exceed four operations. These serve to monitor and evaluate overseas operations by maintaining records and assisting in personnel functions. These departments arose from pressures to coordinate, establish communications links, create departments for promotion, and provide specialized training for expertise in international business. The development of this overseas division was slower and, as a result, has lasted longer than its American counterparts—and has less autonomy.

These divisions were not counted as profit centers. In Japan, if profit and less responsibility reside with the overseas divisions, the company uses a credit memo system to make product division contribution more clear. Managers with limited knowledge and expertise, however, were promoted to head these divisions. Given the organizational culture in Japanese firms, these departments needed to develop ties with the subsidiaries, which hesitated to give up control and ties to key figures in the organizational hierarchy. The division had to build power by gaining knowledge, respect, and connections with subsidiaries and corporate groups. The division heads accomplished this initially by maintaining a low profile and taking on service and career-watching functions. Their efforts emphasized cooperation and integration with other divisions, reinforced in turn by the use of a *"ringi system"* for decision making and by the shared values of company culture (e.g., that the whole is more important than the sum of the parts). Such factors have resulted in the longer life of Japanese overseas divisions compared to their American equivalents, which, because of their designation as profit centers and their more competitive nature, eventually broke up into product or other global structures as they became more successful.

As the third stage of development approaches integration, the international division gains acceptance and stability and can play a major role in policy and strategy determination. Only three out of thirty Japanese companies surveyed had reached this stage (Yoshino, 1979). However, the multiple partnerships with trading companies make coordination and control difficult.

Among the general trading companies (*sogo shosha*), 50 out of 5000 are so designated because they are organized on a global scale. Mitsubishu, Mitsui, Marubeni, C. Itoh, and Sumitomo account for over 80% of foreign trade. These firms supply raw materials and manufactured goods to meet worldwide market needs. They are often active partners in overseas joint ventures providing commercial credit, production financing, and marketing and financing information.

The management systems used include many different kinds of activities closely involving senior management. Individual jobs are not narrowly defined; individuals as well as departments often perform overlapping tasks. The concept of formal delegation of authority is foreign, and authority remains ill defined. Tasks are assigned to groups, with the functions and roles of individuals remaining undifferentiated. Ambiguity and elusiveness characterize the organizational climate. Goals and policies are rarely spelled out formally, but are understood implicitly. This understanding is achieved through extensive socialization and training procedures. The decision-making system relies on dynamic, informal interactions based on personal relations, face-to-face contacts, shared understanding and values, and company loyalty. Japanese firms prefer to deal with major decisions on a case-by-case basis (Yoshino, 1979).

These characteristics of Japanese management may create problems in managing overseas subsidiaries. The decision-making system has not changed in the international area despite great distance and physical isolation. This causes difficulty in the ability of subsidiary managers to participate in discussions, negotiations, and bargaining, because they must maintain close ties and personal networks at corporate headquarters to keep up with climate and power relations. This results in longer lead time, which in turn creates a competitive disadvantage. Non-Japanese managers cannot participate effectively in this process—one reason for the attack on Japanese MNCs for their reliance on Japanese nationals as managers. Not using local managerial talent puts heavy strains on management resources. The future will test Japanese MNCs' ability to adapt their decision making and control systems to heterogeneous cultures and environments (Yoshino, 1979).

A useful summary of the comparison between American, European, and Japanese companies was compiled by Gladwin (1984), and the major variables are shown in Table 10.7.

Rise of the Third World MNCs

The rise of Third World MNCs is conspicious in India, Korea, Brazil, the OPEC nations, and the Latin American groups (see Table 10.8). Thirty-four of the Fortune 500 overseas companies are headquartered in developing countries. Between 1978 and 1979, there was a 48% increase. Third World MNCs demonstrate the lessening of the division between the haves and have nots, and they show the benefits of a truly international economy.

There are essentially three sources of the development of multinational status: resource-rich (e.g., Arabic) countries, labor-rich countries (e.g., Korean engineering), and market-rich countries (e.g., Brazil, Mexico, and the Philippines). Third World governments have promoted development through their pro-business stance and commitment to growth and development of overseas trade and investment. Third World solidarity—a sort of supranationalism—has provided collective self-reliance; similarly, a strong preference for MNC investments by similar countries, seen as less threatening (no sell-out to imperialism), has created greater interdependence. Recent demands for access to technology, the development of successful and exportable technology appropriate to labor-intensive environments, and the provision of services (e.g., banking) have also promoted regional success.

Note, however, some barriers to continued success: sluggish demand in advanced nations because of economic decline, rising protectionism in the United States and the European Economic Community, growing public debt, and rising political instability resulting from the growing gap between the rich

Table 10.7 Comparisons Between American, European, and Japanese MNCs

		American	European	Japanese
Social environment	Cultural composition	Heterogeneous	Heterogeneous	Homogeneous
	Human relationships	Individualism, egalitarianism, confrontational	Individualism, elitism, confrontational	Collectivism, elitism, consensual
	Dominant motivation	Achievement	Security	Obligation/duty
	Labor/management mobility	High	Moderate	Low
	Human thinking	Analytical	Theoretical	Relational
Political environment	Industrial policy	Implicit, welfare oriented	Explicit, welfare oriented	Explicit, productivity oriented
	Business–government relations	Formal adversary	Informal, negotiable	Informal, collaborative
	Regulatory logic	Market rational	Market/plan rational	Plan rational
	State-owned enterprise	Low	High	Low
	Protectionism	Low	High	High
Economic environment	Natural resources	Abundant	Scarce	Scarce
	Foreign trade dependence	Low	High	High
	Debt–equity ratios	Low	Moderate	High
	Top management expertise	Financial legal	Financial technical	Technical
	Interorganizational relations	Arms length	Close	Symbiotic
International orientation	Degree of internationalization	Low/moderate	High	Low
	Mode of involvement	Investment	Exports, investments	Exports
	Growth rate of foreign content	Low	Moderate	High
Organization structure	Divisionalization	High	High	Moderate
	Lateral relations	Formal	Formal/informal	Informal
	International operations	Global structure	Global structure	Overseas division
Control and performance evaluation	Control character	Tight, explicit, formal	Loose/tight, explicit, formal/informal	Tight, implicit, informal
	Control mechanisms	Impersonal, output, complex	Personal, output/behavioral, simple	Personal, behavioral, simple
Goal orientation	Importance of profitability	High	Moderate/high	Low
	Importance of market share/growth	Moderate	Moderate/high	High

Table 10.7   (Continued)

		American	European	Japanese
	Breadth of objectives	Narrow	Broad	Broad
	Impact of corporate philosophy	Small	Moderate	Large
Innovation orientation	Innovation approach	Leaping	Incremental	Incremental
	Innovation stimulus	Market driven	Market technology driven	Market technology driven
	Innovation origin	Top/outside	Top/outside	Bottom/inside
	Innovation character	Labor saving, income saving	Material and capital saving	Material and capital saving
Business development orientation	Acquisition propensity	High	Moderate	Low
	Divestment propensity	High	Low	Low
	Merger propensity	High	Moderate	Low
Strategic planning systems	Formalization	High	Moderate	Low
	Standardization	High	High	Low
	Comprehensiveness	High	Moderate	Low
Participation in strategy making	Strategic decision making	Participative	Collegial	Consultative
	Top management role	Decision making	Decision making	Guiding
	Top management effort	Back-end	Back-end	Front-end
	Reliance on staff planners	High	Low	Moderate
	Influence of board	Moderate	High	Low
Reliance on strategy concepts	Use of ROI	High	Moderate	Low
	Use of portfolio	High	Moderate	Low
	Use of management consultants	High	Moderate	Low
Time and resource orientation	Time horizons	Near term	Near and long term	Near and long term
	Risk-taking burden	Individual	Collective	Collective
	Resource management emphasis	Utilization, integration	Accumulation, integration	Accumulation, integration

Source: T. N. Gladwin, "Strategic Management Across Cultures: Some American, European and Japanese Comparisons." Unpublished manuscript, New York: New York University, 1984.

Table 10.8 Partial Listing of Major Third World Multinationals

Company	Country of Incorporation	Industry	1977 Sales in Estimated Millions of Dollars
National Iranian Oil	Iran	Petroleum	22,315.3
Petróleos de Venezuela	Venezuela	Petroleum	9,628.1
Petrobrás (Petróleo Brasileiro)	Brazil	Petroleum	8,284.3
Pemex (Petroleos Mexicanos)	Mexico	Petroleum	3,394.5
Haci Ömer Sabanci Holding	Turkey	Textiles	2,902.7
Hyundai Group	South Korea	Shipbuilding, transportation	2,590.7
Indian Oil	India	Petroleum	2,315.5
Schlumberger	Neth. Antilles	Measuring and scientific equipment	2,160.3
Chinese Petroleum	Taiwan	Petroleum	1,920.1
Zambia Industrial & Mining	Zambia	Mining and metal refining—copper	1,862.3
The Lucky Group	South Korea	Petroleum, electronics, appliances	1,744.3
Steel Authority of India	India	Metal refining—steel	1,447.6
Turkiye Petrolleri	Turkey	Petroleum	1,376.7
Kuwait National Petroleum	Kuwait	Petroleum	1,376.3
Korea Oil	South Korea	Petroleum	1,341.1
Samsung Group	South Korea	Industrial equipment, electronics, textiles	1,305.3
Thyssen-Bornemisza	Neth. Antilles	Shipbuilding, farm equipment	1,258.7
CODELCO-CHILE	Chile	Mining and metal refining—copper	1,231.2
Koc Holding	Turkey	Motor vehicles	1,207.6
Philippine National Oil	Philippines	Petroleum	986.2
Daewoo Industrial South	South Korea	Textiles	851.8
Siderúrgica Nacional	Brazil	Metal refining—steel	847.5
USIMINAS	Brazil	Metal refining—steel	826.4
General Motors do Brasil	Brazil	Motor vehicles	824.4
Vale do Rio Doce	Brazil	Mining—iron	824.0
Ford Brasil	Brazil	Motor vehicles	758.7
SANBRA	Brazil	Food products	707.3
Indústrias Reunidas F. Matarazzo	Brazil	Chemicals, food products, textiles	675.3
Grupo Industrial Alfa	Mexico	Metal refining—steel, chemicals	603.2
ICC	South Korea	Metal products, rubber, textiles	580.6
Bharat Heavy Electricals	India	Industrial equipment	525.4
Ssangyong Cement Industrial	South Korea	Chemicals	598.0
Sunkyong	South Korea	Textiles	467.6

Source: D. A. Heenan and W. J. Deegan. "The Rise of Third World Multinationals." *Harvard Business Review,* January–February 1979, p. 104.

and the poor in these countries. Conflicting priorities between internal development and the recognition of global interdependence hampered expansion. Sacrificing of sensible investments for glamour (e.g., the Philippine hotel industry) and excessive defense spending have also hurt. Forces for interdependence and the rise in symmetry have lessened the threat of nationalist takeovers. These have also lessened hostilities (Heenan & Keegan, 1979).

CONCLUSIONS—CURRENT AND FUTURE TRENDS

Recently, perhaps mostly as a result of advanced communication technologies and increasing environmental hostility, the trend has been to increase centralization to maximize benefits for the whole organization. Yet many firms have adopted a mixed-mode approach, that is, they have centralized some decisions (e.g., finance, research, product planning) while decentralizing others (marketing, purchasing, industrial relations) (*Business International,* 1981; Duerr & Roach, 1979). Philips, for example, centralizes long-range planning, budgets, accounting, and product development while decentralizing advertising and personnel activities. The choice of combinations depends on the industry. Given a shortage of raw material supplies, the purchasing function may become more centralized to better rationalize resources (Prasad & Krishna Shetty, 1976; Alpander, 1978).

The student should by now realize that different subunits in the organization have different status and different influences on decision making. The financial function, for example, is usually more centralized both because it is important and because money is a generalized mode of exchange.

Use of executive committees tends to increase the trend to centralization, as the vice-president general manager reports to committee members. The influence of American boards of directors in overseas management of operations is growing, whereas in Europe the trend is toward greater influence but less than in the U.S. companies. European MNCs tend to have boards of management with a collective function rather than individual CEOs. Each board member is responsible for specific staff or line functions. Divisions of responsibility and coresponsibility deliberately are drawn. Control is achieved through board membership, not through chain of command (Duerr & Roach, 1979).

Headquarters remains responsible for basic principles: maintaining product image, quality, corporate identity, planning, and business systems (*Business International*, 1981). Top management is responsible for overall planning, coordination, and control and can be divided into two groups: general operating executives, who supervise, coordinate, and plan operational elements; and general staff executives, who provide essential functional services and overall coordination and control. Nine functional categories have been identified, in all of which American firms have developed staff units (whereas non-American firms do not): finance, legal, personnel, R&D, marketing, manufacturing-engineering, public relations, purchasing, and planning (Stieglitz, 1965).

The central office is staffed for in-depth understanding of all products and geographic areas. European MNCs prefer this arrangement; however, each

European subsidiary tends to have its own finance department, which wants more responsibility and resents data requests from headquarters, leading to the danger of noncompliance and misinformation (*Business International*, 1981; Alpander, 1978; Daniels & Arpan, 1972).

The following tables (Table 10.9a and b) relate the structure of MNCs to the number of countries in which they operate and the relative importance of foreign sales. The greater the size and extent of operations, the greater the emphasis on planning, control, and decentralization—and on integration by functional or product structure (as in export sales). The foreign operators of some European MNCs are integrated into domestic structures, whereas others are separated into international units, most often depending on familiarity. Some operations (Ford, e.g.) are not integrated.

Those companies that have grown through acquisition tend to allow the acquired operations greater autonomy than those that did not grow in this manner. Strategies of diversification and concentration—both long and short term—also affect the choice of structure. Crucial strategy elements for the MNC are the volume of activities, geographic dispersion of effort, research and development initiatives, and extent of product diversification (Stieglitz, 1965; *Business International*, 1976).

Multinationals face increasing complexity and diversity not only in the *external environment* but in the *internal environment* as well. Internal pressures are as numerous and as difficult to manage as the external ones. Among the internal factors that affect international structure are the size and type of operations, the extent and duration of international activity, the corporation's traditional culture and history, the CEO's interests and personality, technology and product characteristics, strategy, growth patterns, and the organization's capacity for change (*Business International*, 1976; 1981; Budde et al., 1982).

The growing role of *corporate staff* has created certain problems. The staff role is expanding in efforts to control and coordinate; as a result of modern communication technology, executives tend to believe that they can understand and control worldwide operations. Local personnel have seen increasing dotted line relationships to division or corporate staff. Local managers are needed to gather data, interpret, and take action. However, they tend to spend inordinate amounts of time preparing or meeting, which detracts from normal duties. The problems of increased central control also include CEO-approved recruiting and are involved in compensation systems, all of which require more corporate staff and subsequent higher costs. Clear lines of responsibility (staff versus line) are muddled.

Several alternatives have been suggested:

1. The Russian army model—a large corporate and divisional staff but no subsidiary staff.
2. Large corporate–subsidiary staff, no divisional staff.
3. Large subsidiary staff, small divisional and corporate staffs.

Which of these alternatives is selected depends on the role of function in the organization, that is, how important it is and at what level (*Business International*, 1981).

Table 10.9a Multinational Enterprises, Classified by Structure and by Relative Importance of Foreign Sales

Structure	Total Number of Firms	Number of Firms, Classified by Foreign Sales (as % of total sales)*		
		0–20%	21–39%	over 39%
International division with:				
Domestic Stage 2	8	6	2	0
Domestic Stage 3	82	53	26	3
Area divisions	17	0	4	13
Worldwide product divisions	30	21	9	0
Mixed	22	6	14	2
Grid	3	0	2	1
Total	162	86	57	19

* Foreign sales include exports from the United States but exclude sales of foreign licensees and foreign subsidiaries in which the parent firm owned less than 25% of the equity: includes estimates of foreign sales for a few firms.

Given the increasing complexity and hostility of the environment, MNCs need to adopt structures that are readily responsive to changing environmental conditions. Current economic conditions—zero growth rates, floating exchange rates, recession, and inflation—have dramatically lowered profitability. In response, MNCs have worked to upgrade the role of the functional (e.g., financial) specialist and to establish joint ventures that reduce financial risk. Reacting to shortages of raw materials and the fluctuating availability of energy sources, MNCs have centralized the purchasing function and have recognized the increasing importance of international specialized trading companies (Japanese style). Another trend—growing nationalism—has led host country governments to control economic development through trade barriers and protec-

Table 10.9b Multinational Enterprises, Classified by Structure and by the Number of Foreign Countries in Which They Had Manufacturing Subsidiaries in 1966

Structure	Total Number of Firms	Number of Firms, Classified by Number of Foreign Countries in Which They Had Manufacturing Subsidiaries*			
		6–9	10–13	14–17	18 or more
International division with:					
Domestic Stage 2	8	5	2	1	0
Domestic Stage 3	82	22	19	26	15
Area divisions	17	6	3	2	6
Worldwide product divisions	30	4	14	4	8
Mixed	22	6	3	4	9
Grid	3	0	0	0	3
Total	162	43	41	37	41

Source: From *Managing the Multinational Enterprise* by John M. Stopford and Louis T. Wells, Jr. © 1972 by Basic Books, Inc., Publishers. Reprinted by permission of the publisher.

*The figures include assembly or packaging operations but exclude agricultural, mining, and other extractive operations.

tionist policies that would effectively constrain multinational operations. The MNC has thus had to be more responsive to regional issues and has relied on regional divisional format, matrix and joint-venture structures, and greater decentralization. Other conflicts, whether separate movements within nations, generalized hostility toward capitalism, or increasing competition between companies, have heightened the need for astute political analysis and public relations (Fouraker & Stopford, 1968; Prasad & Krishna Shetty, 1976; *Business International*, 1981).

In light of these growing external pressures, the American MNC has tended to respond to augmenting coordinative and control mechanisms by more narrowly defining discrete business units and reinforcing the functions of headquarters. The European response has been to decentralize operations, in order to grant subsidiaries more autonomy, and to reduce the size and power of headquarters. These contrasting responses are a function not only of cultural differences but also of differences in the historic development of international business (*Business International*, 1981).

Overall trends have been toward an increased use of worldwide product divisions, increased influence of local managers, the use by European MNCs of more mechanistic and impersonal management and control systems (as in the United States), and increased use of local nationals in management positions.

Given increasing diversity and interdependence, the future focus will be on determining an optimal size and scope of mission for both the corporation and its units, analyzing the impact of communications technology in designating responsibility, and more narrowly defining and decentralizing worldwide product formats. The major issues to be solved are the adequate internal cohesion of the firm (given local constraints), selective decentralization, the integration of company purpose with societal needs, and a comprehensive analysis of responsibility.

The organization of the future is likely to shift from worldwide product formats to regional product matrices, managed internationally from different locations instead of from one world headquarters. The corporate headquarters' chief role will be to define and develop major strategy issues, technology, and the monitoring of goals. In view of increasing nationalism, there will probably be a trend toward withdrawal from ownership commitments, especially in some LDCs. As a result, licensing departments will increase in size with the creation of management services or contracting of functional expertise.

Other models include the following: the federal structures, characterized by local decentralization with overall corporate guidance from a council whose members include management representatives, the Japanese general trading company model, a multinational association, and the free-form management model, characterized by task forces, project teams, and mission-oriented practices, which gives free reign to operating executives as independent entrepreneurs. These models enhance flexibility and imagination to cope with change. The traditional chain of command is deemphasized to promote overall responsiveness (e.g., Litton Industries).

Supernational structures provide another alternative, with headquarters placed in more than one country. In the early 1970s, this trend toward transna-

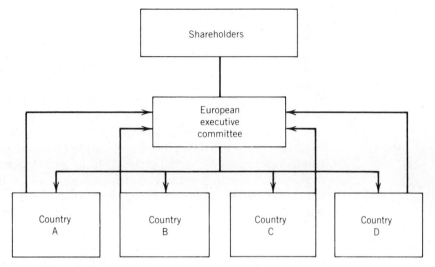

Figure 10.11   Federal structure.

Source: Business International Corporation. *New Directions in Multinational Corporate Organization.* New York: Business International Corporation, 1981.

tionally merged companies (particularly in Europe) was seen in the example of Dunlop-Pirelli, Royal Dutch Shell, and Unilever. However, use of this model is unlikely, given the increasing complexity of regulations, the rise in regional nationalism, public image and public relations problems, and cultural diversity. This model has not proven to help the companies compete more effectively (*Business International*, 1981; Duerr & Roach, 1979).

A truly international company has a global outlook, which integrates its domestic and foreign operations into regional complexes, whose functional services are globally oriented, and develops "internationally minded" managers. Larger MNCs differ less according to nationality; they integrate their international operations through a more geocentric philosophy because the diversity of the international environment demands the adoption of less ethnocentric views.

EXAMPLES OF CORPORATE STRUCTURE

The following section introduces six different MNCs' structures and discusses their operations briefly. The intention here is to highlight the geographic format, the integration of geographic product and functional interrelationships, examples of matrix operations, and finally two examples of general trading companies.

Source: The cases in this section are from Business International Corporation and are used with permission.

PROBLEMS IN GEOGRAPHIC/REGIONAL ORGANIZATIONS

The principal difficulties of the geographic organization arise when the firm has a diverse product range. This is true for both international division structures and worldwide regional organizations. The tasks of coordinating product variations, transferring new product ideas and production techniques from one country to another, and optimizing the flow of product from source to worldwide product markets are not easily handled.

In the geographic organizational framework, companies have traditionally complained that it is difficult or impossible to (1) coordinate R&D programs; (2) conduct planning on a global scale; (3) make a consistent effort to apply newly developed domestic products to international markets; (4) introduce products developed overseas into the domestic markets rapidly, without encountering bureaucratic snarls; and (5) avoid duplication of line and staff managers, especially at the regional level.

The following is a European example of a blend of geography, in the form of country managers, with product, in the form of strong worldwide product divisions.

Saint-Gobain-Pont-a-Mousson

Saint-Gobain-Pont-a-Mousson (SGPM), which celebrated its 317th anniversary in 1980, was created through the merger of a glass company (Saint-Gobain) with an iron pipe manufacturer (Pont-a-Mousson). Corporate headquarters are in Paris. Total sales in 1979 exceeded Ffr35 billion, and over 50% of its business is international.

The organization of SGPM is shown on page 447.

This three-tiered structure, the components of which all report to the chairman and to the CEO, consists of the following:

1. Five corporate staff vice-presidents at headquarters (which is generally understood to be "lean" in staff).
2. Nine worldwide product group presidents, also with limited staffs. For example, the $1.5 billion fiberglass group has a staff of six. Each of these persons heads a department such as R&D or finance, so that the total number of individuals may vary. The group president doubles as chairman of the French operating company.

3. "General delegates," or country managers, whose number varies between seven and nine.

Manufacturing operations in each country are, for the most part, separate companies in each product group. (One of the exceptions is CertainTeed in the U.S.—55% SGPM-owned, with estimated 1980 sales of $1 billion—which operates in several product groups through a single corporate entity.) The country manufacturing operations report in an unequal matrix form to (1) their respective product groups headquartered in France and (2) the country manager, for some administrative reasons. Countrywide finance, tax and legal functions are handled at the country manager level, while each product group has its own marketing staff.

The country manager is responsible for day-to-day management of local operations. He usually intervenes when the manager of a given product facility in his country cannot handle a specific situation, such as a labor dispute. He is the political knowledge center for the country,

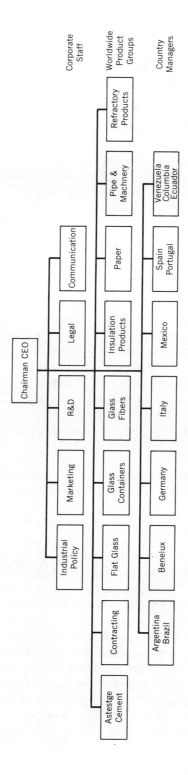

having an understanding of the environment, government controls, pricing, etc. His views on investment decisions are sought, although in a conflict with a product group the latter's views generally prevail. Since planning at SGPM is done primarily by product group, not by country, the country manager's role in that respect is limited. Operationally, his importance appears to grow as a function of geographic distance from the parent.

SGPM's country manager concept is "an intelligent system" in the view of a senior executive with experience on both sides of the table. The country manager must like the country, know the company's businesses there, represent the company, avoid faux pas, and look for the best opportunities.

SGPM does not have a regional structure, although some country managers are responsible for two to three contiguous or otherwise related countries. While in Europe a regional approach is possible for some products, SGPM generally structures its businesses on a national basis—

i.e., the local market must be able to support production on a large scale without excessive reliance on exports.

Most senior line and staff management possess significant international scope—business, cultural, and linguistic—although virtually all are French nationals, including the country managers. This broad scope arises both from assignment rotation and from exposure to international situations.

Examples abound. The current president of the flat glass group was a country manager for 18 years in Italy, the U.S., and Venezuela. The general manager of SGPM's large French fiberglass company used to be the country manager for Benelux. At that time, he felt isolated, uninvolved with international matters beyond his immediate territory. Today, the general manager of SGPM's Belgian fiberglass company heads up a worldwide, groupwide committee on commercial policy. Also, the current director of corporate planning in Paris serves as a member of CertainTeed's board of directors.

PRODUCT, GEOGRAPHICAL, AND FUNCTIONAL INTERRELATIONSHIPS

Below are three brief examples of companies that are wrestling with questions pertaining to decentralization. Product, geographical and functional interrelationships are crucial in each case.

Eaton Corporation, a manufacturer of highly engineered and technologically advanced products, is organized in a worldwide product format. It provides for geographic and functional input in large measure from an international division and from a number of special coordinating committees.

The Dow Chemical Company, the seventh largest chemical company in the world in terms of sales, manages its worldwide operations via a regional structure. Product input is integrated into the geographic framework through several structural techniques. Several firms interviewed by BI referred to Dow as an exceptionally well-managed international company. Some organizational reasons for this are discussed in the case.

Japanese manufacturing companies deal with these issues in a manner that merges traditional Western organizational concepts into their own unique, culturally influenced managerial framework. The Nippon Electric case outlines the manner in which such a fusion takes place in one high-technology firm.

Eaton Corporation

Corporate Overview

Eaton is a manufacturer of highly engineered and technologically advanced products serving world markets in the fields of transportation, industrial automation, electronic and electrical systems, and materials handling. Of $3.3 billion in 1979 sales, $787 million or 23% were outside the U.S. The company employs over 60,000 people in 23 countries.

Eaton is organized in five worldwide product groups, all reporting to the president: (1) automotive components; (2) industrial; (3) investments and diversified products; (4) materials handling; and (5) truck components. Three staff services groups—engineering and corporate development, finance and administration, and law and corporate relations—report directly to the chairman.

Eaton created an international division in the early 1960s, following several overseas acquisitions. Because of product diversity, the division was structured along product, rather then geographic, lines. A direct link was thus forged between each domestic product group and its overseas activities. In fact, the link shortly became strong enough to drop the international division and move to a global product structure. Since then, Eaton has found that a worldwide product format best meets the needs created by its product and customer diversity. As one executive stated, "Our customers are becoming world customers. This means that the company must be able to provide a world perspective on Eaton products and services, which can best be done at headquarters."

While worldwide product structure has proven to be an acceptable format, it was felt that some amount of geographic input was required when, in the 1970s, Eaton had to respond to such common environmental issues as political conditions, codetermination, taxes, labor relations, joint ownership, energy conservation and inflation. Another executive noted, "In a country where there are many company operations and diversified corporate representatives, where there is a variance in performance among the units, and where the government imposes price controls and import restrictions and is somewhat inhospitable to MNCs, a need for corporate assessments and strategies exists." One solution, utilized in Europe and South America, was to create coordinating committees (examined below). While these increased communication among all units, it was still felt that monitoring and assessment of the issues from a corporate perspective was required.

In 1976, therefore, Eaton created the position of vice-president, international, reporting to the executive vice-president, engineering and corporate development. His duties are to keep track of Eaton's investments and evaluate the potential for additional investment outside the U.S.; further the growth of worldwide export sales; represent the company in international organizations and institutions; and maintain direct international coordinating responsibility for Canada and Mexico. He does not have operating responsibilities but serves in an advisory capacity to the company's worldwide operations.

European Coordinating Committee. A need for coordination among Eaton's various European businesses and functions was perceived during the energy crisis of 1973–74, when the UK was forced to adopt a three-day workweek. Eaton's president asked the European managing directors and the director of finance—all based in the UK—to meet regularly to see what could be done about conserving energy and exchanging information about energy requirements among the different organizations in the UK. When the energy crisis passed, the president suggested that the meetings continue to be held not less than four times a year, that the agenda include topics of common interest and that the chairmanship rotate among the four members. Each member was expected to attend in person. This was the genesis of the European coordinating committee.

The committee's purpose was to enhance coordination function; it gave members a chance to exchange useful information. Meetings were held on a monthly basis, and detailed minutes were kept and sent to corporate headquarters in Cleveland. Each of the operating executives delivered a 10-minute report on the state of his particular business and any significant related issues. The director of finance gave a financial forecast and discussed important common financial matters. A different corporate officer (staff or line) always attended and reported on a specific corporate topic. His presence also assured that committee messages would be transmitted back to Cleveland by him personally. The remainder of the agenda was open so that special subjects could be addressed if necessary. The agenda was circulated well ahead of the meeting so that such topics could be included.

After several years of meetings, the European coordinating committee became moribund in the summer of 1979, when a corporate study recommended that it meet on an "as needed" basis. The major reason for this was that the operating divisions did not find it useful. The international division and the corporate planning unit today perform many of the coordination and information functions that the committee was originally intended to handle. Also, the committee's charter did not include the authority to make decisions or recommendations, just to meet. Finally, the historical independence of the product divisions and their marketing differences make regional coordination via a committee impractical.

Country Coordinating Committees. Shortly after the European coordinating committee (ECC) began to function, country coordinating committees (CCCs) were established in most of the European nations in which Eaton had major interests. The CCCs are similar to the ECC in purpose (coordination of and communication among diverse activities) but are more narrowly focused on a specific country basis. The membership includes the head of each product group in the country, senior staff managers, and the relevant international coordinator. The chairmanship rotates among the operating executives. In addition, corporate headquarters used to have one member of the ECC attend CCC meetings.

Unlike the ECC, the CCCs are flourishing. Country executives think they are helpful. In fact, one European manager told BI, "If ours were disbanded, we would still meet informally." Meetings are held bimonthly and are well attended, although no attendance requirements have been imposed by corporate management. The minutes are circulated in Europe and Cleveland.

Reporting to the vice-president, international, are several regional coordinators, the head of Eaton–Japan, an international planning director (who also reports administratively to the head of corporate planning), and a political/ economic information and analysis unit. The regional coordinators have three major responsibilities: (1) to represent Eaton Corporation as a whole within a country or region in various national and international activities and associations, including government and the media; (2) to assist in planning and investment studies and review consolidated plans and profit results for the vice-president, international; and (3) to provide for intercompany cooperation and communication on matters peculiar to one unit but having a potential impact on others, such as labor relations, legal affairs and accounting. Some of the coordinators perform these duties on a full-time basis; others work part-time, depending on the region and the company's needs. The part-time coordinators are mainly line operations managers who are expected to spend about 10% of their time on their coordination duties.

Since it was created four years ago, the international organization has been able to increase the amount of coordination and communication among diverse product operations; factor more comprehensive international elements into functional strategic plans; and provide for better company representation overseas. A key issue is effective planning so that optimal decisions can be made for overseas markets: "Environmental factors are complex and important for Eaton; we must see that they are properly considered in the planning and strategy process." As noted above, an international planner reports to the vice-president, international, as well as to corporate planning. In addition, the company now holds quarterly worldwide operating reviews, at which executives from Asia, Europe and Latin America meet with the product group executives and the president. Such meetings help further the goals of planning and communication.

The international organization is still evolving. Since the need for the kinds of services it provides is increasing, the future may require the creation of more full-time regional coordinator positions. Also, more extensive regional and country plans may come from overseas regional planners rather than from the office of the international planner.

European Coordination

Eaton's first investment in Europe occurred in the late 1940s, when it acquired minority interests in axle and transmission producers in the UK. Eaton's presence in Europe is now substantial, with 35 manufacturing units and 1979 sales of $535 million.

European operations are managed by product group, mostly with a European general manager reporting to a worldwide director of operations

for his product group. The center of Eaton's operations in Europe is in the London area, near Heathrow Airport. With some 150 employees, it houses the European data-processing operations base; financial and accounting personnel, including cash and credit administration; the legal department and directors of personnel, communications and materials management; and the marketing staff for some product groups. Each staff and service operation reports to its functional counterpart at headquarters in Cleveland. The only world headquarters staff functions not represented are planning and corporate development.

The following is a typical CCC agenda:

1. A report on the country's economic conditions;
2. A division-by-division and a countrywide Eaton cash flow report (this provides each manager with an idea of Eaton's present country cash position, which in turn helps them to understand corporate allocation and local bank borrowing);
3. The treasurer's report on the overall financial status of Eaton's country operations;
4. A presentation by personnel executives about a Hay Management Services Ltd. program (corporate headquarters had approved the program and developed a timetable for implementation);
5. A discussion (led by a communications executive) of specific items such as a new Eaton movie, the issuance of a worldwide personnel directory, who should receive the in-house management magazine and the extent to which a new acquisition is to be publicly identified with Eaton over the next few years;
6. A purchasing report; and
7. The business report of each of the product groups.

The meeting was scheduled to begin at 9:30 A.M. and end at 3:45 P.M. (to allow traveling managers to catch a return flight). They try to leave only one major topic for after lunch so that they can close by 3:45.

Functional Meetings

While product coordination is Eaton's main concern in Europe, some of the European staff functions also hold coordinative meetings.

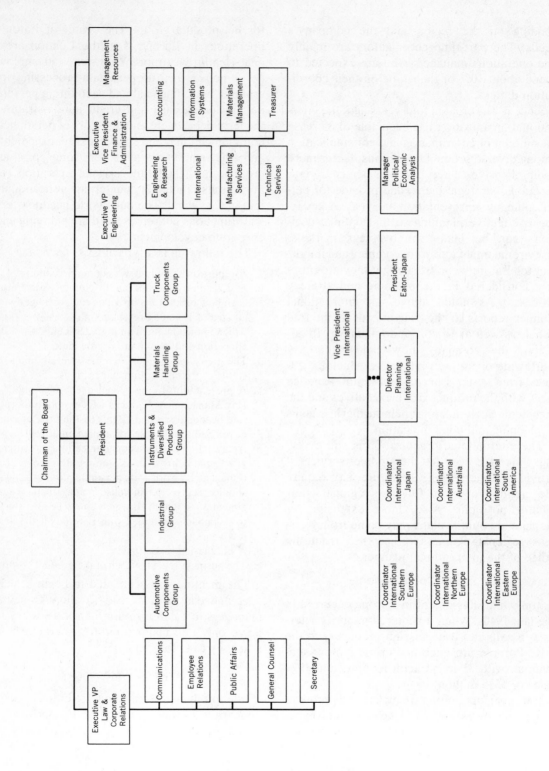

Eaton has two employee relations/management resources directors for Europe, who report respectively to the vice-presidents of personnel and management resources in Cleveland. The personnel coordinators and immediate staff meet about four times a year to review developments in legislation, pensions, salaries, hiring and firing policies, etc. In addition to these, two other types of personnel coordinative meetings are held. About five sessions per year involve the country personnel managers and cover very specific personnel issues in some depth (e.g., policies, legislation, and trends in the area of benefits). Also, there is an annual conference to which personnel managers from all plants are invited. Guest speakers from corporate headquarters also participate.

As a second functional example, the European finance director brings together various country financial managers. The meetings are not scheduled as formally as their personnel counterparts but are held as needed.

The Dow Chemical Company

Corporate Overview

In terms of sales, Dow Chemical is the seventh largest chemical company in the world and the second largest in the U.S. In 1979, net sales totaled approximately $9.3 billion, which placed Dow 24th in sales and 18th in net income among the *Fortune* 500 leading U.S. industrial companies. Sales outside the U.S. in 1979 exceeded 50% for the first time.

Dow makes over 2000 diverse products in the fields of chemicals, plastics, metals, consumer products, and pharmaceuticals. The company is a significant producer in most of its product lines, which are mostly capital-intensive and heavy on technology, generating high profits per employee.

Headquartered in Midland, Michigan, Dow has (directly or indirectly) 121 manufacturing locations and 162 sales offices around the world. Management is organized according to six geographic areas (1979 sales are in parentheses): U.S. ($4.6 billion), Europe/Africa ($2.7 billion), Canada ($600 million), Pacific ($600 million), Latin America ($500 million), and Brazil ($300 million).

Dow has 55,900 employees, 21,800 of them outside the U.S. Sales per employee exceeded $165,000 in 1979. All of Dow's CEOs have been selected from within the company, and the principal officers have been with the firm for an average of 31 years.

Organization

In the 1940s and 1950s, Dow developed an export sales organization, and overseas agents and sales executives were stationed in key locations. The firm also entered into some joint ventures in the plastics field. This period of only gradual offshore involvement came to an end when an international division was created and a strong executive was assigned to head it. Dow spread throughout the world: at first, it created sales organizations and joint ventures (especially in Europe); eventually, however, the joint ventures were eliminated and the company built its own plants. The international division was a classical one, with staff and operating responsibility for all non-U.S. business. The president of Dow International was based at corporate headquarters and traveled about 80% of the time.

The seeds of the next change began to germinate in the early 1960s, when Dow Europe developed its own manufacturing, sales, and technical services under the leadership of a European executive. Subsequently, the Pacific and Latin American areas began to develop as entities. Canadian operations had been strong and had operated quite independently since World War II. A product management overlay existed in the mid-1960s, but it became apparent that worldwide operations needed to be reorganized. Agreement was reached at an important management meeting held in 1968 that the most difficult problem facing Dow was how to transmit geographic and cultural information from headquarters to the field and vice versa. On the other hand, international communication about products or technology was considered not as difficult. Therefore, Dow created a geographic structure, with the U.S. as one of the regions. The headquarters of each region were located in the field. Corporate headquarters remained a distinct operation, so that today fewer than 400 of the company's total 55,900 employees are labeled "corporate." Most of these individuals are found in the financial and legal functions and in the corporate product department.

Up to this point, product department managers had line responsibility in the U.S. and coordination responsibility worldwide. The reorganization meant that these people now had only U.S. responsibility. Life Sciences was the only product division that maintained worldwide reporting control, but in 1975 it was subsumed under each of the geographic operating units.

A corporate product department was created to provide for long-term planning and for worldwide product coordination and communication. Today, it includes six corporate product directors, each of whom is a former line manager and several of whom have had overseas experience. They report to the executive vice-president of the company through two new group vice-presidents, who divide up the product line. Each corporate product director is assisted by one to three operations managers, who are primarily concerned with short-term operations related to the product lines, such as pricing policies and product balances.

While the corporate product department is considered to be a staff unit, the corporate product directors are influential in two important areas. First, they are cosigners with the geographic operating unit heads on every capital project in excess of $1 million that goes to the board in their respective areas of product responsibility. Second, they can move production of a product from one geographic location to another in order to best serve corporate needs. In the recent past, each corporate product director's expenses were allocated across all of the geographic areas on the basis of sales. As of 1980, the department's expenses will be allocated to the corporate budget. The issue of expense allocation is of no practical organizational significance. Dow may just as easily revert to the former method in a few years with no organizational impact.

Until the 1968 reorganization, a number of corporate functional departments with worldwide responsibility had existed. Many of these were subsequently eliminated. Nonetheless, a few key centralized corporate functions remain today: planning, controller, finance/treasurer, legal, economic evaluation, public relations, environment, and salary administration. (There is a marketing executive on staff, but his role is largely coordinative. He schedules marketing meetings every two to three months to coordinate market opportunities, and he interfaces with large industrial clients as needed.) The controller's unit is centralized to the point where it trains and assigns individuals to the regional operating units. The corporate functions report to the office of the president, which is composed of the president and CEO, the chairman of the board and the executive vice-president.

A regional operating unit is typically organized as follows. Vice-presidents of manufacturing, marketing, and business development report to the area president. The latter coordinates functional inputs such as capital planning and distribution; manages the region's existing products; and interacts with government officials and agencies. In some regions, he supervises project business development managers, who seek to initiate projects in places where Dow has not yet established itself. There are variations in this general structure depending on the businesses and conditions involved and the wishes of the regional president. For example, sometimes an area has a vice-president for commercial activity including marketing, purchasing, and business development.

In general, all of the areas have full internal staff support so that they can meet their goals. But they are thin in some highly specialized functions such as market research and therefore must borrow such expertise from the U.S. regional organization or from corporate staff, and foot the bill for it.

Area presidents are responsible for line profit and loss. Profitability, however, is measured according to individual product line. Each product line in a region is managed by a business manager who is head of a product management team composed of marketing, manufacturing, R&D, and technical services managers. The business manager reports to the regional vice-president, commercial (or business development, depending on the area). The teams set strategies and, subsequently, plans and goals for specific products. In their day-to-day jobs, they are expected to implement these strategies. Once the implementation process is under way, the team meets formally every four to six weeks to review developments and provide inputs where needed. Some regions have a team for each major product as well as for many minor ones. Others combine some products.

The teams take three to six months to work effectively, break down functional barriers, establish mutual respect, etc. They work best if they can stay together two or three years—which is difficult in the face of promotions and reassignments. Members are selected because of their product knowledge. Their careers have typically been within the function they represent, although exceptional performers or tech-

nical service people may be promoted across functions. They have two bosses: their own functional supervisor and the business manager. The former has primary responsibility for the individual's compensation but checks up on his team performance with the business manager.

In the U.S. area, each major product line has a technology center manager, who is often a member of a business team. He is a senior manufacturing manager who is the most knowledgeable individual in Dow regarding the specific technology. He is responsible for keeping abreast of current operations; for publishing news about these operations and sending it to the appropriate people; for taking action on trouble spots; for assigning people to start up operations worldwide; and for being aware of technological innovations inside and outside the company.

The product management team is an important component of the management of Dow Chemical. One effect is that many managers work for two bosses at some stage of their career. Since such a situation is quite common within Dow and since this approach has been used for over fifteen years, it is part of the management culture and not regarded as unusual. College graduates who join Dow come in contact with this system early in their careers. It is, of course, difficult to work for two bosses, and a few people (in Dow's experience, one out of ten to fifteen) simply cannot adapt. These are thereafter assigned to positions with a single boss.

It would not have been realistic to switch to the organizational format described above and expect it to be fully operational after, say, a period of three years. The major "shock" of 1968 was the move away from worldwide product to region. The problems created by that shift took four to five years to solve.

Finally, the Dow reorganization was devised and implemented by the firm's own executives—not by outside consultants. The only external assistant was a professor who helped develop certain training programs to deal with behavioral interaction problems.

Reasons for Dow's Success

- Dow has separated its lines of authority and commitment from its lines of communication. Communications are completely free—from top to bottom and laterally. Grade level and functional boundaries do not hinder communications. There is an open-door policy and, conversely, no policy of communicating through channels. Although these conditions are sometimes more difficult to achieve in international operations because of cultural patterns and distance, the company is nonetheless working toward the same goal worldwide that it has achieved at home.

- Living in a city of 40,000, the members of Dow's small central management group know one another very well, and turnover is minimal. Management has broad experience geographically, functionally, and in various product lines. The executive award system is based on the performance of the entire firm rather than its individual segments. Of the nineteen-member board of directors, fourteen are active in the company's management and two of the others are former Dow officers. As one executive told BI, "The excellent communications and unity of purpose made possible by location and management policy allow approaches to management which might not be generally applicable to other organizations."

- Planners must have had prior practical experience in line positions as well as product/business functions. For instance, the executive currently in charge of planning used to manage one of Dow's U.S. product departments.

- Executive management is closely tailored to the firm's needs. Line operations are decentralized geographically, with the six major areas having profit responsibility. The president and CEO, chairman of the board, and executive vice-president form the top-level management group. There are no corporate heads of marketing, manufacturing, purchasing, or distribution. Technology, safety and loss prevention, and ecological matters are important executive management

responsibilities. All corporate activities are linked closely to the president. He has let it be known that he expects disputes to be resolved by the principals below him. If this does not happen and the problem has to go to him for resolution, he feels that the organization has failed. Therefore, only on rare occasions is an appeal made to the top.

- As early as 1950, Dow developed an economic evaluation group that was staffed with engineer MBAs. Its original function was to analyze capital authorization requests, but gradually it came to be used as an in-house consulting group for research, business, and economic matters. Most important, the group has developed over time an objective system of economic evaluation for projects, products, processes, and business opportunities. Dow has become highly centralized in these methods. All parts of Dow's operations throughout the world conduct studies on an almost identical basis. This has given the company a common language for discussing business options.

- Dow is truly an internationally staffed company. Local nationals fill many overseas positions, with a sprinkling of U.S. citizens in various functions. At the corporate level, one product director is a South African, another has significant European experience, and all have traveled widely. The head of personnel has extensive international experience. The executive vice-president has an international business background (e.g., he worked in the former international division) and was president of Dow Pacific. The president and CEO (a U.S. citizen of Italian birth) was regional manager for Dow in Brazil and served as president of both Dow USA and Dow Latin America. Each member of the top management group travels a great deal, visiting each area headquarters several times a year.

- A two-day meeting of the president's staff, including area heads and other senior executives, is held annually for the purpose of reviewing the performance of Dow's top managers. They address such questions as, Who are the exceptional performers? Where should they be assigned next? This exercise also assures that the management committee will be aware of these individuals.

- The planning system at Dow stresses flexibility. Company management has always been concerned lest planning become a straitjacket. Initially, five-year and then ten-year plans were attempted, but these generated too much paperwork, were viewed as sterile exercises, and eventually were discarded. Instead, the following guidelines were established: (1) planning activities should be carried on for the express purpose of setting meaningful goals and encouraging proper and prompt action to carry them out; (2) no single set of numbers can satisfactorily serve the multiple needs of motivating people, making reasonably accurate forecasts, allocating resources, and measuring performance; (3) planning must account for product, geography, and function; and (4) a falsely perceived need to be precise can be too restrictive. Thus, the yearly capital budget should be within ±10% of the targeted number in an individual year but within ±5% over a three-year period. This is close enough for financial planning yet allows enough flexibility to grasp new opportunities.

The ideal to which Dow has moved is characterized as a real-time segmented planning system that is flexible, responsive, nearly continuous, and highly motivating. One executive described this as "the equivalent of distance-measuring equipment on aircraft; you first set the destination and arrival time and then constantly monitor the path and the number of miles to the destination."

The foundation of the system is strategic planning with a seven-year perspective. After some experimentation, this period of time seems best for constructing realistic strategic plans. Dow sets needed goals for each major product line in each operating area of the world, and this determines general capital demands. Exploratory planning is necessary for longer-range goals. The plan relates to approximately eighty-five planning units, which constitute over 80% of total sales. At the core of the planning process is the product's physical growth rate and ROI. Basic product strategies are developed globally by the heads of the product lines and are reviewed at least every year.

Some aspects of the segmented planning system require firm commitment throughout all levels of the organization. An example is the one-year profit performance plan administered by the controller's office. The first three years of the five-year capital plan are likewise in the context of a set budget. Other aspects are more pliable, however. For example, the fourth and fifth years of the capital plan are viewed as subject to improvement—a target that is to be raised if at all possible.

In sum, Dow believes that the planning process should be as nearly continuous as possible and a part of the corporate way of life rather than an annual exercise. Strategic planning that allows for flexibility must be used to balance the rigidities of budgeting and shorter-term operations planning.

Nippon Electric Co. Ltd.

Corporate Overview

Nippon Electric (NEC) was incorporated in Tokyo in 1899 as a joint venture for the manufacture of telephone apparatus with Western Electric of the U.S. Over the years, NEC expanded its operations to include radio communications, electron devices, consumer electronics and electronic data-processing systems.

Today, NEC is one of the largest industrial companies in Japan, with consolidated sales of approximately $4 billion in fiscal 1980. It ranked

87th in sales in *Fortune*'s ranking of manufacturing corporations outside the U.S. The NEC organization, including 29 consolidated subsidiaries, employs about 60,000 persons, and has over 75,000 shareholders.

NEC products are sold in over 120 countries, and the firm has 15 manufacturing facilities in 10 countries and 12 marketing and service affiliates in 7 countries. Overseas sales accounted for almost 30% of its total consolidated sales in fiscal 1979. NEC's overseas plants, together with 36 manufacturing facilities in Japan, supply more than 15,000 products to markets around the world.

Organization

The corporate organization of NEC is portrayed in the chart below. All staff, marketing groups and operating groups report to the president.

The administration staff consists of functions such as administration, comptroller, education, long-range planning, and treasury. Operations

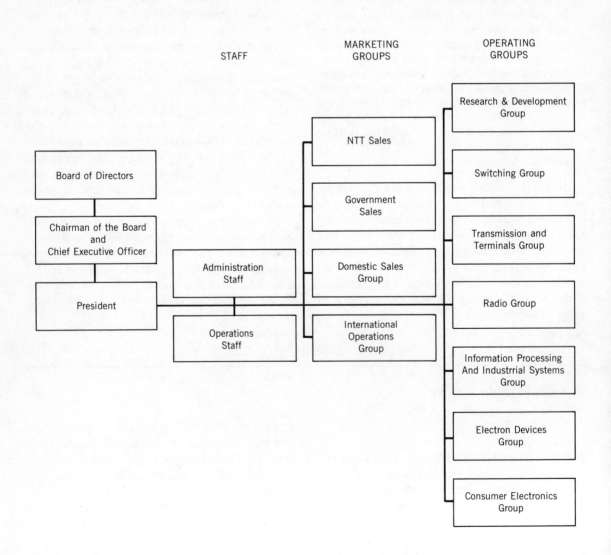

staff includes operations support, community relations, engineering, manufacturing coordination, reliability and quality-control support, and purchasing.

On the marketing side, NEC and its consolidated subsidiaries have more than seventy sales offices in Japan; the country is divided into ten marketing blocks, with each block responsible for developing appropriate marketing strategy for its particular area. Overseas, NEC operates twelve marketing and service affiliates in seven countries; together with these affiliates, the company has more than forty offices in major world cities. "NTT Sales" refers to communications equipment sold to Nippon Telegraph and Telephone Public Corporation. Separate marketing groups for other public-sector and private-sector customers and to the international sector (discussed below) facilitate sales to these markets.

Finally, the six operating groups (plus an R&D unit devoted to basic research) develop, manufacture and sell NEC products.

International Operations

NEC's initial involvement in international business following World War II was via creation of an export department to sell products to foreign customers who were sometimes identified with the help of Japanese general trading companies. Exporting is still important for NEC today. Around 1960, NEC formed an overseas division (*kaigai jigyobu*) to provide sales and staff support to international operations. In time, the staff and marketing sections were each elevated to "division" status because of the remarkable growth of NEC markets, staff, and foreign subsidiaries. Thus, the overseas division evolved into the present international operations group, depicted in the chart on page 460.

The purpose of the international operations group, headed by a senior executive, is to market NEC products overseas, provide components and sales service, and assist all overseas offices in performing their responsibilities.

Licensing, technology transfer, negotiations with foreign governments, and shipping are included in the group's purview. All of the components of this organization—except for the overseas subsidiaries which also report to it—are located at corporate headquarters in Tokyo. The international operations group is considered a profit center.

The subsidiaries' primary mission is to handle sales, sales service, and, in some cases, manufacturing. They gain assistance and support from the parent through the area groupings (e.g., Asia, Latin America) or the product groupings (e.g., EDP, consumer electronics). For example, if a potential U.S. customer has a telecommunications or broadcast equipment project that requires a bid, NEC America Inc. discusses the matter with the relevant area division—in this case, the North America division in Tokyo—which, in turn, interacts with the appropriate product division. Proposals are mostly prepared by NEC America. But sometimes the North America division in Tokyo coordinates the proposal and, when it is completed, sends it back to NEC America. If the customer approves the bid, the North America division coordinates the Japanese portions of its implementation.

Foreign sales of computers and peripherals are managed by the EDP overseas marketing division. Likewise, foreign sales of electron devices and consumer electronics products are handled by the international electron devices division and the international consumer electronics division, respectively.

The area and the product marketing divisions of the international operations group provide technical assistance, information, and sales services (among other things) to the subsidiaries by drawing on the resources of the domestic NEC operations. Informally, they may be considered a "Tokyo branch" for the subsidiaries, as one executive noted. In some countries where no subsidiaries or sales offices exist, the divisions make direct sales to customers.

In sum, it is primarily through this mecha-

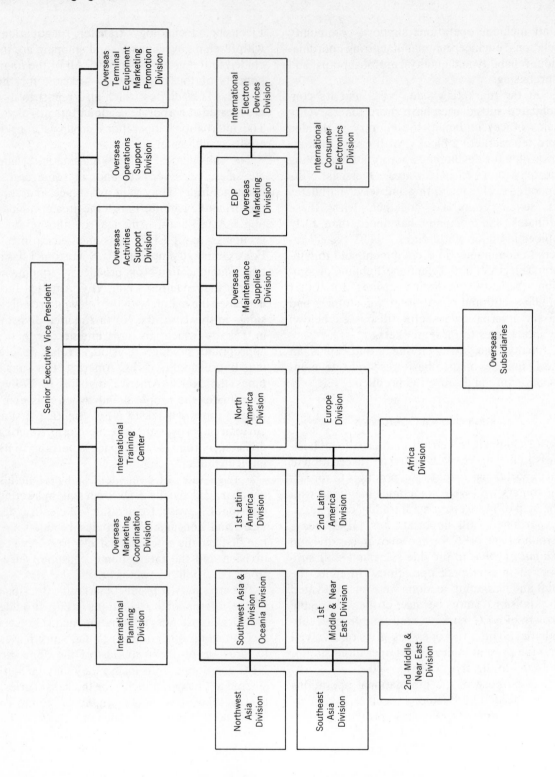

nism for servicing subsidiaries and customers that NEC integrates geography and product. Geographic—regional and country—differences are accounted for by the ten area overseas marketing divisions and also by the fact that some of the product divisions have overseas departments whose primary function is to help with sales and service from the product division side. They do this by providing a link between the product division and the international operations group, by having occasional direct dealings with foreign customers, and by coordinating product modifications to meet special foreign requirements.

Another method of integrating geography and product is through overseas career pathing. Many executives assigned to positions in subsidiaries are selected from jobs in the operating groups. This has an important impact on management because such executives have extensive contacts in the operating groups that they regularly use in their work.

The international operations group supports NEC's overseas business by providing many services. For example, the international planning division assists the subsidiaries in developing their business plans, and it consolidates and analyzes the various international business plans for corporate headquarters. The overseas activities support division helps transfer domestic employees to international assignments and, later, to return them to Japan. This division also administers special compensation and benefits policies for expatriate employees. It coordinates closely with corporate personnel regarding both of these matters. The overseas operations support division works with the operating groups to ensure an adequate and prompt supply of components and subassemblies, as well as special technical assistance to offshore subsidiaries and sales units. Finally, the overseas maintenance supplies divisions provides spare parts for customers and overseas sales offices. In addition to these services, budgeting and investment policies and strategies for NEC overseas operations are handled by the international operations group.

It is not expected that NEC's present organizational structure will change dramatically in the early 1980s. Rather, like the company and its overseas business groups, the organizational format will continue to evolve to meet whatever needs arise. As an example of such evolutionary change, the overseas operations support division's functions were originally handled by each operating group. The division was created to coordinate this effort into a more effective single channel.

COMPANY EXPERIENCES WITH MATRIX

As a means of tying together many of the points covered above and highlighting different ways to utilize matrix, the chapter concludes with cases describing two MNCs' experiences with matrix organization.

Corning Glass Works is an example of a firm whose matrix structure is evolving. The case underscores two points: first, that any organization comprises people and systems as well as structure; and, second, that organizations are constantly changing in order to meet the demands that people, systems, and the business place upon them.

The European case presents a further approach to matrix. Royal Dutch/Shell's structure is complex enough, but is made even more so by its dual headquarters format. Nonetheless, it appears to work smoothly because of a very professional management team and a basically decentralized management arrangement.

Corning Glass Works

Companies moving toward a matrix organization are finding that some tinkering may be needed to make the system succeed for them. Corning Glass Works' experience is a case in point, illustrating the importance of remaining flexible and making organizational adjustments when the original conception does not work out as intended. The company—a $1.4 billion worldwide manufacturer of specialized glass and glass ceramic products for various consumer and industrial uses, with about one-third of its sales international—has spent five years installing and getting the kinks out of its matrix structure. In mid-1980, Corning decided a major modification was necessary since it was not meeting its profit margin and growth goals. This case traces the developments that led to this decision and what the firm hopes to achieve with the organizational restructuring.

The mid-1970s marked a crucial turning point for Corning. In 1975, the company faced a worldwide recession, poor financial results and soaring costs. Foreign competition was beginning to challenge the firm's market shares. Internally, strong intercompany rivalry had developed, with domestic and foreign subsidiaries sometimes selling to and competing in the same markets. At the same time, Corning was attempting to integrate two major foreign acquisitions, Sovirel SA of France and Jobling & Co. of the UK, into its overall organizational framework. The company felt an urgent need for a more coordinated global strategy, and the then-innovative matrix structure seemed to offer a happy solution.

Organizational Setup

At the top of the new organizational structure was a corporate management committee made up of the chairman and chief executive officer, the president, and two vice-chairmen. The product lines were clustered into seven product divisions or macrobusiness units (electrical, electronic, science, medical, consumer, technical, and ceramics products). Since mature businesses and developing ones require different business strategies, the broad product categories were broken down further into about sixty subplanning units, based on items with homogeneous markets. The president was responsible for all domestic operations and a vice-chairman for international. Each business unit overseas was considered a discrete legal entity, and each had its own vice-president and general manager.

The geographic element of the matrix included three regions: Europe, Latin America/Far East, and North America. The regions were responsible for Corning's corporate image and all other geographic matters. The functional component was represented by seven strong staff groups: R&D, engineering, finance, personnel, legal, information systems, and planning. The major responsibilities of these groups were to help the businesses be profitable and to initiate policy changes. Some reported directly to the chairman, some to the president, and others to the vice-chairmen. Their functional counterparts in the areas had strong dotted-line relationships with the corporate staff.

To achieve the coordination required by the new matrix structure, Corning instituted a vigorous planning process. It also developed standard operating procedures, harmonized its accounting system, designed formal and informal communications mechanisms, set up a method of allocating resources, and evolved a worldwide management information system.

Strengths and Weaknesses

Over the 1975–77 period, Corning worked out the decision-making structure for the new sys-

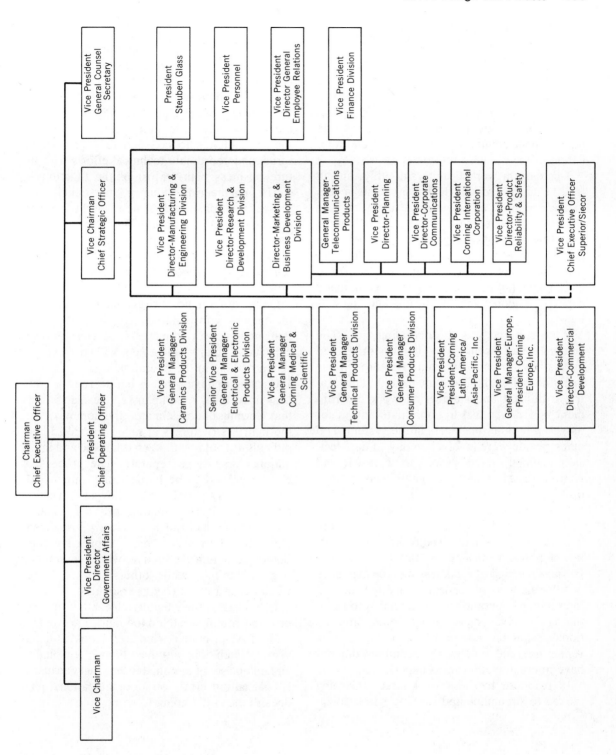

tem and trained the main participants one unit at a time. The planning and budgeting process was the key to holding the matrix together. Strategy meetings were held for the various business units, with the product and regional executives participating. Once a plan was agreed upon, it was presented to the corporate management committee for approval and allocation of the required resources.

This system worked quite smoothly, and in fact the matrix probably had its greatest success in the evolution of long-term strategy. It was the key to developing a worldwide outlook; it raised the level of management competence by getting executives to look beyond their immediate area of responsibility; and it helped to create a pool of personnel experienced in many aspects of global manufacturing and marketing.

What suffered was the operating side. The company had been highly line-oriented, and most division managers came up through the manufacturing arm. These managers found matrix a difficult and smothering work environment, since they had to coordinate any major moves with other managers in the system. Too many people were involved in day-to-day decision making, which slowed to a crawl, and many relatively minor judgments were pushed up to higher hierarchical levels.

Moreover, accountability and evaluation of individual managers was difficult since there was dual responsibility. The result was a shifting of power from line to staff management. Perhaps the biggest weakness was the existence of separate lines of reporting for domestic and international operations, which tended to make the system even more cumbersome. International issues did not receive full attention as senior line and functional executives did not have international business experience.

In response to these weaknesses, Corning moved to streamline and simplify its organiza-

tion. The main change is the separation of the operating and strategic planning sides of the business: global operating responsibilities now come under the president, and longer-term functions and strategic resources are under the vice-chairman and chief strategic officer. The latter is a new title and concept by which the firm intends to consolidate its marketing thrust and coordinate technical efforts with future business plans. Most of the functions—R&D, engineering, finance, personnel, employee relations, and a new marketing and business development division, which oversees planning, corporate communications, the Corning International Corp., and product safety and reliability—all report to the chief strategic officer.

On the other hand, the regional managers and the newly consolidated five macrobusiness units now report to the president. The company expects this major adjustment will speed up decision making in the operating area.

Corning believes that it has learned a great deal since 1975. A company spokesman admits that Corning underestimated the complexity of the matrix structure and failed to realize how difficult it would be to keep domestic and international operations separate. The process of change proved to be harder than anticipated, and too many people were allowed to participate in the decision-making process. Finally, the functions had not been clearly visualized: they needed to play a more supportive role. Some were more effective when centralized (e.g., planning), while others worked better when decentralized (e.g., personnel).

In hindsight, the executive feels that the firm probably attempted to do too much too quickly. "Don't adopt matrix from a textbook," he advises. "Each company has its own personality and unique set of circumstances. Just because it is charted out nicely on an organizational plan doesn't mean it's going to work."

Royal Dutch/Shell Group of Companies

Formed more than seventy years ago, when Royal Dutch Petroleum Company (60%) and The Shell Transport and Trading Company, Ltd. (40%) merged their interests without losing their individual identities, the Royal Dutch/Shell Group of Companies is truly international in structure, ownership, and managerial decision making. The shares of the parent companies are held by about one million shareholders living in many countries. There is no single controlling interest.

Shell companies handle about 8% of the world's oil and natural gas, produce chemicals, produce and trade in metals and coal, and, to a limited extent, engage in nuclear energy. The firm operates in more than 100 countries and employs over 160,000 people. In 1979, Shell companies' revenues totaled £36.5 million.

Organization: Group Corporate Structure

The chart below shows the relationship between the parent companies and the Royal Dutch/Shell Group of Companies.

The parent companies own the shares in the two group holding companies—Shell Petroleum NV and The Shell Petroleum Company Ltd.—but are not themselves part of the group. They appoint directors to the boards of the group holding companies, from which they receive dividend income. Between them, the group holding companies own all the shares in the service companies and, directly or indirectly, the whole group interest in the operating companies.

The five members of the board of management of Royal Dutch and the three managing directors of Shell Transport are also members of the presidium of the board of directors of Shell Petroleum NV and managing directors of The Shell Petroleum Company Ltd. (the group holding companies); as such, they are generally known as "group managing directors." They are also members of a committee of managing directors of service companies.

Operating companies are engaged in various branches of oil and natural gas, chemicals, met-

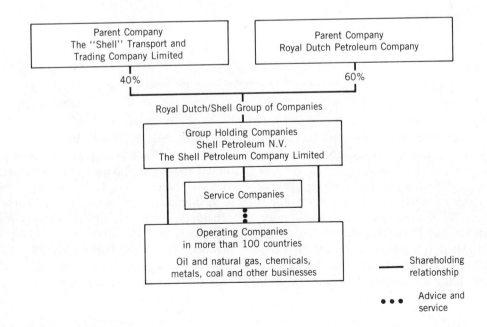

Committee of Managing Directors of The Service Companies

Individual Spheres of Interest

REGIONS	SECTORS	FUNCTIONS	CENTRAL TRADING
UK and Irish Republic	• Upstream Oil and Gas	Finance and Computing	Oil Trading Unit
Europe	• Downstream Oil	Legal	
Africa and South Asia	• Marine	Materials	
East and Australasia	• Natural Gas	Organization	
Middle East	• Chemicals	Personnel	
Caribbean, Central and	• Coal	Planning	
South America	• Metals	Public Affairs	
Eastern Europe	Nuclear	Research	
	(Consumer Products)	Toxicology, Health,	
COUNTRIES	• (Nontraditional	Safety and Environmental	
	Business)	Conservation	
■ Canada			
■ US			

■ Not covered by normal Service Companies organization.
• PANELS: Indicates there are Managing Directors' Panels for these sectors.
Additionally, there are panels for Energy and Oil Operations.

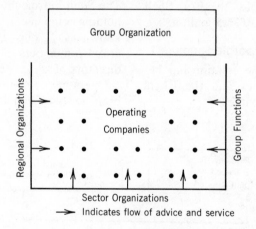

→ Indicates flow of advice and service

als, coal, and other businesses in many countries. Most of the operating companies are managed by local nationals.

There are eleven service companies. Two of these in the Netherlands (Shell Internationale Petroleum Maatschappij BV and Shell Internationale Chemie Maatschappij BV) and two in the UK (Shell International Petroleum Company Ltd. and Shell International Chemical Company Ltd.) are mainly concerned with oil and chemicals; the others are in other business sectors. The "group managing directors" mentioned above are also managing directors of service companies, and they are appointed to a joint committee of managing directors, which considers, develops, and decides upon overall objectives and long-term plans to be recommended to operating companies. The main business of the service companies is to provide advice and services to other group and associated

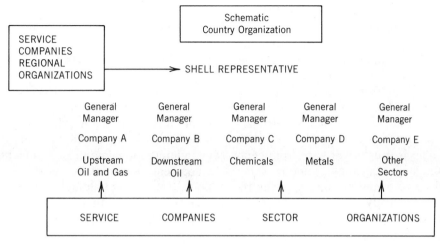

Indicates flow of advice and service

companies. In this regard, it is helpful that many service company managers have had work experience in several foreign countries and also in varying functional assignments. Actual management decisions are made by the boards and the management of each operating company. Thus, Shell is decentralized in part because of the belief that the companies can do best if they are left to manage themselves without interference from the service companies and if they can identify with their own national environments while benefiting from being members of a group, particularly in relation to finance, supply, technology, research, and qualified personnel.

In sum, the Royal Dutch/Shell Group of Companies is a uniquely decentralized operating system within an overall framework of objectives that are worked out with the center. It is a consultative arrangement.

The service companies involve three main types of organization, concerned with regions, business sectors and functions (see charts). These form a three-dimensional support matrix for the operating units.

- **Regions.** Each of the six regions has a regional coordinator who reports to the service companies and acts as a shareholder's representative. He

closely monitors the operating companies' profits, dividends, and investments; studies environmental matters such as local politics, laws, and unions; and helps operating management produce annual business plans for individual countries. Each regional coordinator has a small skeleton staff. Shell's decentralized approach is therefore unlike that of Exxon, for example, whose regional organizations are fully staffed and which seeks to manage its regional business. The regional coordinator's central contact is the "Shell representative" in the country—usually the senior operating company head. (See chart on schematic country organization; some of the larger countries may have several operating companies, including oil, chemicals, metals, coal, and consumer products.)

- **Business sectors.** There are ten business sectors. For planning purposes, the committee of managing directors has set up a number of sectoral panels, each of which includes some managing directors and senior service company executives. The sectoral organizations are concerned with strategy and plans for the country, regional, and worldwide businesses.

- **Functions.** Eleven functions interact with all regions and sectors to provide specialized advice and assistance. For example, operating personnel may call on functional experts to help them develop the business plans which they later review with their regional coordinator.

An example of how the Royal Dutch/Shell matrix works is as follows. The chief executive of each operating company is responsible for preparing a business plan for submission to his company's board, to which he is accountable. In devising the plan, he may seek advice or assistance from specialized functional divisions or from the appropriate business sector organization in the service companies. The extent to which such help is sought will vary from company to company depending, among other things, on the size of the business and the resources available locally.

The senior executive regarded as the "Shell representative" in the country concerned is responsible for coordinating the individual sectoral plans in an overall country plan and for ensuring that the various sectoral activities in his country are harmonized to the extent necessary.

Country plans and performance are considered from a shareholder viewpoint by the regional organizations in the service companies, while individual sectoral plans are considered, in an international context, from a business development viewpoint by the sectoral organizations. The group holding companies therefore receive advice on their investments from both an individual country and a business sector viewpoint.

GENERAL TRADING COMPANIES (*Sogo Shosha*)

Japanese general trading companies (*sogo shosha*) are receiving greater attention from governments, executives, and students of international business and organization. This section will sketch some reasons for the interest; note some of the companies' unique organizational features; and present some organizational problems and possible remedies. It will close with case examples of two of the largest and most successful *sogo shosha*: Mitsubishi Corporation and Mitsui & Co.

Interest in the Japanese General Trading Company Model

Put simply, general trading companies offer services for which the international private- and public-sector need is likely to increase. Governments and companies alike may wish to capitalize on the world's growing trade and investment markets (such as the Pacific Basin and China); to widen their own capacity to scan for new technologies, conclude licensing agreements and arrange for technology transfer; and to help firms expand exports, which will in turn increase domestic jobs and production and encourage a favorable balance of trade.

The longevity and success of Japanese general trading companies has made them models for other firms. Most general trading companies began as marketing arms of industrial groups and later became fully independent firms when the *zaibatsu* (large industrial combines) broke up after World War II. There are at present about fifty such firms in Japan organized on a worldwide scale.

The general trading company model has been adopted by other nations and by non-Japanese companies. Korea has several that trade a wide variety of industrial and consumer goods. Two Brazilian general trading companies—Companhia Brasileira do Entrepostos e Comercio and Petrobras Comercio Internacional SA—were established through government/business collaboration in the 1970s; they specialize in the trade of manufactured goods and foodstuffs. The model is attractive to LDCs in Southeast Asia and to the developed world as well. On April 14, 1980, Canada's Liberal government announced that "to improve the ability of Canadian industry to compete abroad in order to create jobs at home [it] will establish a national trading company." And in the U.S. congressional moves have been made to encourage trading operations.

Unique Organizational Features

The distinctive features of Japanese general trading companies can best be understood by a comparison with Western corporate structure. Western companies are usually organized into profit centers and cost centers. These tend to operate independently, and their leadership is rewarded according to their ability to achieve individual organizational objectives. Matrix structures cut into this traditional format by requiring higher levels of interaction between units and by assigning joint or multiple responsibility for results.

Japanese companies, and Japanese general trading companies especially, are not so compartmentalized. Organizational concepts are ideologically related to the cultural belief that the whole is greater than the sum of its parts. Corporate structure is characterized by shared goals and responsibilities that overlap individuals and departments. Cooperation and interaction between employees and among units is reinforced by a strong common cultural heritage and by company loyalty and esprit de corps. These features act as the lubricants of organization—they make it click.

Decision making is more collective than it is in many Western firms. The *ringi seido* (consensus) system, which has been documented extensively, is a formal mechanism whereby a proposal is routed both horizontally and vertically throughout the company hierarchy for comment and approval.

It follows that rewards are more likely to be distributed along group than individual lines. Hence job security is available to almost everyone in the company. Also, promotions and salary increases are, for many employees, based upon factors such as age and seniority.

Organizational Challenges and Future Formats

No one regards the present structure of the Japanese general trading company as the final, perfect model. The companies are in a state of transition; they have already modified the original structure and are likely to undergo further change. The crucial question is what format will best serve their growing worldwide business. The number and sophistication of the products they handle has increased dramatically: some firms trade between 10,000 and 20,000 products. Also, the number of overseas affiliates mushroomed in the 1970s, and the trend is expected to continue. Finally, special projects, industrial plant exports, national-resource-development deals, and financial and informational services have increasingly cut across traditional product lines.

In the face of these developments, the Japanese general trading companies have retained their flexible worldwide product format but nevertheless have made three major organizational modifications. First, they have created overseas regional offices, such as Mitsui & Co (USA), some of which have become global affiliates in their own right. Second, the trading companies are making greater use of project teams, made up of specialists drawn from various departments and divisions, to handle complex assignments that require various company resources. (See the description of the development division in the Mitsui case.) Finally, the coordinating and planning roles of headquarters staff have been strengthened.

A somewhat longer-range management problem with organizational implications is the difficulty that Japanese companies are beginning to experience—hardly news for U.S. firms—in employing foreign nationals in middle- and top-level management positions abroad. This is taking place for well-known reasons: host-country laws, local employee pressure for meaningful careers in MNCs, and the costs associated with the use of expatriates. When the problem assumes dangerous proportions, the shared responsibility and system of management by consensus—each based in large measure on cultural background—that have worked so effectively to bind a diverse organization together will require modification. Perhaps a more formalized and traditionally Western hierarchy will eventually find some application in such an environment. In fact, the following changes in the organizational format of Japanese general trading companies are highly likely:

1. The continued evolution of staff functions—especially corporate—concerned with new business offshore;
2. Creation of regional headquarters to coordinate and facilitate overseas operations; and
3. Establishment of divisions that organizationally integrate related products.

These changes represent departures from more narrowly structured product lines and are designed to serve the diverse needs of major customers. Several executives interviewed by BI speculated that matrix arrangements may evolve such that products, functions, regional and country offices, overseas affiliates, and special projects are interrelated via strong corporatewide planning, coordination and control systems. In the course of the present decade, according to one expert:

The *sogo shosha* will become global traders of commodities, capital, technologies, managerial skills and labor. Their head offices in Japan will eventually become global operating, investment and management companies. Their major overseas regional headquarters, such as those in North America and Europe, if not hindered by local laws, will develop into holding companies chiefly concerned with investment, management and control of subsidiaries. Operations will be left largely to subsidiaries. Many more service departments, such as financing, processing, packaging, warehousing, transportation, insurance, real estate, and even today's commodity groups, will spin off from the parent company to become independent businesses. The weight of manufacturing business, too, will rise as more manufacturing subsidiaries are established. A few general trading companies might eventually evolve into integrated global conglomerates possessing global production, marketing, financing, information and other capabilities.[1]

General Trading Company Cases

The following organizational studies of Mitsubishi Corporation and Mitsui & Co. provide concrete examples of the general discussions above. The two firms represent the largest and best-managed of the Japanese *sogo shosha*.

Mitsubishi Corporation

Corporate Overview

Mitsubishi Corporation is Japan's largest *sogo shosha*, or general trading company, and its functions and capabilities extend to all corners of the globe. The firm's trading transactions for the year ended March 31, 1980, totaled $50.9 billion, equal to about one-fourth of Japan's national budget. Employees number 14,000; the company handles some 25,000 categories of products. Mitsubishi and its locally incorporated subsidiaries have offices in more than 140 cities worldwide.

Approximately 42% of the company's business is in domestic transactions, 17% in exports, 32% in imports, and 9% in transactions outside Japan. One of its outstanding functions is that of business organizer: in such projects as oil exploration, mineral resources development, airport construction and heavy chemical plant construction, the company is involved in initial surveys, planning, funding, and material procurement, as well as construction and operation, to ensure the project's smooth consummation.

One example of Mitsubishi Corporation's global activities is that of Mitsubishi International GmbH in the Federal Republic of Germany. Mitsubishi International GmbH is a wholly owned, locally incorporated entity encompassing the Dusseldorf Head Office, the Hamburg Branch, and the Russelsheim Automobile Office. Its activities are centered in Germany, extend to the Swiss and Austrian markets, and sometimes, depending on the commodity transacted, expand to cover all of Europe.

In its dealings with Japan, the Dusseldorf Head Office imports such items as steel, autos, machine tools, chemicals, and industrial materials and equipment; it exports machinery and chemicals. It also engages in international transactions in such goods as steel, machinery, and chemicals. Construction of industrial plants is currently increasing in Eastern European countries. In contracting for these projects, financing and product-sharing systems have become important factors. Taking advantage of its trans-European network of business activities, Mitsubishi International GmbH is engaging actively in business with these nations.

The company is also promoting technology transfer. This involves the introduction and licensing contract promotion of superior technologies and know-how possessed by various research institutions and manufacturers. Cen-

---

[1] Alexander K. Young. *The Sogo Shosha: Japan's Multinational Trading Companies* (Boulder, CO: Westview Press, 1979), p. 232.

tering on Germany's Battelle Frankfurt Laboratory, this enterprise makes full use of Mitsubishi's worldwide network of communications and operations.

As a locally incorporated company, Mitsubishi International GmbH has set down solid roots in Germany. Internally, for example, 80% of the staff, including the General Manager of General Affairs and Personnel Division, are locally hired, and thorough employee training systems are being implemented.

The Hamburg Branch engages in transactions outside Germany, primarily in food products, which account for some 70% of total transactions. The branch conducts its business to meet demands for soybeans in various European markets. It also handles materials for vegetable fats and oils, feedstuff, marine products, and canned goods. As for consumer goods such as electrical appliances and cameras, the branch has achieved solid growth in transactions over the years through the establishment of a local sales network. It is also involved in purchasing commodities of European origin, like hops for beer, for shipment to Japan. Taking full advantage of its strategic location, the branch is emphasizing the ocean transport business.

While maintaining effective liaison, both the Dusseldorf Head Office and the Hamburg Branch Office are involved in activities that make the fullest possible use of the advantages of their respective locations.

The Russelsheim Automobile Office is located in the suburbs of Frankfurt, set up in the same building as MMC Auto Deutschland GmbH, an automobile sales joint venture of Mitsubishi Corporation and local interests. The office handles sales of cars manufactured by Mitsubishi Motors Corporation.

Organization

The organization of Mitsubishi Corporation appears on p. 473.

As shown in the preceding chart, there are five functional groups in the general administration division. These furnish staff support to top management, as well as to the nine trading divisions. The groups play an important policy-making and problem-solving role and are well staffed to do so. Their heads are members of the board of managing directors. The general affairs personnel group is concerned with policies and problems dealing with personnel matters, office administration, and communications. The coordination group carries out corporate planning, corporate marketing, and corporate business operation assistance functions. It also assesses potential projects and determines which company resources should be utilized to meet project needs. The administration group includes corporate finance and accounting units. Finally, the credit group sets corporate credit policies and works on specific credit-related projects.

Since most of Mitsubishi Corporation's actual business is done by the trade divisions, each division forms its own business policy within corporate guidelines. At the same time, some divisional decisions are large enough to require the "consensus" approval of some groups in the general administration division. If, for example, the steel division desires to make a large investment, it must clear it with corporate financial units in the administration group. If the machinery division wishes to grant special credit levels to a customer, the approval of the credit group is necessary. Some matters that may have substantial effects on corporate planning and administration, however, require approval from the board of managing directors. Thus, within corporate guidelines, the company is fairly decentralized at home and overseas.

The basic business of each of the trade divisions is, of course, trading. But they also undertake financing, joint ventures (as related to trading), export operations, etc. as needed. Each operates worldwide and involves a number of products and services. Thus, the foods division includes grains and agricultural products; oils and fats; livestock feedstuffs; meat and livestock; sugar; marine products; and processed

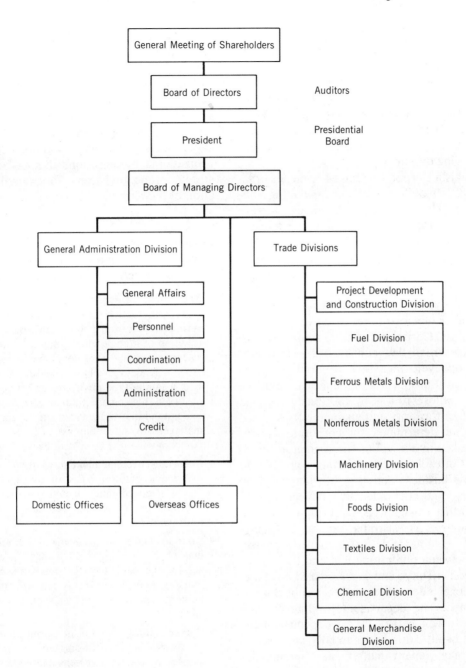

foods. The general merchandise division covers wood and wood products; pulp, paper, and packaging materials; and general merchandise (e.g., asbestos, cement, flat glass, footwear, conveyor belts, rubber products, tobaccos, beer, cameras, electronic goods and electrical home appliances, and other sundries). The head of each trade division is a member of the board of managing directors.

Mitsubishi Corporation has 64 branches in Japan and 140 overseas offices (including subsidiaries). The large domestic and overseas offices have organizational structures similar to that of headquarters, with corresponding nontrading and trading departments. For example, the U.S. subsidiary, Mitsubishi International Corporation, contains a general administration division, several trading divisions, and a number of offices located in major cities.

Mitsubishi Corporation has no actual regional divisions abroad that control overseas operations. However, there are regional directors located in Europe, Latin America, and the Mideast, whose role is to coordinate regional operations. Capacity and character of overseas offices are determined by corporate policy, which takes into account the regulatory environment of each country. Certain countries do not allow business activities but allow liaison activities. A number of legally independent subsidiaries that engage in general trading exist in such countries as Australia, France, Germany, Hong Kong, and the U.S. Contact and coordination between nontrading unit and trading organization in Tokyo and overseas may be made, but the legal independence of each subsidiary is maintained. The department (trading or nontrading) to which they report depends on the issue at hand. Thus, a potentially large-scale, project-management matter may require interaction with the coordination division, while a machinery matter might call for liaison with the machinery division. Medium- to long-range planning documents are taken up directly on the executive level, whereas the nontrading coordination division will often assist with short-term

planning. In fact, Mitsubishi has consistently effected worldwide coordination and control through a vertical (product-oriented) system—unlike other general trading companies that have shifted between vertical (product) and horizontal (regional) approaches. The company feels its approach is fundamentally and historically rooted. Changing conditions induce organizational modifications that help the basic structure function better—for example, the creation of a committee or special task force.

Organizational Coordination

Mitsubishi Corporation is a large and complex company. The following are a few important means by which coordination is achieved.

- **The nature of Japanese companies** provides for close, interactive relationships. This perhaps springs in part from a homogeneous society with a tradition of lifetime employment. "Our divisional system is not like a big conglomerate whose parts are independent. We have a sense of togetherness. It is a family-type environment." One executive observed that some U.S. managers do not seem to understand matrix management but that Japanese managers do, since they live and operate within a companywide matrix system every day.

- **Consensus decision making.** Without the above-mentioned cultural basis of management, high levels of coordination would not exist. Without coordination, consensus decision making could not operate.

- **An individual's job specifications** are not constricting or tightly defined. Each manager is expected to act for the benefit of the company. Since each manager knows how the system operates and has numerous personal contacts, such actions are possible.

- **Career-pathing.** Mitsubishi Corporation transfers executives between trading and nontrading divisions and between overseas and domestic assignments. This helps familiarize a large number of executives with the firm's different operations and increases their base of personal contacts.

- **Training.** The basic system is on-the-job training. An expert in a certain product is assigned to help a newcomer. An individual may change commodities in the course of his career in a division and require new training. There are many other kinds of training programs. The company has, for example, a system for sending selected young employees to business schools such as Stanford and Harvard for intensive studies of business administration and corporate management, and to various countries to learn about the peoples and cultures and to attain linguistic skills, for two or three years. In addition, twice a year, dozens of the overseas staff are brought to the Tokyo headquarters for a two-week orientation session.

Mitsui & Co.

Corporate Overview

Mitsui & Co. is Japan's oldest, most experienced trading house. Older than either the House of Rothschild or the Bank of England, it has played a leading role in Japan's industrial and commercial development since the latter half of the 17th century.

Beginning as a small, family operation, Mitsui prospered and expanded throughout Japan, eventually winning national recognition as a mercantile and banking house. After the Meiji Restoration in 1868, the mercantile company evolved into a trading company, and the banking function became the Mitsui Bank. With these two vehicles, Mitsui invested vigorously in other industries, such as mining and manufacture of a wide variety of products. Then the new trading company set out to provide its many services to businesses abroad.

Mitsui opened its first office outside Japan in Shanghai in 1877 and followed it one year later with offices in Paris and Hong Kong. Its New York office opened in 1879. By World War II, Mitsui had become the largest trading organization in Japan. After the war, the Mitsui family-owned industrial combine was dissolved into over one hundred smaller companies, by order of occupation authorities. As Japan's industry recovered and international trade grew, the new Mitsui opened representative offices throughout the world. More recently, the company has accelerated its global business plan in the following ways:

1. Transferring control over foreign investments and extending loans (with certain limitations) to overseas offices;
2. Transferring existing joint ventures to the accounts of incorporated subsidiaries overseas;
3. Establishing and strengthening the primary control system of joint ventures by incorporating subsidiaries overseas and speeding the autonomy of overseas offices through establishment of fund-raising bases; and
4. Backing up global business from domestic divisions and offices.

In 1979, consolidated net sales were approximately $43 billion.

Mitsui's fundamental goal today is to promote the expansion of free trade and provide an impetus for continued international economic development. Although the company's numerous functions are closely interrelated, they can be classified into two general types: (1) basic trading services and (2) services for commercial development. Basic services include four primary functions:

a. **Conduct of transactions.** Mitsui offers a broad range of support services for companies interested in exporting to or importing from Japan or engaging in trade transactions among the company's worldwide network of offices.
b. **Arranging for the distribution systems,** including insurance, for each transaction. In some cases, distribution can be arranged using Mitsui's own vessels and warehousing facilities around the world.

c. Financing. To augment the financial resources of client firms, Mitsui provides extensive trade credit for companies in the domestic market. It also purchases equity, makes direct loans, guarantees client obligations and provides assistance in obtaining finance from other financial institutions. The company's services in this area center around encouraging the flow and development of trade and commercial activity and therefore extend beyond those provided by financial institutions. Leasing services are also available. However, unlike conglomerates and merchant bankers, Mitsui makes such financial arrangements mainly in connection with trading activities to stimulate trade flows and the market—not for handling funds per se.

d. Information. Through its network of domestic and overseas trade affiliates, the company is in a position to obtain basic information on virtually any market or business opportunity.

These services are augmented by four additional activities:

1. Mitsui has been an active partner in joint ventures in Japan and elsewhere. The new president, Toshikuni Yahiro, recently stated: "We plan to continue to improve the position of our subsidiaries in Japan and overseas. The company's purchase and leasing of grain storage facilities in the U.S. and other investments in this area are one example of the types of investments in key businesses that Mitsui will undertake."

2. The company has invested extensively in resource development.

3. To assist in industrial development at home and abroad, particularly in the developing nations, Mitsui is an active intermediary in the export and import of technology, combining this activity with assistance in transactions and finance for new industries set up through technology transfer.

4. The company also plays the composite role of organizer, in which it draws upon its full range of services—from marketing to finance to technology transfer—to put together major industrial projects.

In sum, Mitsui cannot be categorized as a company in the traditional mold, divided between domestic and foreign operations. It is a true multinational enterprise.

Organization

The organizational structure of Mitsui & Co. may be portrayed as in the following chart.

The head office is very important in Mitsui. The staff divisions—corporate secretary, personnel, legal, planning, finance, and systems—gather necessary information (information gathering is a high-priority activity in Japanese companies), draft corporate policies and see that they are approved via the *ringi* decision-making system, and coordinate policies and information for the operating divisions and geographic regions worldwide. The overseas planning division at headquarters is crucial for Mitsui's worldwide business. It coordinates the international policies, plans, and operations of each of the divisions and overseas subsidiaries. It aims to eliminate conflict and duplication while providing for broad, synergistic action. This coordinative role is in itself a matrix of communications and shared responsibility among the various units.

The traffic division tries to arrange optimal distribution, including insurance, for each transaction. The development department draws upon the firm's full range of services to define and meet the needs of industrial development projects. It conducts feasibility studies and surveys and organizes ad hoc task forces to undertake certain projects. After the corporate role is defined, most projects are then transferred to the appropriate product divisions for implementation.

Mitsui's operating divisions (or business groups) cover: iron and steel; nonferrous metals; fuels; chemicals; textiles; foodstuffs; and machinery. They may be thought of as "business groups," because each contains a number of related divisions. For example, iron and steel is subdivided into iron ore and other ferrous minerals, pig iron, ferroalloys, semifinished steel, steel products, and coal. Other divisions include construction and related materials, lumber, forestry, pulp and paper, rubber, and general merchandise. The divisions operate

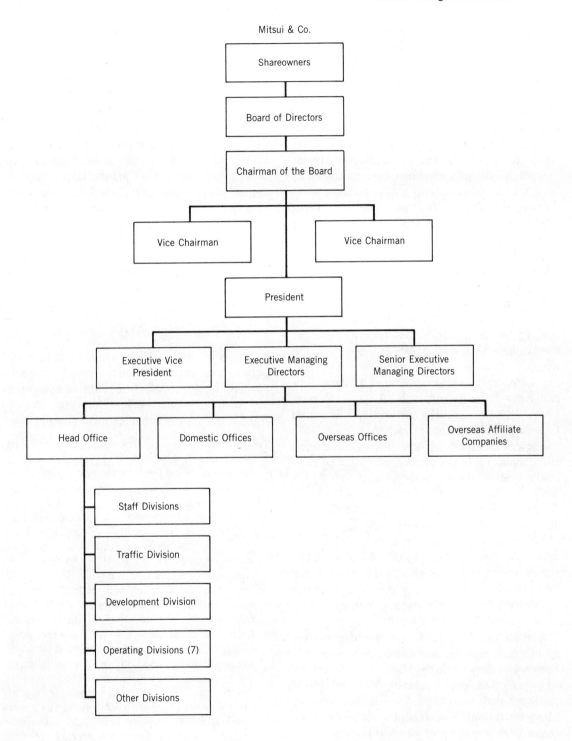

Mitsui & Co.

worldwide. They do not manufacture: as explained in the introduction, their role is trade—worldwide export and import. Each operating division has its own administrative division, which administers the group's interests worldwide and provides staff support in the form of long-range planning and policies, accounting, credit, shipping, and personnel. Most division heads are executive managing directors of Mitsui.

Some of Mitsui's divisions have an overseas department and others do not, depending upon the business. Typically, those that have them began their business after World War II, were successful domestically, then exported and subsequently created an overseas department. The departments' initial task was exporting, and almost all of them later became active in a line (P&L) role overseas.

The firm has fifty-one domestic offices, seventy-five overseas offices, and twenty-eight companies. Sixty-seven offices constitute the overseas trading subsidiaries. Five of these are considered *major* overseas trading subsidiaries—Mitsui & Co: USA Inc., Europe Ltd., Europe GmbH, Australia Ltd., and Canada Ltd. The affiliates include consolidated and unconsolidated subsidiaries and associated companies. The head of each office and of each trading subsidiary has responsibility for all Mitsui business—covering all company divisions—in his geographic location. Many of these divisions are represented by a separate department. Each office and trading subsidiary also has its own administrative division and some staff functions, such as credit and accounting. Each office, affiliate, and trading subsidiary has full authority to conduct business, within certain limits set by the head office.

Completing the matrix are four overseas regions: America (includes North, Central, and South America), Europe, Mideast, and Oceania (Australia and New Zealand). Management of Asia as a region is diffused throughout all head office operations. The executive officer of each region is responsible for all Mitsui operations in that region and is delegated authority to conduct business, within certain limits. The regional executive officers of America, Europe, and Oceania are either executive vice-presidents or executive managing directors of the parent organizations. The head of Mideast is at a lower level, but has special management authority.

Finally, the shareowners of Mitsui differ from those of many Western firms in two respects. First, they are companies rather than individuals. Over the years, Mitsui has helped to create many Japanese companies and owns shares in them. The companies, along with other commercial enterprises, simultaneously own shares in Mitsui. Second, these corporate shareowners are primarily interested in long-term business development, compared with the unremitting focus on short-term return on investment commonly found in the West.

Organizational Coordination

Mitsui is a vast and diverse company. Coordination can prove difficult enough in much smaller, homogeneous firms. Mitsui executives told BI that there are several important keys to their attainment of organizational coordination:

1. The communications network of the trading company, including telexes, computers, special departments, procedures, and personal contacts;
2. Delegation of authority to domestic and overseas units (for example, Mitsui & Co USA Inc. has been delegated responsibility for more than forty business items from the head office; the U.S. subsidiary, in turn, delegates responsibility to its regional organizations in the U.S. and to its Latin American operations); and
3. Education and lifetime employment. For the first three years following employment, a college graduate is given assignments that help him learn a great deal about the company. From that point, programs such as delegation of responsibility, on-the-job training, and job rotation continue the education process. Internationally, about fifty employees each year receive a scholarship to study at a foreign college for a year, followed by a work assignment at company operations within that country. In these ways, over periods of time, many managerial employees are exposed to different aspects of Mitsui business.

CHAPTER 11
Subsidiary–Host Country Relations

In formulating organizational strategy, managers must remain constantly aware of the relationship between the organization and elements in its environment. This is no minor challenge, however. The international business environment tends to be highly complex. For the expatriate manager—someone raised and trained in the home-country culture—the host country may even seem bewilderingly complex. The plethora of environmental factors facing the manager of a foreign subsidiary simply does not fit into the perceptual scheme that seemed appropriate and useful for domestic assignments. The manager's old "cognitive map" no longer applies. Consequently, the new environment often appears unfamiliar and dangerous—a tangle of unrelated events, conditions, and trends.

One of the challenges facing the manager in a foreign subsidiary is to make order out of this chaos. To do so, he or she must develop a new set of cognitive tools for understanding the relationship between the subsidiary and the host country. Part of this task involves learning the particulars of the host country: demographics, economics, politics, culture, and so forth. The task, however, also requires a generally broader view of the new environment.

This chapter serves to outline the issues affecting MNC subsidiary–host country relations in general. As an overview, it cannot delve into all aspects of the subject, but rather examines the fundamental questions and their implications. We begin by examining the historical context of MNC subsidiary–host country interaction. From this historical analysis, we can derive a model for subsidiary–host countries relations. Finally, we suggest a code of conduct—a set of standards for corporate social responsibility—to govern these interactions.

479

HISTORY OF MNCS' RELATIONS WITH HOST GOVERNMENTS

Despite the increases in production that have resulted from the Industrial Revolution, the MNCs' development is a recent phenomenon. This is not to say that international trade itself is new. As early as the second century A.D., merchants traded internationally by means of roads, galleys, and caravans, and trade has continued to develop over the millennia. By 1870, companies that were smaller than modern-day MNCs but not radically different from them engaged in international business (Glynn, 1984). However, some fundamental social, political, and economic changes in the structure of the world community had to open new markets before business could expand.

What MNCs needed to thrive was (and still is) a stable sociopolitical environment within which they could safely invest and then reap the benefits of their investment. Only after the Second World War did the social and political environments stabilize enough to encourage the formation of a world economy. Most major countries agreed to move toward free trade; ultimately, they created a stable international monetary system (Glynn, 1984). This trend toward cooperation coincided with the decline of colonialism, with the consequent fall of colonial trade barriers and the opening of a host of new markets within which MNCs could expand. In addition, the revolution in transport and communication after the war allowed for integration of markets and coordination of activities worldwide.

The Rise of American MNCs

The Second World War itself created another set of forces that resulted in the emergence and expansion of large multinational corporations. American industrial capacity, unlike that of most European or Asian countries, remained intact after the war. The United States had achieved huge increases in productive capacity; now the country needed new markets and cheap natural and human resources for its new industrial ventures. These various needs coincided nicely. The reconstruction needs of many war-ravaged countries, as well as the needs of most developing nations (or any of which had just escaped colonial domination), fit the American need for development and expansion. American MNCs could provide the managerial and technological knowledge necessary to build or rebuild these countries, who, in exchange, could provide cheap labor, natural resources, and new markets.

We should note, however, that in this exchange the cards were (and in some countries still are) heavily stacked in favor of the American MNCs. The companies set the terms for the exchange in whatever way was most advantageous. For the subsidiary manager, the task was simple: the manager set the rules. Consequently, the sociopolitical environment seemed simple and stable.

This period (1946–1958) was one of hegemony for U.S. and British MNCs. The United States owned 60% of all MNCs and the United Kingdom another 20%. MNCs therefore focused primarily on the worldwide acquisition of raw materials—for instance, foreign petroleum. During the next period (1958–1971) continental Europe, now rebuilt and revitalized through the Marshall Plan, became a new market for the American MNCs' expansion.

The Birth of International Competition

Economic domination frequently leads to political domination. The rapid expansion of American MNCs raised people's fears in many nations that the United States might dominate the world economically. The international reaction was prompt. Servan-Schreiber, a Frenchman, published a book in 1968 warning of the American challenge and its economic and political consequencies. The menace of American economic imperialism, spearheaded by American multinationals, is an image still vivid throughout most of the world (Franko, 1978).

The period from 1958 to 1971 also saw a resumption of economic activity in European and Asian countries (notably Japan). Despite the postwar advantages from which American MNCs had benefited, the gap separating them from their European competitors narrowed rapidly. By 1971, American MNCs no longer controlled a majority share of the world market. The period from 1971 to the present has involved an acceleration in non-American firms' activities. During the 1970s American direct investment only doubled, whereas Germany's quadrupled and Japan's increased fivefold during the same period. The era of international competition had arrived.

First Europe, then Japan, and now perhaps Third World countries have responded to the American challenge. Western industrialists started to recognize the potential for competitive challenge from Third World MNCs.

The Rise of the Third World MNCs

Heenan and Keegan see three different kinds of competitive challenges arising from developing countries. First, there is the challenge from the resource-rich developing countries. Many of these nations, particularly those in the Organization of Petroleum Exporting Countries (OPEC) bloc, are anxious to use their vast oil revenues to purchase the technology and managerial talent necessary for international competition. The second class includes the labor-rich, rapidly industrializing countries. For such countries (Hong Kong, the Republic of China, Taiwan, and Korea) rapid and effective industrialization is the only way to support large populations in small countries that lack abundant natural resources. Heenan and Keegan assert that by "combining a cheap, but industrious and well-motivated work force with astute political leadership, developing countries in this category have evolved from basic trading nations to more complex production based economies" (Heenan & Keegan, 1979, p. 103). Finally, a third type of developing country—the market-rich, rapidly industrializing nations—have used the experience developed in their large internal markets to launch effective forays into the world economy.

The developing nation is a new type of competitor but it may still represent a competitive challenge to the American MNCs. The governments of these developing countries are often supportive of their businesses and aggressive about the expansion and development of their enterprises overseas. Precisely this kind of effective and aggressive economic competition has led authors like Heenan and Keegan to assert that "the prevailing image of the developing countries as impoverished, unstable and in a general state of despair deserves reconsideration" (Heenan & Keegan, 1979, p. 101).

The international environment surrounding American MNCs is therefore increasingly competitive. European, Japanese, and Third World MNCs now exert strong competitive forces. American multinationals must adapt global strategies to check their competitors' advance. As Doz and his associates have asserted, "A company wishing to be successful in the increasingly competitive global market needs to take full advantage of its global resources and multinational position" (Doz et al., 1981, p. 64). By concentrating its worldwide manufacturing resources, for example, an MNC may obtain important global cost savings. By protecting its product and process technologies, it can retain its competitive advantages in cost or product characteristics. "Ideally, a clear global strategy ensures maximum leverage of a company's skills and capabilities" (Doz et al., 1981, p. 64). To compete effectively in the world market, it may therefore be necessary for an MNC to subordinate its subsidiaries' actions to those of the multinational as a whole.

Politicization of Relations Between MNCs and Third World Host Countries

Despite the rise of Third World MNCs, we should note that in both their potential and their actual development the developing nations are a heterogeneous group (La Palombara & Blank, 1979). Brazil, for example, has the tenth largest economy in the world. However, only a few developing countries have the capacity to follow a Western model of industrial development. The development of many such countries is slow and difficult. Many of them remain stalled in severe poverty. The hard fact remains that roughly one-fourth of the world's population—largely located in industrialized countries—controls about nine-tenths of the world's gross national product.

The position of impoverished Third World countries in the global economy is another factor that we should examine from a historical perspective. This will provide a context for understanding the relations between MNCs and host countries.

The nineteenth century was a period of empire building. Foreign investment flowed abundantly from Western Europe into Asia, Africa, and the Americas. However, each country's investment always occurred within the political structure that the country's colonial government had already established. As Jacoby put it, "Rare was the profit seeking business corporation that ventured outside the imperial realm to make a commitment in brick and mortar under an alien regime" (Jacoby, 1984, p. 6). Moreover, a policy of armed intervention— "gunboat diplomacy"—was the official Western governments' stance to protect foreign investments. Colonial empires guaranteed the stability necessary for international production and trade; they reinforced it with military power when necessary.

The post-World War II period corresponded with the collapse of these large colonial empires. This period marked the emergence of many politically independent countries led by nationalistic political leaders. In 1950, only 37 developing countries were members of the United Nations. Thirty years later, this number had grown to 110.

The movement toward sovereignty and self-government occurred concurrently with a rapid expansion of foreign MNCs. Generally, it focused Third World leaders' attention on the positive and negative roles that foreign investment played in their countries' development. Their heightened sensitivity led some of these leaders to demand more concessions from MNCs. Discontent with merely supplying raw material and cheap labor prompted leaders in many developing countries to pressure the MNCs. The mere presence of MNCs was not enough; the developing nations now wanted MNCs to contribute to their economic and technological well-being.

Developing nations could exert such pressure because several factors had strengthened their bargaining power. First, MNCs were no longer the only source of development capital. Institutions such as the World Bank and the International Monetary Fund existed as alternative sources. Moreover, the increased competition between MNCs gave host governments the opportunity to select which MNCs to allow into their countries, and on what terms (La Palombara & Blank, 1979). Furthermore, as a result of the Cold War, these governments could choose between (and, if necessary, manipulate) Communist and non-Communist investors. Most important, Third World nations were able to form local associations constituting stronger bargaining blocks. Some of these wielded considerable power. In 1964, for instance, the "Group of 77" was formed; later, this group numbered as many as one hundred developing countries. It has been active within the United Nations in promoting guidelines and rules for international trade and investment. At a more regional level, groups like OPEC have also been able to bargain effectively. Much as European countries had banded together within the Common Market, Third World nations did so to find economic and political strength.

In short, the relations between American MNCs and their host countries have become increasingly politicized. Third World nations are now acutely aware of the costs and benefits that MNCs can bring to their development, and this awareness has been one of the factors contributing to politicization of MNC–host country relations. Another factor is the birth of MNCs in countries whose governments jealously protect their newborn industries. Under both circumstances, an American MNC subsidiary can present a direct challenge to defensive governments.

THE CONFLICT MATRIX

The MNC subsidiary's host country represents a unique set of political, social, and economic forces. In one way or another, the MNC must adapt to these forces. Consequently, its global needs may, in certain instances, have to be subordinated to its subsidiary's local needs. However, it may also be necessary for an MNC to subordinate the subsidiary's actions to those of the multinational overall to compete effectively in the international arena.

When it arises, conflict generally occurs between the strategy necessary for response to the global market and that necessary for response to a host government. Because the host government's needs are not likely to coincide with the MNC's needs, the strategy of adapting to global and national contingencies is also unlikely to coincide with host country preferences. As Doz et al. have stated, "The ideal of a clear, consistent, well-integrated global strategy is limited by powerful forces that push MNCs in the direction of a more ambiguous, less well-integrated strategy that responds to national differences. Since national responsiveness can be achieved only at the expense of global consistency and clarity, tensions are created" (Doz et al., 1981, p. 64). We will refer to these conflicting national and local interests as the "conflict matrix" (see Figure 11.1).

Form of the Conflict Matrix

Two general structural forces collide within the subsidiary; these are the sources of conflict. On one hand are the pressures for global rationalization that have emerged from international competition, and on the other the pressures for national responsiveness that emerged from host countries' heightened sensitivity to the economic, social, and political impact of MNCs. These general-

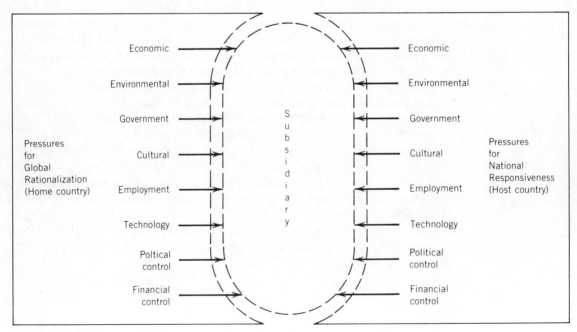

Figure 11.1 Conflict matrix.

ized forces clash within the MNC on several levels (economic, environmental, cultural, etc.). We will devote the following sections to exploring briefly these different levels of conflict.

Conflict over Inflation

Host countries have accused MNCs of raising levels of inflation. The Canadians, for instance, claim that the fluctuation in inflow of capital that MNCs provoke has seriously affected the country's economic planning: namely, it has complicated the problem of attaining stable economic growth without inflation (Jacoby, 1984).

Conflict over Trade Balance

MNCs have another distorting effect on the host country's macro-economy: by increasing the local employees' income, MNCs tend to increase demand for imported consumer goods. As a result, the developing countries' already unfavorable trade balance is destabilized still further.

Inflation rate and trade balance are only two economic indicators that signal the health of the economy to a host country. They are symptoms by which the host country diagnoses itself. Consequently, the MNC manager must monitor these indicators, since ultimately the globally determined strategic decisions (investment patterns, wage rates, etc.) will affect these indicators.

Conflict over State Planning

MNCs have also been criticized for complicating or disturbing economic planning in planned economies. Because they are independent financially from the host government, MNCs cannot be controlled. These circumstances are a source of uncertainty for economic planners. Some countries in which the government has considerable control over the economy through nationalized organizations (e.g., France) have objected to the MNCs' capacity for escaping economic control (Jacoby, 1984).

It is therefore advisable that the MNC manager be aware not only of developmental trends favorable to the host country but also of trends that the host country favors. The challenge facing the subsidiary's management is to integrate as smoothly and discreetly as possible the MNC's global policy and the country's planned industrial policy. Failure to do so will frequently result in the host government's countering the subsidiary's strategy with its own.

Conflict over MNCs' Domination of Key Industrial Sectors

Host governments have sometimes accused MNCs of invading the fastest growing industrial sectors in developing countries. By smothering the emergence of nationally based industry, MNCs harm these countries' economic development. Such accusations often claim that MNCs discourage local entrepreneurs and stifle innovation and initiative (Gabriel, 1977).

Moreover, some host countries have accused MNCs of entering markets by taking over existing local firms. In such cases, nothing changes in the country's state of development. The MNC gains control of local industry; no new productive investment is added to the local economy (Mason, 1974). Even when they are not actually taking over local industry, MNCs have been accused of making local industry noncompetitive (Pahlman et al., 1976). MNCs can pay higher wages than the local rate and can therefore attract the most qualified host-country nationals, which gives them a competitive advantage. Moreover, MNCs can also divert indigenous capital from local industry because of their superior credit (Gabriel, 1977).

Of course, such actions may not be inadvertent. Driven to compete effectively on a global level, MNCs may act aggressively to develop a particular industry within the host country. However, MNCs should undertake such drives only with great sensitivity, because their competitive challenge may represent a potential threat to the host country's economy. Ignoring these dimensions may have negative consequences not only for the host country, but for the MNC itself. The host country may take strong countermeasures to protect its home industry.

Only recently, for example, IBM came under fire from Common Market countries because of its competitive challenge to the European high-technology industries. IBM successfully managed the conflict. However, such successes are not inevitable; even when they occur, it is often at great cost to the subsidiary. Host-country organizations therefore constitute an important dimension that the subsidiary's management must monitor.

Conflict over MNCs' Monopolistic Role

If MNCs divert capital and trained labor from the host country's industries, that country's government or business leaders may feel that companies engage in monopolistic practices. Critical observers claim that the effect of MNCs on many countries is detrimental to their long-term development. The developing country's economy may become entirely dependent on the export of one particular commodity. When the commodity is no longer in high demand on the international market, the MNC withdraws; but by then the agricultural sector of the host economy may have so thoroughly atrophied that the country is unable even to feed itself.

Admittedly, global strategy may dictate that an MNC invest in only one type of business within a host country, and only for a limited period of time. The availability of a single type of natural resource or the cost saving that an economy of scale permits within a country may dictate such strategic choices. However, the MNC managers should realize that they may come under host-country pressure to adopt a more balanced investment package—typically, one that fosters balanced industrial development for the host country.

Long-run development trends that are advantageous to the host country are another environmental dimension that subsidiary managers should understand. Unlike strategies that foster a less balanced short-term gain, investment strategies that are consistent with these trends are more likely to avoid attention from the host country, thus avoiding potential conflict as well.

Conflict over Environmental and Cultural Changes

Environmental standards, for example, limits on pollution, have frequently been more lax in developing countries than elsewhere. However, citizens in many such countries have increasingly objected to the environmental ravages that industrialization can cause. Material damage to a nation is not the only source of criticism; cultural damage resulting from rapid change also inspires considerable outrage in undeveloped countries. Gabriel (1977) points out that strong negative feelings are a common response to the cultural consequences of industrialization, and MNCs often receive the blame.

For these reasons, MNC managers should examine the alternatives before them. From the point of view of a global strategy, it may initially appear advantageous to exploit investment opportunities rapidly; this will preserve a competitive advantage over other international firms. Dropping many of the environmental controls that have constrained MNCs in their home country but not overseas may likewise seem advantageous. However, MNC managers should consider the long-term effects of such strategies as well.

The host-country government (not to mention the citizens) may react negatively to any environmental problems that the MNC creates. Moreover, because of the MNCs' size and potentially monopolistic position in developing economies, companies frequently create the environment in which they will have to function. If short-term strategies produce excessive social change, cultural disintegration, and political unrest, then not only the host country, but also the subsidiary, will pay the price.

Conflict over Employment

Two general areas of conflict emerge around staffing decisions in MNCs: (1) whether expatriates or host country nationals should be employed and (2) whether the industry should be capital or labor intensive. These two types of decisions are conflictual because staffing decisions beneficial to the MNC are frequently detrimental to the host country.

Conflict over the Substitution of Capital for Labor

Conflict arising from the MNCs' capital–labor ratio occurs primarily in developing countries, particularly during the early years of MNC expansion. In this early stage, developing countries were exploited primarily for their natural resources. Extracting these resources was highly capital intensive. The developing nations thus found themselves in the position of having their natural resources depleted while large segments of their populations remained unemployed (Mason, 1974). The developing countries' employment needs contradicted the cost reduction that machine production offered the MNCs. As developing countries have begun to gain strength in negotiating with MNCs, their impact on the employment situation in these countries has become more hotly contested.

At present, MNCs are not held entirely accountable for the developing countries' employment situation. However, the heightened sensitivity to the MNCs' impact on employment has resulted in host country–subsidiary conflict when the companies adopt measures that increase unemployment. Host countries may resist MNC decisions such as shutting down plants, cutting back the number of work hours, and mechanizing facilities.

Obviously, some decisions concerning technology or output levels that corporate headquarters makes after considering competition or market size may conflict with host-country needs. For instance, new technology could give a company advantages over its international competitors because it reduces labor costs. However, MNCs may find such a move politically unfeasible in certain labor-rich developing countries.

Conflict over the Hiring and Training of Indigenous Managers

Another sensitive area concerns the training of indigenous managers. Host countries sometimes accuse MNCs of staffing their subsidiaries' upper echelons with home-country nationals. Under these circumstances, an MNC's investment does little for the development of an indigenous managerial elite. Moreover, under these circumstances, the managerial knowledge imported by the MNC can never "trickle down" into the local economy. The implication that MNCs hoard knowledge and skills for themselves angers many people in host countries.

Another accusation concerns MNCs' tendencies to preserve control over the decision-making processes. Because corporate headquarters is outside the host country, even indigenous managers within the subsidiary cannot make important managerial decisions (Jacoby, 1984). These managers end up missing the opportunity to develop some important managerial skills and often resent the situation.

However important it is for headquarters to preserve a level of centralized control, home-country executives should remember that the benefits of such a strategy must be weighed against the costs of failing to grant some degree of control to indigenous managers. One such cost is the potential for conflict with the host country resulting from the failure to train host-country personnel. We will examine other consequences when we look at political dimensions of the conflict matrix.

Conflict over the Transfer of Technology

The transfer of technology from home to host country causes similar tensions. Of a group of experts in thirty-three countries, one-third of them considered technology transfer a major source of conflict between subsidiaries and host countries. Almost half believe a speedier transfer of technology is desirable (Newman, 1979).

These figures indicate one fear of developing countries—the fear of being relegated to the role of merely supplying raw materials. Citizens of these countries express concern about becoming an integral part of the productive process. Generally speaking, home-country executives see the transfer of technology as the key to their nations' gaining a foothold in the world economy. Only such transfers can let developing countries raise their economies from a stage of small, inefficient companies catering solely to the local economy to one in which larger industries manufacture products for international markets (Mason, 1974).

Some specialists argue that the Third World has taken technology as a symbol of greater income per capita or the availability of modern conveniences (Newman, 1979). Given this perception, a country's relative technological status is therefore of paramount importance; speeding up the transfer of technology becomes an important criterion for measuring economic progress. This preoccupation with transfer of technology may help explain a common suspicion in developing countries: that the MNCs are intentionally slowing the transfer of technology. According to some observers' claims, American MNCs tend to centralize their scientific research and engineering in the United States precisely to restrict the developing nations' access to modern technology. These companies purportedly license their subsidiaries to use only existing or outmoded technologies (Mason, 1974).

Jacoby (1984) has argued, however, that conflicts over transfer of technology and R&D usually resolve themselves over time. When a subsidiary establishes itself in a new country, it will probably depend on the parent company for technological innovation. However, as the subsidiary comes to know its environment, it begins to discover local problems and needs and to develop local research facilities. Whether these facilities can generate sufficiently advanced technological development to satisfy developing countries' aspirations is a matter for debate.

Political Dimensions of the Conflict Matrix

There is another dimension to the conflict matrix that does not arise from contradictions between the MNC's global and national obligations but from the dual national sovereignty or jurisdiction under which the MNC operates. The MNC's headquarters are located in the home country, but the subsidiary resides in the host country. As Jack Behrman has stated, "Every MNC serves several sovereigns " (1969). Political conflict develops when either the host or the home country influences the MNC's actions in ways that are unfavorable to the other country. In such situations, the sovereignty, laws, or ethical principles of one or the other party are violated. The home country may resent a loss of control over its companies, or the host country may fear a loss of control over the economic activity within its own borders. Whatever the validity of these claims, the MNC gets caught in the middle—and the subsidiary manager pays the price.

The MNC as a Conduit for Foreign Policy

Both home- and host-country governments often fear that MNCs will become a tool for foreign policy intervention (Blake & Walters, 1976) and that one or the other country's sovereignty may be jeopardized. Various cases indicate that this fear is not unfounded.

In 1982, for example, the Reagan Administration attempted to bar the construction of a pipeline linking the Soviet Union and Western Europe. As part of its policy, the administration blocked the exports of American goods, services, and technology to a French subsidiary of Dresser Industry, Inc. The European outcry at this intervention in their national affairs was so intense that the Reagan Administration eventually reconsidered its policy. Yet compared with others, the Dresser incident is relatively minor. For instance, the U.S. government attempted to block the French from building their own nuclear force by prohibiting IBM from selling needed equipment. An even more extreme example is the alleged 1973 collaboration by the CIA and ITT in toppling Salvador Allende's government in Chile (Blake & Walters, 1976).

On other occasions, host countries have attempted to use MNCs in affecting foreign policy. In August 1971, the Nixon Administration imposed a 10% surcharge on imports. A large number of American firms with subsidiaries in Latin America pressured the U.S. government to repeal this tariff (Blake & Walters, 1976). In this particular instance, it is unclear whether the MNCs were acting out of self-interest or bowing to pressure from Latin American host countries. However, incidents such as these, in which American MNCs lobby for measures that are favorable to host countries, provide evidence that host countries do, in fact, use MNCs to affect home government policy.

Whether used by the home or the host country for these purposes, the MNC is placed in a delicate position. By obeying one government, the MNC can easily come into conflict with the other. For instance, during the 1973 oil crisis, a major oil company complied with a Saudi Arabian order not to supply oil to the American military. A U.S. senator charged this company with "flagrant corporate disloyalty" (Robock, 1974). However, as a company spokesperson explained later, "The embargo action was taken by a sovereign state and Aramco's compliance came as a result of a direct order and had nothing to do with patriotism" (Robock, 1974, p. 75). In this instance, the MNC was successful in managing the conflict that the Saudi government orders had created. But MNC managers must always remain aware of the danger that political conflict represents for the company.

Conflict from Juridical Control of MNCs

MNCs are not only under the sovereignty of two states; they are also under double jurisdiction. One state's legal constraints on the MNC can force it to act in ways that conflict with the other state's interests. These juridical constraints are a frequent source of conflict between states, and once again, the MNC finds itself in the middle.

For instance, conflict can emerge between home-country and host-country laws concerning investment. As Jacoby (1984, p. 24) asserts, "A Canadian subsidiary of a United States corporation, under instruction from its home office to obey United States law, clearly cannot serve Canadian interests in expanding exports.''

Other juridical sources of conflict arise from American antitrust provisions or acts prohibiting trade with the enemy. If an American firm decides to invest abroad, and if this investment reduces competition within American markets, the company may face an antitrust violation. It may be forced to divest itself of a particular subsidiary. On a lesser scale, the U.S. government may also move to bar such practices as price fixing or market sharing. The host government may, in turn, interpret any compliance with the home government laws as interference in its internal affairs. The MNC may then find itself in a political conflict between home and host states—a conflict that could endanger some of its other subsidiaries located in the host country.

Fortunately, antimonopoly law enforcement has not proved to be a common source of conflict (Jacoby, 1984). Subsidiaries have generally followed American antitrust laws voluntarily, and most host countries have adopted antitrust statutes similar to those in the United States. The U.S. government has therefore avoided intervention in host countries' affairs.

FINANCIAL DIMENSIONS OF THE CONFLICT MATRIX
Conflict over Control of the Subsidiary

Conflict over the financial control of the subsidiary has two interrelated dimensions. First, equity control of the subsidiary results in control of the subsidiary's major decisions. The clash between the host country's attempt to control the subsidiary for its own developmental needs and the MNC's attempt to control the subsidiary to preserve its global competitive position can therefore center on the issue of equity control. Second, conflict may flare up around the issue of profit sharing. How much of the subsidiary's profit should be repatriated? How much should be reinvested in the home country to promote its development? These are intensely debated questions.

Conflict over Equity Ownership

When MNC managers engage in foreign direct investment, they often attach a high priority either to majority or total ownership of equity in the subsidiaries they acquire. Psychologically, this is predictable. A strong equity position affords the parent company a sense of security—a sense that it controls and directs the destiny of its subsidiary. This sense of security holds true even if this subsidiary must operate in a foreign environment subject to the vagaries of unfamiliar market practices and bureaucratic demands. In effect, it seems important to command one's ship even if one cannot control the sea. Strategically, corporate headquarters assumes that the lion's share of equity ownership will be sufficient to guarantee it the right to allocate human and other resources as it sees fit. Its control of seats on the subsidiary's board of directors and in other key management positions will make this possible.

Finally, from a financial perspective, foreign direct investors prefer majority equity ownership so that they can maximize their return on investment. They move abroad with a specific investment project in mind, and they expect to make a profit from this particular investment or at least to integrate it with and improve the profitability of other already existing projects. Thus, they wish to realize a financial reward on as broad an equity base as possible to compensate for their particular anticipated risk.

From the point of view of a host country—particularly a developing country—the perception is very different. At a symbolic level, the country's ownership of the firm connotes power and privilege (Newman, 1979). At a psychological level, a developing country may react negatively to the loss of autonomy that comes with foreign control of the subsidiary. Second (and most important), the amount of equity controlled is often directly proportional to the control a developing country exerts over the company's actions. Because the company's actions affect its economic development, equity control becomes an effective means of subordinating the MNC's action to national development plans.

A number of approaches can manage the conflict over equity control. These approaches consist of different legal and financial structures to apportion the control of the subsidiary. Full MNC ownership, licensing technology to a company in the host country, joint ventures linking host and home country firms, and state-owned enterprises all are alternative ways of sharing control of the subsidiary available to the MNC manager and to the host country.

The relative bargaining power of the host country and the MNC has usually determined the outcome of the conflict over equity control. As already discussed, there seems to be a historical trend toward greater host-country autonomy and control. As the MNCs' bargaining power erodes in developing countries, equity control of the subsidiary may have to be renegotiated in the host countries' favor.

Conflict over Profit Sharing

Another source of conflict, which can occur for a number of reasons, is profit sharing. Conflict may arise over long-term versus short-term profitability. Perhaps the MNC's global strategy is to develop a specific industry in the host country. The company therefore needs to reinvest most of the subsidiary's profits generated into its own operations. This goal, however, may be inconsistent with the host country's immediate cash flow needs. The host country may prefer to take the profits and use the revenue for its own purposes.

Profit repatriation creates other issues. For instance, the host country may want to develop a subsidiary's operations; however, the MNC's global strategy may be inconsistent with this goal. The strategy may dictate that profits be repatriated or reinvested in another subsidiary or location. This scenario is not uncommon. As Robock has asserted, "In maximizing global profits, the multinational enterprise frequently uses transfer pricing and other strategies to position profits in those countries with the lowest tax rates" (Robock, 1974, p. 76).

Clearly, profit sharing can become a controversial issue. On the one hand, the host country may want to control profits to foster industrial development or to gain immediate access to tax revenues. On the other hand, the MNC seeks to control profits to carry out a well-integrated global development strategy or to benefit from the international tax system. MNC and host-country needs may be congruent when both parties want to develop a certain industry, but on other occasions, conflict may erupt.

We should note in passing that the problem of profit sharing is closely linked to that of equity control. Corporate treasurers assume that the ability of host-country bureaucrats to monitor or regulate multinationals' repatriation of profits depends directly on the amount of equity an MNC owns. (This is, however, usually subject to specific negotiations with a local ministry or to contract provisions.) The more equity a parent firm owns in its subsidiary, the more operational latitude it expects in moving capital without first consulting with local partners. Developing countries' governments, well aware of the relationship between equity and decision control, will attempt to gain equity control, if possible, and thus control of profit-sharing decisions.

Consequences of Failing to Negotiate Conflict

What is the price of failing to resolve the conflict matrix? There are a variety of possible outcomes. First, the host country government may institute regulations constraining the MNC's strategy. In Spain, for instance, the government imposed quotas on the Ford company to govern the volume of sales and exports (Doz & Prahalad, 1980). These regulations do not impinge on the managerial autonomy of the MNC; however, the failure to manage the conflict matrix can lead to a second type of host country intervention, which directly affects the MNC's process of strategy formulation. The host government may force the subsidiary into a joint venture or even take complete control of the subsidiary. As Doz and Prahalad assert, "This type of intervention most commonly occurs when MNC subsidiaries are involved in industries perceived by the host government as critical to national, economic, social, or political objectives. In such cases, the usual demand is for multinationals to decentralize decision making to autonomous subsidiaries, and for those subsidiaries to share that process with one or another local constituency" (Doz & Prahalad, 1980, pp. 150–151).

A CODE OF CONDUCT FOR DECISIONS IN THE CONFLICT MATRIX

Our discussion of subsidiary—host country relations thus far has been, and ought to be, somewhat disquieting. We have conceptualized these relations as political and conflictual. Whichever side has more power will get its way. Whoever is the strongest sets the rules of the game. Before the Second World War (and to this day in many poor developing countries) the MNCs held most of the bargaining chips. In those days, the MNCs could lay down the law.

Recently, however, many countries have gained enough power to dictate the conditions for resolving the conflict matrix. The roles are now reversed.

Is there a hidden meaning here—perhaps a moral of some sort? For decades, the MNCs went about their business without regard for the consequences of their actions. Executives in some firms were, of course, well-intentioned. But others were simply unconcerned with what their companies' actions did to people—even to whole populations—in host countries. Too many MNCs abused the power they possessed. Abused power, however, tends to be effective only in the short run, and it frequently creates a reaction. The formerly powerless come to wield their own power. Needless to say, the formerly strong may end up suffering the consequences.

What would it take to move beyond a short-sighted use of power? How can MNCs act more fairly toward all parties concerned? In the next section, we suggest a set of rules specifying corporate social responsibility in a cross-cultural perspective. This can hardly eradicate a long heritage of conflict. However, it can go part of the way toward resolving the conflict matrix and resolving it not only ethically but also economically for both parties involved. It should be emphasized, of course, that other, sometimes competing, considerations also exist, including economic and technological factors.

CORPORATE SOCIAL RESPONSIBILITY; A CROSS-CULTURAL PERSPECTIVE

The Nature of Corporate Social Responsibility

Issues of social responsibility have become a topic of wide discussion and of growing concern to many firms, both domestic and multinational. Indeed, many corporations now have entire departments devoted to developing policy and implementing programs in this area. Such departments would have been unheard of thirty years ago. For example, research by Eilbirt and Parnet (1973) indicates that in the early 1970s, 90% of the largest American corporations had assigned formal responsibility for such issues to either an officer or a high-level committee. Before 1965, fewer than 20% of these companies had had any such position. McAdam (1976) considers three developments responsible for stimulating so many companies to take action:

1. Pressures on corporations to deal with social responsibility issues—from both the public and legislation—have intensified.
2. Many of the arguments against some form of corporate involvement have, for the most part, been refuted by persuasive counterarguments.
3. Corporate managers are adopting new attitudes about the kinds of activities their companies should undertake.

What are the social responsibilities of business? To offer a comprehensive definition of social responsibility is a difficult task. Certainly the concept has many meanings in today's business world; it connotes different ideas to thousands of managers within a wide variety of industries throughout various countries. However, a definition of social responsibility that captures the essence of the concept is the obligation of businessmen to pursue those policies, to make those decisions, or to follow those lines of actions which are desirable in terms of the objectives and values of society (Bowen, 1953). Yet operationally this definition is vague. Can we identify society's values? What are "those lines of actions which are desirable," and can we assume that managers are able to identify them? This is clearly not an operational definition of social responsibility. It is therefore beneficial to review various aspects of the term through the various parties' perspectives.

The Historical Evolution of Social Responsibility

In the late 1800s and early 1900s, the predominant view of corporate social responsibility was that business should provide the consumer with a product or service at the lowest possible price. Business served solely as a profit maximizer. Making money was the firm's only objective. Business viewed labor as a commodity to be bought and sold. The attitude toward the consumer was *caveat emptor* ("let the buyer beware"). Most businesspeople believed that making as much profit as possible, regardless of social costs, was beneficial to society. As a former president of General Motors said, "What's good for GM is good for America."

The post-World War II era gave rise to increasing affluence in the United States. This affluence, along with other rapidly changing socioeconomic conditions, forced businesses to reevaluate their corporate attitudes toward the biological and cultural environments. Yet despite growing affluence, poverty persisted in the United States. In addition, new social issues (pollution, poverty, depletion of resources, etc.) began to arise and demand attention. Indeed, prosperity coexisted with many social problems in postwar America. What became readily apparent was that a nation's affluence in some way heightened the need for social action.

However, American businesses lagged in their attention to social problems. This was largely a consequence of concern about internal efficiency, a concern that was in turn driven by competition. Additionally, companies had ignored the public for years; no existing authority required corporate social responsibility (Luthans & Hodgetts, 1976). The business community saw its role in a very limited context: one of hiring people and producing products or services. Through legislation, the effects of various pressure groups, and the subsequent spread of "enlightened self-interest," however, businesses realized that the environment of the 1970s and 1980s had changed. The new attitudes required not only an awareness of social problems, but also the responsibility of attending to them. The changes came as a shock in some quarters. Others adjusted more imaginatively.

Through a sense of enlightened self-interest, many executives saw benefits such as enhanced corporate reputation and goodwill, increased job satisfaction among all employees, and increased long-run profitability as some of the many benefits predictable from their firms' social involvement. Companies evolved slowly from a profit-maximizing mentality to one that stresses the quality of life. This new attitude emphasizes the great importance of societal interests—that what is good for society is good for the company. Rather than separating business from the environment, this attitude places it in the *context* of its environment. Executives soon came to realize that they are accountable not only to the owners and stockholders but to their employees and society as well.

This corporate philosophy has evolved as a result of many factors. One is the existence of pressure groups—environmentalists, consumer advocates (Nader's Raiders), civil rights activists, and others. These groups, as well as society as a whole, perceived that governmental regulation had not solved many of the most pressing social problems. Consequently, the various activists pressured businesses directly. As society became increasingly aware of the decade's many social ills, people wanted business, like other major institutions, to assume significant social responsibility. Values had changed—now businesses had to change, too. Business institutions have therefore realized that they must move vigorously toward integrating social values into their decision-making processes. The firm that chooses not to take its social responsibilities seriously may find itself losing favor not only with the public at large but even its own customers.

Public pressure on firms has increased steadily over the years. One study by Dierkes and Coppock (1973) analyzed the pressure exerted on American firms' social activity. The researchers found that between 1965 and 1971, government pressure decreased and public pressure increased. In 1965, most pressure for social responsibility originated with the government regulatory bodies, such as the Equal Employment Opportunity Commission (EEOC) and the Food and Drug Administration (FDA), which demanded (and continue to demand) compliance with a plethora of regulations. But the newest sources of pressure are increasingly special interest groups. As federal regulatory agencies have proliferated (e.g., Environmental Protection Agency, Occupational Safety and Health Administration, Consumer Product Safety Commission, all formed during the 1970s), businesses have complied with regulations to a point that compliance is no longer an issue; it is merely part of the firm's standard operating procedures. Instead, businesses have been finding that they must continually monitor their environment for emerging and often highly visible special interest groups that demand their attention to social concerns.

Multinational corporations are of particular interest in the domain of social responsibility. Because they function in a global context, large MNCs should be concerned with taking a proactive stance regarding social responsibility. As in the domestic sphere, there are growing pressures to make such responsibilities second nature. MNCs should therefore assume a role in handling worldwide social and economic problems—important societal issues such as hunger, political oppression, disease, and economic development. These are not theoretical issues but a reality in many Third World markets. As such, they will invariably affect MNCs, directly and indirectly. Yet these problems present not only responsibilities, but opportunities as well. An MNC that can alleviate unfavorable social conditions may not only increase its goodwill but simultaneously create markets for its products and services.

The Social Issues

The following list presents the key issues that have been brought to the attention of business in recent years, not only in the United States, but also in France, West Germany, the United Kingdom, Canada, and Japan:

1. Poverty and equal opportunity.
2. Environment (air, water, and resource use).
3. Consumer concern (product safety).
4. Occupational safety.
5. Employees' welfare.

This list is by no means exhaustive, of course, and these issues vary in importance from industry to industry and from country to country. A firm's list of its own key issues depends on whether it belongs to the manufacturing or nonmanufacturing sector. A steelmaking firm, for instance, obviously must be more concerned about pollution control than a bank; an auto manufacturer must be more concerned about product quality than an insurance company. Each firm should consider the issues most relevant to its own activities.

Before considering the various factors that influence a firm's involvement with social responsibility, we should examine a two-stage model of corporate development in terms of these issues. This model also considers the variables affecting each stage.

The first stage involves the decision to initiate social policy and the variables affecting this stage, that is, (1) public/community pressure and (2) personal/managerial values. Values—the beliefs and attitudes that form a person's frame of reference—help to determine an individual's behavior. All managers and executives have values, which affect their decisions. As indicated earlier, England (1978) believed a value system to be a "permanent perceptual framework which shapes and influences the general nature of an individual's behavior." He found that individual differences accounted for most of the variations that he observed between countries. From this statement, we can infer that managerial values partially account for corporate social policies. (Chapter 6 in this book compared managers' attitudes toward social responsibility.)

The second stage involves the selection of social policy issues. Variables affecting this stage are the size and type of a firm, government action, and the level of the country's industrialization.

VARIABLES AFFECTING THE LEVEL AND EXTENT OF CORPORATE SOCIAL RESPONSIBILITY

Industrialization

A country's level of industrialization appears to affect the degree of corporate social responsibility. Gaedeke and Udo-Aka (1974) have offered an explanation of the differences between consumerism in industrialized and nonindustrialized countries. In industrialized countries, the marketing mechanism is more sophisticated than elsewhere; competition and brand proliferation are intense. This has resulted in the formation of consumer protection groups supported by government or by private industry. Their role is to bridge the gap between the producer and the consumer. In contrast, nonindustrialized countries have little consumer-protection activity because the distribution channel is much shorter. Fewer brands exist to encourage product differentiation. Moreover, nonindustrialized countries lack the facilities, expertise, and resources necessary to certify and test products.

In his study of Japanese businesses, Sethi (1975) showed how economic growth has stimulated the growth of consumerism. During the 1950s and 1960s, Japan realized great economic growth without improving its standard of living. Sethi believes that this stimulated the growth of consumerism in Japan because consumers felt that their well-being had been neglected during the economy's rapid growth. Simultaneously, Japan experienced a high degree of industrialization, characterized by heavy investments in steel and petrochemicals. This industrialization coincided with high population density and concomitant environmental problems.

We can therefore view industrialization as a factor in corporate social responsibility because (1) industrialization can stimulate greater competition and product proliferation, which in turn demands a sophisticated appraisal system to protect consumer interests; (2) industrialization manifests itself in production processes that create environmental problems requiring the corporation's attention; and (3) most industrialized countries have more resources, which provide a higher standard of living for their citizens.

Government Regulation and Spending

Environmental laws in the United States provide a good example of legal pressure as a prime motivating factor in corporate social responsibility. Highly industrialized countries such as the United States, Japan, the United Kingdom, France, and Germany tend to have more environmental laws (e.g., concerning water, air, wastes, etc.) than less industrialized countries such as Turkey, Portugal, and Spain. For example, the Environmental Protection Agency (EPA), which was founded in 1970, develops and enforces standards for clean air and water, controls pollution from pesticides and other toxic substances, and regulates noise and other environmental hazards. It also approves state pollution abatement plans and rules on environmental impact statements. Another federal agency that affects business activities is the Consumer Product Safety Commission. Established in 1972, this agency is responsible for reducing product-related injuries to consumers by mandating better design, labeling, and instruction sheets. These and many other regulatory bodies have forced businesses to enter the realm of social awareness and responsibility. However, we should note that although legislation will undoubtedly stimulate corporate action, a firm that responds to legislation is not necessarily responsive to the community. At times the boundary between these concerns is fuzzy: consider, for example, the regulation in some countries that MNCs cannot fire employees and therefore cannot close a plant (e.g., in Venezuela).

A government's spending patterns can also affect corporate attention to social issues. Countries whose governments spend money in such areas as social security, health, and education take on responsibility for these areas, thus reducing the pressure placed on the private sector to help solve these problems. In France, for example, a number of areas that could fall under the domain of corporate social responsibility are in fact regulated by the government (Preston, Rey, & Dierkes, 1975; 1976). French firms are legally obligated to contribute a percentage of their total payroll to education. Education is therefore no longer a social responsibility issue for French firms. Because the government regulates various social policies, social responsibility in France is much different from that in other countries. That is, by legislating governmental policies that French business must accept, the French government makes potential programs involving business requirements rather than issues.

Managerial Attitudes and Environmental Issues

One variable that affects a firm's attention to environmental issues is the attitudes of individual managers. While a firm's ability to implement policy—not to mention the firm's size, sales volumes, and product type—will probably affect an executive's attitudes, there may be a weak cause–effect relationship between corporate policy and individual opinions. Gidengil's (1977) study of British executives' attitudes toward the environment showed no significant association between executives' answers and the nature of their firms. Rather, the study showed that the nature of the executives themselves—their age, education level, title, and so on—had a more pronounced effect on environmental attitudes than did the nature of their firms. This study also indicated that many executives who favored high levels of ecological responsibility did so more out of enlightened self-interest than out of genuine moral conviction. This conclusion is consistent with those of several other studies concerning executives' attitudes about a wide variety of social issues (Bass & Burger, 1979; 1981 a, b). That is, executives exhibited a pragmatic viewpoint. They felt that a firm should voluntarily enact antipollution standards either to forestall government standards or to create a more pro-business attitude in society.

Corporate responses to environmental issues have been diverse. To meet the challenge of resource depletion, for instance, businesses are joining together to explore for new raw materials. Other methods to increase supplies of raw materials involve research into the development of synthetic products. Several companies are currently trying to develop alternative services of raw materials, such as crude oil, which is expensive and rapidly being depleted. In regard to air pollution, many businesses have taken important steps toward reducing smokestack pollution by installing expensive "scrubbers" and other forms of antipollution equipment. This scrubbing technique appears to be useful in fossil-fuel power plants, which create sulfur dioxide as they burn high-content sulfur fuels.

Because governmental regulation is often the motivating force for the responsibility of firms in the environmental area, we might expect that manufacturing firms would be more active in this field. The type of firm may therefore be another key variable in this analysis. Preston, Rey, and Dierkes (1978), for example, reviewed studies conducted in France, Germany, and Canada; they found that manufacturing firms in Germany and Canada had both a high environmental protection and human resource development index, whereas French food and agricultural firms had a low human resource development index. (See Table 11.1 for more detailed data.) This study also found that the firm's size affected a corporation's commitment to social responsibility. The Canadian survey indicated that attention to corporate social responsibility was clearly related to the firm's size; the larger the firm, the more attention and effort it directed toward social issues. As Table 11.2 illustrates, larger Canadian firms committed more resources to pollution abatement, whereas the largest German firms dedicated the highest percentage of new investment to environmental protection. Table 11.2 also illustrates the effect of firm size on an em-

Table 11.1 Human Resource Development and Environmental Protection Indexes, by Type of Economic Activity

Type of Economic Activity	Human Resource Development Index*			Environmental Protection Index	
	Germany	France	Canada	Germany	Canada
Primary manufacturing—includes iron and steel; stone-clay-glass; petroleum and chemicals; building materials	121 (high)	104	95	187 (high)	148 (high)
Secondary manufacturing—includes metal fabricating, automobiles, and machinery; electric and electronic manufacturing; textiles and leather; rubber and plastics	100	84	103	49	93
Service—includes distribution	—	138	80 (low)	—	86
Transportation and communication	—	163 (high)	119 (high)	—	148 (high)
Finance—includes banking and insurance	—	140	122 (high)	—	66 (low)
Food and agriculture	98	74 (low)	96	40	121
Other—miscellaneous *not* comparable among countries	80	83	72	126	118

Source: L. E. Preston, F. Rey, and M. Dierkes. ''Comparing Corporate Social Performances.'' *California Management Review* 20:44 (1978).
*The national sample average in each case equals 100; numbers are not comparable across columns.

Table 11.2 Indicators of Corporate Performance in Philanthropy, Environmental Protection, and Employee Training, by Size of Firm

| | Environmental Protection | | Employee Training Activity Index* | | | Philanthropy | |
Size Class	Germany: Environmental Expenditures as Percentage of New Investment, 1970–1974	Canada: Percentage of Firms with Pollution Abatement Activity above Legal Requirements	Germany: Expenditures per Worker, DM	France: Percentage of Total Payroll	Canada: Percentage of Firms with Personal Development Programs	Germany: Contributions per Worker (maximum)	Canada: Percentage of Firms with Contributions above 1% Pretax Profit
I (Less than $100 million)	3	34	61	64	85	1208	21
II ($100–500 million)	5	58	114	107	98	1157	13
III (over $500 million)	7	78	125	144	181	409	14
Overall average	5	46	100	100	100	1208	28

Source: L. E. Preston, F. Rey, and M. Dierkes, "Comparing Corporate Social Performances." *California Management Review* 20:43 (1978).
*The national sample average in each case equals 100; data are not comparable across columns.

ployee's training activities. It appears that firm size may be related to personnel training programs as well. Once again, the larger firms performed at higher levels than the smaller ones.

Another issue in Table 11.2 is philanthropy. Firm size is an important variable for this activity, too, but now an inverse relationship appears: smaller German and Canadian firms are relatively more generous in their philanthropic activities than the larger firms.

Equal Opportunity

Over the past twenty years, numerous federal laws have been enacted to address the problem of discrimination in employment in the United States. The establishment of the EEOC—the agency created by the Civil Rights Act of 1964 to facilitate equal employment opportunity—has forced corporations to pay closer attention to their hiring and promoting practices. Since its inception, the EEOC has enforced regulations and guidelines such as the Equal Pay Act of 1963 and the Equal Employment Opportunity Act of 1972. Corporations must strictly adhere to these governmental regulations; failure to do so can result in multimillion dollar fines, government control of certain internal company operations, loss of lucrative government contracts, and a poor public image (Starling, 1980). Additionally, federal contractors are required to have affirmative action programs. These programs, aimed at women, minorities, and the handicapped, are designed to ensure these groups' proportional representation. Affirmative action programs may encompass an extensive set of recruiting programs; in general, however, affirmative action requires a company to take positive steps through its hiring programs to ensure that women, minorities, and the handicapped are hired, developed, promoted, and integrated into all levels and parts of the organization.

Overall, the empirical data on the size and type of firm suggests that both contribute to the firm's socially responsive actions. Larger firms generally participate in more social programs. Manufacturing companies tend to be active in environmental programs, whereas service industries focus on employee development. Additionally, the size and type of firm appear to contribute more to the *selection* of specific issues than to the general decision for social responsiveness.

In summary, there is a great variety of social issues that require a corporation's response today. MNCs respond to them in several ways—voluntarily, in response to government pressure, and in response to public or special interest pressure. No single response can deal with all current issues. Whatever else, however, MNCs must at least *begin* to respond. In today's troubled world, social responsibility is not an option but a necessity.

CONCLUSION

This chapter has touched on a vast range of issues—virtually the whole range of sociopolitical and economic issues facing the world today—and summarizing them inevitably risks some degree of oversimplification. However, the most salient issues are fairly straightforward.

Multinational corporations formerly went about their business with few constraints on subsidiary operations. Particularly in the years just after the Second World War, MNCs expanded rapidly and easily, because the postwar world needed the economic stimuli that the companies provided and the companies, mostly American and relatively unaffected by the war, needed new markets and sources of labor. These circumstances changed, however, as the years passed. As Europe and Asia recovered from the aftereffects of war, and as Third World countries began to industrialize, the American MNCs faced new competition from rivals and new resistance from previously acquiescent host countries. Gradually, the balance of economic power shifted. MNCs now function in a drastically different world from that of their early years.

The reality of international business today is that MNC subsidiary managers must contend not only with great complexity, but with the constant possibility of conflict. Some of the potential for conflict stems from the host countries' newfound powers. With multiple sources of capital and a wide array of companies with which to engage in operations, host countries can select their partners more carefully. MNCs almost invariably face more difficult negotiations with these countries—both when proposing projects and when following their implementation. Moreover, there is also potential for conflict stemming from old resentments. In the past, MNCs often treated host countries in a heavy-handed, even exploitative fashion. Some host countries have accordingly chosen to play a tougher game than the immediate conditions may seem to warrant. Either way, subsidiary managers have a difficult role.

How should managers respond to the challenges facing them in host countries? The circumstances vary from place to place, of course, but the general issues are clear.

First, managers should attempt to perceive and understand the sources of conflict between MNCs and host countries. These sources include not only specific historical resentments—for example, the United Fruit Company's harsh treatment of workers in Central America—but also general concerns about how MNCs affect a country's inflation rate, trade balance, and technological development. Only by shedding ethnocentric attitudes and by seeing conflicts from the other culture's perspective can managers hope to resolve these intricate issues.

Second, managers should understand the consequences of failing to negotiate these conflicts. In the past, MNCs could simply lay down the law, but that time is long gone. Companies must now interact with host countries more imaginatively. Failure to do so may result not just in jeopardizing specific operations but also in harming the company's worldwide reputation.

Third, managers can implement policies that reflect an awareness of corporate social responsibility. MNCs have done considerable good throughout the world, but also great damage. Some of the damage has been material—pollution, depletion of resources, economic disruption; some has been cultural—too rapid industrialization, demographic disruption, and excessive social change. As a result, subsidiaries must consider the consequences of their actions. The weight of social responsibility need not be a burden, however. If managers look to the long-term, they will undoubtedly perceive that wiser, more humane attitudes work to their advantage. Treating workers and consumers well almost invariably enhances a company's economic health as well as its reputation.

The issues of MNC subsidiary-host country relations are obviously complex. The likelihood is that they will grow more so during the years to come. Managers of MNCs will find themselves dealing with a wide range of social and cultural issues in addition to the economic and management issues that seem to be their appropriate terrain. Many of these issues are difficult. Managers' reactions—bafflement, astonishment, even exasperation—are certainly understandable during efforts to provide solutions. However, the circumstances provide the opportunity for creativity as well as frustration. The world situation demands more imagination than it did even twenty years ago, but managers can respond in ways that will benefit them both personally and professionally.

The truth of the matter is that multinational corporations have the potential for collaborative relations with host countries. If they rise to the challenge of collaboration, the consequences will more likely benefit all parties than the old competitive attitudes ever did.

CHAPTER 12
Staffing the MNC Foreign Subsidiary

Multinational corporations continue to grow, as do their international operations. Accordingly, we should examine the issues associated with staffing these firms.

Staffing is particularly important in the realm of multinational business for three reasons (Megginson, 1967; Miller, 1973; Prasad & Krishna Shetty, 1976; Teague, 1970). First, MNC activities are physically dispersed, so that the problem of effective top management attention and control becomes more difficult than it would be in a consolidated setting. The MNC manager must be able and willing to make on-site decisions without continual consulting or reliance on the home office for advice. Second, personnel recruiting, selection, and education and development procedures in countries outside the Western world may be unsatisfactory. Third, multinational operations may involve ventures, products, and markets new to the parent company.

Staffing issues in MNCs are often culturally complex. The host-country nationals' skills may be inadequate for the company's needs, at least in the initial stages; the firm may therefore send home-country nationals (expatriates), or perhaps third-country nationals, to staff key positions in foreign operations. Such staffing decisions may address the MNC's management situation adequately; however, other issues may arise. The issue of the nationality mix within multinational management has received surprisingly little attention in the management literature. Managers in international enterprises face an intricate set of managerial problems that differ drastically from those confronting them in domestic positions. The distinguishing characteristics of these problems are closely related to the external factors (economic, political, social, cultural, legal) found in the firms' various environments. Moreover, international managers are expected to cope with all problems at a distance from the parent company.

Clearly the staffing of foreign operations presents a variety of challenges both to the multinational organization and to the individuals placed in multinational management positions. The present chapter will therefore focus on these challenges and on the consequences for multinational companies that fail to meet them. In particular, we will consider the specific human resource management functions—recruiting, selection, and management education and development—that may aid MNCs and their subsidiary managers.

Note that, although we recognize that multinational companies are headquartered in countries other than the United States, we will present the following discussion from a primarily American point of view. That is, because the majority of international firms are based in the United States, and most of the empirical work we present includes samples of managers from these companies, we will generally refer to the United States as the "parent" or home country. Likewise, we will refer to the foreign subsidiary as the local or host country. Any other foreign location we will refer to as the third country.

CHOOSING AN INTERNATIONAL MANAGEMENT STAFFING POLICY
Factors Influencing the Choice

As a consequence of the diversity of MNCs' environments, many factors, both external and internal, influence managerial staffing. These factors affect the choice of an effective management staffing policy (e.g., the nationality mix of multinational management).

Prasad and Krishna Shetty (1976) have identified a number of these factors, some of which relate to the characteristics of the *company itself,* some to the *individual manager,* and some to the *host country.* Company characteristics that influence the choice of staffing policies include the following:

1. Ownership of foreign subsidiaries. A different policy (and a different kind of person) will be required depending on whether the investment is short or long term.
2. Industry group. Policies will vary at least between manufacturing and service industries.
3. Technology. The level of sophistication and the amount of research needed to sustain it will affect the policies of both the technical and the marketing departments, particularly when the transfer of knowledge virtually requires the transfer of staff.
4. Market influences. Policies will vary according to whether the market for the product is purely local or international, and whether the techniques employed are within the capacity of local management or more global.

5. Age of investment. This will determine the degree to which policies are established and resistant to change.
6. Organization structure. Policies will vary according to whether companies have product-group worldwide structures or matrix structures.
7. Commitment to international business. Policies will vary according to how substantial a portion of the company's business is abroad.
8. Cost factors. These are debatable; there is no standard formula for working out the costs and benefits of the possible policy decisions.
9. Style of management. Companies will settle for a distinctive style that suits their business or their personalities.

In addition to company factors, the choice of a staffing policy is also influenced by the characteristics of available individuals. These include the individuals'

1. Qualifications and experience.
2. Record of previous performance.
3. Commitment to international business, including aspirations for international promotion.
4. Suitability for international business, including ability to adapt to new environments and to show sensitivity to new situations.
5. Family commitments.

Finally, there are the host-country characteristics, which include the following:

1. Level of economic and technological development. This affects the company's ability to recruit in a given country, for either local or international management posts.
2. Political stability and nationalist sentiments, including the propensity to nationalize or expropriate companies.
3. Control of foreign investment and immigration politics. This affects the control of ownership and the issue of work permits.
4. Availability of qualified and experienced managerial personnel, and the need to develop and promote local managers.
5. Sociocultural setting. As mentioned throughout this book, there are potential problems in employees' adjustment across cultural, racial, language, religious, and political boundaries.
6. Geographical location.

These three sets of individual, company, and host-country factors may interact to affect the choice of one particular management staffing policy rather than another. In the next section, we will consider the advantages and disadvantages of choosing a particular staffing policy (sometimes referred to as human resource management policy).

Making the Policy Choice

The key problem in managerial staffing for international assignments is that of selecting personnel. Would home-country personnel, host-country nationals, or third-country nationals be best suited to the needs and demands of the particular multinational operation? Each alternative has advantages and disadvantages.

The various attitudes of MNCs to the management of foreign assignments can be differentiated by the ethnocentric, polycentric, regiocentric, and geocentric approaches (Perlmutter & Heenan, 1974; Heenan & Perlmutter, 1979). The ethnocentric attitude holds that prime positions in the subsidiaries should be staffed by citizens of the parent (home) country. The polycentric attitude holds that prime positions in the subsidiary should be staffed by local nationals (host country). The regiocentric attitude holds that prime positions in the subsidiaries should be staffed by regional citizens; and finally, the geocentric attitude promotes the approach that nationality should not make any difference in the assignment of key positions in the subsidiaries, but competence should be the prime criterion. These differences are further elaborated in Figure 12.1.

Using home-country nationals, or *ethnocentric* staffing, is the most desirable way to obtain personnel with detailed knowledge of company policies, procedures, and people (Holmen, 1980; Prasad & Krishna Shetty, 1976). Traditionally, MNCs have staffed foreign subsidiaries with expatriates—at least when first establishing operations abroad. (To some extent, this is true at later stages, especially in higher-level positions) (Brooke & Remmers, 1978). Companies may adopt this policy because top management perceives a deficiency in the qualifications, experience, and competence of local nationals available to fill middle management positions. Home-country nationals may appear to be more familiar with the parent company's management techniques and methods, as well as with relevant technology and product development. Home-country nationals may also be needed to train and develop local managers, to maintain communications with the home office, to facilitate control, and to ensure that the subsidiary's operation follows overall company policy. Selecting this policy may result in selecting people loyal to the company and influential at company headquarters. Some proponents even suggest that a conflict between national policy and the company's interests would prompt native personnel to favor national policy over company interests (Prasad & Krishna Shetty, 1976). Home-country nationals, in contrast, would probably favor the company.

Yet the strategic advantages of giving assignments to host-country personnel are becoming increasingly obvious. Because host-country nationals are already familiar with the local language, culture, and customs they do not require training in language proficiency or acculturation. Nor do they need time to adapt to the environment, because they are already adapted. Likely as not, they have an intimate knowledge of the local business situation—a vital aid in establishing good relationships with customers, clients, government agencies, employees, and the general public. Having local nationals in management positions, especially at higher levels, may minimize the company's "foreign image" and make it more acceptable in strongly nationalistic countries. This may also enhance other host-country nationals' morale; they probably appreciate working for a boss of the same nationality. Moreover, employing host-country na-

Aspects of the Enterprise	Orientation			
	Ethnocentric	Polycentric	Regiocentric	Geocentric
Complexity of organization	Complex in home country, simple in subsidiaries	Varied and independent	Highly interdependent on a regional basis	Increasingly complex and highly interdependent on a worldwide basis
Authority; decision making	High in headquarters	Relatively low in headquarters	High regional headquarters and/or high collaboration among subsidiaries	Collaboration of headquarters and subsidiaries around the world
Evaluation and control	Home standards applied for persons and performance	Determined locally	Determined regionally	Standards which are universal and local
Rewards and punishments; incentives	High in headquarters; low in subsidiaries	Wide variation; can be high or low rewards for subsidiary performance	Rewards for contribution to regional objectives	Rewards to international and local executives for reaching local and worldwide objectives
Communication; information flow	High volume of orders, commands, advice to subsidiaries	Little to and from headquarters; little among subsidiaries	Little to and from corporate headquarters, but may be high to and from regional headquarters and among countries	Both ways and among subsidiaries around the world
Geographical identification	Nationality of owner	Nationality of host country	Regional company	Truly worldwide company, but identifying with national interests
Perpetuation (recruiting, staffing, development)	People of home country developed for key positions everywhere in the world	People of local nationality developed for key positions in their own country	Regional people developed for key positions anywhere in the region	Best people everywhere in the world developed for key positions everywhere in the world

Figure 12.1   Four types of headquarters orientations toward subsidiaries in a multinational enterprise.

Source: D. A. Heenan and H. V. Perlmutter. *Multinational Organization Development.* Reading, MA: Addison-Wesley, 1979, pp. 18–19.

tionals will be far less expensive than employing home-country or third-country nationals. This will almost certainly be true even if the company pays a salary above local scales to attract and retain more capable people. Finally, the MNC provides better employment opportunities for the host-country nationals because of its size and prestige. In fact, national laws may actually require that a certain proportion of the subsidiary's top managers, if not the chief executives themselves, be citizens of the country.

A third personnel policy that has come into use recently is employment of third-country nationals. Some companies with fairly extensive multinational operations may transfer managers from other overseas subsidiaries when unable to identify and attract competent local personnel. For example, several American firms have utilized personnel of Cuban origin effectively in managerial positions throughout Latin America. Other American firms have used British citizens in Asian countries. European-based MNCs have often employed third-country nationals as a matter of course. This policy has similar advantages to using expatriates, but there are some notable differences. First, third-country nationals form an additional source of recruitment for MNCs. This source is especially advantageous and important where the shortage of qualified host-country nationals is critical, especially if it is further aggravated by a lack of home-country nationals able or willing to take foreign assignments. Second, the costs of maintaining third-country nationals are generally less than the costs of maintaining expatriates abroad. For instance, if the manager's salary is tied to the third-country pay scale and that scale is lower than the home-country scale, the MNC can achieve a substantial saving. Savings from differential payments of fringe benefits and other compensations may also be significant. Firms may also save money in transferring executives from countries other than the home office. Finally, and often most important, third-country nationals may be capable of greater cultural flexibility and ease of adjustment than home-country personnel if the third country and the subsidiary country share a common language and similar cultural background.

In theory, MNCs move from using expatriates to using local and third-country nationals as international activities expand. In practice, however, whichever staffing policy a company adopts involves a mixture of nationalities. We can term this *geocentric* (or at times regiocentric) staffing. To some extent, the proportion of other nationalities (other than the home country) represented in overseas management often provides a good measure of the extent to which the company is internationalizing its executives (Brooke & Remmers, 1978).

To illustrate the actual implementation of current MNC staffing policies, Table 12.1 presents the foreign staffing patterns of 144 American, Western European, and Japanese-based companies. Researchers asked the respondents in these three samples to identify whether management personnel at three different levels (senior, middle, and lower) in each of eight subsidiary regions were primarily "parent-country nationals," "host-country nationals," or "third-country nationals" (Tung, 1982). The frequency distributions show that American and European samples use host-country nationals more often at all levels of

Table 12.1 Extent (in %) to Which Foreign Affiliates Are Staffed by Parent-Country Nationals (PCN), Host-Country Nationals (HCN), and Third-Country Nationals (TCN)

	U.S. MNCs	European MNCs	Japanese MNCs
United States			
Senior management PCN	NR*	29	83
Senior management HCN	NR	67	17
Senior management TCN	NR	4	0
Middle management PCN	NR	18	73
Middle management HCN	NR	82	27
Middle management TCN	NR	0	0
Lower management PCN	NR	4	40
Lower management HCN	NR	96	60
Lower management TCN	NR	0	0
Western Europe			
Senior management PCN	33	38	77
Senior management HCN	60	62	23
Senior management TCN	7	0	0
Middle management PCN	5	7	43
Middle management HCN	93	93	57
Middle management TCN	2	0	0
Lower management PCN	0	4	23
Lower management HCN	100	96	77
Lower management TCN	0	0	0
Canada			
Senior management PCN	25	28	33
Senior management HCN	74	67	67
Senior management TCN	1	5	0
Middle management PCN	1	11	33
Middle management HCN	99	89	67
Middle management TCN	0	0	0
Lower management PCN	3	0	17
Lower management HCN	96	100	83
Lower management TCN	1	0	0
Middle/Near East			
Senior management PCN	42	86	67
Senior management HCN	34	14	33
Senior management TCN	24	0	0
Middle management PCN	27	50	83
Middle management HCN	63	29	17
Middle management TCN	10	21	0
Lower management PCN	9	7	33
Lower management HCN	82	86	67
Lower management TCN	9	7	0
Eastern Europe			
Senior management PCN	15.5	100	NR†
Senior management HCN	69	0	NR
Senior management TCN	15.5	0	NR
Middle management PCN	8	100	NR
Middle management HCN	92	0	NR
Middle management TCN	0	0	NR

(Continued)

Table 12.1 (*Continued*)

	U.S. MNCs	European MNCs	Japanese MNCs
Lower management PCN	0	100	NR
Lower management HCN	100	0	NR
Lower management TCN	0	0	NR
Latin/South America			
Senior management PCN	44	79	83
Senior management HCN	47	16	17
Senior management TCN	9	5	0
Middle management PCN	7	37	41
Middle management HCN	92	58	59
Middle management TCN	1	5	0
Lower management PCN	1	0	18
Lower management HCN	96	100	82
Lower management TCN	3	0	0
Far East			
Senior management PCN	55	85	65
Senior management HCN	38	15	35
Senior management TCN	7	0	0
Middle management PCN	19	25	41
Middle management HCN	81	75	59
Middle management TCN	0	0	0
Lower management PCN	2	5	18
Lower management HCN	96	95	82
Lower management TCN	2	0	0
Africa			
Senior management PCN	36	75	50
Senior management HCN	47	15	33
Senior management TCN	17	10	17
Middle management PCN	11	35	0
Middle management HCN	78	65	100
Middle management TCN	11	0	0
Lower management PCN	5	0	0
Lower management HCN	90	95	100
Lower management TCN	5	5	0

Source: R. L. Tung. "Selection and Training Procedures of U.S., European, and Japanese Multinationals." *California Management Review* 25(1):60, 61, 1982.
*Data were collected on staffing policies of foreign affiliates only. Hence, no statistic was gathered for home country of MNC.
†None of the Japanese MNCs included in this study has affiliate operations in Eastern Europe.

management in developed nations of the world than in less developed nations. The Japanese MNCs employ considerably more parent-country nationals at the senior and middle management levels in their overseas operations. They do not use third-country nationals at any level of management in their overseas affiliate operations except in Africa.

A smaller survey of thirty-six U.S.-based MNCs employing over one million management, professional, or senior technical employees outside the United States, and comparison samples of ten American subsidiaries of Japanese com-

Table 12.2   Foreign Staffing Patterns of Multinational Companies

Industry	Employed Outside Parent Country (in thousands)	Percentage of PCN	Percentage of TCN	Percentage of HCN
Banks (7)[a]	35.0	5.0	1.2	93.8
Petroleum (3)	12.4	3.8	0.6	95.6
Construction and design (3)	60.1	1.0	0.1	98.9
Industrial chemicals (4)	22.8	0.3	0.5	99.2
Electronics and communication	318.0	0.2	0.3	99.5
Pharmaceutical and personal care (7)	91.6	0.2	0.2	99.6
Automotive products (5)	488.0	0.2	0.1	99.7
Total	1007.9			
U.S. subsidiaries of Japanese companies (10)	7.4	2.4%	0.1	97.5
Volkswagen of America	10.0	0.5	0	99.5

Source: Milton G. Holmen. "Organization and Staffing of Foreign Operations of Multinational Companies." Paper presented at a meeting of the Academy of International Business, New Orleans, October 25, 1980.
[a]Numbers in parentheses indicate the number of companies studied.

panies and one subsidiary of a German company, provides additional evidence for the overwhelmingly high representation by host-country nationals (Holmen, 1980). Only in the banking and petroleum industries do parent-country nationals represent even a minimally significant proportion of the subsidiary workforce (Table 12.2). These studies provide further evidence of the reduced reliance on ethnocentric staffing.

Before leaving this topic, however, we should discuss a recent development in international staffing policies: the emergence of the "international grade of executives." In principle, this policy allows for the unrestricted movement of executives of any nationality to anywhere within the MNC's operations. These career international managers are not tied to one particular home-base; thus, the company has a ready reservoir of expertise available for assignments anywhere in the world. We may consider the international grade as an avenue of promotion for local nationals beyond the host-country operations. In itself, this is a big step toward the internationalization of the company. It may reduce parochialism and give the company a more international image (Brooke & Remmers, 1978). Although the purported advantages of this policy may lead to its acceptance on an equal footing with the other three policies discussed, its brief existence precludes a fuller understanding of the practical limitations involved in its implementation (e.g., cost factors, relocation pressures, necessity of a central workforce plan for monitoring requests from subsidiaries, conflict with host-country governments, etc.).

CHALLENGES TO THE ORGANIZATION ASSIGNING AN INTERNATIONAL MANAGER

Whichever managerial staffing policy the MNC finally chooses, the firm must face the task of implementing it. Because our concern in this chapter is the process of transferring personnel to a foreign subsidiary, and the vast bulk of literature concerned with policy implementation has focused on the advantages and disadvantages of expatriation, the implications of this policy (from both the organization's and the international manager's perspectives) will be the focus of attention in succeeding sections. If the MNC can succeed in employing expatriates to manage its foreign operations, then it must overcome several challenges. These include (1) the nationalistic resistance to expatriation and to the imposition of the parent company in the managerial style that expatriates bring along, (2) the great expense involved in maintaining this policy, (3) the initially lower productivity of the new manager (and possibly subsequent productivity losses among the new manager's subordinates), and (4) the special problem of cultural resistance to women managers. We will discuss each of these challenges below.

Nationalistic Resistance to Expatriates

Expatriation goes against the nationalistic trends in most countries today. MNCs build up the expectation of local management by host-country nationals (or, in the case of European firms, by expatriates who are generally assimilated into the local milieu). Local managers build up the MNC's business only to find that one day their business operations transcend national boundaries. Their long-established expectations about who will manage the enterprise are now reversed (Franko, 1973).

The resistance to expatriates may be a matter not only of how well the MNC fulfills the host-country nationals' expectations for local management but also of the expatriates' managerial style. When the MNC reserves the top managerial positions in its subsidiaries and regional headquarters for parent-country nationals, it commits itself to maintaining a managerial style similar to that of the multinational headquarters. Instead of managers adapting their style to conform to the new environment's demands, the MNC expects host-country subordinates to adjust to managerial patterns prevalent in the parent country. Zeira and his associates' studies of foreign subsidiaries in England, Holland, Belgium, and West Germany have examined the resistance engendered in host-country nationals by an inappropriate managerial style for that particular country's culture (Harari & Zeira, 1978; Zeira, 1976, 1979; Zeira & Banai, 1981; Zeira & Harari, 1979; Zeira, Harari, & Izraeli, 1975). These investigators found that an overwhelming majority of host-country national respondents believed that subsidiaries should be headed by host-country managers, and that, when they are not, foreign (expatriate) managers are expected to possess qualifications that only host-country managers would be likely to possess—such as proficiency in the host country's "silent" (nonverbal) language, and adaptability of managers' social and business behavior to the various client and host-country employees' specific expectations. This finding appears to be true across countries and industries. In this situation, host-country subordinates question the desirability of expatriates' dominating top positions and, moreover, the fairness of personnel policies that typically grant greater benefits to expatriates. Locals' desire for vertical mobility in the subsidiary is often frustrated, which may eventually reduce morale.

Cost of Employing Expatriates

Expatriates are expensive to employ. Although a full explication of international compensation systems is beyond the scope of this chapter, we should note several considerations. International managers typically earn their home salaries plus substantial allowances (e.g., cost-of-living, "swamp pay," shelter, education, home leave), usually in the form of premiums for overseas assignments (Brooke & Remmers, 1978). These allowances may increase base salaries by 25 to 100% (Franko, 1973). Schollhammer (1969) has indicated that average recruit compensation of U.S. executives working abroad is roughly twice as high, and three times as high in some cases, as the remuneration he or she would receive in a comparable position at home. When these expenses are combined with relocation costs, tax equalization expenses, the cost of travel between the subsidiary and the parent company headquarters, and the expense involved in reintegrating the expatriate into the home-country operations on completion of the foreign assignment, the MNC is making a substantial investment in its international managerial personnel. It has been estimated that expatriates who "fail" (i.e., return from foreign service prematurely because they, or their families, were unable to cope in a different environment) may cost a company over $200,000 (Chesanow, 1984).

Loss of Productivity

A dominant theme throughout this text has been the variety of adaptation problems—including the effect of the so-called culture shock—when managers cross cultural boundaries. These adaptation problems may affect the international manager's ability to settle quickly into the new job; they may even impair job performance (Brooke & Remmers, 1978). One study found that 80% of European managers of American subsidiaries took more than a year to reach a level of productivity comparable to what they had maintained in their home environment (Leontiades, 1973). Another study has shown that nine out of ten expatriates were significantly less successful in Japan than in their previous home-country assignments (Seward, 1975). Expatriates have reported feeling pressure to justify being stationed abroad, and thus have tended to refrain from seeking information and advice from their subordinates. They consequently often made errors with negative repercussions for the organization (Zeira et al., 1975).

In addition to decreasing their own productivity, expatriates may exhibit managerial behavior that significantly decreases their host-country subordinates' productivity. The use of an expatriate staffing policy may disrupt organizational effectiveness and the integration of parent company policy, primarily as a consequence of the incompatibility between host-country nationals' expectations and the expatriates' managerial role performance (Zeira, 1976).

Cultural Resistance to Women Managers

As of 1977, 22% of American managers were women (U.S. Department of Labor, 1978). As more women enter business, economics, and related disciplines (Grant & Lind, 1976), and as their enrollment in graduate programs of administration and management increases (*Business Week,* 1975), more women will be available for international managerial positions. This trend presents a significant challenge to the MNC. Cultural biases in the subsidiary host countries (especially in the Middle East, Japan, and Latin America) may preclude the acceptance of women as managers (Thai & Cateora, 1979). Host-country subordinates may consider the assignment of a woman executive an affront and an indication of headquarters' low regard for its business with the subsidiary. Host-country subordinates may also worry that a woman will have less influence over headquarters, that she will be less autonomous in negotiations or less able to represent the MNC in local transactions (Izraeli et al., 1980).

These circumstances suggest that changing attitudes toward women in business within foreign countries are not keeping pace with changes in the United States (Thai & Cateora, 1979). Laws and government pressures for affirmative action that are beginning to change attitudes in the United States are either minimal, unenforced, or nonexistent in foreign countries. Without question, the differing attitudes toward women in other cultures must affect MNCs' decisions to station women managers in affected regions. This is not to suggest that corporations should rule out placing women managers overseas, but rather that selection of personnel should be based on consideration of all the relevant factors.

CHALLENGES TO THE INTERNATIONAL MANAGER

In addition to the general challenges the organization faces when implementing a staffing policy, there is another likely significant challenge: the difficulties that individual managers face in the international management setting. International assignees frequently operate in an environment that is stressful for them personally and also resistant to their leadership. Research suggests that drastic changes in one's cultural environment generally create an experience of stress or emotional disturbance (e.g., Coelho & Ahmed, 1980; Mostwind, 1976). International management positions certainly fall within the category of such change. It is not surprising, then, that studies of MNC staffing practices indicate that expatriates develop symptoms of transfer anxiety, culture shock, social dislocation, "exile complex" (feeling abandoned by headquarters), insufficient influence, adaptation problems, and reentry trauma (Brooke & Remmers, 1977; Robock, Simmonds, & Zwick, 1977; Zeira & Harari, 1977). Neither should it surprise us that more than one-third of all expatriates return from foreign services prematurely—many having paid a personal price in the form of alcoholism, drug abuse, or divorce (Chesanow, 1984).

The reasons for expatriates' failure derive from the cultural, political, economic, legal, and other factors in a host country—factors that are often radi-

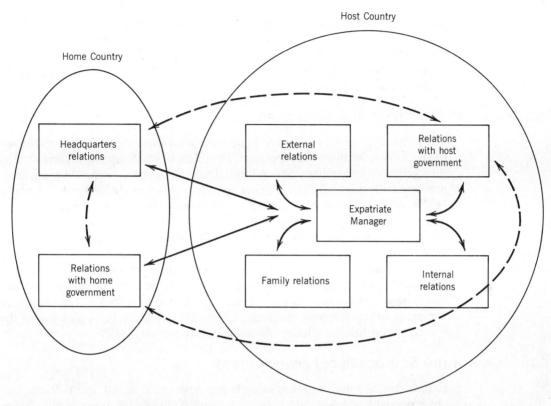

Figure 12.2 Major relations between the expatriate manager and other parties interested in international business.

Source: A Model for Developing Key Expatriate Executives, by Afzalur Rahim, copyright April 1983. Reprinted with the permission of PERSONNEL JOURNAL, April 1983, pp. 312–317, Costa Mesa, California; all rights reserved.

cally different from those in the home country. Such differences are a potential cause for conflict among the major parties interested in international business. A diagram of the relationships between these parties appears in Figure 12.2.

Note that the manager's major functions within the host country are compounded by the expatriate's unfamiliarity with aspects of the local culture that interact significantly with these functions (Rahim, 1983). The broken lines in the figure show the indirect relations between the parent company headquarters and the parent and host country governments. Clearly the challenges that expatriate managers face are substantially greater than what they faced in their home country. They must deal with new personal, professional, and operational relationships within the subsidiary and with relationships between the subsidiary and the host country's community-at-large. They must establish relations with the host government to obtain the necessary permits, licenses, and approvals. They must serve as a liaison between the host government, headquarters, and the home government. Perhaps most significant, they must be sensitive to the changing structure and function of their familial relationships as they adapt to the host culture. The implications of all these challenges are great, and, of course, managers must deal with them all simultaneously—which is in itself part of the challenge. But to perceive them accurately, we should consider them one by one.

Challenges of the Physical Environment

The physical environment provides expatriate managers with their introduction to the foreign setting. Managers and their families will almost invariably find themselves in unfamiliar surroundings. They may even be exposed to an environment with markedly lower living standards, inadequate medical and public health facilities, inferior educational institutions, climatic discomforts, and perhaps even physical dangers—this despite what is typically an entry into the upper-class social life of the local community (Brooke & Remmers, 1978; Zeira et al., 1975). In any case, a major challenge will be the disorientation of living far from home. This geographical distance conflicts with the family's need to feel secure in the community (Heenan, 1970). Removal from family, friends, and familiar environments may result in "separation anxiety" for expatriate managers and their family members. Ultimately, such reactions may impair the managers' on-the-job effectiveness and family morale.

Challenges of the Sociocultural Environment

Expatriates and their families often face a new world of cultural patterns that are potentially at odds with their own value systems and living habits. When expatriates face host-country nationals and their different behavioral assumptions and expectations, tensions may rise. Even performing the simplest actions—shopping, traveling, visiting friends—may produce unexpected and seemingly unintelligible responses from the new cultural environment. As pressures mount, expatriates will presumably start to realize that the assumptions that guided behavior in the past are no longer applicable (Hayes, 1972). Yet such realizations do not necessarily solve the basic expatriates' dilemma.

Unfortunately, the inappropriateness of expatriate managers' assumptions and internal rules is only part of the problem. Another problem is the common inability to communicate with the local employees in their language (Almaney, 1974). This problem not only adds to expatriates' difficulties, but compounds them. Because the expatriates' own frame of reference now seems inadequate, and they have not yet developed a new set of behavioral reference points, they are left with a void in their assumptions about appropriate behavior. Obviously this creates confusion. Moreover, it limits the individual's ability to communicate confusion. This impasse frequently causes a high level of disorientation anxiety, more familiarly termed *culture shock* (Hayes, 1972).

The inadequacy of expatriate managers' frame of reference will probably extend beyond the personal realm. It may also affect managers' ability to deal with individuals and business groups outside the subsidiary, including local partners, trade unions, bankers, and important customers (Rahim, 1983). In many societies, business interactions are quasi-social and occur after normal working hours, a dimension that expatriate managers may fail to acknowledge (Heenan, 1970). American expatriate managers may insist on using their own standards to judge others' behavior. For example, American standards for promptness and attentiveness to scheduled appointments may be severely at odds with the host-country nationals' expectations (Hayes, 1972). A second example relates to protocol for "getting down to business." In the United States, businesspeople briefly exchange amenities before dealing with official matters at hand. In many foreign cultures, however, what seem like endless social amenities and "unnecessary" (by American standards) niceties often precede the "real" business interaction. (The reader should refer to Chapter 4 for further elaboration on communication issues.)

Challenges of the Technical Environment

Managers may also encounter differences in technical sophistication that conflict with their expectations. Operational variations may exist in the subsidiary—scaled-down plants and equipment, differing standards of productivity, nonavailability of credit, inefficiency of internal distribution, restricted communications, and so forth. Moreover, the foreign-based manager, when exposed to countries in varying stages of economic development and industrialization, may view the technical differences as insurmountable (Heenan, 1970). As discussed earlier in this chapter, the manager's attempts to apply the well-established managerial and organizational principles once successful in the home country may produce considerable frustration, because differences in the local culture prevent effective implementation (Cotton, 1973).

Challenges Stemming from Government and Corporate Relations

The expatriate manager must conduct the subsidiary's operations within the constraints imposed by the local government. In host countries with predominant political and economic centralism, the government's involvement in business requires that expatriate managers consider the government as a conegotiator (along with unions in labor relations), a supplier (where public utilities are state-owned), a competitor (in the form of the quasi-public enterprise), or even a marketer (when distribution facilities are government-owned). Unfortunately, the MNC and the local government often disagree over ideologies, objectives, and policies (Behrman, 1970). No matter what expatriate managers do, they will remain vulnerable to hostility and criticism by the host government (Vernon, 1967). This situation raises the possibility that expatriates will experience greater role conflict than their colleagues at home.

Expatriate managers must also act as a link between corporate headquarters and the overseas subsidiary. They are responsible for implementing the objectives and policies that headquarters formulates—even though those objectives and policies may conflict with the managers' ways of handling local problems.

Such differences of opinion may also generate role conflict for expatriate managers (Rahim, 1983).

Another area of conflict may arise when the MNC overcentralizes its decision making. If the managers' authority is visibly constricted, their chances for establishing and maintaining effective relationships with local associates diminish. Indeed, in host environments in which a high value is placed on authority the recognition of the expatriate managers tends to be obscured (Heenan, 1970).

Besides limiting managers' autonomy, headquarters may also overlook the need for communication with its overseas personnel. The expatriates' exclusion from the mainstream of corporate life makes informational support all the more necessary to lessen the many uncertainties of foreign assignments. Some researchers have called this phenomenon the "information gap" (Chorafas, 1967). Its salient features are (1) failure to inform managers abroad about activities at home and (2) a lack of understanding among corporate executives about the differences between conditions abroad and at home. Moreover, the MNC's inability to structure an ongoing dialogue with their expatriate managers may obstruct the managers' needs for personal recognition. It may even increase their difficulty in adapting (Heenan, 1970). In addition, it may force managers to decide whether to work quietly for long-run effectiveness or more earnestly for personal promotion (Rahim, 1983).

There is another challenge to the expatriate manager in this regard. This is the ability to satisfy not only the host government's needs and requirements, but also the home government's. After all, the home government establishes constraints on the overseas operations—constraints that may create conflicts of interest between the corporation and the home government or between the home and host governments (Behrman, 1970). The expatriate manager may end up caught in the middle.

All of these various challenges stemming from government and corporate relations will probably affect the expatriate manager's personal needs. Expatriates may ultimately regard their roles as undefined, dysfunctional, and too expensive in personal and professional terms. Yet their waning enthusiasm for their work may often lead to even more extensive company controls, which will reinforce the managers' sense of incompetence (McKenzie, 1966; Rahim, 1983).

The Special Problem of Repatriation

The March 3, 1978, issue of *Business International* identified reentry as a major personnel issue for international corporations.

Repatriating executives from overseas assignments is a top management challenge that goes far beyond the superficial problems and costs of physical relocation. . . . The crux of the matter is the assumption that since these individuals are returning home—that is, to a familiar way of life—they should have no trouble adapting to either the corporate or the home environment. However, experience has shown that repatriation is anything but simple. (p. 65)

Dun's Review (Smith, 1975) highlighted the reentry issue as the toughest assignment of all for a returning executive:

Few, if any, executives ever come out ahead financially in a transfer back to the U.S. . . . An even more serious shock than the financial shock, because it can have a long-range impact on the executive's career, is the re-adaptation to corporate life. . . . A foreign assignment tends to . . . keep the executive out of the mainstream of advancement. . . . In some respects the more outstanding a performer the executive was overseas, the more uncomfortable his return will be. (p. 72).

Because many key MNC management personnel are on foreign assignment, we might expect to find corporations paying particular attention to the problems they face on returning to the parent country, but in light of the dearth of published research or anecdotal reports, this does *not* appear to be the case.

Three exploratory studies, however, have surveyed former expatriate managers and their families with the objective of helping MNCs and their expatriate managers to plan for and adapt to the reentry process. Each of these studies is concerned with the repatriation of managerial personnel in North America. Their foreign assignments covered the globe, although most frequently included Africa, Asia, Australia, the Caribbean, England, Europe, Mexico, the Middle East, and South America.

Murray (1973) observed that expatriates and their families returning to the United States after an average 4½-year assignment experienced a "cultural shock in reverse." According to Murray, only a few of the participating companies had a formal repatriation policy. Companies that tried to formalize their procedures for implementing a repatriation program appeared to follow the same guidelines as those for their domestic personnel transfer procedures, that is, they provided relocation assistance only for transportation of the family and compensation for setting up the new household. Returning executives had little or no choice in selecting domestic assignments. The salary levels and fringe benefits the executives and their families had on the foreign assignment were lost. The MNCs did not recognize or take full advantage of the skills that managers had developed, nor of the experience acquired, during their foreign assignments. Illustrative of two specific situations are the case studies presented in Cases A and B at the end of the chapter.

Adler (1980) observed that employees found reentry into their home country and home company more difficult than the initial move to the foreign culture. This was true for employees returning from all areas of the world and from all types of assignments. Moreover, upon their return, the managerial skills that expatriates had enhanced abroad generally were neither recognized nor utilized by home-country organizations, thus confirming Murray's earlier finding. Also, home-country managerial colleagues' perceptions of effective reentry behavior differed from that of the returning expatriates. Home-country managers evaluated returnees most highly when they did not have characteristics of "foreigners" and did not use their cross-cultural learning in their domestic job. These domestic managers evaluated as most effective those returnees who had the least overseas experience and least contact with non-home-country cultures. In contrast, returnees saw themselves as most effective when integrating the foreign and the home-country experiences and actively using the skills gained overseas.

Howard's (1980) investigation of the returning overseas managers' problems found that the high rate of inflation and the increasing cost of living in the United States hit the returnees especially hard. The very high cost of housing was particularly shocking. Other returning managers encountered the problem of no job or no suitable job. Many expatriates expressed resentment and dismay over the type of job and career opportunities offered. Others found themselves coming back to an organization in which important career and professional opportunities had passed them by. Howard attributed this phenomenon to an "out-of-sight, out-of-mind" mentality, as well as to top management's continued apathy toward the company's international operations and expatriate personnel.

Returning executives mentioned other problems as well. A number reported a loss of managerial authority and major functional responsibilities. Others reported that uncertainty about the length of their overseas stay adversely affected their life-styles, their ability to plan for their future professional careers, and their children's education. A number of returnees reported experiencing something akin to what Murray termed "culture shock in reverse" (1973); this led to a variety of adjustment problems to the social and moral environments, and to the tempo of American life. Finally, all returnees complained about losing social and professional prestige on returning home. In most cases, they had to give up a company-supported "high style" of living that included fringe benefits, chauffeur-driven company cars, company-paid domestic help, and so forth. They had reverted to a less glamorous social life following their return to the United States.

The similarity of results from these three studies indicates the importance of MNCs' taking a critical look at repatriation programs to avoid traumatizing their returning overseas executives. A properly designed and implemented repatriation program—one that encompasses the professional, financial, and personal facets of the repatriation process and has the blessing of top management—can begin to help expatriates meet the challenges facing them on returning home.

In summary, both the MNC and the managers in foreign assignments face difficult challenges from the chosen staffing policy's effectiveness. Whether or not these challenges are met successfully is largely based on the MNC's ability to locate and tap sources of managerial workforce, to select those applicants with the highest potential for international management success and prepare them for their foreign assignments, and to continue to develop their skills and abilities while they are abroad. The critical importance of these human resource management functions (recruiting, selection, and education/development) will become apparent as we examine their general purposes for developing an effective strategy in staffing the MNC foreign subsidiary.

HUMAN RESOURCE MANAGEMENT APPROACHES FOR MEETING THE CHALLENGES OF INTERNATIONAL ASSIGNMENT

Having identified the major challenges of an international assignment, we might next logically consider how these challenges should be met. Yet it would be premature to seek solutions without clearly marking off the parameters of the international manager's job, as well as the parameters of the organizational and cultural climates in which that job exists. In developing an effective staffing strategy, the next consideration should therefore be assessment of the job, the subsidiary organization, and the host-country culture.

Job, Organizational, and Cultural Analyses

Analyses of the job, the organization, and the culture are necessary as a basis for any human resource program; after all, these factors describe the work setting in human terms. Assuming that the operation had identified its overseas human resource needs, these analyses represent the foundation of any staffing function (see Figure 12.3).

Job analysis serves as a basis for identifying the human behaviors necessary for adequate job performance. As a consequence of identifying such behaviors, hunches or theories about the kinds of people the job requires can be formulated and procedures for identifying, or training, such people can be developed. Analysts can then test the effectiveness of these procedures (by either *predictive* or *concurrent* validation). Another outcome of identifying necessary human behaviors is the development of standards against which the behavior of employees (and therefore the effectiveness of the staffing program) can be evaluated. If we know what behaviors are required for adequate performance, we can evaluate performance against those standards. This also allows us to develop means for responding to performance deficiencies.

Organizational analysis is necessary because research shows that several features of the organization in general—and not just the job in particular—affect human behavior in the work setting. Leadership, supervision, organizational reward systems, and organizational style (or corporate culture) all have both direct and indirect effects on employee behavior.

Last, *cultural analysis* is analogous to examining the characteristics of various domestic geographical regions before marketing a new product. In a cross-cultural context, cultural analysis provides the invaluable service of identifying and categorizing the situational variables in the host-country environment that influence the manager's adjustment and performance. In some cross-cultural circumstances, for example, individuals are assigned to work for a short time in cultures resembling their own. They deal almost exclusively with individuals from their own company: they live in company housing and interact socially with members of the expatriate community. The requirements for success in

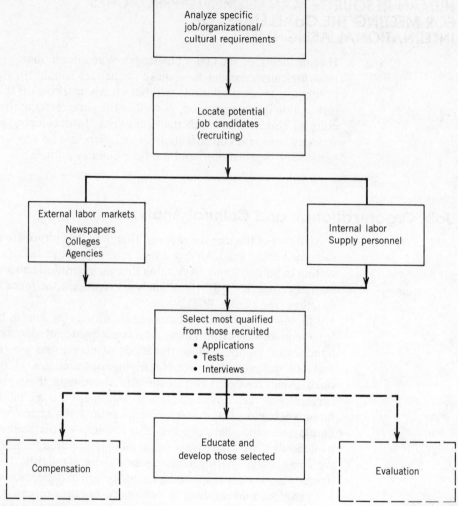

Figure 12.3 Staffing functions.

this environment would be considerably different from the requirements for individuals assigned to unfamiliar cultures for a longer duration and working and living primarily with host-country nationals.

Job, organizational, and cultural analyses serve to determine the *criteria* for recruiting, selecting, educating, and developing potential international managers. For example, in the first of the two cross-cultural circumstances described above, technical skills might count more heavily than behavioral, social, or communicative skills, and adjustment and effectiveness might be more important than transfer of skills or participation in the culture. In the second situation, the weighting scheme would probably be the reverse. These two extreme situations illustrate the potential value of systematically accounting for job, organizational, and cultural factors when forming an effective international staffing system. A number of empirical investigations have examined the criteria that MNC personnel use when making international staffing decisions. Other research has considered views of expatriate managers themselves. A sampling of this research and a summary of the findings appears in the following sections.

Criteria for Human Resource Management

Views of MNC Staffing Personnel   In-depth interviews and surveys of MNC personnel responsible for staffing decisions have identified a number of factors that are potentially critical for managers' effectiveness overseas. These "selection managers" appear to discount the significance of the candidate's ability to live and work successfully in a foreign environment; instead, they consider technical and managerial skills to be of primary importance (Miller, 1972; 1973). Kapoor and McKay's (1971) study of training for multinational marketing also shows that technical knowledge and past performance are primary considerations for overseas assignments.

Past achievement has also emerged as one of two general criteria (the other is professed willingness to be transferred) typically used to select third-country national managers for key overseas jobs (Zeira & Harari, 1977). The research points out, however, that these two selection criteria are not sufficient, because they do not predict the individual's success in coping with the variety of problems that international managers encounter.

Tung's research (1979; 1981; 1982a; 1984) suggests that criteria for selecting international managerial candidates may vary according to managerial level. From Table 12.3, we can see that in positions requiring more extensive contact with the local community (i.e., chief executive officer, responsible for overseeing and directing the entire foreign operation, and functional head, responsible for establishing functional departments in a foreign subsidiary), attributes such as "adaptability, flexibility in new environmental settings," "maturity and emotional stability," and "communication" were cited more frequently as very important. Compare these results with those for positions that are more technically oriented (i.e., troubleshooter, responsible for analyzing and solving specific operational problems, and operative, responsible for first-level management).

The work of Zeira et al. referred to earlier (Zeira, 1979; Zeira & Harari, 1979) has stressed the importance of very similar selection criteria for prospective senior international managers. These criteria include the ability to learn the host environment's characteristics, to adapt behavior to the host-country organization's expectations, and to withstand pressures of conformity to the corporate headquarters' expectations when such pressures conflict with legitimate expectations of the host-country organization. These authors advocate using additional selection criteria inferred from certain personal and managerial patterns of behavior, the absence of which host-country organizations find disturbing. These criteria include politeness, punctuality, tactfulness, integrity,

Table 12.3 Selection Criteria Used for Different Job Categories

Criteria	Chief Executive Officer, %			Functional Head, %			Trouble-shooter, %			Operative, %		
	Criterion Not Used	Used, Not Important	Used, Very Important	Criterion Not Used	Used, Not Important	Used, Very Important	Criterion Not Used	Used, Not Important	Used, Very Important	Criterion Not Used	Used, Not Important	Used, Very Important
Experience in company	1	16	83	1	31	68	11	31	58	39	24	37
Technical knowledge of business	0	21	79	1	8	91	0	11	89	11	21	68
Knowledge of language of host country	24	50	26	7	51	42	13	62	25	16	38	46
Overall experience and education	1	12	87	2	17	81	10	21	69	7	41	52
Managerial talent	0	4	96	0	14	86	30	54	16	41	41	18
Interest in overseas work	6	29	65	10	28	62	17	43	40	16	25	59
Initiative, creativity	5	11	84	5	13	82	4	14	82	16	32	52
Independence	11	25	64	16	37	48	10	33	57	30	48	22
Previous overseas experience	24	51	25	23	55	22	31	56	13	45	43	12
Respect for culture of host country	24	8	68	22	8	70	25	25	50	18	11	71
Sex	68	19	14	69	22	9	75	23	2	74	19	7
Age	70	20	10	64	31	5	80	14	6	70	20	10
Stability of marital relationship	33	32	35	42	24	34	59	25	16	49	22	29
Spouse's and family's adaptability	11	28	61	13	24	63	37	23	40	22	29	49
Adaptability, flexibility in new environment	5	12	83	5	19	76	16	38	46	7	31	62
Maturity, emotional stability	1	9	94	1	1	98	8	17	75	1	11	86
Communicative ability	5	8	97	7	8	85	9	32	59	5	42	53
Same criteria as other comparable jobs at home	8	16	76	6	16	88	12	20	49	5	24	71

Source: R. L. Tung. "Selection and Training of Personnel for Overseas Assignments." *Columbia Journal of World Business* 16:68–78 (Spring 1981).

sensitivity, reliability, tolerance, empathy, self-confidence, self-educability, and orderliness.

Considered together, the research to date points to the continuing gap between the opinions and behaviors of managers selecting individuals for management positions abroad and, on the other hand, the recommendations of international management researchers concerned with candidates' qualifications for overseas management jobs. By accenting technical knowledge and work experience, Miller's study and Kapoor and McKay's work represent the typical position that managers take when involved in making overseas selection decisions. Alternatively, Tung and Zeira's emphasis on the manager's personal qualifications is typical of the international management scholars' perspective.

Views of Expatriate Managers   When interviewed, expatriate managers have expressed views more in line with management scholars than with selection managers. Early work by Gonzalez and Negandhi (1967) examined the views of a large sample (1161) of U.S. expatriates in forty countries. They found that the wife and family's adaptability and the manager's leadership were the most important contributors to an ideal background for an overseas career (see Table 12.4). The importance of the manager's personal characteristics also showed up as significant in Rubin, Askling, and Kealey's (1977) study—one of the few empirical studies on the effectiveness of North Americans (in this case, Canadians) overseas. These researchers found that beyond technical competence, successful and unsuccessful expatriate managers differed in their ability to engage in meaningful two-way communication, empathy, respect for host-country nationals, ability to be subjective, openness, integration of task and relationship dimensions of the job, tolerance for ambiguity, and goal-directed persistence in the face of setbacks.

Similarly, a pilot study of multinational corporations conducted by the Chase World Information Center (Haemmerli, 1978) found that the ability to adapt to the environmental context, to notice and absorb details, to form sincere and trustful personal relations that inspire confidence, to demonstrate a capacity for sensitivity and empathy, and to demonstrate reliability by avoiding excessive promises were all necessary qualities for effective functioning in a foreign country. These studies also clarify the personal abilities required for effective international management, and they suggest a wide range of attitudes and behaviors than those commonly associated with domestic management.

Almost never mentioned in the literature are the criteria used to recruit and select women managers. Although this may not be an issue in U.S.-based MNCs, where the candidate's gender is not considered an important selection criterion, it seems particularly salient for West European and Japanese MNCs, which acknowledge that there are problems in assigning women as expatriates because of some societies' attitudes toward working women (Tung, 1982a).

Table 12.4   Ideal Background for an Overseas Career

Wife and family adaptable	20%
Leadership ability	19
Knowledge of job	14
Knowledge of language of host country	13
Well educated	13
Respect for laws and people of host country	12
Previous overseas experience	4
Desire to serve overseas	4
Miscellaneous	1
Total	100%

Source: Richard F. Gonzalez and Anant R. Negandhi. *The United States Overseas Executive: His Orientation and Career Patterns.* East Lansing: Michigan State University, Graduate School of Business Administration, 1967, p. 113.

One study of a small mixed sample of male and female expatriates has suggested that a woman expatriate manager must have accumulated considerable managerial experience at headquarters, including a list of achievements and proven qualifications (Izraeli et al., 1980). She should be in midcareer, "mature," and not ambivalent about becoming the top authority in the subsidiary, moving her children, or changing her husband's status in his own family or career (assuming that she has a husband and children). These criteria appear to accentuate a relatively equal mix of personal and professional qualifications, perhaps representing a compromise between the views of MNC staffing personnel and expatriate managers.

Comparative Views   The distinction between MNC selection managers criteria and those considered essential by expatriate managers becomes even more blurred when we examine research investigations comparing the two types of managers in the same study. Ivancevich's 1969 study of 127 U.S.-based MNCs showed that American executives in charge of selection considered three factors very important: (1) independence and ability to achieve results with limited resources, (2) sincerity, and (3) technical knowledge of the potential job. Selection managers rated a person's previous overseas experience and youthfulness as least important. In contrast, American expatriate managers chose the following three criteria as most important: (1) the wife's opinion about undertaking a foreign assignment, (2) sincerity, and (3) attitude and adaptability. This study seems to verify the difference between the MNC selection managers' expectations and the expatriate managers' pragmatic considerations; yet its findings have failed to receive confirmation in two more recent investigations.

Hayes (1972) showed that both chief personnel officers of MNCs and expatriate managers ranked job ability (technical skill, organizational ability, belief in mission) as of primary importance for success in an expatriate assignment. Both groups of managers also ranked relational abilities (ability to deal with local nationals, cultural empathy) and family situation (adaptiveness and supportiveness) as more important than language ability and local environment. Personnel managers ranked relational abilities ahead of family situation. No clear difference between the rankings of the two criteria appeared among the expatriate managers. Russell and Dickinson (1979) found no difference in the weighting of criteria between American managers involved in selecting employees for foreign assignments and American managers recently or currently overseas on assignment. Both groups of managers weighted the acceptability of the assignment to the candidate and his or her family significantly greater than all other criteria. Similarly, both groups weighted skill in interpersonal relations significantly greater than skill in planning and organizing, host language proficiency, and technical ability, and adaptability greater than host language proficiency and technical ability.

Several tentative conclusions may be drawn from this research. First, the criteria of technical ability, interpersonal-relational skills, adaptability, and family support appear to be the most critical variables that must be considered in developing an effective managerial recruiting, selection, and education/ development strategy for international assignments. The research reported here supports typical nonempirical views (see Boxes 12.1 and 12.2; also, Blue & Haynes, 1977; Heller, 1980; Noer, 1975). It is in general agreement with the actual selection policies of U.S.-based MNCs (Table 12.5). Second, it is unclear whether selection managers and managers on recent or current assignments overseas differ significantly in their perspectives regarding the most important job criteria. It may be that the factors critical to expatriate success actually resemble the factors used in the selection of individuals for these positions. More comparative research seems advisable before definitive conclusions can be reached.

With an understanding of the criteria necessary to staff the international managerial ranks of an MNC effectively, we should now consider how such criteria guide each component of the staffing process.

Recruiting

Sources for Recruiting Recruiting is a process of identifying people who fit the configuration of the job and the organization in terms of (1) intelligence, (2) aptitudes, (3) interests, (4) desired rewards, and (5) organizational goals. The recruiting activity itself may be preselective, through choosing among the various sources of supply, and through the decision about which candidates should be permitted to go through subsequent screening procedures. In the present context, recruiting concerns the MNC's ability to attract available candidates, both within the organization and from outside, whose capabilities and desires match the organization's present or future needs for international operation management, or both.

Candidates for overseas assignment originate both within the organization and outside. The vast majority of American managers overseas have generally come from within the organization (Baker & Ivancevich, 1971; Prasad & Krishna Shetty, 1976). A survey of sixty-four U.S.-based MNCs and their government agencies has found this to be particularly true in the automotive and machinery, electronics and communications, banking, construction, and consulting/research industries (Holmen, 1980). Furthermore, the key managerial positions in subsidiaries generally go to insiders (Brooke & Remmers, 1978; Prasad & Krishna Shetty, 1976). These individuals typically receive recommendations from fellow managers or other colleagues; they are either expatriates located in other regional divisions of the company or managers in domestic divisions (Miller, 1973). One of the reasons for this practice is that successful insiders take the corporate presence abroad; this is difficult for an outsider. However, if the sole criterion for recruitment from within is the manager's success in domestic operations, then overlooking the special challenges of overseas assignments can lead to increased managerial job failures. We will address this issue further in the discussion of selection criteria.

When an MNC uses outside people, they are generally from other companies (Prasad & Krishna Shetty, 1976), typically expatriate managers who have es-

Box 12.1

Selecting Foreign Executives

The success of any foreign operation is contingent upon the caliber of its manager. Choosing the right man to fill the top managerial posts abroad requires special talent, but talent that can be assisted by a list of the characteristics and skills that a successful overseas manager should have.

The editors of BI, with the assistance of many experienced international firms, have put together a 60-point checklist of factors that should be considered in picking the right man for the right job. What counts most is not the possession of an excellent score on each of them but the total composite—plus, at least, a passing score on all of them.

Even a perfect score may not mean success. Many firms have thought they had the ideal man only to find some psychological quirk explode when the executive found himself in a strange new land. One basic rule that might be followed: do not send a man to a top foreign managerial assignment until he has served abroad in a minor capacity for some time. The list:

Basic Characteristics

1. Zeal for work.
2. Ability to get along with other people.
3. Ability to develop others.
4. Persuasiveness.
5. Resourcefulness.
6. Initiative and imagination.
7. Self-sufficiency.
8. Ability to make decisions.
9. Alertness.
10. Foresight.
11. Ability to plan ahead.
12. Ability to judge people.
13. Intellectual curiosity.
14. Responsibility.
15. Objectivity.
16. Flexibility.
17. Salesmanship.
18. Self-discipline.
19. Honesty.

20. Ability to learn new facts.
21. Ability to learn foreign languages.
22. Adaptability to new ideas, new cultures, and new challenges.

Experience Factors

23. Technical competence.
24. Professional, business, and management experience.
25. Past performance.
26. Knowledge of company markets, products, policies, and goals.
27. Willingness to conform to corporate policies.
28. Previous exposure to foreign cultures and markets.
29. Efficiency.
30. Knowledge of job to which he is to be assigned.
31. Record of ability to delegate.
32. Record of success at hiring others.
33. Record of evaluating and developing others.
34. Ability to express himself, orally and in writing.
35. Profit-mindedness.
36. Open-mindedness to new ideas.
37. Attitude toward foreigners.
38. Toleration of foreign cultures.
39. Lack of fixed prejudices.
40. Corporate loyalty.
41. Cooperativeness.

Environmental Factors

42. Knowledge of firms' international operations and methods.
43. Knowledge of local language.
44. Knowledge of foreign market to which he is to be assigned.
45. Contacts in foreign market to which he is to be assigned.

Personal Factors

46. Motivation for seeking or accepting a foreign assignment.

47. Age.
48. Health.
49. Ethnic origin, insofar as it bears on the country to which the man will be sent.
50. Nationality.
51. Family status.
52. Nationality and attitude of wife.
53. Number and age of children.
54. Health of wife and children.
55. Personal appeal.

56. Personal habits, traits, and attire.
57. Dignity and integrity.
58. Emotional stability.
59. Sociability.
60. Sense of humor.

Source: Business International Corporation. *151 Check-lists—Decision-Making in International Operations.* New York: Business International Corporation, 1974.

tablished themselves in their industries and are host-country or third-country nationals (Brooke & Remmers, 1978). Host-country nationals are recruited within their own country but may be appointed by some central or regional authority if the management position is sufficiently high level. Third-country nationals may come from a wide variety of sources; for example, some companies use worldwide job advertising.

Colleges and universities are, of course, the major source for recruiting candidates for company operations at home and abroad. Japanese and European-based MNCs follow similar practices. This practice is much less prevalent in less-developed countries, where newspaper advertising, employment exchanges, and word-of-mouth are the most popular means of attracting new workers. Private employment agencies are common in European countries, and a number of American management recruiting and consulting firms have also established offices in major European cities to help MNCs in their recruiting endeavors. In Japan, establishing close contact with higher educational institutions and making requirements known to authorities is an acceptable practice.

Another source that some American and European firms have tapped is foreign students and trainees temporarily residing in their countries. This source may provide well-qualified applicants for future managerial positions in a firm's international operations. For example, the large number of foreign students who are pursuing advanced studies in science, engineering, and business in the United States may represent the proper combination of understanding of the host-country environment and exposure to American management processes and behavior. This recruitment source, however, has remained surprisingly underutilized despite these individuals' willingness to be employed by U.S.-based MNCs (e.g., Alpander, 1973).

Yet another surprisingly (or not so surprisingly) underutilized resource are female managerial candidates from either the home country or abroad. It appears that women are implicitly and explicitly excluded from overseas assignment through (1) self-selection (i.e., not applying for available positions or turning down positions when offered) (2) corporate selection (i.e., failing to receive initial consideration or being rejected during the selection process), and (3) foreign country selection (i.e., rejection by foreign country officials and

Box 12.2

How to Pick a Good Expatriate

Almost every international company knows how much easier it is to transfer an executive from city to city within a country than to send him across borders to work in a foreign environment. A company that transfers a manager to a foreign post invests more money and time on that move than any five domestic moves—and it wants its decision on the man to send to be a right one.

But there are no perfected techniques available to management to ensure that the individuals chosen for an overseas assignment will succeed in it. Most companies agree that the tests designed for this purpose by industrial psychologists do not adequately provide the predictive measures needed. Extensive interviews of candidates (and their wives) and evaluations by senior executives still ultimately provide the best method of selection.

But the process is still not easy. Competence and success at home do not always guarantee an individual's success in a foreign environment. Domestic success may be an important and necessary factor, but it rarely suffices. It is evident that in addition to ability, the executive, who is to be posted abroad, must possess many extra characteristics and attitudes.

The checklist below focuses on those factors considered by the managements of many international companies to be the most crucial when considering a candidate for a foreign assignment. It is not intended to be an exhaustive list. The first part indicates those general characteristics considered essential, and the second part focuses on ones related more specifically to business.

I. General Characteristics

What is his motivation? A candidate for an expatriate executive position should have a positive and constructive reason for seeking or accepting an overseas assignment (e.g., wishing to act as a bridge between cultures). Firms should be skeptical of those candidates who ask for an assignment overseas simply to escape domestic problems or difficulties, either on-the-job or personal, in an attempt to seek a new identity elsewhere. (Detailed interviews may be necessary to determine the exact reasons, and negative motivation may not always be apparent at first glance.)

One indication of positive motivation is evidence of the candidate's previous concern with and commitment to foreign interests (e.g., study of a foreign language; courses taken in international affairs, economics; vacation travel to foreign countries, etc.).

Is he independent? Can he make and stand by his own decisions? He cannot rely on the home office for support and guidance in every situation. He must be willing to be held accountable for the consequences (both favorable and unfavorable) of his actions.

Is he resourceful? He must be able to reach objectives and produce results with whatever personnel and facilities he has available, regardless of the limitations and barriers that may arise. Even the simplest tasks, easily accomplished at home, may be difficult to perform in a strange environment.

Is he resilient? Can he bounce back after major and minor setbacks? The executive in a foreign country has less control over factors that may directly or indirectly affect business operations. He has to function with a greater degree of uncertainty, and is subject to the whims of the host country. Nevertheless, he must be able to function effectively and to avoid demoralization under these conditions.

Does he have the intellectual capacity? The expatriate executive has to deal with several dimensions simultaneously, and complex situations often arise. He should have a good analytical mind, and be able to collect and organize factual data (often incomplete) needed to make necessary conclusions and judgments.

Is he tolerant? He must maintain a noncritical attitude toward foreign culture patterns, and avoid judging others by his own values and standards. However, he should not carry this to the extent where it becomes impossible to accomplish objectives. He should be able to "work around" the constraints in a foreign country rather than passively accepting them.

What is his wife's attitude? Her attitudes toward his assignment and foreign cultures generally, and her ability to adjust to the new environment deeply affect the executive's success or failure.

II. Business Factors

Does he have technical competence? He should have the necessary business knowledge and skills to accomplish company goals. His past performance should demonstrate his capacity to achieve objectives.

Can he represent the company to foreign governments, banks, etc.? The expatriate executive, by virtue of his position as liaison between the home company and foreign operations, acts as an official representative of the company in the foreign location. For this reason, his demeanor should exemplify the positive characteristics that the company wishes to project.

Is he good at judging people? He should be able to evaluate, for example, local nationals working in the company and their potential for transfer to the parent company's headquarters operations or third country.

Is he imaginative in business dealings? He should be able to find new ways of doing things if the conventional methods are inappropriate or unacceptable in the foreign environment (e.g., arranging barter deals in Eastern Europe).

Will he be able to train successfully a local national to replace him? This factor becomes more crucial as companies develop policies that emphasize more participation of local nationals at all company levels.

Will he be able to explain cogently the aims and company philosophy to the local manager and workers? Conversely, he must be able to communicate effectively to company headquarters the views of local management.

Will he be able to make and develop contacts with his peers (i.e., nationals of the country who are counterparts in local companies) in the foreign country? This may be a crucial factor that determines proper social adjustment not only for the executive but also for his wife.

Source: Business International Corporation. *151 Checklists—Decision-Making in International Operations.* New York: Business International Corporation, 1974.

Table 12.5 Criteria for Selecting Executives for Overseas Operations: How Seventy Companies Make Selections

Criterion	Number of Times Mentioned	Percentage of Companies Citing
Experience	30	42.9
Adaptability, flexibility	28	40.0
Technical knowledge of business	24	34.3
Competence, ability, past performance	24	34.3
Managerial talent	16	22.9
Language skills/ability	8	11.4
Potential	7	10.0
Interest in overseas work, executive ambition	7	10.0
Appreciation of new management, sensitivity	5	7.1
Education	4	5.7
Initiative, creativity	4	5.7
Independence	3	4.3
Communication	3	4.3
Maturity, emotional stability	2	2.9
Same criteria as for other comparable jobs	2	2.9

Source: Business International Corporation. *Compensating International Executives.* New York: Business International Corporation, 1978, p. 2.

managers at either the predeparture stage—refusing visas—or in the country, by ignoring them or sending them home) (Adler, 1983). Most "deselection" decisions appear to be based on the assumption that women will not be effective overseas or that they do not want to travel or be relocated overseas. Apparently both the corporate managers responsible for overseas assignments and the potential women candidates themselves hold these assumptions (Adler, 1983).

Managers' Willingness to Accept an International Assignment   Simply identifying viable candidates for present or future positions is not enough; firms must consider the candidates' willingness to accept an international assignment as well. This becomes a particularly critical variable when one considers that despite high salaries, fewer people are now willing to work abroad (Freemantle, 1978; see Figure 12.4). Miller and Cheng (1978) describe the results of a study designed to examine the reasons American expatriates chose to accept their current overseas assignment. Although respondents considered an opportunity to go overseas a mixed blessing (because of the "challenges" presented earlier in this chapter), they considered the assignment a necessary step for preparing themselves for future moves into the MNC's top management positions. They were attracted by the opportunities for increased pay and the display of their technical competence under different circumstances.

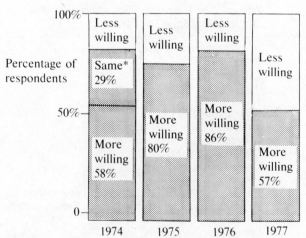

*Note. In 1974 the question was worded differently with "same" being a choice.

Figure 12.4   Willingness to work overseas.

Source: "Working Abroad 1977." Business Division Consultant Ltd. Cited in D. Freemantle. "Foreign Assignment: A Recruiter's Nightmare." *Personnel Management*, October 1978, pp. 33–37.

The results also support the conclusions of earlier research (Cleveland, Mangone, & Adams, 1960; Gonzalez & Negandhi, 1967) that motives for *remaining* overseas are related to, but not the same as, those for expatriates who have accepted an overseas assignment for the first time. Apparently, American expatriate managers who have experience overseas and have chosen to accept additional international assignments perceive the additional overseas experience as an opportunity to improve their careers and promotion potential in the international business arena; they also consider it an opportunity to gain greater job responsibility. These motives resemble those of inexperienced expatriates. The sharpest distinction between the two groups is that experienced expatriates consider the additional international assignments as contributing little to their future advancement into the ranks of the MNC's top management. It appears that the experienced expatriate managers have made the career choice to remain in the international business arena, and the possibility of future promotions into the company's upper management is no longer a viable option or has little interest or appeal.

Successfully recruiting international managerial candidates—whether from inside or outside the MNC, or experienced or inexperienced in foreign assignment—is the first step toward an effective strategy for staffing the MNC. The second step is to develop the means of selecting the "best" recruits.

Selection Methods

Once the recruiting process is completed, the primary screening activity is the examination of recruited candidates by collecting and analyzing additional specific information. This stage involves predictions about the desirability of hiring each candidate and the probability of the candidate's meeting the performance requirements and other expectations of a specific position. In the present context, selection refers not only to the particular methods or techniques used in assessing candidates for international management positions but also to the conceptual system underlying the categories of variables to be assessed—for example, how one assesses "willingness" and "ability."

Interviews with human resource executives have indicated their agreement that selecting the candidate for an overseas position is *the* deciding factor in the assignment's success or failure (Heller, 1980). However, there appears to be relatively little variation among the methods used by MNCs for international selection and no systematic application.

What are the predominant methods of selection? The most common are tests, interviews, and assessment centers.

Tests   The use of tests in the screening process appears to be an almost "outmoded" approach, especially for higher-level positions (Brooke & Remmers, 1978). Since the early 1970s, 79.5% of foreign operations managers of 127 large American firms operating overseas reported that their companies had not used tests for technical competence in the selection process (Baker & Ivancevich, 1971). As we enter the 1980s, this figure has increased to 97% for 80

U.S.-based MNCs, 95% for 35 Japanese-based MNCs, and 86% for 29 West European-based MNCs (Tung, 1982a). The lack of explicit criteria for overseas success, as well as the time and cost factors involved, have been suggested as the primary reasons for the decreasing use of tests (Heller, 1980).

It appears that this decline in testing extends even to the examination of the candidate's *relational abilities*. In the Tung investigation (1982), only 5% of the U.S.-based MNCs and 21% of the West European-based MNCs reported using such tests. None of the Japanese firms was using them. The figure for U.S.-based MNCs is particularly surprising, considering these firms' recognition that relational abilities are important criteria for overseas work, and also considering the extant research showing relational abilities to be crucial for success in overseas assignments. The American firms that did test candidates' relational abilities described such tests as including judgment by seniors, psychological appraisal, and interviews by a consulting psychologist with both candidate and spouse. In the European sample, the most common device was psychological testing, which appeared even more often than in the U.S.-based MNCs.

The value of psychological tests, however, may be particularly questionable, given their potential for cultural bias and their relatively low validity. However, an indication of attitudinal or personal sensitivity to differing cultural environments may give at least an indication of managers' adaptability to their new environment (Brooke & Remmers, 1978). The most promising of these measures is perhaps the California Test (the Indirect Scale for Ethnocentrism), because current (though limited) data suggest that high ethnocentrism correlates with overseas job failure (Robinson, 1978). Various thematic apperception tests (TAT) may be useful in disclosing such characteristics as prejudice, stereotyping, and a compulsion to view things in terms of absolute universal values. These characteristics are undesirable for overseas managers; they suggest an incapacity or unwillingness to perceive the cultural relativity of either personal behavior or corporate strategy.

Interviews   Selection managers generally agree that extensive interviews of candidates (and their spouses) by senior executives still ultimately provide the best method of selection (Heller, 1980). Interviews may be particularly useful for filtering out candidates who are especially likely to fail abroad. An interview worksheet, similar to that in Box 12.3, can serve to structure the candidate's evaluation. Selection managers should rate a potential expatriate as either satisfactory or unsatisfactory on each of the criteria listed in the table. Although there is no agreement concerning the positive features that differentiate an international manager from a domestic one, two negative norms have appeared: (1) the executive who likes to go abroad for short trips but does not want to live outside his home country and (2) the executive who professes an interest only in certain subsidiary locations but not in others. The former should not be selected. The latter, though perhaps better motivated for overseas assignments, may not be sufficiently international-minded (Heller, 1980).

Moreover, it appears that interviewing candidates (or candidates and their spouses) for international assignment is not only the best but also the most

Box 12.3

Interview Worksheet for International Candidates

Motivation
- Investigate reasons and degree of interest in wanting to be considered.
- Determine desire to work abroad, verified by previous concerns such as personal travel, language training, reading, and association with foreign employees or students.
- Determine whether the candidate has a realistic understanding of what working and living abroad requires.
- Determine the basic attitudes of the spouse toward an overseas assignment.

Health
- Determine whether any medical problems of the candidate or his family might be critical to the success of the assignment.
- Determine whether he is in good physical and mental health, without any foreseeable change.

Language Ability
- Determine potential for learning a new language.
- Determine any previous language(s) studied or oral ability (judge against language needed on the overseas assignment).
- Determine the ability of the spouse to meet the language requirements.

Family Considerations
- How many moves has the family made in the past between different cities or parts of the United States?
- What problems were encountered?
- How recent was the last move?
- What is the spouse's goal in this move?
- What are the number of children and the ages of each?
- Has divorce or its potential, death of a family member, etc., weakened family solidarity?
- Will all the children move; why, why not?
- What is the location, health, and living arrangements of grandparents, and the number of trips normally made to their home each year?

- Are there any special adjustment problems that you would expect?
- How is each member of the family reacting to this possible move?
- Do special educational problems exist within the family?

Resourcefulness and Initiative
- Is the candidate independent; can he make and stand by his decisions and judgments?
- Does he have the intellectual capacity to deal with several dimensions simultaneously?
- Is he able to reach objectives and produce results with whatever personnel and facilities he has available, regardless of the limitations and barriers that might arise?
- Can the candidate operate without a clear definition of responsibility and authority on a foreign assignment?
- Will the candidate be able to explain the aims and company philosophy to the local managers and workers?
- Does he possess sufficient self-reliance, self-discipline, and self-confidence to overcome difficulties or handle complex problems?
- Can the candidate work without supervision?
- Can the candidate operate effectively in a foreign environment without normal communications and supporting services?

Adaptability
- Is the candidate sensitive to others, open to the opinions of others, cooperative, and able to compromise?
- What are his reactions to new situations, and efforts to understand and appreciate differences?
- Is he culturally sensitive, aware, and able to relate across the culture?
- Does the candidate understand his own culturally derived values?
- How does the candidate react to criticism?
- What is his understanding of the U.S. government system?
- Will he be able to make and develop contacts with his peers in the foreign country?

Continued on page 538

- Does he have patience when dealing with problems?
- Is he resilient; can he bounce back after setbacks?

Career Planning
- Does the candidate consider the assignment anything other than a temporary overseas trip?
- Is the move consistent with his progression and that planned by the company?
- Is his career planning realistic?
- What is the candidate's basic attitude toward the company?
- Is there any history or indication of personnel problems with this employee?

Financial
- Are there any current financial and/or legal considerations which might affect the assignment, e.g., house purchase, children and college expenses, car purchases?
- Are financial considerations negative factors, i.e., will undue pressures be brought to bear on the employee or his family as a result of the assignment?

Source: D. M. Noer. *Multinational People Management: A Guide for Organizations and Employees.* Washington, DC: Bureau of National Affairs, 1975.

frequently employed method of selection. Tung's investigation of U.S.-, Japanese-, and West European-based MNCs (1982a) revealed that 52% of the U.S.-based firms conducted interviews with both candidate and spouse; 47% conducted interviews with the candidate only; and 1% did not conduct any interviews at all. West European-based firms were similar, with 41% of the companies interviewing both candidate and spouse; and the remaining 59% interviewed the candidate only. The relatively high percentage of MNCs who interviewed both the candidate and the spouse lends support to other researchers' contention that MNCs are becoming increasingly aware of the significance of the spouse's adjustment to a foreign environment and its contribution to managerial performance abroad (Borrman, 1968; Harris & Harris, 1972; Hayes, 1974).

An example of an optimal interviewing format that includes at least one interview involving the spouse is Mobil's "Four-Hour Environmental Interview." At Mobil, the manager of international placement and staffing, along with two assistants (each with twenty or more years of foreign experience) conduct these interviews (Alexander, 1970). The first part of the interview covers actual living conditions in the host country. Interviewers show slides and undertake a discussion of the culture. The second part of the interview focuses on the interaction between the participants, particularly between the employee and the spouse. The interviewers attempt to get beyond many spouses' natural inclinations to make reassuring statements about living abroad—statements that represent a desire to help their partner despite real doubts about their own reactions. Some of these doubts usually emerge in the discussion. In the later stages of the interview, the give and take between the husband and wife provides the personnel executives with a sense of the chances of successfully resolving any interpersonal conflict. Additionally, the candidate undergoes at least one interview regarding the technical aspects of the job. The firm makes a job offer (including a description of salary and benefits) after a few days, and the candidate has about two weeks to respond.

A growing number of companies are adapting an interview assessment technique called adaptability screening (*Business Week,* 1979). Its objective is to make the expatriate's family aware of the different types of stresses and crises that could arise overseas and to prevent failure by giving the family a chance to say no before the transfer. The interview is conducted either by a professional staff psychologist or psychiatrist or by a personnel director trained in the techniques. The interviewer tries to alert the expatriate manager and the spouse to personal issues (e.g., their bonds to church or civic organizations) involved in a transfer; the interviewer also highlights the frustrations of adjusting to a strange culture and learning to communicate in a new language. The two factors generally measured during the screening are (1) the family's success in handling transfers in the United States and (2) the reactions to discussions of stresses caused by transfer abroad and life in a particular foreign country.

Assessment Centers   One of the most promising developments in international managerial selection methodology has been the use of assessment centers. These centers typically include individual and group exercises, individual interviews with managers or psychologists, and perhaps some personality and mental ability tests. Group exercises may be competitive (e.g., a leaderless group discussion) or cooperative (e.g., a manufacturing business game). Individual exercises may involve an in-basket test to simulate the manager's administrative requirements, or they may include an individual talk or presentation. The situational exercises are qualitatively different from domestic managers' normal activities (i.e., they reflect situations particular to the potential host culture). Six observers (usually specially trained line managers) observe about a dozen candidates at a time. The use of assessment centers has been shown to have high face validity and to be an effective tool for selecting from a large pool of international managerial candidates (Kraut, 1973).

We should sound a note of caution, however, about the merits of any given international selection procedure. Selection has *not* been found to be the panacea for international executives' adjustment problems (Adler & Kiggundu, 1983). Indeed, Tucker's extensive review of the selection literature (1974) found that *none* of the fully operational selection programs was based on proven criteria of success! It is therefore not surprising that most MNCs do not use scientific methods in selecting personnel for foreign assignments (Baker & Ivancevich, 1971). They may even rely on selecting candidates personally known to the selection manager—former subordinates or colleagues, perhaps (Miller, 1973).

With this caution in mind, we may proceed to discuss a third way to meet the challenges of international staffing: the education and development of managers who accept a foreign assignment. The managers' predeparture preparation, their postarrival development, and their orientation to repatriation are the subjects of our next discussion.

Education and Development

Even the most careful selection does not eliminate the need for education and development. People are not molded to specifications; processes of organizational, technological, and human change always occur. The organization's basic problem in management education and development is to unite the individual's achievement motivation, capabilities, and self-interest with the organization's goals.

In the present context, we should define *education* as the international manager's preparatory sociocultural development, which provides an orientation to the host country, its people, and its culture that will facilitate the manager's adjustment to the foreign environment. Noer (1975) has referred to this as "front-end programming." We shall define *development* as the processes by which international managers acquire not only skills and competencies in their present jobs but also capacities for future managerial tasks of increasing difficulty and scope (thus, we include preparation for repatriation as a development activity). Both education and development are subsumed here under the general rubric of training.

Box 12.4 and Table 12.6 indicate the relative importance of training needs perceived by fairly large samples of both American expatriates and host-country nationals in Asia (Johnson & Carter, 1972). As Table 12.6 indicates, both groups rank human relations skills, understanding the host culture, and the ability to adapt as most important, but American expatriates view orientation for overseas assignment as much less important than host-country nationals. The low rating by both groups of language ability is also notable. These findings illustrate that education and development programs for expatriate managers must be particularly attentive to the managers' sensitivity to nuances of the host-country culture.

Objectives   Rahim (1983) has presented a model for the development of multinational managers that considers predeparture, postarrival, and reentry training as *development* activities; for the present purpose, we can dichotomize his model's objectives and methods into educational and developmental activities (see Figure 12.5). We can see that the basic goal of education and development for international assignment is to foster the manager's attitudinal and behavioral changes so that he or she can perform overseas operations effectively and efficiently, and can make a smooth transition back to a domestic or another foreign assignment. Ideally, this goal is accomplished by program components that include the following:

1. A review of the terms and conditions of the assignment.
2. Orientation regarding the host-country culture.
3. Awareness of the social, political, economic, business, and legal environments of the host country.
4. Development of a working knowledge of the host-country language.
5. Awareness of the relationship among the needs and expectations of the international manager, headquarters staff, and the host and home governments.

Box 12.4

Training Needs for Americans Overseas (*N* = 403)

1. *A sense for politics* (awareness of political conditions in assigned country; alertness to political consequences of everyday behavior)
2. *Skill as change agent* (the ability to work toward change)
3. *Ability to keep records* (skill in keeping simple records and accounts)
4. *Human relations skills* (ability to work with others, based on understanding oneself and the structure and dynamics of human society)
5. *Teaching skills* (an understanding of and ability to apply the principles of learning and teaching)
6. *Understanding of mission* (having a sense of the purpose of and enthusiasm about one's job and organization)
7. *Technical competence* (ability to do the job: knowing the subject matter and techniques in one's field)
8. *Health knowledge* (an understanding of the principles essential for maintaining physical and mental health)
9. *Orientation for service* (an understanding of the value of all human life and potential, such that one is motivated to serve fellow human beings)
10. *Organizational ability* (ability to combine personnel and resources into dynamic self-sustaining enterprises: ability to "work oneself out of" the job by developing self-sustaining institutions and by training local national personnel to manage them)
11. *Ability to adapt* (flexibility: ability to adapt learning to unlike situations; ability to adjust oneself to change)
12. *Understanding of other cultures* (cross-cultural understanding: the skill to understand the inner logic and coherence of other ways of life, plus the restraint not to judge them as "bad" because they are different from one's own ways; cultural empathy)
13. *Understanding of American culture* (insight into Western values, mores, attitudes, behavior patterns)
14. *Language ability* (a growing ability to express oneself in, and to understand, the language of the adopted country)
15. *Sensitivity training* (self-insight, self-understanding, sensitivity to feelings of others)

Source: M. B. Johnston and G. L. Carter, Jr. "Training Needs of Americans Working Abroad." *Social Change,* 1972, reprinted in Mary B. Johnston. "Training Needs of Overseas Americans as Seen by Their National Co-Workers in Asia," *IDR/Focus,* No. 4, 1974, p. 22.

Assessing the prospective international manager's past experience, proficiency in foreign languages, personal attitudes, values, and beliefs about foreign cultures will determine how much and what type of education and development the individual needs. Although programs should be tailored to fit individual needs, each of the components listed above is applicable to all international assignees. Most MNCs provide some type of preparation or orientation for the manager who is going abroad (although typically there is insufficient cross-cultural input). However, postarrival and reentry training have not kept pace. This section therefore focuses on the orientation and preparation process, with special consideration of postarrival and reentry concerns when information is available.

Table 12.6 Ranks of Importance of Training Needs for Americans Working Overseas as Determined by Ratings by Respondents

Training Need	Ranking by Responses of Americans ($N = 403$)	Ranking by Responses of Nationals ($N = 131$)
Human relations skill	1	1
Understanding of other culture	2	2
Ability to adapt	3	3
Technical competence	4	6.5*
Sensitivity training	5	6.5
A sense of politics	6	12.5[†]
Language ability	7	9
Understanding of mission	8	5
Understanding of American culture	9	15
Orientation for service	10	4

Source: M. B. Johnston and G. L. Carter, Jr. "Training Needs of Americans Working Abroad." *Social Change,* 1972, p. 23.
*The two training needs that tied for sixth place are both ranked 6.5.
[†]The two training needs that tied for twelfth place are ranked as 12.5.

The Education Process From the discussion thus far, it should be apparent that the skills necessary in a domestic position are not sufficient in their own right to achieve success in an international assignment. Indeed, an inquiry into the practices and policies of 77 American managers of foreign operations reported that 60% agreed with a statement that "the overseas American must have a broader and deeper professional training than he needs to perform the same kind of work in his familiar home environment" (White, 1971). Whetton and Cameron's extensive survey of the literature (1984) and the results of their own study of more than 400 practicing managers in domestic positions has led them to develop a list of nine critical skills that domestic managers require (Box 12.5). Each of these skills would clearly require modification in a new cultural context. For example, the ability to establish supportive communication by using the appropriate response formats entails a full understanding of which response formats are specific to the particular culture. Without understanding the dominant cultural patterns of worldview, activity orientation, time sense, attitudes toward human nature orientation, perception of the self, and social organization, the manager may be severely restricted in ability to apply domestic management skills (Samovar, Porter, & Jain, 1981).

For these reasons, it seems almost self-evident that preparation for overseas assignment should be part of an MNC's ongoing process. If the process of

Figure 12.5 A model for the development of multinational management.

Source: A Model for Developing Key Expatriate Executives, by Afzalur Rahim, copyright April 1983. Reprinted with the permission of PERSONNEL JOURNAL, April 1983, pp. 312–317, Costa Mesa, California; all rights reserved.

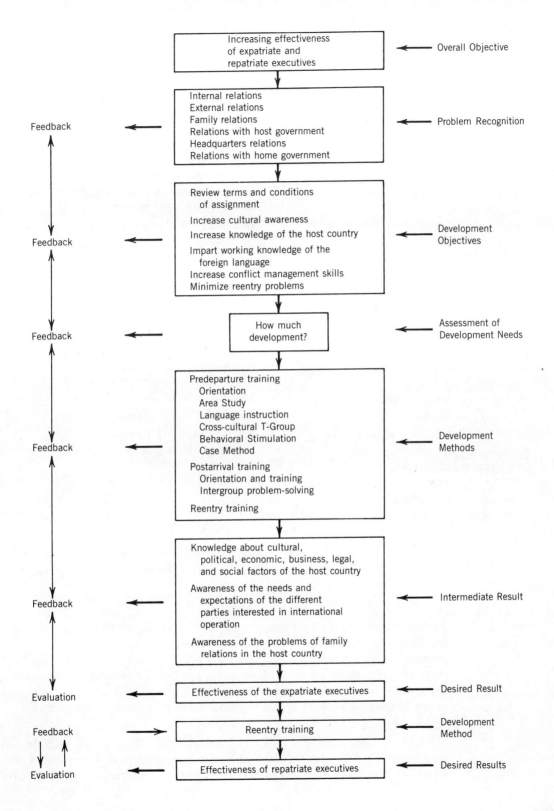

Box 12.5

Critical Management Skills and Subskills

1. Developing Self-Awareness

   Determining cognitive style, level of values development, and interpersonal orientation

   Becoming aware of personal strengths and weaknesses

   Understanding the impact of your interpersonal style on others

2. Managiang Personal Stress

   Developing effective time management techniques

   Identifying major stressors in daily life

   Developing effective coping mechanisms for stress

3. Solving Problems Creatively

   Developing competence in rational problem solving

   Overcoming conceptual blocks

   Creating flexibility in thinking

4. Establishing Supportive Communication

   Becoming adept at active listening

   Developing the ability to be empathetic

   Using the appropriate response formats

5. Gaining Power and Influence

   Establishing a strong power base

   Converting power into influence

   Avoiding abuses of power

6. Improving Employee Performance Through Motivation

   Distinguishing between problems of ability and motivation

   Providing highly valued incentives

   Making rewards contingent on performance

   Timing rewards for maximum impact

7. Delegating and Decision Making

   Developing competence in assigning tasks to others

   Fostering successful task completion in others

   Determining when to involve others in making decisions

8. Managing Conflict

   Balancing assertiveness and sensitivity

   Handling personal criticisms

   Registering complaints effectively

   Mediating conflicts between subordinates

9. Conducting Effective Group Meetings

   Making adequate preparations

   Effectively managing both task and process aspects of meetings

   Making effective presentations

Source: D. A. Whetten and K. S. Cameron. *Developing Management Skills.* Glenview, IL: Scott, Foresman, 1984.

preparing employees for overseas work is an integral part of managerial training, then the recruitment, selection, and preparation for the overseas job is relatively easy. Otherwise, the manager's preparation must be tailor-made to suit individual needs, no matter how costly and time-consuming. Preparation is the keynote for success overseas (Blue & Haynes, 1977). A program composed of the following elements stands a good chance of assuring such success:

Review of Terms and Conditions for Assignment   Preparation often begins with what is perhaps the easiest and least expensive part of the orientation process—a series of discussions between an MNC representative and the prospective international manager (and spouse). Typically included in these discussions are the following:

1. Details of the MNC's expatriate policies and procedures regarding such issues as compensation, taxes, and allowances.
2. Details concerning the housing, transportation, and schools in the host country.
3. A review of moving arrangements, locations, and length of stay.
4. Consideration of the readjustment process to the corporate structure on return to the home country.

Many companies provide the new expatriate with exposure to employees already familiar with the subsidiary's host country—perhaps a recently repatriated manager. Recent studies indicate that a large number of companies permit a trip to the host country either before or after the assignment is offered (Business International Corporation, 1982). One Swedish firm, for example, allows the expatriate and spouse to visit the new location for a period of one to two weeks. The visits, supervised by the top subsidiary executive or the personnel director, are not highly structured. The prospective manager and spouse see housing, schools, and the town; they review the job; they meet with other expatriates and their families. Frequently, the subsidiary appoints a manager (and spouse) to act as the newcomers' hosts for a period of a month or so after their arrival. Some MNCs have attempted to achieve similar acculturation at less cost by sending the candidate and spouse to live for a short time in a nearby "micro-culture," such as an Indian reservation (Tung, 1979).

Cultural Education The next phase of the preparation process often covers the host country, its people, and its culture to familiarize the prospective manager and the spouse with the host country's cultural, political, economic, business, legal, and physical environments. A wide variety of methods provide this education, and several excellent compendiums are available for the practitioner who wishes to apply them (Casse, 1981; 1982; Landis & Brislin, 1983; Miller, 1979; Weeks, Pederson, & Brislin, 1975). These methods have included both traditional academic techniques for cognitive learning and experiential techniques for learning at the interpersonal level.

The academic techniques, or area studies programs, have utilized books, maps, brochures, films, slides, and even lectures by local university professors on the history, culture, and socioeconomic patterns of the host country. The content is factual and prepares the individual for the particular environment under assignment. We should note, however, that these programs appear to be inadequate when used alone to prepare prospective international assignees for environments requiring extensive contact with the host-country community (Harrison & Hopkins, 1967; Lynton & Pareek, 1967; Textor, 1966).

The interpersonal techniques have tended to apply much organizational development (OD) technology. The essence of these techniques is for managers to become aware of the motivations and values that condition their own behavior, as well as people's behavior in the host-country culture. Cross-cultural sensitivity training, for instance, can increase insight concerning one's behavior, sensitivity to others' behavior, and awareness of the process that will facilitate or inhibit group functioning. Although some observers have questioned the effectiveness of sensitivity training, it appears to be a powerful technique for reducing ethnic prejudice (Rubin et al., 1977). Similarly, behavioral simulation (the "culture assimilator") is a programmed learning experience designed to expose members of one culture to some of the basic concepts, attitudes, role perceptions, customs, and values of another culture. Behavioral simulation consists of a series of individual and group decisions through role playing and other simulated activities (e.g., cases on international business) concerning critical intercultural encounters. Studies designed to test the validity and effectiveness of this educational device have generally shown that "these programs provide an apparently effective method for assisting members of one culture to interact and adjust successfully with members of another culture" (Fiedler & Mitchell, 1971, p. 95). In assignments in which time is not a critical factor, and which require extensive contact with members of the local community, this technique should be supplemented by more rigorous training (Tung, 1981).

Language Education   We should give special emphasis to language education, not only because it addresses the basic problem of communication but also because it is an effective indirect method of learning about a country. It is possible, of course, to go through an expatriate assignment without learning the host-country language, yet language may be the most important thing an MNC can provide to an expatriate to ensure a successful assignment (Noer, 1975). Lectures, records, cassettes, or formal classroom instruction may be used in language education. We strongly recommend that the language be taught by a host-country native (Blue & Haynes, 1977; Noer, 1975). It may take months (sometimes years) of language education for the prospective manager to achieve mastery, but as little as twenty hours of instruction may make a significant difference (Rahim, 1983).

Educating Women Expatriates   In addition to the technical and managerial training given to all departing expatriates, an opportunity for women managers to explore problems resulting from their encounter with male host-country subordinates and clients is needed (Izraeli et al., 1980). The purposes of such training are to increase their awareness of when and how their sex is relevant in business interaction and to develop their skills for handling situations when sexual status interferes with effective leadership.

Izraeli et al. recommend basing the training material on actual case studies from other women managers' field experience, as well as on diagnostic studies of host-country attitudes and behaviors toward women executives. Such training may be conducted most effectively in small groups, in which women can provide mutual support, using role playing and other simulation methods found effective in learning new behavioral responses.

Implementing the Education Program MNCs use various methods to prepare managers for their overseas operations. For example, Goodyear hires junior executives with an interest and educational background in multinational business. These men and women then receive a year or two of preparatory training in the company's operating divisions—training which includes coaching by their future superiors. They are then sent to acquire practical experience at one of the Goodyear foreign subsidiaries. Having completed their on-the-job training, they then move upward within the same subsidiary or within another company in another country, depending on their success (Prasad & Krishna Shetty, 1976). This intense education may prove highly productive because the company can link its own policies and procedures (and its own special concerns) with the ongoing program. Moreover, the company can tailor the program to each manager's specific assignments and abilities.

Many companies, however, may not have the internal resources to provide an effective program. Thus, outside programs—those provided by universities and consulting firms—may be useful as well. Their main goal is to enrich the participants' knowledge of a wide variety of topics potentially relevant to their future jobs and to help them translate abstractions into effective actions (Livingston, 1971; Zeira, 1973). For example, various universities and institutions in the United States have educational programs for multinational managers, which are aimed at developing an understanding of the business system, social environment, and language of foreign countries. The best known among these are the Institute of the Business Council for International Understanding at American University (Washington, D.C.), the International Council to Management at the American Graduate School of International Management (Phoenix, Arizona), the Business International Institute of the Business International Corporation (New York City), and the Monterey Institute of International Studies (Monterey, California). The Japanese have established what is reportedly one of the most effective cultural training institutions for prospective Japanese national expatriates: the Institute of International Training and Studies near Fuji. The students—young managers about age thirty—are sent by their companies for an extensive year-long program. The curriculum includes general management, international management, English and another language, study of the United States and one other area, and a two-month study tour to some part of the world.

Some organizations have programs dealing with expatriate relocation and training for international assignments that are especially geared for clients short on time and funding. These resemble the extensive education offered by the management institutes. Among these are the American Society for Personnel Administration (Berea, Ohio), Family Relocation Services Worldwide (New York City), and Overseas Briefing Associates (New York City). These programs are tailored to specific countries and particular company needs. Such organizations as the Asia Society, the Japan Society, and the Middle East Institute (all in New York City) also hold briefing sessions periodically for all executives.

These types of programs have the advantage of taking prospective international managers away from their present job so that they can concentrate on the subject matter, thus exposing them to the most recent international management theories and research findings and increasing the managers' prestige and self-confidence (Zeira, 1976). Despite these important advantages, however, some observers have strongly recommended that U.S.-based expatriate managers travel overseas to educational institutions rather than attend those in America (e.g., Blue & Haynes, 1977). INSEAD in France and IMEDE in Switzerland are examples of institutions that have been recognized for the excellence of their courses. The major benefit of such programs is the opportunity to meet expatriates from other MNCs for a productive exchange of ideas. In addition, the case work at the overseas institution will invariably involve the analysis of foreign companies or foreign business problems from a perspective other than American. Equally important, the experience of putting American managers in a group learning situation, in which they are in the minority, should encourage a rapid and deeper understanding of other business cultures (Bass & Thiagarajan, 1972; Blue & Haynes, 1977; Hughes & Flowers, 1973; Zeira, 1976). The main shortcoming of these programs is that they are not tailor-made, and thus cannot meet the specific needs of managers assigned to overseas positions. Moreover, they are not designed to achieve the specific changes in the participants' managerial behavior to fit the needs of any particular corporation.

Actual MNC Practices   Despite the clear need for MNCs to minimize their prospective expatriate managers' culture shock, only about one-third of U.S.-based MNCs administer formal predeparture preparation programs (Baker & Ivancevich, 1971; Tung, 1982a). This figure has remained virtually unchanged over the last two decades even though large numbers of overseas managers indicating that proper predeparture preparation is absolutely necessary to improve overseas performance. Some of these managers' typical statements regarding preparation appear in Baker and Ivancevich's study:

My adjustment to the overseas transfer could have been smoother if I knew something about the people, their political system, and their government. I was shocked at my ignorance once I knew something about the people.

There is no substitute for actually being abroad. However, a better-than-nothing substitute would be some form of people training (i.e., host nationals). I was selected and shipped so fast to Thailand that I knew absolutely nothing about the people and culture. My ignorance led to many mistakes back in the old days. (p. 42)

The reasons cited for omitting preparation programs center primarily on the trend toward employing local nationals, the temporary nature of international assignments, the difficulty of determining who should receive such education and who should not (those with previous successful overseas experience may not need it), and doubt about the effectiveness of such programs (Business International Corporation, 1982; Tung, 1982a). To make matters worse, many of the existing preparation programs may be deficient in certain respects. For example, Zeira and his associates (Zeira, 1975, 1979; Zeira & Harari, 1977) have indicated a near-total absence of tailor-made in-house training programs for equipping prospective expatriate and third-country managers with adequate expertise to apply in the subsidiaries. In addition, many programs seem to ignore potential morale problems stemming from expatriate managers' ethnocentrism.

Before sounding the death knell for cross-cultural preparation programs, however, we should contrast the practice of U.S.-based MNCs with that of other cultural samples. In the 1982 Tung study cited earlier, approximately two-thirds of West European-based MNCs and three-fifths of Japanese-based MNCs *did* sponsor training programs to prepare their managerial candidates for overseas assignment. Representatives of West European firms that omitted preparation programs indicated that the temporary nature of overseas assignments and the lack of time for implementation were the key reasons for their reluctance to introduce formalized preparation programs. Representatives of Japanese-based firms that omitted such programs also cited lack of time as the primary prohibitive factor.

The Tung study also revealed differences among U.S.-based, West European-based, and Japanese-based MNCs in the types of training programs used for preparing personnel in each of four job categories (as described in the previous section on selection issues). Table 12.7 presents the relative frequencies for using a particular program for each of the job categories in all three samples. The programs appear in ascending order of their rigor in imparting knowledge and understanding of a foreign country. The results show that both

Table 12.7   Frequencies of Training Programs Used for Each Job Category in U.S., European, and Japanese Samples (%)

Training Programs	Job Category											
	CEO			Functional Head			Troubleshooter			Operative		
	U.S.	Eur.	Jap.	U.S.	Eur.	Jap.	U.S.	Eur.	Jap.	U.S.	Eur.	Jap.
Environmental briefing	52	57	67	54	52	57	44	38	52	31	38	67
Cultural orientation	42	55	14	41	52	14	31	31	19	24	28	24
Culture assimilator	10	21	14	10	17	14	7	10	14	9	14	19
Language training	60	76	52	59	72	57	36	41	52	24	48	76
Sensitivity training	3	3	0	1	3	0	1	3	5	0	3	5
Field experience	6	28	14	6	24	10	4	3	10	1	7	24

Source: R. L. Tung. "Selection and Training Procedures of U.S., European, and Japanese Multinationals." *California Management Review,* 25(1):57–71, 1982.

the U.S. and West European firms that established preparation programs regarded rigorous education for CEOs and functional heads as more important than for troubleshooters and operatives. In contrast, the Japanese firms that sponsored training programs appeared to provide slightly more rigorous preparation for operatives. Clearly the level of management receiving education makes a difference; the relatively infrequent use of programs by U.S.-based MNCs may not be representative of MNC education efforts on a global basis.

The Development Process   Predeparture preparation is insufficient to prevent the adjustment difficulties that most new expatriate managers experience. With the great variety of challenges facing the new international manager (e.g., see Box 12.6), it seems clear that postarrival development programs are useful as a complement to front-end preparation. For the most part, a foreign subsidiary must expect to do most of its managerial development within its own organization, because outside facilities are usually limited (Ivancevich, 1969). Typically, line executives organize these programs within the subsidiaries abroad. The principle involved is generally one of learning by doing (Bowen, 1973; Stolz, 1966). Programs may encompass any number of methods—coaching, job rotation, assistant to junior boards, meetings with host-government officials or with managers and employees of the operation, and intergroup problem solving.

Off-the-Job Programs   On-the-job programs can fit each manager's specific assignments and abilities. Furthermore, because the expatriate is being trained by his or her actual superior, this approach eliminates the frequent conflict between external programs' theoretical practices and the realities of the subsidiary. Expatriates receive training according to both their individual needs and the subsidiary's. The manager's immediate supervisor provides constant reinforcement for new managerial behavior (Mahler, 1967; Mahoney, 1961; Zeira, 1976). An additional advantage of such programs is that they can show expatriates how to handle unanticipated managerial problems. Whereas external programs can teach expatriates a great deal about managing, on-the-job programs can actually teach them to manage. Prolonged on-the-job practice can effectively develop skills in problem solving abilities and empathy for host-country subordinates.

Intergroup problem solving is a technique used for managing intergroup conflicts (Rahim & Bonoma, 1979). It is designed to deal with the tasks and behavioral issues of expatriate and headquarters managers. Under this approach, the overseas managers and the home office staff concerned with international business define the two groups' interface problems, formulate alternative solutions to problems, prepare a plan to implement the solutions, select representatives for implementing the plan, and prepare a schedule for reviewing the implementation. This intervention minimizes intergroup conflict and improves the relationship between expatriate and headquarters managers (Rahim, 1983).

Off-the-Job Programs   Off-the-job development programs have recently come into vogue. The American Management Association has management

Box 12.6

Sixty-four Points in Developing International Executives

Management Factors

1. Managing geographically dispensed operations.
2. Managing operations over language barriers.
3. Adjusting to cultural differences.
4. Coping with different business philosophies.
5. Overcoming communications problems in general management, technology, finance, and marketing.
6. Operating in countries with strong government control over the private sector.
7. Managing the activities of personnel unfamiliar with or opposed to the parent company's business techniques.
8. Adapting to the need for extensive travel.
9. Adapting to requirements for making quick decisions in areas without precedent in company operations.
10. Familiarity with foreign politics and economics.
11. Familiarity with general legal framework and company laws in foreign countries.

Controllership Factors

12. Translation and consolidation of foreign subsidiary accounts (P&L and balance sheet).
13. Installation of uniform accounting procedures and use of standard chart of accounts in foreign subsidiaries.
14. Selection and training of foreign accountants.
15. Administration of reporting and control systems.
16. Foreign accounting procedures and requirements.
17. Administration of an international audit program.
18. Relations with foreign public accounting firms.
19. Review and modification of foreign sub-budgets.

Treasury Factors

20. Arranging export financing from commercial banks.

21. Arranging export insurance and financing through local official institutions.
22. Finding foreign sources of capital.
23. Relations with foreign banks.
24. Familiarity with foreign exchange operations.
25. Arranging protection of foreign financial assets.
26. Familiarity with procedures for repatriation of capital and earnings.
27. Arranging asset, fire, and other necessary insurance coverage for foreign subsidiaries.
28. Administration of multicountry credit operations.

Tax Factors

29. Familiarity with foreign tax systems.
30. Familiarity with domestic country's taxation of foreign-source income.
31. Familiarity with provisions of double-tax treaties.
32. Eliminating penalties under audit reallocations.

Marketing Factors

33. Working with foreign distributors and agents.
34. Arranging patterns of distributor compensation.
35. Knowledge of foreign markets and marketing.
36. Adapting to unusual forms of distribution abroad.
37. Coordinating multicountry advertising.
38. Knowledge of tariff and nontariff barriers.
39. Knowledge of export incentives available to foreign subsidiaries.
40. Product modification for foreign acceptability.
41. Setting intercorporate and distributor prices.
42. Policies in price control and cartel situations.
43. Preventing reexport by foreign distributors.

Personnel and Labor Factors

44. Compensating expatriates, third-country nationals, and local nationals.

Continued on page 552

45. Setting policies for overbase allowances and fringes.
46. Pension and profit-sharing plans for foreign nationals.
47. Tax and profit-sharing plans for expatriates.
48. Selection and training of personnel for foreign assignment (where cultural and business differences require a special outlook and discipline).
49. Familiarity with foreign labor laws governing wages, fringe benefits, and dismissal.
50. Adapting to unusual work procedures abroad due to cultural differences.
51. Dealing with unions, including Communist ones.

Production Factors

52. Administering multicountry quality control and assurance programs.
53. Producing under low-volume conditions, with modification of plant design and process engineering.
54. Dealing with local suppliers unaccustomed to domestic purchasing requirements.
55. Originating an international procurement program to reduce costs.

56. Rationalizing production for operations in a common market area.
57. Standardizing product specifications for manufacture of identical products by plants in several foreign countries (involves shifts between metric and English systems, close quality control).
58. Operating with unskilled or semiskilled labor in some foreign countries.

Investment Factors

59. Negotiating investment proposals with foreign government and agencies.
60. Negotiating investment and licensing proposals with prospective foreign partners.
61. Selecting and cooperating with foreign joint venture partners.
62. Making investment decisions in a multicountry framework with greater complexity of factors to be selected in allocating funds.
63. Facing up to problems of nationalism.
64. Operating in socialistically oriented countries.

Source: Business International Corporation. *151 Checklists—Decision-Making in International Operations.* New York: Business International Corporation, 1974.

development centers in Latin America and Europe modeled on American business schools. Several American universities conduct summer programs on other continents. However, many of these programs are tailored to groups rather than to individual international managers and may suffer from being too concise.

Reentry Preparation   With adequate predeparture education and postarrival development, expatriates and their families generally adjust to working conditions abroad (Rahim, 1983). However, the managers' later realization that they are returning to a somewhat unfamiliar home country, and perhaps to an unreceptive company, could come as a shock. This is culture shock in reverse (Murray, 1973). If the company has an effective workforce planning system, the expatriate will have been kept in cultural contact with the home country through home leaves, internal communications, and compensation practices. These practices should minimize the need for reentry orientation (Noer, 1975). Based on the current practices of many MNCs, however, reentry orientation is still a necessary part of an effective staffing policy.

Although planning for an expatriate's eventual return should start at the time of a domestic manager's selection for overseas assignment (e.g., by providing specific information about the length of stay), it is also necessary when the expatriate approaches the end of his or her foreign assignment. An appropriate time is six months before the actual return home. Providing counseling and orientation may help the repatriates adjust to the corporate structure back home and to deal with personal finances. Sensitivity training and role-playing techniques may be useful in helping repatriates and their families to overcome reverse culture shock. It is critically important, too, that repatriates be prepared for "new" professional careers that are attractive and challenging, regardless of whether they return to previously held positions or to different ones. (See Howard, 1980, for suggested elements necessary for any repatriation program.) This process is difficult under normal business conditions but far more so in circumstances of staff cutbacks and high national unemployment. According to a recent survey by Korn, Ferry International (cited in Business International Corporation, 1982), fewer than half of American expatriates receive a promotion on their return home. Some are put in a temporary job and others in a "lateral" position that neither builds on their experiences nor enhances their careers.

With MNCs' expansion into new foreign subsidiaries, and with the increasing likelihood of expatriate managers relocating abroad, it seems essential that companies devote time to planning for repatriation. However, the lack of concerted repatriation research or even anecdotal reports about MNC repatriation programs indicates that the repatriation process had not received the attention it demands. For the most part, MNCs repond to this situation by continuing to expect expatriates to initiate their own repatriation program. Returning managers have little alternative but to seek out benefits, business briefings, and personal information on their own. Supervisors, mentors, or the personnel department may offer help, as well as the unit responsible for the original assignment or repatriation (Business International Corporation, 1982). But generally speaking, returning managers must improvise their own repatriation.

To summarize, there is a clear need for MNCs to have a well-planned strategy for educating and developing their managers for overseas operations. (See Case C at the end of the chapter for the rigorous plan of Mitsui Corporation.) Given the different degrees of contact required within the local culture, varying durations of stay in the foreign country, and the differences between home and other cultures, no one program is appropriate regardless of the management task and the subsidiary environment. These considerations apply to recruiting and selection as well. We should therefore address their implications for MNC staffing policy in the final section of this chapter.

CONCLUSION—IMPLICATIONS FOR STAFFING FOREIGN SUBSIDIARIES

By now it should be apparent that the staffing practices of MNCs—particularly those that are U.S.-based—are generally unsystematic and unsophisticated. The unfortunate result of these practices is that less rigorous recruiting, selec-

Box 12.7

What Is the Failure Rate?

No one knows what the average company's failure rate is in selecting expatriates. Some companies report 10%; a 1981 U.S. study shows 20%; but one company executive confided to BI that it is actually "30% or higher" for his firm, and some managers reported rates as high as 50% in companies that use very poor selection techniques. Of course, there is no clear definition of what is a failure and what is not. There seems to be general agreement that the failures result mainly from the inability of the family as a whole to adapt to living abroad. Research also indicates that among those who serve one or two tours, overseas placement is typically not a preconceived career goal.

Chance is an important factor in selecting who goes abroad. Many managers feel it is damaging to one's career to leave company headquarters and to sever ties with one's sponsors and work networks (both internal and external to the firm). They further perceive that the financial benefits of offshore work have diminished, and that repatriates are frequently not rewarded with promotions or good assignments upon return.

Source: Business International Corporation. *Worldwide Executive Compensation and Human Resource Planning.* New York: Business International Corporation, 1982.

---

tion, and education and development procedures leads to a higher failure rate of international assignments (Tung, 1982a; see Box 12.7 for a discussion of this failure rate). With an estimated 35,000 American managers presently living in foreign countries (Presidential Commission, 1979), managing these human resource functions is perhaps *the* most serious operational challenge for MNCs. To meet this challenge effectively, changes in present staffing policies are necessary.

This chapter has identified several ways to make these changes. A longer, more deliberate program appears necessary for recruiting, selecting, educating, and developing candidates for overseas management positions. It should be based on a thorough analysis of the job, the subsidiary organization, and the host-country culture that explicitly defines the criteria or dimensions for success in the assignment. Which individuals are best suited for specific assignments depends on whether the objective is personal and family adjustment, effectiveness in dealing with host-country nationals, transfer of skills, or some combination of these elements. Clarity in these objectives directly influences the recruiting pool accessed, the selection methodology chosen, and the types of education and development programs required.

This chapter has highlighted the particular importance of the manager's family situation in successful overseas performance. MNCs should consider the prospective expatriate manager's spouse in determining the manager's suitability for overseas work, and should involve the spouse in the education and development activities that precede and follow the departure. This becomes extremely important when we consider that the spouse's inability to adjust to a different physical or cultural environment most often becomes the primary reason for the failure of American and West European expatriates overseas (Hayes, 1974; Tung, 1982a). We have also emphasized women's special staffing concerns in international management. As the number of women gaining managerial experience grows (Haemmerli, 1978), as the percentage of business conducted overseas dramatically increases, and the concomitant demand for top executives rises (Perham, 1977), MNCs must develop more effective and sophisticated ways to include women in their human resource planning.

For these reasons, the traditional belief that a manager who performs well domestically can perform equally well abroad is both overly optimistic and highly simplistic. The transition that an international assignee must make to a new job in a foreign environment encompasses many challenges, which cannot be met simply by transferring previously developed technical and managerial skills. MNCs that recognize this reality and act on it may well see improvement in the rate of success in their international managerial assignments.

Cases A and B: Repatriation

Illustrative of two specific situations are the following case studies.

In the first case, it was reported that Bill Stevenson received a letter from the director of international personnel services of his company, Dayton Dynamics, Incorporated. He had requested an assignment in the United States and was extremely frustrated by his company's response. A short letter from the home office advised him: *"Your request has been considered and at the present time we do not have an assignment at the same level as your present one in Nigeria. However, consideration has been given to your fine employment record and you will be posted at a slightly lower level in the New York area, with comparable remuneration. Details will follow."*

Bill Stevenson had been plant manager in Nigeria for nearly four years for the Dayton Company, which was in the plastic extrusion field. He had set up the plant, organized the labor force, and orders were beginning to come in from other emerging West and Central African countries using plastics in building and other fabrications. For three years Bill and his family had lived at what many people might

consider a material living standard lower than that of the United States. However, they had found the experience both educational and exciting. Their stay was made more attractive by a special hardship premium and extensive allowances. His three children had reached high school age, however, and he was well aware that the educational system in Nigeria and West Africa was not comparable to that in the United States. And since all of his children eventually would be living in the United States—a return assignment was desirable.

Because he had substantial proof of his good performance during his foreign assignment, he felt that his request would get special consideration. The president of the company, for example, had written letters on two occasions—commending his growth in sales for a two-year period, and also, his solving of a production problem which saved the company some 20% in material cost. The negative response he received from the personnel department was all the more astonishing since he felt that he not only hadn't received special consideration for his past performance, but also was being treated the same as if he had requested the move while operating in the United States. His wife was disappointed with his new job location because she didn't want to go back to the New York area. She had come from a small Mid-

Source: J. A. Murray, "International Personnel Repatriation: Cultural Shock in Reverse." *MSU Business Topics* 2(3):59–66 (1979).

western town and hoped that possibly Bill would be moved to the Midwest regional office or the northern California area. The thought of moving to New York conjured up tremendous anxieties. She felt Bill had been discriminated against because he asked for a return home assignment at an inconvenient time. However, they both felt that they had to make a move right at that time—even if it meant quitting his company and looking for a new job in the United States.

A second case study involves Owen Klein, financial officer for the Phayton Chemical Company in Western Europe. He had been headquartered in Paris, as overseer of financial operations of the company in six common market countries. He and his family had enjoyed their four-and-a-half years stay in Paris and had become accustomed to the advantages of French culture and cuisine along with the higher cost of living. Their children had been enrolled in private schools outside of Paris and had liked the more relaxed pace of European life. A return to the Chicago office of the company as assistant to the vice-president of finance had much less responsibility and authority than the European post where Owen reported directly to the president of the European operations. Consequently, he found his new job strange and less challenging.

Although his salary had not been reduced, he was not happy in the Chicago area. Owen Klein felt that the company was not appreciative of the experience he had gained as a key European financial officer in the company. He previously had to operate in the number of different currencies and was quite familiar with the whole European Community. However, the European operations were handled under a vice-president of international affairs, and after a short debriefing session with this vice-president, Owen Klein was not called upon again to give his opinion on any other occasion although he had acquired considerable expertise while in Europe.

In addition, the whole family was upset about having to move back to the United States. One of his children, a daughter, stayed in Europe to complete her education. This forced him to consider looking for a job in another European company. But, since most of his experience had been in the chemical industry, there were limited opportunities for him in this field. He planned to take a vacation in Paris in order to renew acquaintances with his friends there.

Phayton Pharmaceutical had a policy of recalling executives to the home office after a four-year assignment, and they had never deviated from this policy. Their feeling was that executive mobility would give the company the needed communications and training that the key personnel required. The chances that Owen would be returned to his European post were very slim. Although the company had several smaller plants in South America, it only had the one large European operation.

Bill Stevenson and Owen Klein are fictitious names, but their cases are very real. The frustrations facing these two expatriates of international companies represent only a sample of the circumstances faced by a number of individuals who return each year to the United States.

Case C: Mitsui K. K.

The Mitsui method of identifying and grooming potential international managers starts before a candidate leaves school. Each September, Mit-

Source: Business International. July 18, 1975, pp. 228–29. Reprinted with permission.

sui receives a thousand or so applications from seniors in Japan's top-ranking colleges who will graduate the following March. It runs these candidates through a culling procedure which weeds out about half of them: a careful analysis of school records; a battery of "yes or no" tests that check out factual knowledge; an essay-type test that reflects both common sense and business sense; and a multi-tier personal interview system that starts with in-company peer groups—junior executives who have been with the company two or three years—and works up the corporate ladder to a designated senior executive who puts his final "chop" on a candidate's eligibility.

Five to ten years of rotation. The process also produces the first indications of what direction the candidate's career path in the company should take. That direction, however, is not final. For five to ten years after these carefully screened candidates are hired, they are rotated within the company and systematically monitored to make sure they wind up in slots that best conform to their abilities.

The monitoring system includes an annual evaluation by the supervisor in direct daily contact with the executive, which is checked by the section chief and double-checked by the general manager of the department. In addition, an elaborate, written report provides detail under two headings: business ability and work attitude. The former contains such items as ability to administer staff, decisiveness, prejudices, perception, judgment, concentration, planning and negotiating ability, and business knowledge. Work attitudes are measured by such criteria as following proper reporting procedures, keeping apart personal and professional matters, accepting responsibility, maintaining required office hours, and obeying company regulations.

As a general rule, home-base executives are not moved into international jobs until they have been thoroughly pretested within the Mitsui system, i.e., at the middle management level. Three general criteria are applied: character—a combination of strength of character and adaptability; professional rating (Mitsui rates its executives on an A-through-D scale; candidates for service abroad must rank C or higher and for the major overseas posts B or higher); and language ability.

In addition, personal characteristics are put into the selection hopper. Example: Is the executive's temperament right for the post? (Under Mitsui rules, a quick-tempered executive may be sent to North America but would not be assigned to a post where he might have to deal with *manana* attitudes.)

Finally, physical factors are weighed. Can the executive adapt to the food patterns of the country to which he is sent? Can he adapt to the lack of oxygen if the place of assignment is located at elevations of 5000 feet or higher, such as Mexico City or Bogota?

Having met all criteria, the executive is put through a concentrated training and briefing process. He takes a three-month intensive language course at corporate expense and is briefed by in-house experts—staff and line—on political, economic, and business conditions in the country to which he has been assigned.

At the same time, the executive's wife is put through an appropriate language and culture course. A number of independent organizations offer such courses in Japan, with varying degrees of intensity and comprehensiveness. Mitsui picks the course and pays for it.

Once the executive is in his overseas post, Mitsui insists on intensive language training for another year. In some locations, the company finances university training, combining exposure to language with substance of valid interest to the firm. In the past, Mitsui has allowed its executives to choose these courses and take them on an audit basis. The new trend is to have executives take MBA degrees where the academic facilities are available.

Mitsui also takes care of the special schooling needs of executives' children. In Japan, high schools and universities are sharply competitive and inordinately decisive in shaping careers. Japanese executives are therefore particularly anxious to channel their children into the school system early and under the best auspices. Mitsui provides dormitory facilities for children of its executives, boys and girls, at both the high school and the university level. These facilities are situated in the company's residential quarters at various locations in Tokyo and Osaka, and are tightly supervised. Room and board are subsidized, but students pay their own transportation costs (daily travel can be two hours and more) and provide for tuition out of their own resources.

Two routes to overseas duty. At Mitsui, the assignment process for service abroad has two channels. Requests can initiate from the field, with specific requirements, or can be "self-initiated" with specific motivation. A typical example of the first would be Mitsui's North American manager, foreseeing substantial growth in the petrochemical industry in Houston, asking corporate headquarters for a candidate who knows the petrochemical industry, has a workable base of English, and is temperamentally suited to function in Texas. Such a request is fed into the Mitsui personnel computer, which currently has a pool of some 600 executives considered eligible for international service. Once the computer comes up with its choices, a negotiating-selecting process is set in motion between headquarters and the field. Depending on the urgency of filing the slot, this works by letter, telex, or telephone.

An example of self-initiated assignment is the executive who asked for—and quickly got—a post in Saudi Arabia. His main argument was that the country represented an important opportunity for the company.

Most Mitsui executives return to Japan—and the computer pool—after assignments of three years' duration. Hardship posts have shorter stints, and some of the plum assignments tend to last longer; but the general policy is to pull executives back to headquarters regularly to make sure they do not lose touch with how things are done at Mitsui and to make certain they continue to feel part of the mainstream. Occasionally, a particularly adaptable and well-regarded executive, especially at the higher echelons of middle management, is transferred directly from one overseas post to another international assignment, but that is rare.

The new concept at Mitsui—still very much in an embryonic state—is to "nationalize" ex-patriate executives, i.e., leave them in a post in which they are effective and which they find congenial for as long as they like.

At the senior management level, selected executives are sent each year to advanced management courses in the U.S. and Europe to such institutions as Harvard, the Sloan Management School at MIT and IMEDE in Switzerland.

The "inbound" program. Mitsui also has a training system for "inbound" executives, i.e., non-Japanese executives with upward corporate mobility. That system has three channels. In one, candidates are selected from their home country's top universities and rotated in various departments of the local Mitsui subsidiary. London-based Mitsui & Co. Europe, for example, gets graduates from Oxford and Cambridge and, for about three years, trains them in-house, focusing at the same time on plotting long-term career paths. Career opportunities include staff and line positions, as well as the more specialized managerial activities in the commodity divisions of the Mitsui Trading Company.

A second channel sends promising foreign executives to the Mitsui office that commands a particular expertise. For example, a German executive with a career path in Mitsui's production division is sent to the New York office for a training stint of two to three years.

The third Mitsui channel for foreign managerial talent is reserved mainly for young executives from the developing countries, who are pulled into Tokyo for two to three years of training before a career path is plotted for them, preferably in their own countries or contiguous areas.

Mitsui pays particular attention to these young executives from the LDCs because it knows that LDC governments will increasingly insist on local managers as well as on local equity. As a Mitsui executive put it, "Sooner or later, we'll have to ask them to hold our company shares."

For its non-Japanese senior managers, Mitsui

organizes a two-week in-house seminar once a year in Tokyo, at which key employees are immersed in company policies and techniques. Some thirty to fifty executives attend these seminars each year. English is the working language, with executives chosen from any and all of Mitsui's global operations, including its 230 joint ventures.

Mitsui policy in managing joint ventures is to recruit top local management wherever possible. In the U.S. and Canada, for example, the pattern is to have an American or Canadian serve as president of the venture, with a Japanese vice-president. In countries with fewer top managerial resources, the pattern is reversed. The newest trend at Mitsui is to look for top non-Japanese executives to serve on the boards of Mitsui companies in Japan.

Discussion Questions

1. Analyze the strengths and weaknesses of the Mitsui system.
2. Would this system have to be modified in any way for a U.S.-based corporation? How?
3. What do you think of Mitsui's policy of nationalizing expatriate executives?
4. What personnel problems might Mitsui have that U.S.- or European-based firms possibly would not have?

CASES FOR PART III

Case A: Polaroid in South Africa

On Monday, November 21, 1977, Polaroid Corporation announced its decision to terminate its distributorship in South Africa thereby ending the "Experiment in South Africa" which it had begun six years earlier. In making this announcement, an official of Polaroid stated:

> We were presented on Wednesday, November 16, with information which suggested that Frank & Hirsch Pty. Ltd., the independent distributor of Polaroid products in South Africa, has been selling film to the government of South Africa in violation of a 1971 understanding. That understanding stipulated that the distributor refrain from selling any Polaroid products to the South African government.

As a consequence of this new information, we initiated that same day an investigation from

Source: This case was prepared by Dr. Dharmendra T. Verma, professor of Marketing, Bentley College, as a basis for class discussion. It is not intended to illustrate either correct or incorrect handling of administrative problems. Copyright © 1978 by Dharmendra T. Verma, Bentley College, Waltham MA 02154.

which we have now learned that Frank & Hirsch has not fully conformed to the understanding with regard to sales to the government.

Accordingly, Polaroid is advising Frank & Hirsch that it is terminating its business relationship with that company.

In 1971, when the question arose as to whether it was appropriate for Polaroid to continue to sell to a distributor in South Africa, we examined the issue carefully. We abhor the policy of apartheid and seriously considered breaking off all business with South Africa. We felt, however, that we should consider the recommendations of black Africans before making a decision. They urged us to maintain our business relationship and try to accomplish improvements in the economic and educational opportunities for black workers. We did succeed in persuading our distributor to give to black employees responsibilities much greater than they had had in the past and substantially to improve black salary rates. We also made contributions, which aggregate about one-half million dollars, to black African scholarship funds and other programs. In much of this activity our distributor cooperated effectively. We were therefore shocked to learn that the understanding not to sell to the government was not followed.

With the termination of this distributorship in South Africa, we do not plan to establish another one.

The South African Distributor: Reaction

Polaroid Corporation's 1977 sales were over $1 billion. The South African business was worth between $3 million and $4 million. This amounted to about half of the revenues of Frank & Hirsch (Pty.) Ltd., the South African distributorship. Helmut Hirsch, the owner of the distributorship, is a "66-year-old German-Jewish emigree who escaped to South Africa from Nazi Germany. In the South African political scene he is considered a liberal. He is a member of the Progressive Party and a friend of Helen Suzman, a well-known critic of the Vorster regime. He has been the chairman of Dorkay House" (*The Boston Globe*, November 23, 1977). The company has distributed Polaroid products for the past eighteen years and it also handled Japanese cameras, watches, and other imported equipment.

Following Polaroid's announcement, Helmut Hirsch issued a statement in Johannesburg on Tuesday, November 22, 1977, that said:

> On hearing allegations that Frank & Hirsch have supplied Polaroid products directly to departments of the South African government, we made an immediate investigation that revealed over the past several years a very small number of isolated cases where unbeknownst to us there were deliveries to the South African government. Frank Hirsch regrets these isolated instances because they are not in keeping with the agreement between Frank & Hirsch and Polaroid. Immediate steps have been taken to avoid any recurrences.

The Boston Globe reported that in a telephone interview Hirsch confirmed that some

sales of Polaroid products to the South African government violated the agreement with Polaroid. According to Hirsch, his investigation of the records showed three sales in 1975, two deliveries in 1976, and 12 transactions so far in 1977. The records do not go back further. However, he insisted that other sales to South African government agencies had not been restricted by the ban agreed upon in 1971. Hirsch claimed that "only some agencies were restricted—the Security Department, the Bantu (black) Reference Bureaus, and the military. Muller's Pharmacy (a large Johannesburg drugstore) was officially permitted to supply anyone. They were tendering government contracts. Polaroid was well aware of it. They knew the government was putting orders through pharmacies" (*The Boston Globe*, November 23, 1977).

In the same interview, Hirsch explained to the Globe that his firm supplied many government agencies, including hospitals, water supply agencies, and airports. These transactions apparently were prearranged with the government agencies through Muller's Pharmacy. Other deliveries were done as a favor. "It's possible the customers phoned, and I was not aware of it." . . . he "begged" Polaroid management not to sever the relationship. . . . Hirsch said he is planning a trip to the United States this weekend to try and repair his relationship. "If they give us an opportunity to talk to them, we have a good case for not abandoning Polaroid from South Africa. It's become a way of life here." Hirsch was planning to bring Sidney Kentridge, a prominent South African attorney, to represent him in discussions with Polaroid over the weekend. (Kentridge represented the Biko family at the inquest into the death of Steve Biko, a well-known black political activist.)

Circumstances Leading to the Polaroid Decision

Polaroid products were sold through the distributor to drugstores and photographic supply houses in South Africa. Polaroid management had known the South African government was using its film, but believed the purchases were made in the open market and not from its distributor. A 1971 agreement between Polaroid and its distributor had specified that no sales were to be made to the South African government.

Allegations of secret sales of Polaroid cameras and film to the South African military and Bantu (black) Reference Bureau that issue identification documents "passbooks" to blacks (an instrument of apartheid) were made by Indrus Naidoo, a former employee of Frank & Hirsch. Naidoo made a photostat of a delivery note covering one shipment of Polaroid film going to the Bantu Reference Bureau on September 22, 1975. This photostat copy was passed on to Paul Irish, an official of the American Committee on Africa (ACOA) in New York City. Irish released the copy to the press in mid-November 1977, only after Naidoo had left South Africa as an exile.

The Boston Globe (November 21, 1977) reported that Naidoo was interviewed by telephone while in Bonn, Germany, where he was on a speaking tour for the African Liberation Movement and he detailed the transactions between Frank & Hirsch and the South African government:

> Frank & Hirsch billed all the shipments to the South African government through Muller's Pharmacy, a drugstore in downtown Johannesburg. The films and cameras were placed in unmarked cartons and then transferred to unmarked transport vans for the drive to their destination. . . . There were regular deliveries to the Voortrekker Hoogte military headquarters outside Pretoria, periodic deliveries to several local reference bureaus, and at least one large shipment of sunglasses to the Air Force. . . . Since all billing was done through Muller's Pharmacy, there would be no record of funds being received from the South African government.

Polaroid management was informed of the charges on Wednesday, November 16, and they dispatched Hans Jensen, the Export Sales Manager and a British auditor, to South Africa to investigate. Polaroid officials stated:

> Helmut Hirsch told us many times he was not selling to the South African government. As far as we were able to determine he had stuck to the agreement. However, we never took for granted they would follow our stipulation. That's why we have sent people there every year.

Mr. Jensen found several deliveries to the South African government in his examination of Frank & Hirsch records. In his telephone conversation with Polaroid officials, Jensen reported that Hirsch, the owner of Frank & Hirsch, was shocked: "He claimed he had no idea this was going on."

On Monday, November 21, 1977, in announcing Polaroid's decision to discontinue the distributorship, Robert Palmer, director of community relations at Polaroid, described Polaroid officials as distressed.

> People are upset and disappointed. . . . Over the past 6 years Polaroid influenced Frank & Hirsch to substantially raise its black employees' wages and we have contributed almost half a million dollars to several black groups in South Africa. Hirsch followed the program we outlined—equal pay for equal work, and black employees were moved into jobs the whites held. The distributor had only 200 black employees but I think our influence had a ripple effect on other U.S. corporations. . . . Now this "Experiment in South Africa" has come to an end.

Polaroid's Experiment in South Africa and Consequences: A Perspective

In late 1970, internal (corporate) and external (community) questions were raised regarding Polaroid Corporation's involvement in South Africa.[1] Specifically, questions focused on the

---

[1] For details describing the initial protest demonstrations and Polaroid's response, see the author's case. "Polaroid in South Africa (A)," ICH 9-372-624. The Polaroid "experiment," along with local and worldwide reaction, are described in the sequel case "Polaroid in South Africa (B),"

use of Polaroid's ID system by the government of South Africa in its passbook program. These passbooks had to be carried by all nonwhite South Africans and were seen as a means whereby the government enforced its apartheid system. In response, a Polaroid team was sent to South Africa to study the problem firsthand. Based on its report, Polaroid management stated that they had reviewed their operations in South Africa and in January 1971 announced an "Experiment in South Africa." The announcement included the following statements:

- We abhor apartheid.
- We want to examine the question of whether or not we should continue to sell our products in South Africa.
- We do not want to impose a course of action on black people of another country merely because we might think it was correct.

A group of Polaroid employees, both black and white, then toured South Africa and returned with a unanimous recommendation to undertake an experimental program for one year with these goals:

- To continue our business relationship there except for any direct sales to the South African government.
- To improve dramatically the salaries and other benefits of the nonwhite employees of our distributor there.
- To initiate through our distributor well-defined programs to train nonwhite employees for important jobs within that company.
- We would commit a portion of our profits earned there to encourage black education.

At the end of the year, in December 1971, Polaroid management issued their report outlining the benefits of their year-long experiment (see Exhibit 1). The report concluded:

In a year's time the visible effects of the Polaroid experiment on other American com-

panies had been limited, but the practical achievements in increased salaries, benefits, and education had shown what could be done. Therefore, the company decided to continue the program for the present.

In November 1977, following a series of reviews and audits, Polaroid issued a report specifying some of the consequences of the six years following the initial decision to undertake the "Experiment" (see Exhibit 2). In conclusion, the report pointed out:

We believe that it is still too soon to make a final judgment on our relationship to South Africa. We have found that the lack of knowledge concerning American business in South Africa has been as difficult to deal with as has the complexity of issues surrounding business practices in that country.

We will continue to press, as constructively as possible, for change in South Africa. We will not, however, decide for black Africans what they need. The final determination will have to come from South Africans themselves. We intend to stay as long as black South Africans and moderate whites feel that progress is being made and that our presence there is helpful. We should acknowledge that our decision to continue is made easier by the fact that our South African distributor has been a willing participant in the changes affecting his workforce.

We agree with our thoughtful critics that the specific accomplishments of the Polaroid experiment affect relatively few black people. A growing number of people, however, are beginning to share our hope that the possibility of change in South Africa is real.

U.S. Corporations and South Africa: A Different Perspective

The nonprofit Investor Responsibility Research Center (IRRC), Washington, D.C., released a study indicating that about 320 American companies have operations in South Africa. Some of the largest (with 1976 sales in South Africa) are Mobil Corporation (over $500 million); Caltex, a joint venture of Standard Oil of Cali-

---

ICH 9-372-625. Both are distributed through the Intercollegiate Case Clearing House, Harvard University.

Exhibit 1
Polaroid's "Experiment in South Africa," 1971

October 1970—Frank & Hirsch (Pty.) Ltd., South African distributor, pay and benefits, black employees:

- Range R303 to R56, average salary R75 per month (South African Rand = $1.15).
- Pension plan applied to both blacks and whites.
- No medical plan for black Africans.
- Interest-free loans for all employees.
- Christmas bonus of one month's salary after three years.
- A black employees' committee in existence.

May 1971—Report to Congressional Sub-Committee on South Africa:

- We decided whatever our course should be it should oppose the course of apartheid.
- Polaroid is a small economic force in South Africa, but we are well-known and, because of our committee's visit there, highly visible. We hope other American companies will join us in this program.
- South Africa articulates a policy exactly contrary to everything we feel our company stands for. We cannot participate passively in such a political system. Nor can we ignore it.
- Both our distributor and one of his suppliers have granted wage increases to all their nonwhite employees ranging from 13 to 33%.
- An additional increase of 28% for a group of twenty nonwhite Frank & Hirsch employees was announced last week (April 25, 1971).
- Frank & Hirsch and one of their suppliers have agreed to guarantee the educational expenses for the children of their nonwhite employees through the high school level including the cost of school tuition, transportation, and books.
- The first installment of a financial grant to the Association for the Educational and Cultural Advancement of the African People of South Africa (ASSECA) has been completed.

- A grant has been made to the U.S. South African Leader Exchange Program (USSALEP).
- We have been working to set up an educational foundation in South Africa. The foundation will be charged with selecting 500 black students and providing financial assistance to them. Administration of this program will be handled by the Institute of Race Relations.
- We are not sure what the longer-term decision will be regarding Polaroid's relationship with South Africa, but we are convinced that the basic approach of working for change from within deserves this kind of trial.

December 1971—End-of-the-year report:

- The average salary including bonus for black employees (at Frank & Hirsch) had now been increased by 22%.
- Individual increases had ranged from 6 to 33%— the average pay was now R91 up from R75 of a few months earlier.
- Eight black supervisors were appointed during the course of the year in the Computer, Administration, Services, and Distribution Departments. Some of these positions had been formerly held by whites and they were being paid on the same pay scale as their predecessors.
- The pension plan with death benefits and the employee education plan were in full operation.
- A grant of $15,000 was completed to the ASSECA.
- A second grant of $10,000 was made to the USSALEP.
- A third grant of $50,000 was used to establish a foundation to underwrite educational expenses of black students and teachers in South Africa—The American–South African Study and Educational Trust (ASSET).
- A fourth grant of $1000 was made to the American–S.A. Institute.

Exhibit 2
Polaroid's "Experiment" Update, November 1977

- Our contributions are continuing to ASSECA, though some concern has been expressed as to the slow pace of programs of this organization based mostly on the problem of a lack of full-time leadership. ASSECA has requested a full-time person from the United States.

- Our financial contributions have also continued to ASSET. In addition we made up for the loss suffered by the recent devaluation of the dollar. Several other companies have also made substantial contributions to ASSET.

- We have also made additional contributions to the U.S. South African Leader Exchange program, the African-American Institute, and a contribution to AIESEC in South Africa—an organization of students in economics and business administration.

- With our encouragement and assistance, the Addison-Wesley Publishing Company of North Reading, Massachusetts, donated over 22,000 new textbooks for use in black South African schools.

- Training programs, medical benefits, legal aid, bursaries (scholarships) and loans have also been expanded at Frank & Hirsch.

There are some who sincerely believe that complete cessation of business with South Africa is the only solution to the existing problems. We respect that view, though we continue to disagree with it. We believe that constructive engagement is the responsible course of action for an American company already there. Though Polaroid does not have plants, investments, subsidiaries, or employees in South Africa, we have for a number of years sold our products through a local distributor, Frank & Hirsch (Pty.) Ltd. We feel for that reason alone we have a responsibility not to walk away from the problem.

We are pleased that some major U.S. (and other) employers in South Africa have initiated affirmative action programs. The company's general feeling continues to be hopeful. We are aware of a number of companies with large investments there who have started serious new programs in the country. We will continue to review our efforts with our distributor and the programs to which we are making financial contributions on an annual basis. Visitors from South Africa and many other people with whom we have corresponded have encouraged us to continue. Press reports of the effects of our experiment have reinforced our decision to proceed.

---

fornia and Texaco ($500 million), Ford ($288 million), General Motors ($250 million), Chrysler (through a 24.9% interest in Sigma Motors, $190 million), IBM ($163 million or less). The U.S. Commerce Department estimates book value of U.S. investments in South Africa at $1.7 billion in 1976. For most American companies, South Africa represents 1% or less of their total sales. However, in the South African economy, some are significant. IRRC reported that American companies control 43% of the country's petroleum market, 23% of its auto sales, and 70% of its computer business (*The Wall Street Journal*, December 5, 1977).

The article further stated that some companies, such as General Motors, Ford, and

Control Data, have indicated they will limit further expansion there. Chrysler, International Telephone, and Phelps Dodge have merged their subsidiaries into South African companies. Burlington Industries, Weyerhaeuser, Halliburton, and Interpace have completely closed down their South African operations.

The call by a number of groups for complete withdrawal of U.S. investments in South Africa has been voiced on numerous occasions. Following the Polaroid announcement, a church group introduced a shareholder's resolution calling on the Eastman Kodak Company to ban all direct and indirect sales to the South African government. This was seen as a first step in a phased withdrawal of Kodak from South Africa. The resolution called on the corporation not to "make or renew any contracts or agreements to sell photographic equipment, including cameras, film, photographic paper and processing chemicals to the South African government."

Eastman Kodak Corporation has been in South Africa since 1913. It employs 470 people, half of them black, and has sales of about $27 million in South Africa out of total sales of $5.4 billion. *The Boston Globe* (December 14, 1977) reported that a Kodak spokesman, Ian Guthrie, had confirmed sales to the South African government. However, it was pointed out that Kodak had no equipment that could be used to make passbooks or ID cards. Moreover, Kodak's policy was to stay in business in South Africa because of "strong" commitment to the 470 employees in its subsidiary, Kodak (South Africa) (Pty.) Ltd.

Kodak and fifty-three other U.S. companies to date have signed a "Statement of Principles" regarding their operations in South Africa (see Exhibit 3). These companies point to steps they have taken to improve the lot of their black employees and express confidence that in time the existing racial barriers can be pulled down. This "Statement of Principles" was drawn up by Reverend Leon Sullivan, a black minister from Philadelphia and a director of General Motors Corporation. *The Los Angeles Times* (December 29, 1977) reported:

> South Africa's Minister of Information, Connie Mulder, officially approved it (Statement of Principles). "In expressing a desire to contribute to the well-being of the black workers in South Africa, these American companies are to be commended," he said.

In a press release issued September 15, 1977, Dr. Leon Sullivan commented on the fifty-four corporate endorsements and the situation in South Africa:

> We are pleased with the response to date, but we will continue to invite other companies to participate. . . . Some encouraging progress has been made during the last six months. I have been informed that racial signs are coming down; in some instances walls are being broken out to end segregation and new integrated facilities are being constructed; blacks are being selected and promoted to supervisory positions; and all companies are developing plans for aggressive future implementation of the six points. Within the next year we shall see if the effort is only a "ripple" or becomes a "tide for change."

At a business recognition dinner on October 5, 1977, attended by many senior corporate officials, Dr. Sullivan informed the executives that the Statement of Principles was being endorsed by non-U.S. groups such as the Federation of Swedish Industries and expressed the hope that "a worldwide effort against segregation and discriminating practices will be developed by businesses on a global scale." He pointed out that the European Economic Community recently announced its South African code of ethics which are very similar to the American Statement of Principles. (The EEC Code goes further in pushing companies to recognize black trade unions and to practice collective bargaining as pointed out in *Business Week*, October 24, 1977.)

At the same dinner, U.S. Secretary of State Cyrus R. Vance said:

> . . . I think that all of you recognize by your presence here tonight the international business community operating in South Africa has an extremely important role to play. By adopting progressive employment practices for your South African Subsidiaries, you not only enhance the lives of those who work for you, you also demonstrate the promise of a society based on racial justice. . . . We believe that you efforts will set an example which will hasten the day when all the people of South Africa will realize their full human and spiritual potential. . . .

Exhibit 3
Statement of Principles

Each of the firms endorsing the Statement of Principles have affiliates in the Republic of South Africa and support the following operating principles:

1. Nonsegregation of the races in all eating, comfort, and work facilities.
2. Equal and fair employment practices for all employees.
3. Equal pay for all employees doing equal or comparable work for the same period of time.
4. Initiation of and development of training programs that will prepare, in substantial numbers, blacks and other nonwhites for supervisory, administrative, clerical, and technical jobs.

5. Increasing the number of blacks and other nonwhites in management and supervisory positions.
6. Improving the quality of employees' lives outside the work environment in such areas as housing, transportation, schooling, recreation, and health facilities.

We agree to further implement these principles. Where implementation requires a modification of existing South African working conditions, we will seek such modification through appropriate channels.

We believe that the implementation of the foregoing principles is consistent with respect for human dignity and will contribute greatly to the general economic welfare of all the people of the Republic of South Africa.

Companies Endorsing "Statement of Principles"*

Abbott Laboratories	Hoover Company
American Cyanamid	Hublein, Incorporated
American Hospital Supply Corporation	Inmont Corporation
Avis, Inc.	IBM Corporation
The Bendix Corporation	International Harvester Company
Burroughs Corporation	Kellogg Company
Caltex Petroleum Corporation	Eli Lilly & Company
The Carborundum Company	Masonite Corporation
Carnation Company	Merck & Company, Inc.
Caterpillar Tractor Company	Minnesota Mining & Manufacturing Company
Citicorp	Mobil Corporation
Colgate-Palmolive Company	Nabisco, Incorporated
Control Data Corporation	Nalco Chemical Company
CPC International	NCR Corporation
Deere & Company	Otis Elevator
Del Monte Corporation	Pfizer, Inc.
Donaldson Company, Incorporated	Phelps Dodge Corporation
Eastman-Kodak Company	Phillips Petroleum
Envirotech Corporation	Rohm & Haas Company
Exxon Corporation	Schering-Plough Corporation
Ford Motor Company	The Singer Company
Franklin Electric	SmithKline Corporation
Gardner-Denver Company	Sperry Rand Corporation
General Motors Corporation	Squibb Corporation
The Gillette Company	Sterling Drug, Inc.
Goodyear Tire and Rubber Company	Union Carbide Corporation
Hewlett Packard Company	Uniroyal, Inc.

* As of September 26, 1977.

Case B: Maple Leaf Tobacco (Kush) Limited (B)

The June 1970 nationalization decree had created a new state corporation called the Nationalized Tobacco Corporation (NTC)—Maple Leaf Tobacco (Kush) Ltd. no longer existed. An army general and a Kushite lawyer were chosen to run the new corporation, assuming the positions of joint managing directors. Unfortunately for NTC, neither had any experience in the tobacco industry. Obtaining a position in the management of NTC appeared to be a reward for faithful service to the party in power. One of the better trained Kushite executives who was Maple Leaf Tobacco's (MLT's) auditor became president of the Kush Central Bank.

Maple Leaf Tobacco headquarters' response to the Kushite government was underlined by respect for the new regime and a strategy of maintaining cordial relations and cooperation. No attempt was made to coerce the government into returning the firm, and no real attempt was made to obtain full payment for the nationalization.

The lack of experience of the new senior executives soon began to show. Cigarette production declined while employment levels rose. The retail stores were neglected and often did not have enough cigarettes to sell. Profits plummeted and soon the corporation was operating at a loss. The nationalization of MLT had failed to produce income for the government and, instead, was becoming a drain on the treasury.

After considerable efforts by MLT headquarters, in 1977 (seven years after the nationalization) the Canadian firm received 51% of the firm back. The government was the minority joint-venture partner. By 1980, however, production was at a low level and the joint venture was still losing money (see Exhibit 1). However, estimates for 1981 showed a small profit.

The MLT Response

After the nationalization events of 1970 and 1971, the Maple Leaf Tobacco Organization (MLTO) had assumed a posture of cooperation toward the Kushite government. A MLTO executive explained:

> We felt we had absolutely nothing to gain from any other stance. The matter of restitution was still up in the air and we didn't want to burn any bridges. Further, we felt we would still like to do business in Kush. It's a matter of company philosophy—we see ourselves as "cigarette makers to the world." What was happening in Kush was the result of political pressures which could calm down or disappear at any time. We wanted to be ready and available to resume control if the opportunity presented itself. There were still a lot of employees who were loyal to MLTO.

So unlike MLTO's response to the Tanzanian expropriation, no ultimatum was given to the Kush government. This behavior was typical of most, but not all, of the other nationalized firms.

The first official communiqué from the government on the matter of financial restitution was received in October 1971, sixteen months after the nationalization. Signed by the president of the Valuation Commission (a position created by the Companies' Nationalization Act 1970), it contained an audited balance sheet of MLT (Kush) Ltd. as of June 18, 1970, a report of the Valuation Committee, and a valuation statement (see Exhibit 2 for a summarized version). The government of Kush offered FrK 1,227,014 for the subsidiary. This compares with MLT's valuation of at least FrK 4 million

Exhibit 1

Maple Leaf Tobacco (Kush) Limited (B) Performance Data

Year	Cigarette Production (thousands of cartons)	Sales* (thousands of FrK)	No. of Employees	Profit Before Taxes/Sales, %
1968	8012	3328[†]	1250	18.3
1969	6537	3127	1130	16.7
1970	6700	3373	1312	13.1
		Nationalization		
1971	7715	4338	1575	14.6
1972	7118	4250	1736	17.4
1973	5804	4296	1675	1.1
1974	4724	4864[†]	1599	(2.8)
1975	4730	5583	1428	(1.8)
1976	5060	6267	1519	(1.9)
1977	4060	5988	1616	(9.3)
		Joint Venture		
1978	2589	4364	1539	(8.2)
1979	4078	7128	1424	(3.9)
1980	2702	8626[†]	1228	(0.5)
1981	3056	—	—	—

*1 Kush Franc (FrK) is worth approximately $3 Canadian.
[†]The market share *in units* for all cigarettes sold in Kush (including imports) for the years 1968, 1974, and 1980 are 50, 28, and 11%, respectively.

(see Exhibit 3). Included in the communiqué was a description of the procedure for appealing the valuation.

MLTO appealed the decision immediately, stating that the valuation statement and balance sheet increased some liabilities retroactively, reduced some assets such as inventories arbitrarily (for example, by increasing the amount deemed to be obsolete), undervalued some fixed assets such as land, and ignored the earnings potential of the company. Further, MLTO felt that there was an additional claim to be made with respect to intercompany loans, directors' fees, and dividends. Exhibits 3 and 4 outline the MLTO submission.

In spite of the fact that MLT's valuation was nearly four times that of Kush's, no real pressure was put on the Kushites to increase their offer. Neither did MLT reduce their "asked" price or push for the early payment of a smaller

sum. Most other nationalized firms, on the other hand, accepted book value in the form of government of Kush long-term bonds nominated in Kush francs.

MLT, in effect, was not interested in being paid for the company. In fact, they actively *avoided* being placed in a position where payment could be made. "If you are paid for a company," an executive argued, "you give up the right to ask for it back." "So we say to the Government, let's forget about payment, just give it back to us."

In line with this strategy, MLT continued to assist the nationalized subsidiary. Nationalized Tobacco Company executives were still invited to MLT courses in Europe and North America, while three expatriates stayed on in Kush for a year to help with the operation. In March 1972, a technical services agreement was signed which provided that MLTO would supply ser-

Exhibit 2
Government of Kush's Valuation Commission Report (October 1971)

A. Balance Sheet of MLT (Kush) Ltd.—June 18, 1970

Assets			Liabilities		
Cash	FrK	104,667	Bank overdraft	FrK	69,394
Accounts receivable		82,778	Accrued charges		540,894
Other current assets		1,120,401	Other current liabilities		399,391
Total current assets		1,307,846	Total current liabilities		1,004,679
Fixed assets (net)		958,396	Provident fund, indem-		
Goodwill		22,015	nity, and pension		53,043
			Long-term loans		170,460
			Share capital		988,000
			Retained earnings for		
			1969 and 1970		72,075
Total assets	FrK	2,288,257	Total liabilities	FrK	2,288,257

B. Government of Kush Valuation Statement

Shareholder net worth = FrK   166,218 (long-term loans)
                             394,543 (accrued dividends)
                             666,253 (excess of assets over liabilities)

                     FrK 1,227,014

Note: FrK 1 = $3 Canadian.

Exhibit 3
MLTO's Valuation Bases for Compensation

1. Book value of net assets as of December 31, 1969	FrK	1,000,473
Increase for adjustment to correct values of fixed assets		261,570
Net earnings after tax from 1 January to 18 June 1970		59,602
Additional 5 years' earning value		2,383,685
Total asset value of company	FrK	3,705,330
2. Alternative pure earnings value	FrK	4,000,000
Plus additional current liability claim (as of 18 June 1970)		
Past due dividends to foreign corporate shareholders	FrK	394,543
Claims of directors (dividends plus fees)		39,571
Loans (previously long-term) from MLTO companies		166,218
Associate MLT companies current accounts		47,672
Total claim	FrK	648,004

Exhibit 4
MLTO Valuation Appeal

Points

1. We agree with the stated amount of dividends which are due (FrK 394,543), however, we object to the classification of this item as part of the compensation for the valuation of the Company.

2. The values for the provident fund, staff indemnity, and pensions have all been increased retroactively.

3. There is an unsubstantiated 30% reduction in the value of the raw material and finished goods inventories based on the fact that these are "dead" items.

4. The valuation report does not take into account the very considerable appreciation in values which has taken place in every country of the world over the past few years, therefore, the fixed assets are undervalued.

5. The value of a company cannot be set based solely on assets, but must also take into account the earning power of that company.

---

vices such as locating sources of supply, product development, and electronic data processing in exchange for $65,000 (Cdn) or 0.5% of the gross turnover of the company, whichever is greater. Foreign exchange approval for this transaction was applied for and approved. This contract was MLTO's first concrete step toward reinvolvement in Kush.

Throughout this period, MLTO had continued to maintain relationships with the Kushite civil service. John Moore, head of the area office in Beirut and responsible for coordinating African activities, was the main character in the activity. A Canadian citizen, he, like Jenssen, the ex-managing director in Kush, had been with MLT most of his working life and was, in fact, Jenssen's predecessor.

By 1972, MLT had accumulated a fair degree of experience at both the headquarters and Africa Area Group level in the operation of joint ventures. Headquarters' staff had been able to successfully negotiate one of the few Western joint ventures in Japan; a process which made them one of the more knowledgeable multinationals in the very difficult area of reducing joint venture instability. The Africa Area Group had, at the same time, successfully negotiated a joint venture in Uganda with the government as partner, but this was never implemented.

As a consequence of this background of success, MLTO headquarters proposed a joint venture to the Kushite government as a politically expedient and face-saving way to reacquire at least some of their subsidiary. MLTO suggested that they and NTC engage in a joint venture to produce cigarette paper and filters which also had a limited market in other industrial applications. The idea was that an addition to the NTC factory could produce this material, which would reduce the loss of foreign exchange incurred in importing these products. MLTO was to get 51% of the manufacturing plant *and* the cigarette plant, in consideration of which MLTO would offset the investment amount against the restitution debt. After some initial discussion with Moore, the government decided *not* to proceed with the proposal. MLTO executives felt that it may have been "too soon"—two years—for the still sensitive government to take these serious steps.

Returning its attention to the valuation of the subsidiary, MLTO's negotiations with the government concerning restitution continued for another year. Finally, in a letter to the Minister of the Treasury dated April 20, 1973, MLTO confirmed that it would accept a valuation in the amount of FrK 1,150,000 plus interest charges, and FrK 643,000 in claims due to the MLTO group (loans, dividends, and fees). The government made no effort to agree to this and MLTO, in line with its strategy, did not push for agreement and payment.

Kush

The situation in Kush immediately following the takeover by Mazrui was anything but quiet. Tensions between nationalists and communists in the government began to show as early as November 1970, when Mazrui attempted to remove a number of influential communists from their positions in government. The situation came to a head in July 1971, when the communists arrested Mazrui and formed a new government. A countercoup supported by one of Kush's neighbors followed three days later and Mazrui was reinstated. The communist leaders were executed. Two months later Mazrui was elected president by an overwhelming majority. All parties remained outlawed, however, with only the official Kush Socialist Union permitted to exist.

This did not solve Mazrui's political problems, however. The successionist movement in the south of the country was gaining strength. Kush's relations with two of its neighbors continued to deteriorate over ideological differences. Refugees from neighboring states poured in over the borders. Compounding these problems was the financial damage resulting from seventeen years of strife and the hastily implemented nationalization program of the early 1970s.

Mazrui realized that to cement his government's position he must improve economic conditions. That he could not do so alone is summed up in an article by *Le Monde* of Paris (March 1973):

> Last August, President Mazrui ordered the return of some 30 expropriated companies to their former [Kushite] owners. "Development cannot be shouldered by the state alone," says Mr. Ibrahim Moneim Mansour, National Economy Minister, "it would mean postponing the prosperity of our present generations to give the public sector time to generate capital and train managers."
>
> There are groups within the Kush Socialist Union, the only authorized political organization, which are skeptical of and even hostile to

this philosophy, but the economic pundits at present in control have plenty of evidence to support their arguments that the over-riding need is to attract capital investment.

> The fundamental need of Kush is to win back the confidence of both foreign and domestic private capital. This has produced a change in priorities toward projects which would give quick returns, supplemented, it is hoped, by foreign institutional aid for the improvement of the transport infrastructure. Without this basic opening-up of communications, the marketing problem would deter most investors attracted by Kush's agricultural potential.
>
> The need to improve transport was cruelly underlined last year when farmers produced a bumper crop of dura (millet) which could not be moved to export markets.
>
> The result has been that Agriculture Ministry statisticians forecast a drop from 2.1m tons to 1.3m tons in this year's dura crop, the only decline expected in Kush's main crops. Encouragement for private investment has been substantial. Mr. Mansour has two new laws on the stocks to supplement the 1972 Development and Promotion of Industrial Investment Act, which provides generous tax and capital repatriation terms for foreign investors, numerous other privileges and even allows for the negotiation of further exemptions for projects deemed to be of national strategic value.
>
> Foreign businessmen with experience in Kush are cautiously optimistic. They feel the Government has at last got its priorities right but they worry about implementation.

Few if any foreign investors took up this opportunity, however. Furthermore, none of those nationalized firms formerly owned by foreign companies were returned to private hands. Although by this time most of the nationalized firms had accepted restitution from the Kushite government.

Roughly two years later the economy was still in bad shape. In a follow-up article from *Le Monde* it was stated:

> The basic facts about the Kushite economy are depressing. In 1973–74 (the financial year runs from July to June) Kush had a GNP at current

prices of FrK 698m, a five percent improvement on the year before. But taking into account the rate of inflation one is forced towards the conclusion that there was probably little or no real growth in these years. It is generally considered that the same conditions, or worse, prevailed throughout the 1960s.

Imports have usually slightly outrun exports overall, and there has usually been a fairly big deficit on the balance of payments' current account. The Government has not always been able to finance all its expenditures out of revenue, so it has borrowed internally, increasing the money supply without a corresponding amount of growth, and thus increasing inflation. Kush has been tragically unable to pull itself up by its bootstraps. But the country is now in the throes of a massive change in an attempt to break out of the no-growth cycle. The immediate result of this courageous policy has been to cause a general economic crisis: a rate of inflation of between 20 and 25 percent, massive congestion on the infrastructure and severe balance of payments problems.

However, the development schemes in the pipeline looks promising: the infrastructure is being improved, and other economic policies initiated by the Government since 1971 are beginning to pay off. Food production is growing fast and self-sufficiency is not far off. Denationalization has improved the business climate and raised efficiency. The State trading corporations, a constant drain on the exchequer, have been severely warned that they cannot keep running up deficits, and there are even hints that some of them might be returned to the private sector.

Finally, the recent reopening of the Suez Canal is a good boost for Kush: it will speed up and may even cheapen the supply of imports, since in the past seven years tramp ships have rarely visited Port Kush. (In the short term, however, it will probably only add to congestion.) Also, Kush has this year become an associate member of the EEC. This will mean price support in exports of sugar, ground nuts and hides and skins to the EEC, as well as the chance of extra aid.

By 1976, three years later, the world press was viewing the Kushite situation with the same optimism, as this article from *Le Monde* indicates:

> Until economic development begins to pay off, which cannot be much before the end of the decade, Kush will continue to go through difficult times. There is little doubt that the security forces are playing an important role in keeping potential opposition under control, by close observation, questioning, and occasional imprisonment. But the Government has several important factors in its favour. By divesting himself of some of the offices which he previously held, including the Prime Ministership, President Mazrui has shown that the Government of Kush is not a one-man affair and that there would be a good chance of continuity if anything happened to the President. Secondly, the resounding defeat of the coup has made it very unlikely that the opposition will again try to remove Mazrui by violence. [There was a coup attempt in 1976.] Thirdly, the army remained entirely loyal to President Mazrui during the coup and is in the last resort the force that keeps him in power. Finally, there is no sign that the confidence of foreign investors has been shaken: businessmen were arriving and important deals being signed with the Government within a few days of the coup attempt. The Government rightly interprets that as a sign of real stability. (See Exhibit 5 for economic data on Kush.)

It is this political and economic climate of 1977 in which the Maple Leaf Tobacco executives offered to form another joint venture with the Kush government.

The Joint Venture

A senior MLTO headquarters' executive comments:

> How we got from being nationalized in 1970 to participating in a joint venture with the Kush government in 1977 is an interesting story. As you know, we wanted to get back into Kush if circumstances were right. We had a technical services agreement with the nationalized company but there wasn't a lot of action taking place on that, so the real first move was in 1972 when we suggested to the government that we

Exhibit 5
Kush Economic Data (millions of FrK)

	1969	1970	1971	1972	1973	1974	1975	1976	1977	1978	1979	1980
Exports	86	104	114	124	152	122	152	193	230	220	210	N/A
Imports	89	100	115	118	152	228	333	341	369	475	455	N/A
Balance of trade	(3)	4	(1)	6	0	(106)	(181)	(148)	(139)	(255)	(245)	N/A
Balance of payments	2	(11)	(20)	(10)	9	(70)	(166)	(168)	(160)	(160)	(44)	N/A
Consumer price index (base 1956)	146	152	154	175	202	254	315	320	374	418	500(est)	N/A
GDP (millions of current FrK)	517	517	532	632	665	698	1422	1570	1845	2324	2133	N/A

participate in a joint venture to build and operate a cigarette paper and filter plant in conjunction with the cigarette factory. We would supply expertise, and our capital investment would take the form of forgiving part of the debt owed to us by the government. We, of course, wanted control. It was possible that government would not be prepared to take such a move at the time, however, we knew that the idea of offsetting the debt as a capital investment did have some appeal for them.

Well, that deal didn't work out and the restitution discussions continued. We figured that it was too soon for Mazrui to make such a move in favor of a foreign firm. We reached tentative agreement on the compensation amount in 1973 but as the years dragged by we still hadn't received any money. (Although we didn't really push for it either.) The government people were very polite and understanding, but we still weren't receiving the funds. You always hear how multinationals have so much power and influence over host governments, but most of the time that just isn't true. The governments do what they want when they want to. At any rate, it was 1977 and we still hadn't received any compensation. Finally, one of our executives met with the Prime Minister of Kush and requested his intervention in this matter. He spoke to the Minister of Industry and within a month we had received a communication inviting us to meet with the Minister to discuss another joint venture. The joint venture, of course, was to be in the ownership and operation of Nationalized Tobacco Corporation.

The executive in question had been Mr. Moore, the head of the Africa and Mid-East Area Group. Mr. Moore had continued to visit Kush at least twice a year since the nationalization. He used these occasions to maintain contact with the Nationalized Tobacco Corporation executives, the Kush civil servants who were in ministries important to the future of MLTO in Kush, and persons close to the president's office.

The senior MLTO executive continued:

Through our correspondents in Kush we had a pretty good idea of the state of the nationalized corporation: production was down, employment was up, and profits had disappeared. The government wanted our expertise to "get the show back on the road" so we knew we had some negotiating room. On the other hand, we saw this as an opportunity to get back into Kush and to get our money back. There was something in this deal for everybody.

The first major problem was how to structure the deal so that the government wouldn't suffer any political embarrassment. When dealing with any government you must be sensitive to how things will look politically, but it is even more important in a situation such as this where the government has to sacrifice political philosophy for economics. What we were talking about doing was, in effect, denationalizing the company. However, it couldn't look that way. The first step to doing this was to have NTC sold to another corporation in which MLTO and the Kush government were shareholders. This procedure made things less obvious because what we were really doing was buying back a share of NTC.

The next problem was that of control. During the initial discussion several possible shareholdings and shareholders were proposed, but the bottom line was that we had to have more than 50% or nothing [see Appendix 1 for an internal MLTO memorandum on the advantages and disadvantages of the proposals]. This was not only company policy, but good sense in a situation where we were going to have to exercise a lot of management power to get the operation back on its feet. *We had to have control.*

This was a contentious point but eventually the government gave in and we got 51%. Of course, who owned the majority of shares was just the first step in getting control. The Memorandum and Articles of Incorporation of the new company had to be negotiated. Here I'm talking about things like the power of the board of directors, quorum requirements, notice for meetings, and things like that. Having 51% of the shares does you no good if you can't exercise real control. Let me give you a very simple but extreme example. Over 51% allowed us to elect 3 out of the 5 directors. Suppose the company documents allowed the board of directors to convene a meeting with 5 minutes' notice, and 2 directors were considered a quorum. The 2 government directors, who live in Kush, could phone the other directors who might be anywhere in the world, inform them that a meeting is taking place in 5 minutes and that a quorum is present. Effectively, the government would have control of the board of directors. We spent quite a bit of time going over the documents to ensure that this kind of thing couldn't happen.

The next question was, how much was 51% going to cost us? We had to have a consensus of what NTC was worth. It was an amusing situation in a way because the tables were reversed—when we were nationalized we wanted a high valuation of the company and the government wanted a low valuation; now we were striving for exactly the opposite. The government's opening position was that NTC was worth 3.5 million Kush Francs, a figure

they had reached after some very liberal asset revaluations. We felt the real worth to be about half of that, even less under the current management. We opened by offering 460,000 Kush Francs. Our experience dealing with the valuation of Maple Leaf Tobacco (Kush) Ltd. had set the groundwork for this kind of discussion and within a short period of time, I think it was a month, we had agreed on a value of FrK 1.7 million. That meant our 51% was going to cost FrK 867,000.

Tied very closely to this issue was payment to Maple Leaf Tobacco Organization for the nationalization. We were going to pay for our 51% out of the funds which the government owed us—we certainly weren't going to invest any outside funds for a while. We had agreed in 1973 that compensation, with interest, was FrK 1,533,000. After the set off against the 51% we were still owed 668,000 francs. We worked out a deal whereby we would be paid this amount over 5 years, with 1 year's grace, at 9% interest. Getting the money in a lump sum was out of the question, but it was payable in *French Francs*.

These points were solved fairly quickly, as were such matters as a trademark agreement to prevent the government from ever using our name again without our permission. What took longer to settle were four issues: foreign exchange availability for raw materials, dividends, machinery, etc.; the technical services fee; payment terms for the current liabilities (dividends, loans, directors fees) still owed by NTC to the MLT group; and what to do about trimming down the workforce at NTC.

MLTO essentially gained little on two of the four issues, with the current liability issue and improved technical services fees being the only bright spots. On the foreign exchange issue, Kush offered to approve foreign exchange ". . . when foreign funds are available." The slightly over FrK 0.5 million in current liabilities owed to MLTO and individuals for loans, fees, and dividends was to be paid over *four years in foreign currency*. The management services fee took awhile to agree on because MLTO felt that NTC was ". . . really in a mess and it was going

to take a lot of management effort to fix.''
MLTO finally agreed on 6% of the first FrK
500,000 profit before tax, plus 3% of the rest.
There was to be a yearly minimum of
$Cdn80,000. This was an improvement over the
prenationalization fee.

The excessive workforce was probably the
most important issue for MLTO (see Exhibit 1
for employee data). As the senior negotiator
noted:

> This was the only issue which we really lost.
> We felt the workforce was too large by about
> 400 or 500 employees, and that it was totally
> undisciplined. We wanted the power to move
> our efficiency experts in and make whatever
> changes were necessary. The issue was just
> too political though, and the government
> wouldn't give in. Natural attrition was to be
> the only method we could use.

The Outcome

The forecast economic progress of Kush did not
materialize by 1981. Serious organizational and
trade problems seemed to push the country further and further into trouble. The following international bond underwriter's report sums it
up:

> Kush has been under severe balance of pay-
> ments pressure for several years as a con-
> sequence of mismanagement, expansionary
> policies, serious lack of absorbtive capacity,
> depressed export earnings and soaring oil
> prices. The current account deficit widened
> from $US65 million in 1973 to $US690 million
> in 1975 and this pattern has not changed much
> since. Export earnings managed to cover only
> a third of the import bill in 1980.
>
> Hence, external debt arrears accumulated so
> that by mid-1979 they were around $US1.1 bil-
> lion. An unprecedentedly generous debt re-
> scheduling took place in the Paris Club involv-
> ing $350 million worth of arrears and $150
> million of future debt service. Long negotia-
> tions with the banks rescheduled another $600
> million over 7 years with 3 years grace and
> included a new Euroloan of $100 million for

> vital imports. Without the Paris Club agree-
> ment the debt service ratio would have been
> 50%. With that agreement it will still be 35% or
> more, so Kush's debt problem remains severe.
> Long-standing economic and administrative
> conditions will cause the external problems to
> continue with little prospect of real im-
> provement despite the government's efforts.
>
> No [debt] exposure (short, medium, or long-
> term) can escape this morass or have any
> chance of being repaid without long delays. We
> consider Kush totally uncreditworthy for any
> loans.

The problems Kush was experiencing were
reflected in the state of the new joint venture.
Projected production and profit figures simply
did not materialize (Exhibit 6). An internal
MLTO review memorandum dated early 1981
summed the situation up:

MLT Kush

- MLT is the only sizable cigarette manufacturer in
  Kush apart from cottage industry.
- Substantial part of Kush's market demand supplied from smuggling—excessive Kush excise
  taxes on local production precludes MLT expansion.
- Experiencing lack of working capital and delays
  in foreign exchange remittances to foreign suppliers. Foreign exchange situation in Kush serious.
- MLTO does not wish further exposure in Kush so
  will solve MLT Kush problems in light of this.

Points:

1. *None* of compensation yet received. MLTO suggests that government consider amount currently
   due as a capital investment by MLT, which
   would reduce government shareholding from
   49% to 35%. The possibility of MLTO collecting
   these funds in any other way would be minimal.
2. Minimum management fee of $80,000 is being
   received but about one year in arrears.
3. MLT Kush to make representation in respect of
   the excessive excise duties on cigarettes produced in Kush, which directly results in high
   levels of cigarette smuggling.

Exhibit 6
Maple Leaf Tobacco (Kush) Limited Performance

	Projected (1977)	Actual
Production (cartons of cigarettes)		
1977	4,269,000	5,060,000
1978	6,500,000	2,589,000
1979	7,500,000	4,078,000
1980	8,400,000	2,702,000
1981	9,200,000	3,056,000
1982	10,100,000	—
Profit Before Taxes (in thousands of FrK)		
1977	(225)	(557)
1978	60	(357)
1979	505	(278)
1980	820	(41)
1981	1,222	102(est)
1982	1,743	—

4. There is strong pressure to clear up MLT Kush's foreign exchange remittances to foreign suppliers for which local currency has all been deposited with the Bank of Kush. Remittances have not been made since April 1980 and $5 million falls into this category with maturities from 1977–79. All *new* shipments are being made on letters of credit confirmed abroad or at free market exchange rate, so backlog should not increase.

5. The World Bank is considering an industrial development support scheme similar to the successful agricultural support scheme. If and when enacted, MLT Kush must be certain that they can obtain assistance for machinery imports and hopefully also in respect of foreign exchange for raw materials and spare parts.

By early 1982 MLT Kush's fortunes were still at a very low level but with some optimism in the air. Production was almost at 1963 levels due to both the low volume of unit sales and the resulting high buildup of inventory. But during 1981 the firm made its first substantial profit (FrK 102,000) since 1973. There was a new general manager in late 1980 replacing one who ". . . didn't seem to be able to generate a successful relationship with the Government . . ." according to a senior MLTO executive. MLTO headquarters felt that the firm has been substan-

tially "turned around" and that the end of 1982 will show a profit as well.

Economic conditions in Kush were, if anything, getting worse. The lack of foreign exchange was preventing almost all repatriations and foreign purchases. The government wasn't even paying its local currency debts to firms like MLT. MLT *unsuccessfully* attempted in 1981 to convert some of the government debt into a sale of the government shares in MLT Kush. Conditions were so bad that MLT thought that it was the only foreign firm in Kush by mid-1981 that was truly manufacturing a product and not just importing. The new manager, a Pakistani citizen who was in MLT Iran until coming to Kush, was optimistic, however, and reported that in operating terms, MLT Kush will soon be a successful firm.

Conclusion

Eric Walton, senior vice-president of MLTO, read the memo on MLT Kush and reflected on the history of this joint venture. "What did we learn," he wondered, "and, in light of the present situation, should we have done something differently? More immediately, what should we do now with this joint venture?"

Appendix 1
Internal MLTO Brief on the 1977 Joint Venture

July 14, 1977

People Met by Mr. Moore, Head MLTO Mid-East Africa

H. E. Abdel Rahman Abdullah—Minister of Industry

Abdel Latif Widatallah—Undersecretary, Ministry of Industry

Abdel Gadir Mansour—Director of Executive Office, Ministry of Industry

Initial Discussions

- We [MLTO] took the approach that the best all-round solution would be to return 100% to MLTO or at minimum 60%.

- The Minister expressed the following views:

    (a) the desire of the government to have a more meaningful relationship between Nationalized Tobacco Corporation and Maple Leaf Tobacco Organization.

    (b) there were no clear-cut policy restrictions regarding return of MLT to the government private sector. But it would be a precedent for a foreign nationalized enterprise.

Options—Proposed by MLTO

1. 100% MLTO
2. 60% MLTO; 40% government
3. 60% MLTO; 40% private sector
4. 60% MLTO; 20% government; 20% private sector
5. 60% MLTO; 20% government; 20% IFC*
6. 60% MLTO; 20% private sector; 20% IFC
7. 60% MLTO; 15% government; 15% private sector; 10% IFC

Options—Added by Government

8. Continuation of existing ownership situation; MLTO management
9. 30% MLTO; 70% government; MLTO management

Advantages to Government of NTC's Return (MLTO's Perspective)

1. Secure best international cigarette expertise to enable profitable operation, efficiency, and expansion of present NTC operations.

2. Free government of operational problems of operating a complex cigarette business.

3. Reduce or eliminate government obligations for compensation/foreign exchange.

*IFC is the International Finance Corporation, a subsidiary of the World Bank.

Continued on page 578

Appendix 1 (*Continued*)

4. Promote Kush's (a) international image for encouragement of foreign investment; (b) local image for encouragement of private sector.

5. Development of Kushite personnel to international industrial standards.

6. Freeing government managerial manpower resources for necessary public sector activities.

Exchange of Opinions Regarding Option 1—100% MLTO

MLTO:

- Maximum positive image for government encouragement of private enterprise and foreign investment.
- Maximum advantages of private enterprise system.
- Maximum incentive for MLTO involvement and support.
- Relieves government of responsibility/involvement in problems of the business.

Government:

- Government has existing plans for expansion of activity in paper industries (sic), thus inconsistent with divestment of NTC.
- Political implications of 100% divestment, particularly NTC considering its size as a substantial industry.
- Government maintains share to participate in profits.

Exchange of Opinions Regarding Option 8—100% Government–MLTO Management

MLTO:

- Impossible to implement *effective* management and authority when MLTO manages but government remains as owner/employer.
- No MLTO precedent or willingness to participate in such arrangement, which MLTO feels will be unsatisfactory to both sides.
- Least incentive for MLTO employment of full resources.
- Lacks implication of credibility.

Exchange of Opinions Regarding Option 9—J/V Government Majority–MLTO Management

MLTO:

- Implies that government intends to exercise management control, which would almost certainly create conflicts with the managing partner.
- MLTO concern that government direction not effective toward private enterprise–oriented economy.
- Minimizes MLTO financial return for efforts.

Conclusion

100% or majority MLTO—good chance and we should fight strongly.

100% government and MLTO management—not acceptable to us.

References and
Selected Bibliography

Ackoff, R. Toward a behavioral theory of communication. *Management Science* (1957) 4:218–234.

Ackoff, R. and Emery, F. *On Purposeful Systems*. Chicago: Aldine-Atherton, 1972.

Adler, N. J. Cross-cultural management research: The ostrich and the trend. *Academy of Management Review* (1983) 8(3):226–232.

Adler, N. J. Cultural synergy: The management of cross-cultural organizations. In *Trends and Issues in OD: Current Theory and Practice,* W. W. Burke and L. D. Goodstein (eds.). San Diego: University Associates, 1980.

Adler, N. J. Re-entry: Managing cross-cultural transitions. Paper presented at the Academy of International Business Meetings, New Orleans, October 25, 1980.

Adler, N. J. A typology of management studies involving culture. *Journal of International Business Studies* (Fall 1983) 6:29–47.

Adler, N. J. Understanding the ways of understanding: Cross-cultural methodology reviewed. In *Comparative Management: Essays in Contemporary Thought,* R. N. Farmer (ed.). Greenwich, CT: JAI Press, 1982.

Adler, N. J. Women as androgynous managers: A conceptualization of the potential for American women in international management. *International Journal of Intercultural Relations* (1983) 3:407–436.

Adler, N. J. and Kiggundu, M. N. Awareness at the crossroad: Designing translator based training programs. In *The Handbook of Intercultural Training Methodology,* Vol. II, D. Landis and R. Brislin (eds.). New York: Pergamon Press, 1983, pp. 124–150.

Adler, N. J. and de VillaFranca, J. Epistemological foundations of a symposium process: A framework for understanding culturally diverse organizations. *International Studies of Management and Organization* (Winter 1982–1983) XII(4):7–22.

Aharoni, Y. On the definition of a multinational corporation. *Quarterly Review of Economics and Business* (1971) 2:14.

Aiken, M. and Hage, J. Organizational interdependence and intra-organizational structure. *American Sociological Review* (1968) 33:912–930.

Aiken, M. and Hage, J. Organizational permeability. Paper presented at the Meeting of the American Sociological Association, NY: 1972.

Ajiferuke, B. and Boddewyn, J. Culture and other explanatory variables in comparative management studies. *Academy of Management Journal* (1970) 13:153–165.

Ajiferuke, M. and Boddewyn, J. Socioeconomic indicators in comparative management. *Administrative Science Quarterly* (1970) 15:453–458.

Ajzen, I. and Fishbein, M. *Understanding Attitudes and Predicting Social Behavior*. Englewood Cliffs, NJ: Prentice-Hall, 1980.

Alderfer, G. P. *Existence, Relatedness and Growth: Human Needs in Organizational Settings*. New York: Free Press, 1972.

Aldrich, H. E. *Organizations and Environments*. Englewood Cliffs, NJ: Prentice-Hall, 1979.

Aldrich, H. E. Organizational boundaries and interorganizational conflict. *Human Relations* (1971) 24:279–287.

Aldrich, H. E. and Herker, D. Boundary spanning roles and organization structure. *Academy of Management Review* (April 1977), pp. 217–230.

Aldrich, H. E. and Pfeffer, J. Environment of organization. In *Annual Review of Sociology,* Vol. 2. Palto Alto, CA: Annual Review (1976), pp. 79–105.

Alexander, William, Jr. Mobil's four-hour environmental interview. *Worldwide P&I Planning* (1970) 4(1):18–24, 26–27.

Al-Issa, I. (ed.). *Culture and Psychology*. Baltimore: University Park Press, 1982.

Allport, G. W., Vernon, P. E., and Lindzey, G. *A Study of Values*. Boston: Houghton Mifflin, 1960.

Almaney, A. Intercultural communication and the MNC executive. *Columbia Journal of World Business* (1974) 9(4):23–28.

Almond, G. A. and Verba, S. *The Civic Culture: Political Attitudes and Democracy in Five Nations*. Princeton: Princeton University Press, 1963.

Alpander, G. G. Drift to authoritarianism: The changing managerial styles of the U.S. executives overseas. *Journal of International Business Studies* (1973) 4(2):1–14.

Alpander, G. G. Foreign MBA: Potential managers for American international corporations. *Journal of International Business Studies* (1973) 4(1):1–13.

Alpander, G. G. Multinational corporations: Homebase affiliate relations. *California Management Review* (Spring 1978) XX (3):47–56.

Alsop, R. Foreign ventures. *The Wall Street Journal,* March 30, 1981.

Anastasi, A. Evolving trait concepts. *American Psychologist* (1983) 38(2):175–183.

Ansoff, H. I. and Brandenburg, R. G. A language of organization design: Parts I and II. *Management Science* (August 1971) 17(12):705–731.

Aram, J. and Piraino, T. The hierarchy of needs theory: An evaluation in Chile. *Interamerican Journal of Psychology* (1978) 12:179–188.

Argyris, C. *Managerial Thinking* by Mason Haire, E. E. Ghiselli and L. W. Porter, Book Review. *Administrative Science Quarterly* (1967) 12:177–179.

Argyris, C. and Schon, D. A. *Organizational Learning: A Theory of Action Perspective*. Philippines: Addison-Wesley, 1978.

Aronoff, J. *Psychological Needs and Cultural Systems*. New York: Van Nostrand, 1967.

Aronoff, J. Psychological needs as a determination in the formation of economic structures: A confirmation. *Human Relations* (1970) 23:123–138.

Arpan, J. S., Ricks, D. A., and Patton, D. J. The meaning of miscues made by multinationals. *Management International Review* (1974) 14:3–11.

Asante, M. K., Newmark, E., and Blake, C. A. (eds.). *Handbook of Intercultural Communication*. London: Sage, 1979.

Athos, A. G. and Gabarro, J. J. *Interpersonal Behavior: Communication and Understanding in Relationships*. Englewood Cliffs, NJ: Prentice-Hall, 1978.

Ayal, I. and Zif, J. Market expansion strategies in multinational marketing. *Journal of Marketing* (Spring 1979) 43:84–94.

Azumi, K., Hickson, D., Horvath, D., and McMillan, C. Trust and organizational structure: A cross-national comparison. Presented at the Conference on Cross-Cultural Studies in Organizational Functioning, Hawaii, 1977.

Badawy, M. K. Managerial attitudes and need orientations of Mid-Eastern executives: An empirical cross-cultural analysis. Proceedings of the Thirty-ninth Annual Meeting of the Academy of Management, Atlanta, GA, August 1979.

Badawy, M. K. Styles of Mideastern managers. *California Management Review* (1980) 22:51–58.

Baker, J. C. and Ivancevich, J. M. The American executives abroad: Systematic, haphazard, or chaotic? *California Management Review* (1971) 13(3):39–44.

Ballon, R. J. Non Western work organization. *Asia Pacific Journal of Management* (September 1983) 1(1):1–4.

Banks, R. F. and Stieber, J. *Multinationals, Unions and Labor Relations in Industrialized Countries*. Ithaca: New York State School of Industrial and Labor Relations, Cornell University, 1977.

Barrett, G. V. and Bass, B. M. Cross-cultural issues in industrial and organizational psychology. In *Handbook of Industrial and Organizational Psychology,* M. D. Dunette (ed.). New York: Rand McNally, 1976, pp. 1639–1686.

Barrett, G. V. and Frank, R. H. Communication preference and performance: A cross cultural comparison. MRC Technical Report 29, August 1969.

Barry, M. Cross cultural research with matched pair of societies. *Journal of Social Psychology* (1969) 79:25–33.

Bartlett, C. A. How multinational organizations evolve. *Journal of Business Strategy* (1982) 3:20–32.

Basche, J. R. *International Dimensions of Planning*. New York: Business International, 1976.

Basche, J. R. and Duerr, M. *Experiences with Foreign Production Work Forces*. New York: Conference Board, 1975.

Baskin, D. W. and Arnoff, C. E. *Interpersonal Communication in Organizations*. Santa Monica, CA: Goodyear, 1980.

Bass, B. M. Leadership in different cultures. In *Stogdill's Handbook of Leadership*, B. M. Bass (ed.). New York: Free Press, 1981, pp. 522–549.

Bass, B. M. *Leadership, Psychology and Organizational Behavior*. New York: Harper & Row, 1960.

Bass, B. M. Participative vs. directive leadership. In *Stogdill's Handbook of Leadership*, B. M. Bass (ed.). New York: Free Press, 1981, pp. 309–330.

Bass, B. M. A preliminary report on manifest preferences in six cultures for participative management. Technical Report 21, Contract No. 00014-67 (A), Management Research Center, University of Rochester, Rochester, NY, 1968.

Bass, B. M. and Burger, P. C. *Assessment of Managers: An International Comparison*. New York: Free Press, 1979.

Bass, B. M. and Eldrige, L. D. Transnational differences in the accelerated manager's willingness to budget for ecology. Technical Report No. 50, University of Rochester, Rochester, NY, 1972.

Bass, B. M. and Farrow, D. L. The importance of manager and subordinate personality in contingency leadership analysis. Proceedings of the Western Academy of Management, 1977.

Bass, B. M. and Franke, R. H. Societal influences in student perceptions of how to succeed in organization. *Journal of Applied Psychology* (1972) 56: 312–318.

Bass, B. M. and Thiagarajan, K. M. Preparing managers for work in other countries. *Journal of European Training* (1972) 1(2):117–132.

Bass, B. M., Valenzi, E. R., Farrow, D. L., and Solomon, R. J. Management styles associated with organizational, task, personal, and interpersonal contingencies. *Journal of Applied Psychology* (1975) 60:720–729.

Bedeian, A. G. Organizational socialization: A cross-cultural comparison. *Management International Review* (1976) 16:73–79.

Bedeian, A. G. *Organizations: Theory and Analysis*. New York: Dryden Press, 1984.

Beeman, D. R., Simonetti, J. L., and Simonetti, F. L. Management policies/ managerial attitudes and task environment agents: A cross-cultural empirical examination. *Management International Review* (1981) 21:67–77.

Beer, M. *Leadership, Employee Needs and Motivation*. Columbus: Ohio State University, Bureau of Business Research, 1968.

Behrman, J. N. Multinational corporations, transnational interests and national sovereignty. *Columbia Journal of World Business* (1969) 4:15–21.

Behrman, J. N. *National Interests and the Multinational Enterprise*. Englewood Cliffs, NJ: Prentice-Hall, 1970.

Bendix, R. Contributions of the comparative approach. In *Comparative Man-*

agement and Marketing, J. Boddewyn (ed.). Glenview, IL: Scott Foresman, 1969, pp. 10–13.

Bennett, M. Testing management theories cross culturally. *Journal of Applied Psychology* (1977) 62(5):578–581.

Beres, M. E. and Portwood, J. D. Explaining cultural differences in the perceived role of work: An intranational cross-cultural study. Paper presented at the Conference on Cross-Cultural Studies in Organizational Functioning, Hawaii, 1977.

Berry, J. W. A functional approach to the relationship between stereotypes and familiarity. *Australian Journal of Psychology* (1970) 22:29–33.

Berry, J. W. Independence and conformity in subsistence level societies. *Journal of Personality and Social Psychology* (1967) 7:415–418.

Berry, J. W. Introduction to methodology. In *Handbook of Cross Cultural Psychology,* Vol. 2, H. C. Triandis and J. W. Berry (eds.). Boston: Allyn & Bacon, 1980.

Berry, J. W. Research in multicultural societies: Implications of cross cultural methods. *Journal of Cross Cultural Psychology* (1979) 10(4):415–434.

Berry, J. W. Textured contexts: Systems and situations in cross cultural psychology. Paper presented at a symposium at the conference on Human Assessment and Cultural Factors. Kingston, Canada, August 16–21, 1981.

Bhagat, R. S. and McQuaid, S. J. An assessment of recent theory and research in the cross cultural study of individual behavior in organization. Paper presented to the Thirty-ninth Annual Meeting of the Academy of Management, Atlanta, GA, 1979.

Bhagat, R. S. and McQuaid, S. J. Role of subjective culture in organizations: A review and direction for future research. *Journal of Applied Psychology Monograph* (1982) 67(5):635–685.

Bhatt, L. J. and Pathak, N. S. A study of functions of supervisory staff and the characteristics essential for success as viewed by a group of supervisors. *Manas* (1962) 9:25–31.

Bherer, H. and Tixiec, P. E. The integration-differentiation process in collective enterprises. Paper presented at the Forty-first Annual Meeting of the Academy of Management, San Diego, CA, August 16–19, 1981.

Birdwhistell, R. L. *Kinesics and Context.* Philadelphia: University of Pennsylvania Press, 1970.

Blake, D. H. and Walters, P. S. The politics of global economic relations. Englewood Cliffs, NJ: Prentice-Hall, 1976.

Blake, R. and Mouton, J. *The Managerial Grid: Key Orientation for Achieving Production Through People.* Houston: Gulf Publishing, 1964.

Blue, J. L. and Haynes, V., Jr. Preparation for the overseas assignment. *Business Horizons* (1977) 20:61–67.

Boddewyn, J. J. (ed.). *Comparative Management and Marketing.* Glenview, IL: Scott Foresman, 1969.

Boddewyn, J. J. (ed.). *European Industrial Managers: West and East.* White Plains, NY: International Arts and Sciences Press, 1976.

Borrman, W. A. The problem of expatriate personnel and their selection in international business. *Management International Review* (1968) 8(4–5):37–48.

Boucher, J. Display rules and facial effective behavior: A theoretical discussion and suggestions for research. In *Topics in Cultural Learning,* Vol. 2, R. Brislin (ed.). Honolulu: East-West Center, 1974, pp. 87–102.

Bourgeois III, L. J. and Boltvinik, M. OD in cross cultural settings: Latin America. *California Management Review* (Spring 1981) XXIII(3):75–81.

Bowen, C. P., Jr. Let's put realism into management development. *Harvard Business Review* (1973) 5(4):86–87.

Bowen, H. R. *Social Responsibilities of Businessmen.* New York: Harper & Row, 1953.

Brandt, W. K. Determinants and effects of structural design in the multinational organization. Columbia University, Graduate School of Business Working Paper, New York, 1978.

Brandt, W. K. and Hulbert, J. M. Patterns of communication in the multinational corporation: An empirical study. *Journal of International Business Studies* (1976) 7(1):57.

Brief, A. P., Nord, W. R., and Atieh, J. The questions we ask, the answers we accept: The impact of work values on the conduct of management research. Unpublished manuscript, New York University, New York, 1985.

Brislin, R. W. *Cross Cultural Encounters: Face to Face Interaction.* Elmsford, NY: Pergamon, 1981.

Brislin, R. W. Cross cultural research in psychology. *Annual Review of Psychology* (1983) 34:363–400.

Brislin, R. W. Translation and content analysis of oral and written materials. In *Handbook of Cross Cultural Psychology—Methodology,* Vol. 2, H. C. Triandis and J. W. Berry (eds.). Boston: Allyn & Bacon, 1980, pp. 389–444.

Brislin, R. W., Bochner, S., and Lonner, W. J. *Cross Cultural Perspectives on Learning.* New York: Wiley, 1975.

Brooke, M. Z. and Remmers, H. L. (eds.). *The International Firm.* London: Pitman, 1977.

Brooke, M. Z. and Remmers, H. L. *International Management and Business Policy.* Boston: Houghton Mifflin, 1978.

Brooke, M. Z. and Remmers, H. L. *The Strategy of Multinational Enterprise.* New York: Elsevier, 1970.

Brossard, M. and Maurice, M. Is there a universal model of organizational structure? *International Studies of Management and Organization* (1976) 6:11–45.

Brown, E. and Sechrest, L. Experiments in cross cultural research. In *Handbook of Cross Cultural Psychology—Methodology,* Vol. 2, H. C. Triandis and J. W. Berry (eds.). Boston: Allyn & Bacon, 1980, pp. 297–318.

Brown, J. L. and Schneck, R. Structural comparison between Canadian and American industrial organizations. *Administrative Science Quarterly* (March 1979) 24:24–47.

Budde, A., Child, J., Francis, A., Kieser, A., and Burgleman, R. Corporate goals, managerial objectives, and organizational structures in British and West German companies. *Organization Studies* (1982) 3(1):1–32.

Burack, E. H. and Smith, R. D. *Personnel Management: Human Resource Approach*. St. Paul, MN: West, 1977.

Burgleman, R. A. A process model of internal corporate venturing in the diversified major firm. *Administrative Science Quarterly* (1983) 28:223–244.

Burger, P. and Doktor, R. Cross cultural analysis of the structure of self-perception attitudes among managers from India, Italy, West Germany, and the Netherlands. *Management International Review* (1976) 6(3):71–78.

Burns, T. and Stalker, G. M. *The Management of Innovation*. London: Tavistock, 1961.

Burnstein, E. An analysis of group decision involving risk. *Human Relations* (1969) 22:381–395.

Business International Corporation. *151 Checklists—Decision Making in International Operations*. New York: Business International Corporation, 1974.

Business International Corporation. Controlling an MNC—II: Decentralizing tendencies among European firms. *Business International* (March 27, 1981) XXVIII(13):101–102.

Business International Corporation. Corporate staffs are playing greater roles in control of the MNC. *Business International* (April 3, 1981) XXVIII(14):105–107.

Business International Corporation. *Designing the International Corporate Organization*. New York: Business International Corporation, 1976.

Business International Corporation. How tightly should a widespread MNC be run? *Business International* (March 20, 1981) XVIII(12) 89–91.

Business International Corporation. *New Directions in Multinational Corporate Organization*. New York: Business International Corporation, 1981.

Business International Corporation. *Organizing the Worldwide Corporation*. New York: Business International Corporation, 1970.

Business International Corporation. Mitsui's big machine for choosing, grooming its international managers. *Business International* (July 18, 1975), pp. 228–229.

Business International Corporation. Successful repatriation demands attention, care, and a dash of ingenuity. *Business International* (March 3, 1978), pp. 65–67.

Business International Corporation. *Worldwide Executive Compensation and Human Resource Planning*. New York: Business International Corporation, 1982.

Business Week. Gauging a family's suitability for a stint overseas. *Business Week* (April 16, 1979), pp. 127–130.

Business Week. Up the ladder, finally. *Business Week* (1975), pp. 58–68.

Campbell, D. T. Distinguishing differences in perception from failures of communication in cross cultural studies. In *Cross Cultural Understanding: Epistemology in Anthropology*, P. S. C. Northrop and H. H. Livingston (eds.). New York: Harper & Row, 1964.

Campbell, D. T. Stereotypes and the perception of group differences. *American Psychologist* (1967) 22:817–829.

Campbell, D. T. Variation and selective retention in socio-cultural evolution. *International Journal of General Systems* (1969) 16:69–85.

Campbell, J. P., and Pritchard, R. D. Motivation theory in industrial and organizational psychology. In *Handbook of Industrial and Organizational Psychology,* M. D. Dunnette (ed.). Chicago: Rand McNally, 1976.

Cascino, E. How one company "adapted" matrix management in a crisis. *Management Review* (1979) 68(11):57–61.

Casse, P. *Training for the Cross-Cultural Mind.* Washington, DC: Society for Intercultural Education, Training and Research, 1981, pp. 125–136.

Casse, P. *Training for the Multicultural Manager.* Washington, DC: Sietar Pub., 1982.

Caves, R. E. Industrial organization, corporate strategy and structure. *Journal of Economic Literature* (March 1980) XVIII:64–92.

Chandler, A. D. The multi-unit enterprise: A historical and international comparative analysis and summary. In *Evolution of International Management Structures,* H. F. Williamson (ed.). Newark: University of Delaware Press, 1975, pp. 225–254.

Chandler, A. D. *Strategy and Structure: Chapters in the History of the Industrial Enterprise.* Cambridge, MA: MIT Press, 1962.

Channon, D. F. The strategy and structure of British enterprise. Unpublished DBA thesis, Graduate School of Business Administration, Harvard University, Cambridge, MA, 1973.

Channon, D. F. and Jalland, M. *Multinational Strategic Planning.* New York: Amacom, 1978.

Chesanow, N. Getting cultured: Class acts for the foreign-bound. *Savvy* (April 1984), pp. 72–77.

Child, J. Culture, contingency and capitalism in the cross national study of organizations. In *Research in Organizational Behavior,* Vol. 3, L. L. Cummings and B. M. Staw (eds.). Greenwich, CT: JAI Press, 1981, pp. 303–356.

Child, J. Organizational structures, environment and performance: The role of strategic choice. *Sociology* (1972) 6:2–22.

Child, J. Parkinson's progress: Accounting for the number of specialists in organizations. *Administrative Science Quarterly* (1973) 18:328–348.

Child, J. and Kieser, A. Contrasts in British and West German management practice: Are recipes for success culture-bound? Paper presented at the Conference on Cross-Cultural Studies on Organizational Functioning, Hawaii, 1977.

Child, J. and Kieser, A. Organization and managerial roles in British and West German companies: An examination of the culture-free thesis. In *Organizations Alike and Unlike,* Lammers, C. J. and Hickson, D. J. (eds.). London: Routledge & Kegan Paul, 1979, Chapter 13.

Chorafas, D. N. *Developing the International Executive.* AMA Research Study No. 83, American Management Associations, 1967.

Chowdhry, K. and Tarneja, R. *India Is Developing Better Managers: An Eight Nation Study.* New York: National Industrial Conference Board, 1961.

Chukwumah, P. A. L. Developments in the search for higher productivity in Africa, 1974.

Clark, A. W. and McCabe, S. Leadership beliefs of Australian managers. *Journal of Applied Psychology* (1970) 54:1–6.

Clark, R. *The Japanese Company*. New Haven, CT: Yale University Press, 1979.

Clausen, G. Risk taking in small groups. Doctoral dissertation, University of Michigan, Ann Arbor, 1965.

Clee, G. H. and Sachtjen, W. M. Organizing a worldwide business. *Harvard Business Review* (November–December 1964), pp. 55–67.

Cleveland, H., Mangone, G., and Adams, J. *The Overseas Americans*. New York: McGraw-Hill, 1960.

Coch, L. and French, J. R. P., Jr. Overcoming resistance to change. *Human Relations* (1948) 1:512–532.

Codes of conduct: Worry over new restraints on multinationals. *Chemical Weekly* (July 15, 1981), pp. 48–52.

Coelho, G. and Ahmed, P. I. *Uprooting and Developments*. New York: Plenum, 1980.

Cole, M., Gay, J., and Scribner, S. *Culture and Thought*. New York: Wiley, 1974.

Cole, M., Gay, J., and Sharp, D. *The Cultural Context of Learning and Thinking*. New York: Basic Books, 1971.

Collins, B. E. and Guetzkow, H. *A Social Psychology of Group Processes for Decision Making*. New York: Wiley, 1964.

Condon, J. C. and Yousef, F. S. *An Introduction to Intercultural Communication*. Indianapolis: Bobbs-Merrill, 1975.

Connolly, T., Conlon, E. J., and Deutsch, S. J. Organizational effectiveness: A multiple-contingency approach. *Academy of Management Review* (1980) 5(2):211–217.

Contractor, F. J. and Sagafi-Nejad, T. International technology transfer: Major issues and policy responses. *Journal of International Business Studies* (Fall 1981), pp. 43–135.

Cotton, F. E. Some interdisciplinary problems in transferring technology and management. *Management International Review* (1973) 13(1):71–77.

Cowley, W. M. Traits of face to face leaders. *Journal of Abnormal and Social Psychology* (1931) 26:304–313.

Crozier, M. *The Bureaucratic Phenomenon*. Chicago: University of Chicago Press, 1964.

Cummings, L. L., Harnett, D. L., and Stevens, O. J. Risk, fate conciliation and trust: An international study of attitudinal differences among executives. *Academy of Management Journal* (1971) 14:285–304.

Cummings, L. L. and Schmidt, S. M. Managerial attitudes of Greeks: The roles of culture and industrialization. *Administrative Science Quarterly* (1972) 17:265–272.

Cuttman, A. W. and Knudson, H. R. (eds.). *Management Problems in International Environments*. Englewood Cliffs, NJ: Prentice-Hall, 1972.

Cyert, R. N. and March, J. G. *A Behavioral Theory of the Firm*. Englewood Cliffs, NJ: Prentice-Hall, 1963.

Dalton, G. W. *Economic Development and Social Change: The Modernization of Village Communities*. New York: Natural History Press, 1971.

Daniels, J. D. International mobility of people: A summary and classification of the issues. *Essays in International Business.* No. 1, March 1980.

Daniels, J. D. and Arpan, J. Comparative home country influences on management practices abroad. *Academy of Management Journal* (September 1972) 15:305–317.

Daniels, J. D., Pitts, R. A., and Tretter, M. J. Strategy and structure of U.S. multinationals: An exploratory study. *Academy of Management Journal* (1984) 27(2):292–307.

Darwin, C. *The Expression of the Emotions in Man and Animals.* New York: Appleton-Century-Crofts, 1872.

Davey, W. G. *Intercultural Theory and Practice: A Case Method Approach.* Washington, DC: Sietar, 1981.

Davidson, W. H. *Experience Effects in International Investment and Technology Transfer.* Ann Arbor, MI: UMI Research Press, 1980.

Davis, S. M. Basic structures of multinational corporations. In *Managing and Organizing Multinational Corporations.* Elmsford, NY: Pergamon, 1979.

Davis, S. M. *Comparative Management: Organizational and Cultural Perspectives.* Englewood Cliffs, NJ: Prentice-Hall, 1971.

Davis, S. M. *Managing and Organizing Multinational Corporations.* Elmsford, NY: Pergamon, 1979.

Davis, S. M. Trends in the organization of multinational corporations. *Columbia Journal of World Business* (1976) 11:59–71.

Davis, S. M. and Lawrence, P. R. Problems of matrix organizations. *Harvard Business Review* (May–June 1978) 56(3):131–142.

Deci, E. L. The effects of contingent and noncontingent rewards and controls on intrinsic motivation. *Organizational Behavior and Human Performance* (1972) 8:217–229.

Deci, E. L. The effects of externally mediated rewards on intrinsic motivation. *Journal of Personality and Social Psychology* (1971) 18:105–115.

De la Torre, J. and Toyne, B. Cross-national managerial interaction: A conceptual model. *Academy of Management Review* (July 1978) 3(3):462–474.

Deutscher, I. Asking questions cross-culturally: Some problems of linguistic comparability. In *Institutions and the Person,* H. Becker, B. Goer, D. Reisman, and R. Weiss (eds.). Chicago: Aldine, 1968.

DeVos, G. A. Achievement and innovation in culture and personality. In *The Study of Personality: An Interdisciplinary Approach,* E. Norbeck, D. Price-Williams, and W. M. McCord (eds.). New York: Holt, Rinehart and Winston, 1968.

DeVos, T. *U.S. Multinationals and Worker Participation in Management. The American Experience in the European Country.* Westport, CT: Quorum Books, 1981.

Deyo, F. C. The cultural patterning of organizational development: A comparative case study of Thailand and Chinese industrial enterprises. *Human Organization* (Spring 1978) 37(1):68–72.

Dickson, J. Top managers' beliefs and rationales in participation. *Human Relations* (1982) 35(3):203–217.

Douglas, S. P. and Craig, C. S. Examining performance of U.S. multinationals in foreign markets. *Journal of International Business Studies* (1983) XIV (3):51–62.

Dowey, W. G. *Intercultural Theory and Practice: A Case Method Approach.* Washington, DC: Sietar, 1981.

Doz, Y. L. Multinational strategy and structure in government controlled businesses. *Columbia Journal of World Business* (Fall 1980), pp. 14–25.

Doz, Y. L. Strategic management in multinational companies. *Sloan Management Review* (Winter 1980), pp. 27–46.

Doz, Y. L., Barlette, C. A., and Prahalad, C. N. Global competitive pressure and host country demands: Managing tensions in MNCs. *California Management Review* (1981) 23(3):72–84.

Doz, Y. L. and Prahalad, C. K. Headquarters influence and strategic control in MNCs. *Sloan Management Review* (Fall 1981), pp. 15–29.

Doz, Y. L. and Prahalad, C. K. How MNCs cope with host government intervention. *Harvard Business Review* (March–April 1980) 58.

Duerr, M. G. and Roach, J. M. Organization and control in European multinational corporation. In *Managing and Organizing the Multinational Corporation,* S. M. Davis (ed.). Elmsford, NY: Pergamon, 1979, pp. 341–352.

Duncan, R. B. Characteristics of organizational environments and perceived environmental uncertainty. *Administrative Science Quarterly* (1972) 17: 313–327.

Duncan, R. B. What is the right organization structure? Decision tree analysis provides the answer. *Organizational Dynamics* (Winter 1977) 7:63.

Dunkerley, M. D. A statistical study of leadership among college women. *Studies in Psychological Psychiatry* (1940) 4:1–64.

Dyaz, G. P. and Thanheiser, H. T. *The Emerging European Enterprises: Strategy and Structure in French and German Industry.* London: Macmillan, 1976.

Dyer, L. and Parker, D. F. Classifying outcomes in work motivation research: An examination of the intrinsic-extrinsic dichotomy. *Journal of Applied Psychology* (1975) 60:455–458.

Dymsza, W. A. and Negandhi, A. R. Introduction to cross cultural management issues. *Journal of International Business Studies* (Fall 1983), pp. 15–16.

Eckensberger, L., Lonner, W., and Poortinga, Y. H. (eds.). *Cross Cultural Contributions to Psychology.* Lisse: Swets and Zeithinger, 1979.

Eden, D. Intrinsic and extrinsic rewards and motives: Replication and extension with kibbutz workers. *Journal of Applied Social Psychology* (1975) 6:348–361.

Edgerton, R. B. *The Individual in Cultural Adaptation: A Study of Four East African Peoples.* Berkeley: University of California Press, 1971.

Edgerton, R. B. and Langness, L. L. *Methods and Styles in the Study of Culture.* San Francisco: Chandler and Sharp, 1974.

Edstrom, A. and Galbraith, J. Alternative policies for international transfers of managers. *Management International Review* (1977) 17:11–22.

Egelhoff, W. Strategies and structures in the MNC: An information processing approach. *Administrative Science Quarterly* (1982) 27:435–458.

Eilbirt, H. and Parnet, I. R. The current status of corporate social responsibility. *Business Horizons* (1973) 16:5–14.

Eisenstadt, S. N. *Tradition, Change, and Modernity*. New York: Wiley, 1973.

Ekman, P., Friesen, W. V., and Ellsworth, P. *Emotion in the Human Face*. New York: Pergamon Books, 1971.

El Dorado at last. *World Business Weekly* (September 8, 1980), pp. 30–37.

Elder, J. W. Comparative cross national methodology. *Annual Review of Sociology* (1976) 2:209–230.

Emery, F. E. and Trist, E. L. The causal texture of organizational environments. *Human Relations* (February 1965) 18(1):21–32.

Endruweit, G. Relations between organizational goals and structures: A comparison of German and U.S. police organization. Paper presented at the Nineteenth International Congress of Applied Psychology, Munich, Germany, 1978.

England, G. W. Managers and their value system. *Discussion Paper Series*, International Institute of Management, Berlin, February 1978.

England, G. W. Managers and their value systems: A five country comparative study. *Columbia Journal of World Business* (Summer 1978) 13(2):35–44.

England, G. W. Personal value systems and expected behavior of managers: A comparative study in USA, Japan, Korea, Australia and India. Paper presented at the Eighteenth International Congress of Applied Psychology, July 1974, Montreal, Canada.

England, G. W., Dhingra, O. P., and Agarwal, N. C. *The Manager and the Man*. Kent, OH: Kent State University Press, 1974.

England, G. W. and Lee, R. Organizational goals and expected behavior among American, Japanese and Korean managers—A comparative study. *Academy of Management Journal* (December 1971), pp. 425–438.

England, G. W. and Lee, R. The relationship between managerial values and managerial success in the United States, Japan, India, and Australia. *Journal of Applied Psychology* (1974) 59(4):411–419.

England, G. W. and Negandhi, A. R. National context and technology as determinant of employee's perceptions. In *Organizational Functioning in a Cross-Cultural Perspective*, G. W. England, A. R. Negandhi, and B. Wilpert (eds.). Kent, OH: Kent State University Press, 1979, pp. 175–190.

England, G. W., Negandhi, A. R., and Wilpert, B. (eds.). *The Functioning of Complex Organizations*. Cambridge, MA: Oelgeschlager, Guin and Hain, 1981.

Europa Yearbook, 1983, A World Survey, The. London: Europa Publications, 1983.

Evan, W. Measuring the impact of culture on organizations. *International Studies of Management and Organization* (1975) 5(1):91–113.

Evans, M. G. The effects of supervisory behavior on the path goal relationship. *Organizational Behavior and Human Peformance* (1970) 5:277–298.

Everett, J. E., Stening, B. W., and Longton, P. A. Some evidence for an international managerial culture. *Journal of Management Studies* (1982) 19: 153–162.

Farmer, R. N. How to forecast a revolution. *World Wide Projects* (April–May 1979), pp. 28–36.

Farmer, R. N. and Lombardi, J. V. (eds.). *Readings in International Business.* Bloomington, IN: Cedarwood Press, 1983.

Farmer, R. N. and Richman, B. M. *Comparative Management and Economic Progress.* Homewood IL: Irwin, 1965.

Farmer, R. N. and Richman, B. M. A model for research in comparative management. *California Management Review* (1964) 4(2):55–68.

Farrace, R. V., Monge, P. R., and Russell, H. M. *Communicating and Organizing.* Reading, MA: Addison-Wesley, 1977.

Fayerweather, J. A conceptual scheme of the interactions of the multinational firm. International issues. *Journal of Business Administration* (Fall 1975) 7(1):67–89.

Fayerweather, J. *The Executive Overseas.* Syracuse: Syracuse University Press, 1959.

Fayerweather, J. *International Business Policy and Administration.* New York: International Executive, 1976.

Fayol, H. *General and Industrial Management.* London: Pitman, 1949.

Feather, N. T. Educational choice and student attitudes in relation to terminal and instrumental values. *Australian Journal of Psychology* (1970) 22:127–144.

Feather, N. T. Test-retest reliability of individual values and value system. *Australian Psychologist* (1971) 6:181–188.

Feather, N. T. Value importance, conservatism, and age. *European Journal of Social Psychology* (1977) 7:241–245.

Fiedler, F. E. *A Theory of Leadership Effectiveness.* New York: McGraw-Hill, 1967.

Fiedler, F. E. and Chemmers, M. *Leadership and Effective Management.* Glenview, IL: Scott Foresman, 1974.

Fiedler, F. E. and Mitchell, T. The cultural assimilator: An approach to cross-cultural training. *Journal of Applied Psychology* (1971) 55(2):95–102.

Fishbein, M. and Ajzen, I. *Belief, Attitude, Intention and Behavior.* Reading, MA: Addison-Wesley, 1975.

Fiske, S. and Linville, P. What does the schema concept buy us? *Personality and Social Psychology Bulletin* (1980) 6(4):543–557.

Fleishman, E. A. Twenty years of consideration and structure. In *Current Developments in the Study of Leadership,* E. A. Fleishman and J. G. Hunt (eds.). Carbondale: Southern Illinois University Press, 1973.

Ford, D. L., Jr. Cultural influences on organizational behavior. In *Organization and People: Readings, Cases and Exercises,* J. B. Ritchie and P. Thompson (eds.). New York: West, 1976.

Foreign Investment in the United States: Policy, Problems and Obstacles. Conference Board Report No. 625. New York: Conference Board, 1974.

Fouraker, L. E. and Stopford, J. M. Organizational structure and the multinational strategy. *Administrative Science Quarterly* (1968) B(1):47–64.

Fox, W. M. Traditional Japanese management: Upside down and inside out. Paper presented at Division 14 Symposium on an International View of Motivation, American Psychological Association Convention, Chicago, 1975.

Franko, L. G. *The European Multinationals: A Renewed Challenge to American and British Big Business*. Stamford, CT: Greylock, 1976.

Franko, L. G. *Joint Ventures Survival in Multinational Corporation*. New York: Praeger, 1971.

Franko, L. G. The move toward a multidivisional structure in European organizations. *Administrative Science Quarterly* (1974) 19:493–506.

Franko, L. G. Multinationals: The end of U.S. dominance. *Harvard Business Review* (November–December 1978) 56:93–101.

Franko, L. G. Who manages multinational enterprises? *Columbia Journal of World Business* (1973) 8(2):30–42.

Freemantle, D. Foreign assignments: A recruiter's nightmare. *Personnel Management* (October, 1978), pp. 33–37.

Friedmann, W. G. and Benguin, J. P. *Joint International Business Ventures in Developing Countries*. New York: Columbia University Press, 1971.

Gabriel, P. MNCs in the third world: Is conflict unavoidable? *Harvard Business Review* (July–August, 1977), p. 50.

Gaedeke, R. M. and Udo-Aka, U. Toward the internationalization of consumerism. *California Management Review* (1974) 17:86–91.

Galbraith, J. K. *The New Industrial State*. Boston: Houghton Mifflin, 1967.

Galbraith, J. R. Organization design: An information processing view. *Interfaces* (May 1974) 4:28–36.

Gallie, D. *In Search of the New Working Class: Automation and Social Integration within the Capitalist Enterprise*. Cambridge: Cambridge University Press, 1978. (Discussed in Child, 1981.)

Geertz, C. Thick description: Towards an interpretative theory of culture. In *The Interpretation of Cultures*. New York: Basic Books, 1973.

Gibson, E. J. *Principles of Perceptual Learning and Development*. New York: Appleton-Century-Crofts, 1969.

Gidengil, B. Z. The social responsibilities of business: What marketing executives think. *European Journal of Marketing* (1977) 11:72–84.

Gladwin, T. N. *Environment, Planning and the Multinational Corporation*. Greenwich, CT: JAI Press, 1977.

Gladwin, T. N. *MNC and the Natural Environment*. New York University, New York, Graduate School of Business Administration, working paper, pp. 75–100.

Gladwin, T. N. Strategic management across cultures: Some American, European and Japanese comparisons. Unpublished manuscript, New York University, New York, 1984.

Gladwin, T. N. and Terpstra, V. Introduction. In *The Cultural Environment of International Business,* V. Terpstra (ed.). Cincinnati: Southwestern, 1978, pp. x–xxiv.

Gladwin, T. N. and Walter, I. *Multinationals Under Fire*. New York: Wiley, 1980.

Glaser, W. Cross-national comparisons of organizations. *International Studies of Management and Organization* (1975) 5(1):68–90.

Glynn, L. Multinationals in the world of nations. In *The Multinational Enterprise in Transition,* P. O. Grub, F. Ghadar, and D. Khambata (eds.). Princeton: Darwin Press, 1984.

Goggin, W. C. How the multi-dimensional structure works at Dow Corning. *Harvard Business Review* (1974) 55(1):54–65.

Gonzalez, R. and Negandhi, A. *The United States Overseas Executive: His Orientation and Career Patterns*. East Lansing: Michigan State University Press, 1967.

Goodman, P. S. and Moore, B. E. Critical issues of cross cultural management research. *Human Organization* (1972) 31(1):39–45.

Gordon, L. V. *The Measurement of Interpersonal Values*. Chicago: Science Research Associates, 1975.

Gordon, L. V. *Survey of Interpersonal Values—Revised Manual*. Chicago: Science Research Associates, 1976.

Gordon, L. V. *Survey of Personal Values—Manual*. Chicago: Science Research Associates, 1967.

Graham, W. K. and Roberts, K. H. *Comparative Studies in Organizational Behavior*. New York: Holt, Rinehart and Winston, 1972.

Granick, D. International differences in executive reward systems: Extent, explanation and significance. *Columbia Journal of World Business* (Summer 1978) 13:45–55.

Granick, D. *Managerial Comparisons of Four Developed Countries: France, Britain, US and Russia*. Cambridge, MA: MIT Press, 1972.

Grant, W. V. and Lind, C. G. *Digest of Educational Statistics,* 1975 ed. Washington, DC: U.S. Government Printing Office, 1976.

Graves, D. The impact of culture upon managerial attitudes, beliefs and behavior in England and France. In *Management Research: A Cross Cultural Perspective,* D. Graves (ed.). San Francisco: Jossey-Bass, 1973, pp. 282–304.

Greenblatt, S. L., Wilson, R. W., and Wilson, A. A. *Organizational Behavior in Chinese Society*. New York: Praeger, 1981.

Griffeth, R. W., Hom, P. W., DeNisi, A., and Kirchner, W. A multivariate, multinational comparison of managerial attitudes. Paper presented at the Fortieth Annual Meeting of the Academy of Management, Detroit, August 1980.

Grosset, S. *Management: European and American Styles*. Belmont, CA: Wadsworth, 1970.

Grub, P. D., Khadar, F., and Khambata, D. (eds.). *The Multinational Enterprise in Transition*. Princeton: Darwin Press, 1984.

Gruenfeld, L. W. Field dependence and field independence as a framework for the study of task and social orientations in organizational leadership. In

Management Research: A Cross Cultural Perspective, D. Graves (ed.). San Francisco: Jossey-Bass, 1973, pp. 5–23.

Gruenfeld, L. W. and MacEachron, A. E. A cross national study of cognitive style among managers and technicians. *International Journal of Psychology* (1975) 10(1):27–55.

Guion, R. M. Industrial morale: The problem of terminology. *Personnel Psychology* (1958) 11:59–64.

Guttman, L. A general nonmetric technique for finding the smallest coordinate space for a configuration of points. *Psychometrika* (1968) 33:461–469.

Guttman, L. Order analysis of correlation matrics. In *Handbook of Multivariate Experimental Psychology,* R. D. Catt (ed.). New York: Rand McNally, 1966.

Hackman, J. R. Group influence on individuals. In *Handbook of Industrial and Organizational Psychology,* M. D. Dunnette (ed.). Chicago: Rand McNally, 1976, pp. 1455–1525.

Haemmerli, A. *Women in international business.* Paper presented at the Women in International Business Conference, New York, July 11, 1978.

Hagen, E. E. *On Theory of Social Change.* Homewood, IL: Dorsey, 1962.

Haire, M., Ghiselli, E. E., and Porter, L. W. *Mangerial Thinking: An International Study.* New York: Wiley, 1966.

Hall, E. T. *Beyond Culture.* New York: Doubleday, 1976.

Hall, E. T. *The Silent Language.* Greenwich, CT: Fawcett, 1959.

Hall, E. T. The silent language in overseas business. *Harvard Business Review* (May–June 1960) 38(3):87–95.

Hall, R. H. Transorganizational structural variation: Application of the bureaucratic model. *Administrative Science Quarterly* (1962) 7:295–308.

Hannan, M. T. and Freeman, J. H. Environment and the structure of organizations: A population ecology perspective. Paper presented at the annual meeting of the American Sociological Association, Montreal, Canada, August 1974.

Hannan, M. T. and Freeman, J. H. The population ecology of organizations. *American Journal of Sociology* (1977) 82:926–964.

Harari, E. and Zeira, Y. Limitations and prospects of planned change in multinational corporations. *Human Relations* (1976) 29(7):659–676.

Harari, E. and Zeira, Y. Training expatriates for managerial assignments in Japan. *California Management Review* (1978) 20(4):56–63.

Harbison, F. and Myers, C. *Management in the Industrial World: An International Study.* New York: McGraw-Hill, 1959.

Harbron, J. D. The dilemma of an elite group: The industrialist in Latin America. *Inter-American Economic Affairs* (1965) 19:43–62.

Harnett, D. L. and Cummings, L. L. *Bargaining Behavior: An International Study.* Houston: Dame Publications, 1980.

Harpaz, I. H. The meaning of working: MOW international research team. In *Management Under Different Value Systems: Political, Social and Economical Perspectives in a Changing World,* G. Olugos, N. Weiermair, and W. Dorow (eds.). New York: Walter de Gruyter, 1981.

Harris, P. R. and Harris, D. L. Training for cultural understanding. *Training and Development Journal* (May 1972), pp. 8–10.

Harris, P. R. and Moran, R. T. *Managing Cultural Differences*. Houston: Gulf Publishing, 1979.

Harrison, R., and Hopkins, R. The Design of Cross Cultural Training: An Alternative to the University Model. *Journal of Applied Behavioral Science* (1967) 3(4):431–460.

Hartigan, J. A. *Clustering Algorithms*. New York: Wiley, 1975.

Hasenfeld, Y. People processing organizations: An exchange approach. *American Sociological Review* (1972) 37:256–263.

Havatny, N. and Pucik, V. An integrated management system: Lessons from the Japanese experience. *Academy of Management Review* (1981) 6:469–480.

Hawkins, R. G. and Walter, I. Planning multinational operations. In *Handbook of Organizational Design,* P. C. Nystrom and W. H. Starbuck (eds.). New York: Oxford University Press, 1981, Chapter 12, pp. 253–267.

Hayden, S. J. Problems of operating overseas: A survey of company experience. *Personnel* (1968) 45(1):8–21.

Hayes, R. D. The executive abroad: Minimizing behavioral problems. *Business Horizons* (June 1972) 15:87–93.

Hays, R. D., Korrth, C. M., and Roudiani, M. *International Business: An Introduction to the World of the Multinational Firm*. Englewood Cliffs, NJ: Prentice-Hall, 1972.

Heenan, D. A. The corporate expatriate: Assignment to ambiguity. *Columbia Journal of World Business* (May–June 1970), pp. 49–53.

Heenan, D. A. Multinational management of human resources: A systems approach. In *Studies in International Business No. 2,* G. M. Scott and R. Moore (eds.). Austin: Bureau of Business Research, University of Texas at Austin, 1975.

Heenan, D. A. and Keegan, W. J. The rise of third world multinationalism. In *The Multinational Enterprise Intransition,* P. O. Grub, F. Ghadar, and D. Khambata (eds.). Princeton: Darwin Press, 1984.

Heenan, D. A. and Keegan, W. J. The rise of third world multinationals. *Harvard Business Review* (January–February 1979), pp. 101–109.

Heenan, D. A. and Perlmutter, H. V. *Multinational Organization Development*. Reading, MA: Addison-Wesley, 1979.

Hein, J. *International Outlook, 1982: The Corporate Perspective*. New York: Conference Board, Report No. 105, 1981.

Heller, F. A. The role of business management in relation to economic development. *International Journal of Comparative Sociology* (1979) 10:292–298.

Heller, F. A. Some problems in multinational and cross cultural research on organizations. Paper presented at the thirty-ninth annual meeting of the Academy of Management, Atlanta, GA, 1975.

Heller, F. A. and Porter, L. W. Perceptions of managerial needs and skills in two national samples. *Occupational Psychology* (1966) 40:1–13.

Heller, F. A. and B. Wilpert. *Competence and Power in Managerial Decision Making*. New York: Wiley, 1981.

Heller, F. A. and Wilpert, B. Managerial decision making: An international comparison. In *Organizational Functioning in a Cross Cultural Perspective*, G. W. England, A. R. Negandhi, and B. Wilpert (eds.). Kent, OH: Kent State, 1979.

Heller, F. A. and Yukl, G. Participation, managerial decision-making, and situational variables. *Organizational Behavioral Human Performance* (1969) 4:227–241.

Heller, J. E. Criteria for selecting an international manager. *Personnel* (1980) 57(3):47–55.

Heneman, H. G., Jr. Work and non-work: Historical perspectives. In *Work and Non-Work in the Year 2001*, M. Dunnette (ed.). Monterey, CA: Brooks/Cole, 1973.

Henry, E. R. What business can learn from Peace Corps selection and training. *Personnel* (1965) 42(4):36–42.

Herbert, T. T., Popp, G. E., and Davis, H. J. Australian work reward preferences. Paper presented at the thirty-ninth annual meeting of the Academy of Management, Atlanta, GA, August 1979.

Herman, J. B. and Hulin, C. L. Managerial satisfaction and organizational roles investigation of Porter's need deficiency scale. *Journal of Applied Psychology* (1973) 57:118–124.

Herzberg, F., Mausner, B., and Snyderman, B. B. *The Motivation to Work*. New York: Wiley, 1959.

Hesseling, P. and Konnen, E. E. Culture and subculture in a decision-making exercise. *Human Relations* (1969) 22:31–51.

Hickson, D. J., Hinings, C. R., McMillan, C. J., and Schwitter, J. P. The culture-free context of organization structure: A tri-national comparison. *Sociology* (1974) 8:59–80.

Hickson, D. J., Pugh, D. S., and Phesey, D. C. Operations technology and organization structure: An empirical reappraisal. *Administrative Science Quarterly* (1969) 14:378–397.

Hildebrand, H. W. Communication barriers between German subsidiaries and parent American companies. *Michigan Business Review* (July 1973), p. 6.

Hines, G. H. Cross-cultural differences in two factor motivation theory. *Journal of Applied Psychology* (1973) 56(3):375–377.

Hines, G. H. and Wellington, V. U. Achievement and motivation levels of immigrants in New Zealand. *Journal of Cross-Cultural Psychology* (1974) 5:37–47.

Hinrichs, J. R. Cross national analysis of work attitudes. Paper delivered at the American Psychological Association Meeting, Chicago, IL, 1975.

Hinrichs, J. R. and Ferrario, A. A cross-national study of manager's job attitudes. Paper presented at the Eighteenth International Congress of Applied Psychology, Montreal, Canada, August 1974.

Hodges, M. *Multinational Corporations and National Government. A Case Study of the U.K.'s Experience 1964–1970*. Lexington, MA: Saxon House/Lexington Books, Heath, 1974.

Hofstede, G. The color of collars. *Columbia Journal of World Business* (September–October 1972), pp. 72–80.

Hofstede, G. The cultural relativity of organizational practices and theories. *Journal of International Business Studies* (1983) 14(2):75–90.

Hofstede, G. *Culture's Consequences: International Differences in Work Related Values.* Beverly Hills: Sage, 1980.

Hofstede, G. Measuring hierarchical power distance in thirty-seven countries. Working paper 76-32, European Institute for Advanced Studies in Management, 1981.

Hofstede, G. Motivation, leadership and organization: Do American theories apply abroad? *Organization Dynamics* (1983) 9:42–63.

Hofstede, G. Nationality and espoused values of managers. *Journal of Applied Psychology* (1976) 61 (2):148–155.

Hoijer, H. (ed.). *Language in Culture.* Chicago, IL: University of Chicago Press, 1954.

Hoijer, H. The Sapir-Whorf hypothesis. In *Intercultural Communication: A Reader,* L. A. Samovar and R. E. Porter (eds.). Belmont, CA: Wadsworth, 1976, pp. 150–158.

Holmen, M. G. Organization and staffing of foreign operations of multinational corporations. Paper presented at the Academy of International Business Meeting, New Orleans, LA, October 25, 1980.

Holsti, J. J. Change in the international system: Interdependence integration and fragmentation. In *Change in the International System,* R. Holsti, R. M. Siverson, and A. L. George (eds.). Boulder: Westview Press, 1980, pp. 23–53.

Hornstein, H. A. and Tichy, N. M. Developing organization development for multinational corporations. *Columbia Journal of World Business* (Summer 1976), p. 136.

Horovitz, J. H. Management control in France, UK and Germany. *Columbia Journal of World Business* (1978) 13:16–22.

Horvath, D., McMillan, C., Azumi, K., and Hickson, D. The cultural context of organizational control: An international comparison. *International Studies of Management and Organization* (1976) 6(3):60–86.

House, R. J. A path goal theory of leader effectiveness. *Administrative Science Quarterly* (1971) 16:556–571.

House, R. J. and Mitchell, T. R. Path goal theory of leadership. *Journal of Contemporary Business* (1974) 3:81–97.

Howard, C. G. The expatriate manager and the role of the MNC. *Personnel Journal* (October 1980), pp. 840–844.

Howell, I. Theoretical directions for intercultural communication. In *Handbook of Intercultural Communication,* M. K. Asanti, E. T. Newmark, and C. E. Blake (eds.). Beverly Hills: Sage, 1979.

Hughes, C. L. and Flowers, V. S. Shaping personnel strategies to disparate value systems. *Personnel* (March–April 1973) 50(2):8–23.

Hulbert, J. M. and Brandt, W. K. *Managing the Multinational Subsidiary.* New York: Holt, Rinehart and Winston, 1980.

Huseman, R. C., Lahiff, J. M., and Hattfield, J. D. *Interpersonal Communication in Organizations.* Boston: Holbrook Press, 1976.

Hutchinson, J. Evolving organizational forms. *Columbia Journal of World Business* (Summer 1976) 2:48–58.

Illman, P. E. *Developing Overseas Managers—and Managers Overseas*. New York: Amacom, 1980.

Inkeles, A. The modernization of man. In *Modernization,* M. Weiner (ed.). New York: Basic Books, 1976.

Inzerilli, G. and Laurent, A. Managerial views of organization structure in France and USA. *International Studies of Management and Organization* (1983) XIII:97–118.

Ivancevich, J. M. Perceived need satisfactions of domestic versus overseas managers. *Journal of Applied Psychology* (1969) 53(4):274–279.

Ivancevich, J. M. Selection of American managers for overseas assignments. *Personnel Journal* (1969) 48(3):189–193.

Ivancevich, J. M. and Baker, J. C. A comparative study of the satisfaction of domestic U.S. managers and overseas U.S. managers. *Academy of Management Journal* (1970) 13:69–79.

Iwawaki, S. and Lynn, R. Measuring achievement motivation in Japan and Great Britain. *Journal of Cross-Cultural Psychology* (1972) 3:219–220.

Izraeli, D. N., Banai, M., and Zeira, Y. Women executives in MNC subsidiaries. *California Management Review* (1980) 23(1):53–63.

Jacoby, N. H. The multinational corporation. In *The Multinational Enterprise in Transition,* P. O. Grub, F. Ghadar, and K. Dara (eds.). Princeton: Darwin Press, 1984, pp. 3–37.

Jaggi, B. Job satisfaction and leadership style in developing countries: The case of India. *International Journal of Contemporary Sociology* (July–October 1977), pp. 230–236.

Jain, S. C. and Puri, Y. Role of multinational corporations in developing countries: Policy makers' views. *Management International Review* (1980) (2):57–66.

Jamieson, I. Capitalism and culture: A comparative analysis of British and American manufacturing organizations. *Sociology* (1980) 14:217–245.

Jamieson, I. The concept of culture and its relevance for an analysis of business enterprise in different societies. *International Studies of Management and Organization* (1982–1983) 12(4):71–105.

Janger, A. R. *Matrix Organization of Complex Businesses*. New York: Conference Board, Report No. 763, 1979.

Janger, A. R. *Organization of International Joint Ventures*. New York: Conference Board, Report No. 787, 1980.

Jelinek, M. Organizational structure: The basic conformations. In *Organizations by Design: Theory and Practice,* M. Jelinek, J. A. Litterer, and R. A. Miles (eds.). Plano, TX: Business Publications, 1981.

Johnson, E. and Johnson, G. Walking on two legs: Rural development in South China. Ottawa: International Development Center, 1976.

Johnson, H. C. *Risk in Foreign Business Environments: A Framework for Thought and Management*. Cambridge: Arthur D. Little, 1980.

Johnston, M. B. and Carter, G. L., Jr. Training needs of Americans working abroad. *Social Change,* 1972.

Jurkovich, R. A core typology of organization environments. *Administrative Science Quarterly* (September 1974) 19(3):380–394.

Kakar, S. Authority patterns and subordinate behavior in Indian organizations. *Administrative Science Quarterly* (1971) 16(3):298–307.

Kanungo, R. N. Work alienation: A pancultural perspective. *International Studies of Management and Organization* (1983) 13:119–138.

Kanungo, R. N. and Wright, R. A cross-cultural comparative study of managerial job attitudes. *Journal of International Business Studies* (Fall 1983), pp. 115–129.

Kanungo, R. N. and Wright, R. W. A cross-cultural comparative study of managerial job attitudes. Paper presented at the Eastern Academy of International Business Meeting, New York, April 1981.

Kao, H. S. R. and Levin, D. A. Worker motivation in South East Asia: A study of spinning workers. Paper presented at the Nineteenth International Congress of Applied Psychology, Munich, Germany, 1978.

Kaplan, H. R. and Tausky, C. Humanism in organization: A critical appraisal. In *A Sociological Reader on Complex Organizations,* A. Etzioni and E. W. Lehman (eds.), 3rd ed. New York: Holt, Rinehart and Winston, 1980, pp. 44–55.

Kapoor, A. and McKay, R. J. *Managing International Markets: A Survey of Training Practices and Emerging Trends.* Princeton: Darwin Press, 1971.

Karni, E. S. and Levin, J. The use of smallest space analysis in studying scale structure. *Journal of Applied Psychology* (1972) 56:341–346.

Kassem, S. Organization theory: American and European styles. *Management International Review* (1977) 17:11–18.

Kast, F. E. Scanning the future environment: Social indicators. *California Management Review* (1980) 23(1):24.

Kast, F. E. and Rosenzweig, J. E. *Organization and Management,* 3rd ed. New York: McGraw-Hill, 1979, p. 131.

Katz, D. Survey research center: An overview of the human relations program. In *Groups, Leadership and Men,* H. Guetzkow (ed.). Pittsburgh: Carnegie Press, 1951.

Katz, D. and Kahn, R. L. *The Social Psychology of Organizations,* 2nd ed. New York: Wiley, 1978.

Katzell, R. A. and Yankelovitch, D. *Work Productivity and Job Satisfaction.* Cleveland, OH.: Psychological Corporation, 1975.

Kauffman, D. L., Jr. *Systems: An Introduction to Systems Thinking.* Minneapolis: Future System, 1980, pp. 16–37.

Kelley, D. R., Stunkel, K. R., and Wescott, R. R. *The Economic Superpowers and the Environment: The United States, the Soviet Union and Japan.* San Francisco: Freeman, 1976.

Kelley, L. and Worthley, R. The role of culture in comparative management: A cross-cultural perspective. *Academy of Management Journal* (1981) 24(1): 164–173.

Kenis, I. A cross-cultural study of personality and leadership. *Group Organizational Studies* (1977) 2:49–60.

Kerr, C., Dunlop, J. T., Harbison, F. H., and Meyers, C. A. *Industrialism and Industrial Man.* New York: Oxford University Press, 1960.

Kervasdoue, J. de, and Kimberly, J. R. Are organization structures culture-free? The case of hospital innovation in the U.S. and France. Paper presented at the Conference on Cross-Cultural Studies in Organizational Functioning, Hawaii, 1977.

Killing, J. P. How to make a global joint venture work. *Harvard Business Review* (1982) 60:120–127.

King, N. Clarification and evaluation of the two-factor theory of job satisfaction. *Psychological Bulletin* (1970) 74:18–31.

Kitano, H. *Japanese-Americans: Evolution of a Subculture.* New York: Prentice-Hall, 1968.

Klineberg, O. Emotional expression in Chinese literature. *Journal of Abnormal and Social Psychology* (1983) 33:517–530.

Kluckhohn, F. R. and Strodtbeck, F. *Variations in Value Orientations.* Westport, CT: Greenwood Press, 1961.

Kobrin, S. J. *Managing Political Risk Assessment.* Berkeley: University of California Press, 1982.

Kobrin, S. J. Political risk: A review and reconsideration. *Journal of International Business Studies* 10:67–80 (Spring–Summer 1979).

Kobrin, S. J. Political assessment by international firms: Models or methodologies? *Journal of Policy Modeling* (1980) 3(2):251–270.

Kobrin, S. J. When does political instability result in increased investment risk? *Columbia Journal of World Business* (Fall 1978) 13:113–122.

Kobrin, S. J., Basek, J., Blank, S., La Palombara, J. The assessment and evaluation of noneconomic environment by American firms: A preliminary report. *Journal of International Business Studies* (Spring–Summer 1980) 11:32–47.

Kochan, T. Determinants of the power of boundary units in an interorganizational bargaining relation. *Administrative Science Quarterly* (1975) 20:434–452.

Kolde, E.-J. *Environment of International Business.* Boston: Kent Publishing, 1982.

Kornadt, H. J., Eckensberger, L. H., and Emminghaus, W. B. Cross cultural research on motivation and its contribution to a general theory of motivation. In *Handbook of Cross-Cultural Psychology:* Vol. 3. *Basic Processes,* H. C. Triandis and W. Lonner (eds.). Boston: Allyn & Bacon, 1980.

Korten, F. E. The influence of culture and sex on the perception of persons. *International Journal of Psychology* (1974) 9:31–44.

Kotter, J. P. Managing external dependence. *Academy of Management Review* (1979) 4(1):87–92.

Kraar, L. The multinationals get smarter about political risks. *Fortune* (March 24, 1980), pp. 186–200.

Kraut, A. I. Management assessment in international organizations. Symposium: cross-national research. *Industrial Relations* (1973) 12:172–182.

Kraut, A. I. Some recent advances in cross-national management research. *Academy of Management Journal* (1975) 18:538–549.

Kraut, A. I. and Ronen, S. Validity of job facet importance: A multinational multicriteria study. *Journal of Applied Psychology* (1975) 60(6):671–677.

Kroeber, A., and Kluckhohn, C. *Culture: A Critical Review of Concepts and Definitions.* Cambridge, MA: Papers of the Peabody Museum of American Archeology and Ethnology, Harvard University, 1952, pp. 1–223.

Kroeber, A. and Parsons, T. The concepts of culture and of social system. *American Sociology Review* (1958) 23:582–583.

Krus, D. J. and Rysberg, J. A. Industrial managers and nAch: Comparable and compatible? *Journal of Cross-Cultural Psychology* (1976) 7:491–496.

Kohls, R. L. *Developing Intercultural Awareness.* Washington, DC: Sietar, 1981.

Kumar, K. Economics falls short: The need for studies on the social and cultural impact of transnational enterprises. In *Functioning of the Multinational Corporation,* A. R. Negandhi (ed.). Elmsford, NY: Pergamon, 1980.

Kumar, U. Desirable and actual modes of conflict resolution of Indian managers and their organizational climate. Paper presented at the Nineteenth International Congress of Applied Psychology, Munich, Germany, 1978.

Laaksonen, O. J. The power structure of Chinese enterprises. *International Studies of Management and Organization* (1977) 7:71–90.

Lall, S. *The New Multinationals: The Spread of Third World Enterprises.* New York: Wiley, 1983.

Lammers, C. J. and Hicksen, D. J. (eds.). *Organizations Alike and Unlike: International Studies in the Sociology of Organizations.* London: Routledge & Kegan Paul, 1979.

La Palombara, J. and Blank, S. *Multinational Corporations in Comparative Perspective.* New York: Conference Board, Report No. 725, 1977.

La Palombara, J. and Blank, S. *Multinational Corporations and Developing Countries.* New York: Conference Board, 1979.

La Palombara, J. and Blank, S. *Multinational Corporations and National Elites: A Study in Tensions.* New York: Conference Board, Report No. 702, 1976.

Landis, D. and Brislin, R. W. *Handbook of Intercultural Training,* Vols. I, II, and III. Elmsford, NY: Pergamon, 1983.

Lau, S. Managerial style of traditional Chinese firms. Unpublished dissertation, University of Hong Kong, Hong Kong, 1977.

Lawler, E. E., III. *Motivation in Work Organization.* Monterey, CA: Brooks/Cole, 1973.

Lawrence, P. R. and Lorsch, J. W. Differentiation and integration in complex organizations. *Administrative Science Quarterly* (1967) 12(1):1–47.

Lawrence, P. R. and Lorsch, J. W. *Organization and Environment.* Homewood, IL: Irwin, 1967.

Lee, J. A. Cultural analysis in overseas operations. *Harvard Business Review* (1966) 44:106–114.

Leontiades, J. The uprooted European manager. *European Business,* Winter 1973.

LeVine, R. A. *Dreams and Deeds: Achievement Motivation in Nigeria.* Chicago: University of Chicago, 1966.

Levinson, H. *Emotional Health in the World of Work*. New York: Harper & Row, 1964.

Lewin, K. *Field Theory in Social Science*. New York: Harper & Row, 1951.

Lewin, K. and Lippitt, R. An experimental approach to the study of autocracy and democracy: A preliminary note. *Sociometry* (1938) 1:292–300.

Lewis, P. V. *Organizational Communication*. Columbus, OH: Grid, 1980.

Likert, R. An emerging theory of organizations, leadership and management. In *Leadership and Interpersonal Behavior,* L. Petrullo and B. M. Bass (eds.). New York: Holt, Rinehart and Winston, 1961.

Likert, R. *New Patterns in Management*. New York: McGraw-Hill, 1961.

Lincoln, J. R., Hanada, M., and Olson, J. Cultural orientations and individual reactions to organizations: A study of employees of Japanese-owned firms. *Administrative Science Quarterly* (1981) 26:93–115.

Lingoes, J. C. An IBM-7090 program for Guttman-Lingoes smallest space analysis-I. *Behavioral Science* (1965) 10:183–184.

Lingoes, J. C. Identifying regions in the space for interpretation. In *Geometric Representations of Relational Data,* J. C. Lingoes (ed.). Ann Arbor: Mathesis Press, 1977.

Livingston, J. S. Myth of the well-educated manager. *Harvard Business Review* (1971) 49(1):79–89.

Lorsch, J. W. Organization design: A situational perspective. *Organizational Dynamics* (Autumn 1977), pp. 2–14.

Lowe, C. A. and Goldstein, J. W. Reciprocal living and attributions or ability: Mediating effects of perceived intent and personal involvement. *Journal of Personality and Social Psychology* (1970) 16:291–297.

Luthans, F. and Hodgetts, R. M. *Social Issues in Business*. New York: Macmillan, 1976.

Lynton, R. P. and Pareek, U. *Training for Development*. Homewood, IL: Dorsey Press, 1967.

Macarov, D. Work patterns and satisfactions in an Israeli kibbutz: A test of the Herzberg hypothesis. *Personnel Psychology* (1972) 25:483–493.

Machungwa, P. D. and Schmitt, N. Work motivation in a developing country. *Journal of Applied Psychology* (1983) 68:31–42.

MacIver, R. M. *The Web of Government*. New York: Macmillan, 1947.

Maehr, M. L. Sociocultural origins of achievement motivation. *International Journal of Intercultural Relations* (1977) 1:81–104.

Mahler, W. R. Coaching. In *Training and Development Handbook,* R. L. Craig and L. R. Bittel (eds.). New York: McGraw-Hill, 1967.

Mahoney, T. A. *Building the Executive Team*. Englewood Cliffs, NJ: Prentice-Hall, 1961.

Maisonrouge, J. G. The education of the modern international manager. *Journal of International Business Studies* (Spring–Summer 1983), pp. 141–146.

Malpass, R. S. Theory and method in cross cultural psychology. *American Psychologist* (1977) 32(12):1069–1079.

March, J. G. and Simon, H. A. *Organizations*. New York: Wiley, 1958.

Marquis, D. G. Individual responsibility and group decisions involving risk. *Industrial Management Review* (1962) 3:8–23.

Marsh, R. M. and Mannari, H. Lifetime commitment in Japan: roles, norms, and values. *American Journal of Sociology* (1971) 76:795–812.

Maruyama, M. Paradigmatology and its application to cross disciplinary, cross professional and cross cultural communication. *Dialectica* (1974) p. 28.

Maslow, A. H. *Motivation and Personality*. New York: Harper & Row, 1954.

Mason, A. K. and Maxwell, S. R. Changing attitudes to corporate social responsibility. *Business Quarterly* (1975) 40:42–50.

Mason, R. H. Conflict between host countries and the multinational enterprise. *California Management Review* (1974) 17:5–14.

Mason, R. H., Miller, R., and Weigel, D. *International Business*. New York: Wiley, 1981.

Matheson, R. *People Development in Developing Countries*. New York: Wiley, 1978.

Maurice, M. Introduction: Theoretical and ideological aspects of the universalistic approach to the study of organizations. *International Studies of Management and Organization* (1976) 6(3):3–10.

Maurice, M., Sorge, A., and Warner, M. Societal differences in organizing manufacturing units: A comparison of France, West Germany and Great Britain. *Organizationl Studies* (1980) 1(1):59–86.

Mayes, B. T. Some boundary considerations in the application of motivation models. *Academy of Management Review* (1978), pp. 51–58.

Mayo, E. H. and the Western Electric Company. In *Organization Theory*, D. Pugh (ed.). Middlesex, England: Penguin Books, 1971, pp. 215–229.

McAdam, T. W. How to put corporate responsibility into practice. In *Social Issues of Business,* F. Luthans and R. Hodgetts (eds.). New York: Macmillan, 1976.

McCann, E. C. An aspect of management philosophy in the United States and Latin America. *Academy of Management Journal* (1964) 7:149–152.

McClelland, D. C. *The Achieving Society*. Princeton: Van Nostrand Reinhold, 1961.

McClelland, D. C. and Winter, D. G. *Motivating Economic Achievement*. New York: Free Press, 1969.

McFie, J. The effect of education on African performance on a group of intellectual tests. *British Journal of Educational Psychology* (1961) 31:232–240.

McKenzie, C. Incompetent foreign managers. *Business Horizons* (1966) 9(1): 83–90.

McMillan, C., Hickson, D., Hinings, C., and Schneck, R. The structure of work organizations across societies. *Academy of Management Journal* (1973) 16:555–569.

Meade, R. An experimental study of leadership in India. *Journal of Social Psychology* (1967) 72:35–43.

Megginson, L. C. *Personnel: A Behavioral Approach*. Homewood, IL: Irwin, 1967.

Melikian, I., Grinsberg, A., Guceloglu, D. M., and Lynn, R. Achievement motivation in Afghanistan, Brazil, Saudi Arabia, and Turkey. *Journal of Social Psychology* (1971) 83:183–184.

Metcalfe, J. L. Systems models, economic models and the causal texture of organizational environment: An approach to macro-organizational theory. *Human Relations* (1974) 27(7):639–663.

Meyer, M. W. and associates. *Environments and Organizations*. San Francisco: Jossey-Bass, 1978.

Michels, R. *Political Parties: A Sociological Study of the Oligarchical Tendencies of Modern Democracy*. New York: Free Press [1915] 1962.

Miles, R. H. *Macro Organizational Behavior*. Santa Monica: Goodyear, 1980.

Miles, R. E., Snow, C. C., Meyer, A. D., and Coleman, H. J., Jr. Organizational strategy, structure and process. *Academy of Management Review* (July 1978), pp. 546–562.

Miller, E. L. The international selection decision: A study of managerial behavior in the selection decision process. *Academy of Management Journal* (1973) 16(2):234–252.

Miller, E. L. The selection decision for an international assignment: A study of the decision-maker's behavior. *Journal of International Business Studies* (1972) 3(2):49–65.

Miller, E. L. and Cattaneo, R. J. Some leadership attitudes of West German expatriate personnel. *Journal of International Business Studies* (1982) 13:39–50.

Miller, E. L. and Cheng, J. L. C. A closer look at the decision to accept an overseas position. *Management International Review* (1978) 18: 25–33.

Miller, S. W. and Simonetti, J. L. Culture and management: Some conceptual considerations. *Management International Review* (1974) 11(60):87–100.

Miller, V. A. *The Guidebook for International Trainers in Business and Industry*. New York: Van Nostrand Reinhold (American Society for Training and Development), 1979.

Mills, T. Europe's industrial democracy: An American response. *Harvard Business Review* (November–December 1978), pp. 143–152.

Miner, J. B. and Dachler, H. P. Personnel attitudes and motivation. In *Annual Review of Psychology* (1973), Vol. 24, P. H. Mussen and M. R. Rosenzweig (eds.). Palo Alto, CA: Annual Reviews.

Mintzberg, H. Patterns in strategy formation. *Management Science* (1978) 24(9):934–948.

Mintzberg, H. *The Structuring of Organizations*. Englewood Cliffs, NJ: Prentice-Hall, 1979, Chapter 15.

Misami, J. and Seki, F. Effects of achievement motivation on the effectiveness of leadership patterns. *Administrative Science Quarterly* (1971) 16:51–59.

Mitchell, R. E. Survey materials collected in developing countries: Sampling, measurement and interviewing obstacles to intra and international comparisons. In *Comparative Management and Marketing,* J. Boddewyn (ed.). Glenview, IL: Scott Foresman, 1969, pp. 232–252.

Moore, R. The cross-cultural study of organizational behavior. *Human Organization* (1974) 33:37–45.

Moran, R. T. and Harris, P. R. *Managing Cultural Synergy*. Houston: Gulf Publishing, 1982, p. 81.

Morey, N. and Luthans, F. An emic perspective and ethnoscience methods for organizational research. *Academy of Management Review* (1984) 9(1):27–36.

Morris, C. *Varieties of Human Value*. Chicago: University of Chicago Press, 1956.

Morsbach, H. A cross-cultural study of achievement motivation and achievement values in two South African groups. *Journal of Social Psychology* (1969) 79:267–268.

Mostwind, D. Uprootment and anxiety. *International Journal of Mental Health* (1976) 5(2):103–116.

Mouton, J. and Blake, R. Issues of transnational organization development. In *Managing for Accomplishment*, B. M. Bass, R. Cooper, and A. H. Hass (eds.). Boston: Heath, 1970, pp. 208–224.

Mozina, S. Management opinion on satisfaction and importance of psychosocial needs in their jobs. *Proceedings*, Sixteenth International Congress of Applied Psychology. Amsterdam: Swets and Zeitlinger, 1969, pp. 788–794.

Mulder, M. *The Daily Power Game*. Leyden: Martinus Nijhoff, 1977.

Mulder, M. Reduction of power differences in practice: The power distance reduction theory and its applications. In *European Contributions to Organization Theory*, G. Hofstede and M. S. Kassem (eds.). Assen: Van Gorcum, 1976.

Multinationals in Contention. Conference Board Report No. 749. New York: Conference Report, 1978.

Murdock, G. P. Common denominator of cultures. In *The Science of Man in the World Crises*, R. Linton (ed.). New York: Columbia University Press, 1945, pp. 12–142.

Murray, J. A. Intelligence systems of the MNCs. *Columbia Journal of World Business* (September–October 1972), p. 63.

Murray, J. A. International personnel repatriation: Cultural shock in reverse. *MSU Business Topics* (1973) 2(3):59–66.

Muttayya, B. C. Personality and value orientations of panchayat leaders, informal leaders and non-leaders: A comparative study. *Behavioral Science Community Development* (1977) 11:1–11.

Nambudiri, C. N. S. and Saiyadain, M. S. Management problems and practices: India and Nigeria. *Columbia Journal of World Business* (1978) 13:62–70.

Naroll, R. *Data Quality Control*. Glencoe, IL: Free Press, 1962.

Naroll, R. Galton's problem. In *A Handbook of Method in Cultural Anthropology*, R. Naroll and R. Cohen (eds.). New York: Natural History Press, 1970.

Naroll, R. Some thoughts on comparative methods in cultural anthropology. In *Methodology in Social Research*, H. M. Blalock and A. B. Blalock (eds.). New York: McGraw-Hill, 1968, pp. 236–277.

Nath, R. A methodological review of cross-cultural management research. *International Social Science Journal* (1968) 20:35–61.

Negandhi, A. R. Comparative management and organization theory: A marriage needed. *Academy of Management Journal* (1975) 18(2):334–344.

Negandhi, A. R. Convergence in developing countries. In *Organizations Alike and Unlike,* C. J. Lammers and D. J. Hickson (eds.). London: Routledge & Kegan Paul, 1979, Chapter 17.

Negandhi, A. R. Cross cultural management research: Trends and future directions. *Journal of International Business Studies* (1983) 14(2):17–28.

Negandhi, A. R. Cross-cultural studies—Too many conclusions, not enough conceptualization. *Management International Review* (1974) 14:59–67.

Negandhi, A. R. *Functioning of the Multinational Corporation: A Global Comparative Study.* Elmsford, NY: Pergamon, 1980.

Negandhi, A. R. (ed.). *Modern Organizational Theory.* Kent, OH: Kent State University Press, 1973.

Negandhi, A. R. and Baliga, B. R. *Quest for Survival and Growth: A Comparative Study of American, European, and Japanese Multinationals.* New York: Praeger, 1979.

Negandhi, A. R. and Baliga, B. R. *Tables Are Turning: German and Japanese Multinational Companies in the United States.* Cambridge, MA: Odgeschlages, Quin and Hani, 1981.

Negandhi, A. R. and Prasad, S. B. *Comparative Management.* New York: Appleton-Century-Crofts, 1971.

New CPI tactics reduce risk of investing abroad. *Chemical Week,* February 25, 1981, pp. 38–44.

Newcomb, T. M. Stabilities underlying changes in interpersonal attraction. *Journal of Abnormal and Social Psychology* (1963) 66:376–386.

Newman, W. H. Adapting transnational corporate management to national interests. *Columbia Journal of World Business* (1979) 14:82–88.

Newman, W. H. Is management exportable? *Columbia Journal of World Business* (January–February 1970), pp. 7–18.

Noer, D. M. *Multinational People Management: A Guide for Organizations and Employees.* Washington, DC: Bureau of National Affairs, 1975.

Nord, W. R. Culture and organizational behavior. In *Concepts and Controversy in Organizational Behavior,* 2nd ed., W. R. Nord (ed.). Santa Monica: Goodyear, 1976, pp. 197–211.

Nord, W. R. Social exchange theory: An integrative approach to social conformity. *Psychological Bulletin* (1969) 71:174–208.

Nowotny, O. H. American vs. European management philosophy. *Harvard Business Review* (1964) 42:101–108.

Orpen, C. Market conditions, decentralization and managerial effectiveness in South African and American corporations. *Management International Review* (1978) 1:61–67.

Orpen, C. The relationship between job satisfaction and job performance among Western and tribal black employees. *Journal of Applied Psychology* (1978) 63(2):263–265.

Orpen, C. The relationship between managerial success and personal values in South Africa: A research note. *Journal of Management Studies* (May 1976), pp. 196–198.

Orpen, C. The work values of Western and tribal black employees. *Journal of Cross-Cultural Psychology* (1978) 9:99–112.

Ouchi, W. G. *Theory Z, How American Business Can Meet the Japanese Challenge*. Reading, MA: Addison-Wesley, 1981.

Owarish, F. Management development in less developed countries: Lessons, results, evaluation (the UN experience). Paper presented at the Nineteenth International Congress of Applied Psychology, Munich, Germany, 1978.

Pahlman, R. A., Ang, J. S., and Ali, S. I. Policies of multinational firms: A survey. *Business Horizons* 19: December 1976.

Palmer, D. D., Veiga, J. F., and Vora, J. A. Managerial value profiles as predictors of policy decisions in a cross-cultural setting. Unpublished manuscript, undated.

Pareek, U. N. and Kumar, V. K. Expressed motive of entrepreneurship in an Indian town. *Psychologia* (1969) 12:109–114.

Parner, S. H. and Smith, M. A. Work and leisure. In *Handbook of Work Organization and Society,* R. Dubin (ed.). Chicago: Rand McNally, 1976.

Parsons, T. Culture and social system revisited. In *The Idea of Culture in the Social Sciences,* L. Schneider and C. Bonjean (eds.). Cambridge: Cambridge University Press, 1973.

Parsons, T. *Structure and Process in Modern Societies*. New York: Free Press, 1960.

Pascale, R. T. Communication and decision making across cultures: Japanese and American comparisons. *Administrative Science Quarterly* (1978) 23:91–110.

Pascale, R. T. and Athos, A. G. *The Art of Japanese Management: Applications for American Executives*. New York: Warner Books, 1981.

Patterson, M. L. *Nonverbal Behavior: A Functional Perspective*. New York: Springer-Verlag, 1983.

Paven, R. D. J. The strategy and structure of Italian enterprise. Unpublished DBA thesis, Graduate School of Business Administration, Harvard University, Cambridge, MA, 1973.

Payne, R. Factor-analysis of a Maslow-type need satisfaction questionnaire. *Personnel Psychology* (1970) 23:251–268.

Pazam, A. and Reichel, A. Cultural determinants of managerial behavior. *Management International Review* (1977) 17:65–72.

Penn, R., Sheposh, J. P., and Riedel, J. A cross-cultural investigation of organizational functioning. Paper presented at the Nineteenth International Congress of Applied Psychology, Munich, Germany, 1978.

Pepper, S. C. *The Source of Value*. Berkeley: University of California Press, 1958.

Perham, J. C. The boom in executive jobs. *Dun's Review* (1977) 110(5):80–95.

Perlmutter, H. V. The tortuous evolution of the multinational corporation. *Columbia Journal of World Business* (January–February 1969) 4:9–18.

Perlmutter, H. V. *Towards a Theory and Practice of Social Architecture: The Building of Indispensable Institutions*. London: Tavistock, 1965.

Perlmutter, H. V., Root, F. R., and Plante, L. V. Responses of U.S.-based

MNCs to alternative public policy futures. *Columbia Journal of World Business* (Fall 1973), p. 78.

Perlmutter, H. V. and Heenan, D. A. How multinational should your top managers be? *Harvard Business Review* (November–December 1974) 52: 121–132.

Perlmutter, H. V. and Heenan, D. A. *Multinational Organization Development: A Social Architectural Perspective.* Reading, MA: Addison-Wesley, 1979.

Perrow, C. A. A framework for the comparative analysis of organizations. *American Sociological Review* (1967) 32:194–208.

Perrow, C. A. *Organizational Analysis: A Sociological View.* Belmont, CA: Wadsworth, 1970.

Peterson, R. B. and Shimada, J. Y. Sources of management problems in Japanese-American joint ventures. *The Academy of Management Review* (1978) 3:796–804.

Pezeshkpur, C. Challenges to management in the Arab world. *Business Horizons* (1978) 21:47–55.

Pfeffer, J. Management as symbolic action: The creation and maintenance of organizational paradigms. In *Research in Organizational Behaviors,* Vol. 3, L. L. Cummings and B. M. Staw (eds.). Greenwich, CT: JAI Press, 1981, pp. 1–52.

Pfeffer, J. and Leblebici, H. The effect of competition on some dimensions of organizational structure. *Social Forces* (December 1973) 52(2):268–279.

Pfeffer, J. and Nowak, P. Joint ventures and interorganizational interdependence. *Administrative Science Quarterly* (1976) 21:398–418.

Pfeffer, J. and Salancik, G. R. *The External Control of Organizations: A Resource Dependence Perspective.* New York: Harper & Row, 1978.

Phatak, A. V. *International Dimensions of Management.* Belmont, CA: Wadsworth, 1983.

Phillips, G. M. *Communicating in Organization.* New York: Macmillan, 1982.

Piaget, J. *The Moral Judgement of the Child,* M. Gabain, trans. London: Routledge & Kegan Paul, 1970.

Poblador, N. S. The structure of authority and the distribution of rewards in Philippine and American banks. *International Studies of Management and Organization* (1975) 5(1):48–67.

Poortinga, Y. H. (ed.). *Basic Problems in Cross Cultural Psychology.* Lisse: Swets and Zeitlinger, 1977.

Porter, L. W. A study of perceived need satisfaction in bottom and middle management jobs. *Journal of Applied Psychology* (1961) 45:1–10.

Porter, L. W. and Lawler, E. E. Properties of organizational structure in relation to job attitudes and job behavior. *Psychological Bulletin* (1965) 64:23–51.

Porter, L. W. and Roberts, K. H. Communication in organizations. In *Handbook of Industrial and Organization Psychology,* M. D. Dunnette (ed.). Chicago: Rand McNally, 1976, pp. 1553–1590.

Porter, L. W. and Siegel, J. Relationships of tall and flat organization structure to the satisfaction of foreign managers. *Personnel Psychology* (1965) 18: 379–392.

Porter, M. E. *Competitive Strategy: Techniques for Analyzing Industries and Competitors.* New York: Free Press, 1980.

Porter, M. E. How competitive forces shape strategy. *Harvard Business Review* (March–April 1979), pp. 137–145.

Prahalad, C. K. and Doz, Y. L. An approach to strategic control in MNC's. *Sloan Management Review* (Summer 1981), pp. 5–13.

Prasad, S. B. and Krishna Shetty, Y. K. *An Introduction to Multinational Management.* Englewood Cliffs, NJ: Prentice-Hall, 1976.

Presidential Commission on Foreign Language and International Studies. *Strength Through Wisdom: A Critique of U.S. Capability.* Washington, DC: U.S. Government Printing Office, 1979.

Preston, L. E., Rey, F., and Dierkes, M. Comparing corporate social performance. *California Management Review* (1978) 20:40–49.

Preston, L. E., Rey, F., and Dierkes, M. The social examination. *L'Expansion* (April 1975), pp. 75–97.

Preston, L. E., Rey, F., and Dierkes, M. The social examination. *L'Expansion* (April 1976), pp. 93–122.

Pugh, D. S., Hickson, D. J., Hinings, C. R., and Turner, C. The context of organization structures. *Administrative Science Quarterly* (1969) 14:91–114.

Pugh, D. S., Hickson, D. J., Hinings, C. R., and Turner, C. Dimensions of organizational structure. *Administrative Science Quarterly* (1968) 13:65–105.

Punnett, B. J. and Ronen, S. Operationalizing cross-cultural variables. Paper delivered at the Forty-fourth Annual Meeting of the Academy of Management, Boston, MA, 1984.

Rahim, A. A model for developing key expatriate executives. *Personnel Journal* (April 1983), pp. 312–317.

Rahim, A. and Bonoma, T. V. Managing organizational conflict: A model for diagnosis and intervention. *Psychological Reports* (1979) 44:1323–1344.

Raveed, S. and Sekaran, V. Executives' attitudes toward foreign equity investment. *ASCI Journal of Management* (1979) 9(1):68–80.

Raypolov, G. I was a Soviet manager. *Harvard Business Review* (1966) 44: 117–125.

Redding, S. G. Cognition as an aspect of culture and its relation to management processes: An explanatory view of the Chinese case. *Journal of Management Studies* (1980) 17:127–148.

Redding, S. G. Some perceptions of psychological needs among managers in South East Asia. In *Basic Problems in Cross-Cultural Psychology,* Y. H. Poortinga (ed.). Amsterdam: Swets and Zeitlinger, 1977, pp. 338–343.

Redding, S. G. and Casey, T. W. Managerial beliefs among Asian managers. In *Proceedings of the Academy of Management,* R. L. Taylor et al. (eds.), pp. 351–355.

Redding, S. G. and Martyn-Johns, T. A. Paradigm differences and their relation to management, with reference to South-East Asia. In *Organizational*

Functioning in a Cross-Cultural Perspective, G. W. England, A. R. Negandhi, and B. Wilpert (eds.). Kent, OH: Kent State University Press, 1979, pp. 103–125.

Redding, S. G. Some perceptions of psychological needs among managers in South-East Asia. Paper presented at the Third International Conference at the International Association for Cross-Cultural Psychology, Tilburg, Holland, July 1976.

Reischauer, E. O. *The Japanese.* Cambridge, MA: Harvard University Press, 1977.

Reitz, H. J. The relative importance of five categories of needs among industrial workers in eight countries. *Proceedings of the Academy of Management* (1975), pp. 270–272.

Rice, G. E. On cultural schemata. *American Ethnologist* (1980) 7(1):153–171.

Richman, B. and Orpen, M. Management techniques in the developing nations. *Columbia Journal of World Business* (1973) 8:49–58.

Ricks, D. A. *Big Business Blunders.* Homewood, IL: Dow Jones–Irwin, 1983.

Ricks, D. A., Fu, M. Y. C., and Arpan, S. *International Business Blunders.* Columbus, OH: Grid, 1974.

Roberts, K. H. On looking at an elephant. An evaluation of cross cultural research related to organizations. *Psychological Bulletin* (1970) 74(5):327–350.

Roberts, K. H. and Boyacigiller, N. Issues in cross national management research: The state of the art. Paper delivered at the National Meeting of the Academy of Management, New York, NY, 1982.

Roberts, K. H. and Snow, C. C. (eds.). A symposium: Cross national organizational research. *Industrial Relations* (1973) 12(2):137–247.

Roberts, K. H., Walter, G. A., and Miles, R. E. A factor analytic study of job satisfaction items designed to measure Maslow need categories. *Personnel Psychology* (1971) 24:205–220.

Robinson, R. D. *International Business Management—A Guide to Decision Making,* 2nd ed. Hinsdale, IL: Dryden, 1978.

Robinson, R. D. *International Business Policy.* New York: Holt, Rinehart and Winston, 1964.

Robinson, R. D. *Internationalization of Business: An Introduction.* New York: Dryden, 1984.

Robock, S. H. The case for home country controls over multinational firms. *Columbia Journal of World Business* (1974) 9:75–79.

Robock, S. H. and Simmonds, K. International business: How big is it? *Columbia Journal of World Business* (May–June 1970).

Robock, S. H. and Simmonds, K. *International Business and Multinational Enterprise,* 3rd ed. Homewood, IL: Irwin, 1983.

Robock, S. H., Simmonds, K., and Zwick, J. *International Business and Multinational Enterprises.* Homewood, IL: Irwin, 1977.

Rogers, J. *Global Risk Assessments: Issues, Concepts and Applications.* Riverside, CA: Global Risk Assessments, 1983.

Rohner, R. P. and Ness, R. C. Procedures for assessing the validity and reliability of data in cross-cultural research. Document MS 856, American Psychological Association, Washington, DC: 1974.

Rokeach, J. *The Nature of Human Values*. New York: Free Press, 1973.

Ronen, S. *Alternative Work Schedules: Selecting, Implementing and Evaluating*. Homewood, IL: Dow Jones–Irwin, 1984.

Ronen, S. Applying nonmetric multivariate analysis in cross cultural research. Paper presented at the annual meeting of the Academy of Management, New York, NY, 1982.

Ronen, S. A comparison of job facet satisfaction between paid and unpaid industrial workers. *Journal of Applied Psychology* (1977) 62(5):582–588.

Ronen, S. Cross-national perspective of the image of I/0 psychology by personnel executives. *Professional Psychology* (Special Issues: Industrial/organizational psychology—An overview) (1980) 11(3):399–406.

Ronen, S. Cross-national study of employees work goals. *International Review of Applied Psychology* (1979) 28(1):1–12.

Ronen, S. *Flexible Working Hours: An Innovation in the Quality of Work Life*. New York: McGraw-Hill, 1981.

Ronen, S. Personal values: A basis for work motivational set and work attitudes. *Organizational Behavior and Human Performance* (1978) 21:80–107.

Ronen, S. and Kraut, A. I. An experimental examination of work motivation taxonomies. *Human Relations* (1980) 33(7):505–516.

Ronen, S. and Kraut, A. I. Similarities among countries based on employee work values and attitudes. *Columbia Journal of World Business* (1977) 12(2):89–96.

Ronen, S., Kraut, A. I., Lingoes, J. C., and Aranya, N. A nonmetric scaling approach to taxonomies of employees' work motivation. *Multivariate Behavioral Research* (1979) 14:387–401.

Ronen, S. and Punnett, B. J. Nation or culture: The appropriate unit of analysis in cross-cultural research. Paper presented at Northeast Meeting of the Academy of International Business, NY, Spring 1982.

Ronen, S. and Shenkar, O. Clustering countries on attitudinal dimensions: A review and synthesis. *Academy of Management Review,* 1985 (in press).

Rose, S. Why the multinational tide is ebbing. *Fortune* (August 1977), pp. 111–120.

Ross, M. H. and Homer, E. Galton's problem in cross-national research. *World Politics* (October 1976), pp. 1–28.

Rowthorn, R. *International Big Business 1957–1967*. London: Cambridge University Press, 1971.

Rubin, B. D., Askling, L. R., and Kealey, D. J. Cross-cultural effectiveness: An overview. In *Intercultural Communication: State of the Art Overview,* D. S. Hoopes (ed.). Pittsburgh: Society for Intercultural Education, Training and Research, 1977.

Ruhly, D. *Orientation to Intercultural Communication*. Chicago: Science Research Associates, 1976.

Rumelt, R. P. *Strategy, Structure, and Economic Performance*. Boston: Division of Research, Graduate School of Business Administration, Harvard University, 1974.

Rummel, R. J. and Heenan, D. A. How multinationals analyze political risk. *Harvard Business Review* (1978) 56:67–76.

Russell, P. W. and Dickinson, T. L. *Factors affecting the selection of American managers for overseas assignment.* Unpublished manuscript, Colorado State University, 1979.

Rutenberg, D. P. *Multinational Management.* Boston: Little, Brown, 1982.

Ryterband, E. C. and Barrett, G. V. Managers' values and their relationship to the management of tasks: A cross-cultural comparison. In *Managing for Accomplishment,* B. M. Bass, R. Cooper, and J. A. Hass (eds.). Lexington, MA: Heath, 1970, pp. 226–260.

Sadler, P. J. and Hofstede, G. H. Leadership styles: Preferences and perceptions of employees of an international company in different countries. *Mens en Onderneming* (1972) 26:43–63.

Salmans, S. Total productivity hours increase involvement. *International Management* (1978) 33:131–141.

Samovar, L. A., Porter, R. E., and Jain, N. C. *Understanding Intercultural Communication.* Belmont, CA: Wadsworth, 1981.

Sarnoff, I. *Society with Tears.* Secaucus, NJ: Citadel Press, 1960.

Schaupp, D. and Kraut, A. I. A study of the communality of industrial values across cultures. *Proceedings of the Academy of Management* (1975), pp. 291–292.

Schein, E. H. Does Japanese management style have a message for American managers? *Sloan Management Review* (1981) 23:55–68.

Schlesinger, I. M. and Guttman, L. Smallest space analysis of intelligence and achievement tests. *Psychological Bulletin* (1969) 71(2):91–100.

Schollhammer, H. The comparative management theory jungle. *Academy of Management Journal* (1969) 12:81–97.

Schollhammer, H. The compensation of international executives. *MSU Business Topics* (Winter 1969).

Schollhammer, H. Current research on international and comparative management issues. *Management International Review* (1975) 15:29–45.

Schollhammer, H. Strategies in comparative management theorizing. In *Comparative Management Teaching, Training and Research,* J. Boddewyn (ed.). New York: New York University Comparative Management Workshop, 1970, pp. 13–44.

Schramm, W. and Roberts, D. F. (eds.). *Process and Effects of Mass Communication.* Urbana: University of Illinois Press, 1971.

Schriesheim, C. A., Mowday, R. T., and Stogdill, R. M. Crucial dimensions of leader-group interactions. In *Cross-Currents in Leadership*, J. G. Hunt and L. L. Larson (eds.). Carbondale: Southern Illinois University Press, 1979.

Scott, B. R. The industrial state: Old myths and new realities. *Harvard Business Review* (March–April 1973), pp. 133–148.

Scott, W. A. *Values and Organizations: A Study of Fraternities and Sororities.* Chicago: Rand McNally, 1965.

Sechrest, L. On the dearth of theory in cross cultural psychology: There is madness in our method. In *Basic Problems in Cross Cultural Psychology*, Y. H. Poortinga (ed.). Amsterdam: Swets and Zeitlinger, 1977, pp. 73–82.

Segall, M. H. *Cross Cultural Psychology: Human Behavior in Global Perspective*. Belmont, CA: Wadsworth, 1979.

Segall, M. H., Campbell, D. T., and Herskovitz, M. J. *The Influence of Culture on Visual Perception*. Indianapolis: Bobbs-Merrill, 1966.

Sekeran, U. Are U.S. organizational concepts and measures transferable to another culture? An empirical investigation. *Academy of Management Journal* (1981a) 24(2):409–417.

Sekaran, U. The dynamics of job involvement. Unpublished doctoral dissertation, University of California, Los Angeles, 1977.

Sekaran, U. Methodological and analytic considerations in cross-national research. *Journal of International Business Studies* (Fall 1983) 14(2):61–73.

Sekaran, U. Methodological and theoretical issues and advancements in cross cultural research. *Journal of International Business Studies* (1983) 14(2):61–73.

Sekaran, U. Nomological networks and the understanding of organizations in different cultures. *Forty-first Academy of Management Proceedings* (1981b), pp. 54–58.

Sekaran, U. and Martin, H. J. An examination of the psychometric properties of some commonly researched individual differences, job and organizational variables in two cultures. *Journal of International Business Studies* (1982) 13(1):51–65.

Sekaran, U. and Trafton, R. S. The dimensionality of jobs: Back to square one. *Twenty-first Midwest Academy of Management Proceedings* (1978), pp. 249–262.

Serpell, R. Cultural validation in psychological research. Paper presented at the Nineteenth International Congress of Applied Psychology, Munich, Germany, 1978.

Servan-Schreiber, J. J. *The American Challenge*, R. Steel, trans. New York: Atheneum, 1968.

Sethi, S. P. *Japanese Business and Social Conflict*. Cambridge, MA: Ballinger, 1975.

Sethi, S. P. A research model to study the environmental factors in management. *Management International Review* (1970) 10(6):75–79.

Sethi, S. P. Coca-Cola and the Middle East crisis: International politics and multinational companies. In *Advanced Cases in MNB Operations*. Pacific Palisades, CA: Goodyear, 1972, pp. 69–73.

Sethi, S. P. and Sheth, J. N. *Multinational Business Operations I: Environmental Aspects of Operating Abroad*. Santa Monica, CA: Goodyear, 1973.

Seward, J. Speaking the Japanese Business Language. *European Business* (Winter 1975), pp. 40–47.

Shaw, M. E. Communication networks. In *Advances in Experimental Social Psychology*, Vol. 1. L. Berkowitz (ed.). New York: Academic Press, 1964, pp. 111–147.

Shaw, M. E. *Group Dynamics: The Psychology of Small Group Behavior*. New York: McGraw-Hill, 1971.

Sheridan, M. Young women leaders in China. *Signs* (1976) 2:59–88.

Shetty, Y. K. and Vernon, M. B. Corporate responsibility in large-scale American firms. *Management International Review* (1976) 16(1):25–33.

Simon, H. A. *Administrative Behavior*. New York: Macmillan, 1961.

Simonetti, S. H. and Weitz, J. Job satisfaction: Some cross-cultural effects. *Personnel Psychology* (1972) 25:107–118.

Singh, N. P. N-Ach among agricultural and business entrepreneurs of Delhi. *Journal of Social Psychology* (1970a) 81:145–149.

Singh, N. P. N-Ach, risk-taking and anxiety as related to age, years of schooling, job experience, and family: Commitment among progressive-traditional, successful-unsuccessful agricultural entrepreneurs of Delhi. *Psychologia* (1970b) 13:113–116.

Singh, N. P. and Wherry, R. J., Sr. Ranking of job factors by factory workers in India. *Personnel Psychology* (1963) 16:29–33.

Sinha, D. Study of motivation in a developing country: Concept of happy life among Indian farmers. *Journal of Social Psychology* (1969) 79:89–97.

Sinha, J. B. P. The authoritarian leadership: A style of effective management. *Indian Journal of Industrial Relations* (1976) 2:381–389.

Sinha, J. B. P. Power in superior-subordinate relationships: The Indian case. *Journal of Social and Economic Studies* (1978) VI(II):205–218.

Sirota, D. The multinational corporation: Management myths. *Personnel* (1972) 49:37.

Sirota, D. and Greenwood, J. M. Understand your overseas work force. *Harvard Business Review* (1971) 49(1):53–60.

Sitaram, K. S. and Cogdell, R. T. *Foundations of Intercultural Communication*. Columbus, OH: Merrill, 1976.

Sitaram, K. S. and Haapanen, L. W. The role of values in intercultural communication. In *Handbook of Intercultural Communication,* M. K. Asante, E. Newmark, and C. A. Blake (eds.). Beverly Hills: Sage, 1979.

Slocum, J. W. A comparative study of the satisfaction of American and Mexican operatives. *Academy of Management Journal* (1971) 14:89–97.

Slocum, J. W. and Topichak, P. W. Do cultural differences affect job satisfaction? *Journal of Applied Psychology* (1972) 56(2):177–178.

Slocum, J. W., Topichak, P. M., and Kuhn, D. G. Cross-cultural study of need satisfaction and need importance of operative employee. *Personnel Psychology* (1971) 24:435–445.

Smith, A. J. Similarity of values and its relation to acceptance and the projection of similarity. *Journal of Psychology* (1957) 43:251–260.

Smith, B. E. and Thomas, J. M. Cross-cultural attitudes among managers: A case study. *Sloan Management Review* (1972) 13:34–51.

Smith, E. C. and Fiber, L. *Towards Internationalism: Readings in Cross Cultural Communication*. Rowley, MA: Newbury House Publishers, 1979.

Smith, H. L. and Krueger, L. M. *A Brief Summary of Literature on Leadership*. Bloomington: Indiana University, School of Education Bulletin, 1933.

Smith, L. The hazards of coming home. *Dun's Review* (1975) 106(4):71–73.

Smith, P. C., Kendall, L. M., and Hulin, C. L. *The Measurement of Satisfaction in Work and Retirement*. Chicago: Rand McNally, 1969.

Sorge, Arndt. Cultured organizations. *International Studies of Management and Organization* (1982–1983) 12(14):106–138.

Starbuck, W. H. Organizations and their environment. In *Handbook of Industrial and Organizational Psychology*, M. D. Dunnette (ed.). Chicago: Rand McNally, 1976, pp. 1069–1106.

Starling, G. *The Changing Environment of Business: A Managerial Approach*. Boston: Kent Publishing, 1980.

State in the market, The. *The Economist* (December 30, 1978), pp. 37–58.

Steinger, G. A. *Business and Society*. New York: Random House, 1971.

Stening, B. W. and Everett, J. E. Direct and stereotype cultural differences. *Journal of Cross-Cultural Psychology* (1979) 10:203–220.

Stieglitz, H. *Organization Structures of International Companies*. New York: Basic Books, 1972.

Stieglitz, H. *Organization Structures of International Companies*. Studies in Personnel Policy, Report No. 198. New York: Conference Board, 1965.

Stolz, R. K. Executive development: New perspective. *Harvard Business Review* (1966) 44(30):133–143.

Stopford, J. M. and Wells, L. T., Jr. *Managing the Multinational Enterprise*. New York: Basic Books, 1972.

Subsidies trade. *Financial Times of London* (November 23, 1977).

Sullivan, J., Peterson, R. B., Kameda, N., and Shimoda, J. The relationship between conflict resolution approaches and trust—A cross-cultural study. *Academy of Management Journal* (1981) 24:803–815.

Swartz, M. J. and Jordan, D. K. *Culture, the Anthropological Perspective*. New York: Wiley, 1980.

Sylvestre, J. Industrial wage differentials: A two country comparison. *International Labour Review* (1974) 110:490–514.

Tajfel, H. Social and cultural factors in perception. In *The Handbook of Social Psychology*, G. Lindsay and E. Aronson (eds.). Reading, MA: Addison-Wesley, 1969.

Tajfel, H., Jahoda, G., Nemeth, C., and Campbell, J. D. The development of children's preference for their own country: A cross national study. *International Journal of Psychology* (1970) 5(4):245–253.

Takane, Y., Young, F. W., and De Leeuw, J. Nonmetric individual differences in multi-dimensional scaling: An alternating least squares method with optimal scaling features. *Psychometrika* (1977) 42:7–67.

Tannenbaum, A. S. *Hierarchy in Organizations: An International Comparison*. San Francisco: Jossey-Bass, 1974.

Tannenbaum, A. S. Organizational psychology. In *Handbook of Cross Cultural Psychology—Social Psychology*, Vol. 5, H. C. Triandis and R. W. Brislin (eds.). Boston: Allyn & Bacon, 1980, pp. 281–334.

Tannenbaum, R. and Schmidt, W. H. How to choose a leadership pattern. *Harvard Business Review* (1958) 36:95–101.

Taylor, F. W. *The Principles of Scientific Management*. New York: Harper & Row, 1911.

Taylor, S. and Crocker, J. Schematic basis of social information processing. In *Social Cognition: The Ontario Symposium,* Vol. 1, E. T. Higgins, M. Zana, and C. P. Herman (eds.). Hillsdale, NJ: Erlbaum, 1981, pp. 89–134.

Teague, F. A. International management selection and development. *California Management Review* (1970) 12(2):1–6.

Terpstra, V. *The Cultural Environment of International Business*. Cincinnati, OH: Southwestern, 1978.

Terpstra, V. *International Marketing*. Hinsdale, IL: Dryden, 1978.

Textor, R. B. (ed.). *Cultural Frontiers of the Peace Corps*. Cambridge, MA: MIT Press, 1966.

Thai, N. L. and Cateora, P. R. Opportunities for women in international business. *Business Horizons* (1979) 22(6):21–27.

Thayer, L. *Communicating and Communication Systems*. Homewood, IL: Irwin, 1968.

Thiagarajan, K. M. and Deep, S. D. A study of supervisor subordinate influence and satisfaction in four cultures. *Journal of Social Psychology* (1970) 82:173–180.

Thompson, A. and Strickland, A. J. *Strategy Formulation and Implementation*. Dallas: BPI, 1980.

Thompson, J. D. Organizations and output transactions. *American Journal of Sociology* (1962) 68:309–325.

Thompson, J. D. *Organizations in Action*. New York: McGraw-Hill, 1967.

Tichy, N. M. Organizational innovations in Sweden. *Columbia Journal of World Business* (Summer 1974), pp. 18–27.

Tilgher, A. Work through the ages. In *Man, Work and Society,* S. Nosaw and W. H. Forms (eds.). New York: Basic Books, 1962.

Toyne, B. Host country managers of multinational firms: An evaluation of variables affecting their managerial thinking patterns. *Journal of International Business Studies* (Spring 1976), pp. 39–55.

Triandis, H. C. *The Analysis of Subjective Culture*. New York: Wiley, 1972.

Triandis, H. C. Dimensions of cultural variations as parameters of organizational theories. *International Studies of Management and Organization* (1982–1983) 12(4):139–169.

Triandis, H. C. *Interpersonal Behavior*. Monterey, CA: Brooks/Cole, 1977.

Triandis, H. C. Subjective culture and interpersonal behavior. In *Applied Cross-Cultural Psychology,* J. W. Berry and W. J. Lonner (eds.). Amsterdam: Swets and Zeitlinger, 1975.

Triandis, H. C. Toward an analysis of the components of interpersonal attitudes. In *Attitudes, Ego, Involvement and Change,* C. Sherif and M. Sherif (eds.). New York: Wiley, 1967.

Triandis, H. C. and Brislin, R. W. (eds.). *Handbook of Cross-Cultural Psychology: Methodology,* Vols. 1–5. Boston: Allyn & Bacon, 1980.

Triandis, H. C. and Martin, G. Etic plus emic versus pseudo etic. *Journal of Cross-Cultural Psychology* (1983) 14(4):489–500.

Triandis, H. C. and Vassiliou, V. A comparative analysis of subjective cultures. In *The Analysis of Subjective Culture*, H. C. Triandis et al. (eds.). New York: Wiley, 1972, pp. 299–335.

Triandis, H. C. and Vassiliou, V. Interpersonal influence and employee selection in two cultures. *Journal of Applied Psychology* (1972) 56:140–145.

Triandis, H. C., Vassiliou, V., Vassiliou, G., Tonaka, Y., and Shanmugam, A. V. (eds.). *The Analysis of Subjective Culture*. New York: Wiley, 1972.

Trist, E. L. and Bamforth, K. W. Some social and psychological consequences of the long wall method of coal getting. *Human Relations* (1951) 4: 3–38.

Tsurumi, Y. *Multinational Management: Business Strategy and Government Policy*. Cambridge, MA: Ballinger, 1984.

Tucker, M. F. Screening and selection for overseas assignments: Assessment and recommendation to the U.S. Navy. Denver, CO: Center for Research and Education, 1974.

Tung, R. L. *Key to Japan's Economic Strength: Human Power*. Lexington, MA: Lexington Books, 1984.

Tung, R. L. Selection and training of personnel for overseas assignments. *Columbia Journal of World Business* (1981) 16:68–78.

Tung, R. L. Selection and training procedures of U.S., European, and Japanese multinationals. *California Management Review* (1982a) 25(1):57–71.

Tung, R. L. *US–China Trade Negotiations*. Elmsford, NY: Pergamon, 1982b.

Tung, R. L. *U.S. Multinationals: A Study of Their Selection and Training Procedures for Overseas Assignments*. Paper presented at the Thirty-ninth Annual Meeting of the Academy of Management, Atlanta, GA, August 8–11, 1979.

Tushman, M. L. and Scanlan, T. J. Boundary spanning individuals: Their role in information transfer and their antecedents. *Academy of Management Journal* (1981) 24:289–305.

Tzeng, O. C. and Osgood, C. E. Validity tests for componential analysis of conceptual domains: A cross cultural study in methodology. *Behavioral Science* (March 1976), pp. 69–85.

Utterback, J. M. Environment analysis and forecasting. In *Strategic Management*, D. E. Schendel and C. W. Hofer (eds.). Boston: Little, Brown, 1979, pp. 134–144.

U.S. Department of Labor. *Working Mothers and Their Children*. Washington, DC: Bureau of Labor Statistics, Women's Bureau, Office of the Secretary, August 1978.

VanFleet, D. and Al-Tuhaih, S. A cross-cultural analysis of perceived leader behaviors. *Management International Review* (1979) 19:81–88.

Vardi, Y., Shirom, A., and Jacobson, D. A study on the leadership beliefs of Israeli managers. *Academy of Management Journal* (1980) 23:367–374.

Vernon, R. International investment and international trade in the product cycle. *Quarterly Journal of Economics* (May 1966), pp. 190–207.

Vernon, R. Multinational enterprise and national sovereignty. *Harvard Business Review* (1967) 45(2):156–172.

Vernon, R. *Sovereignty at Bay: The Multinational Spread of U.S. Enterprises.* New York: Basic Books, 1971.

Vernon, R. *Storm over the Multinationals: The Real Issues.* Cambridge, MA: Harvard University Press, 1977.

Vernon, R. and Wells, L. T. *Manager in the International Economy.* Englewood Cliffs, NJ: Prentice-Hall, 1981.

Vickers, Sir G. *Value Systems and Social Process.* New York: Basic Books, 1968.

Vogel, E. F. Guided free enterprise in Japan. *Harvard Business Review* (May–June 1978), pp. 161–170.

Vozikis, G. S. and Mescon, T. S. Convergence or divergence? A vital managerial question revisited. *Columbia Journal of World Business* (1981) 16(1): 79–87.

Vroom, V. H. Leadership. In *Handbook of Industrial and Organizational Psychology,* M. D. Dunnette (ed.). Chicago: Rand McNally, 1976, pp. 1527–1551.

Vroom, V. H. *Work and Motivation.* New York: Wiley, 1964.

Vroom, V. H. and Yetton, P. W. *Leadership and Decision Making.* Pittsburgh: University of Pittsburgh Press, 1973.

Wahba, M. A. and Bridwell, L. G. Maslow reconsidered: A review of research on the need hierarchy theory. *Organizational Behavior and Human Performance* (1976) 15:212–240.

Wallach, M. A., Kogan, N., and Bem, D. J. Group influence on individual risk taking. *Journal of Abnormal and Social Psychology* (1962) 65:75–86.

Wallin, T. O. The international executive baggage: Cultural values of American frontier. *MSU Business Topics* (Spring 1972), pp. 49–58.

Walters, R. D. and Monsen, R. J. State-owned business abroad: New competitive threat. *Harvard Business Review* (March–April 1979), pp. 160–170.

Waters, L. K. and Roach, D. A factor analysis of need fulfillment exams designed to measure Maslow need categories. *Personnel Psychology* (1973) 26(4):185–195.

Weaver, J. L. Value patterns of a Latin American bureaucracy. *Human Relations* (1970) 23:225–233.

Webber, R. H. Convergence or divergence. *Columbia Journal of World Business* (1969) 4(3):75–83.

Weber, M. *Theory of Social and Economic Organization.* New York: Free Press, 1947.

Weber, R. J. and Hadd, T. A. A factor analytic examination of the internal structure of a Maslow-type need satisfaction instrument. Paper presented at the Eighty-second Annual Convention of Division 14, American Psychology Association, New Orleans, 1974.

Weeks, W. H., Pederson, P. B., and Brislin, R. W. (eds.). *A Manual of Structured Experiences for Cross-Cultural Learning.* La Grange Park, IL: Intercultural Network (Society for Intercultural Education, Training, and Research), 1975.

Weick, K. E. Cognitive processes in organizations. In *Research in Organiza-*

tional Behavior, Vol. 1, L. L. Cummings and B. M. Staw (eds.). Greenwich, CT: JAI Press, 1979, pp. 41–74.

Weick, K. E. *The Social Psychology of Organizing.* Reading, MA: Addison-Wesley, 1969.

Weick, K. E. *The Social Psychology of Organizing,* 2nd ed. Reading, MA: Addison-Wesley, 1979.

Weinshall, T. D. *Culture and Management.* Middlesex, England: Penguin, 1977.

Weissenberg, P. A comparison of the life goals of Austrian, German-Swiss and West German managers. *Economics et Societies* (1979) 13:683–693.

Weitzel, W., Pinto, P. R., Davis, R. V., and Jury, P. A. The impact of the organization on the structure of job satisfaction: Some factor analytic findings. *Personnel Psychology* (1973) 26(4):545–558.

Welge, M. K. A comparison of managerial structures in German subsidiaries in France, India and the United States. *Management International Review* (1981) 21(2):5–21.

Westly, B. and Maclean, M. A conceptual model of communication research. *Journalism Quarterly* (1957) 34:31–38.

Whetten, D. A. and Cameron, K. S. *Developing Management Skills.* Glenview, IL: Scott Foresman, 1984.

White, A. F. Preparation of managers for cross cultural assignment. Unpublished master's thesis, Sloan School of Management, MIT, Cambridge, MA, 1971.

White, L. *The Science of Culture.* New York: Grove Press, 1949.

Whitehill, A. M. Cultural values and employee attitudes: United States and Japan. *Journal of Applied Psychology* (1964) 48:68–72.

Whitehill, A. M. and Takezawa, S. *The Other Worker.* Honolulu: East-West Center Press, 1968.

Whitely, W. A cross national test of England's model of manager's value systems and their relationship to behavior. In *Organizational Functioning in Cross Cultural Perspective,* G. W. England, A. R. Negandhi, and B. Wilpert (eds.). Kent, OH: Kent State University Press, 1979, pp. 19–47.

Whitely, W. and England, G. W. Managerial values as a reflection of culture and the process of industrialization. *Academy of Management Journal* (1977) 20(3):439–453.

Whitely, W. and England, G. W. Variability in common dimensions of managerial values due to value orientation and country differences. *Personnel Psychology* (1980) 33:77–89.

Whitely, W. and England, G. W. Variability in managerial values as a result of country and value orientation differences. *Proceedings of the Academy of Management* (1975), pp. 267–269.

Whiting, B. B. The problem of the packaged variable. In *The Developing Individual in a Changing World,* Vol. 1, K. Riegal and J. Meacham (eds.). Den Haag: Mouton, 1976.

Whiting, J. W. M. and Child, I. *Child Training and Personality.* New Haven, CT: Yale University Press, 1953.

Whitsett, D. Obstacles to implementing structural changes in job design in MNCs. *Columbia Journal of World Business* (Summer 1976), pp. 85–92.

Whorf, B. L. *Language, Thought and Reality*. Cambridge, MA: MIT Press, 1967.

Whorf, B. L. A linguistic consideration of thinking in primitive communities. In *Language, Thought, and Reality: Selected Writings of Benjamin Lee Whorf*, J. B. Carroll (ed.). Cambridge, MA: MIT Press, 1956.

Whorf, B. L. The relation of habitual thought and behavior to language. In *Language, Culture and Personality*, L. Sapir (ed.). Menasha, WI: Sapir Memorial Publication Fund, 1941, pp. 75–93.

Whyte, W. F. and Williams, L. K. Supervisory leadership: An international comparison. Symposium BB, paper B3C, C10S XIII, 1963.

Wiener, N. *The Human Use of Human Beings*. Boston, MA: Houghton Mifflin, 1954.

Wilkins, M. *The Emergence of Multinational Enterprise: Colonial Era to 1914*. Cambridge, MA: Harvard University Press, 1970.

Wilkins, M. *The Maturing of the Multinational Enterprise, 1914–1970*. Cambridge, MA: Harvard University Press, 1974.

Williams, C. R. Regional management overseas. *Harvard Business Review* (1967) 45:87–91.

Williamson, H. F. *Evolution of International Management Structures*. Newark: University of Delaware Press, 1975.

Wilpert, B., Kudat, A., and Ozkan, Y. *Workers' Participation in an Internationalized Economy*. Kent, OH: Comparative Administration Research Institute, 1978.

Witkin, H. A., Dyk, R. B., Faterson, H. F., Goodenough, D. R., and Karp, S. A. *Psychological Differentiation*. New York: Wiley, 1962.

Wofford, J. C. The motivational basis of job satisfaction and job performance. *Personnel Psychology* (1971) 24:501–518.

Woodward, J. *Industrial Organization: Theory and Practice*. London: Oxford University Press, 1965.

World Bank. *World Tables, 1983*. Baltimore: Johns Hopkins University Press, 1983.

Wright, G. N. et al. Cultural differences in probabilistic thinking: An extension into South East Asia. Technical Report 77-1, Decision Analysis Unit, Brunel University, 1977.

Wright, P. Organizational behavior in Islamic firms. *Management International Review* (1981) 21:86–94.

Wrightsman, L. S. *Social Psychology*. Belmont, CA: Brooks/Cole, 1976.

Wrigley, L. Divisional autonomy and diversification. Unpublished DBA thesis, Harvard Business School, Harvard University, Cambridge, MA, 1970.

Yoshino, M. Y. Emerging Japanese multinational enterprises. In *Managing and Organizing the Multinational Corporation*, S. M. Davis (ed.). New York: Pergamon, 1979, pp. 474–494.

Yousef, F. S. Cross cultural communication: Aspects of contrastive social values between North Americans and Middle Easterners. *Human Organization* (1974) 33:357–383.

Youssef, S. M. Integration of local nationals into the managerial hierarchy of American overseas subsidiaries: An exploratory study. *Academy of Management Journal* (1973) 16:24–34.

Yuchtman-Yaar, E. and Seashore, S. E. A system resource approach to organizational effectiveness. *American Sociological Review* (1967) 32:891–903.

Yun, C. K. Role conflicts of expatriate managers: A construct. *Management International Review* (1973) 13(6):105–113.

Zaidi, S. M. H. Applied cross-cultural psychology: Submissions of a cross-cultural psychologist from the Third World. Paper presented at the Nineteenth International Congress of Applied Psychology, Munich, Germany, 1978.

Zald, M. The power and functions of boards of directors. *American Journal of Sociology* (1967) 75:97–111.

Zaltman, G., Duncan, R., and Holbek, J. *Innovation and Organizations*. New York: Wiley, 1973.

Zeira, Y. Ethnocentrism in host-country organizations. *Business Horizons* (1979) 22(5):66–75.

Zeira, Y. Is external management training effective for organizational change? *Public Personnel Management* (1973) 2(6):400–407.

Zeira, Y. Management development in ethnocentric multinational corporations. *California Management Review* (1976) 18(4):34–42.

Zeira, Y. Overlooked personnel problems of multinational corporations. *Columbia Journal of World Business* (1975) 10:96–103.

Zeira, Y. and Banai, M. Attitudes of host-country organizations toward MNC's staffing policies: Cross-country and cross-industry analysis. *Management International Review* (1981) 21(2):38–47.

Zeira, Y. and Harari, E. Managing third country nationals in multinational corporations. *Business Horizons* (October 1977), pp. 83–88.

Zeira, Y. and Harari, E. Managing third-country organizations and expatriate managers in Europe. *California Management Review* (1979) 21(3):40–50.

Zeira, Y., Harari, E., and Izraeli, D. Some structural and cultural factors in ethnocentric multinational corporations and employee morale. *Journal of Management Studies* (1975) 12(1):66–82.

Zurcher, L. A. Particularism and organizational position: A cross cultural analysis. *Journal of Applied Psychology* (1968) 52:139–144.

Zurcher, L. A., Meadow, A., and Zurcher, S. Value orientation, conflict and alienation from work: A cross cultural study. *American Sociological Review* (1965) 30:539–548.

Index